HANDBOOK
TO LIFE
IN ANCIENT
MESOPOTAMIA

HANDBOOK
TO LIFE
IN ANCIENT
MESOPOTAMIA

STEPHEN BERTMAN

OXFORD
UNIVERSITY PRESS

OXFORD
UNIVERSITY PRESS

Oxford University Press, Inc., publishes works that further
Oxford University's objective of excellence
in research, scholarship, and education.

Oxford   New York
Auckland   Cape Town   Dar es Salaam   Hong Kong   Karachi
Kuala Lumpur   Madrid   Melbourne   Mexico City   Nairobi
New Delhi   Shanghai   Taipei   Toronto

With offices in
Argentina   Austria   Brazil   Chile   Czech Republic   France   Greece
Guatemala   Hungary   Italy   Japan   Poland   Portugal   Singapore
South Korea   Switzerland   Thailand   Turkey   Ukraine   Vietnam

First published by Facts On File, Inc., 2003

First issued as an Oxford University Press paperback, 2005
198 Madison Avenue, New York, New York 10016
www.oup.com

Oxford is a registered trademark of Oxford University Press

Library of Congress Cataloging-in-Publication Data
Bertman, Stephen.
Handbook to life in ancient Mesopotamia / Stephen Bertman.
p. cm.
Originally published: New York : Facts on File, c2003, in series:
Facts on File library of world history.
Includes bibliographical references and index.
ISBN-13: 978-019-518364-1
ISBN-10: 0-19-518364-9
1. Iraq—Civilization—To 634.   I. Title.
DS69.5.B47 2005
935—dc22
2004030582

1 3 5 7 9 8 6 4 2
Printed in the United States of America
on acid-free paper

CONTENTS

"Y" know—Babylon once had two million people in it, and all we know about 'em is the names of the kings and some copies of wheat contracts and . . . the sales of slaves. Yes, every night all those families sat down to supper, and the father came home from his work, and the smoke went up the chimney, —same as here."

— Thornton Wilder, *Our Town*

ACKNOWLEDGMENTS

For rescuing the ancient civilizations of Mesopotamia from oblivion we are indebted to generations of travelers and explorers, archaeologists and philologists, whose love of the past gave that past new life and whose words and work inspired and shaped this book. I remain personally indebted to Leonard Cottrell and others whose popular books on archaeological discovery pointed the way for me when I was young, and to the teachers—Jotham Johnson, Casper J. Kraemer Jr., Lionel Casson, and Cyrus Gordon—I was later lucky to find as guides.

For this project, special thanks for bibliographical help go to Elaine Bertman, William W. Hallo, Angeline Sturam, and Dr. Fred Wassermann, and to Diana Wu, Margie Prytulak, and Biljana Barisic for giving my manuscript electronic form. I am also indebted to the following individuals for assisting me in obtaining photographic illustrations: Carla Hosein, Sylvia Inwood, Tory James, Ryan Jensen, Ulla Kasten, and Charles Kline.

Ultimately, my greatest debt is to those who are now nameless but were human like ourselves, those whose long-ago hopes and dreams still swirl in the dust of Iraq. In writing this book, it is with those ancient ghosts I seek to keep faith, for to be remembered is to be alive.

In Memory of

Cyrus H. Gordon
(1909–2001)

who looked across artificial borders
and bravely reported a wider truth

INTRODUCTION

Along with Egypt, ancient Mesopotamia was the birthplace of civilization. But, unlike Egypt, Mesopotamia was the home of not one but a succession of glorious civilizations—the civilizations of Sumer, Babylonia, and Assyria—that together flourished for more than three millennia from about 3500 to 500 B.C.E.

It was Sumerian mathematicians who devised the 60-minute hour that still rules our lives. It was Babylonian architects who designed the fabled Tower of Babel and the Hanging Gardens of Babylon, one of the "Seven Wonders of the Ancient World." And it was Assyrian kings and generals who, in the name of imperialism, conducted some of the most ruthless military campaigns in recorded history.

The civilizations of Mesopotamia are united by many common denominators: the land of the twin rivers—the Tigris and Euphrates—and the resources it possessed; the gods and goddesses that lorded over it; the cities—the world's first—that rose and fell with their towers and temples; the lawmakers and empire-builders; the farmers, merchants, and artisans who lived out their daily lives; the scribes who told their story in the world's oldest writing; and the works of literature that still survive that speak of a search for meaning in a land that so often saw the hopes of humankind frustrated by nature's raw power or man's voracious greed.

Handbook to Life in Ancient Mesopotamia presents a panorama of human striving painted on a broad geographical and historical canvas, a story of the struggle to create civilized life in a fertile land racked by brutal conquest, a tale of universal human aspirations written in the dust and recaptured by archaeology. In retelling this tale the author has produced English versions of ancient texts designed to convey their underlying humanity.

In the main, yesterday's Mesopotamia is today's Iraq, a war-torn land where people still struggle to eke out their daily lives as did their ancestors thousands of years ago. Yet buried in Iraq's barren desert there also lie the ruins of an earlier glory and splendor that once shone for all to see.

LIST OF MAPS

LIST OF ILLUSTRATIONS

1

GEOGRAPHY OF MESOPOTAMIA

THE LAND AND ITS RIVERS

It was ancient Greek travelers and historians who first gave the land the name by which we know it: Mesopotamia. The name means "the land between the rivers" (from *mesos*, the Greek word for "between" or "in the middle"; *potamos*, the Greek word for "river"; and *ia*, a suffix that the Greeks attached to the names of places). The ancient Mesopotamians did not have a name for the whole land; instead, their

1.1   A century-ago view of the Euphrates River from a point south of the site of ancient Babylon. (Robert William Rogers, A History of Babylonia and Assyria, 6th ed. [New York: Abingdon Press, 1915])

mental horizons were limited to the names of the cities and kingdoms where they lived. Today, most of ancient Mesopotamia lies within the borders of modern Iraq, with some parts—to the west and north—in Syrian and Turkish territory.

The rivers that defined Mesopotamia were the Tigris and the Euphrates. Like the name Mesopotamia itself, the spelling of the rivers' names is something we owe to the Greeks. The original name of the Tigris was the Idiglat; the original name of the Euphrates, the Buranum—names that were first used by the inhabitants of the land in prehistoric times and which survive in their earliest records.

In the Bible, the Tigris was called the Hiddekel, the Hebrew pronunciation of the river's authentic name, while the Euphrates was simply called the Prat. The book of Genesis describes them as two of the four rivers that flowed out of Eden and watered its famous garden. Biblical tradition thus connects Mesopotamian geography with the beginnings of the human race.

The river valleys of Mesopotamia are framed by the desert, the mountains, and the sea. To the west is the Syrian Desert; to the north and east, the mountains of Turkey and Iran; to the south, the Persian Gulf.

Rising in the mountains, the rivers descend through foothills and steppe and flow toward the southeast through a flat, alluvial plain until they empty through marshes into the sea.

Reading as we do from left to right, upon hearing the phrase "Tigris and Euphrates," we may think of the Tigris as the one farther west. In actually, the Euphrates lies to the west and the Tigris to the east. Of the two rivers the Euphrates is the longer (about 1,740 miles in length) compared to the Tigris (about 1,180 miles). Each is fed by tributaries: the Euphrates by the Balikh and Khabur Rivers; the Tigris, by the Great Zab, the Little Zab, and the Diyala.

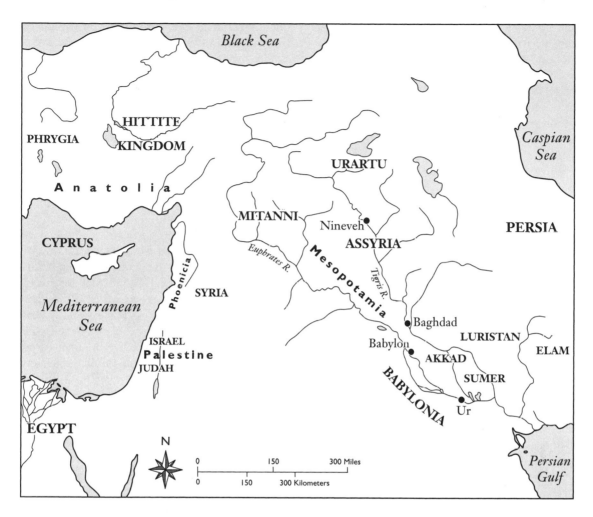

Map 1. *The Ancient Near East*

Today, in the south, the Tigris and Euphrates merge into the Shatt al-Arab before jointly emptying into the sea; but in ancient times they flowed into the Persian Gulf separately. In those days (during the fourth and third millennia B.C.E.) the Gulf extended as much as 150 miles farther inland than it does today, making ancient cities like Ur and Eridu (inland today) virtual seaports. Over the centuries, heavy accumulations of silt deposited by the rivers along with the sea's own retreat pushed the coastline south.

When the winter snows in the mountains melted (sometime between April and early June), the rivers flooded unpredictably and often violently, destroying everything in their path. Their propensity for destructive fury and the uncertainty of their will, it is argued, draped much of Mesopotamian thought in pessimism. On the other hand, it was their life-giving waters—channeled by the technology of irrigation—that made urban civilization possible in the flood-prone plain. Yet even when the rivers were not guilty of short-term caprice, their long-term behavior could undermine everything that civilization had built: an otherwise vital city could literally be left high and dry economically when a meandering river altered its course and cut it off from trade and transportation.

In the steppe to the north, life was less erratic. There the rivers coursed through a rocky terrain that made their paths more permanent. Unlike the subtropical south where summer temperatures could average 120°F., the climate in the north was temperate. There rainfall, rather than artificial irrigation, watered farmers' fields and sustained their livestock. Indeed, from the wild grains that grew in the north, agriculture itself may have begun. Yet the south was the more fertile land, thanks to the richness of its alluvial soil, a richness that—when watered—could support large population centers and material prosperity.

The geographic differences between north and south—between Assyria in the north and Babylonia in the south—bred differences in temperament between their peoples and generated political division and tension. At times, greed or vindictiveness ignited war.

Meanwhile, there were also ethnic differences within the south. In the deepest south lived the Sumerians, who created the world's first civilization. Though the Sumerians were united by a common language and common traditions, the control of the lands and waterways inspired intercity rivalries and war. To their north dwelt the Semitic Akkadians, who coveted what the Sumerians possessed and conquered them, joining Sumer to Akkad. With the rise of the city and kingdom of Babylon, the whole of the south came to be called Babylonia.

Babylon, Babylonia's largest city, lay on the Euphrates; Nineveh, Assyria's largest city, on the Tigris. Baghdad, Iraq's modern capital, is situated midway down the Tigris at the point where it veers closest to the Euphrates.

The name "Mesopotamia" is, in fact, a misnomer: many of the land's ancient cities were located not *between* the two rivers but just outside the edge of the irregular spearpoint they form as they aim southeast to the sea.

NATURAL RESOURCES

Mesopotamia's major resources were its water and fertile soil. If, as the ancient Greek historian Herodotus claimed, Egypt was the gift of the Nile, Mesopotamia was the gift of the Tigris and Euphrates. This was especially true of the alluvial plain to the south, where the well-watered fertility of the land nurtured such staples of the people's diet as barley, sesame, and dates.

From riverine clay the Mesopotamians not only made bricks but also fashioned clay tablets to write on with the help of pens cut from the reeds that grew along the rivers' banks.

A unique resource of the land was bitumen, a natural asphalt that seeped from beds in the ground, especially in the area around Hit on the Euphrates. Bitumen had many uses: as an adhesive for bricks, as a waterproof coating in construction, and as a cement to create works of art.

The critical resources that Mesopotamia largely lacked were building stone (except in Assyria where gypsum was available), construction-grade timber, and minerals, including copper and tin (needed to make bronze), iron, silver, and gold.

Combined with the demands of an increasingly affluent society and the desires of its rulers for splendor, the scarcity of these resources encouraged foreign trade and the rise of a merchant class as the Mesopotamians exchanged agricultural produce and textiles for the commodities they lacked. As a result, caravans plied regular overland trade routes throughout the Middle East and ships sailed up and down the Persian Gulf. Timber was hauled in from the Zagros Mountains and Lebanon; copper and tin from Anatolia, the Caucasus, and Iran; silver from the Taurus Mountains; and gold from Egypt and even India. From Afghanistan came a precious blue mineral called lapis lazuli. Ships were sailing as early as the fifth millennium B.C.E. between Mesopotamia and ports in Bahrain and Oman, and as early as the third millennium B.C.E. between Mesopotamia and the Indus Valley. So great was the influence of Babylonian merchants that their Akkadian language and cuneiform script became tools for international commercial and diplomatic correspondence throughout the ancient Near East.

SURROUNDING COUNTRIES

As we have seen, commerce brought Mesopotamia into contact with other lands, both near and far.

At almost the same time that civilization was born in Sumer (near the end of the fourth millennium B.C.E.), it also was born to the west in Egypt, land of the Nile. Indeed, scholars still debate where it was born first. And when Sumer's monarchs were later laid in their graves surrounded by their royal retinues and splendor, the pyramids of Egypt's pharaohs were just being built. How much these two classic eras of civilization knew of each other's existence is likewise a subject for debate. Striking cultural parallels between them exist (their nearly simultaneous invention of writing and monumental architec-ture, for example), but are offset by equally striking differences in style and intent.

About five centuries after the earliest civilizations of Egypt and Mesopotamia arose, yet another civilization was born, the civilization of the Indus Valley, represented by the ruined cities of Mohenjo-Daro and Harappa. Artifacts and inscriptions point to commercial contact between Mesopotamia and this land, which the Mesopotamians called Meluhha. Whether the contact was more than commercial we cannot yet say.

In the second and first millennia B.C.E., the imperialistic ambitions of the Assyrians and Babylonians brought them into military conflict with an array of other nations that vied for the control of the lands known today as Syria and Israel. These lands were important because of the trade routes that passed through them and the tribute that could be exacted from their cities.

During the second millennium B.C.E. Egypt fought for the control of this region against two other superpowers: the Hittites, who were based in Turkey, and the Mitanni, who occupied northwestern Mesopotamia.

By the first millennium B.C.E. direct strikes were made against cities in ancient Israel by Assyrian and Babylonian armies. Assyrian armies went so far as to invade Egypt, and a Babylonian army under Nebuchadnezzar captured Jerusalem and took Jewish prisoners of war back to Babylon. The emotional turmoil of these times resonates in the writings of the Hebrew prophets and the biblical book of Lamentations.

By the sixth century B.C.E., the armies of Babylon were defeated by a new player that had stepped on the stage of world politics, the Persians, who were to amass the largest empire the world had ever seen, one that stretched from Turkey in the west to India in the east and south into Egypt. The kings of Persia even invaded Greece, but they were valiantly rebuffed there in a series of battles fought in the early fifth century B.C.E.

In the late fourth century B.C.E. a charismatic leader named Alexander the Great led an army of Macedonian and Greek soldiers in a war against Persia fought for revenge and greater glory. After defeating the Persians, Alexander made Babylon the capital of his new empire, seeking to create a new multicultural society on a global scale, one in which the European heritage of Greece would be blended with the legacy of the Orient. Though Alexander died before he could see his dream fulfilled, the forces he set into motion brought West and East closer together than they had ever been before, or would ever be again.

Evidence of over three millennia of cultural development and change lie buried in the cities of the ancient Tigris and Euphrates. It is time we visited each of these cities and listened to their tales.

GAZETTEER

Names of Cities

Listed below in alphabetical order are the names of ancient sites in Mesopotamia that have special archaeological and historical significance. Where the original name of a site is known, it is listed alphabetically; where only the modern name of its ruins survive, the modern name appears in its stead. In cases where a Mesopotamian city is mentioned in the Bible, the biblical spelling of its name is provided as well.

Original Name	Modern Name	Biblical Name
	Abu Salabikh	
Adab	Tell Bismaya	
Agade		Akkad
Akshak	Tell Mujeilat	
Arbil	Erbil	
Ashur	Qalat Shergat	Asshur (=Assyria)
Babil(a)	Babylon	Babel
Bad-tibira	Tell Madain	
Borsippa	Birs Nimrud	
Carchemish	Jerablus	Carchemish
	Chagar Bazar	
	Choga Mami	
Ctesiphon	Tell al-Ma'aridh (?)	
Dilbat	Tell Dulaim	
Dur-Katlimmu	Sheikh Hamid	
Dur-Kurigalzu	Aqar Quf & Tell al-Abyad	
Dur-Sharrukin	Khorsabad	

Original Name	Modern Name	Biblical Name
Dura-Europos		
Eridu	Abu Shahrain	
Eshnunna	Tell Asmar	
Girsu	Tello	
Guzana	Tell Halaf	
Hatra	Al-Hadr	
Imgur-Enlil	Balawat	
Isin	Ishan Bahriyat	
	Jemdet Nasr	
Kalhu	Nimrud	Calah
Kar-Tukulti-Ninurta	Telul al-Aqar	
Kish	Tell Ingharra & Tell Uhaimir	
Kutha	Tell Ibrahim	
Lagash	Tell al-Hiba	
Larak		
Larsa	Tell Senkereh	
Mari	Tell Hariri	
Neribtum	Tell Ishchali	
Nina-Sirara	Zurghul	
Ninua	Kuyunjik & Tell Nebi Yunus	Nineveh
Nippur	Nuffar	
Nuzu (Nuzi)	Yorghun Tepe	
Puzrish-Dagan	Drehem	
	Qalat Jarmo	
	Samarra	
Shaduppum	Tell Harmal	
Shubat-Enlil	Tell Leilan	
Shuruppak	Fara	
Sippar	Tell Abu Haba	
Sippar-Amnanum (Sippar-Anunitu)	Tell ed-Der	
	Tell Arpachiyeh	
	Tell Brak	
	Tell Fakhariyeh	
	Tell Hassuna	
	Tell al-Oueili	
	Tell Qalinj Agha	*(continues)*

(continued)

Original Name	Modern Name	Biblical Name
(Karana or Qatara?)	**Tell al-Rimah**	
	Tell es-Sawwan	
	Tell Taya	
	Tell al-Ubaid	
	Tell Uqair	
	Tepe Gawra	
Terqa	Tell Ashara	
Til Barsip	Tell Ahmar	
Tuttul	Tell Bi'a	
Tutub	Khafaje	
	Umm Dabaghiyah	
Umma		
Ur	Tell Muqayyar	
Uruk	Warka	Erech
	Yarim Tepe	

Descriptions of Cities

Abu Salabikh Abu Salabikh contains the remains of a city that flourished in the fourth and third millennia B.C.E. In antiquity, the city was situated on a branch of the Euphrates, about halfway between the ancient cities of Kish and Nippur in the southern part of Mesopotamia known as Sumer. Its original name may have been Kesh, a Sumerian city whose patron goddess was Nisaba, the goddess of the reeds that grew abundantly in the riverbanks and marshes. Because the reeds were used by scribes to make their pens, Nisaba was their patron deity as well. Today, the ruins of the city lie about 75 miles southeast of Baghdad.

Abu Salabikh was first excavated in the 1960s. The excavations uncovered the oldest city walls that have ever been found in southern Mesopotamia, the land where the world's first cities arose. In what may have once been a temple complex, the archaeologists unearthed some 500 fragments of clay tablets inscribed in cuneiform. Among them were portions of literary works: the character-building advice of a father to his son (called "The Instructions of Shuruppak") and a hymn praising the temple of the Sumerian mother-goddess Ninhursag.

Adab This Sumerian city once lay on the ancient path of the Euphrates River, 25 miles southeast of Nippur. When the river changed its course, the city began to die. Today its ruins are called Tell Bismaya.

Agade Around 2300 B.C.E., the Semitic king Sargon conquered Sumer and made the city of Agade his capital. There he built his palace and erected temples to honor the gods of war, Ishtar and Zababa. For over a century, Agade served as the seat of an empire whose reach extended to Iran in the east and Syria in the

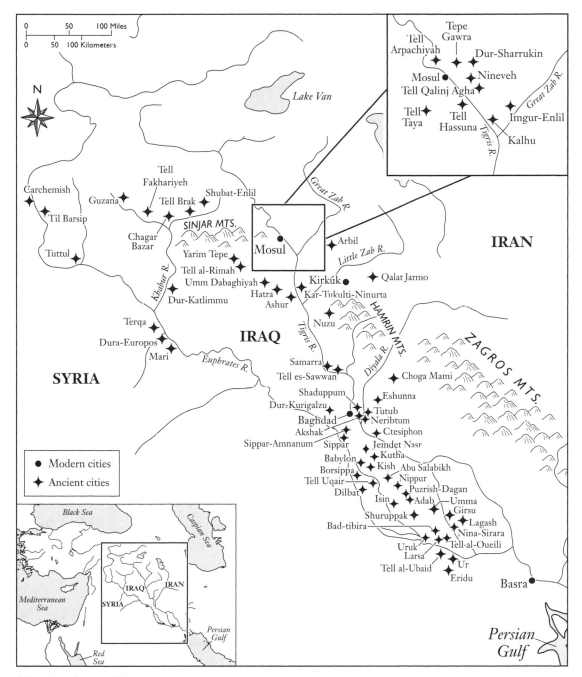

Map 2. *Cities of Mesopotamia*

west. Agade prospered from imperialism, and foreign ships bearing exotic cargo docked in its harbor.

Historians call Sargon's native land Akkad, from the Hebrew spelling of the city's name (Genesis 10:10). Likewise, the Semitic language of its people is called Akkadian. A later form of this language was spoken by the Babylonians and Assyrians, and for a time became an international language of commerce and diplomacy.

About 2200 B.C.E. the city and its empire fell to an invading horde called the Guti, who swept in from the Zagros Mountains of Iran. According to a poem entitled "The Curse of Agade," the city's destruction was the consequence of divine vengeance because Sargon the Great's grandson, King Naram-Sin, had desecrated a temple. In fulfillment of the divine curse, the city's freshwater turned to salt, and its lands were abandoned.

The gods must have been forgiving, however, if Babylonian inscriptions are to be believed, for Babylon's kings were constructing buildings there as late as the sixth century B.C.E.

To the frustration of archaeologists and historians, the ruins of Agade have never been located. Perhaps the curse of the gods is still in effect after all.

Akshak   Forty miles north of Babylon lay the northern Akkadian city of Akshak, later called Opis. In 539 B.C.E., Cyrus, king of Persia, met and defeated the Babylonian army here before going on to capture Babylon itself. The Greek historian Herodotus reports that when a white horse belonging to Cyrus drowned in the nearby Tigris, Cyrus punished the river by draining off its water. Today the remains of Akshak are known by the name of Tell Mujeilat.

Arbil   Arbil was a major Assyrian city located in the country's heartland between the Great and Little Zab Rivers, tributaries of the Tigris.

A canal, partly underground, was engineered by King Sennacherib in the seventh century B.C.E. to supply the city with more water. Ishtar, the goddess of love and war, was revered here from early times. In later times, Arbil became famous because of a battle that was fought in 331 B.C.E. at nearby Gaugamela, when Alexander the Great defeated Darius III, king of the Persians. Alexander's decisive victory there (in the so-called Battle of Arbela) marked the end of the Persian Empire and the beginning of the Hellenistic Age.

Ashur   Called Qalat Sherqat today, the ruins of Ashur lie on a plateau high above the Tigris in northern Iraq, about 60 miles south of the modern city of Mosul. In ancient times it lay on a caravan route that connected the Levant with Iran, and prospered from its location.

Though the site had been explored by Europeans as early as 1821, scientific excavation did not commence until the beginning of the 20th century under the direction of the German archaeologist, Walter Andrae.

In the second millennium B.C.E., Ashur became the first royal capital of the Assyrian nation. Its name was the same as the country's name as well as the name of the country's divine protector, the god Ashur. The names "Assyria" and "Syria" still echo this name. Even when the Assyrian Empire's political capital was moved (to Kalhu, Dur-Sharrukin, and Nineveh), Ashur remained its religious capital and the last resting place of its kings. In 614 B.C.E., the city was sacked by the Medes and Babylonians, who simultaneously brought to an end Assyria's dreams of imperial glory.

At its height, Ashur boasted 34 temples. The oldest, indeed the oldest public building in the entire city, was the temple of Ishtar, goddess of both war and love. In its ruins, archaeologists found a carving of a naked woman on a bed, and erotic images fashioned from lead and dedicated by worshipers whose sexual powers had been restored by the god-dess' intervention. The city's patron god Ashur was also honored with a temple as well as with a nearby ziggurat, a lofty stepped platform sur-mounted by a shrine.

In addition to religious structures, the city contained two palaces, an old and a new. In their basements in vaulted tombs, the mon-archs were laid to rest in stone sarcophagi together with their treasure. None of their riches were to escape the hands of plunderers.

Babil(a)   See Babylon

Babylon   Babylon is the most renowned city of ancient Mesopotamia and one of the most famous urban centers of antiquity. Despite its ruined state, Babylon retained a permanent place in Western consciousness because of its role in the Bible. It was the site of the Tower of Babel, scriptural symbol of humanity's hubris, as well as the internment site for the pious Hebrew captives who were marched into exile by King Nebuchadnezzar II in the sixth cen-tury B.C.E. In addition, it was described with eyewitness detail by the "father of history," Herodotus, and it was home to the "Hanging Gardens," one of the legendary Seven Won-ders of the Ancient World.

Today, the remains of Babylon are spread out over a cluster of mounds, or tells, located on the Euphrates about 59 miles southwest of Baghdad. Early European travelers were drawn to the locale by accounts of the city's former glory, by the extent of its ruins, and by the presence—there and nearby—of architectural remains that suggested the fabled tower. Some returned to Europe in the 17th and 18th cen-turies with artifacts, including the very first samples of cuneiform writing. Excavations did not begin in earnest, however, until the 19th century. The major expedition, which lasted from 1899 to 1914, was directed by German archaeologist Robert Koldewey.

1.2   During Koldewey's excavation of Babylon, a basket brigade clears rubble from the site.   (Rogers, *A History of Babylonia and Assyria*, 1915)

The name Babylon is itself a bit of a mys-tery. The biblical Hebrews traced its origins to a word in their own language *(bavel)* that meant "confusion," deriving the name of the tower from the linguistic confusion God visited upon its builders so they could no longer communi-cate to complete their work (an explanation, incidentally, for how the world's many lan-guages came into being). In the Semitic lan-guage of the Babylonians themselves, the name of their city may have meant "Gate of God" or "Gate of the Gods" *(bav il* or *bav ilim)*. But the real root and its true meaning may even ante-date the Babylonians, and perhaps their Sumerian predecessors as well.

Sumerian inscriptions tell us the city existed in the third millennium B.C.E. Its first age of glory, however, was in the 17th century B.C.E., when it was ruled by the conqueror and lawgiver Hammurabi. After a thousand years during which it suffered decline and destruction, it rose again in the sixth century B.C.E. to become the capital of Nebuchadnezzar and the Neo-Babylonian Empire. Liberated from the Persians in the fourth century B.C.E. by the charismatic Alexander the Great, Babylon went on to become the capital of Alexander's worldwide kingdom and the city where in 323 B.C.E. he died. By the days of the Roman Empire, Babylon was deserted, an urban memory in the dust.

1.3   Excavations at Babylon uncover the bricked pavement of the audience hall of Nebuchadnezzar II's royal palace. An inscribed brick can be seen in the foreground. (Rogers, *A History of Babylonia and Assyria*, 1915)

However, with the help of archaeological discoveries and ancient literary accounts, it is possible to resurrect Babylon, at least in our imaginations. Besides Herodotus's fifth century B.C.E. account (whose complete accuracy some doubt), we possess a detailed cuneiform guide to the city as it looked in the 12th century B.C.E., complete with the names of its major buildings. Though the high level of groundwater has inhibited archaeologists from excavating this deeply into Babylon's past, a reliable picture of the later sixth century B.C.E. city has emerged as it might have looked in the days of Nebuchadnezzar, a century or so before Herodotus's visit.

The shape of the city was delineated by the Euphrates, which in ancient times divided it into two unequal parts: an "old city" to the east and a smaller "new city" to the west. Between them flowed the Euphrates from north to south, and the river fed main canals that watered each half.

In the eastern half of the city stood the king's palace and the city's main religious buildings.

Called by Nebuchadnezzar "the marvel of mankind, the center of the land, the shining residence, the dwelling of majesty," the royal palace was located at the northern edge of the old city beside a fortress. Rising from the palace's northeastern corner may have been the Hanging Gardens of Babylon, a series of earthen terraces that supported a forest of trees—supposedly an architectural gift from Nebuchadnezzar to his Persian wife who pined for the landscape of her mountainous homeland.

South of the palace and adjoining the Euphrates were two structures dedicated to the gods. The first was a mighty ziggurat, a 300-foot-tall stepped platform on a square base that measured about 300 feet on each side. The core of the structure was made of sun-dried brick encased in a 49-foot-thick layer of oven-baked brick. The platform ascended in seven stages or stories of diminishing size and was crowned by a shrine approached by a broad staircase. On the

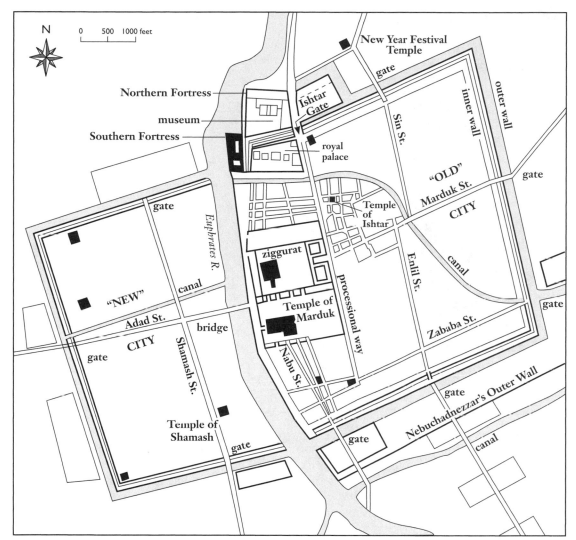

Map 3. *Babylon*

heights of the ziggurat, priests performed rituals and uttered prayers on behalf of the multitudes assembled below. The ziggurat's name was Etemenanki, "the House of the Foundation of Heaven and Earth."

Just south of the ziggurat was a temple complex dedicated to Babylon's patron god Marduk and his divine consort. Called Esagila, "The House That Lifts Its Head," its sanctuary had walls and a ceiling plated in gold.

Throughout the city were hundreds upon hundreds of altars and shrines so that the Babylonians might serve their gods, who in turn would show them favor.

Girding the entire city was a defensive moat and a brick wall 85 feet thick surmounted by

1.4 An artist's rendering of Babylon's Ishtar Gate as it would have appeared in the sixth century B.C.E. (Oriental Institute, University of Chicago)

1.5 Façade of the Ishtar Gate, built by Nebuchadnezzar II and housed in a museum in Berlin. (Bildarchiv Foto Marburg/Art Resource, N.Y.)

towers at 65-foot intervals. The wall was about five miles long and, according to Herodotus, was wide enough to permit a four-horse chariot to make a U-turn on its elevated roadway. Separate walls lined the banks of the Euphrates as it wound its way through the city.

Nine stoutly fortified gateways, each named for a god, gave pedestrians access to the city's grid-pattern of streets and neighborhoods and to the countryside beyond. Recovered by Koldewey, the Ishtar Gate now stands reconstructed in the Berlin Museum, resplendent with sculpted bulls and dragons gleaming in colorful glazed brick.

Outside the city walls to the northeast lay a special temple used to celebrate the New Year's Festival. Connecting it with the city was an avenue for celebrants called the Processional Way, which passed through the Ishtar Gate and alongside the palace and ziggurat before turning west to cross over the Euphrates by bridge to the residential quarters of the new city.

Before his death, Alexander the Great ordered the superstructure of Babylon's ziggurat pulled down in order that it might be rebuilt with greater splendor. But he never lived to bring his project to completion. Over the centuries, its scattered bricks have been cannibalized by peasants to fulfill humbler dreams. All that is left of the fabled Tower of Babel is the bed of a swampy pond.

Bad-tibira Before the days of the Great Flood, Sumerian tradition recounted, Bad-tibira was one of the five most important cities in the land. According to the literary record, the other major cities of earliest Sumer were Eridu, Larak, Shuruppak, and Sippar. Today, the ruins of Bad-tibira go by the name of Tell Madain.

Balawat See Imgur-Enlil.

Borsippa Seven miles southwest of Babylon lie the remains of ancient Borsippa, referred to today as Birs Nimrud. Occupied from the late third millennium B.C.E., Borsippa was the sacred home of the god Nabu and the site of his most renowned temple, the Ezida, or "Enduring House." At first a patron god of scribes, over the course of time Nabu rose in preeminence to stand beside Marduk and to be thought of as his son. At the time of the New Year's Festival, the cult statue of Nabu was transported from Borsippa to Babylon so that he might visit his divine father. From the Ezida temple the statue traveled down the Processional Way of Borsippa, through its Lapis Lazuli Gate, and onto the road toward Babylon.

Because of its nearness to Babylon and because the core of its brick ziggurat still towers 150 feet above the surrounding plain, many early visitors believed that Borsippa, rather than Babylon, was the true location of the biblical Tower of Babel.

Excavations at Borsippa were carried out sporadically during the 19th century and, most recently, by an Austrian expedition in the 1980s. Besides the remains of the ziggurat and the temple precinct, the ruins of a palace built by Nebuchadnezzar have been found.

Carchemish Strategically situated on a busy Near Eastern overland trade route at a vital crossing on the Euphrates and fortified in the second millennium B.C.E., Carchemish played an important role for more than a thousand years and profited from its location. Its wealth, however, attracted the covetous eye of its imperialistic neighbors, and it was successively dominated by the Mitanni, the Hittites, and the Assyrians. Carchemish was also the setting for a key battle in 605 B.C.E. that marked the end of the Assyrian Empire, when Nebuchadnezzar of Babylon triumphed over the Assyrian army and its Egyptian allies.

Today, the ruins of Carchemish lie about 280 miles west of Mosul in Turkish territory across the border from the Syrian village of Jerablus.

The first to identify their archaeological significance was George Smith in 1876. Smith had earlier found fragments of the Babylonian Flood Story in the ruins of Nineveh. After surveying the site of Carchemish and sketching some of its surviving monuments, Smith died en route to Aleppo. Further explorations and excavations followed under the leadership of the British Museum, where Smith had worked. Assisting in the digging for five seasons was T. E. Lawrence ("of Arabia"). Archaeological discoveries included the citadel, the temple of the storm god, and an elaborate series of sculptural reliefs, most of which are now on exhibit at the Museum of Anatolian Civilization in Ankara.

Chagar Bazar The ruins known as Chagar Bazar lie in the northern part of present-day Syria in the basin of the Khabur River, one of the tributaries of the Euphrates. In the burnt remains of a second millennium B.C.E. administrative building, an archive was uncovered. One tablet recorded how a potentate named Yasmah-Addu showed up in the city with 3,000 soldiers and draft animals and demanded food. Elsewhere in the city ruins, a clay pendant has been found impressed with a banqueting scene showing diners entertained by a musician. One of the most curious objects discovered in Chagar Bazar was a knife from a third millennium B.C.E. grave deposit. The knife-blade was made of smelted iron, one of the earliest artifacts of man-made iron ever found.

1.6   Pictured by a 19th-century artist, this 120-foot-tall arch still soars over the site of ancient Ctesiphon.
(George Rawlinson, *The Seven Great Monarchies of the Ancient Eastern World* [New York: Alden, 1884])

Choga Mami   About 70 miles northeast of Baghdad in the foothills of the Zagros Mountains lie the remains of Choga Mami. The prehistoric site may be as old as the sixth millennium B.C.E. and was a thriving village before the emergence of complex urban life. The site offers some of the oldest evidence of irrigation canals. Scattered among the remains of the village were baked clay figurines of women, their bodies tattooed with paint and their elongated eyes shaped and split like coffee beans. Prehistoric means preliterate, and so we have no inscribed words to give these women (goddesses?) voice or to describe their life in this long-ago time. Foundations of houses, regularly planned with as many as 12 rooms, survive, but no walls that reverberate with the sounds of everyday activity. Broken pottery litters the ruins.

Ctesiphon   Ctesiphon was founded by the Parthians on the Tigris when they wrested Mesopotamia from the Hellenistic Seleucid dynasty in the second century B.C.E. It then became their capital, the place where their treasures were kept and their kings were crowned. Successively sacked by the legions of Rome, it was finally taken in the second century C.E. by the Sassanians, who replaced the Parthians as masters of Mesopotamia. Under Sassanian rule, Ctesiphon retained its place as a capital and center of culture. Plagued by malaria and mosquitoes, it eventually fell in the seventh century to an Arab army whose soldiers were dazzled by the splendor of its palace. In chapter 51 of his monumental history of the Roman Empire, Edward Gibbon re-creates the scene:

> The naked robbers of the desert were suddenly enriched beyond the measure of their hope or

knowledge. Each chamber revealed a new treasure secreted with art, or ostentatiously displayed; the gold and silver, the various wardrobes and precious furniture surpassed . . . the estimate of fancy or numbers . . . One of the apartments of the palace was decorated with a carpet of silk, sixty cubits [90 feet] in length, and as many in breadth: a paradise or garden was depictured on the ground: the flowers, fruits, and shrubs were imitated by the figures of the gold embroidery, and the colours of the precious stones; and the ample square was encircled by a variegated and verdant border. (Gibbon 1845: 4, 409–10)

As a new city called Baghdad arose 22 miles to the north, the buildings of Ctesiphon were demolished and their bricks hauled away for reuse. No one, however, dared to dismantle the grand arch covering the palace's great hall, a brick-built arch over 80 feet wide and 120 feet high, in Seton Lloyd's words "the widest single-span vault of unreinforced brickwork in the world."

Dilbat   Located about 27 miles south of Babylon, Dilbat was the home of a Sumerian earth-goddess named Urash. Today, the city's fruitless ruins are named Tell Dulaim.

Drehem   See Puzrish-Dagan.

Dur Katlimmu   At a point 140 miles southwest of Mosul stand the remains of Dur Katlimmu, a provincial capital of the Assyrian Empire. Called Sheikh Hamid today, the remains lie in Syria on the river Khabur, the main tributary of the Euphrates. The site was first investigated in 1879, but no systematic excavations were undertaken until another hundred years had passed. Some 500 cuneiform tablets have been found, some of which show that Assyrian laws were being obeyed even after the collapse of the Assyrian Empire.

Dur-Kurigalzu   In the late 15th or early 14th century B.C.E., a Kassite king, Kurigalzu, named this city for himself and made it his capital. With the fall of his dynasty two centuries later, the city was soon abandoned and its soil used for a cemetery. Today, the remains of Dur-Kurigalzu occupy two mounds—Aqar Quf and Tell al-Abyad—located 18 miles west of Baghdad. On one mound, Tell al-Abyad, are the ruins of a palace. One room features a painted procession of officials. Running along a corridor are the pillaged chambers of a treasury. Elsewhere, a terra-cotta hyena silently howls. Towering over desolate Aqar Quf is the 187-foot-tall twisted and eroding hulk of a ziggurat

1.7   This mud-brick hulk is all that remains of Dur-Kurigalzu's once-proud ziggurat.   (Rogers, A History of Babylonia and Assyria, 1915)

once dedicated to Enlil, chief god of the Sumerian pantheon. All that is left is the mud-brick core, the reed mats that were laid between the layers of brick still visible in the sun.

Dur-Sharrukin   Near the end of the eighth century B.C.E., the Assyrian king Sargon II founded Dur-Sharrukin ("The Fortress of Sargon") as his new capital city. Located about seven miles northeast of the northern Iraqi city of Mosul and more commonly called Khorsabad, the site of Dur-Sharrukin witnessed the first large-scale excavations in the history of Near Eastern archaeology. Initiated in 1843 by Paul-Émile Botta and renewed a decade later by Victor Place, these excavations yielded the first

examples of monumental Assyrian sculpture. As the discoveries were unearthed they were meticulously sketched by Eugène Flandin and, later, Félix Thomas before being shipped to the Louvre. The drawings proved invaluable because of the fragile nature of the stone and an attack (by hostile Bedouin tribesmen) on two barges transporting the works of art, works which as a result still lie sunk in the muddy bottom of the Tigris. The Place expedition also employed photography, possibly its first use in the service of archaeology.

Sargon's capital city was over a mile square and its design became his preoccupation. The city's dimensions, for example, were based on the numerological value of Sargon's name.

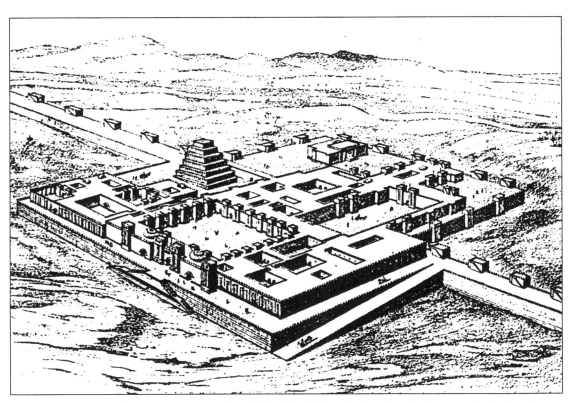

1.8   Bird's-eye view of Sargon's palace at Dur-Sharrukin (Khorsabad) as it might have once looked.   (Gaston Maspero, *The Passing of the Empires*, ed. A. H. Sayce [New York: Appleton, 1900])

Tablets describing the story of the palace's construction were deposited in its cornerstone with the identical text repeated on individual tablets of copper, lead, silver, gold, limestone, magnesite, and lapis lazuli, while paintings illustrated how cedarwood was imported from Lebanon to provide needed timber. Colossal stone bulls with wings and human heads guarded its entranceways. And the walls of the palace were decorated with so much sculpture that the panels, if laid end to end, would stretch for a mile.

Besides having a "palace without rival" (as Sargon dubbed it), the city also included temples dedicated to the gods of the sun and moon and to Nabu, god of writing and wisdom. In addition, a four-story ziggurat was erected that featured on the outside a spiral staircase for priests, with each of the four levels of the building painted a different color: white, black, red, and blue.

A later expedition by the University of Chicago's Oriental Institute recovered a document prized by historians, namely, the "Khorsabad King List," a list naming the rulers of Assyria from early antiquity down to Sargon's day, including the lengths of their reigns. Numbered among other significant finds were carved ivories (like those discovered in Nimrud), embossed bronze bands for door decoration (like those found in Balawat), curious weights in the shape of ducks, and small corroded bronze bells.

In his annals (that were also found), Sargon declared himself "Lord of the Four Quarters of the Earth" and bragged he had turned his enemies' cities into forgotten ruins. Today, his own city is a ruin, his winged bulls are corralled in Paris, and the bronze bells no longer ring.

Dura-Europos In 1921 while taking cover in a deserted ruin and digging in for a firefight with local Arabs, a company of British soldiers stationed in Syria hit upon some buried wall paintings. Subsequent investigations by the British, French, and Americans revealed the remains of an ancient city known to the natives as Dura and to the Hellenistic Greeks as Europos. The city was founded around 300 B.C.E. by a successor of Alexander the Great named Seleucus I. Located on a promontory overlooking the upper Euphrates, Dura-Europos became an important caravan station that was successively ruled by the Greeks, Parthians, Romans, and Persians. In the fourth century C.E., tradition tells, the Roman emperor Julian hunted lions among its otherwise lifeless remains.

Although archaeologists uncovered the remains of a typical Near Eastern city from Greco-Roman times—houses and temples, a marketplace, and public baths—their most sensational discoveries were a Jewish synagogue and a Christian church. Both date to the third century C.E. and are among the oldest ever found. Both are also decorated in murals such as those unearthed by the British army. The themes of the synagogue murals are drawn from the Old Testament and depict Abraham preparing to sacrifice Isaac, Moses standing before the burning bush, and King David playing on his harp, as well as other biblical scenes. The themes of the church murals come from both the Old and the New Testament: the sinful story of Adam and Eve, the image of Jesus as Savior and the Good Shepherd, and the story of the Good Samaritan.

The finds from Dura-Europos are now in the collections of the Yale University Art Gallery and the Damascus Museum.

Eridu Set in the marshes of the lower Euphrates, Eridu was Sumeria's most southern city and possibly its first. Tradition made it the earliest city to have a king before the days of the mythical Great Flood. Eridu's archaeological story can be traced back to at least the sixth millennium B.C.E. If the tradition of its antiquity is true, Eridu may well have been the first city on earth.

Eridu was a religious center sacred to Enki (or Ea, as he was known in Akkadian), the god of underground freshwater. A benefactor of humanity, Enki warned Ziusudra, the Sumerian equivalent of Noah, of the coming flood. The god's temple has been found and shows that it was rebuilt over the course of thousands of years. In its earliest phase (dating back to about 5500 B.C.E.), it measured about 12 by 15 feet, was made of mud brick, and featured a simple podium or altar for sacrifices and a niche meant to hold a statue of the god. To judge by evidence found in a later niche—fish bones and ashes scattered on the floor around the altar—the god's favorite meal was freshwater fish. The temple's antiquity makes it the oldest in Mesopotamian architectural and religious history.

The citizens of ancient Eridu were also proud of another structure: a mighty ziggurat dedicated around 2100 B.C.E. by Ur-Nammu, king of Ur, and his son. Though its eroded platform stands only about 30 feet high today, its base of oven-baked brick measures over 150 by 200 feet and once supported a far more imposing superstructure.

The exploration of Eridu began with diggings by J. E. Taylor in 1854 and continued briefly after World War I and World War II. The site consists of a cluster of seven mounds, the largest of which is called Abu Shahrain, and lies about 14.5 miles southwest of the ancient city of Ur.

Eshnunna In the middle of Mesopotamia on the Diyala River, a tributary of the Tigris, the city of Eshnunna prospered during the third and second millennia B.C.E. Today its deserted remains lie about 48 miles northeast of modern Baghdad.

The excavations of Eshnunna were carried out in the 1930s under the auspices of the University of Chicago's Oriental Institute. The expedition was led by Henri Frankfort.

The major discovery was that of a temple, possibly dedicated to Abu, a god of vegetation. Buried in its floor was a cache of gypsum figurines, representing how the Sumerians saw themselves when in the presence of a god. With large round eyes wide open, they stand attentively, their hands clasped over their chests. The statues may have functioned as votive figurines or miniature sculptural surrogates for actual worshipers, which by their eternal presence in the temple would symbolize the perpetual piety of the Sumerian men and women they portrayed. The largest statue, some 30 inches tall, may in fact represent the god Abu himself, and another his divine wife, though this is by no means certain.

In another temple lay pottery vessels decorated with images of serpents. These vessels may have once held real serpents that figured in ritual.

Other discoveries at Eshnunna include a horde of artifacts of silver and lapis lazuli buried under the floor of a palace (to safeguard them from vandals?). Elsewhere seal-stones were found that suggest trade between Mesopotamia and the Indus Valley: the seals are carved in the Indian style and depict elephants and other animals like the crocodile and rhinoceros, not native to Iraq. Less exotic but no less illuminating are some small children's toys that remind us that the ancient Mesopotamians were not artifacts in a museum but human like ourselves. In the streets of Eshnunna 5,000 years ago the sound of children playing could be heard.

Girsu Called Tello today, the ruins of ancient Girsu were the first in Mesopotamia to offer evidence of Sumerian civilization. In addition, Girsu became the first Sumerian site to be thoroughly investigated by archaeologists. Exploration by the French began in 1877 and continued for a total of 20 seasons. Sadly, the site was also persistently raided by looters.

Girsu is located in southern Mesopotamia midway between the Tigris and Euphrates. In the third millennium B.C.E. it was allied with two nearby cities connected by waterway: Nina-Sirara (modern Zurghul) and Lagash (modern Al-Hiba), the latter of which served as leader.

Girsa's patron god was Ningirsu ("Lord of Girsu"), whose temple was lavishly renovated by Lagash's leader, Gudea. The exact location of the temple has not been identified, but its ornate construction—employing cedar wood, gold, and precious stones—is described in detail by Gudea in a surviving celebratory inscription. Besides the inscription, the city yielded a grand total of over 40,000 cuneiform tablets.

Two striking works of sculptural art have also been found: a stone relief portraying Ur-Nanshe, ruler of Lagash, piously carrying a basket on his head filled with clay to make bricks for a new temple; and the Stele of the Vultures, depicting his son's military triumph. The stele gets its name from a section that shows the heads and limbs of dead enemy soldiers being carried off by hungry vultures.

Today's Tello is a desolate heap picked over by archaeologist and looter alike, hardly a temptation to the contemporary bird of prey.

Guzana Situated at the headwaters of the Khabur River near the foothills of the Taurus Mountains and close to the modern border between Syria and Turkey, Guzana was first settled in the sixth millennium B.C.E. Its inhabitants produced a distinctive style of pottery marked by lustrous geometric designs painted in red, black, and white. The style is called Halaf from Tell Halaf, the Arabic name for the settlement's ruins. Samples of this pottery have been found widely distributed in sites in northern Syria and northern Iraq, the result either of trade or of multiple settlements by a common culture.

By the first millennium B.C.E., Guzana had become the capital city of an independent Aramaean state but was soon absorbed into the Assyrian Empire. Dating to these historical times are the remains of a palace elaborately decorated by sculpted panels of stone and adorned with full-scale figures. Alternating between black basalt and white limestone, the slabs show a variety of action scenes depicting hunting and war. Mythological images also appear. The desert scorpion was a special source of inspiration: one of the panels features a fantastic creature half-scorpion, half-man; while at the entrance to the palace stands a human-headed bird with a scorpion stinger.

The Aleppo Museum now houses this mythic menagerie.

Hatra The people of the desert city of Hatra worshiped the sun, to whom they erected a glorious temple, a god who watched over them in times of siege. Under the protection of the Parthians, the city grew rich between 100 and 300 C.E. In the second century it was twice besieged by Roman armies that endured the blistering heat and suffered from swarms of flies that attacked their food and drink. The defenders were also adept at using the ancient equivalent of napalm, pouring down from their walls flaming bitumen or naphtha on the enemy troops below. Roman determination motivated by greed, however, eventually won the day, and the temple of the mighty sun was sacked.

The city was captured again in the third century C.E. by the Sassanians. According to the story, the daughter of Hatra's king revealed to the king of the Sassanians the talisman that magically protected her father's city. After Hatra's capture, the Sassanian king—who had first intended to marry the princess—had second thoughts when he reflected on how readily she had betrayed her own father. So instead of marrying her, he killed her by tying her hair to the tail of a wild stallion.

It still takes a trek across the desert to reach Hatra, or Al-Hadr as its ruins are known today.

Imgur-Enlil Imgur-Enlil, or Balawat as it is better known, lies in northern Iraq about nine miles northeast of ancient Nimrud and about 20 miles southeast of modern Mosul. In 1878, following a chance discovery by a local gravedigger, archaeologist Hormuzd Rassam unearthed a series of bronze bands that once decorated two sets of monumental doors from a ninth-century B.C.E. Assyrian palace. According to their inscriptions, the bands from one set date to the days of Ashurnasirpal II; the bands of the other, to the time of his son, Shalmaneser III. Embossed and incised on the bands are detailed scenes from the monarchs' military campaigns. A further set of bronze-banded doors was found by archaeologist Max Mallowan digging in the 1950s in the ruins of a Balawat temple dedicated to the god Mamu. Ashurnasirpal had piously installed them in the god's honor.

Isin Beginning in 2017 B.C.E. and continuing for two centuries, Isin was one of the leading imperialistic states of southern Mesopotamia, until its conquest by Hammurabi in 1787 B.C.E. Dating to its Golden Age is the Sumerian law code of its 19th-century B.C.E. ruler, Lipit-Ishtar. Almost every one of the surviving statutes of Lipit-Ishtar's code is echoed in the later, but more famous, code of Hammurabi. Today the ruins of Isin lie about 124 miles south-southeast of Baghdad.

The city of Isin was home to the goddess Gula, the Mesopotamian goddess of healing. Archaeologists have found her temple, which stood at the highest point of the city. Like Epidaurus in ancient Greece and Lourdes in France, the city attracted individuals in search of miraculous cures. A figurine was found near the temple that showed a man kneeling and holding his back. The statuette may have been a gift to the goddess given in gratitude for her divine intervention in alleviating his pain. Some skeletons found at the site bear signs of stroke and of traumatic injuries to the skull. A deliberate opening in the right parietal bone of one skull points to an operation called trepanation that may have optimistically been performed to cure a persistent and severe headache.

One of the most curious discoveries at Isin is a whale bone, reminiscent of the story of Jonah, whose missionary activity took place in Mesopotamia.

Eventually, the ruins of Isin were swallowed not by a whale but by a marsh, and they were called Ishan Bahriyat, "The Monument Drowned by the Sea."

Jemdet Nasr The last cultural era of southern Mesopotamia prior to the full flowering of urban life is called the Jemdet Nasr period (about 3500–3000 B.C.E.). The term stems from the Arabic name for a two-mound site located about 62 miles south of Baghdad and first explored in 1925.

At the site there were discovered some of the earliest inscribed tablets ever found in Mesopotamia, second in age only to tablets uncovered at Uruk. The style of writing is called proto-cuneiform, the world's oldest writing system and the ancestor of the more developed style that came to dominate the Mideastern world for three millennia. A monogram found on many Jemdet Nasr artifacts—a five-pointed star with the phonetic value "UB"—may point to the original name of the site. The tablets are administrative in nature and concern the management of agricultural property, probably by temple officials. Different counting systems are used, including the sexigesimal (based on the number 60) that became fundamental to Sumerian mathematics and is the origin of our 60-minute hour and 360-degree circle. On some tablets, a seal-stone impression gives a list of southern Mesopotamian cities (including Larsa, Nippur, Ur, and Uruk), evidence of economic cooperation among urban centers, reinforced by the prevalence of a common style of pottery once used by the people who lived in the area.

Kalhu Better known by its Arabic name Nimrud, Kalhu was founded in the 13th century B.C.E. and in the ninth became the capital of the Assyrian Empire, a position it held for 150 years. Even when the capital was eventually moved, Kalhu on the Tigris remained a city of prominence, covering 16 square miles and girded by a wall over 4.5 miles long composed of 70 million bricks. It is still one of the largest ancient cities in Iraq.

Austen Henry Layard was the first European to recognize the historic importance of the city's ruins. Excavations commenced in the mid 1800s and were renewed by a British expedition between 1949 and 1963 under the leadership of Max Mallowan. Digging and restoration

has continued under the auspices of the Iraq Department of Antiquities.

After Ashurnasirpal II chose Kalhu as his capital, he lavished great attention upon the city, building the defensive walls and a magnificent canal. The construction of his palace (the so-called Northwest Palace) took 15 years and was celebrated by a 10-day party. As Ashurnasirpal himself tells in an inscription, he invited from all corners of the land 69,754 guests who consumed 2,200 oxen, 16,000 sheep, 10,000 skins of wine, and 10,000 barrels of beer. The palace was occupied by later Assyrian kings and, until recently, still held their queens, buried beneath the floor in tombs along with 1,500 pieces of golden jewelry weighing a total of 100 pounds. Later kings also built separate palaces in Kalhu. Among them was Shalmaneser III who built one to the southeast. Dubbed "Fort Shalmaneser" by the

1.9   A view of the Assyrian capital of Kalhu (Nimrud) in the days of its splendor, as conceived in a reconstruction by artist James Fergusson.   (Austen Henry Layard, *A Second Series of the Monuments of Nineveh* [London: John Murray, 1853])

British, it featured an armory and a parade ground for reviewing troops as well as a residence for the royal harem.

Temples at Kalhu include a ziggurat and a temple dedicated to the hero Ninurta, and a separate temple dedicated to the god Nabu and his consort built by Queen Sammu-ramat, the inspiration for the legendary Semiramis.

Recovered from the bottoms of wells where they were mysteriously hurled were panels of masterfully carved ivory that once decorated wooden furniture. One portrays a woman's face with a Mona Lisa smile.

Numbered among miscellaneous but fascinating discoveries are wooden "writing boards" that were once coated with wax and inscribed with a stylus (the ancient equivalent of a reusable "magic slate"), bronze fittings from a horse's bridle, and a miniature bronze and iron fortress (a toy for a prince?) fashioned with turrets and wheels like the portable machinery used in a siege.

Real soldiers, not toy ones, however, were responsible for Kalhu's fall when the city was captured and destroyed by the Medes in 612 B.C.E.

Today, the ruins known as Nimrud stand on a bluff 21 miles southeast of Mosul. By a kind of poetic justice, this former capital of armed Assyrian might now goes by the name of a mighty hunter who once roamed the earth and whose fame is recalled in the Bible and Koran: Nimrod.

Kar-Tukulti-Ninurta   When the 13th-century B.C.E. Assyrian king Tukulti-Ninurta triumphed over Babylon, he built a new city on the Tigris and named it for himself. To thank Assyria's national god, Ashur, for giving him victory, he built the god a great temple and ziggurat, but he also took time out to build himself a palace on an imposing terrace, a palace resplendent with mythological friezes and frescos painted in red, white, blue, and

black. The city was abandoned when he died. The Tigris still flows nearby, 85 miles south of Mosul.

Khorsabad   See Dur-Sharrukin.

Kish   In Mesopotamian memory, the first kings who ruled after the primordial flood were the kings of Kish. That there was a devastating flood early in the city's history is demonstrated in the depths of the mound by a 1.5-foot-thick layer of river mud. Such layers are indeed found at other sites in Mesopotamia but, because they date to different time periods, they point to localized floods rather than a universal one such as is described in Mesopotamian literature and the Bible.

About 85 miles south of the present-day city of Baghdad, ancient Kish rose from its flood to become one of the leading city-states of early Sumer. Graves have been found like those at Ur in which the dead were interred with chariots, garaged for their enjoyment in the afterlife.

A temple and ziggurat dating to the first half of the second millennium B.C.E. honored Kish's patron deity, the warrior god Zababa. Dating to the same period also are the remains of a school for scribes.

Kutha   Situated 25 miles northeast of ancient Babylon, Kutha was one of Babylonia's most important religious centers. Home of the cult of the dead, its chief temple honored the netherworld god Nergal. Today the city's ruins go by the name of Tell Ibrahim.

Lagash   Covering over two square miles, the mound known as Tell al-Hiba constitutes one of the largest ghost towns of the ancient Near East. Located approximately 120 miles northwest of Basra, the site was once the Sumerian city of Lagash. Through wars of conquest waged during the second half of the third millennium B.C.E., the state of Lagash held sway over most of Sumer. Among the leaders of its imperialistic adventures were Ur-Nanshe, his grandson Eannatum, and the "photogenic" and ego-driven Gudea, whose sculptured portraits abound. Appropriately, the patron deity of Lagash was Ningirsu, the war god. The remains of his temple as well as those of the temple of Inanna were found in excavations begun by German archaeologists in 1887 and renewed by an American expedition in the 1960s. Lagash was allied with the nearby cities of Girsu (Tello) and Nina-Sirara (Zurghul).

Larak   Along with Bad-tibira, Eridu, Shuruppak, and Sippar, Larak was one of the great cities of Sumer before the days of the flood recalled in Mesopotamian legend. The city was also the earthly home of Pabilsag, divine husband of Ninisina, the Sumerian goddess of healing.

Larsa   Ancient Larsa was located near the Euphrates between Uruk and Ur. Following the fall of Ur's Third Dynasty, the city-states of Larsa and Isin vied for control of southern Mesopotamia, a rivalry that occupied the first two centuries of the second millennium B.C.E. Larsa finally conquered Isin but was in turn conquered by Hammurabi of Babylon. Hammurabi's siege of Larsa lasted six months until the city fell. Its king, Rim-Sin, had ruled for 60 years.

The rising and setting of Larsa's power was ironically presaged by its largest sanctuary, the temple of Shamash, god of the sun. The transience of its glory is also symbolized by the 19th-century B.C.E. palace of King Nur-Adad, a palace that was built but never occupied.

Today the ruins of Larsa go by the name of Tell Senkereh. Excavations by the French ended in 1991 with the outbreak of the Gulf War.

Mari   In 1933, Syrian peasants digging a grave in a deserted mound found a headless statue. The mound where the peasants dug that first fortuitous grave is today called Tell Hariri, almost midway between Damascus and Baghdad. Probing the mound for more artifacts, French archaeologists later found the remains of an ancient city called Mari, the capital of a kingdom that had flourished between the beginning of the third millennium B.C.E. and the beginning of the second. Situated on the upper Euphrates, it had grown rich by exacting taxes from caravans and river traffic that flowed between Syria and Babylonia.

At its height, its king was Zimri-Lim, who resided in an elaborate two-story palace that contained more than 250 rooms on the ground floor alone. Decorated with wall paintings showing scenes of royal investiture and ritual sacrifice, the building featured an open courtyard with a symbol of fertility and abundance as its centerpiece: an artificial palm tree fashioned of bronze and silver plates attached to an armature of natural wood. In one room stood a stone statue of a robed goddess holding a vase. Hidden within the statue was a channel that permitted piped-in water to cascade down from the vase, emblematic of water's life-giving blessings and the favor of the gods that made it available. A special chapel was reserved for Ishtar as was another sanctuary dedicated to a divine champion whose identity is lost but who was represented by an almost life-sized warrior's head carved from alabaster, dressed for battle with a tight-fitting helmet and chinstrap. In the palace archives, more than 20,000 cuneiform tablets were found, revealing details of everyday life in the kingdom and including correspondence between Zimri-Lim and his self-styled "brother," Hammurabi of Babylon.

In unbrotherly fashion, Hammurabi captured the city in 1760 B.C.E. and destroyed the palace after first looting it. Ironically, the walls he knocked down buried and preserved many paintings and other artifacts the archaeologists would later find.

Nevertheless, despite the ravages of man and nature, the palace is—in the words of its latest excavator, Jean-Claude Margueron—"the best known, the best preserved, and the richest . . . of all the palaces . . . of the entire Bronze Age" in the Near East (Margueron 1995: 885), affording us a vision not only of Zimri-Lim's world but also the world of his contemporary rival, Hammurabi, whose own palace suffered far more at the hands of time. Indeed, as Margueron noted of Mari, "no other site has been so rich in evidence of a millennium of Mesopotamian civilization" (Margueron 1997: 416).

Neribtum Tell Ishchali, 10 miles east of Baghdad on the Diyala River, bears the remains of ancient Neribtum. Excavations in the 1930s by the University of Chicago's Oriental Institute uncovered the ruins of the temple of Ishtar-Kititum. Ishtar, called Inanna in Sumerian, was the goddess of sexuality and war and the most important goddess in Mesopotamian religion. The name Kititum may connect her worship with another city in Mesopotamia. An alternative is that it echoes the name of Kition, a city on Cyprus, the island that was the home to the cult of Aphrodite, the Greek goddess of the erotic and the Hellenic equivalent of Ishtar/Inanna.

Discovered in the temple was a curious three-inch-tall figurine of a monkey carved out of alabaster. Monkeys were not native to Mesopotamia, so the artist either saw one when he was traveling (in India or Egypt, where monkeys existed, or in the Aegean, where they are pictured in Minoan art) or saw one that had been imported as an exotic pet. The statuette dates to sometime between 2000 and 1800 B.C.E.

Another work of art traceable to Neribtum is a 6.5-inch-tall bronze figurine of an unknown god. He had four bearded faces and stands with his foot on a sacrificial ram.

Nimrud See Kalhu.

Nina-Sirara Nina-Sirara (or, more simply, Nina) together with the nearby Sumerian cities of Girsu and Lagash formed the city-state of Lagash, which played a dominant role in the politics of southern Mesopotamia during the early third millennium B.C.E. The ruins of Nina, now called Zurghul, lie about 114 miles northwest of Basra. Digging there in 1887, German archaeologist Robert Koldewey found the remains of a temple to Nanshe. Sumerian hymns tell us Nanshe was a goddess who cared passionately about social justice. She looked out for the helpless, especially poor widows and orphans, and she hated those who stole and cheated others. Though her temple was ultimately abandoned, the ethical principles she stood for were eventually incorporated into Mesopotamian law.

Nineveh See Ninua.

Ninua Encroached upon by the urban sprawl of modern Mosul, the remains of ancient Nineveh (or Ninua, as it was originally named) lie just east of the Tigris. There are two prominent mounds: Tell Kuyunjik to the north and Tell Nebi Yunus to the south. Since the earliest excavations in the 1840s and 1850s (by Botta, Layard, Rassam, and Loftus), digging has focused on Kuyunjik and uncovered two palaces. Probes have shown that Nebi Yunus was very likely the site of a royal arsenal, but full-scale excavation has been precluded because the site is revered by Muslims (as its Arabic name denotes) as the tomb of Jonah, the reluctant biblical prophet who came to save the Ninevites from their sins.

At the end of the eighth century B.C.E., Sennacherib chose Nineveh to be the new capital of the Assyrian Empire. He proceeded to surround it with a seven-mile-long wall designed to terrify and deter any enemy. Within, he constructed a palace "without rival." The building's main axis was one-third of a mile in length. It featured a portico consisting of solid bronze columns resting on the backs of solid bronze lions and bulls, each of which weighed 43 tons. Inside, the palace was adorned with carved reliefs showing the king in the process of erecting colossal monuments or waging war against Assyria's enemies (including a depiction of his siege of the Judaean city of Lachish, replete with a gory portrait of Jewish captives impaled on stakes). Because of exposure to the elements and the depredations of modern looters, many panels still at the site have crumbled beyond recognition or have been broken into profitable pieces for sale on the illicit antiquities market. The sculptures of Sennacherib's throne-room suite have been violated in this way. Indeed, in lieu of tight on-site security, the best way to safeguard pieces not already in museums is, paradoxically, to rebury them.

North of Sennacherib's palace, his grandson, Ashurnasirpal, built another. It too was decorated with sculptural reliefs, including a powerful series that shows the monarch hunting lions from his chariot and, with his sword, stabbing one in hand-to-paw combat. Ashurnasirpal's royal library was also discovered. Comprised of 24,000 cuneiform tablets, it is a priceless compendium of Assyrian diplomacy, science, and literature. Transported to the British Museum, some of the tablets were deciphered by a specialist named George Smith, who found an epic account of a great flood that strikingly paralleled the flood story in Genesis. Regrettably, because of a cracked tablet, the end of the story was missing. Sponsored by a London newspaper, Smith traveled to Nineveh and within days recovered the missing piece—a needle in a Nineveh haystack.

Ancient Nineveh must have been a wonder to behold. The biblical book of Jonah says the city took three days to cross on foot. And the annals of Nineveh's kings tell how they enriched the city with marvelous botanical and zoological gardens and parks.

But in the summer of 612 B.C.E. despite its splendor and wealth (or perhaps because of them), the city was attacked by the Babylonians and Medes. Despite its "terrifying" wall, it fell after a three months' siege and was sacked. In its ransacked palace, the victorious Babylonian king held court, before ordering the city flooded by river water to pay back the Assyrians for what Sennacherib himself had done to Babylon decades before. He then marched proudly home with an urn of Nineveh's ashes in his luggage.

The fall of Nineveh teaches how tenuous, despite all outward signs, a nation's power is, and how brutal its end can be. The biblical prophet Nahum (3:1–3) visualized the final scene:

> The whip cracks and the wheel rattles,
> The horse bolts and the chariot bounds,
> The driver soars through air.
> The sword flashes and the spearpoint gleams.
> The body count rises and the cadaver heap
>   mounts.
> There is no end to corpses.
> They stumble on the pile.

Skeletons still lay tangled in the dust beside a yawning gate 26 centuries later.

Nippur Unlike other cities that were guided by rulers who often had imperialistic ambitions, the Sumerian city of Nippur never possessed a ruling dynasty of its own. Instead, Nippur maintained a position of political neutrality while acting as a religious center to which other cities and rulers turned. Nippur enjoyed this preeminence because it served as the site of the most important temple of the god Enlil, regarded from the third millennium B.C.E. as the head of the Sumerian pantheon. Enlil's temple was called the Ekur, or "Mountain House," a name that suggests the god's worship emanated from the mountainous region north and east of Sumer's alluvial plain. Indeed, of the major cities of Sumer, Nippur was the farthest north. A mountain-like ziggurat stood near Enlil's temple. In addition, Nippur contained a temple to Enlil's divine daughter, Inanna.

Besides finding the remains of these sacred structures, archaeologists unearthed a campus for student scribes and their teachers. Called "Tablet Hill" by its discoverers, this scribal quarter has yielded 60,000 cuneiform tablets that contain extracts from every major work of Sumerian literature, including a Sumerian version of the Great Flood story. Another remarkable document is a map (in clay) of the city of Nippur itself, marking the locations of various monuments.

Founded as a settlement in the early sixth millennium B.C.E., Nippur's longevity extended to 800 C.E. Because of its lengthy habitation and the buildup of occupational debris, the ruins of Nippur now rise up almost 70 feet above the surrounding plain, some 100 miles southwest of Baghdad. Longevity made the city itself a minor mountain of civilization's past.

Nuzu Today a cluster of tells set among the oil fields of northeastern Iraq, the community of Nuzu (also spelled Nuzi) was once a flourishing town in the empire of the Mitanni, an imperialistic people who vied with the Egyptians for the riches of the Levant. Its population was mostly Hurrian.

As a center for provincial administration, it boasted an impressive government house, adorned with frescoes and paved in marble. In addition, the building had a system of drainage and plumbing advanced for its time, including flush toilets with marble seats. Doors were studded with copper nails plated in silver.

Metalwork found elsewhere at the site includes bronze scales that comprised armor for the men and horses of Nuzu's chariot corps, and a bronze dagger with a hilt inlaid with iron, in those days a rare and precious metal.

The most notable finds, however, proved to be cuneiform tablets. Numbering more than 20,000, these tablets revealed the public and private life of the community over the course of five or six generations, from the mid-15th to the mid-14th centuries B.C.E. They encompass information about workers and salaries, commodities and taxes, and the active role of freeborn women in business. The customs that these tablets shed light on also illuminate the social milieu of the world in which the Hebrew patriarchs lived.

One of the most poignant discoveries comes from a private home: the burial of an infant beneath a jar shaped like a mother's breast.

Puzrish-Dagan Known to archaeologists as Drehem, this Sumerian city served as a livestock depot for nearby Nippur. Some 100,000 cuneiform tablets have been unearthed recording orders, sales, and shipments of animals.

Qalat Jarmo The principles of agriculture may have been discovered not in the alluvial plains of the southern Tigris and Euphrates but in the hill country, well watered by rain, to the north where cereal grain grew wild. Just such a site was investigated by Robert and Linda Braidwood between 1948 and 1955. At Jarmo, located in the foothills of the Zagros Mountains east of Kirkuk, they found evidence of an early agricultural community that had been founded in the seventh millennium B.C.E. The village was small, measuring only about 300 by 450 feet. There the inhabitants had cultivated emmer wheat, barley, peas, and lentils, and they raised domesticated sheep and goats. They lived in multiroom houses with pre-brick walls of packed mud (known as *tauf* or *pisé*) supported on stone foundations. By the sixth millennium B.C.E. they were making pottery; before that, they had waterproofed baskets with sticky bitumen and decorated them with colored stones.

Among the most intriguing discoveries were small pieces of clay fashioned into geometric shapes. The villagers of Jarmo may have used them as tokens for the purpose of primitive accounting. Some scholars believe that from the shapes of such early tokens came the symbols that became the basis of writing some 2,500 years later.

Samarra   Like Jarmo, Samarra began as a prehistoric farming community in the seventh millennium B.C.E. But because it was located in central Mesopotamia where rainfall was too scant to grow crops, Samarra used irrigation canals to draw upon the adjacent waters of the Tigris. Samarra ware is its most distinctive artifact: pottery with precisely painted geometric bands on the outside, and animate figures on the inside, including human beings (some dancing) and insects such as spiders and scorpions arranged in bands.

Samarra's Golden Age, however, would have to wait another 8,000 years. It became a major urban center in Islamic times, serving in the ninth century C.E. as the capital of the Abbasid caliphs, a distinction it held for over 50 years. Today the ruins of that city are still impressive, covering 35 square miles and stretching for 31 miles along the Tigris. For a time Samarra was the proud home of what was then the largest mosque in Islam, marked by a 170-foot-tall minaret wrapped in a spiral ramp. This minaret's inspiration may have been the ziggurat of ancient Dur-Sharrukin, which also featured a spiral ramp. The minaret, in turn, became a source of inspiration for later European painters, who, in the absence of a towering structure at Babylon, modeled Babel's Tower on Samarra's.

The mosque and minaret still stand 60 miles north of Baghdad, and they constitute an enduring symbol of both aesthetic continuity and spiritual evolution.

Shaduppum   Founded during the days of Sargon of Akkad in the late third millennium B.C.E., the city of Shaduppum rose to prominence during the second. A twin temple with an entrance flanked by terra-cotta lions stood just inside the city's main gate. The temple was dedicated to Nidaba, the Sumerian patron goddess of writing and recordkeeping, and her divine consort, Haia. Fittingly, numerous cuneiform tablets have been found in the houses of the city. Among them are two that contain the text of a law code promulgated by Bilalama, the ruler of Eshnunna, who lived during the first half of the 18th century B.C.E., two centuries before the great Hammurabi. Notwithstanding its earlier date, Bilalama's code is the more progressive, accepting monetary compensation for violent acts rather than Hammurabi's "eye for an eye." Today, the ruins of ancient Shaduppum, called Tell Harmal, lie on the outskirts of Baghdad.

Shubat-Enlil   Called Shekhna when the Akkadians used to administer the upper Tigris, the city was later chosen as capital by the Amorite empire-builder Shamshi-Adad I around 1800 B.C.E. He then renamed it Shubat-Enlil. According to the archives at Mari, he beautified this and other cities in his kingdom with transplanted palms, cypresses, and myrtles. The archives of Shubat-Enlil contain tablets concerned not with trees but with beer—specifically, the maintenance of an adequate stock of royal beer for the king's pleasure. When Shamshi-Adad was not drinking, he was conquering, and boasted of having set up a stele with his name on it in far-off Lebanon on the shore of the Mediterranean Sea. About 50 years after his death, his capital city was destroyed by another man of ambition, the Babylonian king Samsuiluna. Shubat-Enlil would remain deserted until the early 20th century C.E., when a Kurdish village, Tell Leilan, grew up on its ruins.

Shuruppak In the Sumerian version of the flood story, the role of Noah is played by a prince named Ziusudra. According to a Sumerian chronicle, Ziusudra's father was the last king to rule Shuruppak before the deluge came. Evidence of such a deluge was found by archaeologists digging at the site: a two-foot-thick layer of mud dating to about 2750 B.C.E. that once covered the entire city—though not all of Sumer, let alone the world. The memory of the Shuruppak flood, however, may have been vivid enough to cause a poet to cast a Shuruppaker in the starring role in that diluvian drama.

Besides mud, the archaeologists found post-disaster real estate documents and grain-storage silos, showing that life went on.

The remains of Shuruppak are today called Fara, situated about halfway between Baghdad and Basra.

Sippar The worship of the sun gave ancient Sippar its claim to fame, for the city was the home of the most revered temple to the sun-god (Utu in Sumerian, and Shamash in Akkadian). Called the "White Temple" because of the exterior whitewashing that reflected the sun's gleaming rays, it was linked to a convent for the priestesses who served the god. Archaeologists have found rows of two-room houses on parallel streets in the city's religious quarter that may well be the remains of their residence. Tradition records that wealthy Mesopotamian families and even kings sent their daughters to serve the god. The everyday spiritual and commercial activities of the temple are illustrated by tens of thousands of cuneiform tablets that have been uncovered, many still stacked in the brick wall-cabinets where they were stored. Thousands more crumbled when they were unearthed, partly because the early methods used to excavate them were crude but also partly because the scribes of Sippar had never baked them in ovens to make them hard. Instead, ironically, they had relied on Shamash to dry them.

Before the Great Flood, Sumerian chronicles tell us, Sippar was one of five cities chosen by divine providence to rule the land of Sumer. The city was strategically located on the Euphrates where it comes closest to the Tigris; indeed, the Euphrates was often called "the Sippar River." To better fortify his capital city of Babylon, Nebuchadnezzar constructed an east-west wall from river to river just north of Sippar. Today, the remains of this city of the sun bleach in its rays at a place called Tell Abu Habah, 16 miles or so south of modern Baghdad.

Sippar-Amnanum Close by Sippar was its twin city, Sippar-Amnanum (modern Tell ed-Der), where a goddess named Annunitum was worshiped. Though no convent was found, archaeologists did discover the home of the goddess' chief singer of dirges, one Ur-Utu. Two thousand tablets from the house detail the religious duties and lucrative business dealings of this cleric. The building was destroyed by fire in 1629 B.C.E. to judge by the latest date on the documents. By a twist of fate, the heat of the fire baked the tablets and thus preserved them. We may not have a CD of Ur-Utu's plaintive droning, but at least we have his diary written in clay.

Tell Arpachiyeh Near ancient Nineveh is a small prehistoric site that flourished between 6000 and 5000 B.C.E. Its people lived in igloo or keyhole-shaped huts that were made of clay. The villagers were adept at making a fine type of pottery with multicolored linear decoration. On the floor of what seems to have been a craftsman's shop were found bone tools used for sculpting clay, palettes for mixing colors, a piece of red ochre, and fragments of shattered bowls, some of which were adorned with painted flowers and dancing girls. These remains were intermingled with the ashes of a fire that had destroyed the shop and caused its abandonment. As at another prehistoric site, Yarim Tepe, some of the graves at Tell

Arpachiyeh are puzzling because the buried skeletons were found headless.

Tell Brak On the upper Khabur 120 miles west of modern Mosul, Tell Brak prospered from its location on the ancient trade route for metals. Its main temple featured an altar decorated with alternating bands of colored stone and gold. The gold bands were attached with silver nails with gold-plated heads. The temple itself has been dubbed the "Eye" Temple because of the votive figurines it contained. Sculpted from clay or stone and measuring one to four inches tall, these hauntingly abstract statuettes have heads dominated by large hollow-pupiled eyes. Though 300 of these figures have been unearthed intact, there are enough fragments to suggest some 20,000 may have once stood in the shrine. The temple and its contents have been dated to the fourth millennium B.C.E., but what god or goddess they honored we do not know. Even the ancient name of Tell Brak is a mystery.

Tell Fakhariyeh Tell Fakhariyeh is located in present-day Syria near the springs that feed the Khabur River, in what was once northern Mesopotamia. For a time, archaeologists believed that the ruins might be the site of Washukanni, the capital of the empire of the Mitanni, a people who were once the imperialistic rivals of the Egyptians for the control of the Levant. In 1979, however, a tractor plowing near the edge of the tell dislodged a 5.5-foot-tall basalt statue of an Aramaean king. On the statue was an inscription stating that it had been dedicated to the god Hadad of Sikani. Sikani was thus very probably the ancient name of the tell. Where the lost city of Washukanni is remains a mystery.

Tell Hassuna Situated 22 miles south of Mosul, Tell Hassuna is typical of small farming communities that existed in northern Mesopotamia and, indeed, much of the Near East during the late seventh and early sixth millennia B.C.E. In an age before metal, tools and weapons were made from stone. Grain was stored in bins, ground between flat rubbing stones, and baked into bread in clay ovens.

Like their contemporaries, the inhabitants of Tell Hassuna had learned how to construct high-temperature kilns. They found that pottery baked at higher temperatures lost its porosity and so could hold liquids, something not possible before.

Simple graves have been found in which the bodies of infants were interred in pottery jars, with other jars of food and drink set nearby to serve their childhood needs in the afterlife.

Tell al-Oueili Like Tell Hassuna, this site located near Larsa offers evidence of Neolithic life before the emergence of urban centers. But, unlike most Mesopotamian sites, people stopped living at Tell al-Oueili before the urban revolution began. As a result, archaeologists do not face the formidable task of having to dig down through the superimposed debris of later eras in order to reach the remains of Neolithic times. Besides evidence of the community's agricultural lifestyle, excavators have discovered bricks that amazingly bear the imprints of the ancient brickmakers' fingers. The earliest remains of Tell al-Oueili's life, however, lie submerged below the river valley's present water table.

Tell Qalinj Agha The northern Mesopotamian city now known as Tell Qalinj Agha prospered during the late fourth millennium B.C.E. The man-made terrace that supports its temple may be the north's earliest. One of the city's residential streets featured houses with outdoor ovens, a practical precaution against fire.

Tell al-Rimah Thirty-nine miles west of Nineveh lay a small city that thrived on trade in the late third and second millennia B.C.E. Its original name may have been Qatara or Karana. Its most prominent feature was a religious complex set atop a walled terrace, including an elaborate temple and an adjoining ziggurat. The exterior wall of the temple was enlivened with engaged columns of mud brick sculpted to resemble the trunks of palm trees. The braid-like columns of a temple at Shubat-Enlil (Tell Leilan) are in the same style. Inside Tell al-Rimah's temple are reliefs, including one with the grimacing Gorgon-like face of the monster Humbaba.

The remains of a small palace were also discovered at the site, and within it a cuneiform list enumerating the stores of wine in the royal wine cellar.

Tell es-Sawwan This agricultural community on the Tigris north of Baghdad was contemporary with the Neolithic villages of Jarmo and Hassuna. A total of 130 graves was found beneath the floor of one building, containing a disproportionately high number of children's burials. The building may have had special spiritual significance, but the high rate of infant mortality is unexplained.

Tell Taya Terra-cotta figurines of chariots, wheels, a horse's head, and a naked charioteer have been unearthed at this northern Iraqi site, which served as an important center for surrounding villages during the third millennium B.C.E. Its vitality continued into the next millennium as well, and on into Parthian and Sassanian times. Though part of the wall of its citadel collapsed into a dry river-bed and the site itself was deserted, the mound was resettled by villagers around 1000 C.E., but later abandoned. About 1940, a homesteader built a solitary house on top of the ruins, but when he died, it too was abandoned, and ownership of the site reverted to the descendants of the snakes and scorpions, which still slither across Taya's ancient potsherds.

Tell al-Ubaid Tell al-Ubaid was once a prosperous Sumerian city on the Euphrates 3.5 miles west of Ur. Like ancient Tutub (modern Khafaje), Tell Ubaid possessed a temple set on a terrace enclosed within an oval wall. The temple was dedicated in 2500 B.C.E. to Ninhursag, the Sumerian goddess of childbirth. Guarding the entranceway were eight fierce copper-skinned lions with shining, inlaid eyes. On the façade of the temple over its door hung an eight-foot-wide frieze hammered out of copper that showed a lion-headed eagle with wings outspread and flanked by antlered stags. Columns stood to either side, coated with black bitumen and inlaid with contrasting triangles of red limestone and mother-of-pearl, while the walls bloomed with an appliqué of flowers made of clay—altogether the most elaborate decoration to survive from any Sumerian temple. Less imposing but no less informative is another frieze, inlaid with shells, that shows the milking of cows, one of the mainstays of the community's economy.

From the early pottery of Tell al-Ubaid, which resembles the pottery of other sites of the same era, archaeologists developed the term "Ubaid" to describe the art and culture of Mesopotamia during the millennium and a half before 4000 B.C.E.

Tell Uqair Tell Uqair, northwest of ancient Nippur, is significant because of its "Painted Temple." Dating to the fourth millennium B.C.E., the temple gets its name from the wall paintings it contains. Especially striking are the pictures of powerful animals that decorate its altar: a bull, a leopard, and possibly a lion. Elevated on a high platform approached by steps, the temple was later demolished and filled in with mud brick so it could serve as the foundation for a still higher structure. Paradoxically, the bricks that it was packed with helped to preserve the colors on its interior walls and the endangered species in its sanctuary. Leopards, incidentally, still prowl the mountains of nearby Iran.

Tepe Gawra Tepe Gawra is located in the foothills of Kurdistan about 15 miles northeast of Mosul on a tributary of the Khosr River. The term "tepe" means mound in Kurdish or Turkish just as "tell" does in Arabic.

Tepe Gawra arose as a farming community around 6000 B.C.E. and was continually inhabited until about 1800 B.C.E. Thus its material remains provide archaeologists with an unbroken story of cultural development in northern Mesopotamia from the beginnings of agriculture down through the middle of the Bronze Age.

It is the dead who are the principal witnesses and their wordless testimony comes from their graves. Tepe Gawra's affluence is evident in the jewelry found on skeletons, worn on their heads and necks, their wrists and hands, their ankles and even knees. Unstrung by the disintegration of their strands, the beads lie in scattered heaps—25,000 beads in one tomb alone, shaped from turquoise, jadeite, and carnelian; from white faience, ivory, and shell; and from gold and electrum, an alloy of silver and gold. Five hundred of the beads are carved from precious blue lapis lazuli, a mineral imported from Afghanistan across a distance of 1,200 miles. Also notable among the grave goods is a miniature wolf's head fashioned from electrum, with ears attached by copper pins and a movable lower jaw jointed with pins of electrum.

A massive "Round House" may have served as a community center and grain storage bin as well as a storage depot for weapons: the pear-shaped mace-heads found on the floor date to the early fourth millennium B.C.E. and are among the earliest tools of war ever discovered in Mesopotamia. They lay among the embers of a fire that destroyed the structure, evidence perhaps of wartime conflagration.

Terqa Tell Ashara, the ruins of ancient Terqa, lie on the Euphrates in present-day Syria west of the Iraqi border. Politically subject to Mari, 42 miles to the southeast, Terqa became the capital of an independent kingdom after Mari's fall in 1761 B.C.E.

When Terqa was struck by a horde of locusts, the city's governor scooped them up and sent them to Mari's king as a gastronomic delight.

Terqa owed much of its fame to its temple to Dagan, the god of grain. Ninkarrak, the goddess of good health, also had a temple there. The goddess' pet was a dog, and a dog was found fittingly buried beside the altar of her sanctuary.

A school for scribes was also unearthed in the city. It featured a brick platform where the scribes knelt to shape tablets from the clay stored in an adjacent jar. A jar found in a private home was filled not with clay but with cloves, proof of trade between Mesopotamia and the Far East, where cloves were grown. Alas, the aroma of that household's cooking has long since vanished.

Til Barsip Many cities of Mesopotamia possessed palaces, but very few had wall paintings which survive. Til Barsip is just such an exception. The city was located about 70 miles northeast of Aleppo, Syria. Originally the capital of an Aramaean state, it was conquered by the Assyrians in the ninth century B.C.E. The conqueror, Shalmaneser III, then built an elaborate palace on the city's acropolis and ordered it decorated with murals. We can still see the king receiving tribute from his subjects or hunting lions from his chariot. Other scenes show prisoners of war being led to execution. The pictures are lent immediacy by vigorous sketching and colors that retain their vividness despite the passage of almost 3,000 years.

Tuttul Northwest of Terqa at the confluence of the Euphrates and the Balikh Rivers lay ancient Tuttul, called Tell Bi'a today. Here Sargon of Akkad (2334–2279 B.C.E.) worshiped Dagan and thanked him for giving him victory in his western campaigns. A later king, Shamshi-Adad I of Assyria (1809–1766 B.C.E.), built a palace here. His archives have been found along with scores of unburied skeletons, victims of war or epidemic. One tablet in the archives contained a Hurrian magic spell, but neither the right one to save the victims nor one potent enough to save the city itself: almost half of Tuttul has been washed away by the Euphrates.

Tutub Better known as Khafaje, the ancient city of Tutub lies nine miles east of Baghdad on the Diyala River, a tributary of the Tigris. The city is notable because its temple (once thought to be dedicated to the moon-god Sin) was constructed atop a double terrace, each level of which was enclosed within an oval wall. The "Temple Oval" dates to the fourth millennium B.C.E.

Umm Dabaghiyah At this site some 55 miles south-southwest of Mosul lie the remains of a Neolithic village dating to the late seventh and early sixth millennia B.C.E. From the large quantity of bones found there, the villagers seemed to have made a living slaughtering and processing onagers for their hides, sinews, and tail-hair. The animals are also pictured on the walls of the villager's houses. Judging by the hundreds upon hundreds of sling-shot pellets uncovered, the villagers also kept an ample store of weapons on hand in case of attack.

Umma The Sumerian cities of Umma and nearby Lagash clashed over territory in the third millennium B.C.E. Lagash's triumph is depicted on the Stele of the Vultures, where its soldiers tread over the corpses of Umma's men. Thousands of clay tablets have been unearthed at Umma, including one of the earliest of Mesopotamian calendars.

Ur Located along the Euphrates River in what is now southern Iraq, Ur was the setting for the most sensational discovery in the history of Mesopotamian archaeology, the discovery of "the Royal Graves of Ur" by Sir Leonard Woolley. Ranking in importance with the discovery of King Tut's tomb by Howard Carter in Egypt, the revelations at Ur were the result of meticulous excavations that began in 1922 (the year of Carter's achievement) and continued through 1934 under the joint sponsorship of the British Museum and the Uni-

1.10 Arab tribesmen sit before the remains of ancient Ur prior to its excavation by Woolley. (Rogers, A History of Babylonia and Assyria, 1915)

1.11 *Workmen stand on the stairways of Ur's ziggurat at the end of the second season of excavations.*
(University of Pennsylvania Museum Archives)

versity of Pennsylvania Museum, institutions that today, along with the Iraq Museum, share the treasures.

Digging in a 2,000-grave cemetery that had been turned into a rubbish heap in antiquity, Woolley unearthed the last resting place of a Sumerian warlord, Mes-kalam-dug. On his head was a gold helmet fashioned in the form of a wig backed by a golden chignon, a helmet fitted with earholes so the warlord could hear as well as command. At his waist lay a golden dagger and a lapis lazuli whetstone to keep it sharp. His vanity in the afterlife was served by a skin care kit that included golden tweezers.

Nearby rested the skeleton of a king guarded by spear-carrying sentries whose skulls were crushed by the weight of the earth that had borne upon them. Nine women (members of his harem?) lay there too with ornate headdresses of golden beech-leaves on their heads, and earrings like huge crescent moons. On the buried ramp that once led into the collapsed tomb were the remains of two four-wheeled wagons, the oldest wheeled vehicles in history ever found, along with their leather tires.

A later tomb had allowed Queen Puabi (or Shub-ad, as an earlier decipherment spelled it) to be interred near her husband. Inside was a game board for her eternal amusement and a disintegrating lyre held by a court musician. The lyre, its deep-toned sound box fashioned with a wooden bull's head covered in gold foil, was like two others found in her husband's tomb. The queen had a golden straw buried with her so she could sip a cooling drink while the music played.

In the largest burial pit of all, called the "Great Death Pit," Woolley found six armed guards and 68 serving women. They wore ribbons of gold or silver in their hair, except one woman who still held in her hand the coiled-up silver ribbon she was unable to fasten before the sleeping potion took hold that painlessly carried her away to the afterworld with her master.

More historically revealing than any other single artifact from Ur was the "Royal Standard of Ur," a pair of two inlaid panels set back to back that illustrated a battle in progress and the victory celebration that followed it. On one side, donkey-drawn chariots rumble over the bodies of the enemy dead; on the other, Ur's leaders drink beer and listen to music as captured livestock and prisoners of war are paraded by.

Altogether, Woolley uncovered the graves of 16 kings and queens who ruled Ur and its empire in the middle of the third millennium B.C.E. when the pyramids at Giza were being built. Though some scholars, given the absence of royal inscriptions, doubt they were really kings and queens, the magnificence of their wealth and the power radiating from it are undeniable.

Though Ur did not possess a pyramid to match Giza's, it did possess a ziggurat, the best preserved in Mesopotamia. Rebuilt at the end of the third millennium B.C.E. and again in the sixth century B.C.E. by later rulers, it rose in seven stages to a total height of 240 feet (half the height of Egypt's Great Pyramid) and featured a triple staircase at the front that enabled priests to ascend and honor Ur's patron deity, Nanna, the god of the moon.

In the course of his excavations, Woolley found an eight-foot-thick layer of mud sand-wiched between layers of occupational debris. Woolley first thought it might be evidence of the biblical flood, but later studies revealed other flood layers at other Mesopotamian sites dating to different time periods—proof of devastating local floods but not a simultaneous and universal one.

Another possible biblical tie-in is Ur's identification as the patriarch Abraham's hometown, called "Ur of the Chaldees" (i.e., the Chaldaeans) in Genesis. Other scholars, however, argue for a location of this city in northern Mesopotamia closer to Abraham's ancestral city of Harran; indeed, such an ancient city, called Ura, did once exist.

Even if stripped of its biblical claims to fame, Woolley's Ur is still a glittering example of Sumeria's golden age. Though its original lyres no longer sound, with our inner ear we can still hear their melodies.

Uruk Situated about 50 miles northwest of ancient Ur, the southern Mesopotamian city of Uruk is the home of a number of "firsts" in the country's archaeological story: the oldest examples of monumental stone architecture (made of imported limestone), the earliest cylinder seals, and the oldest examples of writing (a pictographic script that was the ancestor of later cuneiform)—all dating to the fourth millennium B.C.E. In addition, Uruk was the hometown of mythic heroes including Gilgamesh, who, tradition said, built its mighty walls that measured six miles in length. In the Old Testament the city is called Erech.

Founded in the late fifth millennium B.C.E., Uruk became Sumeria's most important urban center during the next millennium, exerting political and economic influence that reached throughout Mesopotamia. Its religious life was centered in two areas: the temple complex of Inanna, the goddess of love and war and the city's renowned patron; and the temple complex of the sky-god Anu, each with its own ziggurat. Sanctuaries to other gods have been found as well.

Discoveries in sculpture include the Warka Vase, carved with a procession of offerings to Inanna, and a life-size limestone "mask" portraying the now wigless head of a now eyeless goddess (perhaps Inanna herself).

Abandoned in the seventh century C.E., Uruk had a life-span of 5,000 years. Its oldest layers lie virtually unexplored, submerged deep in the mud of the alluvial plain from which its life once sprouted.

Yarim Tepe Southwest of Mosul lie a cluster of mounds called Yarim Tepe containing prehistoric remains dating between 7000 to 4500 B.C.E. Most striking are the graves. As in the graves of Tell Arpachiyeh, some 75 miles away, there is evidence that corpses were dismembered with the heads sometimes buried separately. One grave seems to be that of a hunter, judging by the buffalo skull and maceheads that were laid beside his body. As at Arpachiyeh, the inhabitants lived in igloo- or keyhole-shaped dwellings made of mud, brick, or stone.

Besides the many archaeological sites whose ancient names are known, many others stand in anonymous desolation. At the same time, ancient hymns celebrate the names of numerous cities whose locations have never been identified. It will remain for a future edition of this gazetteer to find these urban orphans a name and geographic home.

Indeed, archaeologists have uncovered only a tiny fraction of what still lies buried. As eminent archaeologist Robert McC. Adams points out: "We probably have some knowledge, other than having walked over the surface, of less than one percent and it may be one-tenth of one percent of existing sites. I myself must have mapped 5,000 mounds or something in that neighborhood. So the treasures to be unearthed over thousands of years to come are enormous."

READING

The Land and Its Rivers

Boiy 1999, Rowton 1969: watercourses; Butzer 1995: environmental change; Jacobsen 1982: agriculture and salinity; Lloyd 1955: landscape; Roaf 1990: geology and topography; Roux 1992: geographical setting.

Natural Resources

Forbes 1955–58: raw materials and their uses; Landsberger 1960, 1962: fauna; Oppenheim 1977: economic facts; Postgate and Powell 1992: timber; Potts 1997: material resources; Roaf 1990: agricultural resources.

Surrounding Countries

Cottrell 1957, Gordon and Rendsburg 1997: historical perspective; David 1998: Egypt; Ghirshman 1954: Iran; Roaf 1990: maps; Sasson 1995: historical, archaeological, and cultural studies of major nations of the ancient Near East.

Gazetteer

Amiet 1980: detailed descriptions of selected sites with plans and bibliography; Beek 1962:

atlas; Bienkowski and Millard 2000: concise descriptions of selected sites with bibliography; Lloyd 1978 and 1980: narrative description of selected sites; Meyer 1997: detailed descriptions of selected sites and bibliography; Pfeiffer 1966: descriptions of selected sites; Ravn 1942: Herodotus's description of Babylon; Roaf 1990: maps and precise locations; Sasson 1995: cultural studies of various sites and indexed references to those and others.

2

ARCHAEOLOGY
AND HISTORY

THE DISCOVERERS

The lost world of Mesopotamia would not have been found had it not been for the curiosity of travelers, the zeal of archaeologists, and the diligence of philologists. Without their efforts and writings, the ruined sites, buried treasures, and dead languages of the Sumerians, Babylonians, and Assyrians would have remained forgotten.

In the 19th century the field of archaeological exploration was dominated by the British and French because of the diplomatic influence and commercial interests they had in the area. In the late 19th and early 20th centuries, German and American archaeologists began to dig, inspired—as had been the British and French before them—by the prospect of unearthing impressive works of art and written records from the days of the Old Testament. In still later decades, the Iraqis themselves came to the fore, both to safeguard their national heritage from being carried off to foreign lands and to uncover for themselves the glories of their cultural past.

Listed below in alphabetical order are the names of some of the major explorers of ancient Mesopotamia to whom we are indebted for our present knowledge. However, because so much lies yet undiscovered or still awaits interpretation, it is a list that will need to be expanded by future generations.

Robert McC. Adams *20th-century American archaeologist.* Adams pioneered the art of surface reconnaissance in Mesopotamia, painstakingly identifying ancient settlement and irrigation patterns from their aboveground features and remains. In 2002, he was awarded the Archaeological Institute of America's Gold Medal for his lifelong work in exploring the evolution of civilization.

Walter Andrae *19th-century German archaeologist.* With the assistance of Julius Jordan and Arnold Noldeke, Andrae excavated the royal city of Ashur. Then, through his talent as an artist, he recaptured its original splendor in a series of drawings and paintings.

Ibn-Battuta *14th-century Berber geographer and traveler.* A contemporary of Marco Polo, Ibn-Battuta traveled to the far-flung corners of the world. In the course of his travels, he visited the ruins of Nineveh and in his writings described its walls and gates.

2.1   *An early 20th-century view of the ruins of Borsippa.* (Rogers, *A History of Babylonia and Assyria*, 1915)

Abbé de Beauchamp *18th-century French cleric.* While serving in Babylonia, he visited the ruins near Al-Hillah and reported that villagers had found buried reliefs and carved "idols."

Gertrude Bell *19th- and 20th-century British scholar and administrator.* Bell professionalized archaeological activities in Iraq following World War I. She established an Iraqi Antiquities Service to supervise excavations by foreigners and to insure the sharing of all finds. She also laid plans for a national museum to house the country's archaeological treasures.

Benjamin of Tudela *12th-century Spanish rabbi and traveler.* He was the first European traveler we know of to visit Iraq. During his visit to the Jewish community at Mosul, he described seeing the ruins of Nineveh.

2.2   *Sketching the palatial sculptures of Nineveh.* (Austen Henry Layard, *Discoveries in the Ruins of Nineveh and Babylon* [London: John Murray, 1853])

2.3   *Workmen uncover colossal winged beasts guarding an entranceway at Nineveh.*   (John P. Newman, *The Thrones and Palaces of Babylon and Nineveh from Sea to Sea* [New York: Harper, 1876])

Berossus *Fourth- and third-century B.C.E. Babylonian priest and scholar.* Drawing upon the archives of the Babylonian temple where he served as priest, Berossus wrote the earliest known comprehensive history of Mesopotamia starting from the time of creation and continuing down to the days of Alexander the Great. Written in Greek, the lingua franca of the Hellenistic world, his three-volume history survives only in fragments quoted by later classical authors.

Paul Émile Botta *19th-century French naturalist, diplomat, and archaeologist.* His discoveries at the royal city of Khorsabad beginning in 1843 mark him as the world's first Assyriologist. The dramatic sculptural panels and colossal statues he unearthed are now on display in the Louvre.

Robert J. Braidwood *20th-century American archaeologist.* With his wife, Linda, Braidwood investigated the beginnings of farming in the ancient Near East, digging at Jarmo and other sites in the Kurdish hills. He was among the first archaeologists to use carbon-14 analysis to date organic remains such as charcoal and bone.

Jean Chardin *17th- and 18th-century French traveler.* Chardin visited Persepolis and other Persian sites. Believing cuneiform inscriptions to be writing rather than mere decoration, he became the first European to study them and publish his research.

Edward Chiera *19th- and 20th-century archaeologist and philologist.* After excavating for the University of Chicago's Oriental Institute, Chiera headed its Assyrian Dictionary project, while specializing in Sumerian.

Frederic Cooper *19th-century British artist.* Cooper accompanied Austen Henry Layard (see below) on Layard's second expedition to Mesopotamia. Cooper's drawings and paintings illustrated Layard's discoveries.

Friedrich Delitzsch *19th- and 20th-century German philologist.* Delitzsch argued in 1902 that the Old Testament was not the world's oldest book but had in fact been influenced by even earlier works of Mesopotamian literature.

John Eldred *16th-century English merchant and traveler.* Eldred visited Baghdad during the reign of Queen Elizabeth. In his memoirs he mentioned seeing the "Tower of Babel."

Henri Frankfort *20th-century Dutch archaeologist and historian.* Prior to World War II,

2.4   *The entrance to an Assyrian temple at Kalhu (Nimrud) at the time of its exploration by Layard.* (Layard, *Discoveries in the Ruins of Nineveh and Babylon,* 1853)

2.5   An entrance passageway at the buried site of Nineveh. (Layard, *Discoveries in the Ruins of Nineveh and Babylon,* 1853)

gated the literary remains discovered at Ebla. His writings stressed the cultural connections between and among the peoples of the East Mediterranean world.

Georg Friedrich Grotefend *18th- and 19th-century German philologist.* Grotefend became the first scholar to decipher part of the Behistun Rock inscription, and thus the first modern scholar to read cuneiform. His 1802 decipherment of words from the Old Persian portion of the inscription was based on an earlier copy made by Karsten Niebuhr (see below).

Herodotus *Fifth-century B.C.E. Greek traveler and historian.* Herodotus, "the father of history," discussed the customs of the Babylonians and described the city of Babylon in the first chapter of his global account of the wars between the Persian Empire and Greece.

Herman Volrath Hilprecht *19th- and 20th-century German philologist.* Hilprecht served as curator of the Mesopotamian collection of the University of Pennsylvania Museum and participated in its excavations at Nippur, where some 30,000 cuneiform tablets were discovered that documented Sumerian civilization.

Edward Hincks *19th-century Irish clergyman and philologist.* A pioneer in the decipherment of cuneiform, Hincks proposed that the script had been adapted by the Babylonians from an earlier system of writing devised by a people whose language was not Semitic.

Mazahim Mahmud Hussein *20th-century Iraqi archaeologist.* Digging in 1989 beneath the floor of the palace at Nimrud, Hussein found the entombed remains of three Assyrian queens draped with golden jewelry.

Engelbert Kämpfer *17th- and 18th-century German traveler.* Noting in 1686 how the

Frankfort organized and directed excavations in Iraq for almost a decade under the auspices of the University of Chicago, where he served as research professor.

Albrecht Goetze *20th-century American philologist.* Goetze founded and edited the *Journal of Cuneiform Studies* and for many years served as director of the American School of Oriental Research at Baghdad.

Cyrus Herzl Gordon *20th-century American philologist.* Gordon authored the first grammar of the Ugaritic language, and he investi-

of the site and the information it could be made to disclose.

Samuel Noah Kramer *20th-century American philologist.* The leading Sumerologist of the 20th century, Kramer classified and deciphered neglected cuneiform tablets in museums around the world. Through his translations and the cultural synthesis he constructed, Kramer gave the Sumerians their rightful place as the creators of what may have been the world's first civilization.

Austen Henry Layard *19th-century British archaeologist.* One of the giants of Assyriology,

2.6   *Excavating in the interior of the mound at Kuyunjik where ancient Nineveh once stood. As native laborers send a basket of debris up to the surface, a god—half man, half scaly fish—acts as overseer.* (Layard, *Discoveries in the Ruins of Nineveh and Babylon*, 1853)

characters in inscriptions at Persepolis looked like wedges or nails, Kämpfer called them "cuneatae," from the Latin word *cuneus*, or "wedge." Kämpfer's observation became the source for the word "cuneiform."

Robert Koldewey *19th- and 20th-century German archaeologist.* A leader in bringing Germany into the field of Mesopotamian archaeology, Koldewey dug at Babylon for 14 seasons, applying a keen eye to the stratigraphy

2.7   *A tunnel at Kuyunjik is strewn with Assyrian sculptures.* (Layard, *Discoveries in the Ruins of Nineveh and Babylon*, 1853)

2.8   *A youthful portrait of Austen Henry Layard (in Albanian dress).* (Rogers, *A History of Babylonia and Assyria*, 1915)

Layard made major discoveries at both Nimrud and Nineveh. At Nimrud, he unearthed almost two miles of sculptural reliefs depicting battles and the hunt together with colossal statues of bulls and lions that guarded the palace's portals. At Nineveh, he uncovered the royal library of Ashurbanipal, totaling 24,000 tablets. Both sets of discoveries now enrich London's British Museum.

Seton Lloyd *20th-century British archaeologist.*   Under the auspices of the University of Chicago's Oriental Institute, Lloyd served as field supervisor for excavations at Tell Asmar, Tell Agrab, and Khafajah. Later, he acted as adviser to Iraqi archaeologists in the large-scale excavations they undertook at Eridu and Hassuna.

William Kennet Loftus *20th-century American geologist and archaeologist.*   Loftus dug at ancient Uruk, the largest archaeological site in what was once Sumer.

Lucian *Second-century C.E. Greek writer.*   Born in Samosata on the Euphrates, Lucian wrote satires in Greek in the days of the Roman Empire. In one, he describes the barren remains of Nineveh.

Agatha Christie Mallowan *19th- and 20th-century British mystery writer.*   As the wife of Max Mallowan (see below), Agatha Christie spent several seasons accompanying her husband on archaeological expeditions. Her visits to the Middle East inspired *Murder in Mesopotamia* (1936), and the memoirs of her adventures, *Come, Tell Me How You Live* (1946). Though she claimed never to have said it, Ms. Christie was quoted as having said the one advantage of being married to an archaeologist is that he gets more interested in you the older you look.

Max E. L. Mallowan *20th-century British archaeologist.*   After excavating at Ur and elsewhere, Mallowan spent 12 seasons at Nimrud. Among his sensational finds were delicate sculpted ivories from the palace of Ashurnasirpal and cuneiform inscriptions on wax.

Al-Masudi *10th-century Arab geographer.*   Al-Masudi visited the ruins of Nineveh in 943 C.E. and described seeing statues covered with inscriptions.

Jacques de Morgan *19th-century French explorer.*   While exploring the ruins of the Persian city of Susa, de Morgan unearthed a large black diorite slab sculpted with a picture and inscribed in cuneiform—the Code of Hammurabi—probably carried to Susa as plunder from Babylonia.

2.9   Lowering a colossal winged bull onto a pallet for transport from the ruins of Nineveh to the British Museum. (Layard, *Nineveh and Its Remains*, 1849

2.10   A colossal Assyrian lion arrives on the steps of the British Museum.   (*The Illustrated London News*, 1852)

Friedrich Münter *18th- and 19th-century Danish philologist.* Münter recognized that royal Persian inscriptions in cuneiform were written in three different scripts and languages that reiterated the same message. He also identified the signs for "king" and "king of kings" in 1802, the same year that they were spotted by George Friedrich Grotefend (see above).

Nabonidus *Sixth-century B.C.E. Babylonian king.* King Nabonidus was an antiquarian who restored buildings that were ancient in his time, and he searched foundations of temples for antique remains. He can lay claim to being the world's first archaeologist.

Karsten Niebuhr *18th-century Danish mathematician and geographer.* Under the sponsorship of the king of Denmark, Niebuhr led an expedition to the Persian capital of Persepolis. His careful copying and publication of the inscriptions he found there led to the decipherment of cuneiform.

A. Leo Oppenheim *20th-century American philologist.* Oppenheim was one of the most productive scholars of the University of Chicago's Oriental Institute, exploring the multiple facets of Mesopotamian culture in his research and writing.

Jules Oppert *19th-century French philologist.* Oppert postulated that a pre-Babylonian civilization had once inhabited southern Mesopotamia and had invented cuneiform. Their land, he argued, was the land known in the Bible as Shinar—the land we now call Sumer.

Jean d'Outremeuse *14th-century French writer.* Under the pseudonym Sir John Mandeville, d'Outremeuse wrote a popular guidebook for pilgrims heading to the Holy Land. Though he had never visited the Middle East himself, he drew upon earlier sources that had described the walls and ziggurat of Babylon.

André Parrot *19th- and 20th-century French archaeologist.* In the 1930s, Parrot excavated the site of Tell Hariri in Syria, the remains of the capital of the ancient kingdom of Mari.

John P. Peters *19th-century American philologist.* While professor of Hebrew at the University of Pennsylvania, Peters in 1887 initiated the first American archaeological expedition to Iraq, an expedition based at the site of the Sumerian city of Nippur.

Pethahiah of Regensburg *12th-century Jewish traveler.* He visited Jewish communities in the Middle East, including Iraq, and he wrote of his travels, describing the ruins he had seen.

Thomas Victor Place *19th-century French archaeologist.* Place dug at Khorsabad and systematically uncovered remains of the palace of Sargon.

Arno Poebel *19th- and 20th-century German philologist.* In 1923 Poebel published a landmark grammar of the Sumerian language.

Robert Ker Porter *19th-century English painter.* Porter's evocative paintings of Mesopotamia's ruins inspired increased interest in its buried civilization.

Hormuzd Rassam *19th-century Chaldaean archaeologist.* An assistant to Austen Henry Layard (see above), Rassam excavated from Nineveh the Creation and Deluge tablets later deciphered by George Smith (see below), as well as the lion-hunt relief from the palace of Ashurbanipal.

Leonhart Rauwolff *16th-century German physician and explorer.* Rauwolff was one of the first Europeans to explore the mounds that held Nineveh's remains.

Henry Creswicke Rawlinson *19th-century English adventurer and philologist.* At great risk to his life, Rawlinson scaled the cliff at Behistun to inspect and copy its 1,200-line inscription, transcribing the characters by hand or using papier-mâché "squeezes" obtained by a Kurdish boy who acted as his death-defying assistant. Rawlinson then succeeded in deciphering the Old Persian portion of the inscription, paving the way for cuneiform's full decipherment. Stored in the British Museum, the historic squeezes were later nibbled away by mice.

Claudius James Rich *18th- and 19th-century English diplomat, explorer, linguist, and archaeologist.* Rich was the first to survey and scientifically excavate the remains of Babylon. His memoirs, published in 1813 and 1818, awakened public interest among other Europeans. In 1820 he also explored the ruins of Nineveh.

Sayid Fuad Safar *20th-century Iraqi archaeologist.* With the guidance of Seton Lloyd (see above), Safar became the first Iraqi archaeologist to conduct large-scale excavations in his own country. He helped found the University of Baghdad's faculty of archaeology, and for over two decades he served as his nation's inspector general of excavations.

Ernest de Sarzac *19th-century French archaeologist.* De Sarzac's excavations at Telloh provided physical evidence for the existence of a pre-Babylonian civilization. His discoveries, including a portrait statue of Gudea and the Stele of the Vultures, became the first works of Sumerian art seen in Europe. They are now in the collection of the Louvre.

Denise Schmandt-Besserat *20th-century French-American archaeologist.* Schmandt-Besserat proposed a theory that writing originated not with drawings but with small clay tokens that were pressed into clay to document exchanges of commodities. She argued that the tokens, many of which have been excavated, lent their shapes to the first Mesopotamian pictographs.

George Smith *19th-century English philologist.* A bank-note engraver by trade who was later employed by the British Museum to piece together broken cuneiform tablets, Smith taught himself to read the script. One day he chanced upon a cuneiform story that resembled the biblical story of the Great Flood. Sponsored by the London *Daily Telegraph* to search for the rest of the story at Nineveh, he found the tablet's missing 17 lines. Later, he found and translated the remains of an Akkadian story of the Creation.

E. A. Speiser *19th- and 20th-century American archaeologist and philologist.* Speiser directed a University of Pennsylvania expedition to Tepe Gawra, 10 miles northeast of Nineveh. In later years, he served as editor of the *Journal of the American Oriental Society* and also produced translations of major Akkadian myths and legends.

Strabo *First-century B.C.E./C.E. Greek geographer.* His surviving writings, the result of extensive travels and research, offer us vivid vignettes of ancient Babylon and Babylonian culture and history.

William Henry Fox Talbot *19th-century British philologist.* In 1857, Talbot suggested that Britain's Royal Asiatic Society challenge four scholars including himself to decipher a previously untranslated passage of cuneiform while working independently. When they all arrived at essentially the same translation, the decipherment of cuneiform was scientifically confirmed.

J. E. Taylor *19th-century British diplomat and archaeologist.* Taylor became the first archaeologist to excavate a Sumerian ruin. Tunneling into the ziggurat at Tell Muqayyar, Taylor found an inscription that, when deciphered, proved the city was ancient Ur.

François Thureau-Dangin *19th- and 20th-century French philologist.* His study of cuneiform established Sumerology as a separate and important field for scholarly investigation.

Pietro della Valle *16th- and 17th-century Italian traveler.* From his travels to Persepolis, della Valle was among the first to return to Europe with samples of cuneiform writing. Soon after setting out on his journey to the East, his new bride died. Della Valle had her body embalmed and took it with him on his travels, burying it only when he returned home to Italy 10 years later.

Charles Leonard Woolley *19th- and 20th-century British archaeologist.* Working between 1922 and 1934 under the joint auspices of the British Museum and the University of Pennsylvania Museum, Woolley unearthed the Sumerian city of Ur, including its astoundingly rich royal graves. Woolley's discoveries confirmed the ancient splendor and importance of Sumerian civilization. Earlier, Woolley had excavated at Carchemish on the Euphrates in the company of T. E. Lawrence, later "Lawrence of Arabia."

Xenophon *Fifth- and fourth-century* B.C.E. *Greek writer.* While serving as a mercenary in an aborted Persian coup, Xenophon marched through Mesopotamia with 10,000 fellow Greek soldiers. The account of their expedition and the story of their perilous escape is told in Xenophon's *Anabasis.*

Juris Zarins *20th-century American geologist.* From satellite photographs and topographical evidence, Zarins identified the location of the rivers Gihon and Pishon, which, along with the Tigris and Euphrates, defined the location of the Garden of Eden, an area currently underwater beneath the Persian Gulf.

DATING THE PAST

Geography is easier to survey than the landscape of time. Past events are invisible except for the imprint they leave on matter or mind, and time itself erases evidence and memory. It is one thing to measure how many miles from modern Baghdad lie the ruins of ancient Ur; it is something altogether different to count how many years from today ancient Ur once flourished. How many suns have risen and set since that day? Was it a thousand, ten thousand, a hundred thousand, or more?

Historians would owe a deep debt of gratitude to the ancients if they had only dated their times in terms of "B.C.E." ("Before the Common Era") and "C.E." ("Common Era"). Alas, the ancient Mesopotamians did not use a Christian calendar, nor were they prescient enough to anticipate Jesus' birth and backdate their doings accordingly! Most of their cultural history, after all, transpired long before the Star of Bethlehem was ever sighted, and even longer before the prophet Muhammed left Mecca on his *hegira*, the starting point of the Muslim calendar. Indeed, Mesopotamia did not even possess a uniform dating system until it was imposed on the land by its Hellenistic conquerors in 311 B.C.E. For a long time, in fact, even the names of Mesopotamian months differed from city to city!

How then did the ancient Mesopotamians date their past, and by what means can we reconstruct it chronologically? As we will see, our chronological understanding of Mesopotamian history is a complex jigsaw puzzle that has been pieced together by many decades of persistent effort, not unlike the investigation of the human genome. And, like the structure of our DNA, many of the components and their correlations have yet to be fully understood.

To track the passage of time, the ancient Mesopotamians used not one but three different dating systems over the long course of their history. The first and the simplest was to name a year after the king who was then ruling, and to number it according to the year of his reign: for example, "the fifth year of King Shulgi." The second system—far richer in the historical data it can provide us with—was to name a year after an important event that had occurred: for example, "the year the temple of Ishtar was built" or "the year the Guti were defeated." The third system, introduced by the Assyrians, was to name a year after the personal name of a royal official, called the *limmu*. In this dating system, the first year was named for the king, and then each successive year for a different *limmu*, the honorary title being passed on annually from one high official to another.

To make sequential sense out of their past, Mesopotamian scribes kept running lists of kings and dynasties and officials as well as chronicles of historical events of major significance. Thanks to the discovery of these cuneiform records and their decipherment, we possess Babylonian and Assyrian King Lists, and even Synchronistic Lists giving the names of the Kings who ruled the south and the north as contemporaries. Copies also survive of a comprehensive Sumerian King List that begins in the mythic days before the legendary Great Flood and continues to the end of the First Dynasty of Isin (about 1800 B.C.E.), enumerating the many rulers of Sumer and the lengths of their reigns. The farther back into the past we go, however, the more history morphs into myth: thus, the eight kings who ruled before the flood are each assigned an average reign of 30,150 years. In attributing the greatest

longevity to its earliest leaders, the Sumerian King List parallels the biblical book of Genesis, where Adam is said to have lived 930 years and Methuselah 969—mere youngsters compared to their antediluvian Sumerian peers.

To their credit as scientific historians, some of the Sumerian chroniclers omitted these mythical kings from their list or attached the details of their reigns as an addendum. Unfortunately for our purposes, however, the various Mesopotamian King Lists are rife with scribal errors and chronological gaps. In addition, dynasties are presented as though they all came one after the other, whereas some may have actually overlapped or functioned simultaneously in different cities and regions.

On the positive side, the Lists give us a firm grasp of Mesopotamia's *relative* chronology: which kings came first, which next, and which last, including how many years each ruled (with all due allowance for mythic exaggeration and clerical discrepancy). What we lack, however, is an equally firm grasp of *absolute* chronology: the actual and precise years when a given king ruled or particular events took place in terms of our own calendar—that is, how many years ago "B.C.E."

It is at this point that heaven can come to our aid. Because the ancient Mesopotamians stood in awe of the sky and its mysteries, celestial phenomena such as lunar and solar eclipses were among the special events they cited in their chronicles. Due to their meticulous observations, today's astronomers can calculate exactly when these events would have taken place. Since the ancient astronomer also noted who was then sitting on the throne, modern calculations can help us date not only heavenly events but terrestrial ones as well. Astronomy thus provides us with the very keys we need to unlock the absolute chronology of the Mesopotamian past.

An Assyrian *limmu* list, for example, records that a complete eclipse of the sun took place in the month of June in the tenth year of King Ashur-dan III's reign. Just such an eclipse would have been visible in the Assyrian capital of Nineveh between 9:33 A.M. and 12:19 P.M. on June 15, 763 B.C.E. Pegging the tenth year of Ashur-dan's reign to 763 B.C.E. generates "B.C.E." dates for all the other kings in the list as well, spanning almost three centuries of Assyrian history. Our chronological chart can be unrolled even farther thanks to the work of the second-century C.E. Alexandrian astronomer Ptolemy, who drew up a list of over four centuries of unusual heavenly phenomena arranged in sequence according to the kings who then governed the Near East, from Nabonassar of Babylon to Alexander the Great. Because these events can be precisely dated by modern astronomers, the kings who then ruled can be dated too. And because the Assyrian *limmu* list (stretching from 911 to 627 B.C.E.) and Ptolemy's "Canon" (stretching from 747 to 323 B.C.E.) overlap, six centuries of Mesopotamian history are covered. In fact, with the additional help of Greek and Roman historians, absolute dates can be assigned to most of the first millennium B.C.E.

If we head farther back to the second millennium B.C.E., it's a planet that comes to our aid—Venus, one of the most important heavenly bodies in antiquity because it was associated (as its Roman name shows) with the goddess of love. During the eighth year in the reign of a Babylonian king named Ammisduqa, an ancient astronomer who had been keeping his eye on Venus for years recorded his observations, including the dates in the Babylonian calendar when she first poked her head out from behind the sun and then later withdrew (her heliacal rising and setting). The "Venus Tablets," as they've come to be called, allow astro-historians to date Ammisduqa's reign—with one wrinkle: because Venus has a 60-year orbital cycle, there are three possible dates for Ammisduqa's accession to the throne—1702

B.C.E., 1646 B.C.E., or 1582 B.C.E.—all of which fit the celestial data. This means that there are also three possible dates for all the other kings of the era! Thus, the problem for historians is to decide which of the three is correct: the so-called High Chronology (which pushes events farther back into the past), the Middle Chronology, or the Low Chronology (which views events as more recent). Ancient records of lunar eclipses seem to support the validity of the High Chronology, though many scholars (including this writer) still abide by the more "middle of the road" Middle one. Today, the Low is least favored.

Though Shakespeare claimed our destiny lies "not in the stars, but in ourselves," it has been the stars—the Sun and the evening star—that have pointed our way to a sharper vision of the Mesopotamian past.

DIGGING FOR HISTORY

The greatest biblical mandate for archaeologists is found in the book of Job (12:8): "Speak to the earth and it shall teach thee." The history of Mesopotamia ultimately resides in the earth, and it is to the earth that the historian must turn, not only to the surviving records of the past that lie among the ruins but to the very ruins themselves that wordlessly but faithfully testify to the passage of time.

Places that are inhabited for a long time grow vertically. As houses, especially those built of impermanent materials like reeds or sun-dried bricks, crumble or are destroyed by fire or war, new ones are built over their leveled remains. As dwelling-places rise, the streets they front are repaved with dirt. When, from time to time, villages are abandoned, wind-blown soil covers their remains; and, when settlers return, new homes are built on top. The increased altitude even gives the villages a strategic advantage—from the ravaging torrents of flood or the assaults of armed invaders, or from the smell of the garbage that they can now conveniently toss off the edge of their town. Finally, when a community is deserted (especially when the wandering course of a river has left it literally high and dry and remote from transport), the mound formed by its accumulated remains becomes what the Arabs call a "tell," its profile silhouetted like a rough-hewn ziggurat against the horizon.

To invite a "tell" to tell its story, the archaeologist must approach it with gentleness, patiently peeling away its layered remains as though turning the fragile pages of an antique book. Each layer that signifies a period of history is known as a *stratum* (plural *strata*), and the process of peeling them away, *stratigraphic excavation*.

But unlike a book, which we begin to read starting at chapter 1, the archaeologist must begin with the final chapter, for strata are superimposed chronologically with the last, and the newest, remains on top, where they were deposited by the settlement's final inhabitants. A tell, then, *is* a book, but one with its back cover facing up. The archaeologist must start at the end of the story and deliberately work back to its beginning, carefully turning each page and meticulously noting each word. But, unlike a book, which remains after the reading is done, an excavated tell ceases to exist once it has been dug up. Therefore the archaeologist must take detailed notes as he reads, and then publish the result of his findings after he has reconstructed the buried tale. For if he does not, the tale will be lost forever. The archaeologist's true mission, after all, is not gold but history.

Within each stratum, or layer of debris, the archaeologist will almost inevitably find arti-facts. Taken collectively, they convey a composite portrait of everyday life, framed by contemporary architectural remains. Of course, much will be missing because, as an ancient poet once said, "time devours all things." But to the practiced eye, much will abide.

Because strata are deposited sequentially, they provide the basis for developing the relative chronology of a site. Simply put: what is lowest is oldest and what is highest is newest, and everything else in between represents a series of progressive stages. In similar fashion, the artifacts at a site represent a progression also, from earlier forms at the bottom to later stylistic forms (of bricks, pottery, weaponry, jewelry, sculpture, and architecture) at the top. After organizing this data, the archaeologist can construct a "typology," or outline of development, for each type of artifact, with some styles notably older and others newer, each denoting the cultural period to which it belongs. And if a particular style of artifact is likewise found at another site, the strata in which both are found can be chronologically linked even though the sites may be many miles apart.

In this effort, pottery becomes the archaeologist's best friend because as an article of daily life it is commonly found and widely dispersed, with a history that begins in the late Stone Age and persists through classical (and later) times. Though a work of pottery is fragile, the broken pieces of a shattered vessel are virtually indestructible and therefore become durable witnesses to changing styles and times.

But, granting that one specimen of pottery or sculpture is older than another, how old is "old"? Are they separated by a year, a century, a millennium? And how far are they—and the cultural periods their strata signify—distant from our own day? Relative chronology may be informative, but for a true understanding of history we need absolute chronology, the measurement of age in years. In short, the archaeologist asks, to what century B.C.E. does my find belong?

Uncovering a dateable inscription would be certain to answer his needs, an inscription—for example—attributable to a ruler whose regnal years have already been established by other means. Such inscriptions do occur (cut into stone or stamped onto brick), but they are rare. More common—from Persian, Greek, and Roman times—are coins, but they need to be found in sufficient quantity to show they were in circulation during the period in question. Second to inscriptions on the archaeologist's "wish list" would be physical evidence of a dateable event—the destruction of a city or the construction of a building—that can be connected to a known figure in history.

But, failing this evidence, the archaeologist can turn to techniques developed by other sciences. Three techniques in particular, all developed in the latter half of the 20th century, have proved valuable for dating the kinds of materials archaeologists unearth. These techniques are carbon-14 analysis, dendrochronology, and thermoluminescence.

Carbon-14 analysis is based upon the fact that all organic material contains carbon, not only regular carbon but a special radioactive isotope of carbon called carbon-14. These two carbons coexist proportionately, with one atom of radioactive carbon for every billion atoms of nonradioactive. As long as a plant or animal is alive, that proportion is maintained. But once an organic being dies, the radioactivity in it begins to degenerate, decaying at a fixed and measurable rate until half of it is gone after 5,730 years. After another 5,730 years, another half disappears. By burning an organic sample and measuring the residual radioactivity left in a gram of its carbon, scientists can determine how long ago the plant or animal died. Thus by analyzing an ancient piece of wood, scientists can tell how long ago the tree from which it came was felled, and thus how old the wood

itself is; or how old charcoal is, or reeds, or bone, or anything else organic.

Carbon-14 analysis can yield dates within a 300-year range of accuracy, useful for coming up with a rough estimate of an object's age and, by extension, the age of its archaeological context, but not useful enough to provide precise historical dates. Another limitation is that—in order to determine the age of a sample—the ancient sample itself must be incinerated! As the technique has been perfected, though, smaller and smaller samples have been required as sacrifices on the altar of chronology.

Another scientific dating technique is dendrochronology, based on the fact that tree rings vary in width. These variations reflect the changing climatic conditions of annual growing seasons—wider for more growth and narrower for less. The unique patterns formed by the rings constitute "fingerprints" that can be used to identify the years during which a given tree grew. Some long-lived trees like the bristle-cone pine have given scientists a tree-ring lifeline that extends for centuries, enabling them to adjust for the variations in atmospheric radiation that for a long time made carbon-14 analysis less than accurate.

A third technique is thermoluminescence, based on the fact that over the course of time the electrons in baked clay are displaced from their atomic orbits and become trapped in the clay's crystalline structure. The longer pottery has been exposed to cosmic radiation, the more of its electrons are displaced. However, if the baked clay is suddenly heated to 500°C, the electrons "break out of jail" and return to their atomic homes. In the process, they give off a faint burst of light that can be measured. The more light, the more electrons that are escaping, the longer their term of past imprisonment, and the older the pot! Not only can pottery be dated this way, but so can any baked clay, including ancient bricks and even cuneiform tablets as long as they were once fired, whether deliberately by a scribe or accidentally by a marauder's torch.

ANCIENT NARRATIVES

Whether they offer firsthand accounts or preserve still older traditions, ancient narratives are the past's own testimony about itself and an authentic witness to history.

To the first category—firsthand accounts—belong the self-congratulatory utterances of monarchs proud of their military victories and domestic accomplishments, which were celebrated on tablets of clay and stelae of stone. To the same category belong the lamentations of those whose cities and homes were destroyed by those very same kings. Such accounts, whether by the victors or the vanquished, are inevitably biased, but taken together convey a composite truth.

To the second category belong works by ancient historians whose writings survive in whole or in part. After the anonymous chroniclers of the Babylonians and Assyrians, two authors come to the fore whose personalities are distinct: Berossus, the third-century B.C.E. Babylonian scholar-priest, and Herodotus, the fifth-century B.C.E. peripatetic Greek traveler. Berossus's multivolume *Babyloniaca* tracked Babylonian history from the Deluge to Alexander. Berossus was a native Babylonian and had access to temple archives, but his history is preserved only in fragments cited by classical authors. Herodotus, on the other hand, was a Greek, and a tourist at that, but an intelligent one, handicapped by language but impelled by a curiosity that still radiates from the first book of his *History* that describes his visit to Babylonia. Nevertheless, he lacked access to the valuable documentary sources Berossus was intimate with. Yet chronological beggars can't

be choosers, and we must remain grateful even for the crumbs from history's banquet table.

It is time now to survey that table and reconstruct from the menu the grand order of the banquet's historic courses.

SURVEY OF HISTORY

Presented below is an overview of Mesopotamian history based on the present state of our knowledge. As more ancient sites are explored, more discoveries made, and more texts deciphered, our knowledge will grow in breadth and depth. The majority of dates below are approximate, especially for those periods most remote in time when historical records were not kept because writing itself had not been invented, and from which other physical evidence is slight.

More details about places can be found in chapter 1, and personalities in chapter 3. Discussions about the literary and artistic evidence for historical periods occur in chapters 5, 6, and 7. For a handy reference, a chronological table is located near the book's end.

The account below has been deliberately kept simple in order to provide readers with an easy-to-comprehend road map across historically complex terrain. Readers desiring a more detailed account should turn to Georges Roux's excellent study, *Ancient Iraq*, or to the more specialized studies included in the bibliography.

The Stone Age (ca. 70,000–5800 B.C.E.)
The longest chapter in humanity's story, the Stone Age is also the sparest in documentation because of the original poverty of man's material culture and the protracted ravages of time. The very name "Stone Age" is an admission of our ignorance, since it is but stones (handless implements) and bones (speechless skeletons) that survive.

For clerical convenience, the Stone Age is divided into a beginning, a middle, and an end: the Palaeolithic ("Old Stone") Period (ca. 70,000–9000 B.C.E.), the transitional Mesolithic ("Middle Stone") Period (ca. 9000–7000 B.C.E.), and finally the Neolithic ("New Stone") Period (ca. 7000–5800 B.C.E.) The hallmark changes in the style of Stone Age tools and weapons demonstrate a progressive sophistication in design. During this era, the only advanced technology was literally "cutting edge."

But the movement from period to period was also marked by an evolution in lifestyle. While the Palaeolithic economy was based on food gathering (through hunting, fishing, and picking wild edible plants), the Neolithic economy was primarily based on food production (through farming and animal husbandry). While Palaeolithic existence was more mobile, the Neolithic was more settled, for agriculture and the domestication of animals went hand in hand with village life. Technologically, the Neolithic also witnessed the birth of domestic architecture (in place of seeking the shelter of caves) and the beginnings of pottery, a boon to archaeologists because ceramics offer abundant evidence of the character of everyday life.

Among the most notable Stone Age sites are Palaeolithic Shanidar Cave and Neolithic Jarmo. both in northern Iraq.

The Chalcolithic Period (ca. 5800–3750 B.C.E.)

The Chalcolithic ("Copper/Bronze-Stone") Period constitutes—as the name suggests—a transition from a time when the principal material for man's tools and weapons was stone to a time when it became copper and (later) bronze. Just as the Stone Age saw the early Mesopotamians move from cave to farm so did the Chalcolithic Period see their descendants' primitive villages grow into nascent cities.

The subperiods of the Chalcolithic derive their names from archaeological sites that have

yielded evidence of progressive developments in communal life. These developments were due to the Agricultural Revolution of Neolithic times, for as the food supply increased, population size grew, and settlements became larger. The names of these Chalcolithic communities are Tell Hassuna, Samarra, Tell Halaf, and al-Ubaid, and the progressive subperiods named for them—Hassuna, Samarra, Halaf, and Ubaid—extend chronologically from the early sixth millennium B.C.E. to the early fourth.

From these Chalcolithic sites come the earliest examples of Mesopotamian temples and statuettes, as well as stamp seals (to mark personal property) and intricately painted pottery.

The Beginning of the Bronze Age (ca. 3750–2900 B.C.E.)

By the middle of the fourth millennium B.C.E., the climate of northern Mesopotamia began to grow cooler and drier, and less hospitable to farming that depended upon rain. As a result, settlers from the north migrated to the south, where, in fertile alluvial plains, water was more plentiful and accessible.

The cultural developments that took place then are named for two early urban sites in the south, Uruk and Jemdet Nasr. Urbanization took place first in Uruk (ca. 3750–3150 B.C.E.) and then in Jemdet Nasr (ca. 3150–2900 B.C.E.), and subperiods are accordingly named for the characteristic finds made at each. But these two sites are not isolated instances of urbanization, but rather merely examples of a profound change that simultaneously took place elsewhere in the south: the birth of civilization, the emergence of a complex form of society characterized by large population centers, the specialization and interdependence of labor, and the growth and concentration of wealth.

Technologically, these changes were accompanied by advances in metallurgy (hence, the "Bronze" Age) and a number of specific and momentous inventions: the plough and the wheel, the chariot and the sailboat, and the cylinder-seal, the single most distinctive art form of ancient Mesopotamia and a pervasive demonstration of the importance of property ownership and business in the country's daily life. But the most important invention of all—not only for our understanding of Mesopotamia but also for its impact on the world—was writing, which first appears in pictographic form at Uruk around 3300 B.C.E.

The Early Dynastic Period (ca. 2900–2334 B.C.E.)

The climatic changes that had begun in the middle of the fourth millennium B.C.E. and had originally affected only the north persisted and now began to affect the south, drying up rivers and streams and making arable land scarce. The environmental problem was solved by building extensive networks of irrigation canals, but their excavation and maintenance demanded a new level of cooperative effort, centralized authority, and governmental control. Cities vied for water rights and quarreled over the borders that set limits to their lands. Some disputes, in fact, led to armed conflict, and to the rise of hegemonies under the leadership of one city-state or another. Nevertheless, southern Mesopotamia was generally blessed with sufficient water and fertile soil for a good life, reason enough to thank the gods and honor civic leaders. Surpluses of agricultural produce, moreover, and manufactured products like textiles enabled southern cities to grow rich through trade and to acquire the raw materials they lacked. From such wealth and such materials, glorious works of art were created to celebrate the splendor of the southern land we call Sumer.

Among the cities that flourished during this era were Kish, Isin, Nippur, Shuruppak, Lagash, Uruk, Larsa, Ur, and Eridu. Because most of these cities were governed by royal dynasties, the period as a whole is called the Early Dynastic Period. Its golden glory is most evident in the discoveries made by Sir Leonard Woolley at the Royal Cemetery of Ur.

The Akkadian Empire (ca. 2334–2193 B.C.E.)

The affluence of the south inspired covetousness among the Semites who lived just north of Sumer. In 2334 B.C.E., a Semitic king named Sargon (Sharru-kin) began a career of military conquest that won him the south and made him the master of the first empire in Mesopotamian history. Sargon ruled it from a city he founded called Agade. From "Agade" comes the name "Akkadian," a descriptive term for the Semitic language of Sargon and his people. Though Sargon respected Sumerian culture and retained Sumerian as the language of his official inscriptions, the Akkadian tongue would eventually become the dominant language of Mesopotamia and much of the Near East.

After reigning for 55 years, Sargon died. Following his death, a general revolt broke out that was quelled by Sargon's grandson, Naram-Sin, who ruled for another 37 years, all the while battling rapacious tribes at his kingdom's frontiers. Soon after his death, the Akkadian empire collapsed, but it had set a precedent for imperialistic expansion that would never be absent from the thoughts of Mesopotamia's future leaders.

The Third Dynasty of Ur (ca. 2112–2004 B.C.E.)

One of the tribes that Naram-Sin had battled was the fierce Guti, who succeeded in dominating Mesopotamia for almost a century following the Akkadian Empire's collapse. Eventually, however, the Guti were driven out by a coalition of Sumerian kings.

In the aftermath, two Sumerian rulers assumed leading roles in the life of their country: Gudea of Lagash, famous for his many pious portraits carved in stone, and Ur-Nammu of Ur, the founder of his city-state's Third Dynasty. Both Gudea and Ur-Nammu were prolific builders, who thanked the gods with temples and ziggurats for the divine favors they had bestowed. It is to Ur-Nammu that we must attribute the ziggurat of Ur, the best preserved of such monuments in all of ancient Mesopotamia.

Ur-Nammu's imperialistic dreams were fulfilled by his son Shulgi and grandson Amar-Sin. Under pressure, however, from the Elamites to the northeast and the Semitic Amorites to the northwest, Ur and its empire fell. A golden age of Sumerian civilization came to an end, as Ur lay in smoldering ruins.

The Era of Isin and Larsa (ca. 2000–1800 B.C.E.)

After the fall of Ur, two city-states rose to ascendancy in southern Mesopotamia—Isin and Larsa—and fought with each other for territorial control. Meanwhile, in northern Mesopotamia, two other states—Ashur and Eshnunna—vied with each other for control of trade routes. During this same period, Amorite tribesmen exercised power in northern Mesopotamia, and ruled the kingdom of Mari.

The First Dynasty of Babylon (ca. 1900–1595 B.C.E.)

A century after the fall of Ur, the Amorites founded the so-called First Dynasty of Babylon. It would endure for three centuries. The sixth and greatest king of the dynasty was Hammurabi (1792–1750 B.C.E.), who rose from being a mere local ruler to becoming the undisputed master of all Mesopotamia, embracing Sumer and Akkad, Mari, and Assyria. Conqueror, statesman, and lawgiver, Hammurabi reigned for 43 years. Just a century and a half after his death, his dynasty ended when the city of Babylon was captured and looted by a Hittite army.

The Dynasty of the Sea-Land (ca. 1730–1460 B.C.E.)

In the aftermath of Hammurabi's death, the marshland of southern Sumer seceded under the leadership of a usurper named Iluma-ilum, who established a dynasty dubbed the Second Dynasty of Babylon. As an independent state, the Sea-Land lasted for almost three centuries.

The Kassite Dynasty (1595–1157 B.C.E.)

With the withdrawal of the Hittites from Babylon, an Iranian tribe known as the Kassites occupied the city. Kassite kings went on to rule Mesopotamia for almost four and a half centuries. Their circumspect policy was to honor and respect the revered literary and religious traditions of the land they now governed. The Kassites were eventually defeated by the Elamites.

The Second Dynasty of Isin (1156–1025 B.C.E.)

After Elamite forces withdrew from Babylonia, leaders from the city-state of Isin founded this dynasty, also known as the Fourth Dynasty of Babylon. When it ended, a succession of foreigners sat on Babylon's throne and the city itself was cut off from the countryside by hostile Aramaeans.

The Neo-Assyrian Empire (911–612 B.C.E.)

With the lands she once occupied and her trade routes held by foreigners, Assyria near the 10th century's end was, as Georges Roux puts it, "at her lowest ebb." But she rallied and rose under the leadership of Adad-nirari II to wage a successful war of national liberation against her enemies. Her multiple successes spawned repeated campaigns of imperialistic expansion under a succession of merciless warrior-kings: Ashurnasirpal, Shalmaneser III. Tiglathpileser III, Sennacherib, Esarhaddon, and Ashurbanipal, monarchs who extended Assyria's conquests across the entire Near East and made Nineveh one of the richest cities of the ancient world. The Assyrian Empire, however, became the victim of its own overvaunting ambition and the jealous resentment of those it had crushed and repressed. In 612 B.C.E., Nineveh fell to a combined military force of Babylonians and Medes.

The Neo-Babylonian Period (625–539 B.C.E.)

Thirteen years before the fall of Nineveh, a Chaldaean dynasty assumed the throne of Babylon. The Chaldaeans, or Kaldu, were an Aramaean tribe that had settled in southern Mesopotamia some three centuries earlier. Under Chaldaean leadership, Babylon filled the imperialistic vacuum left by the collapse of the Assyrian Empire. Babylon's most energetic king was Nebuchadnezzar II (604–562 B.C.E.), whose armies destroyed Jerusalem and whose own capital city, Babylon, became legendary for its magnificence. Under less single-minded and less ruthless successors, however, Babylon's power waned until the city and its remaining empire were conquered by the Persians in 539 B.C.E.

The Persian Period (539–331 B.C.E.)

Under the leadership of the Achaemenian Dynasty, ancient Iran (later called Persia) would become the master of the largest empire in the history of the world, an empire whose territory would stretch from Egypt in the west to India in the east. With Cyrus's conquest of Babylon in 539 B.C.E., the territory formerly ruled by Chaldaean kings was absorbed into the kingdom of the Persians.

During two centuries of Persian domination, the economy and civilization of Mesopotamia declined. During this time, Akkadian was reduced to a language of the learned few (a fate Sumerian had previously suffered), and was replaced by Aramaic as the lingua franca of the Near East. Ironically, it would be an inscription celebrating Persian victories (in the Old Persian, Babylonian, and Elamite languages) that would become the key to the later decipherment of cuneiform.

The Hellenistic Period (331–126 B.C.E.)

In 331 B.C.E., the charismatic Macedonian leader Alexander marched to greatness on the plain of Gaugamela by defeating the army of the Persian king Darius III. Alexander then proceeded to Babylon, where he liberated the city and was hailed as the land's new king. Following the death of Darius and the burning of the royal palace at Persepolis, Alexander made Babylon the capital of his new empire, striving for geographic unity by fostering a cultural fusion of Eastern and Western races and values. His political agenda ended when he died in 323 B.C.E. at the age of 32, but his dream of multiculturalism lived on as the spirit of Hellenistic civilization, the culture of later Greece and the world it transformed.

With Alexander's death, his empire was divided up among the generals who had fought by his side. One of these generals, Seleucus, received Mesopotamia as his share of the spoils and founded a dynasty, the Seleucid, that ruled the country until 126 B.C.E., when it was conquered by the Parthians.

The Parthian Period (126 B.C.E.–227 C.E.)

The Parthians were a Scythian tribe from Turkestan that had migrated and settled in Iran. The Parthians ruled Iran and Iraq (except for two brief incursions into Mesopotamia by the Romans) until 227 C.E., when they were in turn defeated by the Sassanians, a people who traced their ancestry to Persia's Achaemenian kings.

The Sassanian Period (227–651 C.E.)

Under Sassanian domination, Mesopotamia lay in ruins, its fields dried out or turned into a swampy morass, its once great cities made ghost towns. With the Islamic conquest of 651 C.E. the history of ancient Mesopotamia ends.

KEY RULERS OF MESOPOTAMIA

The dates below are the dates of the rulers' reigns. For details about the rulers' careers, see chapter 3.

Akkadian and Sumerian Rulers
Sargon the Great (2334–2279 B.C.E.)
Naram-Sin (2254–2218 B.C.E.)
Gudea (2141–2122 B.C.E.)
Ur-Nammu (2112–2095 B.C.E.)
Shulgi (2094–2047 B.C.E.)

Babylonian Rulers
Hammurabi (1792–1750 B.C.E.)
Nebuchadnezzar I (1124–1103 B.C.E.)
Nebuchadnezzar II (604–562 B.C.E.)
Nabonidus (555–539 B.C.E.)

Assyrian Rulers
Tukulti-Ninurta I (1244–1208 B.C.E.)
Tiglathpileser I (1115–1077 B.C.E.)
Ashurnasirpal II (883–859 B.C.E.)
Tiglathpileser III (744–727 B.C.E.)
Sargon II (721–705 B.C.E.)
Sennacherib (704–681 B.C.E.)
Esarhaddon (680–669 B.C.E.)
Ashurbanipal (668–627 B.C.E.)

Foreign Rulers
Cyrus the Great of Persia (549–529 B.C.E.)
Alexander the Great of Macedonia (336–323 B.C.E.)
Artabanus II of Parthia (128–124 B.C.E.)

READING

The Discoverers

Fagan 1979, Kuklick 1996, Lloyd 1955, Mirsky 1977, Moorey 1991, and Oates and Curtis 1982: history of Mesopotamian archaeology.

Dating the Past

Aström 1987–89, Brinkman 1977, Cryer 1995, Ehrich 1992, Roux 1992, Rowton 1970: chronology; Gasche 1998: fall of Babylon; Grayson 1980: historiography; Jacobsen 1937, Vincente 1995: Sumerian King List; Millard 1997: Babylonian King Lists.

Digging for History

Aitkens 1974: carbon-14 analysis; Bertman 1986, McIntosh 1999, Renfrew 1991, Wheeler 1954: archaeological method; Hole and Heizer 1977: laboratory dating methods; Russell 1998: destruction and looting.

Ancient Narratives

Burstein 1978, Kuhrt and Sherwin-White 1987: Berossus; Hornblower and Spawforth 1996: Herodotus.

Survey of History

Crawford 1991, Kramer 1963: Sumer; Edwards 1975–, Roaf 1990, Roux 1992, Saggs 1995, Snell 1997: general survey; Ghirshman 1954: Persia; Hallo and Simpson 1998, Von Soden 1994 (1985): historical survey of ancient Near East; Kuhrt 1995: detailed survey; Kuhrt and Sherwin-White 1987, Peters 1970: Hellenism; Postgate 1992: early Mesopotamia; Saggs 1962: Babylonia and Assyria.

Key Rulers of Mesopotamia

Bienkowski and Millard 2000, Leick 1999, Sasson 1995: biographies.

3

GOVERNMENT AND SOCIETY

THE STRUCTURE OF CIVILIZATION

Civilization is a social entity defined by its structure, a structure more complex than earlier forms of society.

It is not simply the size of a population or its concentration into large settlements that defines a civilization, but rather the specialized functions of its people and their interdependence and collaboration. Civilization is capable of doing more than earlier forms of society because it represents an amassing of energy that, with leadership, can be directed toward specific ends not feasible, or even conceivable, before. As a by-product of that capability, the individual may, through the use of his or her talents in labor or leisure, achieve a level of productivity or find a degree of fulfillment otherwise not possible.

In exchange, however, for the benefits it bestows, a civilization requires the individual to surrender a portion of his or her freedom and autonomy. As rewards, the civilization provides security, instills purpose, and promises happiness.

All of these essential characteristics can be found in the history of the earliest civilizations, including that of Mesopotamia. Yet, in the process of development, each civilization acquired its own distinctive and unique personality.

THE STRATIFICATION OF SOCIETY

In the same way that the watered soil of Mesopotamia produced its wealth, the land of Mesopotamia generated its class structure.

Though social stratification seems to have been less pronounced during the early centuries of Sumerian civilization, by the time of the Babylonian Empire under Hammurabi (1792–1750 B.C.E.) it was sharply drawn. With the passage of time, the ownership of land—and, with it, the possession of political power—came to be concentrated more and more in the hands of the few.

Social Classes

Our clearest and most detailed picture of the social structure of Mesopotamian civilization is to be found in the Babylonian Code of Hammurabi, dating to the first half of the 18th century B.C.E. According to the code, there were three types of persons in society: the *awilum*, or patrician (a member of one of the landholding families), the *mushkenum*, or plebeian (a citizen who was free but did not possess land), and the *wardum*, or slave (a member of society who neither owned land nor was free). Significantly, the most privileged were also held to the highest standard of responsibility under the law, while those who were less privileged were penalized less for breaking it, unless it happened that their offense was committed against a member of a higher class.

The three classes, however, were not rigidly separated. Were he compelled to surrender his land because of debt, an *awilum* could become a *mushkenum*. Conversely, were a *mushkenum* to acquire land, he would become an *awilum*. Furthermore, a slave could be granted his freedom, and a free citizen in dire financial straits could lose his.

SOCIAL MOBILITY

Significantly, Babylonian law tended to foster upward social mobility. If, for example, a member of one class married a member of another, the children born of their marriage would belong to the higher of the two classes.

PRIESTS AND KINGS

Notwithstanding the real estate holdings of families or individuals, the largest parcels of land were always in the hands of the priests (who were the servants of the gods) and the kings (who were the gods' surrogates on earth). Thus those who held supreme authority also controlled the most property and the wealth it produced.

THE BEGINNINGS

Thanks to the Constitution of the United States, students of America's history can readily understand the main features of its government. Alas, students of Mesopotamian history are not so fortunate. Unlike the United States, Mesopotamia did not become a political entity all at once. Instead, its governmental structure evolved slowly and underwent significant metamorphoses. These events occurred, moreover, not a couple of centuries or so ago but thousands of years earlier, making their reconstruction immensely more difficult. In addition, Mesopotamian government was not defined by a single document crafted by "founding fathers," but rather it is reflected in scattered records surviving from assorted periods, the oldest of which offer only scant testimony.

There is no doubt that Mesopotamia was eventually and for most of its history governed by rulers we might call "kings." Indeed, we even know their names and can catalogue their careers. But exactly when kingship first came into being, under what circumstances it arose, and precisely what its nature was remain matters of scholarly contention. Theories abound, but facts are few.

By comparison, Egyptologists have it easy. The Egyptian nation was born of a single act of unification performed by a single man, and—except for two periods of interregnum—it was ruled by absolute monarchs called pharaohs during the course of its 3,000-year-long history. Each pharaoh was regarded as divine: in life the incarnation of the god Horus and upon death the simulacrum of Osiris, sovereign of the netherworld.

To reconstruct Mesopotamia's constitutional history, however, we must step onto the fog-shrouded landscape of myth and from the misty shapes on the horizon attempt to discern the outlines of historical fact. It won't be easy. But the journey must be undertaken, for at stake is our understanding of how one of the earliest of human civilizations assumed an organizational form that enabled it to achieve great things, some of which—like urban life, law, and imperialism—became for better or worse its legacy to our times.

KINGSHIP

The most prominent mythic document that sheds light, albeit indirect, on the Mesopotamian institution of kingship is the Babylonian *Epic of Creation*. The oldest versions of the *Epic* date to the first millennium B.C.E., but the original story may go back to the early second, when the city of Babylon assumed great power and would have wanted its glory celebrated in song.

The action of the *Epic* revolves around a titanic battle among the gods, a battle that ensued in the primordial days before mankind was created. There were two main deities then: Apsu (the male god of freshwater) and Tiamat (the goddess of salt water). According to the story, Apsu became annoyed at the noise his progeny were making, and he proposed to destroy them. His plans, however, were thwarted by his great-grandson, Ea, renowned for his cleverness. Employing a magic spell, Ea hypnotized both Apsu and his minister, seized Apsu's crown, executed him, and put the prime minister under arrest. Enraged, Tiamat quickly took steps to counter the coup. She convened an assembly of the gods and, with their council's approval, raised an army and appointed a commander in chief to lead them in battle. As soon as Ea heard what was going on, he reported the news to his divine grandfather Anu, who was revered for his wisdom. Anu tried to negotiate with Tiamat to forestall all-out war, but when that failed he called upon Ea's son, Marduk, to stand as champion against Tiamat and her forces. Marduk agreed to fight, but only if the other gods granted him absolute power then and thereafter. Anu agreed to Marduk's terms and invited the other gods to a great banquet. With their consent, Marduk was given kingship over the universe and went on to defeat Tiamat and her minions, establishing his sovereignty forever. In the politics of heaven, the triumph of Marduk over Tiamat validated his father Ea's earlier efforts to end the despotism of Apsu, the universe's former king. In the politics of earth, the ascendancy of Babylon's patron god Marduk as ruler of the universe symbolized and theologically justified Babylon's own ascendancy over the other cities of Mesopotamia and their local gods.

Even earlier than the Babylonian *Epic of Creation* is a Sumerian epic tale about the hero Bilgames (later known as Gilgamesh), a tale called "Bilgames and Agga," or "The Envoys of Agga." According to the story, Agga, ruler of the city of Kish, sent an ultimatum to the city of Uruk demanding its submission. Bilgames, Uruk's ruler, turned to his city's council of elders for advice, and they recommended acceding to Kish's demands. Dissatisfied, however, Bilgames decided to take the matter one

3.1 *Portrait of an Assyrian king, Ashurnasirpal II, dressed in his ceremonial robe and holding a weapon in each hand. The statue is now in the British Museum.* (Franz von Reber, *History of Ancient Art* [New York: Harper, 1882])

step further and turned to the city's popular assembly composed of all men of fighting age. Rejecting the idea of surrender, the assembly urged armed resistance—exactly the answer Bilgames had been waiting to hear. Leading his people into battle, Bilgames defeated the enemy. As we see from the story, the will of Uruk's council of elders was not binding upon its king, who was free to turn to the popular assembly and ask its opinion as well. Whether the assembly's expressed will was then binding, or again merely advisory, we are not told.

Both mythic accounts—one describing divine affairs and the other human—speak of a governmental structure that included a supreme ruler, on one hand, and a legislative body, on the other. The legislature, in turn, consisted of a smaller council and a larger assembly. Collectively, such structural elements comprise what Thorkild Jacobsen termed a "primitive democracy" that existed in ancient Mesopotamia some 4,000 or more years ago.

Of course, the kind of government attributed to heaven may have simply been a divine version of the kind of government the Mesopotamians were already familiar with on earth. In envisioning the world of the gods, human beings are often wont to project images from their own earthly experience onto a larger heavenly screen. In just such a way, the gods of mythology can take on human characteristics in their physical appearance and emotional makeup. Thus the ancient Greeks imagined their gods dwelling as a family in a palace on Mt. Olympus just as royal families in the Mycenaean era inhabited palatial citadels on earthly heights.

It is likely, however, that the ancient Mesopotamians took a less rationalistic view of things, believing instead that the gods were genuine and had instituted government on earth as a terrestrial extension of their own administration of the cosmos. In such a view, the earth was a divine estate and man its caretaker, tending the land on the gods' behalf much as did Adam when he worked as Eden's gardener. Indeed, they would have believed—and their priests would have instructed them—that the service of the gods was humanity's prime function, indeed its raison d'être. As Thorkild Jacobsen observed in *Before Philosophy:*

> The only truly sovereign state, independent of all external control, is the state which the universe itself constitutes, the state governed by the assembly of the gods. This state, moreover, is the state which dominates the territory of Mesopotamia; the gods own the land, the big estates, in the country. Lastly, since man was created especially for the benefit of the gods, his purpose is to serve the gods.

> Therefore no human institution can have its primary aim in the welfare of its own human members; it must seek primarily the welfare of the gods. (Frankfort 1949: 200)

It is for this reason that "kingship descended from heaven," first (before the legendary Great Flood) to the city of Eridu and then later (after the Great Flood) to the city of Kish. So proclaims the "Sumerian King List," a document that purports to list all of Sumer's monarchs from the dawn of civilization, and implies that certain monarchs—those of Eridu and Kish—once exercised sovereignty over the whole land.

Each city-state—the city and the cultivated fields surrounding and supporting it—also needed to be administered on the behalf of its own local god. For this reason there also had to be local government.

In the beginning, sacred and secular authority may have rested in the hands of one individual—a natural enough development since the people of Mesopotamia saw no dichotomy between the two. Thus the earliest ruler of a city-state may have been the *en*, a Sumerian word for "high priest." The *en* would have thus been the local god's representative on earth, managing the temple lands and the people who worked them. At a later stage of development, when the population had grown and society had become more complex, a second office may have arisen, that of *ensi*, or "governor," whose duty it became to manage civic affairs (law and order, commerce and trade, and military matters) while the *en* continued to manage the business of the temple (the supervision of temple lands and the performance of religious rituals). In special times of crisis, a *lugal* (literally, "great man") might be appointed by the people through a council or a popular assembly (much as Marduk had been appointed in the *Epic of Creation*). Indeed, the office of *lugal* seems to have emerged at about the same time as Sumerian cities began to construct defensive walls to protect them from their enemies, and thus needed leaders in time of special emergency. Initially, the *lugal* might have been entrusted with authority only so long as an emergency existed; but if the cirsis persisted or repeated crises occurred, the *lugal*'s supreme authority may have become permanent, especially if, like Marduk, he relished power and exercised it with verve. As individual city-states coalesced into alliances or were conquered by their neighbors, the *ensi* or *lugal* of the dominant city might hold wider sway and govern as king.

To justify this greater power, however, the king would require a divine mandate, especially since he was no longer just the leader of a single community serving a local god but the master of a wider domain. One solution would be to claim he had been chosen by heaven, a claim that could be affirmed by the high priest of a nationally venerated temple such as the temple of the god Enlil at Nippur. Indeed, the king's evident success was the most convincing proof of his divine selection. Both that success and his choice by the gods would then be celebrated in poetry and song. Another solution would be to elevate the king's divine patron from local to higher, national stature. Thus Marduk and Ashur, both originally the gods of specific cities, rose from relative obscurity to become the patron gods of imperial states. Just as was the case with the kings, the success of the gods on the battlefield was the most persuasive evidence that their political majesty was deserved.

Divinity

Though the kings of Mesopotamia sought divine approval, they did not necessarily regard themselves as divine. In inscriptions, only some kings' names are prefixed with the sign DINGIR, that meant "god." Sargon of Akkad's grandson, Naram-Sin, was in the late third millennium B.C.E. the first to use the honorific

title. Shulgi, king of Ur, adopted it during the middle of his reign about two centuries later. Thereafter, it was employed sporadically, though never by Hammurabi of Babylon nor by the Assyrian and Neo-Babylonian kings.

Other means, however, were used to suggest divinity: references to the king's radiant aura or to his being the god's "son"; grand epithets, such as "king of the four quarters [of heaven and earth]"; and artistic devices, such as portraying the king standing in a god's presence (as Hammurabi stands before Shamash on the stela of his famous code, basking in divine light) or making the king taller than the people around him (as Naram-Sin's sculpted stela of victory depicts him, superhuman in size). As a Sumerian proverb put it: "Man is the shadow of god, but the king is god's reflection."

Though royal dynasties flourished, direct descent was not a requirement for succession (though usurpers were quick to call themselves "legitimate"). A king, for example, might be followed to the throne by a brother or by a son other than his first born.

Symbols and Duties

The symbols of kingship in Mesopotamia were three—the crown, the throne, and the scepter—and each had a ceremonial function when a new king was installed, just as such objects have played a role in the institution of kingship in almost every land where it has existed, including ancient Egypt. The duties of the Mesopotamian king were also analogous to the responsibilities of other kings: he participated in religious rituals, guided the administration of justice, and directed the affairs of state in both peace and war. In carrying out these responsibilities he acted as the earthly representative of the gods and, in particular, of the chief god of his city-state or nation, manifesting in the process the royal virtues of strength and wisdom.

3.2 The standing figure of an Assyrian king, carved on the wall of his palace at Kalhu (Nimrud). (Austen Henry Layard, Nineveh and Its Remains [London: John Murray, 1849])

Officials

A variety of officials assisted the king in the exercise of his powers. These included the priestly hierarchy of the temples, including the high priest of the state's principal god; a judiciary to administer the laws; a commander in chief of the army and his subordinates; a prime minister to tender advice and conduct the business of diplomacy; a large staff to maintain the day-to-day operations of the palace, including a chief of staff, or chamberlain, and a royal cup-bearer, as well as servants aplenty; a ready corps of scribes; and the occasional architect or sculptor to execute commissions with the aid of their apprentices.

As the territory of the kingdom grew—especially when it attained the size of empire—the king needed governors—likely drawn from the nobility—to administer its parts, as well as a cadre of royal messengers to transmit reports and deliver his commands.

The Substitute King

One of the most peculiar of Mesopotamian royal customs was that of the "substitute king." If dire omens predicted the king's death, a temporary substitute for him would be chosen. The substitute would be dressed in royal robes, given a "queen," and permitted to live in the palace in the hope that destiny would strike him rather than the real king (who stayed in hiding). Once the danger was passed, the substitute "went to his fate"—an expression that implied death. In this way the Mesopotamians hoped to trick fate. Becoming substitute king was not exactly a career move unless you were dying to sit on the throne.

TAXATION

Nominally, all the lands and waters of a Mesopotamian city-state belonged to its gods and were managed by their surrogates, the rulers and priests. Individuals who used the lands and waters and derived economic benefit from them were, in turn, subject to taxation.

Because coinage had not yet been invented (see Chapter 9), taxes were paid in the form of goods and services. Normally the goods represented a share of what had been produced (such as grain, dates, fish, wool, or livestock) or a percentage of its worth in silver. Services could be rendered through military service or by laboring on communal projects (the excavation and maintenance of irrigation canals; the harvesting of crops grown on communal land; or the construction of temples and palaces). Merchants were also subject to special taxes when they shipped or received goods, or when they passed through cities along trade routes or crossed rivers.

With the growth of cities and the rise of empires, tax collection became a major government activity, employing a corps of civil servants, some of whom regularly traveled to make collections. Those who refused to comply (including subject states) would be threatened with military reprisal. Mesopotamian kings—except for those of Assyria—often sold the right to collect taxes to the highest private bidder, who then reaped a fortune by extorting a far greater sum from the taxpayers than he himself had paid. Occasionally, a king might also grant tax exemption to a favorite in exchange for some past or future service.

As an ancient proverb notes (see chapter 5), the Mesopotamian man most to be feared was the tax collector.

JUSTICE AND LAW

In the Mesopotamian mind, the divine was conceived of as a force that brought order out of chaos. Maintaining cosmic order was the chief responsibility of heaven's sovereign, the sky-god Anu.

The king, in turn, was the representative of Anu on earth. His chief responsibility was to make the divine will manifest on earth by bringing order to human society. This he did by governing firmly and justly: issuing decrees, enacting laws, and administering their enforcement. The divine mandate implicit in a Mesopotamian king's actions enhanced his authority and inspired compliance. It is therefore no accident that kings, as a practical matter, emphasized that they were acting on god's behalf. Their own

divine status, when assumed, only served to reinforce their spiritual mandate. And, despite the existence of "primitive democracy," it was not a legislature but a king who enacted the laws.

Law Codes

We are fortunate to possess, in whole or in part, law codes promulgated by Mesopotamia's ancient kings. Not only are they the world's oldest legal codes; they also contain the world's oldest surviving laws. Three of the codes belong to the rulers of Sumer: Urukagina (ca. 2350 B.C.E.), Ur-Nammu (ca. 2100 B.C.E.), and Lipit-Ishtar (ca. 1930 B.C.E.). The others were written in Akkadian: the laws of the city of Eshnunna dating to the 19th century B.C.E.; the early 18th-century B.C.E. laws of Hammurabi of Babylon; 12th-century B.C.E. Middle Assyrian laws; and even later laws of Neo-Babylonian kings. Of all these, the most famous is the Code of Hammurabi, described by J. N. Postgate as "the most informative single source for legal history before the classical world" (Postgate 1992: 288).

The codes of Lipit-Ishtar and Hammurabi are especially fascinating because their prologues have been preserved. Like the opening of the Declaration of Independence and the preamble to the Constitution, each prologue sets forth the spiritual and moral justification for the text that follows. Each king invokes the names of his country's supreme gods, declaring that they called upon him to act on their behalf so as to make human society more orderly and just. Lipit-Ishtar emphasizes his commitment to family values, while Hammurabi proclaims his mission to "crush the evil-doer and protect the weak from the strong." At the top of Hammurabi's sculpted stela, the king stands before the sun-god Shamash, promising as in his prologue to make "justice rise over the people like the sun and brighten the land with its light." In similar fashion, a seventh- or sixth-century B.C.E. Neo-

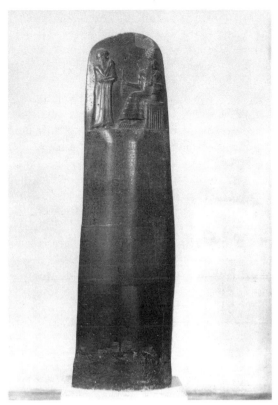

3.3 The code of Hammurabi, carved on a sculpted block of black diorite, stands today in Paris in the Louvre. (Photographie Lauros Giraudon/Art Resources, N.Y.)

3.4 In this close-up, we see the Babylonian god Shamash instructing Hammurabi in the law. Shamash is seated on his divine throne as the king stands before him. (Bildarchiv Foto Marburg/Art Resource, N.Y.)

Babylonian text celebrates the dedication of a now anonymous king to the cause of justice:

> For the sake of due process he did not neglect truth and justice, nor did he rest day and night! He was always drawing up, with reasoned deliberation, cases and decisions pleasing to the great lord Marduk (and) framed for the benefit of all the people and the stability of Babylonia. He drew up improved regulations for the city, he rebuilt the law court. He drew up regulations . . . his kingship forever. (Foster 1995: 209)

Copied onto stone stelae and set up in the cities of the land, the law codes of Mesopotamia made public the standards by which people were expected to live. Such standardization sought to unify a wide territory that might otherwise have been fragmented by diverse practices, and simultaneously solidified the ruler's grasp over his domain. And when reforms were introduced to correct abuses, the level of social justice was universally raised.

The codes cover a lot of ground—crime and punishment, of course, but also matters that are largely economic: wage and price controls, property rights (including slave ownership), and regulations governing inheritance and indebtedness. The codes are by no means comprehensive, but their range is wide. In content, they seem to be rationalized compilations of normal practices elevated by an abiding concern for uniformity and equity. In style, case-form prevails: "If X has done such-and-such, then Y must be the penalty." Indeed, their very specificity serves to illuminate the nooks and crannies of daily life—from who pays for a damaged ox to who gets to keep a divorced wife's dowry.

In the Code of Hammurabi, penalties were assessed based on one's social class: the same act committed against a member of a lower class resulted in a lighter punishment; but against a member of a higher class, a heavier one. The penalty system thus reinforced the existing social order. And, in recognition of economic realities, fines assessed on the poor were lower than fines assessed on the rich.

Mesopotamian law also fostered worker efficiency by severely punishing professional incompetence. A boatman whose negligence sank a boat was responsible for the cost of the boat and its entire cargo. A surgeon who cost a patient his eye had his hand cut off. And if a building collapsed and its owner died, the builder had to pay with his life.

The Administration of Justice

If the law codes of Mesopotamia signify an ideal of justice that should govern society, how was the ideal made an everyday reality?

To begin with, there were no lawyers. Nor was there a regular court system, as we understand it. Nor were there prisons, or even a police force. How then was justice achieved, or even approximated?

The key was an innate compliance to higher authority, a behavioral characteristic that permeated Mesopotamian culture. Society's prime personal virtue was humble and unquestioning obedience—to the gods and their earthly surrogates. Within society, it was the state and its demands rather than the individual and his rights that were supreme.

The Mesopotamians, however, were human beings, and therefore far from perfect. Even when greed and anger didn't rear up their ugly heads, other things—an accident, a basic misunderstanding, or overlapping claims—could provoke controversy. Hence the need for adjudication to settle disputes.

Most controversies were resolved on the local level—the village or neighborhood—by a council of elders whose members were impaneled as judges when circumstances warranted. Though there were judges in ancient Mesopotamia, there were no juries selected from the population at large to hear cases. Instead, the litigants presented their arguments to the judges in oral testimony, witnesses were called (some, if need be, from considerable distances), and evidence (in the form of a written contract, for example) was examined. Those who testified were required to swear an oath, not on a Bible but on a sacred symbol of the local god. (For this reason, trials were often held on the grounds of temples.) Perjury was punished not by law but by divine retribution, for the only way to avoid a curse was to tell the truth, and anyone refusing to take the oath was immediately suspect.

If the judges were unable to reach a decision by rational means, they had recourse to "trial by river." The accused would be thrown into the river. If he surfaced and swam to shore, he was innocent. But if the god of the river swallowed him up, he was guilty as charged.

The eventual verdict would be inscribed on a clay tablet and announced publicly by a herald. If property had to be seized or some other directive of the court carried out, a soldier would act as bailiff.

Cases of serious crime, including murder, were referred to a higher court presided over by one or more officials appointed by the king. A verdict could be appealed to such a higher court, and even the king himself, if authorities deemed it proper.

Penalties

Punishments could be harsh and served as powerful deterrents against unlawful acts. Earlier Sumerian law seems to have been guided by the principle of compensation to a victim who had suffered injury or loss, but the later Babylonian Code of Hammurabi preferred to physically punish the perpetrator, following the principle of "an eye for an eye, a tooth for a tooth," a principle enunciated also in the Old Testament (Leviticus 24:20). Though initially such a practice might seem barbaric, upon closer inspection it can be viewed as an attempt by society to set limits to retribution that might otherwise have taken both the eyes and even the life of a perpetrator. This said, Hammurabi's Code severely punishes crimes that would receive lesser penalties under contemporary Western law. The death penalty, for example, is meted out for breaking and entering, for stealing, or for receiving stolen property; likewise, for falsely accusing another of murder. An adulterous couple was bound and thrown into the river to drown, and a son who struck his father had his hand cut off. And a priestess who was caught entering a bar was burnt alive. By such harsh strictures, Babylonian law sought to preserve the integrity of property, the sanctity of family, and the sacredness of society's institutions.

To the Western eye, Assyrian law seems even more savage. If a man's wife was caught stealing from another man's home, her husband had to pay a penalty and cut off her ears; if he chose not to pay the penalty, the owner could cut off her nose. If a couple were found committing adultery, the man would be castrated and his face mutilated; the woman—again—would lose her nose. There were also severe penalties for showing affection to another man's wife: for touching, the perpetrator would have a finger cut off; for a kiss, his lower lip would be passed across the sharp blade of an ax, slicing it off. Furthermore, if a man saw a prostitute wearing a veil (the sign of a respectable woman) and failed to report her infraction, he would be stripped and beaten with a stick 50 times. Then his ears would be pierced and threaded with a cord and somehow tied to his back, after which he would serve a month at hard labor.

Incarceration was apparently not a sentencing option in Mesopotamia, for imprisonment did neither the injured party nor society itself any good. Using the criminal for forced labor seemed, at least to the Assyrian state, a far more economically productive and socially beneficial alternative.

Assaults upon morality and their reproof were serious subjects in Mesopotamia, precisely because society itself was serious business. Without order and respect for ethical constraint, civilization itself would be doomed.

It would be a facile and self-serving exercise for us who are spectators at our own permissive culture's decline to mock the efforts of ancients, however excessive, to stave off civilization's fall. Perhaps the closer to the end they came, the more desperate they became, hoping—in vain, it turns out—to save the world they knew by toughening the penal code and rounding up the usual suspects. As Mesopotamian history shows, their real enemy was an entropy to which all empires succumb. Ironically today, a similar holding action is again taking place in certain nations of the Mideast, this time against what is perceived as the morally corruptive influence of the West. Only in Islamic law can analogies still be found for the harsh penalties of the Mideast's more ancient codes.

For our understanding of Mesopotamian jurisprudence, we are aided by the survival of court records. Some cases acquired such notoriety or seemed so stereotypical that they became copying exercises for scribal trainees, and were thus preserved in multiple copies. One of the most famous trials involved a murder that took place around 1900 B.C.E. Three men conspired to murder a fourth, and the intended victim's wife found out about the plot, but she did nothing to stop it. The killers were later apprehended, along with the all-too-reticent wife. The transcript goes like this:

> Nanna-sig, Ku-Enlilla the barber, and Enlil-ennam the orchard-keeper, murdered Lu-Inanna the priest. After Lu-Inanna was dead, they told his wife Nin-dada that her husband had been murdered. Nin-dada kept her mouth shut and didn't tell anyone. The case was referred to the city of Isin and presented to the king. King Ur-Ninurta remanded the case for trial before Nippur's Assembly.
>
> Ur-gula, Dudu the bird-catcher, Ali-ellati the noble, Puzu, Eluti, Sheshkalla the potter, Lugal-kam the orchard-keeper, Lugal-azida, and Sheshkalla the son of Shara-har got up and said: "Since they killed a man, they shouldn't be allowed to live. All four should be killed in front of the ceremonial chair where Lu-Inanna used to sit." Then Shuqalilum the soldier and Ubar-Suen the orchard-keeper got up and said: "Nin-dada didn't really kill her husband, so why should *she* be executed?" At that point the Elders addressed the Assembly and said: "If a wife has no respect for her husband's life, it may be because she's already slept with another man. That other man may murder her husband knowing she would never tell. Why else would she keep silent? More than anyone else *she's* the one who caused her husband's death, and *she* bears the most guilt!"
>
> The Assembly having resolved the issue, Nanna-sig, Ku-Enlilla the barber, Enlil-ennam the orchard-keeper, and Nin-dada, the wife of Lu-Inanna, were sentenced to death. Verdict of the Assembly of Nippur.

All that is missing from the account are the tears in Nin-dada's eyes and the downcast expressions on the faces of the condemned, including Ku-Enlilla the barber, who probably wielded the deadly razor that took the unsuspecting priest's life 4,000 years ago.

BIOGRAPHIES OF POLITICAL LEADERS

In chapter 2 we tried to capture the sweep of Mesopotamian history by painting its moving landscape in broad strokes. Now it is time to identify individual figures in that landscape who, for better or worse, may be said to have "made history" by governing the lands of the Tigris and Euphrates and their people.

Our list is alphabetical rather than chronological because Mesopotamia embraced not one country and culture but multiple ones that moved separately on parallel tracks, yet also interacted when one nation or another became dominant and exerted political control over its neighbors. Thus to study Mesopotamian history is to study not one chronology but many that are intertwined like the threads of an elaborate tapestry. To follow these threads, the reader may wish to consult the chronological tables at the back of Georges Roux's masterful book, *Ancient Iraq*, or the streamlined table at the end of our own. There is also a chronological list of Key Rulers of Mesopotamia included in chapter 2.

An alphabetical list like the one that follows has certain intrinsic virtues. The reader who is intrigued by a particular figure in history can readily find the basic facts of his career as well as the period in which he lived and held power. And it is precisely by *ignoring* chronology and reading such a list sequentially that the reader can become sensitized to the common political themes that by their repetition transcend the borders of space and time.

For the reader in a hurry who has no time to read the following directory in its entirety, a summary is in order:

> The kings of Mesopotamia had long names, and sons usually followed them to the throne with equally long names. They all busied themselves fighting over territory against other kings. When they weren't destroying or killing something, they spent their spare time building things. We know a lot about some kings, and precious little about others. Some kings, however, do stand out due to the quality or quantity of their destroying, their killing, or their building. Their wives are seldom mentioned.

The impression such as summary gives comes not only from what the ancient rulers of Mesopotamia did but also from what they and their chroniclers wanted remembered. In short, we are prisoners of the evidence, evidence that is inevitably the biased product of deliberate selection by the participants. Furthermore, the more objective archaeological evidence we *could* have possessed has been winnowed by time and the forces of natural and man-made destruction, leaving us with a pile of historical detritus. Only rarely when we have twin portraits of the same ruler painted from opposing angles—from his nation's side and the enemy's—do we have grounds for constructing an accurate hologram, yet one that—like all holograms—will forever remain not quite alive.

Before taking the true measure of a man, we must also learn to read between the cuneiform lines: to appreciate not only the "killing" but the killed; not only the "destroying" but the destroyed; not only the "building" but the purposes for which things were built, and what—if anything—in the end they achieved.

We will seek in the remainder of this book to fill in those very human blanks as we explore life in ancient Mesopotamia. But let us first give these "makers of civilization" their due.

Note: the dates in parentheses are, where known, the dates of a given king's reign. While historians often differ on matters of ancient chronology, for simplicity's sake I have followed the dating scheme found in Georges Roux's book cited above.

A-annepadda (ca. 2525–2485 B.C.E.) This ruler of Ur's First Dynasty erected a temple at Tell Ubaid near Ur in honor of the goddess Ninhursag.

Abi-eshuh (1711–1684 B.C.E.) Abi-eshuh was the grandson of Hammurabi I and followed his father, Samsu-iluna, to the throne of Babylon. His father had faced the first Kassite attack on Babylonian territory; Samsu-iluna successfully repelled the second, but nevertheless lost a hold on some of the lands he had inherited in the area of the Middle Euphrates. Seeking to regain control over Sumer, Abi-eshuh dammed up the Tigris in a failed attempt to drive out the rebel leader Iluma-ilum from the marshes to the south.

Abirattash (middle of the 17th century B.C.E.) Abirattash ruled the Kassites of Babylonia after the reign of Ushishi.

Abi-sare (1905–1895 B.C.E.) As king of Larsa, Abi-sare triumphed over the rival city-state of Isin after slaying its king in battle.

Adad-apla-iddina (1067–1046 B.C.E.) This Babylonian king was married to an Assyrian princess, but that did not prevent the Assyrians from attacking Babylonia. His reign was also troubled by an Aramaean revolt and Sutean raids. Internally, he wisely concentrated on rebuilding Babylon's fortifications and renovating temples throughout Babylonia to court divine favor.

Adad-nirari I (1307–1275 B.C.E.)   By military force this Assyrian king extended the borders of his empire in every direction. His military campaigns are made vivid by surviving descriptive accounts of his army's actions, something which we do not have in the case of earlier Assyrian kings. Among his achievements was his capture (and, later, generous release) of the Mitanni king Shatturara I after a Mitanni challenge to Assyrian dominion. The Assyrian king's generosity, however, was misplaced: after Shattuara's death, the Mitanni revolted again.

Adad-nirari II (911–891 B.C.E.)   This later Assyrian king continued the mission of his father, Ashur-dan II, to restore his nation's borders against the intrusions of its enemies.

Adad-nirari III (810–783 B.C.E.)   This Assyrian king tried to establish rapprochement with Babylonia consequent to the brutal treatment it had suffered at the hands of his predecessor, Shamshi-Adad V. As a consequence, Babylonian deportees were allowed to return to their homeland, and the statues of Babylonia's gods were restored to the shrines from which they had been taken.

Adad-shuma-iddina (late 13th century B.C.E.)   A Kassite king of Babylon during the period when Babylonia was under the control of Assyria's king Tukulti-Ninurta I.

Adad-shuma-usur (1218–1189 B.C.E.)   A Kassite, Adad-shuma-usur became Babylonia's king after his predecessor, Adad-shuma-iddina, was overthrown. He appears as a character in a late Babylonian epic.

Agga (Akka) (ca. 2650 B.C.E.)   A ruler of Kish, Agga tried to impose his will upon the neighboring city of Uruk, but he was defeated and captured by Uruk's ruler, the legendary Gilgamesh. According to an early epic account, Gilgamesh showed mercy to Agga and released him after the battle.

Agum I (early 18th century B.C.E.)   Agum I became second king of the migrant Kassites after they had established themselves in Mesopotamia.

Agum II Kakrime (ca. 1570 B.C.E.)   Agum II was the first Kassite ruler of the city of Babylon following Babylon's destruction by the Hittites and the termination of its First Dynasty. According to a story, he brought back to Babylon sacred statues of the god Marduk and his divine consort Sarpanitum, statues which the Hittites had earlier carried off when they plundered Babylon in 1595 B.C.E.

Agum III (middle of the 15th century B.C.E.)   Agum III was a Kassite king of Babylonia. During his career he conducted military campaigns in the south against the army of the Sea-Land, a political region so named because of its proximity to the Persian Gulf.

Akalamdug (ca. 2600 B.C.E.)   The tomb of this ruler of Ur was discovered by Sir Leonard Woolley in the city's Royal Cemetery.

Akkia (beginning of the 20th century B.C.E.)   The name of this early Assyrian king suggests that he—like his predecessors Ushpia and Kikkia—was Hurrian.

Akurgal (ca. 2465 B.C.E.)   Ruler of Lagash.

Alexander III the Great (356–323 B.C.E.)   A master strategist and charismatic leader, Alexander became king of Macedonia at the age of 20 following the assassination of his father Philip II. Not content with merely inheriting his father's Hellenic empire but driven instead by a heroic compulsion to prove his own worth and win greater glory, Alexander conceived a plan to

3.5   This ancient Greek coin portrays Alexander the Great (on the left) wearing the lion-skin cap of his hero Hercules. The back of the coin (on the right) shows the king of the Greek gods, Zeus, seated upon his Olympian throne.   (J. Verschoyle, The History of Ancient Civilization [London: Chapman and Hall, 1889])

wage a holy war against Greece's historic enemy, the Persians, then the possessors of the largest empire in the history of the world. After defeating Persia's "king of kings," Darius III, with a combined Macedonian and Greek force, burning the palace at Persepolis, and liberating Egypt from Persian domination, Alexander marched to the Indian subcontinent and might have gone on to China had his men not threatened mutiny. Recognizing that a 3,000-mile-wide empire spanning Europe and Asia could not be held together by military force alone, Alexander envisioned the creation of a racially integrated society on a global scale. To achieve this end, he enlisted Persian officers in his army, encouraged his soldiers to intermarry with native women (as he did himself), and founded cities across the breadth of his kingdom to be partly populated by colonists from Greece to encourage the formation of a unified culture. Babylon was the centrally located city that he chose for his capital, and in Babylon he died—of fever possibly aggravated by alcoholism—just short of his 33rd birthday. Though the empire he had sought to build was divided up after his death by the generals who had fought by his side, his most lasting

legacy was the cultural fusion of West and East known as Hellenistic civilization.

Alexander Severus (222–235 C.E.)   A Roman emperor, he managed to maintain Rome's military hold over Mesopotamia.

Amar-Sin (2046–2038 B.C.E.)   The son of Shulgi and the third member of Ur's glorious Third Dynasty, Amar-Sin presided over a secure and prosperous empire.

Amel-Marduk (Biblical "Evil-Merodach") (first half of the sixth century B.C.E.)   Amel-Marduk was the son and successor of Nebuchadnezzar II, and the third king of the Neo Babylonian dynasty. Tradition records that his royal behavior was tyrannical. After two years he was assassinated by his sister's husband, Nergal-shar-usur.

Ammi-ditana (1683–1647 B.C.E.)   Ammi-ditana was the great-grandson of Hammurabi I and followed his father, Abi-eshuh, to Babylon's throne. He engaged in public works projects inside the city of Babylon and may have briefly regained hold over some of the lands lost to rebels subsequent to Hammurabi's death.

Ammi-saduqa (1646–1626 B.C.E.)   Ammi-saduqa was the son of Ammi-ditana and the tenth king of Babylon's First Dynasty. Like his ancestor Hammurabi, Ammi-saduqa ordered a cancellation of citizens' debts as a way of giving Babylon's economy a fresh start. He is also remembered for having ordered court astronomers to record the rising and setting times of the planet Venus for the purpose of making astrological predictions. Thanks to this database recorded in cuneiform, modern historians can date the reign of Ammi-saduqa and other First Dynasty rulers, including Hammurabi. However, because the planet Venus has a 60-year cycle, the rising and setting the

Babylonians recorded could fit any one of three possible chronological "windows" as much as 120 years apart. The Venus Tablets have thus compelled scholars to chose—and argue—among a "High," a "Middle," and a "Low" chronology for Babylon's kings ("Low" having the lowest B.C.E. numbers). The dating scheme used in this chapter follows the middle road.

Anni (second half of the 18th century B.C.E.) Anni was the last man to rule Eshnunna before its destruction by the Babylonians under Samsu-iluna.

Antiochus I (281–260 B.C.E.) Antiochus was the son of Seleucus I. Following his father's murder, he succeeded him after a long military struggle as Hellenistic ruler of Babylonia. To win the loyalty of his people, he restored the great temples of Babylon and asked the gods for their blessings. His is the last surviving royal inscription in Mesopotamia to be engraved in cuneiform.

Antiochus II (260–246 B.C.E.) Antiochus was the third member of the Seleucid dynasty that ruled Babylonia in Hellenistic times. To make peace with Ptolemaic Egypt, Antiochus agreed to marry Ptolemy II's daughter. Because Antiochus was already married, his plan did not have a happy outcome: his first wife poisoned him.

Antiochus III (222–187 B.C.E.) A member of the Hellenistic Seleucid dynasty, he won territory in Egypt by employing trained elephants in battle, but he was forced out of Turkey by the Roman army.

Antiochus IV (175–164 B.C.E.) Antiochus wielded Hellenistic culture as a device to unify his kingdom. In Israel his efforts sparked a revolt by the Maccabees, who succeeded in capturing and reconsecrating the temple at Jerusalem, which had been dedicated to the worship of Zeus. Their victory is still commemorated in the Jewish holiday of Hanukkah. In Babylon, Antiochus constructed a Greek-style gymnasium and theater, but by that time the city's population had declined as a result of a mass movement to Mesopotamia's popular Hellenistic capital, Seleucia-on-the-Tigris. In Egypt, Antiochus suffered defeat at the hands of the Romans, who compelled him to kill his attack elephants.

Antiochus VII (138–129 B.C.E.) Earlier in the second century B.C.E., the Seleucid dynasty had lost territory to Parthian aggression. Antiochus VII succeeded in reclaiming Babylonia and Media, but only briefly. He died in battle, and after his reign the Euphrates became his kingdom's easternmost border. In less than a century, the Romans laid claim to even that.

Antiochus XIII (69–65 B.C.E.) The last member of the Seleucid dynasty. In 64 B.C.E. under Pompey's leadership the Roman army captured Antioch, which had become the Seleucid's capital after the fall of Seleucia to the Parthians.

Apil-Kin (2126–2091 B.C.E.) Military governor of Mari.

Apil-Sin (1830–1813 B.C.E.) Son of Sabium, Apil-Sin was the fourth king of Babylon's First Dynasty. During his 18-year reign, there is no reference to war. Instead, he seems to have devoted himself to peaceful works, augmenting the city's network of irrigation canals and waterways while shoring up its defensive walls.

Ardeshir (Artaxerxes I) (first half of the third century C.E.) The founder of a dynasty, Ardeshir was the first Sassanian ruler to conquer Mesopotamia. In the process, he destroyed the city of Hatra and made Ctesiphon his capital.

Arik-den-ili (1319–1308 B.C.E.) This Assyrian king led his army into the Zagros Mountains to check the incursions of nomadic tribes on Assyria's northern and eastern frontiers.

Arsaces (Arshak) (250–248 B.C.E.) Arsaces was the founder of the Arsacid Dynasty and the first Parthian to rule Mesopotamia.

Artabanus I (211–191 B.C.E.) The third Parthian ruler of Mesopotamia.

Artabanus II (128–124 B.C.E.) A Parthian king, Artabanus confirmed Parthia's hold over Mesopotamia, a dominion that would endure for three and a half centuries until the triumph of the Sassanians in 227 C.E.

Artatama I (ca. 1430 B.C.E.) Hurrian king of the Mitanni. The pharaoh Amenhotep III of Egypt repeatedly asked (in the Amarna letters) to marry a daughter of Artatama to strengthen diplomatic ties between the two nations in the face of potential Hittite aggression.

Artaxerxes I (464–424 B.C.E.) This king of the Persian Empire was troubled by insurgencies instigated by the Greeks at the western edge of his kingdom.

Artaxerxes II (404–359 B.C.E.) The reign of this Persian king was contested by his younger brother, Cyrus, who marched into northern Mesopotamia at the head of an army that included 10,000 Greek mercenaries. When Cyrus was defeated and killed at Cunaxa in Babylonia, the Greeks were a thousand miles from home and were forced to make a dangerous trek home through hostile territory. The tale was later told by one of their courageous leaders, Xenophon, in his *Anabasis* ("The March Upcountry").

Artaxerxes III (358–338 B.C.E.) A king of the Persian Empire, Artaxerxes III reasserted Persia's control over Egypt before being killed in a coup along with most of his family.

Asharid-apal-Ekur (first half of the 11th century B.C.E.) An Assyrian king.

Ashurbanipal (668–627 B.C.E.) When Esarhaddon was still king of Assyria, he appointed his son Ashurbanipal as his heir to the Assyrian throne and his son Shamash-shum-ukin as his heir to the throne of Babylonia. After his death, the two brothers continued to share power in keeping with their father's wishes. Shamash-shum-ukin, however, chafed under Ashurbanipal's directives and eventually led a rebellion that Ashurbanipal crushed. Ashurbanipal went on to become Assyria's last warrior-king, waging war not only against Babylonia but also against Egypt and Elam. The king prided himself on his learning and established a great library in his palace at Nineveh, a library which—thanks to excavation—became a treasure-house of literary and scientific knowledge for modern scholars. Though his tomb at the city of Ashur was looted long, long ago, Ashurbanipal is still ebullient in London at the British Museum, enjoying a sculpted garden party with his resplendent queen, as the king of Elam's severed head hangs in perpetual adornment from a nearby bough.

Ashurbanipal's name—like those of the monarchs that follow—incorporates the name of Assyria's national god, Ashur, for whom the country itself was named.

Ashur-bel-kala (1074–1057 B.C.E.) An Assyrian king, Ashur-bel-kala spent his leisure time hunting and collecting exotic animals, some of which were sent to him as a gift by Egypt's pharaoh. Another gift he received was a new wife, thanks to the generosity of Adad-apla-iddina, whom Ashur-bel-kala appointed to the throne of Babylon and whose daughter Ashur-bel-kala then wed to strengthen diplomatic ties between Assyria and Babylonia. Militarily,

3.6 Ashurbanipal and his queen enjoy a garden party as the severed head of an enemy king hangs from a nearby tree.   (The British Museum)

Ashur-bel-kala spent time dealing with insurgents on Assyria's borders. His royal tomb was one of five discovered in the lower reaches of the palace at Ashur.

Ashur-bel-nisheshu (late 15th century B.C.E.) This Assyrian king signed a treaty with the Babylonian king Karaindash confirming an earlier agreement between their predecessors (Puzur-Ashur III and Burnaburiash I) defining the border between Assyria in the north and Babylonia in the south, and thereby establishing the historic division of Mesopotamia between the two nations. He also constructed a new wall around his capital city of Ashur to better protect it in case the Babylonians had second thoughts.

Ashur-dan I (1179–1134 B.C.E.) This Assyrian king was renowned for having reached a ripe old age (without dying of natural causes or falling victim to an assassin) and is credited with a 46-year reign. His kingdom's extended prosperity must have contributed to his longevity. On the other hand,

the prosperity was achieved in part by plundering Babylonian cities.

Ashur-dan II (934–912 B.C.E.) This Assyrian king made efforts to restore the losses his nation had sustained for almost a century and a half following the death of Tiglathpileser I. Adding muscle to his army, he recaptured lands Assyria's enemies had seized and returned them to productive use, while regaining control over old trade routes to further stimulate his nation's economy. In one brutal show of force, he flayed an enemy king alive and hung his skin over his city's wall.

Ashur-dan III (772–755 B.C.E.) The reign of this Assyrian king was troubled by rebellion, failed military ventures, the spread of epidemic, and an eclipse of the sun. Despite the king's bad luck, the last of these events proved to be a boon to historians since the calculation of its date, June 15, 763 B.C.E., helped them to date Ashur-dan's reign as well as Mesopotamian chronology in general during the first millennium B.C.E.

Ashur-etil-ilani (second half of the seventh century B.C.E.) Ashur-etil-ilani was an Assyrian king, the son and successor of the great Ashurbanipal. His ascent to the throne wasn't easy: he needed the backing of a powerful court eunuch and, even then, was challenged militarily by his own brother. He also faced a foreign enemy, King Nabopolassar of Babylonia.

Ashur-nadin-ahhe I (ca. 1450 B.C.E.) A congratulatory letter survives sent by this Assyrian king to his international colleague, the pharaoh Thutmose III, complimenting the Egyptian ruler on his military victories in Palestine and Syria. Despite his epistolary skill, Ashur-nadin-ahhe was deposed by his brother, proving the sword is mightier than the pen.

Ashur-nadin-ahhe II (ca. 1400 B.C.E.) This Assyrian king constructed a palace at Ashur that Assyrian kings continued to occupy for centuries thereafter. He was also the recipient of a shipment of gold from Egypt meant to insure good diplomatic relations between Assyria and the land of the Nile.

Ashur-nadin-apli (end of the 13th century B.C.E.) This Assyrian king seized the crown by plotting with courtiers and murdering his father, Tukulti-Ninurta I. Despite his malevolence, he could humbly fall to his knees when it suited his purposes: when the river Tigris began to change its course and seemed bent on flooding his capital city, Ashur-nadin-apli prayed and the disaster was averted.

Ashur-nadin-shumi (699–694 B.C.E.) As crown prince of Assyria, Ashur-nadin-shumi was put on the throne of Babylon by his father, Sennacherib. When Sennacherib attacked southern Elam to drive out Chaldaean rebels who had sought refuge there, the Elamites counterattacked by striking at Babylonia. At Sippar they captured Ashur-nadin-shumi and transported him to Elam where it is probable he was executed.

Ashurnasirpal I (1050–1032 B.C.E.) An Assyrian king. Though he ruled for almost two decades, we know nothing of what he did. He wasn't even the father of the famous Ashurnasirpal II. That honor went to Tukulti-Ninurta II.

Ashurnasirpal II (883–859 B.C.E.) Ashurnasirpal II set a standard for the future warrior-kings of Assyria. In the words of Georges Roux, he "possessed to the extreme all the

3.7 Carved from a 3.5-foot-tall block of hard magnesite, this portrait of Ashurnasirpal greeted Layard when he dug up the king's palace at Kalhu (Nimrud). The inscription below the king's beard gives his name. (Layard, *A Second Series of the Monuments of Nineveh*, 1853)

qualities and defects of his successors, the ruthless, indefatigable empire-builders: ambition, energy, courage, vanity, cruelty, magnificence" (Roux 1992: 288). His annals were the most extensive of any Assyrian ruler up to his time, detailing the multiple military campaigns he led to secure or enlarge his nation's territorial dominion. From one raid alone he filled his kingdom's coffers with 660 pounds of gold and an equal measure of silver, and added 460 horses to his stables. The sadistic cruelty he inflicted upon rebel leaders was legendary, skinning them alive and displaying their skin, and cutting off the noses and the ears of their followers or mounting their severed heads on pillars to serve as a warning to others. Inside his kingdom he constructed a new capital city at Kalhu (Nimrud) with an over 300,000 sq.ft. palace. To celebrate its completion, he invited 69,574 people to a party that lasted 10 days. The menu of the banquet still survives as do the ruins of his palace, the finest such structure in Assyria and one of the first great Assyrian monuments to be discovered in modern times.

Ashur-nirari I (1547–1522 B.C.E.) Inscriptions record that this Assyrian king engaged in building projects at his capital city.

Ashur-nirari II (second half of the 15th century B.C.E.) An Assyrian king, son of Enlil-nasir II.

Ashur-nirari III (end of the 13th century B.C.E.) This Assyrian king's claim to fame is that he was once reprimanded by a Babylonian king in a vitriolic letter.

Ashur-nirari IV (second half of the 11th century B.C.E.) An Assyrian king.

Ashur-nirari V (754–745 B.C.E.) This Assyrian king died during a revolt that began in his capital city, Kalhu.

Ashur-rabi I (first half of the 15th century B.C.E.) Though he was the son of a former Assyrian king (Enlil-nasir I), Ashur-rabi had to depose a usurper to become king. The usurper had warmed the seat only for a month.

Ashur-rabi II (1016–973 B.C.E.) An Assyrian king.

Ashur-rem-nisheshu (late 15th century B.C.E.) An Assyrian king.

Ashur-resh-ishi I (1133–1116 B.C.E.) An Assyrian king, he fought against Babylonia to the south as well as tribal insurgents on Assyria's eastern and western flanks.

Ashur-resh-ishi II (first half of the 10th century B.C.E.) An Assyrian king.

Ashur-uballit I (1365–1330 B.C.E.) During the reign of this Assyrian king, the kingdom of Mitanni collapsed due to civil war within and Hittite pressure without. In consequence, Assyria became the major power in northern Mesopotamia. Ashur-uballit intervened in Babylonian politics, deposing a usurper and putting his own candidate (Kurigalzu II) on the throne. Ashur-uballit's confidence is evident in a pompous letter sent to Egypt's pharaoh, and in the epithet, "king of the universe," he awarded to himself.

Ashur-uballit II (second half of the seventh century B.C.E.) Assyria's last recorded king. After Nineveh fell in 612 B.C.E. to the Babylonians and Medes, Ashur-uballit escaped to the city of Harran and set up a government in exile. Nabopolassar of Babylon viewed Ashur-uballit as a dangerous loose end and accordingly laid siege to Harran. That year, 610 B.C.E., marks the last page in the annals of the Assyrian Empire. As for Ashur-uballit himself, we can only imagine his end at Nabopolassar's hands.

Asinum (second half of the 18th century B.C.E.) An Assyrian king. After his death, anarchy ensued as a series of eight usurpers seized the throne.

Azuzum (second half of the 20th century B.C.E.) Ruler of Eshnunna and rebuilder of the capital's royal palace.

Baba-aha-iddina (late ninth century B.C.E.) Like his predecessor, Marduk-balassu-iqbi, Baba-aha-iddina was captured by the Assyrians and likely executed. He had sat on the throne of Babylon for less than a year.

Balili (middle of the 25th century B.C.E.) A member of Ur's First Dynasty.

Bazaia (1649–1622 B.C.E.) An Assyrian king.

Belakum (beginning of the 19th century B.C.E.) Ruler of Eshnunna.

Bel-shar-usur (Biblical "Belshazzar") (ca. 553–543 B.C.E.) Bel-shar-usur ruled Babylon during his father Nabonidus's 10 year absence from the capital, shortly before it fell to the Persians. In the biblical book of Daniel Belshazzar sees the fateful writing on the wall that forecasts his kingdom's fall.

Belshazzar See *Bel-shar-usur*.

Belu-bani (1700–1691 B.C.E.) An Assyrian king.

Bilalama (first half of the 20th century B.C.E.) This ruler of Eshnunna is credited with developing a code of law, written in Akkadian, over a century before the more famous Akkadian Code of Hammurabi. Bilalama also fought off Amorite chiefs before they became an established force in Mesopotamian politics.

Burnaburiash I (second half of the 16th century B.C.E.) Burnaburiash I was the successor of Agum II Kakrime and thus the second Kassite king to rule Babylon following its fall to the Hittites. To stabilize the northern border of his kingdom, he negotiated a treaty with the Assyrians establishing the territorial limits of their separate empires.

Burnaburiash II (1375–1347 B.C.E.) A Kassite king of Babylonia, Burnaburiash II reigned for 28 years, during which he constructed or renovated a number of religious edifices. The Amarna letters record diplomatic exchanges of gifts between Burnaburiash and the heretic pharaoh Akhenaton: Burnaburiash sending horses and lapis lazuli and Akhenaton reciprocating with gold, ivory, and ebony. Burnaburiash was miffed, however, when the pharaoh sent only five carriages to Babylonia to escort Burnaburiash's daughter to her royal wedding in Egypt. Even so, the wedding went ahead as scheduled, with Akhenaton sending bridal gifts sufficient to fill four columns and 307 lines of a cuneiform inventory. Hopefully, this Nilotic gesture made amends, but Burnaburiash was not an easy father-in-law to please: on an earlier occasion, when the pharaoh had promised to send him 50 lbs. of gold, the Kassite king melted down the artifacts upon their arrival and found they came up short. He then sent a letter of complaint, avoiding direct insult by suggesting that some Egyptian underling must have erred in tallying the shipment.

Bur-Sin (1895–1874 B.C.E.) Ruler of Isin.

Cambyses II (530–522 B.C.E.) When Cyrus II the Great of Persia captured the city of Babylon on his march of conquest, Cyrus appointed his son Cambyses to be Babylon's king. Upon Cyrus's death, Cambyses assumed the throne of the Persian Empire as well and made war on Egypt to complete his father's imperial plans. Hastening from Egypt to Persia to subdue a revolt at home, he accidentally wounded himself with his sword and died of blood poisoning.

Caracalla (198–217 C.E.) This Roman emperor, famous for the baths he completed in Rome, was killed by an assassin in northern Mesopotamia, while he visited the temple of the moon-god Sin at Harran, later called Carrhae. According to one version of the story, he was relieving himself behind a sand dune when the guard who was accompanying him did him in.

Carus (282–283 C.E.) After driving the Persians back, this Roman emperor was supposedly killed near Ctesiphon by an errant bolt of lightning (rare at that time of year) or more likely by the well-aimed blade of an assassin.

Constantius II (337–361 C.E.) This Roman emperor battled the Sassanian king Shapur II for control of northern Mesopotamia.

Cyrus II the Great (559–530 B.C.E.) Cyrus II was an aggressive Persian conqueror and empire-builder who transformed his original kingdom into a formidable world power. After defeating the Medes, he had all of Iran in his grasp. He then won Anatolia from King Croesus of Lydia and Babylonia from King Nabonidus, capturing both rulers. He shrewdly released the Judaeans who had been held captive in Babylonia for half a century, and he allowed them to return home to rebuild the temple in Jerusalem that Nebuchadnezzar had earlier destroyed. As a result, Jewish tradition made "Cyrus" one of the two non-Hebrew names that Jewish boys can be given (the other being "Alexander," the name of another foreign benefactor of the Jewish people, Alexander the Great).

3.8 On this cylinder inscribed in cuneiform, Cyrus describes how the Babylonian god Marduk showed his favor. Because of the Persian king's piety—Cyrus tells us—Marduk allowed him to march into the city of Babylon unopposed. (Rogers, *A History of Babylonia and Assyria*, 1915; picture courtesy Mansell, 1915)

Dadusha (ca. 1805–1780 B.C.E.) A ruler of Eshnunna, he formed an alliance with Elam.

Damiq-ilishu (1816–1794 B.C.E.) He lost his sovereignty—and Isin, its independence—

when he was defeated in war by Rim-Sin, king of the rival state of Larsa. Not to be confused with a later ruler (below) of the same name.

Damiq-ilishu (first half of the 17th century B.C.E.) Ruler of the Sea-Land, the marshland of southern Babylonia.

Darius I (522–486 B.C.E.) Darius's accession to the Persian throne was greeted with rebellions in all quarters of his kingdom. His subsequent triumph over the rebels was celebrated in an inscription carved on the sheer face of a cliff overlooking Behistun (Bisitun) in Media. The inscription—in Old Persian, Elamite, and Babylonian—became the equivalent to Egypt's Rosetta Stone, offering modern scholars the key to the decipherment of Mesopotamia's cuneiform writing system. Darius also built a new capital city and grandiose palace at Persepolis, as well as constructing an arsenal and an expanded royal residence at Babylon. In addition, he reorganized the administration of his empire to give himself greater control, established a system of royal roads and messengers for efficient communication, and imposed a universal code of law and standard of currency throughout his realm. It was he who made Aramaic (instead of Akkadian) the official language of Mesopotamia and the rest of his Near Eastern empire. His greatest foreign policy success was his domination of Egypt; his signal failure, his military defeat at the hand of the Greeks at Marathon in 490 B.C.E.

Darius II (423–405 B.C.E.) This Persian king faced challenges to his authority in Media and Ionia.

Darius III (335–331 B.C.E.) The last king of the Persian Empire, Darius was defeated on the battlefield by Alexander the Great, and later murdered by a Persian general. In keeping with Alexander's wishes, Darius was buried with full honors at Persepolis, the Persian capital, whose palace had earlier been burned following its capture by Alexander.

Diadumenian (218 C.E.) Briefly Roman emperor together with his father Macrinus, Diadumenian fled to Parthia after his father's defeat in battle. There he was caught and executed.

Dumuzi (second half of the 28th century B.C.E.) The last of the four mythical kings of Uruk, Dumuzi is also described in Sumerian mythology as a shepherd who became the lover and husband of the goddess Inanna.

Ea-gamil (ca. 1460 B.C.E.) With his defeat by Ulamburiash, king of Babylon, Ea-gamil became the last ruler of the Sea-Land and the last member of the so-called Second Dynasty of Babylon. From that point forward, Babylon controlled the whole of Sumer.

Eannatum (ca. 2455–2425 B.C.E.) The "Stele of the Vultures" depicts this ruler of Lagash battling his enemies as vultures feast on their corpses. His enemies were legion both within southern Mesopotamia and at its fringes.

Elili (ca. 2445 B.C.E.) A member of Ur's First Dynasty.

Emisum (2004–1977 B.C.E.) Ruler of Larsa.

Enannatum I (ca. 2425 B.C.E.) This ruler of Lagash built a temple in his home city with a distinctive oval shape.

Enannatum II (first half of the 24th century B.C.E.) Ruler of Lagash.

Enbi-Ishtar (ca. 2430 B.C.E.) A member of Kish's Second Dynasty.

En-entarzi (first half of the 24th century B.C.E.)   Ruler of Lagash.

En-hegal (ca. 2540 B.C.E.)   King of Lagash.

Enlil-bani (1860–1837 B.C.E.)   A gardener by trade, Enlil-bani was chosen by Isin's monarch, Irra-imitti, to serve as "substitute king" until the king himself was free of the danger a prophecy had foretold. Irra-imitti, however, ended up choking on some hot soup, and Enlil-bani became Isin's next king, a good one at that to judge by the hymns of praise that were afterward composed in his honor.

Enlil-kudurri-usur (end of the 13th century B.C.E.)   An Assyrian king.

Enlil-nadin-ahhe (1159–1157 B.C.E.)   Enlil-nadin-ahhe was the last Kassite king to rule Babylon. After waging war against the king of Elam, he was captured. The Elamites then ravaged Babylonia and deported large numbers of its people. With this defeat, over four centuries of Kassite rule came to an end.

Enlil-nadin-apli (ca. 1100 B.C.E.)   Enlil-nadin-apli ruled Babylon as the son and successor of Nebuchadnezzar I.

Enlil-nadin-shumi (late 13th century B.C.E.)   Enlil-nadin-shumi was a Kassite king of Babylon during the period when Babylon's fate was in the hands of the Assyrian king Tukulti-Ninurta I.

Enlil-nasir I (ca. 1500 B.C.E.)   Inscriptions record the building projects of this Assyrian king.

Enlil-nasir II (second half of the 15th century B.C.E.)   An Assyrian king who took the throne by unseating his brother, Ashur-nadin-ahhe I.

Enlil-nirari (ca. 1325 B.C.E.)   Enlil-nirari's father and predecessor on the Assyrian throne was Ashur-uballit I, during whose reign the empire of Mitanni ceased to be a threat. During Enlil-nirari's reign, however, Kurigalzu II of Babylon (who had been put on his throne by Enlil-nirari's father) challenged Assyria on the battlefield, after which a peace treaty was signed that historically redefined the borders of the two countries.

Enmebaragesi (ca. 2700 B.C.E.)   The 21st to sit on the throne of Kish after the days of the legendary Great Flood, Enmebaragesi distinguished himself by triumphing over the rival state of Elam.

Enmerkar (second half of the 28th century B.C.E.)   The second of the four mythical kings of Uruk, Enmerkar made war against the distant kingdom of Aratta to obtain supplies of gold, silver, and lapis lazuli for the beautification of his city's temples. In this cause he was aided by the goddess Inanna. Legend says he was also responsible for the invention of writing.

En-shakush-anna (ca. 2430–2400 B.C.E.)   A member of Uruk's Second Dynasty, this king warred against Kish and recovered religious artifacts that had been plundered from Uruk's temples by Kish's king.

Entemena (Enmetena) (ca. 2400 B.C.E.)   Entemena is famous for a canal he built connecting the Tigris with the Euphrates. In the city of Lagash where he was ruler he was popular for issuing a decree that absolved citizens of heavy debts. His piety is documented by an inscribed silver vase that he dedicated to the patron god of the city, Ningirsu.

Eriba-Adad I (1392–1366 B.C.E.)   An Assyrian king who ruled for a quarter of a century and is remembered only in two broken building inscriptions.

Eriba-Marduk (769–761 B.C.E.) Following the death of the Assyrian king Adad-nirari III, Eriba-Marduk seized the Babylonian throne. He then suppressed the incursions of nomads into Babylonian territory and laid the basis for economic growth and prosperity, taking time to thank the gods for renewing their blessings.

Erishum I (ca. 1906–1867 B.C.E.) Erishum I was an Assyrian king who continued the trade policies of his predecessor, Ilushuma. Like his predecessor also, he restored the temples of the gods at Ashur, his capital.

Erishum II (second half of the 19th century B.C.E.) An Assyrian king.

Erishum III (1598–1586 B.C.E.) An Assyrian king.

Esarhaddon (680–669 B.C.E.) The son of Sennacherib, Esarhaddon had to fight his brother for Assyria's throne. At home, he tried to placate the Babylonians by restoring the city his father had destroyed. Though prophecies declared that Babylon could not be rebuilt for 70 years, Esarhaddon had his priests read the cuneiform number upside-down and came up with 11, exactly the number he had wanted to fulfill his plans. Abroad, his major preoccupation was Egypt, which he invaded three times, dying on his third and final march. As his letters attest, no Mesopotamian king before or after had so frequently consulted astrologers to foresee his destiny.

Etana (early third millennium B.C.E.) According to an epic poem entitled *The Adventure of Etana* (see chapter 5), this early ruler of Kish traveled to heaven on the back of an eagle in order to obtain a magic plant that would enable him to father an heir.

3.9 *On this diorite stele, Esarhaddon holds two subject kings on leashes. The smaller figure, kneeling, is Egypt's pharaoh.* (Rogers, *A History of Babylonia and Assyria*, 1915; picture courtesy Mansell, 1915)

Eulmash-shakin-shumi (1003–987 B.C.E.) Eulmash-shakin-shumi founded Babylon's Sixth Dynasty that endured for just three years after his death.

Evil-Merodach See *Amel-Marduk*.

Gandash (ca. 1730 B.C.E.) Gandash is the name given in the Babylonian King List to the founder and first king of the Kassite dynasty. Originating in the Zagros Mountains of Iran, the Kassites swept into Mesopotamia in the second half of the 18th century B.C.E. By the beginning of the 16th century B.C.E., they controlled Babylonia and went on to dominate the land militarily and politically for over four centuries.

Gilgamesh (Sumerian: Bilgames) (ca. 2700 B.C.E.) Gilgamesh is the central character in Mesopotamia's greatest literary work, *The Epic of Gilgamesh* (see chapter 5). His epic exploits are apparently based on the life of a real person, a ruler of Uruk named in the Sumerian King List. Gilgamesh is credited with having built Uruk's mighty walls. In the epic, he begins his career as a self-centered king and ends it searching for, and losing, the secret to eternal life.

Gordian III (238–244 C.E.) This Roman emperor drove the Persians out of Mesopotamia. A mutiny instigated by an ambitious subordinate led to his execution at the city of Circesium in Mesopotamia.

Gudea (2141–2122 B.C.E.) The prosperity that had begun in Lagash under Ur-Baba continued during the reign of Gudea. To thank the gods, Gudea restored or rebuilt over a dozen temples, and commissioned multiple stone portraits of himself to communicate his piety. In two statues he sits with the Mesopotamian equivalent of blueprints resting on his lap. His lengthy dedicatory inscriptions embody the apex of classic Sumerian literary style. In the words of Georges Roux: "This young man sitting calmly, a faint smile upon his lips, his hands clasped in front of his chest, the plan of a temple or a foot rule across his knee, is the finest example of a figure unfortunately soon to disappear: the perfect Sumerian ruler, pious,

3.10   *In this disembodied portrait head in stone, we gaze upon the serene and imperturbable countenance of Gudea. The leader's capacity for control and attention to detail are suggested by the precise sculpting of the multiple spirals in Gudea's cap and the chiseling of his chevron-like brows. The portrait is now in the collection of the Louvre.* (de Sarzec, *Découvertes en Chaldée*, 1884–1912)

just, cultured, faithful to the old traditions, devoted to his people, filled with love and pride for his city and . . . pacific" (Roux 1992: 168).

Gulkishar (second half of the 17th century B.C.E.) Ruler of the Sea-Land.

Gungunum (1932–1906 B.C.E.) Gungunum was an imperialistic leader of Larsa who occupied the lower half of southern Mesopotamia and thereby gained commercial access to the Persian Gulf.

Hammurabi I (Hammurapi) (1792–1750 B.C.E.) Hammurabi, the son of Sin-muballit, was the sixth and greatest of the Amorite rulers who governed Babylon as its First Dynasty.

Hammurabi reigned for 43 years, beginning his career as a local king and ending it as the undisputed master of Mesopotamia. He is most famous for his codification of Babylonian law (see above and chapter 5), an act which exemplified his interest in organization, his preoccupation with detail, and his desire for control, as well as his dedication to the cause of uniform social justice. In addition to these personal qualities, he was also an able administrator, an adroit diplomat, and a canny imperialist, patient in the achievement of his goals. Upon taking the throne, he issued a proclamation forgiving people's debts, and during the first five years of his reign further enhanced his popularity by piously renovating the sanctuaries of the gods, especially Marduk, Babylon's patron. Then, with his power at home secure and his military forces primed, he began a five-year series of campaigns against rival states to the south and east, expanding his territory. This accomplished, Hammurabi spent the next 18 years consolidating his holdings and carrying out public works projects at home, including strengthening the city's fortifications, improving its irrigation system, and beautifying its temples. Then, commencing in the 29th year of his reign, he turned once again to war, conquering in rapid succession all his former rivals: the states of Eshnunna (in the east), Larsa (in the south), Assyria (in the north), and Mari (in the west). In the end, illness compelled him to abandon his dreams and surrender his throne to a successor. It is mainly from the diplomatic correspondence of others (especially the Mari letters) that we get an impression of Hammurabi's character. From the practice of naming Babylon's years after the most outstanding accomplishments of its rulers, we gain a chronological account of his deeds. As to the actual city he ruled, it remains buried beneath the stratified ruins left by his successors, so deep below the water table as to preclude excavation to date. Soaking in the darkness lie the unread archives of one of Mesopotamia's mightiest monarchs.

Hanun-Dagan (2016–2008 B.C.E.) Military governor of Mari.

Harbashihu (second half of the 17th century B.C.E.) Harbashihu ruled the Babylonian Kassites after the days of Urzigurumash.

Hilal-Erra (ca. 2025 B.C.E.) Military governor of Mari.

Iaggid-Lim (Yaggid-Lim) (ca. 1830–1820 B.C.E.) Iaggid-Lim was an Amorite chieftain who founded a dynasty that ruled the kingdom of Mari for a little over a century. Situated on the upper Euphrates, Mari was the main stop for merchants traveling between Syria and Babylonia. As a result of trade and textile manufacture, Mari grew rich and became a principal player in the power politics of the early second millennium B.C.E. After a falling-out with his rival, the king of Ekallatum on the Tigris, Iaggid-Lim's capital was captured and his son taken and held as a hostage. By 1820 B.C.E. the father had died and the son, Iahdun-Lim, became Mari's new ruler.

Iahdun-Lim (Yahdun-Lim) (ca. 1820–1796 B.C.E.) The son of Iaggid-Lim, Iahdun-Lim followed his father to Mari's throne, and he took initiatives to enhance the wealth and power of his kingdom and dynasty. Domestically, he undertook large-scale irrigation projects and strengthened the fortifications of Mari and nearby Terqa. In foreign affairs, he pursued an expansionist policy, marching his army westward to the shores of the Mediterranean, compelling the cities of the Syrian coast to pay him tribute, and securing the trade routes in between. He was killed by order of the king of Terqa, possibly at the hands of his own son, Sumu-Iaman, who briefly succeeded him before being murdered in turn by servants.

Iasmah-Adad (Yasmah-Addu) (1796–1776 B.C.E.) Following the death of Iahdun-Lim's son, Sumu-Iaman, Iasmah-Adad became the third Amorite ruler of the kingdom of Mari. He was appointed to this position by his father, Shamshi-Adad, who then reigned as king of Assyria. The son, however, proved to be a sore disappointment to the father, as the Mari archives reveal, more interested in fast horses and women than the serious business of state. In one letter, Shamshi-Adad sternly reproved his son:

> Here's your brother winning battles and there you are bedding women! When you next head up the army, act like a man. Your brother is earning himself a fine reputation. You have a chance to do the same.

Iasmah-Adad tried to answer the charges, but the tone of his response merely confirmed their accuracy:

> Daddy, I read your letter where you wrote: "How can I let you hold the reins? You're a child, not a grown-up, too young even to shave! When will you learn to manage a household? Can't you see that your brother is commanding huge armies? And you can't even run a palace!" That's what you wrote, Daddy. How can I be the hopeless child you say I am? Aren't you the same person who promoted me? You've known me ever since I was a little boy. Why then do you believe the bad things some people are saying about me? You hurt my feelings, and I'm coming to tell you so.

After Shamshi-Adad's death, Zimri-Lim, a son of Iahdun-Lim, returned from exile and seized Mari's throne.

Ibal-pi-El I (first half of the 19th century B.C.E.)   Ruler of Eshnunna.

Ibal-pi-El II (first half of the 18th century B.C.E.)   Ibal-pi El II ruled Eshnunna in the days of Hammurabi and Babylonian imperialism. He captured Mari and forced its king, Zimri-Lim, to recognize his authority in the region, but the agreement wasn't worth the clay it was written on.

Ibbi-Sin (2028–2004 B.C.E.)   The last member of Ur's Third Dynasty, Ibbi-Sin tried to stave off the inevitability of its collapse from external pressures, but in the end he failed. The brutal attack on Ur by the Elamites and their allies is recalled in a poetic lamentation composed by one of the city's survivors. Ibbi-Sin himself was captured and died in exile.

Ibiq-Adad I (second half of the 20th century B.C.E.)   Ruler of Eshnunna.

Ibiq-Adad II (first half of the 19th century B.C.E.)   Ruler of Eshnunna.

Iblul-il (second half of the 25th century B.C.E.)   This king of Mari tried to encroach upon the Syrian city of Ebla's commercial empire but was stopped short on the battlefield. He was allowed to stay on as Mari's governor subject to the will of Ebla's king.

Iddin-Dagan (1974–1954 B.C.E.)   This ruler of Isin is best remembered for a poem written in his day, which describes the king making love to the city's patron goddess Ninisina as part of the annual New Year Festival to renew the fertility of the land.

Iddin-Ilum (first half of the 21st century B.C.E.)   Military governor of Mari.

Ididish (second half of the 23rd century B.C.E.)   The first to rule Mari with the special title of *shakkanakku* ("military governor") under orders from the king of Akkad.

Ikinum (first half of the 19th century B.C.E.)   An Assyrian king, Ikinum strengthened Ashur's fortifications and maintained commercial colonies in Turkey.

Ikin-Shamagan (second half of the 25th century B.C.E.)   Ruler of Mari.

Ikum-Shamash (first half of the 25th century B.C.E.)   Ruler of Mari.

Ilshu (ca. 2500 B.C.E.)   King of Mari.

Iluma-ilum (Iliman) (ca. 1732 B.C.E.)   Originally a ruler of Isin, Iluma-ilum built a mini-empire based in the marshlands of southern Mesopotamia, founding the so-called Dynasty of the Sea-Land (so named for its proximity to the sea), or Second Dynasty of Babylon. The contemporary king of Babylon, Abi-eshuh, tried to capture him by damming the Tigris and drying out its marshes, but to no avail.

Ilum-Ishtar (first half of the 21st century B.C.E.)   Military governor of Mari.

Ilushu-ilia (ca. 2028 B.C.E.)   Ruler of Eshnunna.

Ilushuma (second half of the 20th century B.C.E.)   Ilushuma was an early Assyrian king who concentrated on expanding trade as a way to create prosperity. He encouraged Assyrian merchants to found colonies in Turkey, which was rich in metallic ores, and he spurred them to act as middlemen, selling metals (especially copper) to Babylonia, which lacked such resources. He also rewarded Assyria's trading partners by exempting them from customs duties. Domestically, he focused on the restoration of temples dedicated to Assyria's gods.

Iptar-Sin (1661–1650 B.C.E.)   An Assyrian king.

Iqish-Tiskpak (second half of the 18th century B.C.E.)   He governed Eshnunna between its conquest by Hammurabi and its destruction under Hammurabi's successor, Samsu-iluna.

Ir-Nanna (ca. 2050 B.C.E.)   Governor of Lagash when it was under the domination of Ur.

Irra-imitti (1868–1861 B.C.E.)   Ruler of Isin.

Ishar-ramashshu (first half of the 20th century B.C.E.)   Ruler of Eshnunna.

Ishbi-Erra (2017–1985 B.C.E.)   This general of Ur used a famine to his personal advantage. When the king of Ur desperately ordered him to secure grain from nearby cities with the help of local governors, he used his newly obtained authority to proclaim himself the ruler of Isin.

Ishkibal (middle of the 17th century B.C.E.)   Ruler of the Sea-Land.

Ishkum-Addu (second half of the 22nd century B.C.E.)   Military governor of Mari.

Ishme-Dagan (1953–1935 B.C.E.)   During his reign, this king of Isin attacked the city of Kish.

Ishme-Dagan I (1780–1741 B.C.E.)   An Assyrian king.

Ishme-Dagan II (first half of the 16th century B.C.E.)   An Assyrian king.

Ishtup-Ilum (ca. 2150 B.C.E.)   Military governor of Mari.

Ishu-Il (ca. 2400 B.C.E.)   Ruler of the northern Mesopotamia city-state of Akshak.

Isma-Dagan (2199–2154 B.C.E.)   Military governor of Mari.

Isqi-Mari   See *Lamgi-Mari*.

Iterpisha (second half of the 19th century B.C.E.)   Ruler of Isin.

Itti-ili-nibi (ca. 1700 B.C.E.)   Ruler of the Sea-Land.

Itti-Marduk-balatu (second half of the 12th century B.C.E.) Itti-Marduk-balatu was the second king of Babylon's Fourth Dynasty, otherwise known as the Second Dynasty of Isin, after the name of the city-state from which its rulers came. Like his father before him, Itti-Marduk-balatu made incursions into Assyrian territory.

Jovian (363–364 C.E.) Under the emperor Jovian, the Romans pulled out of northern Mesopotamia and made peace with the Sassanians, surrendering territory Rome had won decades before.

Julian II the Apostate (360–363 C.E.) Reviled by the Christian Church for his support of paganism over Christianity, the Roman emperor Julian died in battle near Ctesiphon in a campaign against the Persians. According to tradition, as he lay dying from a spear wound he cried out to Jesus, "Though you have defeated me, Galilean, I renounce you still!"

Kadashman-Enlil I (early 14th century B.C.E.) Like his predecessor Kurigalzu I, the Kassite king Kadashman-Enlil I sent a daughter (as well as a sister) to enter the pharaoh Amenhotep III's harem. However, such friendly overtures had their limits. Amenhotep sent Kadashman-Enlil large quantities of gold in recompense, but not one of his own daughters in exchange. The kings' diplomatic correspondence survives in Egypt's Amarna archives.

Kadashman-Enlil II (1279–1265 B.C.E.) Like his royal Kassite predecessor, Kadashman-Turgu, Kadashman-Enlil II maintained correspondence with the Hittite king Hattusilis III. Like his predecessor, also, he devoted his domestic energies to renovating religious structures in the Sumerian city of Nippur.

Kadashman-Harbe I (middle of the 15th century B.C.E.) Kadashman-Harbe I was a member of Babylon's Kassite dynasty and the father of Kurigalzu I.

Kadashman-Turgu (1297–1280 B.C.E.) A Kassite king of Babylon, Kadashman-Turgu was a contemporary of the Hittite king Hattusilis III. In surviving correspondence, the Babylonian king promises to lend military support to the Hittite king if the latter's interests are ever threatened by Egypt.

Kandalanu (647–627 B.C.E.) Kandalanu ruled Babylonia thanks to the Assyrians. They put him on the throne following an Assyrian civil war that led to the death of Babylonia's previous king, Shamash-shum-ukin. Kandalanu was the last member of Babylonia's Ninth Dynasty.

Karahardash (middle of the 14th century B.C.E.) A Kassite king of Babylonia who was also the grandson of an Assyrian king, Karahardash was dethroned and probably murdered in Babylon as part of a Kassite coup.

Karaindash (ca. 1425 B.C.E.) Karaindash was a member of Babylon's Kassite dynasty. Correspondence between him and Egypt's pharaoh, Amenhotep III, has been found in the Amarna archives. Domestically, he erected a new temple to the goddess Inanna in the city of Uruk, deep in Sumer.

Kashtiliash I (first half of the 17th century B.C.E.) Kashtiliash I was the son and successor of Agum I and became the third Kassite ruler of Babylonia. His throne was in Terqa, where he reigned as sovereign of the kingdom of Hana. His rival and enemy was Abi-esuh, Hammurabi's grandson, who defended the throne of Babylon and the territories it controlled.

Kashtiliash II (middle of the 17th century B.C.E.) Kashtiliash II followed Abirattash as king of the Babylonian Kassites.

Kashtiliash III (ca. 1500 B.C.E.) Kashtiliash III was another member of Babylonia's Kassite dynasty.

Kashtiliash IV (middle of the 13th century B.C.E.) The Kassite king Kashtiliash IV was the successor and possibly the son of Shagarakti-Shuriash, during whose reign the Babylonian people faced harsh economic conditions. Perhaps to enrich his nation, Kashtiliash attacked Assyria and Elam, but he was defeated on both fronts. His defeat inspired the only surviving Assyrian epic, the so-called *Tukulti-Ninurta Epic*. Eventually, he was deposed by Assyria's king Tukulti-Ninurta I, who appointed a series of three governors to administer Babylonia in Assyria's name. Before a decade had passed, however, Kassite Babylonia had regained its independence.

Kidin-Ninua (1615–1602 B.C.E.) An Assyrian king.

Kikkia (end of the 21st century B.C.E.) Kikkia is an Assyrian king who was credited in ancient times with having been the first to fortify the city of Ashur with a defensive wall. He may have also been the first ruler to have ended Sumer's dominance over Ashur during the days of Ur's Third Dynasty. His name, which is neither Sumerian nor Akkadian, suggests he may have been a Hurrian.

Kirikiki (first half of the 20th century B.C.E.) Ruler of Eshnunna who formed an alliance with Elam and the Amorites.

Kirta (first half of the 16th century B.C.E.) A Hurrian ruler.

Ku-Baba (ca. 2400 B.C.E.) A queen during Kish's Third Dynasty, Ku-Baba is said to have begun her career as a "woman of wine," that is, a grape grower, wine merchant, or tavernkeeper.

Kudur-Enlil (middle of the 13th century B.C.E.) Not much is known about this Kassite king of Babylonia, except that his name appears in inscriptions on civic monuments and in economic texts. He was succeeded by Shagarakti-Shuriash, who may have been his son.

Kurigalzu I (second half of the 15th century B.C.E.) To enhance his prestige, Kurigalzu I became the first Kassite ruler of Babylonia to declare himself divine. To add to his magnificence, he also constructed a new capital city, Dur-Kurigalzu ("Kurigalzu's Fortress"), about 65 miles north-northwest of Babylon at the site now known as Aqar Quf. His capital included a frescoed palace, a larger-than-life-sized statue of himself, and a mighty ziggurat whose core still rises 187 feet above the desolate desert plain. Under his leadership, Babylonia became a major player in international politics. To firm up good relations with Egypt, he sent his daughter to join Amenhotep III's harem and exchanged gifts and letters with the pharaoh.

Kurigalzu II (1345–1324 B.C.E.) A Kassite, Kurigalzu II was given the throne of Babylon by the Assyrians after they put down a coup and deposed a Kassite usurper. Kurigalzu II went on to become a celebrated warrior, defeating the Elamites of Iran and even challenging the Assyrians. At home, he carried on building projects in Sumer and at the Kassite capital, Dur-Kurigalzu, named for his namesake and earlier predecessor, Kurigalzu I.

Labashi-Marduk (556 B.C.E.) The son of Nergal-shar-usur, Labashi-Marduk had a youthful and malevolent turn on the Babylonian throne for nine months before enemies tortured and murdered him. He was succeeded by Nabu-naid (Nabonidus).

Lamgi-Mari (Isqi-Mari) (first half of the 25th century B.C.E.) Found in the ruins of

Tell Hariri, a statue of this king—with an inscription describing him as Mari's king—enabled archaeologists to identify the site as the capital of one of Mesopotamia's great kingdoms.

Lipit-Enlil (1873–1869 B.C.E.) Ruler of Isin.

Lipit-Ishtar (1934–1924 B.C.E.) The moral sensibilities of this king of Isin were expressed in two ways: through the promulgation of a code of laws that set humane limits to personal debts, and through the construction of a rectory at Ur where his daughter served as temple priestess. Ur was captured by Larsa, and Lipit-Ishtar died that same year.

Libaia (1690–1674 B.C.E.) An Assyrian king.

Lubalanda (first half of the 24th century B.C.E.) Ruler of Lagash.

Lugalbanda (second half of the 28th century B.C.E.) The third of the four mythical kings of Uruk, Lugalbanda is described as a shepherd who attained divinity.

Lugal-dalu (ca. 2500 B.C.E.) Ruler of the southern Mesopotamian city-state of Adab.

Lugal-kinishe-dudu (ca. 2400 B.C.E.) This king of Uruk also held sway over Ur.

Lugal-shag-engur (ca. 2500 B.C.E.) Ruler of Lagash.

Lugal-ushumgal (2230–2200 B.C.E.) Ruler of Lagash.

Lugalzagesi (ca. 2340–2316 B.C.E.) An imperialist, Lugalzagesi began his career as ruler of Umma. He went on to plunder Lagash and make himself king over Uruk. Having conquered Sumer, he boasted of ruling the Near East from sunrise to sunset (east to west) and from the Persian Gulf to the shores of the Mediterranean. After a quarter of a century his dreams of empire were eclipsed when he was defeated by another imperialist, Sargon of Akkad.

Lu-kirilaza (first half of the 21st century B.C.E.) Governor of Lagash when it was under the domination of Ur.

Lullaia (1621–1618 B.C.E.) An Assyrian king.

Manishtusu (2269–2255 B.C.E.) Manishtusu followed his twin brother Rimush to the throne of the Akkadian Empire founded by their father, Sargon of Akkad. During his reign, Manishtusu sent military expeditions across the Persian Gulf in quest of silver ore and other precious natural resources. One text relates that his courtiers murdered him with their cylinder seals—an excruciatingly slow way to go. It is possible, however, that the story alludes to a murder plot that employed forgery.

Mar-biti-ahhe-iddina (941–?B.C.E.) Mar-biti-ahhe-iddina was the third member of the Eighth Dynasty to sit on Babylon's throne.

Mar-biti-apla-usur (ca. 975 B.C.E) Mar-biti-apla-usur was the founder and, to his regret, sole member of Babylon's Seventh Dynasty, also known as the Elamite dynasty.

Marduk-apal-iddina I (1173–1161 B.C.E.) Marduk-apal-iddina was one of the last Kassite kings of Babylon. Four years after he died, the Kassite dynasty fell.

Marduk-apal-iddina II (Biblical "Merodach-Baladan") (721–710 B.C.E.) Marduk-apal-iddina II was a Chaldaean leader who became king of Babylon with the support of

3.11 This so-called boundary stone or kudurru, *marks a real estate transaction in which the Babylonian king Marduk-apal-iddina II gave a noble title to lands formerly held by the king. Note how the king is deliberately made taller than the noble to convey his greater political stature. Indeed, even his walking stick is taller. At the top are symbols of the gods.* (Carl Bezold, *Nineve und Babylon,* 1909)

the Elamites. Sargon, the king of Assyria, tried twice to unseat him militarily, and the second time forced him to flee to Elam for refuge. Seven years later with the support of the Elamites and the Aramaeans of southern Iraq, Marduk-apal-iddina made another bid for power, entering Babylon and declaring himself king. Rightly viewing this as a challenge to Assyrian dominance, the new Assyrian king,

Sennacherib, attacked with his army and forced Marduk-apal-iddina to flee once more. But three years later the Chaldaean leader was at it again, stirring up rebellion. This time he fled by ship, taking with him statues of the country's gods, and he ultimately died in exile. Today, his only surviving portrait is carved on an ancient boundary stone. He is remembered also in the Bible (Isaiah 39) for having sought to enlist King Hezekiah of Judah in his anti-Assyrian cause.

Marduk-apla-usur (early eighth century B.C.E.) Marduk-apla-usur was a Babylonian king of the Eighth Dynasty.

Marduk-balassu-iqbi (second half of the ninth century B.C.E.) Under his reign, the peace that had existed for almost a half century between Babylonia and Assyria came to an end as a new Assyrian king, Shamshi-Adad V, raided Babylonian cities and succeeded in capturing Marduk-balassu-iqbi himself.

Marduk-bel-zeri (early eighth century B.C.E.) Marduk-bel-zeri ruled Babylon as a member of its Eighth Dynasty.

Marduk-kabil-ahhesu (1156–1139 B.C.E.) Marduk-kabil-ahhesu founded Babylonia's Fourth Dynasty, also known as the Second Dynasty of Isin, the city-state that was the home of its members. The dynasty established itself in Babylon once Elamite troops who had been occupying the city were expelled or withdrew. Marduk-kabil-ahhesu made incursions into Assyrian territory as would his two successors, Itti-Marduk-balatu and Ninurta-nadin-shumi.

Marduk-nadin-ahhe (early 11th century B.C.E.) As king of Babylon, Marduk-nadin-ahhe invaded Assyria when it was ruled by Tiglathpileser I. By capturing Ekallatum, he put his forces just 30 miles south of Assyria's royal capital. The Assyrians struck back, attacking cities in northern Babylonia, including Dur-Kurigalzu and Babylon, where the royal palace was targeted for destruction. Later in the king's reign, a famine struck Babylonia and Aramaean tribesmen raided Babylonian territory.

Marduk-shapik-zeri (first half of the 11th century B.C.E.) During his reign the famine that had begun in the days of his predecessor, Marduk-nadin-ahhe, abated, and a peace treaty was concluded with the Assyrians.

Marduk-zakir-shumi I (854–819 B.C.E.) Marduk-zakir-shumi's position as Babylonian king was threatened by his brother Marduk-bel-usate's ambition. His brother, moreover, had the backing of the Aramaeans. To hold the Aramaeans in check, the Assyrian king Shalmaneser III sent in his army and won the day. With the rebellion over, to show his good faith to Babylon's king, Shalmaneser humbly made thanksgiving offerings at the great shrines of the city's gods. For good measure, he then drove south to Sumer and pushed the Chaldaeans (another potential enemy of Babylonia) all the way back to the Persian Gulf.

Marduk-zer-x (ca. 1050 B.C.E.) Little is known of this 10th king of Babylon's Fourth Dynasty, not even the last syllable(s) of his name—hence the "x."

Me-durba (second half of the 26th century B.C.E.) Ruler of Adab.

Melishipak (1188–1174 B.C.E.) Melishipak was king of Babylon during the last century of rule by the Kassite dynasty. Records show he bequeathed land to his son Marduk-apal-iddina I, who succeeded him to the throne.

Merodach-Baladan See *Marduk-apal-iddina II.*

Mesannepadda (ca. 2560–2525 B.C.E.) A bead of lapis lazuli inscribed with the name of this king of Ur was found at Mari in northwestern Mesopotamia. That single bead is about all we know of this Sumerian king.

Meshkiangasher (second half of the 28th century B.C.E.) The first of the four mythical kings of Uruk, Meshkiangasher was—according to tradition—the son of the Sumerian sun-god, Utu.

Mesilim (ca. 2550 B.C.E.) An early and influential ruler of Kish, Mesilim helped resolve a quarrel between two other Sumerian cities. At one of them, Lagash, he built a temple to the city's patron god, Ningirsu.

Meskalamdug (second half of the 27th century B.C.E.) The tomb of this ruler of Ur was unearthed by Sir Leonard Woolley. Among the objects in the tomb were a golden oil lamp shaped like a shell and an extraordinarily detailed helmet of gold that simulated the king's chignon hairstyle, complete with functional ear-holes for hearing.

Meskiagnunna (ca. 2485–2450 B.C.E.) One of the oldest inscriptions in Akkadian is found on a bowl dedicated to this king of Ur by his devoted wife.

Mithridates I (171–138 B.C.E.) A Parthian king, Mithridates marched into Mesopotamia, capturing the cities of Babylon and Seleucia. To make himself more acceptable to the people of Mesopotamia, he described himself as a "king of kings" as had the Persian kings before him, and portrayed himself as sympathetic to the values of Greek civilization to which Hellenistic monarchs before him had subscribed.

Mut-Ashkur (second half of the 18th century B.C.E.) An Assyrian king. His father and predecessor, Ishme-Dagan, had arranged a diplomatically useful marriage for him with a Hurrian princess.

Nabonassar   See *Nabu-nasir*.

Nabonidus   See *Nabu-naid*.

Nabopolassar   See *Nabu-apla-usur*.

Nabu-apla-iddina (887–855? B.C.E.)   Nabu-apla-iddina maintained the peace that his father, Nabu-shuma-ukin, had secured for Babylonia, and he signed an additional peace treaty with the new Assyrian king, Shalmaneser III. In addition, he devoted his energies to reactivating old religious rites and sites to renew his people's spirituality and invite heaven's protection. His leadership fostered an era of cultural rebirth.

Nabu-apla-usur (Nabopolassar) (625–605 B.C.E.)   Nabu-apla-usur was the first member of Babylonia's 10th Dynasty, also known as the Neo-Babylonian or Chaldaean dynasty. Possibly of Chaldaean origin, Nabu-apla-usur made southern Mesopotamia (known as the Sea-Land) his powerbase. Following the death of the Babylonian king Kandalanu, he fought for the mastery of Babylonia for seven years against armed Assyrian opposition. When the Medes captured Ashur, Nabu-apla-usur took advantage of the opportunity to form an alliance with them through a treaty sealed by the marriage of a Median princess to his son, Nebuchadnezzar II. With the fall of Nineveh in 612 B.C.E., Nabu-apla-usur achieved his goal of Mesopotamian sovereignty. Meanwhile, the Egyptians had moved military forces into Palestine and Syria. He unsuccessfully tried to oppose them, but they were finally vanquished by Nebuchadnezzar at the battle of Carchemish in 605 B.C.E. as Nabu-apla-usur lay dying in his palace at Babylon. During his reign he had devoted himself to the restoration of Babylon's monuments, a task that his son continued after his father's passing.

Nabu-kudurru-usur I (Nebuchadnezzar I, Nebuchadrezzar I) (1124–1103 B.C.E.)   Nabu-kudurru-usur I was the fourth king to sit on Babylon's throne after the fall of the Kassite dynasty and the city's brief occupation by the Elamites. Unlike his three predecessors who had made military moves against the Assyrians to the north, he focused on Elam to the east, waging two campaigns, the first of which was unsuccessful and the second of which succeeded thanks to the help of an Elamite defector. The king was proud of having recovered from Elam a statue of the god Marduk that had been looted from its sanctuary in Babylon.

Nabu-kudurru-usur II (Nebuchadnezzar II, Nebuchadrezzar II) (604–562 B.C.E.)   Thanks to the Bible, the most famous Mesopotamian king of all was Nabu-kudurru-usur II. If his name seems unfamiliar, its Hebrew equivalent is not: Nebuchadnezzar (or, as it is sometimes spelled in closer keeping with the Akkadian original, Nebuchad*r*ezzar). Even without the Bible, this king's fame is well deserved: he was one of Babylon's greatest kings and sat on the throne for 43 years, one of the longest reigns in Mesopotamian history. His father was Nabopolassar (Nabu-apla-usur) and his wife was a Median princess named Amytis. But Nebuchadnezzar didn't just sit on the throne. He had extensive military experience even before he became king, including his defeat of Egypt's army at Carchemish. In foreign affairs, his eyes looked to the west, for he coveted the tribute he could exact from the trade-rich cities of Palestine and Syria, and the timber he could harvest from the mountains of Lebanon. Of course, the pharaoh of Egypt wanted the same things, and that put Babylonia and Egypt on a collision course. When the kingdom of Judaea twice rebelled against its Babylonian masters, Nebuchadnezzar twice laid siege to Jerusalem, destroying the city the second time (in 586 B.C.E.), despoiling and burning its Holy Temple, and marching thousands of Jews into captivity. Domestically, Nebuchadnezzar focused on large public works projects in 13 major Mesopotamian cities, completing them in part with slave labor. He devoted the greatest attention to his capital city of Babylon, virtually rebuilding its fortifications, substantially enlarging its palace, adding to the splendor of its temple tower, spanning the Euphrates with a mighty bridge, and constructing a grand processional boulevard and gateway that glistened in glazed brick. The public museum he installed in his palace and filled with antiquities may rank as the world's oldest museum. Nevertheless, despite Nebuchadnezzar's civic efforts and ambitious plans, within a quarter of a century after his death the Neo-Babylonian Empire he had helped fashion fell to the Persians, the consequence of successors who were less determined and ruthless than he.

Nabu-mukin-apli (977–942 B.C.E.) Nabu-mukin-apli founded Babylon's Eighth Dynasty, the so-called Dynasty of E, and he ruled for 36 years. Invasions by Aramaeans were a persistent problem during his reign. For one extended period the city of Babylon was cut off from its fertile countryside and religious processions were unable to commemorate the New Year. Later the Aramaeans settled in Southern Mesopotamia between the Tigris and Elam. During his reign also, a tribe known as the Kaldu (later called the Chaldaeans) invaded and settled in Sumer.

Nabu-mukin-zeri (ca. 730 B.C.E.) After the death of Nabu-nasir, two kings briefly ruled Babylonia. The second assassinated the first and was, in turn, deposed by a powerful sheikh named Nabu-mukin-zeri. Worried over political instability in Babylonia, the Assyrian king Tiglathpileser III made his move and pursued Nabu-mukin-zeri with his army. Failing to capture him, the Assyrian nevertheless secured the support of some Babylonian leaders and declared himself king.

Nabu-naid (Nabonidus) (556–539 B.C.E.) Nabu-naid was the last member of Babylon's Neo-Babylonian dynasty, before the country was conquered by Persia. Nabu-naid's career was distinguished by piety verging on preoccupation at a critical period in Mesopotamia's history. His mother had been a priestess of the moon-god Sin at the northern city of Harran; Nabu-naid would appoint his own daughter high priestess of the god at the southern city of Ur; and he himself devoted time to the reconstruction of both temples. His most radical act, however, was his withdrawal from public life, retreating to the oasis of Tema in Arabia, and absenting himself from his capital city for 10 years. In part, his actions may be explained by his mother's death at the age of 104 during the eighth year of his reign, but we will never know. His absence from Babylon, however, irritated the priests of Marduk since it precluded the celebration of the spiritually important New Year Festival, adding to the rage the priests felt at the king's fixation over the god Sin to the exclusion of Babylon's principal deity and divine patron, Marduk. During his absence, Nabu-naid left his son Bel-shar-usur in charge of the government, a responsibility Bel-shar-usur failed to take seriously enough in view of the looming menace of Persian imperialism. Nabu-naid returned to Babylonia in 539 B.C.E., but it was too late: the Persian army was already on the march. Nabu-naid was captured and his son killed in battle. According to one tradition, Nabu-naid was not killed but instead was awarded a government post in central Iran as part of a Persian policy of amnesty. Nabu-naid and his son are both remembered in Hebrew literature. Nabu-naid's sojourn in the desert is attributed to an extended fit of madness during which he ate grass (according to the book of Daniel, which confuses him with Nebuchadnezzar); also he suffered from a king-sized case of boils (according to the "Prayer of Nabonidus" found among the Dead Sea Scrolls). As for Bel-shar-usur (Belshazzar), he was reviled in the book of Daniel (chapter 5) for the ominous feast at which he saw the divine writing on the wall that foretold his empire's doom. Nabu-naid himself has a more respectable claim to fame as perhaps the world's first archaeologist: while rebuilding temples, he explored their lower reaches for ancient time-capsules called "foundation deposits" put there by his predecessors. The aesthetic and historic objects he found (including inscriptions and works of sculpture) were then deposited by him in a special museum.

Nabu-nasir (Nabonassar) (747–734 B.C.E.) Nabu-nasir ruled Babylonia with the military help of Assyria's king, Tiglathpileser III, who pushed back the Aramaeans and Chaldaeans and used deportation and resettlement as instruments of control. In exchange, Tiglathpileser received the title of "King of Sumer and Akkad." Six years after Nabu-nasir's death, the Assyrian king would declare himself "King of Babylon" as well. Drawing upon Babylonian records, the second century C.E. Greek astronomer Ptolemy drew up a list of Mesopotamian rulers from Nabu-nasir (whom he called "Nabonassar") to Alexander the Great, noting remarkable astronomical events that occurred during their reigns. Calculating when the celestial events would take place, modern historians have been able to accurately date the reigns of Babylonia's kings.

Nabu-shuma-ishkun (760–748 B.C.E.) The last member of Babylon's Eighth Dynasty,

Nabu-shuma-ishkun presided over a time of civic violence and unrest.

Nabu-shuma-ukin (899–888? B.C.E.) Though threatened by the Assyrian army, Nanu-shuma-ukin negotiated a treaty that secured a peace for Babylonia that endured for 80 years, providing the framework for economic stability. The peace treaty was sealed by a double wedding in which each king married a daughter of the other.

Nabu-shum-libur (1032–1025 B.C.E.) Nabu-shum-libur was the 11th and last member of Babylon's Fourth Dynasty. The western provinces of his kingdom were subject to frequent raids by nomadic tribes. A marble weight survives, optimistically inscribed with the title, "King of the World," but priestly omens were already boding disaster, a prophecy fulfilled when his dynasty fell.

Nam-mahazi (2113–2111 B.C.E.) Ruler of Lagash.

Naplanum (2025–2005 B.C.E.) Possibly an Amorite, Naplanum ruled Larsa when Isin was the dominant power in southern Mesopotamia.

Naram-Sin (2254–2218 B.C.E.) The grandson of Sargon of Akkad, Naram-Sin conducted military campaigns along his kingdom's far-flung borders, regaling himself with the title "King of the Four Quarters (of the Earth)" and calling himself divine. A stela now in the Louvre shows him proudly ascending a mountain in triumph over his enemies. Tradition declares that his overweening pride angered the gods, who chastised him for his hubris.

Naram-Sin (second half of the 19th century B.C.E.) An Assyrian king who bore the same name as an illustrious earlier ruler of Akkad. Originally the son of a king of Eshnunna, he

3.12 As the stellar symbols of his patron gods shine above him, the larger-than-life figure of Naram-Sin of Akkad triumphantly towers over a fallen enemy king as Naram-Sin's army looks on from below. (Rogers, A History of Babylonia and Assyria, 1915; photo from a 1900 French work entitled Délégation en Perse)

favored the city and fostered its influence in the affairs of northwestern Mesopotamia.

Naram-Sin (second half of the 19th century B.C.E.) A ruler of Eshnunna, he allied himself with Mari and fought against the Assyrians. He called himself the divine "king of the world." Easily confused with a contemporary Assyrian king of the same name who ruled around the same time.

Narses (end of the third century C.E.) A Sassanian ruler, he challenged the power of Rome in the Near East by invading Mesopotamia. He was eventually defeated on the battlefield and submitted to a peace treaty that ceded territory to Rome as far east as the Tigris.

Nazimaruttash (1323–1298 B.C.E.) Nazimaruttash was a Kassite king of Babylonia and the son and successor of the warrior and builder Kurigalzu II. The Babylonians during his reign clashed with the Assyrians over their mutual interest in Elam. The result was a treaty defining their national borders.

Nebuchadnezzar I (Nebuchardrezzar I) See *Nabu-kudurru-usur I.*

Nebuchadnezzar II (Nebuchadrezzar II) see *Nabu-kudurru-usur II.*

Nergal-shar-usur (Neriglisaros, Neriglissar) (559–556 B.C.E.) Nergal-shar-usur was a businessman who became king of Babylon by killing his sister's husband, Amel-Marduk. During his four-year reign he militarily restored Babylon's control over the Cilician coast in southwestern Turkey and engaged in public works at home. When he died, he was succeeded by his young Nero-like son, Labashi-Marduk, who was tortured and murdered nine months later.

Neriglisaros See *Nergal-shar-usur.*

Nin-kisalsi (first half of the 26th century B.C.E.) Ruler of Adab.

Ninurta-apal-Ekur (1192–1180 B.C.E.) For some reason, the women in this Assyrian king's harem repeatedly squabbled, compelling him to issue decree after decree to maintain order.

Ninurta-apla-x (ca. 800 B.C.E.) Little is known of this Babylonian king of the Eighth

Dynasty, not even the last syllable(s) of his name: hence the "x."

Ninurta-kudurri-usur (ca. 950 B.C.E.) Ninurta-kudurri-usur was the son of Nabu-mukin-apli and became the second king of Babylon's Eighth Dynasty.

Ninurta-nadin-shumi (second half of the 12th century B.C.E.) The third member of Babylon's so-called Second Dynasty of Isin, Ninurta-nadin-shumi made incursions into Assyrian territory as had his two predecessors. He was the father of the next Babylonian king, Nabu-kudurru-usur I.

Nur-Adad (1865–1850 B.C.E.) Nur-Adad, a king of Larsa, expanded his city's territory to the north. When the Euphrates, upon which his kingdom's life depended, changed its course, Nur-Adad set into motion a massive project to reroute its waters, resettle people whose homes had been destroyed, and rebuild structures that had been damaged not only in Larsa proper but also in nearby Eridu and Ur.

Nur-ahum (first half of the 20th century B.C.E.) Ruler of Eshnunna who formed an alliance with the city-state of Isin.

Nur-ili (first half of the 15th century B.C.E.) An Assyrian king.

Nur-mer (ca. 2150 B.C.E.) Military governor of Mari.

Odenath (ca. 250 C.E.) As king of Palmyra in Syria, he made his kingdom a power to be reckoned with. His foreign policy was pro-Roman, and with Roman backing he attacked the city of Ctesiphon. Odenath's wife and successor was the legendary Zenobia.

Orodes II (57–37 B.C.E.) After the disastrous defeat of the Romans at Carrhae (Harran), this Parthian king was awarded the severed head of the Roman general Crassus, supposedly while Orodes was watching a performance of Euripides' savage tragedy, *The Bacchae*.

Parattarna (ca. 1530 B.C.E.) A Hurrian king of the Mitanni.

Pescennius Niger (193–194 C.E.) Pescennius Niger served as governor of Syria under the Roman emperor Pertinax. At news of Pertinax's death, Pescennius's army proclaimed him Rome's new emperor. Defeated by another claimant to the throne, Septimius Severus, Pescennius fled east, but he was caught and killed near Antioch.

Phraates II (139/138–128 B.C.E.) The son of Mithridates I and a king of Parthia, Phraates rebuffed a challenge by the Seleucid king Antiochus VII to take over control of Mesopotamia.

Pirig-me (2117–2115 B.C.E.) Ruler of Larsa.

Puzur-Ashur I (ca. 2000 B.C.E.) This early Assyrian king was the founder of a new dynasty that ruled from the city of Ashur. Unlike his predecessors who had Hurrian names, Puzur-Ashur is the first Assyrian monarch whose language was Semitic Akkadian, a linguistic and ethnic precedent.

Puzur-Ashur II (ca. 1850 B.C.E.) An Assyrian king.

Puzur-Ashur III (1521–1498 B.C.E.) The Assyrian king Puzur-Ashur III concluded a treaty with king Burnaburiash I of Babylonia delineating the border between their two kingdoms (near Samarra), thus establishing the historic geographical division between Assyria in the north and Babylonia in the south. The terms of the treaty were confirmed near the end of the century by Ashur-bel-nisheshu of Assyria and Karaindash of Babylonia.

Puzur-Ishtar (2050–2025 B.C.E.) Military governor of Mari.

Puzur-Nirah (ca. 2400 B.C.E.) Ruler of Akshak.

Puzur-Sin (first half of the 24th century B.C.E.) Founder of Kish's Fourth Dynasty.

Rim-Sin I (1822–1763 B.C.E.) His 60-year reign as ruler of Larsa was the longest of any ancient Near Eastern king except for Egypt's Ramses II, who reigned for 67. Rim-Sin was proudest of his conquest of Isin, Larsa's age-old rival. Eventually, Larsa itself was conquered in 1768 B.C.E. by the combined forces of Mari (under Zimri-Lim) and Babylon (under Hammurabi).

Rim-Sin II (1741–1736 B.C.E.) Ruler of Larsa after its conquest by Hammurabi of Babylon, who stripped the city of its fortifications.

Rimush (2278–2270 B.C.E.) Despite rebellions, Rimush successfully maintained the kingdom he inherited from his father, Sargon of Akkad, which stretched from Syria in the west to Iran in the east.

Sabium (1844–1831 B.C.E.) The son of Sumu-la-El, Sabium was Babylon's third king. He supervised the construction of temples and canals, and he strengthened the city's walls.

Samium (1976–1942 B.C.E.) Ruler of Larsa.

Sammuramat See *Semiramis*.

Samsi-Addu See *Shamshi-Adad*.

Samsu-ditana (1625–1595 B.C.E.) The son of Ammi-saduqa, Samsu-ditana was the last member of Babylon's First Dynasty. His reign ended with a Hittite assault upon the city that led to Babylon's destruction and the king's probable death. Thereafter Babylonia was ruled by a Kassite dynasty.

Samsu-iluna (1749–1712 B.C.E.) The son and successor of Hammurabi I, Samsu-iluna of Babylon spent most of his 38-year reign trying to protect the territory won by his father against foreign invasion (by the Kassites) and internal insurrections in the northern and southern provinces. By the end of his reign, the north and south had been lost, and Babylon only controlled Akkad. In the course of subduing rebellions in Sumer, Samsu-iluna looted and burned the temples of Ur and Uruk, and demolished their cities' walls.

Sargon of Akkad (Sharru-kin) (2334–2279 B.C.E.) Sargon was a Semitic ruler of Akkad who conquered Sumer and united the two lands under his leadership, thereby forming the most extensive kingdom Mesopotamia had ever seen. His capital was founded at Agade, "the only royal city of ancient Iraq whose location remains unknown" (Roux 1992: 152). His imperialistic ambitions carried him and his army to Iran in the east and Syria in the west. As he boasted in an inscription: "Let any king who regards himself as my equal go where I have gone!" A legend (that may have inspired the biblical story of Moses' birth) related that his mother gave birth to him in secret, thereafter placing him in a reed basket and floating him down a river until he was found by someone (a drawer of water) who adopted and raised him. Shown divine favor (by the goddess Ishtar), he went on to fulfill his royal destiny. Sargon's name means "legitimate ruler," implying that he may in fact have been a usurper, a theory supported by another account: that he had served as cup-bearer to king Ur-

3.13 This bronze royal portrait head dates to the late third millennium B.C.E. and is believed to bear the likeness of Sargon the Great. It is housed in the Iraq Museum in Baghdad. (Photographie Giraudon/Art Resource, N.Y.)

zababa of Kish until he seized the king's throne for himself.

Sargon I (Sharru-kin) (first half of the 19th century B.C.E.) Sargon I was an Assyrian king who bore the same name as an illustrious one who earlier ruled Akkad. Like his predecessors in Assyria, he encouraged the founding of trading colonies in Turkey, and he also worked at the never-ending task of repairing his city's fortifications.

Sargon II (Sharru-kin) (721–705 B.C.E.) The name of this Assyrian king, Sargon, means "legitimate king," and indicates that he—like the original Sargon of Akkad—may have been a usurper who used such a title to make people think he deserved the throne. Though Sargon II had his share of military successes, he was continually pressed on all fronts by those nations who coveted Assyria's territory and her tribute-paying vassal states. Among his enemies for a time were the Muski, or Phrygians, an Anatolian people ruled by a king named Mita—the legendary Midas who had the touch of gold. Sargon built a new capital city for himself at a place he called Dur-Sharrukin ("Sargon's Fortress"), later known as Khorsabad. The palace was completed a year before Sargon died in battle, but later kings preferred to rule from Nineveh, so it was never used thereafter as a royal residence. The tomb of Sargon's queen, Taliya, may have been uncovered in yet another palace, an earlier one at Kalhu (Nimrud).

Saustatar (ca. 1500 B.C.E.) Hurrian king of the Mitanni.

Seleucus I (305–281 B.C.E.) Seleucus was one of the successors of Alexander the Great who divided up and ruled Alexander's empire subsequent to his death. After fighting off the challenges of a rival named Antigonus, Seleucus consolidated his hold over Babylonia and extended his dominion so that it included Syria and half of Turkey. He founded a new capital he named for himself, Seleucia-on-the-Tigris, and he maintained a second capital as well farther west at Antioch-on-the-Orontes. The Hellenistic dynasty which he established, the Seleucid, endured for almost two and a half centuries until its defeat by the Romans in 64 B.C.E. Seleucus was succeeded by his son, Antiochus I.

Seleucus II (245–226 B.C.E.) Son of the Hellenistic ruler Antiochus II, Seleucus suffered military defeats and saw the size of his inherited kingdom shrink. In the end, he died of a fall from a horse.

Semiramis (Sammuramat) (ca. 823–811 B.C.E.) Semiramis was the wife of Shamshi-Adad V and the mother of his successor, Adad-nirari III. She took the extraordinary step of accompanying her husband on at least one military campaign, and she is prominently mentioned in royal inscriptions. Thanks to embellishments added to her biography by later Greek historians, she became the most famous queen of Assyria, legendary for her beauty, cruelty, and sexual appetite.

Sennacherib (Sin-ahhe-eriba) (704–681 B.C.E.) Sennacherib was the son of Sargon II of Assyria. The chief problem during his reign was the intransigence of Babylonia, which he eventually dealt with by besieging Babylon and devastating the city after its capture by flooding it with the rechanneled waters of the Euphrates. To force King Hezekiah of Judah to pay him tribute, he laid siege to the kingdom's cities, a campaign that he commemorated in sculptural reliefs and annals in which he boasted of having shut Hezekiah in Jerusalem like a bird in a cage (see also 2 Kings 18). Turning from his father's capital of Dur-sharru-kin (Khorsabad), Sennacherib directed his energies toward the construction of a new capital at Nineveh, adorning it with a palace "without rival." Nineveh would remain thereafter the capital city of Assyrian kings. Sennacherib was stabbed to death by an assassin (possibly one of his sons) or, according to another account, was crushed to death by the monumental weight of a winged bull that he just happened to be standing beneath.

Septimius Severus (193–211 C.E.) This Roman emperor campaigned with his army in Mesopotamia and imposed Roman authority on the northern part of the country with the help of two legions. His campaign and the capture of Ctesiphon were celebrated in sculptural relief on his triumphal arch that still stands at the western end of the Roman Forum.

3.14 Sennacherib on his throne. The king holds a bow and arrows in his hands to signify his martial character. (Newman, *The Thrones and Palaces of Babylon and Nineveh from Sea to Sea,* 1876)

Shagarakti-Shuriash (1255–1243 B.C.E.) Contemporary economic texts suggest that Babylonia faced hard economic times under the reign of this monarch. The level of individual debt was high, forcing many people to sell themselves into slavery as a means of repaying their creditors.

Shallim-ahhe (ca. 1950 B.C.E.) The son of Puzur-Ashur I, Shallim-ahhe was the second member of Assyria's new Akkadian dynasty. He renovated the temple of the god Ashur, the patron god of the city which bore his name and the god of the Assyrian nation. Shallim-ahhe's name turns up in letters uncovered in an Assyrian merchant colony located in northeastern Turkey.

Shalmaneser I (Shulmani-ashared) (1274–1245 B.C.E.)   Shalmaneser I was an Assyrian king and leader in war who viewed himself as the servant of the god Ashur in extending Assyria's dominion over other nations. His was the last reign in which the kingdom of Mitanni challenged Assyrian power. Shalmaneser defeated Mitanni's Hurrian king and appointed governors to rule the kingdom thereafter. He boasted in his inscriptions of having turned his enemies' cities into abandoned ruins. Among other campaigns, his army made a thrust into the territory of Urartu in Armenia.

Shalmaneser II (1031–1020 B.C.E.)   An Assyrian king.

Shalmaneser III (858–824 B.C.E.)   The son of the great Assyrian king Ashurnasirpal II, Shalmaneser III followed in his father's imperialistic footsteps (or chariot tracks). He directed 34 military campaigns, over two times as many as his father had, and he recorded his name and conquests in inscriptions and chronological annals more than any other Assyrian king. At the royal capital of Kalhu (Nimrud) he constructed a treasury and arsenal dubbed "Fort Shalmaneser" by modern archaeologists. Shalmaneser died of old age in the midst of a long civil war instigated by one of his sons.

Shalmaneser IV (first half of the eighth century B.C.E.)   The role of the Assyrian king as commander in chief of the nation's armed forces seems to have been subverted in the reign of Shalmaneser IV by a general named Shamshi-ilu, who boasted of his victories without even mentioning the king's name.

Shalmaneser V (726–722 B.C.E.)   This Assyrian king was the son of Tiglathpileser III, but he lacked his father's acumen. By making formerly independent cities pay taxes, he ignited a revolt that terminated his reign (and life) after four years. The tomb of his wife, Yaba, may have been found beneath the floor of their palace at Kalhu (Nimrud).

Shamash-mudammiq (?–ca. 900 B.C.E.)   During the reign of Shamash-mudammiq, Babylonia was invaded twice by the Assyrian king Adad-nirari II. Each time the Babylonians were vanquished and suffered major territorial losses.

Shamash-shum-ukin (668–648 B.C.E.)   Anticipating his own death, King Esarhaddon of Assyria chose his son, crown prince Shamash-shum-ukin, to govern Babylonia. He appointed his other son, Ashurbanipal, to govern Assyria. After Esarhaddon died, Ashurbanipal insisted that Shamash-shum-ukin be subservient to him. For 16 years, Shamash-shum-ukin tolerated this humiliating arrangement, but he finally plotted his brother's overthrow. Learning of the plot, Ashurbanipal marched on Babylon and a civil war ensued. After a two-year siege, Babylon—ravaged by famine and disease—fell. Shamash-shum-ukin died in a fire that consumed the palace, a fire—legend says—that he set himself.

Shamshi-Adad I (Samsi-Addu) (1809–1766 B.C.E.)   Before the time of Shamshi-Adad, the kings of Assyria had used the title of *ishakkum* ("governor"), equivalent to the Sumerian title of *ensi*. Shamshi-Adad was the first to refer to himself as *sharrum* ("king") and even *shar kishshatim* ("king of the universe"). Significantly, he was not of royal blood, and therefore he probably sought to enhance his prestige through the adoption of more magnificent titles than those used by his predecessors. His reign is documented by the archives of Mari, where his son served as governor. Shamshi-Adad's domain reached to the Mediterranean, and south to the Babylonian empire of his contemporary, Hammurabi, with whom he signed a treaty.

Shamshi-Adad II (1585–1580 B.C.E.) An Assyrian king.

Shamshi-Adad III (first half of the 16th century B.C.E.) Shamshi-Adad III was an Assyrian king who prided himself on repairing the crumbling tops of the temple towers in his capital city.

Shamshi-Adad IV (ca. 1050 B.C.E.) An Assyrian king of Babylonian origin.

Shamshi-Adad V (823–811 B.C.E.) The son and successor of Shalmaneser III, Shamshi-Adad V of Assyria invaded Babylonia despite the good diplomatic relations that had earlier existed between the two countries. Captured, the Babylonian king and his advisers were transported to Nineveh where they were executed by being skinned alive. Shamshi-Adad was also husband to the legendary Semiramis (Sammuramat).

Shapur I (Sapor) (middle of the third century C.E.) Shapur was the successor of Ardeshir and the second Sassanian ruler of Mesopotamia. In his wars against Rome, he destroyed the city of Ashur and surrounded a Roman army commanded by the emperor Valerian. Valerian himself was taken prisoner and died in captivity.

Shar-kalli-sharri (2217–2193 B.C.E.) The son of Naram-Sin of Akkad, this Assyrian king witnessed the collapse of the empire his grand-

father Sargon had built. Though he built temples to the gods, their favor deserted him as nomadic tribes swept across his borders and his authority crumbled.

Sharma-Adad I (1673–1662 B.C.E.) An Assyrian king.

Sharma-Adad II (1601 B.C.E.) An Assyrian king.

Sharria (end of the 20th century B.C.E.) Ruler of Eshnunna.

Sharru-kin See *Sargon.*

Shattuara I (ca. 1300 B.C.E.) After the breakdown of the Mitanni empire, the king of Assyria, Adad-Nirari I, first deported this Hurrian king and then relented and sent him home. But when Shattuara fomented a revolt, Adad-Nirari attacked his capital and killed him.

Shattuara II (ca. 1275 B.C.E.) Possibly the last of the Hurrian rulers of what was left of the once-great Mitanni Empire.

Shu-Dagan (second half of the 23rd century B.C.E.) Military governor of Mari.

Shu-ilishu (1984–1975 B.C.E.) This ruler of Isin became a benefactor of Ur. He built a monumental gateway for the city and retrieved from Elam a purloined idol depicting Ur's patron deity, Nanna, god of the moon.

Shulgi (2094–2047 B.C.E.) Shulgi, the Ur-born son and successor of Ur-Nammu, required that he be worshiped as a god during his lifetime. He had statues of himself set up throughout his empire and decreed that offerings should be placed before them twice a week. As Julius and Augustus Caesar would do two thousand years later (via July and August), he even named a month in the calendar for himself. When he wasn't strengthening his empire's frontiers, Shulgi was bureaucratically tightening his control over its economy, going so far as to tax the temple estates of the gods. He prided himself on his stamina, boasting he could run the hundred or so miles between Nippur and Ur roundtrip in a single day, and he improved public roads, furnishing them with landscaped rest stops. Despite his physique and energy, Shulgi may have died violently from an assassin's blow, along with his consorts Geme-Ninlila and Shulgi-shimti.

Shulmani-ashared   See *Shalmaneser*.

Shushsi (middle of the 17th century B.C.E.) Ruler of the Sea-Land.

Shu-Sin (first half of the 24th century B.C.E.) Ruler of Akshak.

Shu-Sin (2037–2029 B.C.E.) Shu-Sin was a Sumerian king of Ur. Like the Roman emperor Hadrian, Shu-Sin built a long wall to block incursions by barbarians. Hadrian's barbarians were the Scots, who tried to invade Roman Britain in the second century C.E.; Shu-Sin's barbarians were the Amorites, who had their eyes on his fertile lands and their riches. Hadrian's Wall went east to west across England for 73 miles; Shu-Sin's stretched for 170 miles from the Tigris in the east to the Euphrates in the west. Shu-Sin was also the male lead in a series of erotic poems in Akkadian written in dialogue form similar to the later biblical Song of Songs.

Shuttarna I (ca. 1560 B.C.E.)   A Hurrian ruler.

Shuttarna II (ca. 1400 B.C.E.)   A Hurrian king of the Mitanni.

Shu-Turul (2168–2154 B.C.E.) Shu-Turul was the last king to govern the shattered empire that Sargon of Akkad had founded a century and a half before.

Silli-Adad (1842–1835 B.C.E.) He ruled Larsa briefly before dying in a battle against the forces of Babylon.

Simbar-shipak (1024–1007 B.C.E.) Simbar-shipak was the founder of Babylon's short-lived Fifth Dynasty, also called the Second Sea-Land dynasty because its founder may have come from the south. Simbar-shipak, who followed Nabu-shum-libur to the throne, did his best to restore public confidence by lending his support to traditional religious activities, but he fell victim to a coup. Two now nameless kings followed him in quick succession and the dynasty ended in 1004 B.C.E.

Sin-ahhe-eriba   See *Sennacherib*.

Sin-eribam (middle of the 19th century B.C.E.)   Ruler of Larsa.

Sin-iddinam (1849–1843 B.C.E.) A king of Larsa, Sin-iddinam reinforced the imperialistic policies of his predecessors. According to reports, he was killed when a chunk of brickwork fell from the top of his city's temple to the sun.

Sin-iqisham (middle of the 19th century B.C.E.)   Ruler of Larsa.

Sin-magir (1827–1817 B.C.E.)   We know little about this king of Isin except that he was so loved by a concubine, named Nattuptum, that she donated money to construct a building in his honor.

Sin-muballit (1812–1793 B.C.E.) Son of Apil-Sin, Sin-muballit was Babylon's fifth king. Domestically, he engaged in public works projects. Externally, he joined in an alliance to curb the territorial ambitions of Larsa, but he was defeated by its king, Rim-Sin.

Sin-shar-ishkun (second half of the seventh century B.C.E.) Sin-shar-ishkun, a son of Ashurbanipal, vied with his brother, Ashur-etil-ilani, for the crown of Assyria. He succeeded him to the throne, becoming the next to the last king Assyria would have. Under his reign the city of Nineveh was attacked and captured by a combined force of Babylonians and Medes. His life was either spared by the enemy or, according to another source, lost when the palace caught fire.

Sumu-Abum (1894–1881 B.C.E.) Sumu-Abum was one of a number of Amorite sheikhs who led their tribes into Mesopotamia during the early second millennium B.C.E. Sumu-Abum chose as his headquarters a small city on the middle of the Euphrates called "The Gate of the Gods" (Ka-dingir-ra in Sumerian and Bab-ilani in Akkadian), the city that came to be known in the Bible as Babylon. Sumu-Abum became its first king and founded its First Dynasty. To strengthen his position, he fortified the city with defensive walls and fought neighboring kings to establish his supremacy.

Sumu-El (1894–1866 B.C.E.) As king of Larsa, he continued the expansionist policies of his predecessor, Gungunum. Sumu-El diverted water away from Isin and wrested away its authority over Nippur.

Sumu-la-El (1880–1845 B.C.E.) Sumu-la-El was the second king of Babylon's First Dynasty. During his 36-year reign, he strengthened Babylon's defenses and battled Kish and the incursions of nomadic tribes.

Tiglathpileser I (1115–1077 B.C.E.) Active throughout his almost 40-year reign as Assyria's king, Tiglathpileser I led expedition after expedition against his nation's enemies on the north, south, and west. He was the

3.15   Grooms lead the horses to Tiglathpileser III's chariot. As the driver grips the reins, a servant holds a parasol to keep the sun off the king's head.   (Newman, The Thrones and Palaces of Babylon and Nineveh from Sea to Sea, 1876)

3.16   *The military might of Assyria inspired fear and respect. On this limestone relief, the eighth-century* B.C.E. *king Tiglathpileser III (second from the left) receives homage. While the king stands bow in hand conversing with two officials, a groveling ruler kisses his foot in obeisance. On the far right another figure has his hands manacled. Meanwhile, at the far left, a servant whisks flies from Tiglathpileser's head.*   (© 1984 The Detroit Institute of Arts [Founders Society Purchase, Ralph Harman Booth Bequest Fund])

first Assyrian king to record and celebrate his victories in chronological annals, and to ideologically justify his conquests. His annals are also the first to mention the Aramaeans, a tribe that would remain a thorn in Assyria's side for centuries to come. In his military campaigns, he defeated King Nebuchadnezzar I of Babylon and marched westward to the Mediterranean, where he went fishing and caught a narwhal, a cross between a dolphin and a swordfish. His annals also boasted of his having killed 920 lions, 800 from his chariot and 120 on foot. Back home, he set up a palace library, supervised the codification of Assyrian laws and judicial precedents, and planted foreign and domestic flora in luxurious gardens and parks. The lengthy résumé of this Assyrian Teddy Roosevelt ended when

he was murdered and succeeded by a nondescript conspirator.

Tiglathpileser II (967–935 B.C.E.)   During the reign of this Assyrian king, the Aramaeans advanced farther into Assyrian territory.

Tiglathpileser III (744–727 B.C.E.)   This Assyrian king reinvigorated his nation's imperialistic dreams by systematic reorganization. To increase his own power, he decreased the authority of nobles by reducing the size of the territory each controlled and the autonomy they previously possessed. He also restructured the army, making conscripts subordinate to a new permanent corps of professional soldiers. In addition, he strengthened Assyria's hold on conquered lands by deporting patriotic native populations and replacing them with loyal settlers; the deportees were then used as laborers in outlying provinces.

Tiptakzi (end of the 17th century B.C.E.) Tiptakzi was the king of the Kassites at the time of the capture of Babylon by the Hittites. Subsequent to the event, the Kassites assumed the throne of Babylon, which they were to hold for over four centuries.

Tiridates I (248–211 B.C.E.) The second Parthian king to rule over Mesopotamia.

Tiriqan (Tirigan) (?–2120 B.C.E.) Tiriqan, a Gutian tribesman, reigned over Mesopotamia for a little over a month, but his fall marked the end of nearly a century of Gutian domination. When his army was defeated by a coalition led by Uruk, Tiriqan was captured. The king of Uruk then dramatized his victory by forcing Tiriqan to lie on the ground while he put his foot on Tiriqan's neck.

Trajan (98–117 C.E.) Famous for his defeat of Dacian tribes in Romania, the Roman emperor Trajan invaded Mesopotamia, capturing the Parthian capital of Ctesiphon, and marching to the Persian Gulf. He then declared Mesopotamia a province of the Roman Empire, but he was ultimately forced to retreat.

Tukulti-Ninurta I (1244–1208 B.C.E.) Tukulti-Ninurta was a warrior and Assyrian empire-builder in the tradition of his father and predecessor, Shalmaneser I. His defeat of the Babylonian king Kashtiliash resulted in Babylonia being ruled for a time by Assyrian governors. In literature, Tukulti-Ninurta's victory over Kashtiliash was celebrated in an epic, the so-called *Tukulti-Ninurta Epic*, the only Assyrian one we possess. In the end he was murdered in his palace by conspirators led by his son, Ashur-nadin-apli.

Tukulti-Ninurta II (beginning of the ninth century B.C.E.) This Assyrian king completely rebuilt the wall protecting his capital city of Ashur. He toured Mesopotamia with his army, collecting tribute on the way, and he entrenched Assyria's hold on its subject territories by building fortresses and fostering the settlement of underpopulated areas.

Turam-Dagan (2071–2051 B.C.E.) Military governor of Mari.

Tushratta (ca. 1375 B.C.E.) A Hurrian king of the Mitanni, Tushratta sent his daughter to join the harem of pharaoh Amenhotep III as a means of strengthening diplomatic ties between the two nations in the event of Hittite aggression. Tushratta also corresponded, as the Amarna letters show, with Queen Tiye of Egypt and her son Amenhotep IV (later named Akhenaton). When Amenhotep III was ailing, Tushratta sent him a statue of Ishtar of Nineveh in the hope that the goddess' powers would cure him. Tushratta's brother, Artatama II, may have set up a separate ruling dynasty. Whatever the case, Tushratta was in the end murdered by a son he did not choose to succeed him. The other son, Shattiwaza, the rightful heir, sought refuge first in Babylon and then, when refused, fled to the Hittites for asylum, as his father's kingdom disintegrated.

Uhub (ca. 2570 B.C.E.) An early ruler of Kish.

Ulamburiash (ca. 1475 B.C.E.) Ulamburiash defeated the king of the Sea-Land in battle, and thereby regained control over Sumer, which had seceded from the Babylonian Empire after the death of Hammurabi I.

Unzi (second half of the 25th century B.C.E.) Ruler of Akshak.

Ur-Baba (2155–2142 B.C.E.) Ruler of Lagash.

Urdukuga (1836–1828 B.C.E.)   Ruler of Isin.

Ur-gar (2114 B.C.E.)   Ruler of Lagash.

Ur-gigira (2146–2141 B.C.E.)   A member of Uruk's Fourth Dynasty.

Ur-Nammu (2112–2095 B.C.E.)   Ur-Nammu founded the glorious Third Dynasty of Ur that filled the power vacuum left when the Sargonic Empire collapsed. To court the gods' favor and thank them for their blessings, he undertook the construction of towering ziggurats at Eridu, Nippur, Uruk, and Ur, and he ringed Ur with walls "high as a shining mountain." To increase agricultural productivity, he dug new irrigation canals and dredged old ones, at the same time promoting foreign trade. And to bring justice to the land, he (or possibly his son Shulgi) promulgated the oldest surviving code of Mesopotamian law. Praised in hymns for his valor and good works, Ur-Nammu died on the battlefield, where sadly "his body lay tossed aside like a broken urn."

Ur-Nanshe (ca. 2550 B.C.E.)   This ruler of Lagash engaged in building activities and is proudly depicted on a plaque carrying a basket of clay on his head to make bricks for a new temple. Ur-Nanshe also promoted foreign

3.17   Observed by his queen and courtiers, Ur-Nanshe, with his son in tow, proudly commences the construction of a new temple. Below, we see him celebrating with drink in hand.   (E. de Sarzec, Découvertes en Chaldée, 1884–1912)

trade between his own city and far-off Dilmun in the Persian Gulf.

Ur-nigina (2153–2147 B.C.E.) A member of Uruk's Fourth Dynasty.

Ur-Ningirsu (2121–2118 B.C.E.) Ruler of Lagash and successor of Gudea.

Ur-Ningizzida (second half of the 20th century B.C.E.) Ruler of Eshnunna.

Ur-Ninkimara (first half of the 21st century B.C.E.) Governor of Lagash when it was dominated by Ur.

Ur-Ninmar (second half of the 20th century B.C.E.) Ruler of Eshnunna.

Ur-Ninsuna (first half of the 21st century B.C.E.) Governor of Lagash when it was dominated by Ur.

Ur-Ninurta (1923–1896 B.C.E.) A usurper, Ur-Ninurta took the throne of Isin upon the death of Lipit-Ishtar, but he lost it when he was killed in battle some 30 years later. With his defeat, Larsa seized the lands Isin had controlled.

Uruinimgina See *Urukagina*.

Urukagina (ca. 2350 B.C.E.) Ruler of Lagash. Before his military defeat by the ruler of Uruk, Urukagina instituted social reforms to free citizens from the crushing weight of heavy debt and excessive taxation.

Ur-Zababa (ca. 2340 B.C.E.) Ur-Zababa was the last member of Kish's Fourth Dynasty. He was deposed by a usurper who had served as his royal cup-bearer, the ambitious Sargon of Akkad.

Urzigurumash (second half of the 17th century B.C.E.) Urzigurumash was a Kassite king

in Babylonia who took the throne after Kashtiliash II.

Ushpia (ca. 2025 B.C.E.) An Assyrian king who, to judge by his name, was probably Hurrian in origin.

Ushshi (first half of the 17th century B.C.E.) Ushshi became the leader of the Kassites in Babylonia following the death of Kashtiliash I.

Usur-awassu (first half of the 20th century B.C.E.) Ruler of Eshnunna.

Utu-hegal (2123–2113 B.C.E.) During his reign he drove invading Gutian hordes out of Sumer but was replaced on the throne of Uruk by the ruler of another city, Ur-Nammu of Ur. A text says that he died of drowning while supervising an irrigation project.

Warad-Sin (1834–1823 B.C.E.) Warad-Sin was put on Larsa's throne after his father, Kudur-Mabuk, a tribal leader, defeated Larsa's king in battle. To court popular favor, Warad-Sin devoted himself to renovating temples to the gods within his kingdom's borders, making sure to inscribe his name on his public works. He also took charge of reconstructing the fortifications of Ur.

Warassa (first half of the 19th century B.C.E.) Ruler of Eshnunna.

Wasasatta (beginning of the 13th century B.C.E.) One of the Hurrian rulers of what had once been the powerful kingdom of Mitanni.

Xerxes I (485–465 B.C.E.) The son of the Persian king Darius I, Xerxes reasserted Persian authority over Egypt and Babylonia, dividing the latter into two districts for more effective administration. Preoccupied with the conquest of Greece, which his predecessor had failed to win, Xerxes set into motion a massive invasion of Greece involving forces on land and sea—the second "Persian War" recounted by Herodotus in his *History*. Once again, Persia was defeated in a David and Goliath struggle that served to inspire the patriotic Golden Age of Greece. Both Xerxes and his son were later killed in a coup.

Yaggid-Lim   See *Iaggid-Lim*.

Yahdun-Lim   See *Iahdun-Lim*.

Yasmah-Addu   See *Iasmah-Adad*.

Zababa-shuma-iddina (middle of the 12th century B.C.E.) Zababa-shuma-iddina was the next to the last Kassite king to rule Babylonia. After reigning for only a year, he was forcibly deposed.

Zabaia (1941–1933 B.C.E.)   Ruler of Larsa.

Zambia (second half of the 19th century B.C.E.)   Ruler of Isin.

Zenobia (250 C.E.)   Wife and successor of the Palmyran king Odenath, she reversed her husband's pro-Roman policy and drove the Romans out of Egypt, Syria, and Turkey. In vengeance, the Roman emperor Aurelian attacked and ravaged Palmyra, capturing Zenobia and transporting her to Rome to be paraded in his triumphal procession. Tradition says she lived out her days in Rome in exile but with dignity.

Zimri-Lim (1776–1761 B.C.E.)   Exiled when Shamshi-Adad I appointed his own son governor of Mari, Zimri-Lim—the son of Mari's former king Yahdun-Lim—returned follow-ing Shamshi-Adad's death to claim the throne. The Mari letters illuminate his times, revealing how he gathered intelligence about his rivals and used political alliances to strengthen his position, often by giving his daughters in marriage to other potentates and relying on his wife for advice. He added splendor to his six-acre palace, such that it became one of the wonders of the ancient Near East. In a mural, he still stands receiving the symbols of kingship from the goddess Ishtar, while other female deities attend, holding vases from which the waters of life continually flow. The royal family dined on haute cuisine detailed in the palace's surviving culinary archives; Zimri-Lim himself was most proud that he had arranged for ice to be brought from the mountains to the north to cool his guests' drinks. Unfortunately, his diplomatic relations broke down with his longtime ally and friend, Babylon's king Hammurabi. Hammurabi eventually attacked Mari with his army, sacked the palace, and demolished the city's walls. Zimri-Lim's dinner parties ceased, as did probably Zimri-Lim himself.

Zuzu (second half of the 25th century B.C.E.)   Ruler of Akshak. Supported by the forces of Mari and Kish, he marched against king Eannatum of Lagash, but he was defeated.

READING

The Structure of Civilization

Diakonoff 1982: structure of Mesopotamian society; Frankfort 1956: the rise and unique character of Mesopotamian civilization.

The Stratification of Society

Gordon 1953: social stratification; Gordon 1957: role of social classes in Hammurabi's Code; Kramer 1963: social structure of the Sumerian city; Oates 1978: social organization; Van de Mieroop 1999: the city.

The Beginnings

Bottéro et al. 2001: origin of the Sumerians; Frankfort 1948, Klein 2001, Jacobsen 1970: the beginnings and primitive democracy; Frankfort, Wilson, and Jacobsen 1946: the cosmos as a state, the function of the state.

Kingship

Bienkowski and Millard 2000: kings and kingship; Bottéro 1992: the substitute king; Contenau 1954: king and state; Frankfort, Wilson, and Jacobsen 1946: the function of the state; Gibson and Briggs 1987: Near Eastern bureaucracy; Grayson 1999: absolute monarchy in Assyria; Greengus 1995: legal and social institutions of Mesopotamia; Larsen 1976, Liverani 1976: imperialism; Oppenheim 1977: "the great organizations"; Postgate 1995: royal ideology and state administration in Sumer and Akkad; Saggs 1989: the rise of kingship; Saggs 1995: kingship.

Taxation

Bienkowski and Millard 2000: taxation in the ancient Near East; Postgate 1974: taxation in Assyria; Postgate 1992: limitations of evidence for early Mesopotamia; Saggs 1962: taxation in Mesopotamia.

Justice and Law

Bienkowski and Millard 2000: law, river ordeal; Bottéro et al. 2001: trial by ordeal; Driver and Miles 1952 and 1955: Babylonian laws; Gordon 1957: Hammurabi's Code; Greengus 1995: law codes, social justice, and legal education; judges and courts; Nemet-Nejat 1998: administration of justice; Postgate 1994: laws and the law; Pritchard 1969: legal texts; Saggs 1962: law and statecraft; Saggs 1965: law; Sasson 1977; criminals.

Biographies of Political Leaders

Bienkowski and Millard 2000, Leick 1999, Sasson 1995: biographies; Brown 1995: selected kings; Roux 1992: historical context.

4

RELIGION AND MYTH

THE MULTIPLICITY OF THE GODS

Manifold are the divine powers that ruled over Mesopotamia and the minds and hearts of its people.

The multiplicity of these ancient gods can be explained by many factors. What we in our scientific age would describe objectively as "the environment," the ancients viewed as alive with diverse spirits. The spirits were immanent in nature and as numerous as nature's parts: the sky above, the fertile earth beneath, and the waters that nourished the soil; the Moon, Sun, and stars; and the generative powers that helped the creatures of nature, including humanity, reproduce and flourish. The ancients also saw the hand of the divine at work in the arts by which human culture and civilization were sustained: the making of fire, the molding of brick, the raising of crops, the tending of flocks and herds, the healing of the sick, the invention of writing, and the creation of justice and law. To address these numinous powers, to thank them for their beneficence and to appeal to them in time of need, the ancients conceived of their gods in anthropomorphic form with eyes to see them and ears to hear their hymns and prayers. In a naturalistic way, they also endowed them with human emotions because nature seemed alternately compassionate and cruel. They also envisioned the existence of other powers—darker, demonic powers—that lurked in a subterranean realm and were ever ready to rise and to steal from human beings the very things they regarded as most precious.

4.1   As King Ashurnasirpal II looks on, the god Ninurta advances with thunderbolts in hand against a horned monster, part lion, part bird. The relief once adorned a temple at Kalhu that the king built to honor the god.   (Layard, *A Second Series of the Monuments of Nineveh*, 1853)

But there were other reasons that explain the gods' multiplicity. The human institution of marriage, for example, when applied to the major gods automatically doubled their numbers, since most deities were assigned divine spouses.

Mesopotamia's ethnic composition and political history also played their roles. The Sumerians worshiped certain gods by certain names, and the Semitic Babylonians and Assyrians worshiped others by others, though in many ways the pantheons were parallel or grew to be so as a result of cultural assimilation and conquest. In addition, before the rise of empire, the existence of autonomous city-states engendered special gods who were venerated locally as the protectors of their hometowns; whereas, with the rise of empire, certain local gods assumed a nationwide importance they had not previously enjoyed. In a reverse phenomenon, through a process known as syncretism, a major god might absorb the functions and family connections of lesser gods. Yet the force of tradition was often so strong that the names of the so-called lesser gods would still persist.

To the pious Christian, Jew, or Muslim who takes the oneness of god as an article of faith, or even to the secular soul who regards monotheism as a normal state of affairs, Mesopotamian polytheism may come as something of a shock. But it is simply another way—perhaps more primitive—of coming to terms with a world in which there are nameless forces, some seemingly benign and others hostile, that affect an individual's life. If the Mesopotamians used more names to articulate their confusion and their hope, it does not make them less human than we. Indeed, were they to travel by time machine to our world, they might marvel how a human race so hellbent on mutual destruction could naively believe that god is loving and one.

THE GOVERNANCE OF THE WORLD

According to a tradition that began with the Sumerians, human society was patterned on a plan conceived by the gods. To fulfill this organizational plan, operational rules had been devised to govern human activities and behavior. These rules were collectively known as the *me* (a Sumerian plural pronounced "may," and referred to in Akkadian as *parsu*). The *me* defined such aspects of civilization as government and religion, war and peace, sexual intercourse (including prostitution), art and music, and crafts and professions, as well as such abstractions as truth and falsehood, and sadness and joy. The implementation of the *me* was supervised by the gods, especially by An (Akkadian Anu), the god of creation, and Enlil (Akkadian Ellil), heaven's chief executive.

In addition, Babylonian tradition told of the existence of an object called the Tablet of Destinies. This inscribed tablet contained within itself absolute power over the world, and bestowed this power upon its possessor. Held in the hand or worn on the chest, the tablet could be given by one god to another, stolen by guile, or seized by force.

THE NAMES AND FUNCTIONS OF THE GODS

In the following inventory, the gods and goddesses of Mesopotamia are listed alphabetically.

In cases where a deity was worshiped under both a Sumerian and an Akkadian name, the Sumerian name is given first, followed by the Akkadian equivalent. Thus, for example, Utu/Shamash tells us that the god of the sun was worshiped by the Sumerians as "Utu" but by the Babylonians and Assyrians as "Shamash." For convenience, cross-references are also provided. Where gods or goddesses played prominent roles in mythology, their significance is noted by asterisks placed before their names. Their dramatic functions in Mesopotamian literature will be described in chapter 5. The reader will notice the Mesopotamian predilection for having gods starting with the letter "N." This practice is in large part due to their use of the honorific prefix "Nin-," which meant "Lord" or "Lady," not unlike our own use of "St." before the name of a religious figure.

Abba   A Babylonian goddess popular in Mari and Isin; also a divine being created by the goddess Ninhursag.

Abzu/Apsu   A primordial god personifying the subterranean realm from which freshwater emanates.

Adad   See *Ishkur*.

Alala   A god of songs sung at harvest time.

Amurru   See *Martu*.

Anshar and Kishar   A pair of primordial deities who are mentioned in the Babylonian *Epic of Creation*. In Sumerian, the first syllable of the god Anshar's name meant "heaven"; the first syllable of the goddess Kishar's name meant "earth." Their cosmic parents (or possible grandparents) were Apsu, the primordial god of freshwater, and Tiamat, the goddess of salt water. Anshar and Kishar became the parents of the sky-god Anu.

*An/Anu   An was the august and revered "chairman of the board" of the Mesopotamian pantheon. His name literally meant "heaven." He was the supreme source of authority among the gods, and among men, upon whom he conferred kingship. As heaven's grand patriarch, he dispensed justice and controlled the laws known as the *me* that governed the universe. Myths name various goddesses as his wife: the goddess of the earth (Ki/Uras); a female heavenly counterpart (Antum); a mother-goddess (Nammu or Ninmah); and the sex-goddess Inanna/Ishtar, who is sometimes also spoken of as his daughter.

Annunitum   An Akkadian goddess, worshiped in a number of Sumerian cities, whose attributes resemble those of the goddess Inanna/Ishtar.

Annunaki (or Anunnaki)   An assemblage of lesser deities (as many as 60 or even 600) who are frequently mentioned in literature and are always referred to collectively, like a flock of angels. They can pronounce judgment or perform labor at the behest of other gods. In their number and function, they parallel another divine grouping, the Igigi. The Annunaki were worshiped in both Sumerian and Babylonian tradition.

Anu   See *An*.

Anzu   See *Imdugud*.

Apsu   See *Abzu*.

Aruru   A Babylonian mother-goddess.

Asag   A hideous demon that could provoke violence and cause human suffering. A myth relates how Asag was defeated by the hero Ninurta.

Asarluhi   An ancient Sumerian deity worshiped in a temple near Eridu and in the city-state of Lagash. A son of the wise god Enki,

Asarluhi was associated with the magical power of incantations. In Babylonian thought, he took on the heroic stature of Marduk, with whom he was linked.

Ashnan An ancient Sumerian goddess of grain and bountiful harvests. In curses, she was asked to withhold her blessings from the fields of the enemy so as to starve him into submission.

*Ashur (or Asshur) God of the Assyrian nation. Originally a local god of the city of Ashur, he grew to preeminence as the Assyrian state expanded through imperialistic conquest.

Astabi The Hurrian god of war.

Aya See *Sherida.*

Baba A Sumerian deity of great antiquity, Baba was the "Lady of Abundance" whose fertilizing energy helped human beings and herds to generate offspring. In later times, she was associated with the divine power of healing and with the potency of magic spells. She was worshiped as the wife of Ningirsu at Lagash, where their marriage rite was ritually reenacted as part of the New Year Festival.

Bel Meaning "lord" or "master" in Akkadian, this name signified the god Enlil, and later the god Marduk. The biblical equivalent for this honorific title was Baal, the name given to the chief god of the Canaanites. The feminine form of Bel was Belet.

Belet-ekallim A Babylonian goddess whose name meant "Lady of the Great House." At Mari she was the divine patroness of the ruler and his family, and she was known as the "Lady of the Sceptre." Her role there and her titles inform us she was the special protector of the royal household.

Belet-seri A Babylonian goddess who, as the "Lady of the Steppe," served as the wife of Amurru, the god of the nomadic Amorites. She also functioned as a scribe in the netherworld.

Damgalnuna/Damkina Originally a mother-goddess, she was worshiped as the wife of the Sumerian god Enki (Ea), the lord of freshwater, and dwelt with him in his subterranean kingdom. In Babylonian times, she was looked upon as the mother of Babylon's chief god, Marduk.

Damu Taking after his divine mother Ninisini, Damu functioned as a Sumerian god of healing, as did his physician-sister Gunura. Damu was especially worshiped in the city of Isin.

*Dumuzi (Hebrew and Arabic: Tammuz) A Sumerian god of shepherds and their flocks, Dumuzi was chosen by Inanna/Ishtar, the cruel goddess of sexual passion, to be her lover. When Inanna was held captive in the netherworld and needed a substitute to "die" for her, she pointed the demons to Dumuzi. He still lives on today in the Hebrew and Arabic spelling of his name, Tammuz, the name for the Semitic lunar month that laps over July, the time when pastures wither and the god must for a time die again.

Dumuziabzu A Sumerian goddess who represented the life-giving powers of freshwater; also, in Sumerian, the name of a male deity who served Enki, the freshwater god.

Ea See *Enki.*

Ellil See *Enlil.*

Enbililu A son of the water-god Enki/Ea, he went into the family business and became a divine inspector of canals, also supervising the flow of the Tigris and Euphrates.

*Enki/Ea Enki's domain was the Abzu (or Absu), an ocean of freshwater upon which the earth floated and which served as the life-giving source of streams and rivers. Because of water's secret and potent source, Enki/Ea was associated with arcane wisdom, embodied in both skilled crafts and sorcery. He used his cunning to save mankind before the Great Flood, and he was prayed to by those beset by crisis. His holy city was watery Eridu. In art, Enki/Ea is depicted with streams of water cascading from his shoulders or pouring from a vase held in his hands. His divine wife was Ninki, the "Lady (Sumerian: *nin*) of the Earth (Sumerian: *ki*)," just as Enki is its "Lord" (Sumerian: *en*). Elsewhere, his wife is called Damgalnuna (Damkina). Their divine children were Marduk and his sister Nanshe.

Enkimdu Enkimdu went into business with his brother Enbililu as a protector of irrigation systems.

*Enlil/Ellil One of the most important gods of Mesopotamia, Enlil/Ellil was second in authority only to An/Anu. Just as An/Anu ruled the airy realm above the earth and Enki/Ea ruled the watery realm beneath, Enlil/Ellil ruled the earth itself, directing the forces of nature (especially torrential floods) and bestowing kingship upon the leaders of humankind. He was the keeper of the Tablet of Destinies that decreed the fate of gods and men. If An (Enlil's father, according to one tradition) was the divine chairman of the board, Enlil was the heavenly corporation's CEO, or chief executive officer. His cosmic headquarters were based at Nippur. His executive assistant was his son Nuska. Enlil/Ellil was a family man, married to Ninlil (also called Sud), and with her he raised a brood that included—among others—the moon-god Nanna/Sin, the sun-god Utu/Shamash, the weather-god Ishkur/Adad, and the love-goddess Inanna/Ishtar.

Enmesharra A primordial god associated with the realm of the dead.

Ennugi A god associated with both the realm of the dead and the irrigation of fertile land.

*Ereshkigal The queen of the Mesopotamian netherworld. Sexually deprived and jealous of her sister Inanna/Ishtar, she dwelt in a dark and desolate domain. Seduced by her, the god of light Nergal was compelled to spend six months of every year (the months of winter darkness) trapped in her realm as her sexual partner. Compared to an analogous Greek myth, Ereshkigal played the role of lonely Hades and Nergal the role of ravished and forlorn Persephone, though with their mythological genders reversed. The center of the cult of the netherworld was the city of Kutha, famous for its temple of Nergal.

Erra See *Nergal.*

Galla One of a number of like-named underworld demons whose job it was to hunt down the marked souls of the living and drag them down to the infernal regions. The Gallas' most famous victim was Dumuzi.

Gatumdug A daughter of An, she was worshiped in Lagash.

Geshtinanna A Sumerian goddess and the sister of Dumuzi. Because she tried to keep him from the clutches of the Gallas, Geshtinanna was sentenced to spend six months out of every year in the underworld. There she served as a scribe. Each time she was paroled, she spent her freedom weeping for her brother, who took her place. Because she lived in the steppes where she kept sheep, she was identified with a similar divinity, Belet-seri. Tradition also connected Geshtinanna with viniculture.

Gibil/Girra The Mesopotamian god of fire and heat, viewed not only as a destructive force but also as a constructive power. Because he energized the baker's oven, the potter's kiln, and the metalsmith's forge, Gibil/Girra was called the "founder of cities."

Girra See *Gibil.*

Gishbare A god who was worshiped in the city of Girsu.

Gugulanna The Sumerian name for Ereshkigal's husband. By Babylonian times he was referred to as Nergal.

Gula The Babylonian goddess of healing and the patron deity of physicians. Her most important temple was at Isin, but she was honored in other cities as well. Her sacred animal was the dog, and ceramic models of dogs were dedicated to her at her sanctuaries by those who had been blessed by her tender mercies. Her husband was variously named Ninurta, Pabilsag, or Abu. Because at least two of these divinities were connected with agriculture, her marriage to them may symbolically reflect the medicinal use of plants. Gula gave birth to two children, the gods Damu and Ninazu, both of whom dedicated themselves to the healing arts.

Gushkin-banda Patron god of Sumerian goldsmiths.

Hendursanga/Ishum A benevolent Mesopotamian deity who gave wise and calming advice to the gods. He also acted as a divine herald, and as a watchman providing nighttime security.

Humbaba See *Huwawa.*

Huwawa/Humbaba Distinguished by his hideous, Gorgon-like face (which resembled a coiled mass of intestines), this monster was charged with the protection of a mountainous forest of sacred cedar trees. Duped by the hero Gilgamesh into surrendering his magic powers in exchange for trinkets and empty promises, Huwawa was killed by having his head cut off. In Babylonia, clay models of Huwawa's face were hung on walls to ward off evil. If, however, diviners examining a sacrificed animal thought they saw Huwawa's face in its entrails, it was a sure sign the nation would find itself in a dangerous mess.

Igigi (or Igigu) A collective term (like Anunnaki) for a group of assorted, but otherwise nameless, gods. Some believe the Igigi may have been chthonic deities and the Anunnaki celestial ones, but the matter is unresolved, as is the Igigi's number, which may have been as high as 300. According to one myth (contained in the Akkadian tale of *Atrahasis*), the Igigi were forced to do hard labor by the Anunnaki. After 40 days, however, the Igigi had had enough, and they called a strike by burning their tools—the first strike in history by organized labor The strike, however, had an unforeseen and (from our standpoint) unwelcome outcome: to take up the slack, human beings were created to do the gods' work. Unlike the Anunnaki who are first mentioned in Sumerian texts, the Igigi do not appear in literature until Babylonian times.

Ilaba The chief god of Agade. With the military triumphs of Sargon I, the war-god Ilaba (along with Inanna/Ishtar, who always loved a good fight) became the patron deity of the Akkadian Empire's kings.

Imdugud/Anzu (or the "Zu-bird") An immense mythical bird with the head of a lion and the body of an eagle, whose huge wings could stir up horrendous windstorms. According to Mesopotamian legend, its behavior could be benevolent (rewarding a hero for tending its young) or malevolent (stealing the Tablet of Destinies, which gave to its possessor control over the universe). The latter theft by Imdugud/Anzu was thwarted by the heroic god Ninurta.

Iminbi/Sebittu A group of seven chthonic spirits, some good, some evil, led by the god Nergal/Erra.

*Inanna, or Inana/Ishtar (West Semitic: Astarte) The most popular deity of ancient Mesopotamia, Inanna/Ishtar represented the power of sexual attraction and the carnal pleasure that proceeds from it. Focused on the immediate gratification of her own sensual needs, she was neither a goddess of marriage nor of childbirth. Her sexual appetite was inexhaustible and her relationships with men short term. Legion were her lovers but cruel the price they all paid, Dumuzi in particular, whom she consigned to hell. Because of her savagery and her fierce determination to have her own way whatever the cost to others, Inanna/Ishtar was also a goddess of war and a patroness of ruling dynasties. Her animal was the lion and her symbol the star, signifying the morning and evening star Venus, with whom she was astrologically identified. Her major shrines were at Uruk and Kish (in Sumer), Agade (in Akkad), and Arbil and Nineveh (in Assyria), and priestesses are said to have served her as sacred prostitutes. Inanna/Ishtar's divine father was variously listed as An/Anu, Enlil/Ellil, Enki/Ea, or Nanna/Sin (the moon-god); her mother, in certain texts, as the moon-god's wife, Ningal. Inanna/Ishtar herself was also associated with the moon, either because of the moon's changeable mood expressed through its phases or the parallelism between lunar and menstrual cycles. Her only sibling was the dread Ereshkigal, the sexually deprived queen of the netherworld.

Inzak The chief god of the blessed paradise-like land of Dilmun.

Ishhara A goddess who, like Inanna/Ishtar, was associated with love and war. Her worship seems to have been of Semitic origin, and she was popular among the Hurrians. The creatures sacred to her were the snake and scorpion. In astrology, she was identified with the constellation the Greeks would later call Scorpio in remembrance of the scorpion that was her pet.

Ishkur/Adad (West Semitic: Hadad) The god of weather, worshiped in Sumer, Babylonia, and Assyria, and as far west as Syria. The son of An/Anu or Enlil/Ellil, his power precipitated both destructive storms and beneficent rain. His divine symbol was lightning, and his sacred animal the bull, which bellowed like thunder.

Ishtar See *Inanna*.

Ishtaran The patron god of the city of Der in eastern Mesopotamia. Associated with the idea of justice, Ishtaran's minister was a snake-god and his symbol the snake.

Ishum See *Hendursanga*.

Isimud/Usmu A minor god with two faces, who served as minister to Enki/Ea.

Iter-Mer The name of this Babylonian god means "Mer has returned." Since *Mer* is the Sumerian word for rain, the god may have been associated with the seasonal rains that nourished the fields. He was the patron god of the city-state of Mari.

Ki The Sumerian goddess who symbolized the earth.

Kingu (also Qingu) *In* the Babylonian *Epic of Creation*, Kingu serves under Tiamat and commands her military forces. When Tiamat and her minions are defeated, Marduk executes Kingu and uses his blood to create man.

Kulla Patron god of brick-laying.

Kumarbi A Hurrian deity, possible a god of grain, who struggled for power with his divine father Anu.

Kusuh The Hurrian god of the moon.

Lahmu (male) and Lahamu (female) Primordial Mesopotamian gods who were born from Abzu/Apsu (freshwater) and Tiamat (saltwater). Their bodies, according to one text, were half human and half fish.

Lama, or Lamma/Lamassu A female deity of the Sumerians who offered her worshipers protection. In Assyria, the term *lamassu* was applied to the protective statues of winged bulls or lions that guarded the entranceways to palaces.

Lamashtu A gruesome Babylonian demoness who tried to snatch away the lives of fetuses and newborn infants. To ward her off, a pregnant woman or nursing mother would wear a magic charm or hang an amuletic plaque by her doorway.

Lamassu See *Lama*.

La-tarak and Lulal Protective gods who guarded doorways and protected the faithful against sorcery.

Lisin A Sumerian mother-goddess.

Lugal-irra and Meslamta-ea Twin deities who guarded doorways, including the entrance to the netherworld. In astrology, they were linked to the constellation later called Gemini, "the Twins."

Mamitu (abbreviated as Mami or Mame) Named for the Akkadian word for "oath," this goddess stood for the sanctity of the oath and punished those who committed perjury.

4.2 This glazed-brick dragon from Babylon's Ishtar Gate symbolizes the power of the city's patron god, Marduk. (Photograph © 2001, The Detroit Institute of Arts [Founders Society Purchase, General Membership Fund])

*Marduk Originally a patron deity of Babylon and a farmer's god whose symbol was the *marru*, or spade, Marduk rose with the growth of the city's empire to become a national deity and chief god of the Babylonian pantheon. His heroic deeds included the defeat of Tiamat (followed by the organization of the cosmos and the creation of man), the rescue of the Tablet of Destinies from the Zu-bird, and the defense of the moon against the gods who tried to steal its light. As a divine champion of good against the forces of evil, Marduk was frequently invoked in incantations by petitioners who sought his protection. He was described in tradition as the first-born son of Enki/Ea, as the spouse of Sarpanitum, and as the father of Nabu, patron of scribes and god of wisdom. His main sanctuary, the Esagila, was fittingly located in the city of Babylon, his original hometown.

Martu/Amurru The national god of the Amorites, a nomadic Semitic people from the steppes who raided the cultivated lands of Sumer and Babylonia. As the Amorites were integrated into Mesopotamia's civilized population, the god Martu/Amurru joined the Mesopotamian pantheon, where he was "adopted" as An/Anu's son. Among the western Semites, his wife was known as Ashratum; among the Babylonians, as Belet-seri, the "Lady of the Wilderness." A Sumerian tale recounts how the uncultured Martu (who dug up truffles and ate his meat raw) became "civilized" when he married a Sumerian girl from the city.

Meshkilak   Chief goddess of the blessed paradise-like land of Dilmun.

Meslamta-ea   An ancient Sumerian god of the underworld, later identified with Nergal.

*Nabu   Equivalent to the Sumerian goddess Nisaba and revered by the Babylonians and Assyrians, the god Nabu was the patron deity of scribes, literacy, and wisdom. By the first millennium B.C.E., he was spoken of as the son of the great Marduk, a sign of the high esteem in which he, and the written word he stood for, were held. His name was used in Babylonian personal names, including the names of some of Babylon's rulers, such as *Nebu*chadnezzar and *Nabo*nidus. He even appears in the Bible as "Nebo" in a passage (Isaiah 46:1) in which the text refers to the humbling of Babylon's idols, Bel (=Marduk) and Nebo. Nabu was the chief god of Babylon's sister-city, Borsippa, from which his cult statue was ceremoniously borne to Babylon each New Year's so that he might pay his respects to his divine father. At Nabu's temple, votive offerings (no doubt given in gratitude by scribes) included clay tablets imprinted with especial calligraphic skill. Nabu's symbol was a single wedge-shaped cuneiform mark, or a stylus shown resting on a tablet. His divine wife was named Tashmit. Continually worshiped until the second century C.E. (when cuneiform became a lost art), Nabu

was identified in Hellenistic times with the Greek god of prophecy and the arts, Apollo.

Nammu   A primordial Sumerian mother-goddess who originally signified the freshwater that nourishes the soil. It was she who first conceived of the idea of creating man so that he might serve the gods. Her name is contained in the name of the Sumerian ruler and lawgiver Ur-Nammu.

Namtar/Namtaru   The name of an underworld demon and/or the minister of Ereshkigal, queen of the dead.

Nana   A Sumerian goddess, known in Babylonian times as the wife of Marduk or of Nabu. Because of her association with both love and war, she bore similarities to Inanna/Ishtar.

Nanaya   Another Sumerian goddess similar in nature to Inanna, Nanaya was invoked in incantations where the petitioner prayed to become more sexually appealing.

*Nanna/Sin or Suen   First-born son of Enlil/Ellil and Ninlil, Nanna/Sin was the Mesopotamian god of the moon. He was married to Ningal, and through her he bore two children: Utu/Shamash, the god of the sun; and Inanna/Ishtar, the goddess of love. The Mesopotamians thus conceived of day, illuminated by the sun, as emanating from the darkness of night and the lesser light of the moon. As the time of lovemaking, the night and the moon were linked to the goddess of the erotic. As a source of light, the moon was also viewed as humanity's protector against acts of criminality undertaken under the cover of darkness (even as the illuminating and all-seeing sun was looked upon as a guardian of justice). A Mesopotamian myth tells how a cabal of gods (including the god of the sun) plotted to steal the moon's light, until their plot was foiled by

Marduk. Lunar eclipses were a source of great ritual concern. During the new moon when Nanna/Sin's light was not visible, the god was said to be in the netherworld, where he judged the dead. The moon's crescent was viewed alternately as a boat in which he traveled or as the horns of a calf, inspiring the god's connection with the fecundity of herds. The center of moon-worship in Mesopotamia was Nanna's temple at Ur, where the daughters of rulers often served as priestesses. Another center of moon-worship was the city of Harran in northwestern Mesopotamia. King Nabonidus's mother served as chief priestess there, even as his daughter was consecrated to the god's service at Ur. The god's name was sometimes simply written as the number "30," signifying the approximate number of days in the lunar month, the basis of the ancient Mesopotamian calendar. Despite the correspondence of the moon's phases to the menstrual cycle, the god Nanna/Sin was conceptualized as male. In this respect, he was like the moon-gods of ancient Egypt (Thoth, Khensu, and Aah), but unlike the moon-*goddesses* of classical civilization (Artemis and Diana).

Nanshe A Sumerian goddess, worshiped especially in Lagash, who was the divine patron of fishing and divination. Gudea of Lagash sought her oracular guidance. A hymn describes her concern for social justice.

Nergal/Erra A Mesopotamian god of the underworld and husband of Ereshkigal. The center of his cult was located at the city of Kutha. Nergal/Erra was also a destructive god of war and pestilence, associated also with the scorching heat of the sun. In astrology he was identified with the planet Mars, named for the classical god of war.

Ninazu A Sumerian chthonic deity whose mother was Ereshkigal. He is spoken of as a god of healing who brought humanity the gift of grain.

Ningal A Sumerian goddess, wife to the moon-god Nanna, with whom she was venerated at Ur and Harran. Known as Nikkal in Syria, her worship there endured until the first millennium C.E. One of the specialties of the goddess and her priestesses was the interpretation of dreams. An ancient Sumerian lamentation describes how she tried unsuccessfully to intervene with the gods to avert the city of Ur's destruction.

Ningirin A Sumerian goddess whose name means "Lady of Incantations."

Ningirsu A Sumerian god whose name means "Lord of Girsu." He began as the local god who protected the city of Girsu and nurtured the productivity of its fields. His symbol was then the plow. But as the political power and territorial ambitions of Girsu grew, so did his stature. Eventually, his heraldic symbol became the awesome Zu-bird of myth, who sought to steal the cosmic Tablet of Destinies.

Ningishzida A son of Ninazu and, like his father, a Sumerian god of the underworld, Ningishzida was called the "Lord of the Steadfast Tree" perhaps because trees are rooted in and draw their sustenance from a subterranean realm. Gudea of Lagash chose him as his personal patron, and he was honored in other cities as well. The god's wife was Geshtinanna, who—like her brother Dumuzi—spent six months of every year living in the netherworld. Ningishzida's symbol was the dragon, which Mesopotamian astronomers saw in the sky as a constellation. The later Greeks called that same constellation Hydra, their own name for a dragon-like monster.

Ninhursag (or Ninhursaga, or Ninhursanga) A Sumerian mother-goddess, who watched over the wild animals that roam the hills, and nurtured earth's creatures. Many rulers proudly claimed that she loved them and accordingly built sanctuaries in her honor, especially at the city of Kish.

Ninildu   Patron god of carpentry.

Ninisina   A Sumerian goddess of healing and patron deity of the city of Isin. She was praised as the "great physician of the black-headed ones [i.e., the human race]." Her father was the sky-god An and her mother an earth-goddess named Urash. Her husband was Pabilsag. Their son, Damu, also became a doctor, chasing away evil demons and "mending torn sinew."

Ninlil   Originally named Sud, Ninlil became the wife of Enlil/Ellil and together with him jointly administered the cosmos. In the days of the Assyrian Empire, she was spoken of as the wife of Ashur, the god of the Assyrian nation. This mythological adjustment served to divinely justify the temporal power exercised by Assyria's imperialistic monarchs.

Ninmah   A Sumerian mother-goddess who served as "midwife" when the primeval goddess Nammu created man. Later, Ninmah and Enki got drunk on beer and took turns trying to alter how man was designed. Enki won the contest when he invented a design so bad it couldn't be changed. Our gross imperfection as a race, said the Sumerians, was thus the result of a drunken bet.

Ninmar   A local deity worshiped in Lagash.

Ninshubur/Papsukkal   A Mesopotamian deity who acted as a vizier for An/Anu or for Inanna/Ishtar. In texts where he serves An/Anu, he is depicted as male; in texts where he serves Inanna/Ishtar, as female. In stories,

Ninshubur/Papsukkal plays the role of a divine messenger.

Ninsianna   A Sumerian goddess identified with the bright planet Venus and the goddess of love, Inanna.

Ninsun   The wife of Lugulbanda, ruler of Uruk, and the mother of the hero Gilgamesh. In other sources, she is also cited as the mother of Dumuzi, Inanna/Ishtar's star-crossed lover. Ninsun's main sanctuary was at Uruk and she was the patron goddess of the cattle-herder, reflecting Dumuzi's origin as a divine herdsman.

Nintu (also Nintur)   The Sumerian goddess of childbirth.

Ninurta   Ninurta began his divine career as a god of irrigation and agriculture. In fact "The Instruction of Ninurta" is the title of an ancient Sumerian "farmer's almanac." But with the rise of imperialism he too, like Ningirsu, was transformed into a young and vigorous god of war. In this latter role, Ninurta became a favorite of aggressive Assyrian kings. His wife was named Gula or Bau.

Nisaba (also Nidaba)   Especially popular during the second millennium B.C.E., Nisaba was the Sumerian patron goddess of writing, and she worked as a divine scribe for the gods. With the rise of the Semitic god Nabu (also a patron of scribes), she became his mythological bride and lived with him happily ever after in the ancient land of literacy.

Numushda   A son of the Sumerian moon-god Nanna, Numushda had a daughter who married and civilized the cloddish god Martu.

Nungal   A Sumerian goddess of the netherworld who pursued and imprisoned the wicked.

Nusku A Sumerian god of fire and light who served as a high official under the god Enlil. Gibil/Girra, the fire-god, was his son. In incantations, Nusku's powers were invoked to burn sorcerers. His symbol in art was the oil lamp. At Harran, he was worshiped together with his father, the moon-god Sin, and in Syria Nusku's cult endured down to the early centuries of the common era, keeping his sacred fire alive.

Pabilsag A son of Enlil, Pabilsag was the husband of the Sumerian goddess of healing, Ninisina. His cult center was Larak, and his star-cluster the constellation Sagittarius.

Pazuzu A hideous-looking chthonic demon who inhabited the pantheon of the Babylonians and Assyrians. Despite his appearance (see *Samana* below), he could be benevolent: protecting pregnant women from harm (as long as they wore an amulet with his ugly face on it). He did so by restraining the demoness Lamashtu from killing their unborn children by keeping her in the underworld. He could also fight ancient air pollution by diverting foul winds from Mesopotamia's cities. Though short on pizzazz, Pazuzu made it to Hollywood: he is the only Mesopotamian demon to have starred in a movie—*The Exorcist.*

Qingu See *Kingu.*

Samana While Pazuzu had a snake-headed penis, a scaly body, and bulging eyes (not to mention his four wings and bad smile), the demon Samana had dragon's teeth, eagle's talons, and a scorpion's tail. Both inhabited the underworld of the Babylonians and Assyrians. Samana targeted both men and women, but he had a special appetite for infants and prostitutes.

Sarpanitum (or Zarpanitum) As the divine wife of Marduk, Sarpanitum was the preemi-nent goddess of Babylon and shared her husband's temple there. Under the name Erua, she was looked to as a goddess of pregnancy and childbirth.

Sebittu See *Iminbi.*

Shala A Hurrian goddess, the wife of Ishkur/Adad or of Canaanite Dagan. In astrology, she was identified with the constellation Virgo.

Shamash See *Utu.*

Shara A Sumerian warrior-god and protector of the city of Umma.

Shulpae The husband of Ninhursag, this Sumerian god was associated with Ninhursag's generative power over the animal kingdom, but he also had a demonic side. In astrology, he was linked with the planet Jupiter.

Shaushga A Hurrian goddess who shared the attributes of Inanna/Ishtar.

Sherida/Aya Wife of the sun-god Utu/ Shamash and, by association, a goddess of light. Because of the sun's life-giving energy, she was also associated with fecundity.

Shimegi A Hurrian god of the sun.

Sin, or Suen See *Nanna.*

Sud See *Ninlil.*

Tashmetu The wife of the scribal god Nabu, Tashmetu was a benevolent and merciful Mesopotamian deity who interceded with other divine powers on behalf of those who prayed to her. In astrology she was identified with the constellation Capricorn.

Teshub The Hurrian weather-god. His sister was Shaushga.

*Tiamat The primordial goddess of salt water. She and Abzu/Apsu, primordial god of freshwater, produced the next generation of gods. As the leader of a rebellion, she was vanquished by Marduk, who sliced through her body and used her top half to make the sky. Their battle is described in the Babylonian *Epic of Creation*.

Tishpak A warrior-god who became the protector of Eshnunna, a city located near Hurrian territory. Tishpak may have originally been identical to the Hurrian god of the storm, Teshub.

Tutu A Sumerian god of creation.

Urash A Sumerian earth-goddess who is spoken of as the wife of the sky-god An. Urash is also the name of a male deity who was the patron god of the Babylonian city of Dilbat and as such was cited in the prologue to Hammurabi's Code.

Usmu See *Isimud*.

*Utu/Shamash The Mesopotamian god of the sun, whose father was the moon-god Nanna/Sin and whose sister was Inanna/Ishtar. As a source of light that banishes darkness and as a god who, by virtue of his light, sees all things from heaven, Utu/Shamash was looked upon as a god of justice who punishes the unjust. In this guise he is depicted on the Code of Hammurabi as a dispenser of justice. Utu/Shamash traversed the sky in his chariot, emanating from a heavenly gate at the east and departing through a gate at the west. He then rested in the netherworld before commencing another journey. His wife was Sherida/Aya and his symbol was the solar disc.

He was worshiped in Sumer at Eridu and prominently at Larsa, where his temple was called the "Shining House." In Akkad, he was venerated at Sippar, and in Assyria at Ashur, where he shared a sanctuary with the god of the moon.

Uttu The Sumerian patron goddess of weaving. As a weaver of webs, her symbol was the spider.

Zababa A warrior god who was the protector of the city of Kish. Inanna/Ishtar, who in addition to being a goddess of love was also a goddess of war, was said to be his wife.

Zarpanitum See *Sarpanitum*.

Myths

Mesopotamian tradition contained many stories about the gods and their interactions with each other and with human beings. While we may casually refer to these tales as myths, to the ancient people of Mesopotamia they were as real as history itself, only shrouded in mist because of the remoteness of the times in which they took place. As for the gods and goddesses themselves, they were palpable realities, as real as the invisible forces that make plants and animals multiply, human beings yearn for love, and life come to an end.

Preserved through the miracle of writing and the equal miracle of literature, these tales survive, though many have been lost forever and still others wait to be retrieved from the dust. The major tales can be found retold in chapter 5 in the section on epic poetry. For references to specific gods or goddesses, the reader is directed to the index.

PLACES OF PUBLIC WORSHIP

The physical focus of Mesopotamian religion was the temple. The temple, however, was not like a church, synagogue, or mosque—a building whose interior is intended for congregational worship. Instead, the Mesopotamian temple—like the sanctuaries of ancient Egypt, Greece, and Rome—was conceived of as the home of the deity. Inside was the cult statue, the rendering in three-dimensional sculpted form of the god's numinous presence. Inside also was the repository for the votive offerings given by the faithful. Attached to the sanctuary would be the official quarters of the priests or priestesses who acted as the deity's servants, performing rituals at the altar, singing hymns of praise, or uttering prayers on behalf of the community as a whole or on behalf of pious individuals who had sought the god's intercession and aid. Public worship, when it occurred, took place *outside* the temple in a large court-

yard, much as today a crowd will reverently gather in St. Peter's Square as the pope appears on his balcony to lead them in worship. Each Mesopotamian city might have a number of temples dedicated to different gods, but in each city a certain god was usually singled out for special treatment because he or she was looked upon as the city's special patron and protector. It is the sanctuary of that god that would be the largest and most architecturally splendid in all the city. In some cases the same sanctuary or an adjacent one might be dedicated to the worship of a related deity, such as a divine husband or wife.

What distinguishes the Mesopotamian temple from other ancient Mediterranean sanctuaries was the presence of an additional structure that adjoined those temples that were most important: the ziggurat. Called *unir* in Sumerian and *zigguratu* in Akkadian, the ziggurat was a multistoried stepped platform surmounted, it is believed, by a shrine. Staircases enabled priests or priestesses to ascend to the structure's summit to perform rituals and recite hymns and prayers in full view of worshipers gathered below. The height of the shrine,

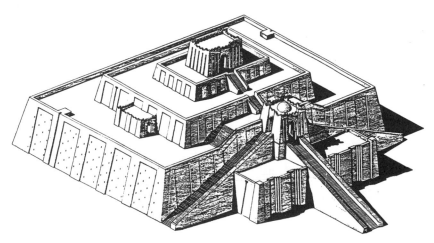

4.3   Reconstructed plan of the ziggurat built by Ur-Nammu at Ur.   (P. R. S. Moorey, *Ur 'of the Chaldees':
A Revised and Updated Edition of Sir Leonard Woolley's Excavations at Ur* [Ithaca, N.Y.: Cornell University
Press, 1982]; © the Estate of Sir Leonard Woolley and P. R. S. Moorey; used by permission of the publisher)

moreover, enabled the deity to descend more easily from heaven both to receive offerings and to bestow divine blessings on his or her earthly devotees. The mountain-like mass and profile of the ziggurat may have constituted a man-made replica of the mountains where the gods were once thought to dwell, mountains that were absent from the flat alluvial plain where civilization itself took root.

Thus a Mesopotamian temple complex might include both a sanctuary and a ziggurat with a large or double courtyard, all enclosed by a wall. The temple, however, was more than just a sacred edifice. It was also an office building of sorts, containing rooms where priestly officials managed real-estate holdings and commercial transactions in the name of the god they served. For in actuality much of the property in the city belonged to the gods, and man was merely a caretaker—not unlike the way God in Genesis planted a garden in Eden and placed man there to tend it. And because writing was so important for recordkeeping, part of the temple complex often functioned as a school where students, including prospective clerics, were instructed in the scribal arts.

Both temple and ziggurat were given honorific names (beginning with the Sumerian *e*, which meant "house"), such as "the Shining House" or "the House that is the Foundation of Heaven and Earth." The story of the architectural design of these structures is told in chapter 6.

PRIESTS AND PRIESTESSES

The management of a temple complex was in the hands of the priesthood. In earliest days, the secular ruler of a Mesopotamian commu-nity may have simultaneously served as its chief priest; indeed, our modern distinction between church and state is not one that an ancient Mesopotamian would have readily understood since the everyday affairs of man were thought of as inextricably intertwined with the will of heavenly and earthly powers who governed human existence and whom human beings were required to serve. Eventually, however, the exercise of sacred and secular duties were separated to a degree, leading to the rise of professional priesthoods who managed the day-to-day operations of temples and the worship of the gods. Each temple might have a temple administrator (known as a *sanga* in Sumerian and a *shangu* in Akkadian) who supervised the business side of the temple's activities. At the same time, a high priest (*en*) or high priestess (*entu*) would govern the performance of the sanctuary's sacred rites and duties. Assisting them were numerous priests and priestesses, some of whom had specialized functions: for example, to ritually slaughter animals, interpret omens, or perform rites of purification. Some priests played a role analogous to that of a Jewish cantor, singing songs of lamentation or joy to the accompaniment of instrumentalists and a choir that might consist of over a hundred voices.

To qualify to train as a priest or priestess a young person would need to come from a good family and have a body that was free of physical defect. Training would include an education in literacy (often at a temple-run school) and an extensive period of apprenticeship. Male novices could look forward to a career serving a god; female novices, to serving a goddess, though there are instances in which a high priestess governed the temple of a male deity, such as the moon-god Nanna/Sin. Priestesses were expected to be celibate. Though they could not bear children, they could, paradoxically, marry, sharing their husband's estate and acting as stepmother to any children he may have fathered. The office of priestess was one of great respect, like that of the Vestal Virgins of ancient Rome (who, incidentally, were also allowed to marry—and even bear children—once they had completed 30 years of service to their goddess).

In Mesopotamian religion perhaps the most curious and salacious custom (at least to the Western mind) was sacred prostitution, that is the practice of women offering sex for pay on the sacred grounds of the temple of Ishtar. The fifth century B.C.E. Greek historian Herodotus was the first to report this custom to a European audience. As Herodotus (*History* 1: 199) tells it:

> The Babylonians have one most shameful custom. Every woman born in the country must once in her life go and sit down in the precinct of Aphrodite [=Ishtar], and there consort with a stranger. Many of the wealthier sort, who are too proud to mix with the others, drive in covered carriages to the precinct, followed by a goodly train of attendants, and there take their station. But the larger number seat themselves within the holy enclosure with wreaths of string about their heads,—and here there is always a great crowd, some coming and others going; lines of cord mark out paths in all directions among the women, and the strangers pass along them to make their choice. A woman who has once taken her seat is not allowed to return home till one of the strangers throws a silver coin into her lap, and takes her with him beyond the holy ground. When he throws the coin he says these words: "The goddess Mylitta prosper thee." (Aphrodite is called Mylitta [=an Akkadian title of Ishtar, meaning "she who brings about birth"] by the Assyrians.) The silver coin may be of any size; it cannot be refused, for that is forbidden by the law, since once thrown it is sacred. The woman goes with the first man who throws her money, and rejects no one. When she has gone with him, and so satisfied the goddess, she returns home, and from that time forth no gift however great will prevail with her. Such of the women as are tall and beautiful are soon released, but others who are ugly have to stay a long time before they can fulfil the law. Some have waited three or four years in the precinct. A custom very much like this is found also in certain parts of the island of Cyprus. (Herodotus, 1942 [1862]: 107–8, trans. George Rawlinson)

The Greek geographer Strabo repeated the tale some four centuries later, and the Greek satirist Lucian described a similar practice in a second century C.E. temple of Astarte in Lebanon. How accurate these accounts are we do not know. It is also possible that certain priestesses of Ishtar functioned as sacred prostitutes, or "hierodules" as scholars sometimes call them. Mesopotamian sources themselves are silent about these matters except for the fact that they inform us of the existence of prostitutes in society (witness the seduction of Enkidu in the *Epic of Gilgamesh* and references to prostitutes in law codes—evidence of the "world's oldest profession" in the world's oldest civilization). There is no doubt, however, that the concept of sacred prostitution would have been consistent with the character of Ishtar, a goddess of carnal pleasure who used men and sex for her own higher purposes.

Because the Mesopotamian temple was a large and complex enterprise engaged in not only religious but also commercial activities, many employees beyond its normal complement of priests and priestesses were required to run it. First of all, there had to be a household staff to accommodate the priesthood's need for food, drink, and clothing, and—even more important—to provide regular offerings of nourishment and refreshment for the deity: usually two meals a day, a two-course breakfast and a big, two-course dinner, set on or near the altar. Among the god's favorite menu items might be bread and beer, and a variety of meats such as mutton, lamb, and beef, as well as sweets such as honey, dates, figs, and cakes. To supply these provisions, herdsmen and butchers were employed as well as millers, oil-pressers, brewers, bakers, cooks, and servers. The divine "leftovers" (a statue doesn't eat much!) may have been diverted for priestly consumption. Also numbered among the temple staff would have been accountants, treasurers, scribes, and messengers; janitors and guards; artisans to create ritual objects; weavers, tailors, and seamstresses to make vestments; and barbers to shave the heads of priests. Some of these positions may have been filled by slaves—dedicated to the temples as orphans or by parents who were too impoverished to raise a child, donated to the temple by wealthy parishioners from slaves in their own household, or consigned to the god's service as prisoners of war.

HOLY DAYS AND FESTIVALS

The greatness of the gods and their manifold blessings were celebrated on special holy days and festivals. The most important of these sacred occasions in a community honored its local god, who was its patron and protector. But on a larger scale across their country, the people of Mesopotamia also expressed their gratitude in common for the fertility of their land whose bounty sustained their lives and derived from divine favor.

The greatest of these agricultural holidays was called, in Sumerian, the *Akiti*, and in Akkadian, the *Akitu*, a word of uncertain meaning that may in fact be pre-Sumerian. The ceremonies connected with the holiday took place principally at a sanctuary in the countryside just outside the city walls, a structure known simply as the *Akiti* or *Akitu* building. In some communities, like Babylon, the ceremonies were conducted once a year immediately after the barley

harvest in March at the time of the spring equinox. (Barley was Mesopotamia's chief grain.) In other communities, like Ur, there were two celebrations a year, one at the time of the harvest and the other in September when new seed was sown. Because the Mesopotamians looked upon the spring equinox as the beginning of their year, the Harvest Akitu was also a New Year's holiday and a time of added celebration.

Thanks to the survival of fragmentary texts that date to between 1000 and 600 B.C.E. and a copy that belongs to the Hellenistic period, we know the main outlines and many of the details of the Akitu festival that took place in ancient Babylon.

The holiday began on the vernal equinox (on the first day [Zagmuk] of the ancient month of Nisan, equivalent to our March 20th or 21st—at least when the eccentric lunar calendar coincided with the solar one!). The holiday then lasted for a total of 12 days, the first six or seven (we're not sure how many) taken up with private religious rituals conducted by the high priest, and the last five or six involving outdoor processions and public rites. During both halves of the holiday the king played an important role. And because the patron god was Marduk, it was Marduk who was the focal deity, along with his first-born son Nabu, who was worshiped both at Babylon itself and at nearby Borsippa.

About Day One we have no information. On Day Two, the high priest prayed alone before the statue of Marduk asking that the god protect his city. On Day Three, the priest instructed craftsmen to make two dolls out of wood simulating worshipers of Nabu. On Day Four, the priest prayed before Marduk and his divine wife Sarpanitum in her adjoining sanctuary. Then, standing in the courtyard, he faced north and uttered a triple blessing over the entire temple complex. Later that same day, the king set out for Borsippa to fetch the sacred image of Nabu and bring it to Babylon. In the evening, the high priest stood before Marduk's statue and recited the entire *Epic of Creation*, the poem that celebrated Marduk's ascendancy among the gods and his creative arts, including the arrangement of the cosmos and the making of man. On Day Five, the high priest again prayed before Marduk and Sarpanitum, addressing them in celestial terms. Their temple was then ritually cleansed, as was a shrine of Nabu located within the temple precinct. The Nabu shrine was then covered with a golden canopy in anticipation of the god's arrival by boat from Borsippa, accompanied by Babylon's king. Then followed a dramatic ceremony: the high priest divested the king of his royal insignia, slapped his face, and forced him to kneel before the god's holy image—an act of humbling debasement that asserted the power of church over state, of god over man. On his knees, the king made confession, swearing that he had not abused the authority entrusted to him and had not sinfully forsaken the interests of Babylon, its people, and its god. (In its negative formulation ["I have not . . ."], this confession is reminiscent of the "Negative Confession" found in the Egyptian *Book of the Dead* by which souls sought to gain entry into paradise, and also of the biblical Ten Commandments, which were also cast in negative terms ["Thou shall not . . ."].) At the conclusion of the royal confession, the high priest again slapped the face of the king until tears flowed from his eyes, a sign of his genuine contrition. Later, just before sunset, the king—his insignia restored—offered up a burnt offering as he and the high priest jointly prayed to the planet Mercury, the "star of Marduk," now visible on the horizon (Nisan being the month of its heliacal rising). On Day Six, statues of the patron gods and goddesses of surrounding communities arrived in Babylon to collectively honor Marduk. It is then that the two wooden dolls had their heads cut off and were burnt in a ritual fire in the presence of Nabu (perhaps symbolic of an ancient human sacrifice or of an unknown episode in mythology).

On Day Seven or Eight, the more public aspect of the holiday began, as the king took the image of Marduk by the hand and led him out of his temple and on to the "Shrine of the Destinies," situated within Nabu's sanctuary. Within the shrine, the king's fate for the coming year (and, with it, the destiny of his people) was divined and decreed as the king, Marduk, and Nabu stood in the company of the other gods. Then, the doors of the shrine were thrown open by the priests and a grand procession began. In his book, *Ancient Iraq*, Georges Roux recaptures the thrilling scene:

> A great solemn cortège was then formed, including the statues of all the gods and goddesses. Headed by Marduk on his chariot glittering with gold and precious stones and led by the king, it went down Procession Street across Babylon in an aura of incense, songs and music, while people were kneeling down in adoration as it passed by. Through Ishtar Gate the cortège left the city, and after a short journey on the Euphrates, reached the *bît akitu*, a temple filled with plants and flowers in the middle of a large park. (Roux 1992: 400)

At that point, a great banquet was held in the Akitu building, where the participants remained for three days, returning to Babylon on Day Eleven, accompanied by the statues of the gods. The grand procession back to the city was accompanied by another round of celebration and festivity, with the cortège arriving at Nabu's temple, where the previously divined destiny of the king was publicly proclaimed, after which a final banquet for dignitaries ensued. On Day Twelve, the sacred image of Nabu was borne home to Borsippa, and the images of the neighboring gods to their respective communities.

Scholarly speculation and debate surround an event that may have taken place in the Akitu building or in Babylon itself upon the return of the holy procession. Two Sumerian literary documents, one referring to Shulgi of Ur and the other to Iddin-Dagan of Isin, speak in poetic terms of each king making love to the goddess Inanna/Ishtar in a reenactment of her copulation with the divine shepherd Dumuzi. In the case of Iddin-Dagan, the liaison took place in his palace on New Year's Eve. Both occasions have been interpreted as symbolic rituals that renewed the fecundity of the land. We also know that in late Assyrian and Babylonian times a ritual was carried out in Babylon in which the statues of Marduk and Sarpanitum were laid in bed side by side as part of the New Year's ceremonies. Herodotus—our entertaining Greek informant on all things Mesopotamian—says (*History* 1:181) that the shrine on top of Babylon's ziggurat was the site of a sacred tryst.

> On the topmost tower there is a spacious temple, and inside the temple stands a couch of unusual size, richly adorned, with a golden table by its side. There is no statue of any kind set up in the place, nor is the chamber occupied of nights by any one but a single native woman, who, as the Chaldaeans, the priests of this god, affirm, is chosen for himself by the deity out of all the women of the land. They also declare—but I for my part do not credit it—that the god comes down in person into this chamber, and sleeps upon the couch. (Herodotus 1942 [1862]: 97–98, trans. George Rawlinson)

In his account, Herodotus does not refer to the New Year's holiday as the occasion for this mating, but instead he seems to describe it as an ongoing activity rather than a once-a-year event. Indeed, even if Herodotus got his information from a personal visit to Babylon, the New Year festival would have been last celebrated there in a formal way in 538 B.C.E., almost a century before the time of his visit. The Persian king Xerxes, in fact, destroyed Marduk's temple in 482 B.C.E. and removed the god's statue from its home, decades before Herodotus's visit.

Some scholars have proposed that during the New Year's festival a "sacred marriage" took place between the king (acting as Dumuzi) and perhaps the high priestess of Inanna/Ishtar. However, the focus of the New Year holiday was on Marduk not Dumuzi, and the two are not identified in Mesopotamian religion. Still, it is possible that the wedding of Marduk and his divine consort Sarpanitum *was* ritually enacted, not only by their statues but in a live reenactment in which the king played the role of Marduk and a priestess of Sarpanitum played the goddess, and that this sacred marriage did take place as part of the holiday, either in the Akitu temple or upon the return to Babylon. But our ancient sources are too slim on the details of the holiday to make this more than an intriguing speculation.

What we do know for sure is that the celebration of the springtime New Year festival in Babylon was Mesopotamia's most elaborate religious holiday, reaffirming the supremacy of Babylon's great god and offering thanksgiving for the fertility of the lands he ruled.

DIVINATION AND EXORCISM

Apart from participating in public festivals, the people of Mesopotamia had access to the gods by other means.

They believed, for example, that the will of the gods is manifest in nature and that, with proper skill, it can be read and interpreted, thus giving the pious petitioner insight into divine intention. Priestly specialists known as *baru* priests were charged with the responsibility of divining heaven's will by inspecting the organs (especially the liver) of sacrificial animals, by studying heavenly bodies and the celestial messages their changes and movements implied, and by analyzing telltale patterns in floating drops of oil or upward-spiraling wisps of smoke. Both

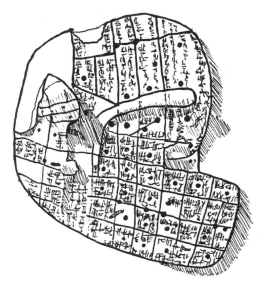

4.4   *Represented in this drawing is an anatomically detailed model of a sheep's liver fashioned out of clay. The zones marked by the grid denote areas of the organ that might portend future events indicated by annotations in cuneiform. The holes may have served to hold pegs used as markers, either for the purpose of priestly instruction or during the examination of an actual liver. Measuring about 6 inches by 6 inches, the model is now in the collection of the British Museum and may date back to between 2000 and 1600 B.C.E.*   (Drawing by the author)

king and commoner turned to these priests for spiritual guidance and sought personal readings to help them see into the future. Because illness was frequently thought to be caused by unexpiated sin or by demonic possession, spiritual healers called *ashipu* priests were summoned to assist the sick by discovering what god they may have offended so he or she could be appeased, or by finding what hostile spirit was possessing them so that it might be expelled by rites of exorcism. Meanwhile, amuletic plaques were hung in the home from walls or by doors to keep out evil spirits who might attempt entry, like the

feared demoness Lamashtu, who tried to steal unborn children from mothers' wombs or infants from their cribs, robbing them of life.

The documented arts of divination and exorcism are described in chapter 5 ("Language, Writing, and Literature"), while their practitioners are discussed in chapter 11 ("Everyday Life").

PERSONAL PIETY

Beyond prayer and ritual, beyond ceremony and magic, lies another dimension of piety: the intent of the heart and its personal expression through moral action. Yet the depth of the heart, especially the ancient heart, is difficult to plumb, for the private recesses of the soul are not as accessible as public demonstrations of faith, nor are they as evident in a culture's monumental remains. To find them we will need to search for the soul's signature in poetry and read between the lines of cuneiform prose.

In his book, *History Begins at Sumer*, Samuel Noah Kramer summarized the ethical outlook of Mesopotamia's first civilized culture:

> The Sumerians, according to their own records, cherished goodness and truth, law and order, justice and freedom, righteousness and straightforwardness, mercy and compassion. And they abhorred evil and falsehood, lawlessness and disorder, injustice and oppression, sinfulness and perversity, cruelty and pitilessness. King and rulers constantly boasted of the fact that they had established law and order in the land; protected the weak from the strong; the poor from the rich; and wiped out evil and violence. . . . The gods, too, according to the Sumerian sages, preferred the ethical and moral to the unethical and immoral, and practically all the major deities of the Sumerian pantheon are extolled in Sumerian hymns as lovers of the good and the just, of truth and righteousness. Indeed,

there were several deities who had the super-vision of the moral order as their main func-tion—the sun-god Utu, for example. Another deity, a Lagashite goddess by the name of Nanshe, is also sporadically mentioned in the texts as devoted to truth, justice, and mercy. (Kramer 1981: 101–2)

Even as the all-seeing eye of the sun looked down from heaven upon the deeds of man, the goddess Nanshe protected widows and orphans and gave comfort and shelter to the weak. The presence of such gods in Sumerian conscious-ness thus instilled in the people a sense of con-science that was reinforced by the ethical standards articulated in law.

It would be too much to imagine that the Sumerians, or the Mesopotamians in general, were morally pure. After all, it was from the blood of a rebellious god that the first human being was made, and many of the rites in Mesopotamian religion were intended to expi-ate man's propensity for sin. Nor would law itself have needed to exist if humanity did not require its instructions and sanctions. In short, the ancient Mesopotamians were human like ourselves.

Nevertheless, they clearly recognized that there is a difference between being merely human and being humane. As J. J. A. Van Dijk has shown, the Sumerian word *namlulu* meant not only "the human race" but also "human-ity," those collective qualities of conduct and behavior that make human beings worthy of the name. It was those qualities that the ancient Sumerians strove to emulate.

THE CONCEPT OF IMMORTALITY

The ethical conduct of the ancient Mesopotamian in this life was not conditioned by the notion of an afterlife where the good were rewarded and the wicked were punished. As the divine bar-maid Siduri tells the soul-weary Gilgamesh, instead of futilely seeking the blessing of an eternal life you should make the most of your own. "The life you're looking for," she says, "you'll never find, for when the gods made man, they reserved death for him, saving life for themselves." These lines from the *Epic of Gilgamesh* highlight what we find imprinted elsewhere in the Mesopotamian mind: the dichotomy between the authority and preroga-tives of the gods and the necessary obedience and humility of man who must remain resigned to his lesser station in the existential order. Indeed, only through such resignation does the hero Gilgamesh ultimately find inner peace.

An even more pessimistic assessment of the human condition occurs in a literary dia-logue between a Babylonian master and his cynical slave:

Master: "Agree with me, slave!"
Slave: "Absolutely, master!"
Master: "I shall make love to a woman!"
Slave: "By all means, my lord. A man who loves a woman forgets his sorrows."
Master: "No, slave, I *won't* love a woman!"
Slave: "Correct, my lord. A woman is a pitfall, a sharp-bladed dagger that can slit your throat!"
Master: "Slave, I shall give alms to the poor!"
Slave: "Oh, do so, my lord. He who gives alms to the poor is blessed by god."
Master: "No, slave, I *won't* give alms!"
Slave: "Just so, my lord. Such charity could only breed ingratitude . . . Climb upon the mounds of bygone cities and walk among the ruins. Behold the skulls of those who died in days of yore. Who, my lord, is the evildoer, who the doer of good?"

Other texts affirm that there is an afterlife, but that it is morally neutral. The souls of the wicked are not eternally punished as in the Christian hell, nor the souls of the good eternally rewarded as in heaven. There is, in short, no spiritual grist for a Mesopotamian Dante's mill—no "Inferno," no "Paradiso," nor even a "Purgatorio" between the two. But the landscape of the netherworld is grim nonetheless: a dark, dusty, and desolate place where souls of the dead gather and must eternally remain, their only hope being that the living will remember them. Ruling over this sombre realm are death's queen, Ereshkigal, and her divine consort Nergal, just as kings and queens rule the sunlit world above. It is a landscape depressingly similar to the one painted by the Greek poet Homer in the 11th book of his *Odyssey*, and one that is alluded to in the Old Testament by the name of Sheol.

The bleak Mesopotamian vision of the afterlife was reinforced, indeed even induced, by the very environment in which the people of Mesopotamia lived, an environment in which nature could sweep away with sudden floods all the works and material possessions of man, burying the sites of the cities in shrouds of mud, making a mockery of humanity's very existence.

What incentive, we may then ask, would the ancient Mesopotamian have had for living a life of piety if he foresaw no final judgment at life's end, no reward for good deeds or punishments for bad?

If some scholars are correct, this very question would have lacked meaning for the average Mesopotamian, who was culturally conditioned to obey the gods' supreme authority and who viewed himself as a necessarily compliant servant of his heavenly master, a servant for whom the very notion of free will would have been a novel—even an unsettling—idea.

But there is another possibility. Despite the darkness of Hades (or even because of it), the ancient Greeks lived passionate lives, fervent in the realization that they must drink this life's wine down to the last drop because there would be only an empty cup in Hades. Nor did that attitude divert them from seeking to build a just society in this world, to enact laws for its construction, and to debate the very definition of justice in order that they might more nearly approximate its philosophical ideal in their private and public lives. Nor did the absence of a clear picture of the afterlife dissuade the ancient Hebrew prophets from proclaiming the imperative of social justice, or Jewish sages from later seeking its realization through acts of everyday piety and righteousness. The same may well be true of the ancient Mesopotamians, who sought to live moral lives without the incentive of heavenly reward in an afterlife. It was in this life that their gods would reward them both as individuals and as communities for their faithful service. And if the gods did not, it was as it should be in accordance with heaven's greater wisdom and will. Paradoxically, Islam—the dominant religion of present-day Iraq—offers a paradise to the faithful and, in doing so, reveals a closer connection to the eschatology of ancient Egypt and of early Christianity than to the ancient traditions of its own land.

READING

The Multiplicity of the Gods

Black and Green 1998, Leick 1991: lists of gods; Bottéro 2001: the pantheon and henotheistic tendencies; Nemet-Nejat 1998: development of the pantheon.

The Governance of the World

Black and Green 1998; Kramer 1963: the *me* and the Tablet of Destinies.

The Names and Functions of the Gods

Black and Green 1998: demons, and symbols; Kramer 1961: mythology of Sumer and Akkad; Kramer 1972: Sumerian mythology; Leick 1991: Near Eastern mythology; McCall 1990: Mesopotamian myths; Saggs 1962: demons; Van Buren 1945: divine symbols.

Myths

Bottéro 2001: general discussion; Dalley 1989: translations and commentary; Kramer 1972: Sumerian mythology; Lambert 1995: myth and mythmaking in Sumer and Akkad; McCall 1990: major Mesopotamian myths; Nemet-Nejat 1998: religious views in early Mesopotamia.

Places of Public Worship

Harris 1963: the cloister; Nemet-Nejat 1998: places of worship and their functions; Roaf 1995: palaces and temples; Robertson 1995: temple organization.

Priests and Priestesses

Bienkowski and Millard 2000: priest and priestess; prostitution and ritual sex; Bottéro 2001: maintenance of cults; Leick 1994: ritual sex; Nemet-Nejat 1998: religious personnel and servants; Saggs 1962: priests and associated temple personnel; Wiggermann 1995: theologies, priests, and worship.

Holy Days and Festivals

Bienkowski and Millard 2000: sacred marriage; Black 1981: New Year ceremonies; Cohen 1993: the cultic calendar; Kramer 1969: sacred marriage; Nemet-Nejat 1998: religious festivals; Roux 1996: New Year festival; Steinkeller 1999: sacred marriage.

Divination and Exorcism

Bottéro 1992: interpretation of dreams, divination, and the scientific spirit; Bottéro et al. 2001: astrology, magic and medicine; Farber 1995: witchcraft, magic, and divination; Jeyes 1980: extispicy; Jones 2000: horoscopes; Nemet-Nejat 1998: sorcerers, exorcists, and diviners; Oppenheim 1977: the art of the diviner.

Personal Piety

Bottéro 2001: religious sentiment; Bottéro et al. 2001: the concept of sin; Buccellati 1995: ethics and piety in the ancient Near East; Contenau 1954: the moral worth of the gods, sin and confession; Frankfort, Wilson, and Jacobsen 1949: the good life; Jacobsen 1976: personal religion; Kramer 1963: the concept of humanity; Kramer 1981: the first moral ideas and the first "Job"; Jacobsen 1976: history of religion.

The Concept of Immortality

Bottéro 2001, Surlock 1995: death and the afterlife in ancient Mesopotamian thought.

5

LANGUAGE, WRITING, AND LITERATURE

LANGUAGE

In 1890, inventor Thomas Edison invited the three most famous people in England to record their voices for posterity on his recent invention, the phonograph. The three people were Queen Victoria, Prime Minister Gladstone, and the poet Tennyson. The queen declined, the prime minister sent some one else to read his message, and Tennyson—who had always been fascinated with science—agreed, and proceeded to make a whole series of recordings on the primitive wax cylinders of Edison's "talking machine." Regrettably, Tennyson stored his records in a box near the heating pipes of his home, and so the waxen hills and dales made by the running needle long ago melted into inaudible plains. But on some tracks still, beyond the hiss of hardened wax, the poet's voice can still be heard, boldly declaiming his spirited verse.

Before the invention of the phonograph, the past stands silent. The great Americans whose faces we know from early photographs or art—Lincoln or Jefferson, for example—are mute. If history is measured in "B.C.E." and "C.E.," another pair of designators ought to be employed to signify the time before which and after which history can be authentically heard. If such were used, we would soon realize how many important voices cannot speak because audio technology came too late.

Of course, their words still remain, even if they can only be recited in the privacy of our minds or aloud with our own 21st-century tongue. But what if these words too had never been preserved, or had faded beyond all recognition?

Such problems are compounded the farther back into time we go: before the phonograph, before the photograph, before the printed word, before the written word itself. Mute human remains and an equally silent art are our only witnesses to these most ancient times before writing's invention.

The present chapter will focus on the written record of Mesopotamian culture; a later chapter, on the testimony of ancient art. Here we will examine Mesopotamia's languages and its invention of writing, which has not only allowed us literally to read the ancient mind but also has given us the world's oldest masterpieces of literature. Next, we will examine the forms of literary expression that Mesopotamian language took: epic poetry, historical chronicles, legal documents, divination texts, hymns and prayers, lamentations, letters, proverbs, social satire, and erotic poetry.

THE GREAT DECIPHERMENTS

Even though ancient artists have provided us with pictures of life in ancient Mesopotamia, those pictures would be silent were it not for our ability to read and understand the "captions," and through literature and written records penetrate deeper into the ideas, emotions, and experiences of the past.

Yet before the ancient writings could be read, they first had to be deciphered, for they were set down in scripts whose sounds and meanings had long ago been forgotten. The decipherment, as we shall see, was the product of an international effort carried out over most of the last two centuries. Though the scholarly achievements were largely incremental and based on dogged persistence, they were energized by flashes of insight and even acts of courage.

In many ways the story of the decipherment of lost languages embodies some of the most admirable qualities of our race: curiosity, dedication, intelligence, and tenacity. But most of all it signifies the spiritual essence of civilization: the realization that we are nothing if we forget our roots.

The Significance of Inscriptions

Before inscriptions can be deciphered, however, they must first be recognized for what they are—writing. Though early travelers had returned to Europe with inscribed artifacts or had copied inscriptions they had seen on monuments, many doubted they were examples of writing. To some, the tablets resembled "bits of pottery decorated in an unusual manner." To others, the peculiar wedge-shaped symbols looked like "bird tracks on wet sand." But still others saw them for what they were: the traces of a mysterious writing system unlike any that was known. One such scholar, Engelbert Kämpfer, called the wedge-shaped characters "cuneatae," or cuneiform, from the Latin word for wedge.

The Challenge of Persepolis

After surviving a disastrous expedition to Arabia, the Danish mathematician Carsten Niebuhr journeyed in 1765 to Persepolis, the ancient capital of the Persian kings. While there he studied the monuments and made detailed copies of the inscriptions he found on the stones. These were published upon his return to Denmark.

The scene now shifts to Germany where, in 1802, a school teacher named Georg Friedrich Grotefend bet some friends he could decode at least part of the Persepolis inscriptions.

Niebuhr had recognized what seemed to be three distinct writing systems based on the

5.1   *Georg Friedrich Grotefend opened the door to the decipherment of cuneiform by discovering royal names in inscriptions found at Persepolis.* (Rogers, *A History of Babylonia and Assyria*, 1915)

number of characters they used. In the belief that it was alphabetic, Grotefend decided to attack the shortest of the systems, thinking it would be the easiest to crack.

Observing how certain clusters of characters repeated themselves in patterns, Grotefend recalled a classic pattern from his study of Persian history: "A, Great King, King of Kings, Son of B, Great King." The Persepolis inscription, however, added what seemed to be a third name: ". . . Son of C," but C was not identified as a king himself. Who then, wondered Grotefend, were A, B, and C? Persian history supplied the answer: A was Xerxes, whose father had been a king. B was the father, Cyrus the Great; and C was Cyrus's father, Hystaspes, who had never sat on the Persian throne.

Grotefend then substituted the names of Xerxes, Cyrus, and Hystaspes for the alphabetic cuneiform characters that spelled out their names. In addition to recognizing three names, he now also knew the phonetic values of 12 cuneiform characters, and he had identified the words for "king" and "great." Moreover, he had won his bet.

But he had also hit a roadblock. He had no other historical formulas to give him a clue as what the other words in the inscription meant, nor even enough letters to help him sound them all out.

Discovered just three years earlier, Egypt's Rosetta Stone would prove far easier to decode. At its bottom was a complete Greek translation of the hieroglyphic text. With the help of Coptic, a living linguistic descendant of ancient Egyptian, the French scholar Jean François Champollion eventually translated all the hieroglyphic words. What cuneiform scholars would need was the Mesopotamian equivalent of Coptic: a living descendant of the language of Persia's ancient kings; with its aid the meanings of other cuneiform words might be deduced. That language would prove to be Parsee, or Avestan, the language of the Zend-Avesta and of the Zoroastrians who cherished it as their sacred scripture. While the key to cuneiform would be Avestan, the key waited to be turned in the linguistic lock by an English adventurer named Henry Creswicke Rawlinson.

The Behistun Rock

On the royal road between Babylon and Ecbatana stands a 1,700-foot-high cliff. Around 520 B.C.E. the Persian king Darius I ordered a monument to be carved on its sheer face celebrating his triumph over insurgents. On a sculpted relief he stands with his foot on a prostrate enemy as defeated chieftains cower before him, their hands tied behind their backs, their necks connected by rope. Accompanying the relief is an immense cuneiform inscription totaling 1,200 lines and measuring about 100 feet high by 150 feet wide. To make the rock face more durable, the entire surface was highly polished by the Persians and then thickly varnished after repairs had been made to cracks with fresh stone set in lead.

5.2   *The carvings on the sheer face of the Behistun Rock proved to be the Mesopotamian equivalent of Egypt's Rosetta Stone. The inscriptions provided the master key for unlocking cuneiform's complexities.* (Maspero, *The Dawn of Civilization*, 1897)

5.3 Sir Henry Creswicke Rawlinson died at the age of 85 after a life of derring-do that included scaling the heights of Behistun. (Rogers, *A History of Babylonia and Assyria*, 1915)

The English soldier, diplomat, and linguist Henry Creswicke Rawlinson had become fascinated with the Behistun Rock, whose precise details were unintelligible from ground level even with the aid of a telescope. Beginning in 1835 Rawlinson climbed the cliff face to get a better look, inching his way across a two-foot-wide ledge. Determined to copy the entire inscription, he brought up a ladder and balanced precariously on its topmost rung, or hung from ropes like a mountain climber. He was still at it by 1847, when he secured the help of a "wild Kurdish boy," who reached the more inaccessible parts of the cliff by driving wooden pegs into the rock and swinging from side to side by rope. Finally, dangling in a makeshift

scaffold, the boy copied the remaining parts of the inscription by squeezing wet papier-mâché into the engravings.

Back home in Baghdad with a pet lion cub often napping beneath his chair, Rawlinson labored over the same alphabetical cuneiform characters Grotefend had worked on years before, and he came up with similar insights about royal names and titles. But then, drawing upon his knowledge of Avestan and Sanscrit (an Indo-European language related to Persian), Rawlinson took the decipherment of cuneiform a giant step further, aided by the fact that the Behistun inscription contained numerous personal and place names that could, by deduction, yield additional phonetic values.

In the end, Rawlinson completely translated the so-called Old Persian part of the Behistun inscription—a third of the whole—and began work on what we now know as the Akkadian part. This section was far more difficult to decipher because it was not alphabetic in nature; instead, it was composed of over 300 characters, many of which had multiple values. By 1845, however, the Swedish philologist Isidor Löwenstern identified its language family as Semitic, and, thanks to parallel vocabulary in known Semitic languages like Hebrew and Arabic, the Akkadian portion of Darius's inscription was eventually decoded.

The middle portion, however, now known as Elamite posed a special challenge because, as it turned out, Elamite is a linguistic orphan with no known parentage that can provide etymological clues. Indeed, even today, the Elamite portion of the Behistun trilingual is not completely understood.

The Secrets of Sumerian

Cuneiform inscriptions found in southern Mesopotamia revealed the existence of yet another language, the language of the oldest of Mesopotamian civilizations: Sumerian. Like Elamite, Sumerian is a linguistic anomaly; its meaning could not be unlocked by comparing its vocabulary to that of other known languages.

Nevertheless, Sumerian *was* deciphered, chiefly because the Babylonians and Assyrians held it in such high esteem as a classical language long after it had ceased to be spoken. As a result of its reputation as a language of learning, Akkadian dictionaries were prepared in ancient times, dictionaries that listed Sumerian and Akkadian synonyms in parallel columns. With their assistance, scholars like the Frenchman François Thureau-Dangin, the German Arno Poebel, and the Americans Thorkild Jacobsen and Samuel Noah Kramer advanced our understanding of the world's oldest classical language and the people who originally spoke it 5,000 years before our time.

Deciphering the Past

In our quest to decipher the meaning of the past, it is the ancients who have helped us the most: first, by inventing writing and giving it lasting form; and second, by developing a multicultural society in which the linguistic traditions of different ethnic groups were acknowledged and preserved. By unlocking one script, we are given the keys to unlock another; by reading one language, we come to better understand them all.

Babylon Online

Because the first major archaeological discoveries in Mesopotamia were made in Assyria, scholars who study cuneiform inscriptions have come to be called "Assyriologists" even though their interests may range beyond that northern land. Today there are some 400 professional Assyriologists working in universities and museums around the world.

Since 1998, their efforts have been aided by the Cuneiform Digital Library Initiative, a project cosponsored by the University of California at Los Angeles and the Max Planck Institute for the History of Science in Berlin, and headed by Robert K. Englund of UCLA.

The CDLI is hoping to scan and digitize the more than 200,000 cuneiform tablets scattered in collections around the globe and make their texts electronically accessible. According to Professor Englund, the online library will become "the single-largest, most organized, and best catalogued repository of cuneiform inscriptions in the world," accelerating our understanding of Mesopotamia's life and thought.

MAJOR LANGUAGES

Sumerian

The oldest texts discovered in Mesopotamia are written in a language called Sumerian. Sumerian was the primary language of southern Mesopotamia, and it was used by the people who, near the end of the fourth millennium B.C.E., created what may have been the world's first civilization. It is from that time that humanity's autobiography begins. Sumerian continued to be a spoken language for two millennia more, but it continued even after to have a vital existence as a classic language of learning for another millennium and a half down to the first century B.C.E.

Sumerian, however, was not the oldest language ever spoken in the valleys of the Tigris and Euphrates. Imbedded in Sumerian vocabulary are words not Sumerian in origin, but instead ones that hark back to earlier

Mesopotamian tongues and cultures. The names of some of Sumeria's most famous cities and even the names "Tigris" and "Euphrates" are pre-Sumerian, belonging to a language scholars have dubbed "Proto-Euphratean" or "Ubaidian" (from the name of a site of great antiquity now called Tell al-Ubaid). The high level of this pre-Sumerian culture can be measured by the words the Sumerians borrowed from this mysterious indigenous population when they first settled in the land, including the very names of basic occupations: farming, herding, and fishing; potterymaking, weaving, basketmaking, and leatherworking; carpentry, masonry, and metalworking; and even the professions of merchant and priest. That the Sumerians learned the arts of agriculture from these people is clear from the non-Sumerian origin of their words for "plow" and "furrow." Likewise, the non-Sumerian origins of their words for "date" and "palm" reveal that the Sumerians were outsiders when they first encountered these plants after migrating and settling in the land.

The Sumerians' language also contains its own mystery: it is linguistically unique, being unrelated to any other world language or language family for which evidence exists. Thus the language of the Sumerians provides no clues as to the country of their origin or their preimmigration ethnic ties. Unlike the Semitic languages of Mesopotamia, Sumerian used two classes—personal or impersonal—to distinguish nouns. Also it was an agglutinative language: its words were based on mono- or bi-syllabic stems that changed their meaning and syntactic function through the attachment of one or more prefixes and suffixes.

Akkadian

The other major language of ancient Mesopotamia was Akkadian, a member of the Semitic language family. Akkadian entered the scene with the migration of Semites from the west during the early third millennium B.C.E. Establishing themselves in northern and central Mesopotamia, the Semites dominated Sumer by 2350 B.C.E. under the leadership of Sargon of Akkad. As a result, "Akkadian" (from Akkad) gradually supplanted Sumerian, even in the south, as Mesopotamia's chief vernacular language. By about 1450 B.C.E. through the widespread activity of Mesopotamian merchants, Akkadian had become an international language of diplomatic correspondence between and among the great nations of the Near East.

Unlike Sumerian, Akkadian—like other Semitic languages—used two genders (masculine and feminine) to distinguish between nouns, and based its vocabulary on three-letter roots, modifying their spelling both externally and internally to convey shades of meaning. Two dialects of Akkadian existed: Babylonian in the south and Assyrian in the north.

In modern scholarly transcriptions, Sumerian words are printed in capital letters and Akkadian ones in italics.

Later Semitic migrations by a people from the west called the Amorites led to the introduction of yet another Semitic language, Aramaic, that began to displace Akkadian in popularity by the late first millennium B.C.E., and it eventually became the dominant Semitic language of the ancient Near East.

Other Languages

Another ingredient in the linguistic mix of Mesopotamia was Hurrian, the language of a people who settled in Mesopotamia—first in the north and later in the south—beginning around 2500 B.C.E., and who developed the powerful kingdom of Mitanni. Like Sumerian, Hurrian is connected to no known language or language family.

Eventually, as Persian and Greek conquerors swept across the landscape of the Tigris and Euphrates, other tongues could be heard in the marketplaces and administrative centers of the land.

Throughout, the one line of continuity was Sumerian, which, like Latin in classical, medieval, and Renaissance Europe, bridged the temporal expanse between the birth of civilization and its later cultural transformations.

WRITING

Our knowledge of the languages that were spoken in ancient Mesopotamia derives from the discovery and decipherment of written texts. The invention of writing was one of Mesopotamia's greatest achievements. It facilitated the organization and management of society and served as the chief instrument by which a complex civilization could come into being. Eventually, it became the medium through which the people's collective experience and wisdom were transgenerationally transmitted. Though Mesopotamia's languages and scripts ultimately became extinct, its invention of writing endured as its most lasting legacy to the modern world.

Origins and Devices

Vast and impressive as its impact was, writing's origins were simple and humble. The earth itself was its birthplace: the clay found beside its rivers was shaped in the hands to form small pillow-like tablets to write on, while the reeds that grew along the rivers' banks became tools. With the upper and lower parts of the stem neatly sliced off, the reed became a stylus and acquired a triangular cross-section that could be pressed into the soft clay. The wedge-shaped indentations later gave rise to a name for this style of writing, "cuneiform," from the Latin word "cuneus" for wedge.

Around the same time in history, writing was invented in the valley of the Nile. There the Egyptians made use of a plant that grew in abundance along the river's banks, the papyrus plant. From its fibrous pulp, hammered flat and dried in the sun, they made the world's first paper. Indeed, our word "paper" comes from the ancient word "papyrus." From the loose fibers at the ends of the plant's stems, the Egyptians made brushes they used to apply ink to paper.

Did the Egyptians learn the concept of writing from Mesopotamia? Did Mesopotamia learn the art of writing from Egypt? Or did the two instances of invention arise independently? Scholars still debate the issue—an important one, since at its heart lies another critical question: Which civilization—Mesopotamia's or Egypt's was the world's first? The real answer may never be found, because the evidence—if it did not disintegrate—probably lies buried deep in the estuaries of the Tigris and Euphrates and the Nile's muddy delta.

One thing is almost certain: necessity was the mother of invention. As each culture became economically and politically complex near the fourth millennium B.C.E., writing was devised as a way of keeping records. Each nation found in its own natural environment the raw materials it needed to become literate.

Style

Both the Mesopotamians and the Egyptians also used the objects of the world around them as the inspiration for the shapes of their written symbols. These were far easier to represent through the use of a brush, and so Egyptian characters became largely recognizable images of such things as animals, plants, and the parts of the human body. But using the blunt end of a reed to do so posed a special challenge, and therefore Mesopotamian written characters tended to look more abstract, being angular assemblages of wedge-shaped marks arranged in different positions (vertical, horizontal, or slanted). The pictographic origins of Mesopotamian writing, as Denise Schmandt-Besserat has argued, may actually lie in small clay tokens that were pressed by merchants into clay to mark the basis of a transaction: so many sheep, so many bushels. From these primitive impressions of animal, garment, food, and vase shapes arose the outlines of the shapes later reproduced, in more sophisticated form, in cuneiform. Long dismissed by archaeologists as trivial finds, these toy-like tokens—some as early as the eighth millennium B.C.E.—may constitute the first baby steps in the slow march toward phonetic writing and literature.

From Pictogram to Phonogram

Initially, each character stood for the object that it pictorially represented: in short, the picture of a sheep meant "one sheep" and two pictures of a sheep meant "two sheep." But such a system has obvious limitations when it comes to expressing actions rather than objects, and even more limitations when it comes to representing abstract ideas and logical relationships. (For example, does a picture of a man next to a sheep mean "the man owns the sheep," "the man sold the sheep," or "the man is sheepish"? And, incidentally, was the sheep white or black, young or old?) The solution was to create some characters that would traditionally stand for certain abstract concepts or ideas. Thus, the ideogram was born. But even pictograms and ideograms left much to be desired, since there had to be a symbol for everything, especially as society became more complex and affluent. Through a leap of imagination, the phonogram was born: a

symbol that stood not for an object or an idea but a sound. Using a finite number of phonograms, the sounds of each and every word in the language could be reproduced and represented in writing, including the names of people and places. This was especially easy to do in Sumerian, where most words were monosyllabic. Thus by joining different syllabic symbols, or syllograms, together, new words could be formed. Of course, in a traditional society like ancient Mesopotamia's or Egypt's, few things were readily discarded, including pictograms and ideograms, especially if they could help clarify meaning through a kind of graphic redundancy. But the basis of each nation's writing system became phonograms. All that was left was to reduce their total number into the makings of a streamlined alphabet, an innovation that first appeared in the second millennium B.C.E. but took many centuries to gain acceptance. Until then, each ancient system was comprised of hundreds upon hundreds of separate characters (for Akkadian, about six hundred), representing individual sounds and syllabic combinations along with more ancient pictographic and ideographic symbols.

Technique

These symbols were impressed on clay tablets, with the writer's hand moving from left to right, or from top to bottom, so as not to smudge the clay with the palm of the hand. When vertical columns were used, the tablets were written and read from left to right. To then "turn the page," the column was flipped over bottom to top. Reading then continued from the column on the farthest right and moved leftward. If the scribe ran out of room, he might write between the lines or even write on the tablet's edge. At the end of the tablet would go what scholars call a colophon, giving the title of the document, the "page" number

Meaning	Pictogram (ca. 3500–3000 B.C.E.)	Early Cuneiform (ca. 2400–1800 B.C.E.)	Later Cuneiform (ca. 700 B.C.E.)	Phonetic Equivalent (in Sumerian)
heaven				an
sun, day				ud
earth				ki
water, stream				a
mountain				kur
plough				apin
grain				she
orchard				shar
ox				gud
cow				ab
pig				sha
donkey				anshe
fish				ku(a)
bird				mushen
bowl, food				ninda
eat ("mouth and food")				ku
drink ("mouth and water")				nag

5.4 (Opposite page)   This chart illustrates the development of cuneiform characters. Characters were originally drawn as pictures, but they were later reproduced in more abstract form by using triangular impressions made in clay by the blunt end of a reed. Over the course of time, the number of impressions was reduced and the shapes simplified in the interest of efficiency. At some point in time, the axis of most characters was rotated 90 degrees, in effect making them "lie on their backs." The reason for this is not clear, but it may reflect a desire on the part of scribes to save valuable space by compressing the characters vertically.

Each character stood for a simple sound. By combining these characters, and the sounds they stood for, more complex words and ideas could be represented.

5.5   This simulation illustrates how cuneiform characters would have been produced using a clay tablet and a stylus.   (Oriental Institute, University of Chicago)

5.6   For purposes of security, cuneiform tablets were often enclosed in clay envelopes. These envelopes, or "case tablets," included a description of the contents. In addition to being so inscribed, the envelopes might also be marked with personal seals. (Babylonian Collection, Yale University Library)

of the tablet, and a "catch-line": the first line of the next tablet. In a legal document, the colophon might include the scribe's name, and the date and place where the tablet was written. Contracts and letters were generally put in clay envelopes marked on the outside with the contents and the seals of the parties involved. When taking dictation or doing rough drafts, a scribe might write with a bronze stylus on a wooden tablet covered with soft wax, which could later be rubbed smooth like a "magic slate" to ready it for the next composition. Texts of permanent significance—like a law code or a royal proclamation—would be painstakingly cut into monumental stone.

The Role of the Scribe

Without doubt, the most important man in the ancient society of Mesopotamia was the scribe. Kings might extend their sway over hitherto unknown regions, merchants might organize the importation of rare commodities from distant lands, the irrigation officials might set the labourers to utilise the bountiful waters of the rivers and bring fertility to the soil, but without the scribe to record and transmit, to pass on detailed orders of administrators, to provide the astronomical data for controlling the calendar, to calculate the labour force necessary for digging a canal or the supplies required by an army, the co-ordination and continuity of all these activities could never have been achieved. Ancient Mesopotamian civilisation was above all a literate civilisation.

With these words H. W. F. Saggs points up the central role of writing and the scribe in Mesopotamia (Saggs 1965, 1987: 72). Mesopotamia's was, as Saggs notes, "above all a literate civilisation." But literacy in Mesopotamia was very limited, making the role of the professional scribe (*dubsar* in Sumerian and *tupsharru* in Akkadian) all the more important. Given the complexity of the cuneiform script, becoming a scribe required a lengthy education.

Though evidence exists for literate women, indeed, for the activity of female scribes, the occupation of scribe was a profession mostly reserved for males. As boys (almost always the sons of socially prominent individuals) they would attend a scribal academy known as a "tablet house" (*edubba* in Sumerian and *bit tuppi* in Akkadian). Initially their training consisted of shaping tablets out of clay, cutting styluses, and learning to manipulate the stylus to produce legible cuneiform characters. Simultaneously, they would practice and practice again, recognizing and reciting such characters aloud. They would then move on to the study of language, including spelling and grammar. After the conquest of Sumer by Akkad, scribes had to be bilingual, and that meant studying vernacular Akkadian and classic Sumerian (sometimes with the help of bilingual dictionaries). Finally came the study of literary style, achieved by the repeated copying of compositional models and perfected by the attentive reading of literary masterpieces. The curriculum would also include mathematics and lessons in the technical vocabulary a scribe might need to know in such fields as medicine, astronomy, and engineering. For the advanced student there would also be instruction in the dialectal differences between Babylonian and Assyrian, and perhaps even training in other languages such as Hurrian and Egyptian.

Archaeologists believe they may have found the remains of scribal academies in the ruins of Ur, Sippar, and Nippur—private houses containing rooms with multiple benches that may have served as classrooms—but schools may have also been attached to temples in various cities. A neighborhood in ancient Nippur had so many tablets scattered on the floors of its houses that archaeologists concluded it may have once been a scribal quarter (which they named "Tablet Hill").

Once a scribal student "graduated" from school, he could look forward to a remunerative career. He might serve on the staff of a palace or temple (keeping records, maintaining inventories, copying documents, taking dictation, managing correspondence, and composing the texts for inscriptions). Or he might work for businessmen (cataloguing merchandise, writing up transactions, and drawing up contracts). Or he might even freelance, setting up shop near a city gate and charging illiterate customers for writing or reading their letters or drawing up the formal documents they needed to arrange such things as a marriage or the legal transfer of property. The enterprising graduate might even go on to further training to become a physician or priest or—equipped with literacy—help his father in an already thriving family business.

Literary Tradition

Beyond meeting the immediate needs of his society, however, the scribe played a critical role in maintaining his culture's spiritual longevity. It was the scribe who by his skills enabled a thirsty present to drink from the reservoir of the past, for literacy was the link that connected the present with the wisdom of the past and its instructional and inspirational power. By making multiple copies of Mesopotamia's literary masterpieces, the ancient scribe—like the monks in the European Middle Ages—preserved a precious literary legacy and made it accessible to later generations. Indeed, were it not for Mesopotamia's scribes, her ghosts would be voiceless today and her ruins silent.

Archives and Libraries

The records of palace and temple were stored in archives. Thanks to this database, we can tap into the everyday life of an ancient world, adding to the information we can elsewhere gain from public inscriptions graven on stone.

By a twist of fate, the destruction of the city of Nineveh by the Babylonians and Medes in 612 B.C.E. buried and preserved the royal library of Ashurbanipal. Containing as many as 1,500 separate works, it represents the private literary preserve of an avid and intellectual collector who once boasted that he had read with his own eyes tablets "written before the Flood." Though other royal libraries may have existed, Ashurbanipal's is the only one to have survived. More than any other single source it has illuminated our understanding of the Mesopotamian mind. Ironically, the burning of cities by enemy armies actually preserved the clay documents by baking them.

It is now time to explore the literary treasures of ancient Mesopotamia: its epic poetry; its historical chronicles; its legal documents; its divination texts, hymns, prayers, and lamentations; its letters and proverbs; its social satire; and its erotic poetry.

LITERATURE

Epic Poetry

The scale of an epic tapestry is broad, for divine myth and heroic legend are the warp and woof from which it is woven. Its themes are the great deeds of human beings and the gods, and the intertwined existence of their worlds. Its length is often long, given the weight of its message: the creation of the universe, the origins of heavenly beings and humanity, the meaning and purpose of life.

Before writing's invention, such tales were recited orally, each storyteller transmitting a traditional narrative core that grew by creative embellishment. Writing tended to fix the story's structure and content, but over the course of generations even these might be reshaped, especially in the hands of a master poet, to form a work of literary art.

The civilization preserved its masterpieces by copying and recopying them; but the literary masterpieces also preserved their civilization by acting as a lifeline that connected the present to the past and the spiritual guidance it could provide.

THE LEGEND OF GILGAMESH

One of the greatest poems of ancient Mesopotamia is the *Epic of Gilgamesh*. Of all Mesopotamian epics, its voice is the most universal for, despite the epic's alien names and settings, it speaks of the human condition: of love and loss, of striving and failure, of innocence and regret, of boundless dreams and reality's cruel limits. The *Epic of Gilgamesh* is thus at once the oldest of mankind's tales and the most perennially modern.

It is also a tale that is incomplete. Only 80 percent of the story survives: 575 of its original 3,000 or so lines are completely lost, and the plot is riddled with holes. But the story's main outlines are clear, and the characters compelling. A "standard version" of the epic has been pieced together from the remains of some 70 clay "manuscripts" found in Mesopotamia, most from the seventh century B.C.E. library of Ashurbanipal at Nineveh. But documents prove the story is many centuries earlier. One tradition attributes its authorship to a scholar from Uruk named Sinleqqiunninni, who perhaps lived in the 13th century B.C.E.. Yet fragments exist of an even earlier version of the text, dating back to the Old Babylonian period (ca. 1800–1600 B.C.E.). And even older than these are samples of the story written in Sumerian: individual heroic episodes that later were integrated into a single grand design transcribed into Akkadian.

As for the hero himself, it looks like he may have actually existed. The Sumerian King-list names a Gilgamesh as the fifth king to rule Uruk after the legendary Great Flood. Working backward from the names and dates of more historic kings, this would put his reign to sometime between 2800 and 2700 B.C.E. From his actual deeds—the conquest of Kish and the construction of Uruk's great walls—grew the stuff of legend. Like England's King Arthur, Gilgamesh became larger than life: a man "2/3 divine and 1/3 mortal," as the story goes, who "probed the depths of existence . . . and finally found wisdom."

Our survey of his legend begins with Sumerian tales (where his name is spelled "Bilgames") and concludes with the great Akkadian epic that bears his name. Like other long Mesopotamian poems, the text of the *Epic of Gilgamesh* is traditionally divided into chapters called tablets because each fills the surface of a single clay document. We begin, however, with the shorter Sumerian tales from which the longer epic grew.

Sumerian Tales of Bilgames

"BILGAMES AND AGGA" OR "THE ENVOYS OF AGGA"

Characters
Agga (Akka), ruler of Kish
Bilgames, ruler of Uruk
Birhurturra, Bilgames's bodyguard

Plot
Through envoys, Agga, the ruler of Kish, delivers an ultimatum to the city of Uruk demanding its submission. Bilgames, the ruler of Uruk, turns to his council of elders, who recommend acceding to Agga's demands. Rejecting their decision, Bilgames then turns to an assembly of young warriors, who choose to fight rather than surrender. With his ultimatum rejected, Agga lays siege to the city. Birhurturra volunteers to go as an emissary to persuade Agga to desist. His body beaten, Birhurturra remains defiant, declaring that Bilgames will ultimately triumph. Bilgames then leads his people into battle, defeats the enemy, and captures Agga. Recalling a past favor, however, Bilgames shows Agga mercy and releases him.

Commentary
This is the best preserved Sumerian tale that features Bilgames as its central character. At 115 lines, it is also the shortest to survive. The story celebrates defiance in defense of civic freedom and praises individual courage. In addition, it extols mercy as an attribute of effective leadership. As a reflection of Sumerian political history, the story documents military conflict between city-states (in particular, Uruk and Kish) and demonstrates the existence of a bicameral legislature in Sumer. The divergent views of the elders and the young warriors is also our earliest literary evidence in history of a politically charged generation gap. The picture of Gilgamesh we see here is that of a brave and resolute military leader who tempers justice with mercy. The content of the epic tale is purely secular and features no gods.

"BILGAMES AND THE CEDAR MOUNTAIN"

Characters
Bilgames, ruler of Uruk
Enkidu, his servant
Utu, god of the sun
Huwawa, guardian of the Cedar Mountain

Plot
Seeing a corpse drifting down a river, Bilgames becomes acutely conscious of his own mortality. In order to secure immortality, he decides to

become famous by journeying to a distant and forbidding mountain covered with sacred cedar trees. His servant, Enkidu, implores him to pray to the sun-god Utu for aid. In response, Utu gives Bilgames seven constellations to act as his guides. Fifty men free of responsibility volunteer to serve under Bilgames's command on this dangerous mission and are armed for combat. After crossing six mountain ranges, the expedition arrives at the seventh—their destination—where they begin to fell sacred cedar trees. The noise, however, awakens the divine guardian of the forest, Huwawa, who attacks them with his magic power and renders them unconscious. Awakened by Enkidu, Bilgames resolves to find and fight Huwawa. When Enkidu tries to dissuade him from going, Bilgames urges that Enkidu join him, since two will be stronger than one. Bilgames eventually succeeds not by might but by craft, offering to give Huwawa one gift after another in exchange for each of his magic powers. The seven gifts include the gift of Bilgames's two sisters in marriage, kinship, flour and cool water, slippers, and precious minerals. Stripped of his powers, Huwawa is then captured by Bilgames, who in an act of generosity releases him, much to the consternation of Enkidu, who proceeds to cut off the dangerous Huwawa's head. Upset over Huwawa's death, the god Enlil distributes the magic powers that were once Huwawa's to other entities in the cosmos.

Commentary

This story draws upon a variety of motifs that occur in the mythologies of other nations, including the myths of the Greeks. Like Achilles in the tale of the Trojan War, Bilgames is driven by a hunger for immortality that he seeks to satisfy by performing unforgettable deeds. Like Ulysses in the cave of the Cyclops, Bilgames uses trickery and the lure of a gift to strip a monster of his power when physical strength alone will not prevail. And like Jason and the Argo-nauts who sought the Golden Fleece, Bilgames and his men quest after something guarded by an awesome and terrifying creature. In the Mesopotamian myth, the recurrence of the magic number seven is also notable.

In the later Babylonian *Epic of Gilgamesh*, the hero is motivated to search for the secret of eternal life after keeping vigil over the dead body of his companion, Enkidu. The later storyteller achieved this effect by intermixing three elements from the tale of Bilgames and the Cedar Mountain: the thought-provoking corpse floating down the river; Enkidu's efforts to awaken Bilgames from a death-like sleep; and Bilgames's underlying compulsion to attain immortality. In this tale, however, Enkidu is merely a servant, not the half-civilized, half-animal creature he later becomes.

Two Sumerian versions of the Cedar Mountain story survive. In one, the potent theme of the fragileness of mortality is positioned in the narrative to give it greater emphasis. In this same version, Bilgames expresses doubts about his ability to defeat his enemy. What we see then in these two versions is evidence of different authorship and a different philosophical perspective on the nature of the hero. The later epic will choose the path of vulnerability and doubt over the path of bravado.

"BILGAMES AND THE BULL OF HEAVEN"

Characters
Bilgames, ruler of Uruk
Ninsun, his goddess-mother
Inanna, goddess of sexual love
An, Inanna's divine father
Lugalgabangal, Bilgames's minstrel
Enkidu, Bilgames's servant

Plot
Seeing the handsome Bilgames rowing a boat in a marsh, the goddess Inanna wants to have sex with him. Later, Bilgames's mother warns her son about Inanna's dangerous and seductive

power. As a result, Bilgames rejects Inanna's advances and thereby enrages her. Bent on revenge, Inanna appeals to her divine father to release the destructive Bull of Heaven (possibly the constellation Taurus) from the sky. When he refuses, she throws a tantrum and gets her way. Bilgames's minstrel, Lugalgabangal, sees the Bull of Heaven coming and warns his master about its approach, but Bilgames dismisses his fears as exaggerated, bidding Lugalgabangal to play and sing while he (Bilgames) drinks beer. Finally, Bilgames rises to the challenge. With his servant Enkidu holding the bull's tail, Bilgames strikes its head with an ax and slays it. Then, he cuts off its hindquarter and hurls the object at Inanna, driving her off. Afterward, Bilgames cuts up the bull's meat and gives it to the orphans of his city to eat. The horns he consecrates to Inanna.

Commentary

The battle with the Bull of Heaven will become a major episode in the comprehensive Babylonian *Epic of Gilgamesh*. The probable astral significance of the episode, however, is regretably unknown to us.

The story clearly illustrates how the Mesopotamians conceived of both the goddess of sexual love and the love she represented: a primal hunger that was seductive and dangerous, self-serving and cruelly destructive. In that regard, Inanna (Babylonian Ishtar) was not unlike Greek Aphrodite, but very unlike the Christianized and chivalric notion of love that would pervade the European Middle Ages and still persists in the popular imagination today as "romance." As the conclusion of the story shows, Inanna's importunings may be temporarily rebuffed, but ultimately her powers must be acknowledged by man.

"BILGAMES AND THE NETHERWORLD"

Characters
Enki, god of subterranean freshwater
Inanna, goddess of sexual love
Utu, god of the sun
Bilgames, ruler of Uruk
Enkidu, Bilgames's servant

Plot
After a comic episode, the story describes how a storm strikes the god Enki as he is sailing to the netherworld. In the aftermath of the storm, the goddess Inanna finds a broken willow tree beside the Euphrates. She plants it in her garden in the hopes of making a throne and bed from its wood after it has grown. The tree, however, is inhabited by evil spirits. They are later driven away by Bilgames, who cuts the tree down so that Inanna will have the wood she needs for her furniture. From the wood Bilgames also makes equipment for a game (perhaps a wooden ball and mallet). The game becomes so popular among the young men of the city that the women are distressed. The sports equipment, however, falls through a hole in the ground into the netherworld. Enkidu volunteers to retrieve it, and Bilgames gives him special instructions on maintaining a humble demeanor when he enters the land of the dead—instructions that Enkidu totally ignores, with the result that he is held captive in the netherworld. Bilgames's pleas for divine help are ignored until Enki asks Utu, the sun-god, to bring Enkidu along as a passenger when he rises at dawn from the darkness. Upon Enkidu's return, Bilgames questions him about what he saw and learned during his visit to the netherworld. Enkidu speaks of the sufferings of those who died childless (and thus have no one to mourn them) and describes the suffering of those who died awful deaths.

Commentary
The story of Bilgames and the netherworld is an imaginative Alice-in-Wonderland tale in which one odd or improbable event generates another. Like Homer's *Odyssey*, Virgil's *Aeneid*, and Dante's *Divine Comedy*, it also takes us on a

tour of the land of the dead, though in more abbreviated form than do the poetic tours conducted by later European authors. To the Sumerian storyteller, the netherworld was an unmitigated horror of sorrow except for those who had male heirs to keep their memory alive. Significantly, the happiest souls are those of stillborn babies; thus the most blessed human beings are those who were never born at all.

The second half of this Sumerian tale (Enkidu's mission and his report) forms the substance of the *Epic of Gilgamesh's* Tablet XII and a now-lost dream sequence in Tablet VII.

"THE DEATH OF BILGAMES"

Characters
Bilgames, ruler of Uruk
Various gods, including Enlil and Enki

Plot
The story begins with Bilgames on his death bed. In a dream he appears before an assembly of the gods who are to decide his fate. Though (like Achilles) his mother was a goddess, his father was a mortal; his mixed parentage thus poses a quandary to the gods: should he be granted immortality or not? After a recitation of his deeds—including his defeat of Huwawa and his visitation with Ziusdra, the Noah-like survivor of the Sumerian Deluge—the gods reach their decision: Bilgames must go to the netherworld, but he will occupy a place of honor there as a semi-divine judge. There he will be reunited with his family and his companion, Enkidu. Meanwhile, he is told, on earth men will honor him with festivities that will include wrestling matches, even as he once wrestled with Enkidu. Awakened from his dream, Bilgames proceeds to plan his tomb. The tomb is to be built of stone and gold in the bed of the Euphrates, after the waters of the river have been diverted to permit excavation. There he will be buried together with mem-

bers of his family and his servants and his possessions along with presents meant for the gods he will later meet.

Commentary
The storyteller reminds his audience that even a demi-god like Bilgames was compelled to dwell in the netherworld after death. As the Babylonian *Epic of Gilgamesh* would make clear, the gods reserved eternal life for themselves. The mass burial described in the text strikingly parallels the discoveries of the Royal Tombs of Ur made by Sir Leonard Woolley. The text itself inspired Tablet VIII of the *Epic of Gilgamesh*, but there it is Enkidu rather than Gilgamesh who is to be buried.

The Babylonian *Epic of Gilgamesh*

Characters
Gilgamesh (= Sumerian "Bilgames"), ruler of Uruk
Ninsun, his divine mother
Enkidu, his friend and companion
Shamhat, a prostitute
Shamash, the god of the sun
Humbaba (= Sumerian "Huwawa"), guardian of the Cedar Mountain
Ishtar (= Sumerian "Inanna"), goddess of sexual love and chief goddess of Uruk
Siduri, a divine barmaid
Urshanabi, a ferryman
Utnapishtim, the Babylonian "Noah" (= Sumerian "Ziusdra")

Plot

Tablet I: Gilgamesh and Enkidu

Gilgamesh, the hero of the epic, is described as handsome, brave, and strong, two-thirds divine and one-third human. As king of Uruk, he had built its great walls. He later searched for the secret of life and, after great effort, ultimately found wisdom. Before he died, he recorded his autobiography on a tablet of lapis lazuli

5.7 The hero Gilgamesh, holding a sword in one hand, with a lion cub tucked under his arm. (Bonomi, Nineveh and Its Palaces, 1875 [after Botta])

secured in a cedar box—the basis of the story that follows.

Early in his reign, Gilgamesh acted arrogantly, harassing young men and sleeping with their brides before they were wed. To alleviate their oppression, the gods created someone to oppose Gilgamesh. His opponent was named Enkidu, a hairy, muscular, and naked creature more at home with the wild beasts than he was with humankind. Enkidu looked after his animal friends by undoing hunters' traps, letting the animals live free.

To stop Enkidu, a hunter hires a prostitute. By having sex with Enkidu, the prostitute strips him of his naïveté and estranges him from the simple animals that had formerly been his friends. She invites him to come to Uruk to challenge Gilgamesh, who had already had a premonition of his arrival.

Tablet II: Conflict, Friendship, and Coming Adventure

After sharing the company of shepherds and learning the ways of man, Enkidu arrives in Uruk and blocks Gilgamesh's path. The two worthy adversaries wrestle and, in recognition of each other's prowess, become friends. Gilgamesh proposes that Enkidu join him on a mission to kill Humbaba, the guardian of the Cedar Mountain. Enkidu expresses reservations about the wisdom of such an adventure. Gilgamesh then proposes his plan to the council of elders, but they too seek to dissuade him. Gilgamesh, however, is undeterred.

Tablet III: Blessings and Instructions

The elders then give Gilgamesh and Enkidu advice to guide them on their mission. Afterward, the two go to visit Gilgamesh's divine mother. Ninsun ceremonially adopts Enkidu as her son, and he and Gilgamesh perform rituals to promote their success. Gilgamesh next instructs his people about what they must do in his absence. Enkidu again seeks to dissuade Gilgamesh from his plan, but finally he offers his aid. The young men of the city cheer the two heroes on.

Tablet IV: A Journey of Dreams

On successive nights of their journey, Gilgamesh has a series of foreboding dreams that are interpreted optimistically by Enkidu. With Shamash urging them to commence their attack on Humbaba, the two heroes bolster each other's courage and arrive at the place of combat.

Tablet V: Encounter with Humbaba

Humbaba demeans Enkidu's heroic stature. Humbaba and Gilgamesh then clash. Shamash aids Gilgamesh by buffeting Humbaba with fierce winds. Defeated, Humbaba begs for mercy. Enkidu argues that he must be slain, and Gilgamesh kills Humbaba with his dagger. Gilgamesh and Enkidu then chop down cedar trees, with Enkidu choosing an especially tall tree to serve as timber for constructing a new door for Enlil's temple in Uruk. The two then load the lumber on a raft for the trip back home. Gilgamesh carries the head of Humbaba home as a trophy.

Tablet VI: Ishtar and the Bull of Heaven

Back home in Uruk, as Gilgamesh bathes and dresses, the goddess Ishtar lusts for him and tries to seduce him with offers of wealth and power. Gilgamesh, however, rebuffs her advances, citing her vices and reciting a litany of her former lovers who paid a high price for her affections. Enraged, Ishtar asks the sky-god Anu to let loose the Bull of Heaven to ravage Uruk and kill its king. Anu at first refuses but then relents when Ishtar threatens to release the dead from the netherworld. The bull begins its rampage but is stopped dead in its tracks by Gilgamesh and Enkidu. When Ishtar throws a fit in frustration, Enkidu tears off the bull's hindquarters and hurls them at the goddess. The heroes then consecrate the bull's horns and celebrate their victory.

Tablet VII: The Death of Enkidu

Enkidu recounts to Gilgamesh a dream he had. In the dream the gods pronounced a death sentence upon him for complicity in the murder of Humbaba and the Bull of Heaven. Enkidu then expresses regret for the cedar temple door he made for an ungrateful Enlil, and he curses the hunter and the prostitute who were his original undoing. In response, Shamash tells Enkidu he should count his blessings for having become civilized: the pleasure from the bread and beer he consumed and the clothes he wore, the friendship he shared with Gilgamesh, and the honors he will receive from humankind after his death (including honors Gilgamesh himself promises to bestow). Humbled by this realization, Enkidu blesses the prostitute he had previously cursed.

In a second dream, the text of which is mostly lost, Enkidu describes what he saw in the dark and dusty realm of the dead.

Growing weaker and weaker from sickness, Enkidu finally dies.

Tablet VIII: The Funeral of Enkidu

Recalling their deeds together, Gilgamesh laments the death of his friend and companion. He orders that a statue of Enkidu be fashioned from precious materials, describes the mourning that will ensue, and recounts the inventory of grave goods to be placed in the tomb as offerings to Enkidu and as presents for the gods whom Enkidu's spirit will meet in the netherworld.

Tablet IX: The Wanderings of Gilgamesh

Driven mad by grief, Gilgamesh wanders across the world seeking light to replace the darkness that has now possessed his soul. The death of Enkidu has awakened in him a realization of his own mortality, and he searches for Utnapishtim, the survivor of the Deluge, who holds the secret to eternal life. Gilgamesh passes through a mountain guarded by scorpion-men, and he travels through a long, dark tunnel to a garden of bright jewels at the edge of the world.

Tablet X: At the World's Edge

Beyond the garden lies the shore of an immense sea. Near the end of his journey, wasted by weariness and harrowed by grief, Gilgamesh comes upon a tavern run by a divine barmaid named Siduri. Frightened by his haggard appearance, she hides, but he finds and accosts her. She listens as he tells her of his love for

Enkidu and the weight of the sadness he carries because of Enkidu's death. He tells her how he kept vigil over Enkidu's corpse until a maggot crawled from the nose and Gilgamesh knew that Enkidu's life was gone forever, that death would one day claim him too, and that he must therefore search for the secret of everlasting life. To this Siduri replies as follows (according to the Old Babylonian version of the *Epic*):

Gilgamesh, where are you going?
The life you're looking for you'll never find.
When the gods made man,
Death is what they reserved for him, but saved
    life for themselves.
Eat and drink your fill, Gilgamesh, and
    celebrate day and night.
Make every day a festival; day and night dance
    and play.
Let your clothes be sparkling fresh; rinse your
    hair and bathe.
Mind the little one that holds your hand, and
    let your wife enjoy your embrace.
For *this* is the proper business of man.

Noting his determination, however, Siduri points Gilgamesh toward a ferryman that could transport him across the vast sea and the Waters of Death to the place where Utnapishtim dwells, the survivor of the Great Flood and the only man ever to have been granted immortality. With the ferryman Urshanabi's help, Gilgamesh lands on the farther shore and finds Utnapishtim.

Tablet XI: The Story of the Deluge, and Immortality Lost

Utnapishtim tells Gilgamesh about the Great Flood that destroyed all of humanity and all living things. Warned by the god Ea to build an ark to save himself and his family and other creatures, Utnapishtim survived the destructive caprice of the other gods who had sent the Deluge. Out of divine repentance for having sent the flood, the god Enlil rewarded Utnapishtim and his wife by making them immortal.

Utnapishtim then puts Gilgamesh to the test. To see if he too deserves immortality, Utnapishtim requires Gilgamesh to stay awake for six days and seven nights. If he can resist sleep, he can resist the bigger sleep that is death. But Gilgamesh falls asleep and thus fails the test. Utnapishtim then tells Urshanabi to take this unwelcome visitor away and never again return. Nevertheless, prompted by the compassion of his wife, Utnapishtim tells Gilgamesh about a magic plant that grows at the bottom of the sea, a plant that can restore youth. Gilgamesh dives and plucks the plant from the sea floor.

Traveling home with Urshanabi, Gilgamesh stops beside a pool to rest and bathe, setting the plant down at the pool's edge. Attracted by the plant's fragrance, a serpent steals the plant away and, with its youth renewed, sheds its skin. The hope of eternal youth has thus slipped from the hero's grasp, and he weeps, grieving over its loss.

As Urshanabi and Gilgamesh come to the end of their journey, Gilgamesh points out to his ferryman Uruk's mighty walls and the city's glorious expanse, the image of grandeur and cultural achievement with which the epic poem began.

Tablet XII: Enkidu and the Netherworld

This tablet reiterates the second half of the Sumerian tale entitled "Bilgames and the Netherworld." For this reason, and especially because Enkidu had already died long before this point in the *Epic's* narrative, some modern scholars believe the tablet represents a scribal addendum that was not integral to the *Epic's* own plan.

Commentary
Like Goethe's Faust, Gilgamesh sought one means after another to satisfy a deep hunger in his soul. In the beginning, he wielded his power as king to dominate others but gained no lasting satisfaction. Then in Enkidu he met his match. Together with Enkidu, he followed

another avenue—aiming for fame—but found it was only a dead end street when the one he sought to share it with was no more. Having once asserted his autonomy by scorning Inanna and carnal pleasure, he had lost Enkidu, the object of his manly love. To fill the void caused by Enkidu's death and the consequent realization of his own mortality, he goes on a quest for eternal life only to find that it too cannot be had. Hoping instead to merely restore his youth, he sees even that wish slip through his fingers and be lost.

In the end, like Faust who dug drainage ditches to reclaim wasteland and by that humble work found satisfaction, Gilgamesh returns to Uruk, the place where his epic journey had begun, and contemplates the city walls he had built. In a world where no one is immortal and nothing is permanent, it is better, he realizes, to give his life to something rather than to nothing, to some constructive act that may, in ways he may never know, benefit others. In an antique anticipation of T. S. Eliot's *Four Quartets*, Gilgamesh returned to where he had begun and knew it now for the first time. The greatest irony is that the immortality Gilgamesh vainly searched for during his lifetime would be bestowed upon him posthumously by the heroic account of his failed struggle.

Beyond the personal implications of the epic is a larger theme: the value of civilization itself. In one of the boldest strokes of originality, the epic transforms Enkidu from a mere servant and companion to an anti-civilizational creature of untamed nature. With a bite of a bitter Eden-like apple, Enkidu loses paradise, surrendering the unself-conscious innocence of natural instinct to contrivance and calculation. It is not sexual experience per se that does him in—for animals have sex too—but cunning deception, a markedly human trait. In exchange, Enkidu gets bread and beer, a haircut, fancy clothes, and an exciting adventure that kills him. Poor brutish Humbaba also pays a price,

and once he succumbs to deceit, it's open season for loggers in the great Cedar Forest. Civilization has triumphed, but the cost has been high.

The Babylonian *Epic of Creation*   Our next epic is called the Babylonian *Epic of Creation*, or *Enuma elish* as it was known to the Babylonians themselves from the first words of the poem that meant "When on high . . ."

Its modern name is a bit of a misnomer since it hardly deals with creation in the way the opening chapters of the Old Testament do. Instead, this thousand-line epic is a patriotic religious tract celebrating the rise to power of Babylon's chief god, Marduk. His ascendancy is set against a background of cosmic events and struggles. In the Babylonian narrative the creation of man, the culminating act of God's six-day workweek in Genesis, is relegated to the role of a cosmic footnote. But that is as it should be in the Mesopotamian worldview: man was a lesser being who only earned his right to live through subservience to the gods—a flawed being at that, since he was manufactured with the blood of a rebel god who was slain for his arrogance. And what a crew these gods are: lusting for power, seething with anger, thirsting for revenge, and rejoicing in slaughter. Enough to make one tremble, and that too is as it should be, so that man would remain humble and mindful of his servile place. Yet there is reason for hope, for most of the poem's rogues' gallery were primal gods, vanquished and put in *their* place by the chosen one, Babylon's own, the great god Marduk, champion of the universe.

Unlike the *Epic of Gilgamesh*, there are no human characters here with lines to speak, and the storyteller is not interested in what an intellectual (ancient or modern) might call "the human condition." The gods are not even anthropomorphic, except by a stretch: Marduk has four eyes and four ears, and Tiamat may have been a verbose dragon. But the gods are anthropo*pathic*: they are endowed with human emotions, including some of the most ugly. And therefore, without meaning to, the epic constitutes an inverse commentary on our own darker side. It is a side that ought to give us pause, for today we possess cosmic powers of destruction that the ancients could only attribute in their imagination to primal gods. Moreover, we are flawed—as they foresaw—for in our veins flows the blood of an angel who lost paradise.

It is now time to recite the litany of tablets that recount this Mesopotamian clash of the Titans.

Characters
Apsu, god of subterranean freshwater
Mummu, primal god and Apsu's vizier
Tiamat, goddess of salt water
Anu, god of the sky
Ea, god of cunning and wisdom and father of Marduk
Marduk, chief god of Babylon and son of Ea
Kingu, divine commander serving under Tiamat

Plot

Tablet I

Before heaven and earth were created, three primordial gods coexisted: Apsu, Mummu, and Tiamat. The male god Apsu and the female god Tiamat mated and produced four offspring. One of these, Anshar, fathered Anu, and he in turn fathered Ea. These gods were a noisy bunch and their noise bothered Apsu. Much to Tiamat's distress, Apsu proposes to destroy his boisterous progeny. He and his ally Mummu are, however, opposed by Ea, who vanquishes them and takes Apsu's crown. Ea then fathers the god Marduk. Ea's revolt, however, provokes Tiamat to seek revenge. To aid her, she creates a number of monsters, including their leader Kingu, to whom she entrusts the "Tablet of Destinies."

Tablet II

Having discovered Tiamat's plan, Ea reports it to his grandfather Anshar, who calls for a champion to oppose Tiamat. Anu and Ea both shrink in fear before her might, but Marduk offers to stand up to her provided the gods grant him absolute power.

Tablet III

Anshar summons the gods to an assembly in order that they may confer supreme authority on Marduk.

Table IV

In a coronation ceremony, Marduk is granted kingship over the universe. He then arms himself for battle. Preceded by storm winds, he rides in his chariot against Tiamat. Seeing him, Kingu and his minions lose heart. For her part, Tiamat is incensed. Charging her with rebellion against the divine order, Marduk challenges Tiamat to single battle. He attacks her with his winds and fires an arrow through her heart, felling her. Next, he ties Kingu up and strips him of the Tablet of Destinies, which he then places on his own chest. Finally, he smashes Tiamat's skull with a club, severs her arteries, and slices her body in two, using the top half to form the sky.

Tablet V

Marduk proceeds to organize the cosmos, stationing the stars and constellations, apportioning the seasons, and fixing the phases of the moon.

Tablet VI

Kingu is charged with inciting a revolt and is executed by having his arteries cut. Kingu's blood is then used by Ea to make man. After mercifully setting free Tiamat's and Kingu's accomplices, Marduk assigns the various gods their realms. The gods in turn sing Marduk's praises.

Tablet VII

Marduk's manifold powers and virtues are celebrated as the poem concludes.

The Descent of Inanna and Dumuzi's Death

Characters
Inanna, the goddess of love
Ninshubur, her faithful servant
Neti, the gatekeeper of the netherworld
Ereshkigal, the queen of the netherworld and
    Inanna's sister
Enlil, the supreme god of heaven
Nanna, god of the moon
Enki, god of cleverness and wisdom
Dumuzi, a shepherd and the husband of Inanna
Utu, the god of the sun
Geshtinanna, Dumuzi's sister

Plot
Inanna decides to leave heaven and earth and journey to the netherworld. After dressing in her regalia, she instructs her servant Ninshubur to get divine help to rescue her if she fails to return. Inanna then travels to the netherworld and demands entrance. Neti, the gatekeeper, informs Ereshkigal of her arrival. Ereshkigal grudgingly agrees to admit her, but she tells Neti to strip Inanna of everything she wears. As Inanna then passes through each of seven gates, she is compelled to remove an article of apparel until finally she stands naked before her sister. Ereshkigal peremptorily orders Inanna killed and savagely hangs her carcass from a hook.

After Inanna fails to return home, Ninshubur follows her instructions and turns to a series of gods for aid. Enlil and Nanna refuse, but Enki agrees to help. Enki then creates two beings and sends them on a mission to the netherworld. When they find Ereshkigal grieving for her lost children, they are to empathize with her pain. They do so, and in gratitude for their concern Ereshkigal offers them a reward. They refuse generous gifts and (as planned) merely ask for the meat they see hanging on a hook. Ereshkigal gladly complies, not realizing their hidden intent. The two creatures then sprinkle Inanna's corpse with the food and

water of life and revive her. But a panel of divine judges announces that, once dead, a person cannot simply leave the netherworld, at least not without providing a substitute. Hence a substitute must be found.

In the company of demons, Inanna returns to earth and goes from city to city searching for a substitute. She rejects a number of her loyal servants who grieved over her death. Coming upon her husband, Dumuzi, however, she finds him sitting on a throne and untouched by mourning. Enraged, she directs the demons to take Dumuzi hostage and haul him off to the netherworld. Dumuzi pleas with Utu, the sun god, for help, and Utu lets Dumuzi change shape to escape his pursuers. Finally, despite attempts by his sister Geshtinanna to protect him, the demons discover Dumuzi in a sheepfold and drag him to the netherworld along with his sister. An agreement is then reached by which each will in turn spend only half a year in the realm of the dead.

Commentary
The texts of these Sumerian myths constitute the components of an epic tale about the goddess of love, Inanna, and the fate of her lover, the shepherd, Dumuzi. The story teaches that death is inexorable, that even the gods cannot escape its grip if they come too dangerously close. And, like the *Epic of Gilgamesh*, the narrative takes us to depths our own human vision cannot penetrate—at least while we are alive—by describing the landscape of death's realm and the dark spirits who inhabit it. It is a portrait more chilling than that painted by Homer in the *Odyssey*'s 11th book and Vergil in the *Aeneid*'s sixth, and, in its brushstrokes if not in the sweep of its canvas, approximates the hand of Dante in the *Inferno*. Significantly, all these works—*Gilgamesh*, the *Odyssey*, the *Aeneid*, and the *Inferno*—see death and love as cruelly intertwined, and the tale of Inanna and Dumuzi is no exception. The details of the story bring other classical myths to mind: King Admetus's search for a substitute to die for

him (dramatized by the playwright Euripides in *Alcestis*) and the eternal bargain struck by Demeter that allows her daughter Persephone to dwell above ground for half the year before returning to Hades' winter embrace.

The Mesopotamian tale is tantalizing because of the questions it leaves unanswered (though the ancients might have thought explicit answers redundant since they already knew them by heart): who were the children for whom the queen of the dead grieved, why did Dumuzi fail to mourn his wife, and—most of all—what was Inanna's motive for descending to the netherworld in the first place? But, then, the universal response to death has always been a series of unanswered questions.

The Romance of Nergal and Ereshkigal

Characters
Anu, the father of the gods
Kakka, Anu's emissary
Ea, god of cleverness and wisdom
Ereshkigal, queen of the netherworld
Namtar, Ereshkigal's vizier
Nergal, a male deity, who becomes Ereshkigal's
   consort

Plot
At a heavenly banquet of the gods, Anu realizes Ereshkigal cannot join the celebrants (nor would the celebrants deign to descend to the netherworld). As a compromise, he sends an emissary down to tell Ereshkigal she can call in an order for carry-out food. The emissary does so, and in turn Ereshkigal sends her vizier up to claim her portion. Upon his arrival in heaven, however, he is insulted by one of the gods, Nergal, who fails to show him proper respect. To make amends, Nergal is instructed by Ea to go down to Ereshkigal's domain. But, lest Nergal be ritually compelled to stay in the netherworld, Ea warns him not to sit in a chair while he is there, not to eat bread or meat, not to drink beer, not to have a foot-bath, and most certainly not to have sex with Ereshkigal.

Yes, you guessed it: after passing through the seven gates of the netherworld, Nergal is able to turn down everything he is offered, except Ereshkigal herself. When Ereshkigal takes a seductive bath and puts on a transparent gown, Nergal can't resist. (Actually, it takes her two baths and two gowns to thoroughly break down his resistance.) Then they have sex for six days. On the seventh, Nergal insists he must leave and ascends a staircase to heaven.

Ereshkigal is disconsolate, and sends Namtar to heaven to fetch Nergal, threatening that she will raise the dead until they outnumber the living unless her demands are met. "When I was a little girl," she says, "I never played with dolls, never knew what it would be like to have a child of my own. Now his seed is in me, and I want to sleep with him again." Anu complies and rounds up the usual suspects, but Namtar fails to pick Nergal out of the lineup. After Namtar reports his failure to his mistress, Ereshkigal sends him back up, ordering him in no uncertain terms to arrest the divine perpetrator. He does so, and Nergal is forced to descend.

Upon arriving in the netherworld, Nergal smashes through its seven gates, confronts Ereshkigal, laughs in her face, grabs her by the hair, pulls her off her throne, and . . . embraces her passionately. Like Rhett Butler standing with Scarlet O'Hara on the landing of Tara's grand staircase, he sweeps her off her feet. At this point—alas—the text breaks off.

In a condensed version of the tale found in Egypt in the 14th century B.C.E. ruins of Amarna, there *is* an ending. After breaking through the gates of the netherworld (as before), Nergal grabs Ereshkigal's hair and pulls her off the throne, intending to cut her head off. "Please don't kill me," she begs. "I have something to say. Be my husband and I will be your wife. Marry me and share the kingdom I rule." Hearing her words, Nergal's grip relaxes. He draws her close, kissing her and wiping away her tears. "You waited for me," he says. "I have come."

Commentary

The story explains how Nergal became the consort of Ereshkigal and shared her dominion over the dead. Beneath the archaic stiffness of traditional narrative form is a tale of emotional deprivation and hunger that shows hot colors can exist even in the unremitting grayness of the netherworld. As the biblical Song of Songs (8:6) proclaims: "Set me as a seal upon your heart, as a seal upon your arm; for love is as strong as death, passion as cruel as the grave." As an inversion of the much later Roman epic, the *Aeneid* (where the hero Aeneas rejects Queen Dido's offer of her body and kingdom only to be shunned by her chill ghost in Hades), the story of Nergal and Ereshkigal eternally joins two hot-blooded protagonists.

The Wrath of Erra

Characters

Erra, god of devastation and lord of the netherworld (=Nergal)
Ishum, Erra's faithful vizier and god of fire
Marduk, chief god of Babylon

Plot

The story opens with the god of war in the grip of lethargy. Even his weapons, gathering dust in storage, complain. Their rebuke rouses him from inertia and he decides, contrary to Ishum's counsel, to conquer Babylon. In order to distract its patron god Marduk, Erra accuses Marduk of dressing shabbily. Chagrined, Marduk repairs to his tailor while Erra offers to mind the store (Babylon). Seizing this opportunity, Erra attacks Babylon and rains down indiscriminate destruction upon its people. Once again, Ishum counsels prudence, but to no avail. Young and old are put to death, fathers bury their sons, and the righteous perish together with the wicked. Sated with bloodshed, Erra

finally relents, prophesying that one day, after an era of universal warfare, a new military leader will arise and unify the people. Now in the company of the other gods, Erra justifies his actions as simply an expression of the kind of god he is ("When I get angry, I break things!"). Ishum then prophesies that, thanks to Erra's restraint, a remnant will remain that will eventually flourish anew. The poem concludes with a paean of praise for Erra, god of war.

Commentary

This poem vividly portrays the savagery of war, and the bloodlust that colored so much of Mesopotamian history. The poem's most horrifying aspect is that it does not condemn war, but instead regards it as an inevitable part of the human condition. Historically, the description of Babylon as disheveled suggests that the events of the poem refer to a time when Babylon and its empire were in decline, but a time (cf. Erra's lethargy) when full-scale aggression against her had not yet broken out. The image of the "remnant" recalls the imagery of the Hebrew prophets who looked toward the day when the survivors of the Babylonian Captivity would be gathered together by God's faithfulness and returned to their homeland. The "Wrath of Erra" may date to the eighth century B.C.E., or about two centuries before the captivity took place.

The Story of Enki and Ninhursag

Characters

Enki, god of subterranean freshwater
Ninhursag, a goddess of the earth

Plot

This mythic story takes place in a watery and fertile paradise-like land called Dilmun, where no one dies. The god Enki impregnates the goddess Ninhursag, who gives birth to a daughter. Enki then impregnates his daughter and, later, his granddaughter. Before he can impregnate his great-granddaughter, she insists upon his first giving her gifts of vegetables and fruit. After receiving them, she sleeps with her great-grand-father, but she does not give birth to a child. Somehow, Ninhursag uses Enki's semen to produce eight different plants that Enki later picks and eats. Angry at him for uprooting the plants, Ninhursag curses him and disappears. Enki pines away for her until a clever fox lures her back to Dilmun. As Ninhursag and Enki have intercourse, she asks him if he feels pain in any part of his body. Eight times he replies in the affirmative, naming the part of his body that hurts, and eight times Ninhursag names a corresponding god that is then born of his pain. Enki appoints the last to rule as lord of Dilmun.

Commentary

The details of this story may seem bizarre (serial incest among the gods, sexual intercourse for the purposes of horticulture, and psychosomatic coitus, not to mention a cameo appearance by Reynard the Fox), but underlying them is a vital theme: fertility and fecundity and the inscrutable power of the divine that generates both. The story also teaches us how different from ours are ancient Mesopotamian sensibilities, at least until we reflect upon the frequent occurrence of serial divorce, child abuse, artificial insemination, psychosomatic illness, and genetically manipulated food production in our own contemporary society. The only difference is that we don't attach these processes to our concept of God.

The Defeat of Zu

Characters
Zu, a divine bird
Enlil, the ruler of the gods
Ea, the god of cleverness and wisdom
Ninurta, a warlike divine champion

Plot
This three-tablet epic from Old Babylonian and Assyrian times is based upon a character who first appears in Sumerian myth, Zu, a god-like bird. According to the story, the Zu-bird steals the Tablet of Destinies from the supreme god Enlil and thus arrogates to himself the control of the universe. The Zu-bird has flown off with the tablet, and now the gods must choose a champion to secure its return. Ninurta, the god who is selected, attacks Zu in the air over a mountain range, but his missile attack fails: because it possesses the Tablet of Destinies, Zu has the power to order Ninurta's weapons to disassemble themselves and revert to the places of their origin: the bow to the woodland, the gut bowstring to a sheep, the shafts of the arrows to a canebrake, and the arrows' feathers to birds. Urged on by the god Ea to launch another attack, Ninurta assails Zu with powerful winds that tear its wings off and render it defenseless. Ninurta then slits the Zu-bird's throat and recovers the precious Tablet of Destinies.

Commentary

In divine terms, the epic describes how the benign order of collaborative government can be threatened by a single individual's arbitrary seizure of power and how, in the end, such treason is inevitably punished. The myth may therefore have served as an object lesson in real life to forewarn potential political traitors of the deadly consequences of their designs.

Fragmentary Epics

The original length of the foregoing epics can only be approximated due to the breakage of the fragile tablets on which they were written. In fact, a number of other Mesopotamian epics once existed, but today they survive only in random fragments like the scattered pieces of incomplete jigsaw puzzles. Belonging to different tablets and even to different chronological periods, the pieces can be arranged on the scholar's worktable to create the semblance of a narrative order, but gaping holes remain, often for those parts of the picture we would most want to see. Yet because the stories themselves are so intrinsically fascinating, they deserve to be heard again despite the tentative quality of their present reconstruction. Perhaps in the future other pieces of these literary puzzles will be found in the dust, making their pictures complete. Here then are their outlines.

The Story of Atrahasis

Characters
Enlil, the supreme god of heaven
Ea, the god of cleverness and wisdom
Atrahasis, a pious man

Plot
Disturbed by mankind's noisiness, the god Enlil determines to eliminate the problem of noise pollution by reducing the earth's population. First he causes devastating famine and disease, but when these are not totally effective, he decides to drown humanity in heavy rains. Anguished at the human suffering and selfishness he has witnessed during the crisis, Atrahasis prays to Enlil for divine help. Ea responds by telling Atrahasis to build a big boat and put food on it along with birds and beasts, men skilled in crafts, and members of his own family.

This Assyrian and Old Babylonian tale is antedated by an earlier Sumerian one in which the character known as Atra(m)hasis is called Ziusdra. Ziusdra is described as a pious king who receives divine instruction to build an ark. After seven days and seven nights of rain, Ziusdra looks out from the ark and sees sunlight. He is then granted immortality and is allowed to dwell in a paradise called Dilmun.

Commentary
The character of Ziusdra and Atrahasis and their stories prefigure Utnapishtim and his narrative of the Deluge in the *Epic of Gilgamesh*,

where the account is longer and richer in detail. The biblical account of Noah and the ark drew upon this Mesopotamian epic tradition for its literary inspiration.

The Story of Adapa

Characters
Adapa, a hero
Anu, god of the sky
Ea, god of cleverness and wisdom

Plot
Drowning in the sea in the midst of a storm, Adapa curses the wind and causes it to stop by breaking its wing. Distressed that the wind no longer blows, the sky-god Anu summons Adapa to heaven. Before Adapa goes, Ea, the god of wisdom, advises him not to eat or drink while he is there or he will die. Adapa complies, not realizing the food and drink he is offered are really a means to become immortal.

Commentary
The myth of Adapa tells us that man was not meant to live forever. Even when the food and drink of eternal life were within his grasp, he chose not to taste them. In the end, he was betrayed by one of the gods (or, in a more humanistic interpretation, by his own flawed intellectual assumptions).

The Adventure of Etana

Characters
A snake
An eagle
Shamash, the sun-god
Etana, a hero

Plot
The city of Kish is in need of a king, and the god Enlil has selected Etana for the job, but Etana lacks a son who could become his royal heir.

Meanwhile, a snake and an eagle make a pact pledging their mutual cooperation: while each in turn hunts for food, the one will not eat the other's young. The eagle, however, breaks the pact by devouring the snake's offspring. The snake appeals to the god Shamash in whose name both creatures had sworn. Shamash advises the snake to hide inside the carcass of a bull; when the eagle crawls inside to pick at the meat, the snake should seize it, sever its wings, and hurl it into a bottomless pit.

Soon after, Etana prays to Shamash for offspring of his own. In response, Shamash tells Etana about the eagle's plight and advises him to seek the eagle's help in securing a magic "birth plant."

Etana finds the pit where the eagle is trapped and, after a long period of physical therapy and rehabilitation, helps the eagle to fly once again. The eagle then in gratitude offers to fly Etana up to heaven so he can get the magic "birth plant" from Ishtar, goddess of sexuality. Etana climbs onto the eagle's back and they go for a test flight. As they reach an altitude of three miles, Etana becomes fearful and asks the eagle to land. Once on the ground, Etana climbs on the eagle's back once again, and again they take off, climbing higher and higher, until they reach heaven.

Though the final tablet ends here, the Sumerian King-list reports that Etana not only ruled Kish but also had an heir, so apparently the second flight was a success and Etana returned to earth with the miracle cure he had sought.

Commentary
This tale blends together an Aesopian fable with the essence of heroic adventure. Particularly graphic is the description of the progressively shrinking landscape as Etana and the eagle look down at first from one mile up, then from two, and lastly from three. Like the view from an ascending rocket, the green Mesopotamian countryside comes to resemble a little garden and the sea a small water-filled bucket. The image of manned flight via eagle recurs in the Greek myth of Ganymede, who

was borne up to heaven, and the Arabic tale of Sinbad and the bird known as the Rukh. The ancient story of Etana is also notable for its literary treatment of the theme of male infertility and the search for a medicinal cure.

Ninurta and Agag

Characters
Ninurta, a heroic king
Sharur, his magic weapon (endowed with speech)
Agag, a rebel leader

Plot
The Sumerian story tells how Ninurta battled Agag, a spirit of nature (possibly a mighty tree) that led a rebellious rabble of plants and stones in an invasion of Ninurta's territory. With the help of his talking weapon, Sharur, he defeats Agag by using rain to quell a dust-storm whipped up by his enemy. Next (in what may originally have been a separate tale), Ninurta raises up foothills to make rain flow south into the Tigris so farmers can thereby use its waters to irrigate their fields. Lastly, Ninurta pronounces judgment upon the various types of stone that had been Agag's accomplices in his rebellion. In a long passage, he assigns a specific function to each of Mesopotamia's minerals. At the fragmentary conclusion of the epic, the god Enlil sings Ninurta's praises; the goddess of writing, Nidaba, through whose powers Ninurta's deeds will be preserved, is celebrated; and Ninurta himself is honored by the poet.

Commentary
The epic begins with an imaginative variation on the theme of military invasion. After its "Sorcerer's Apprentice" opening, the epic then turns etiological, delving into the origins of agricultural irrigation and explaining why different kinds of stones are used for different purposes. The epic's conclusion extols the art of writing's importance.

Lugalbanda and the Thunderbird

Characters
Lugalbanda, a warrior from Uruk
Thunderbird, a divine bird
Enmerkar, king of Uruk
Inanna, the goddess of sexual love

Plot
The beginning of this Sumerian epic presupposes an earlier event: the war between Uruk and Aratta. Recovering from illness in a cave where he has been left behind by his fellow soldiers, Lugalbanda becomes well enough to travel to the front to rejoin his comrades. On the way, he comes upon the nest of a giant bird, and he feeds and cares for the bird's young. When the bird, the Thunderbird, returns, it expresses its gratitude by offering Lugalbanda a reward. Lugalbanda asks for speed and endurance, which are granted to him. When he reaches the army, he finds that its commander in chief, Enmerkar, is about to call off the siege of Aratta. Needing the goddess Inanna's permission to do so, Enmerkar calls upon Lugalbanda to hasten to Uruk to seek the goddess' blessing. The goddess instead sends instructions to Enmerkar to eat a special fish and feed it to his troops. This diet, according to the broken tablet, will bring them victory. Regretably, the text ends before dinner is served!

Commentary
The plot blends wartime realism with fantasy. The theme of a hero who is rewarded by a great bird he has befriended is found in another Mesopotamian epic, *The Adventure of Etana*, though the reward in each case is different. Above all, the story teaches that people can be granted special powers by the divine if they are merciful and obedient.

The Tukulti-Ninurta Epic

Characters
Tukulti-Ninurta I (Assyrian king: 1244–1208 B.C.E.)

Kashtiliash IV (Kassite king of Babylonia and Tukulti-Ninurta's contemporary)
Chorus of Assyrian soldiers

Plot
Ignoring his treaty with Tukulti-Ninurta, Kashtiliash prepares to make war against Assyria. Tukulti-Ninurta seeks rapprochement but is rebuffed. Praying for divine aid, the Assyrian king then launches a preemptive invasion of Babylonia. A fearful Kashtiliash offers resistance, but his army is routed and he himself flees the battlefield. Praising Tukulti-Ninurta's valor, his soldiers urge him to attack again and secure a decisive victory. The Assyrian army then triumphs and plunders Babylonia. The treasure is transported to Assyria's capital, Kar-Tukulti-Ninurta, where it enriches the temples of the gods. The poem concludes with a celebration of Tukulti-Ninurta's piety.

Commentary
This is Assyrian literature's only native epic, and it is significant that it deals with what the Assyrians were most proud of: their capacity to shape history through the exercise of force. Rather than dwell on mythology, the poet chooses recent military events as the material most worthy of his talents and constructs an encomium in praise of his king, a monarch who is portrayed as both pious and brave. Indeed, it is likely the poem was given its first public reading in the palace before Tukulti-Ninurta himself and his courtiers. On a separate note, it is interesting that the poem's inventory of Babylonian plunder includes works of literature as well as gold.

Historical Chronicles

The archaeologist who digs into the earth seeks not gold but history. His quarry, however, is an elusive one, the more so the deeper he digs. No living witnesses remain, and artifacts alone are mute. Even the testimony of literature is suspect, especially when—like epic—it is based more on imagination than on fact.

The archaeologist's quest is made easier by those who in ancient times sought to chronicle their own past. The record they left behind is incomplete and often very subjective. It is usually content to list events in mere chronological order rather than to explore their causal connection. And it is not "scientific," since it assumes the hand of God shapes the affairs of man. But these very limitations teach us how the ancients understood history, and therefore illuminate the Mesopotamian mind in a way that sterile objectivity could not.

The earliest documents we have, from Sumerian times, are written on clay. The later ones, from Old Babylonian, Assyrian, and Neo-Babylonian times, are frequently inscribed on stone. These later documents are more numerous, in part because stone is more durable than clay, but in larger part because the imperialistic kings whose deeds they describe loved to trumpet their accomplishments. Thus their achievements are inscribed on the pavements of temples, the walls of palaces, the bases of statues, and on sculpted cylinders, barrels, multi-sided prisms, and stelae of stone. As a result, the kings have triumphed over their adversaries not only in war but also in remembrance.

Among the oldest Sumerian works we possess is the "Sumerian King-list." Though the text dates backs about 2100 B.C.E., its narrative recalls events that it asserts took place 241,000 years before the primordial Flood. Declaring that kingship came from heaven, it lists the monarchs who ruled Sumer's cities both before and after the cataclysm, beginning with A-lulim of Eridu, who reigned—it says—for 28,800 years. In chronological sequence, the names of other kings and the lengths of their reigns are cited (including the 27th king, Dumuzi, the husband of the goddess Inanna, who ruled for 100 years; and the 28th, the hero Gilgamesh, who ruled for 126). The list also mentions key

military defeats that shifted supreme power from city to city. The larger-than-life reigns, incidentally, are reminiscent of the genealogies in the early chapters of Genesis.

Another important text is the "Sargon Chronicle," which comes down to us in a Neo-Babylonian transcription. The chronicle paints the rise of Sargon of Akkad with broad and dramatic brushstrokes, focusing not on chronology but on action, including an act of sacrilege that brought down upon Sargon the divine vengeance of Marduk.

The career of another famous king, Hammurabi of Babylon, can be reconstructed thanks to the official custom of naming each of the years in a king's reign after a memorable deed he performed. Forty-three surviving "year names" pay special attention to Hammurabi's piety in erecting temples and statues to the gods and to his civic leadership in constructing and restoring canals and walls. His military triumphs are also recounted de rigueur.

For the kings of Assyria, however, military triumphs were the main bill. Supreme egotists as well as conquerors, they composed autobiographies and ordered them inscribed in monumental stone for all to see. One such autobiography contains over 1,300 neatly chiseled cuneiform lines of self-congratulation. We read how monarchs smashed their enemies like clay pots, used blood to dye the mountains red, and leveled cities like torrents of a flood. Conspirators might be punished by having their tongues torn out, or by having their heads crushed with stone idols and their corpses cut into small pieces and fed to dogs, pigs, and vultures. The compliant would be allowed to kiss the king's feet after their tribute had been duly itemized and tallied. The Assyrian autobiographies (of such kings as Tiglathpileser, Shalmaneser III, Sennacherib, and Ashurbanipal) also give step-by-step accounts of their military campaigns and victories (including Sennacherib's siege of

Jerusalem). Needless to say, royal defeats are not highlighted.

Western civilization would have to wait for over two centuries for Greek historians like Herodotus and Thucydides to probe the role that human nature plays in history. Without meaning to, however, the royal chronicles of Mesopotamia have much to say to us about humanity's dark side as well as its occasional conscientious capacity for constructive good.

Legal Documents

The Mesopotamians believed their ruler was an instrument of God who brought justice to an imperfect human society. To organize his divinely inspired vision of an ideal society, the ruler applied the force of law and used the instrument of writing to give it permanent and, eventually, public form. By compiling legal standards and displaying them on inscribed stelae, the ruler gave monumental expression to his desire for civic order and enduring justice.

THE CODE OF HAMMURABI

The most outstanding example of this desire is the 18th-century B.C.E. Code of Hammurabi, king of Babylon. It has been described by Cyrus H. Gordon as "the apex of legal codification prior to Roman Law" (Gordon 1957: 2). But the code's sociological value exceeds its place in the history of jurisprudence. As a summary of everyday life in ancient times, Gordon adds, it is "our chief single source for reconstructing the society of Old Babylonia" and our "best available mirror of Mesopotamian society" (Gordon 1957: 3). Carved on a 6.5-foot-tall monolith of smooth and hard black diorite, the Code of Hammurabi is an imperishable time capsule from a lost civilization.

The code consists of 282 laws in forthright prose framed by a lengthy and elaborate pro-

5.8 *The Code of Hammurabi is preserved on this inscribed and sculpted block of stone housed in the Louvre.* (Rogers, *A History of Babylonia and Assyria*, 1915; picture courtesy Mansell, 1915)

logue and epilogue in verse. The laws are organized into topical categories (such as family law and property rights), with legal principles clearly expounded according to a standard case formula ("If such-and-such happens, then such-and-such will be done.") The poetic prologue and epilogue stylistically elevate the prosaic center section and provide the spiritual rationale for obedience: Hammurabi was mandated by none other than Shamash, god of the sun and justice, and Marduk, chief god of Babylon, to enact these statutes for the betterment of society; he who obeys will be blessed and he who disobeys will be punished by heaven. The divine source of the law is further illustrated at the top of the stela by a relief that shows Hammurabi piously standing before Shamash's throne as he receives the god's instruction—a powerful image meant to impress even the illiterate. By both its visual and literary structure, Hammurabi's stela communicates the imperative of order.

EARLIER CODES

Hammurabi's, however, was not the first Mesopotamian code of law. Another Akkadian code, two centuries earlier, has been found in the city of Eshnunna, but without a formal prologue and epilogue. Somewhat earlier is the Sumerian code of Lipit-Ishtar, copied in clay from the text of a now-missing stone stela. Only 37 laws are legible on the broken tablet along with a prologue and epilogue (with blessing and curse) in prose. Still earlier is the 21st-century B.C.E. Sumerian code of Ur-Nammu, of which only five statutes can be deciphered. The oldest code we know of, however, was promulgated by a Sumerian ruler named Urukagina, who reigned around 2350 B.C.E., over six centuries before Hammurabi. In a fragmentary inscription in clay, the king enumerates various social injustices and cites the legal measures he will institute to correct them. Though not the oldest, Hammurabi's Code is nevertheless the most complete and detailed legal document we possess from Mesopotamia's long history. Later laws on clay tablets have been unearthed dating to Assyrian and Neo-Babylonian times, and other laws—even older that Urukagina's—may even now lie buried in neglected mounds.

CONTRACTS

Though not matching law codes in regal splendor, another category of legal documents surpasses them in sheer abundance: contracts. In fact, of the tens of thousands of cuneiform tablets found in Sumer, nine out of 10 are contractual in nature. Like the codes, the contracts follow a formulaic pattern established by tradition. First the subject is stated (the purchase of a slave, an exchange of property, the arrangement of a marriage), followed by the names of the contracting parties and the details of their transaction. The document concludes with the names and seals of witnesses, the name of the scribe, and the seals of the principals to the agreement, with the place and date of the transaction sometimes appended. Such contracts reveal the highly organized nature of ancient Mesopotamian civilization and the pervasive role of commerce in everyday life. More than the abstract codes, these humble documents disclose by the cumulative weight of their mundane particulars the humanity of the past.

Divination Texts

To many, history is a dull subject because the past lacks excitement. After all, they say, it's all so predictable: this happened in one century, and that happened in the next. In actuality, however, the past was not predictable at all for those who lived it. *We* may know what was going to happen, but *they* certainly did not—not the next century nor even the next day.

In fact, precisely because of their historical myopia, the people of the past passionately cared to know what the future held. This was especially true of the people in ancient Mesopotamia, who used a variety of methods to foretell the future and employed specialists to do the job.

The Mesopotamians' bent for futurism was predicated on the belief that human affairs and the natural environment are interrelated. What was going to happen to human beings on earth, they believed, was already inscribed in the book of nature. By drawing upon arcane knowledge and applying traditional skills, a seer could discern the shape of things to come. By studying the appropriate omens, such a seer could determine in advance whether a contemplated course of action would lead to failure or success.

Divination was based on the idea that association is tantamount to causality: that is, if two unusual events occur in proximity, one is responsible for the other. Thus if a king died after an eclipse, the conclusion was reached that the eclipse foreshadowed his death. Likewise, if a shooting star was sighted the night before a military victory, a later sighting foretold yet another military success.

For most of Mesopotamian history, divination was used to guide the affairs of state. Few rulers would make or act upon an important decision without first consulting their royal fortunetellers.

To predict the future, Mesopotamian seers studied celestial and meteorological phenomena and examined the organs and entrails of sacrificial animals. Though they didn't read tea leaves, they did scrutinize oil (how drops dispersed on the surface of water in a bowl) and smoke (how wisps curled up from a censer) for clues about what lay ahead. In effect, the ancient seer was like the modern weatherman who uses his professional expertise to forecast what the future holds for us.

ASTROLOGY

In Mesopotamia, astrology was the premier means of divination, for the ancient Mesopotamians believed our destinies are written in the skies.

In the 21st century, we are blinded to the luminous stars and planets of a pitch-black night by the ambient light of 24/7 electric cities. The ancients, however, gazing upward at the stars slowly wheeling across the dark expanse of the heavens, stood in the presence of an awesome mystery. In the scattered stellar dots they discerned heavenly images and, by connecting the dots, drew constellations and gave them names. Some of these names—translated into Greek as Hydra, and into Latin as Taurus, Gemini, Cancer, Leo, Libra, Scorpio, Sagittarius, Capricorn, and Aquarius—are the names we still call them by. The Mesopotamians also followed the trails of five "wandering" stars, the planets Mercury, Venus, Mars, Jupiter, and Saturn. The evening and morning star, Venus, held special fascination for them and they named it, as did the later Romans, for the goddess of love.

The outer planets—Uranus, Neptune, and Pluto—were unknown to Mesopotamian astronomers because, though they were drawn to the numinous sky, they lacked a telescope to penetrate its deepest secrets. The best they could do was to use a forked stick or hollow tube, a telescope sans lens, for sighting.

The moon, with its changing phases and stunning Eclipses, became the essence of their cosmic calendar. Yet because a lunar year (12 cycles of about 29.5 days each) is shorter by about 11 days than a solar one, the lunar months and their religious holidays soon grew out of step with the seasons. The solution was to insert extra, or intercalary, months at regular intervals to bring the lunar year back into alignment with the solar. This seemingly awkward lunar calendar was inherited by the later inhabitants of the Near East and is still used by pious Jews and Muslims to mark the sacred passage of the months and their holy occasions. Indeed, to this very day the ancient Babylonian names for the months are echoed in the litany of month-names found in the Jewish calendar.

As a result of their painstaking observation of celestial phenomena over the course of many centuries, Mesopotamian priests accumulated in diaries and almanacs a vast store of mathematical information about the operation of the cosmos: the regular movements of stars and planets, the cycle of eclipses of sun and moon, and the appearance of comets. This written information ultimately served as an invaluable database for the later scientific speculations and theories of the Hellenistic Greeks. The Christian Middle Ages likewise stood in awe of "Chaldaean science" as Mesopotamian astronomy came to be called, in particular because its lore had inspired the Three Magi to follow the "star of Bethlehem."

Like the Magi of the New Testament, the priests of Mesopotamia viewed astronomy not as an end in itself but as a means to a higher spiritual truth. Their concern for most of their history was not with astronomy as a science but with astrology as an art by which the future could be divined through the discovery of omens good and bad to inform political decision making and assure personal success. No less an Old Testament prophet than Isaiah, however, railed against Babylonian kings who dared think that astrology could shield them from Jehovah's vengeance. "Let the astrologists, stargazers, and monthly prognosticators stand up," he said, "and try to save you from what is coming" (47:13). In a latter day, Adolf Hitler too fell under astrology's spell, only to learn its shortcomings in war.

Numerous texts survive that reveal Mesopotamia's fascination with the skies. Most were preserved in Ashurbanipal's library found at Nineveh. They include astronomical diaries, mathematical tables on celestial subjects, and instructional manuals for interpreting heavenly signs.

Three works have special significance. The first is *Enuma elish* ("When on high . . ."), the Babylonian *Epic of Creation*, which can be dated back to at least the first millennium B.C.E. Tablet V describes how Marduk, the god of Babylon, fashioned the heavens and formed the

constellations. Another work, *Enuma Anu Enlil* ("When [the gods] Anu and Enlil . . ."), may be even older, and systematically lists omens under the categories of moon, sun, weather, and stars. Another seventh century B.C.E. treatise, *Mul Apin* (named for the "Plough Star" that begins its narrative), divides the stars and constellations into three parallel belts, each ruled by a different god: Enlil, Anu (in the middle), and Ea. By the fifth century B.C.E., as our texts show, the astrologers had divided the night sky into three belts that were now circular and concentric. These were divided by 12 radii into 12 equal pie-slice segments of 30 degrees, each marked by a sign—the origin of the now-familiar zodiac.

It was in the fifth century also that astrology took a personal turn. Whereas previously astrologers had focused on kings and the fate of nations, now for the first time they began to offer their services to ordinary clients, specifically the parents of newborn babies. A small number of inscriptions, dating between the fifth and third centuries B.C.E. reveal that astronomers were hired to predict a child's future based on the infant's birth date or presumed date of conception. Thanks to the detailed astronomical information contained in the horoscopes, we can actually calculate the month, day, and year a given child began its life. One such horoscope reads:

> In the year 48 of the Seleucid era (=263 B.C.E.) on the night of the twenty-third of Adar (February/March), a child was born. At the same time the Sun was 30 degrees into Aries; the Moon ten degrees into Aquarius; Jupiter at the start of Leo; Venus with the Sun; Mercury with the Sun; Saturn in Cancer; and Mars at Cancer's end. . . . He won't be rich. His appetite won't be satisfied. What he has when he is young he will lose. But then for 36 years he will prosper, and his life will be long . . .

Not all such texts are found on clay tablets. Over 70 years ago a young archaeologist named Jotham Johnson came upon the ruins of a private home in the ancient city of Dura-Europos. Scratched onto the plastered wall was a sketch of the zodiac with astronomical notations in the Greek alphabet, the script then used by Dura's Hellenistic population. Though the plaster was cracked, Johnson labored over the enigma until he had deciphered the names of planets and the signs of the zodiac where they had stood when the child was born.

A horoscope, yes—but what year, what month, what day? On his return to Yale, young Johnson turned to the university's Department of Astronomy. Six weeks later, after a number of celestial calculations to determine when all of the planets could have been aligned the way the sketch portrayed them, Johnson had his answer: July 3, 176 C.E. More than that, the Yale astronomers were able to give him the time of birth: about 10 P.M.

10 P.M. almost two millennia ago. Nighttime in Roman Dura. A baby cries in a bedroom lit by a flickering oil lamp. We still do not know the child's name, or the fortune the stars foretold.

ANIMAL AUTOPSIES

Besides looking up to the sky to predict the future, the priests of Mesopotamia also looked down at the organs and entrails of animals sacrificed, a practice known as *extispicy*. From these ancient biopsies, the priests believed they could tell whether circumstances were auspicious or inauspicious for a course of action their king was contemplating. The most favored organ for these readings was the liver, regarded as the seat of emotions. Next in importance came the animal's lungs and intestines. To guide them in their determinations (and to aid in the training of apprentice diviners), the priests had recourse to clay models of the organs in question, appropriately labeled in cuneiform with the key features of an organ and their spiritual meaning. Finding a malformed organ was a bad omen for sure. In addition to the clay models, we also have texts that enumerate the telltale signs an augur should look for and what his prognosis should be. The formulaic pattern is: "If X is found, then . . . or, with more detail, "If X is found and Y is present also, then . . ."

Besides guiding policy, extispicy was also applied in elections to high office: as each candidate was presented, the omens were taken. If the omens were unfavorable, the next candidate stepped up, and so on until a winner emerged. Such a system led to the election of king Nabonidus's daughter as high priestess of the moon god, Nanna. Of course, it would have been embarrassing if the king's daughter had *not* been chosen, so we have grounds for suspecting some priestly collusion in the outcome—if not a stuffed ballot box, then a stuffed sheep, stuffed with the best-looking liver that had been seen in many a moon. The desire to please at all costs is also evident in reports submitted by royal astrologers, who sometimes go out of their way to show that the stars favor what the king has already done.

For the priest, however, who took his sacred craft seriously, divine will was immanent in the things of this world. Such priestly piety and humility infuse a remarkable ancient poem called "The Prayer to the Gods of the Night," which was composed sometime between 2000 and 1500 B.C.E. In it, a priest readies a lamb so that from its flesh a vision of the future might emerge. Historian Giorgio Buccellati sets the scene: "The suppliant is standing on the roof of a temple, looking at a world asleep. It is a calm and dark night: even the moon and the brightest star (the morning star) are absent. The fire on the roof and the constellations in the sky are the only source of light, and to them the suppliant turns as operative sources of truth" (Buccellati 1995: 1693). Here are the priest's ancient words:

The gods of heaven repose;
the doors of their palace are locked.
The people on earth lie down;
the gates of their cities are shut.
All gods, all goddesses —
Sun and Moon, Morning-Star and Storm —
have gone to sleep,
suspending their judgment,
withholding their verdict.
The curtain of night has fallen;
the shrines and temples are dark.
The traveler murmurs his last utterance;
the litigant stills his plea.
Even Shamash, guardian of justice,
has gone to bed.

O great gods of the night —
of Fire and the Netherworld;
O Constellations and Stars
looking down;
watch over me as I offer
this sacrifice.
Harken to my prayer.

Hymns and Prayers

The "Prayer to the Gods of the Night" printed above belongs to an important genre of poetic literature in which the writer (and speaker) addresses the divine. In such a work, one or more gods may be praised through a commendatory account of the divine attributes they possess and the blessings they bestow. This praise can then be followed by a petition from the worshiper asking for the god's help and concluding with an affirmation of faith. In their sensibility and imagery, these Mesopotamian hymns and prayers remind us of the Psalms of the Old Testament; indeed, the Psalms vividly reflect the historic influence of Mesopotamian spirituality and expression on Hebraic thought, an influence that transcended the difference between the number of gods each people worshiped.

Most of the hymns were probably composed by priests, and they were set down in writing as an act of piety. Once transcribed, the words of praise could then be recopied and recited by others. Such songs of praise may have been accompanied by instrumental music (as when the psalmist, King David, strummed his harp), but we cannot say with certainty.

The hymns provide us with the names of the major divinities the Mesopotamians worshiped and tell us where their chief temples were located. The most elaborate hymns are like spiritual kaleidoscopes, radiant with divine epithets and attributes and illuminated with colorful shards of myth ("O Adad, god of thunder, warrior who wields lightning, whose gentle rain makes the fields rejoice . . .").

If the hymns of Mesopotamia illuminate the gods, it is the prayers that teach us about humanity, for in prayers we encounter the hopes and fears of everyday mortal life. Why such earnest messages should ever have been committed to writing is difficult to explain. Those who uttered and transcribed the prayers may have believed that their sentiments, expressed through the originally sacred medium of writing, might thereby more readily reach the ears (and eyes) of the gods. Another possibility is that prayers set down in writing were deposited in— and thus, like letters, delivered to—the holy temples where the gods dwelled.

What the people prayed for is instructive: to be cured of disease, freed of infirmity, absolved of guilt, safeguarded from enemies, protected from family ghosts, shielded from witchcraft, and to attain professional success. In one striking example, a suffering soul—uncertain of what sin he may have committed or what deity he may have offended—prays to all gods for forgiveness of all possible sins—the first "to whom it may concern" letter in history sent to heaven.

The sin I have committed I know not;
the forbidden thing I have done I do not know.

Some god has turned his rage against me;
some goddess has aimed her ire.
I cry for help but no one takes my hand.
I weep but no one comforts me.
God, Goddess, Whoever you are,
forgive me and I will give you praise.

There are also some prayers from the mouths of Assyria's kings. An ailing Ashurnasirpal I implores Ishtar to restore his vigor; a scholarly Ashurbanipal petitions Nabu, patron of scribes, for divine blessing; and Nabonidus, Assyria's last king, with unconscious irony prays to Shamash for lasting dominion. To make their intent more indelible, such royal prayers were often inscribed on the thresholds and steps of palaces and temples and even on the bricks that paved ceremonial avenues.

Most remarkable of all is a lengthy prayer composed by Enheduanna, daughter of the third millennium B.C.E. monarch Sargon of Akkad. Her father, it seems, had appointed her high priestess of the moon-god Nanna, the patron god of Ur. But political contention and religious turmoil put her position—and perhaps, even, her life—at risk. In her prayer she pleads with the formidable goddess Ishtar to champion her cause, and recounts her suffering:

The day came: I was burned by the sun;
The night came: I was blown by the wind.
My voice fails me;
Pleasure is turned to dust . . .
I have come to a harbor of sorrows.
There I will die with this hymn on my lips.

Lamentations

Grief is raised from a personal to a communal level in another genre of poetry that began in Sumerian times, the genre of lamentation. In this type of literature, the poets' concerns are not with their own suffering and fate but with the suffering and fate of their city-state as a consequence of war. These poems of lamentation decry the destruction of the cities themselves and their temples, and the pain inflicted upon a vanquished people. As the poems reveal, the people's affliction is made all the more intense by the realization that they are being punished by God. Ultimately, however, these "city laments," as they are called, become hymns of redemption, for in their concluding stanzas they tell of how the power and glory of each community were ultimately restored by divine intervention. It is for this reason that the poems were for centuries thereafter publicly recited by priests as patriotic and spiritual anthems.

It is their "happy endings" that make the Sumerian laments so different from the biblical book of Lamentations, which they otherwise resemble and indeed inspired. For the Jewish people the destruction of Jerusalem and its temple in 586 B.C.E. was followed by exile; only in later days under the leadership of Ezra and Nehemiah was a victorious ending appended to their story, an ending that sadly would not be lasting.

As historical documents, the laments over the destruction of such cities as Ur and Nippur graphically illustrate the instability of ancient Mesopotamian life and the capriciousness of gods who, unlike their Hebraic counterpart, offered no moral lesson to justify their wrath. In the verses of these poems, moreover, we encounter a universality of wartime suffering that transcends time.

During the siege:

Inside, outside, is the same:
Only death.
Without, the enemy's spear;
Within, famine's knife . . .
Hunger contorts the belly,
Twists the face.

During the attack:

My eyes can no longer behold
The slashing of mothers' wombs.

In the aftermath:

> Dead men, not potsherds
> littered the way.
> In the wide streets
> where the crowds once gathered and cheered,
> the corpses lay scattered.
> In the fields where the dancers once danced
> the dead were heaped in piles.
>
> Congealed blood plugged up the walls.
> Flesh oozed beneath the rotting sun.
>
> On the boulevards where people used to
>   promenade
> The fat of corpses melts.

*   *   *

> This is my house:
>   where food is not eaten,
>   where drink is not drunk,
>   where seats are not sat in,
>   where beds are not made,
>   where jars lie empty,
>   and cups are overturned,
>   where harps no longer vibrate
>   and tunes no longer sing.
>
> This is my house:
>   without a husband,
>   without a child
>   without even
>   me.

It is images like these that shrink the centuries, putting the lie to the specious claim that in four thousand years humanity's cause has measurably improved. If anything, we have simply amplified suffering's scale.

Letters

ORIGIN

According to a Sumerian tale, the desire to write a letter inspired the invention of writing.

Once upon a time, as the story goes, two kings vied with each other for supremacy: the king of Uruk in southern Iraq and the king of Aratta in Iran. Instead of making war against one another, they engaged in an international battle of wits, using riddles as their weapons. Whoever failed to solve his opponent's riddle would be the loser. A messenger acted as a go-between, memorizing each riddle, reporting it orally, and returning with the recipient's answer. Because the kings were well matched, the intellectual contest wore on and on with each successive riddle becoming more complicated than the last. Finally, the poor messenger's memory circuits overloaded and crashed. Undaunted, the king of Uruk (named Enmerkar) took a piece of clay, patted it flat, and inscribed it with the blunt end of a reed, making the world's first written symbols. He then sent the tablet to his opponent who, in utter bafflement at the meaning of the visual riddle, threw up his hands and admitted defeat.

According to another Sumerian tale, a much darker motive inspired the world's first letter. As the story goes, the king of Kish had an ambitious cupbearer named Sargon whom he feared might someday seize the throne. To prevent this, he wrote a message on a clay tablet and enclosed it in another piece of clay, thus creating the first envelope in history. "Take this to the king Lugalzagesi of Uruk," he said, and gave the sealed letter to Sargon. The message inside: "Kill the bearer of this letter!" Like the Greek hero Bellerophon who was targeted in a similar way, Sargon sidestepped disaster and went on to achieve greatness.

Each of those tales is surely woven on the loom of imagination, but some of the yarn is spun from history. Both stories involve the city of Uruk, where in fact archaeologists have unearthed samples of Mesopotamia's most ancient writing system, a pictographic script that became the ancestor of classic cuneiform. Legend places Enmerkar, the hero of the first story, in the early third millennium B.C.E., close to the time when writing was indeed invented; while history puts Sargon in the latter part of the millennium, the date of our earliest cuneiform letters.

One thing is certain: the letter was to become a major category of Mesopotamian writing.

PRESERVATION

Had they been written on paper, letters from Mesopotamia never would have survived; buried in damp soil, they would have readily disintegrated. But, made of clay, they endured. Unlike a modern letter, a Mesopotamian one couldn't be "torn up" or "crumpled"; tossed into a trash heap, it would still retain its shape. Indeed, even when cracked into pieces, its message can be restored to wholeness by the patience and diligence of the archaeologist and philologist. Some tablets, in fact, are oven-baked after excavation to insure their survival.

DELIVERY

The philatelist is bound to be stymied in his search for ancient postage stamps! The Mesopotamians never used stamps, but instead simply addressed the envelope with the name of the intended recipient (and sometimes the sender's own name) and entrusted the missive to a servant or peripatetic merchant to deliver with careful instructions as to where the addressee lived. Regretably, most of these clay envelopes are lost because they were immediately broken apart to get to the letters inside and then thrown away. The closest thing to a government postal service was the royal mail, but this was reserved for diplomatic and military communiqués transported by special messengers. Such a system was the product of imperialism and the territorial expansion of empire. For the average person, life was lived out mostly in one's home and neighborhood where formal letters were not needed because communication was more intimate and personal. Besides, given the complexity of cuneiform and the low level of popular literacy, composing a letter—or even reading one—normally required the paid services of a scribe.

STYLE

Instead of beginning with "Dear X" and concluding with "Yours truly, Y," an ancient Mesopotamian letter generally began with a single line naming the sender and the one to whom the message was directed ("Y says the following. Tell X that . . ."). Sometimes the addressee was named in the first line ("Tell X") and the sender simply signed the letter at the bottom with his seal.

Next might come an expression of respect for the recipient and a wish for his good health and the welfare of his household (assuming that the intent of the letter was reasonably friendly).

This then would be followed by the main body of the letter, a detailed statement outlining the writer's concerns and any actions he wished the recipient to take in response to them.

TONE

The tone of a letter reflected the relative status of the sender and the recipient. If someone of lower social status were writing to someone of higher social status (an underling corresponding with a ruler, for example), the tone would tend to be flattering and subservient ("I am but dirt beneath your feet.") If social equals were corresponding (for example, one king to another), the tone would tend to be proud but respectful, with one referring to the other as "brother" ("I and my household, my horses and chariots, and my officials and subjects are well. I trust things are well with my brother and his household, his horses and chariots, and his officials and subjects.") When a superior, however, was writing to an inferior, the tone could be direct and brusk and bereft of formal pleasantry ("Mark this urgent!" "I don't want to have to remind you about this matter again!" "Don't eat, drink, or even sit down till you get here!" "I don't want excuses!") A brief perusal of some of these Mesopotamian memos is enough to persuade us that stress must not have been an exclusively modern phenomenon.

CONTENT

Mesopotamian letters fall into a number of categories based on their subject-matter.

Royal Correspondence Among the historical treasures of Mesopotamia are letters from the archives of its kings. From the palace of Zimri-Lim at Mari come documents that detail the political uncertainty and shifting alliances that prevailed in the days before Hammurabi unified Babylonia. Communiqués concern the sending of ambassadors and the movement of troops, including intelligence reports on the enemy. Some letters contain advice offered by oracles and prophets to guide foreign policy. From Mari and elsewhere come letters that illuminate Hammurabi's own reign, especially in the correspondence he exchanges with subordinates. Other letters discovered in the ruins of Nineveh portray the life and times of Ashurbanipal and the later kings of Assyria and offer insights into their diplomatic, military, and domestic activities. These letters further reveal how omens and divination could determine the direction of government policy.

Here are some examples:

To his majesty, universal sovereign, from his servant, Nabu-shum-lishir:
May the gods Nabu and Marduk grant your royal majesty everlasting life.
When I sent soldiers from Birat on reconnaissance into the Babylonian marshland, they were attacked by Babylonian troops. They killed four of the enemy and took nine prisoners that are on their way to you.

To his royal majesty from his servant Bel-ikisha:
May Nabu and Marduk bless your royal majesty.
The members of your royal household whom you have chosen to promote (Tabzuai to the rank of captain, Nabu-sakip to the rank of adjutant, and Emur-ilishu to the rank of bodyguard) are all drunks and will be too drunk to stop a potential assassin from stabbing you. Because of what I know, I felt I had to write to you. Feel free, though, to use your own discretion.

To his royal majesty from his servant Kisir-Ashur:
Greetings!
When I went to Khorsabad, people there told me there had been an earthquake on the ninth of Adar. They said you'd want to know if it had done any damage to the city walls.
I'm pleased to report that the shrines and ziggurats, the palace and fortifications, and the houses of the city are in good shape.
I knew that when you heard about the earthquake in a day or two you'd want the latest report.

To his majesty, universal sovereign, from his servant, Bel-ushezib:
May Bel, Nabu, and Shamash bless your Majesty.
An eclipse is supposed to have occurred but was not visible here in the capital because of cloud cover. Your majesty should send messengers to various cities to find out if anyone sighted it.
Be sure to recite the necessary incantations to secure forgiveness for any sin.
The great gods who dwell in your city caused the clouds to obscure the eclipse as a way of saying that the eclipse would not bring harm to you or your country. Therefore rejoice!
The thunder-god Adad will be loudest during the month of Nisan, but the harvest will be unaffected.

To his royal majesty from your servant Nabu-nasir:

In response to your request for an official diagnosis, I have concluded you are suffering from an inflammation. An inflammation of the head, hands, and feet is dental in origin. Therefore your teeth should be extracted. Your pain will then subside, and your condition will improve.

Letters from the sands of ancient Egypt have also shed light on Mesopotamia. The 14th century B.C.E. was an age of internationalism in which various rulers of the Near East corresponded with Egypt's pharaohs: Amenhotep III, Amenhotep IV (better known as Akhenaten, the heretic pharaoh), and the boy-king Tutankhamun. Beginning in 1887, almost 400 letters were recovered from the deserted capital city of Akhetaten (modern Tell el Amarna). Known as the "Amarna letters," these documents underscore the tenuous and tense relationship that existed between and among the military superpowers of the day—the Egyptians, the Hittites, and the Mitanni—as a distracted Egypt began to lose its military grip on its vassal states in the Levant. Lesser players, eager to inflate their roles, also appear on the stage: the Babylonians and the Assyrians. All the while, Egypt's enemies hover like covetous vultures. "Send me more gold," they say. "In Egypt, gold is as plentiful as dirt."

Most striking is the fact that the letters are written in cuneiform on clay tablets, almost all in the Akkadian cuneiform, proof of the pervasive influence of Mesopotamian culture throughout the East Mediterranean world.

Business Correspondence The widespread use of the cuneiform script and Akkadian was due in considerable part to the international activity of Mesopotamian businessmen and the trading routes and colonies they established. The bulk of these letters concern commodities and payments due. The commodities include textiles, livestock, and grain—Mesopotamia's chief exports.

Scribal Exercises Except for merchants who kept their own books and were therefore literate, most letters we have come from the hands of professional scribes who took dictation from their masters and clients. Part of a scribe's education consisted of practicing the writing of formal letters. To give their students such practice, some scribal schools maintained collections of sample letters to serve as models for their students' work. Thanks to the repeated copying of such models, the texts of some historical letters have come down to us even though the originals have long since disappeared. Most notable among these are letters from some of the kings of Ur's glorious Third Dynasty.

Letters to Gods Comprising what may be the most unusual category of correspondence are letters written to gods. Composed by rulers, they were probably intended to be read aloud by priests to the assembled populace. A number of such letters are known to have been written by Assyrian kings, but the practice is documented as far back as Sumerian times and continued down through the days of the Neo-Babylonian Empire. By composing such a letter, a king expressed his gratitude for divine guidance and aid. Of course, having his subjects as an audience for such a pious recitation served to enhance his popularity. The nearest modern equivalent to such an occasion—albeit in a secular setting—would be a U.S. president's "State of the Union" address.

Sometimes, however, the letter to a god was cast in the form of a question, whereby the king sought divine guidance in choosing the right course for the ship of state. The god's answer came in the form of a sign read by priests from the entrails (usually the liver) of a sacrificed animal.

In two documented cases from Assyrian times, a god actually sent a letter to a king expressing his divine displeasure at something the king had done. No doubt the letter was penned by a priestly ghostwriter who used the opportunity to make a political statement. No doubt also the priest was later transferred by a knowing king to a remote desert parish.

Personal Letters Most letters mailed in Mesopotamia are not addressed to us. They speak of remote gods and kings, of an alien world we may intellectually understand but can never emotionally know. But then there are other ancient letters, ones inscribed in a more human hand. By their simplicity and immediacy they achieve a velocity that permits them to escape the orbit of their times and enter our own.

Curiously, in one way or another they all treat the subject of material possession. Therein perhaps lies the secret of their potency: as we read the letters we realize that the fragile things that mattered most to the writers are, like the writers themselves, no more, even as we ourselves and the things we cherish will someday cease to exist.

Here, then, are one humorous and two poignant examples. The first is written by a spoiled young man; the last two, by vulnerable women.

> From Iddin-Sin to his mother, Lady Zinu:
> Every year my friends dress better, and every year my own clothes get worse. It seems this is the way you want it. I know you have plenty of wool at home, but all you send me is rags. My friend, whose father works for my father, dresses better than I do: he has two sets of everything. My friend's mother adopted him; yet you gave me birth. But it looks like she loves him more than you love me.

> From the slave-girl Dabitum to her Master:
> I told you what might happen, and it has. I carried the baby for seven months. The baby has been dead for a month now, and no one will

help me. Do something before I die. Just come, Master, so I can see you. You said you were sending me something, but nothing has arrived. If I must die, let me only see your face.

> From the priestess Awat-Aja to her dear Gamillum:
> When my eyes beheld you, I filled with joy like that first day when the door of the dark chapel closed behind me and I saw the face of the goddess shining down. I know it made you happy to see me too. "I'll be here for a week," you said. But I couldn't tell you then what I once wrote to you about from a distance. And then all of a sudden you were gone, and for three days I went mad. No food touched my lips, no water, only memory. Send me what you can so I can feed those who are depending on me. The winter cold draws near. Help me. No one did I ever love more.

Proverbs

An essential function of writing was to preserve a record of the past, for from the experiences of the past the ancient reader could draw lessons to guide his life in the present and future. Even before the invention of writing such lessons were passed on, but by word of mouth from one generation to the next. The shorter the lessons were, the easier they were to remember and recite, and so the proverb was born. Eventually, when writing became popular, these nuggets of cultural wisdom were recorded and organized into anthologies. Sumerian anthologies have been found that date back to the second millennium B.C.E., though their entries no doubt derive from even earlier times. They are, in fact, the oldest documented proverbs in the world. By the first millennium B.C.E., bilingual anthologies were being composed with parallel versions of the same proverb in Sumerian and Akkadian.

In one respect, these proverbs are culture-specific: in their imagery and references they reflect the largely agrarian society from which they grew. But in another respect, they are universal: they provide insights into life that can be translated into the language of any age—at least, any age willing to listen.

Despite natural destruction and war (or possibly because of them), the ancient Mesopotamians valued the reassuring constancy of tradition. They saw no necessary disconnect between the past and the present; because change came slowly, the experience of older generations remained relevant and useful and was shown respect. It is for this reason that proverbial wisdom was revered. This respect and reverence is evident in the very fact that Sumerian was preserved as a classic language long after the glory days of Sumer were gone.

A word of caution. Proverbs are by definition pithy. But over the course of millennia, some of the "pith" has disintegrated, much to the consternation of cuneiform scholars who seek to divine the exact meanings of uncommon words and phrases. Many Mesopotamian proverbs, therefore, still elude translation. The samples below, though, are among the clearest that have come down to us.

> "If I threw you in the river, you'd pollute the water."
>
> "If you're poor, you're better dead than alive; if you've got bread, you can't afford salt; if you've got salt, you can't afford bread."
>
> "Take your enemy's land and your enemy comes and takes yours."
>
> "There are lords and there are kings, but the real person to fear is the tax collector."
>
> "If you don't shut your mouth, a fly will get in."
>
> "Tell me what you found, not what you lost."

Social Satire

As far back as Sumerian times, class structure inspired satire. The satire took the form of brief humorous tales, animal fables, and fictional letters. The common theme is class conflict: in some of these works, representative members of different classes vie with one another, proclaiming their own virtues even as they demean their rivals; while, in others, social injustices are depicted. Many have happy endings in which the weak put down or gain the upper hand over the strong.

In one short story, a well-to-do and demanding customer hectors a cleaner on how to properly launder his robe; the cleaner responds by telling the customer to take his own clothes and wash them in the river. In a second story, a poor man cleverly repays the ingratitude of an arrogant mayor. And in a third, a supposedly learned doctor is shown up as a fool by a simple gardener.

Over a thousand years before Aesop, Sumerian fables used talking animals to point up human truths. Significantly, the lowly dog is the most common character in those stories, and even a powerful lion can be outwitted. Animals also take part in debates (as do trees), each singing the praises of its own class (dog, wolf, or fox; tamarisk or date-palm) while berating the deficiencies of others.

Mesopotamian satire could also take the form of fictional letters or contracts. One letter, which purports to be written by none other than the hero Gilgamesh, ridicules the pretentiousness of royal correspondence. Another letter, written by a trained monkey to his mother, bemoans how animals in show business are mistreated and pleads for a "care package" from home. Most curious of all is a cuneiform real estate contract for the purchase of worthless land. The unusual thing is that the contract is drawn up by a bird and is witnessed at the bottom by his feathered friends whose "signatures" appear in the clay as bird-tracks!

Behind the Mesopotamian humor, of course, is a serious message about social injustice: how a poor peasant (the bird) might not be able to afford a decent plot to work; how the talents of a worker (the monkey) might be taken advantage of by an unfeeling boss; and how the rich and powerful (the demanding customer, the arrogant mayor) might lord it over the humble. Despite the legal codes of Ur-Nammu and Hammurabi, unlegislated (and perhaps unlegislatable) inequities still lurked between the lines—even as they still do today despite all our laws. By wearing an animal mask or wielding the blade of wit, an ancient social critic could help his fellow citizens see the glaring gaps.

Erotic Poetry

Separated as they are by space and time, it is easy to be insensible to the unity that binds civilizations together. Since cultures are more readily distinguished from one another by their differences, their inner likenesses may escape us. Yet surely such likenesses exist, and have existed throughout all time.

One of them is the human capacity to love. Sexual love has been primarily responsible for the perpetuation of the human race, but it has also been responsible for the creation of literature—more so than any other category of love except, perhaps, the love of God.

The erotic poetry of different nations is similar in the psychophysical source of its inspiration. But love poets are also conditioned by the places and times in which they live. The Egyptian love poet speaks of nature and eternity, the Greek poet of beauty and transience, the Roman poet of slavery and mastery. Even the imagery of erotic poems varies with geography.

When the ancient Mesopotamians were moved by love, what did they write about and by what tokens did they express their passion?

To begin with, writing about love did not come naturally. Writing in cuneiform was not a spontaneous process but a laborious one, requiring calligraphic skill and the command of a complex script. And, because literacy was not common, especially among women, it was highly unlikely that a Sumerian Juliet could have understood a note from her Romeo without asking for help from a scribe. Moreover, since Mesopotamian literature was governed by tradition, there would have been age-old traditional norms of form and theme an amorous writer would have been expected to observe.

These challenges, in fact, are evident in surviving Sumerian examples of erotic poetry: they echo the hallowed halls of temple and palace. A long work celebrates the courtship and wedding of the sex-goddess Inanna and her shepherd-lover Dumuzi; another, the mourning that attended his death. Elsewhere, lyrics lavishly praise the handsomeness of king Shu-Sin of Ur and the dutifulness of his queen. These two sets of poems may indeed be related, for in an annual rite on New Year's Day it may have been customary for a Sumerian ruler to play the role of Dumuzi in a ceremony of "sacred marriage." In this wedding, the role of Inanna would have been played by the goddess' high priestess, who may have also been the queen. Examples of bawdy lyric also occur, no doubt intended for the titillation of the royal court. One is a dialogue in which a customer at a tavern propositions an all-too-willing barmaid.

In these poems, erotic experience is described through the use of similes and metaphors designed to evoke the senses. Paramount among the senses here are taste and smell. The sweetness of the beloved is compared to the sweetness of honey and dates, of butter and beer; the pleasantness of the beloved to the fragrance of woods such as juniper and pine. The sense of sight is addressed through visible imagery reflecting the sky (the Moon and moonlight, and the stars) and the colors of precious minerals (gold and silver, carnelian and topaz, alabaster and obsidian, and lapis lazuli) that adorn or delineate the lover's body. Touch is awakened by references to temperature: the coolness of water and ice; the shade of a cedar tree. Of all the senses, hearing receives the least overt attention, perhaps because it was already implicit in dialogue and underlay the poet's very mission.

The origin of the poetic similes and metaphors was the agrarian society in which the Mesopotamian poet lived and the rich material culture that grew from it. This reservoir of imagery is evident in the examples above, but also in the poetic terms of reference applied to the body's sexual organs. Thus the penis "sprouts" and, when erect, is compared to a straight stalk of barley, the trunk of an apple tree, a stout pillar of hard alabaster, or the taut string of a lyre. Pubic hair is called wool or tufted lettuce. The vagina is described as wet, either as an irrigated garden watered by semen or as an incense-bearing tree flowing with sap. And the clitoris is spoken of as a little bird. As these illustrations show, Sumerian poetry could be sensually explicit and anatomically graphic.

Passion, for its part, was likened to a hunger for bread or beer; infatuation, to the sticky pitch that clings to a boat's hull; and intercourse, to digging a canal or ploughing a field. In coarse love charms (short poems recited to secure a woman's affections by magic power), the copulation craved by the sorcerer's clients was gleefully compared to the activity of rutting swine or dogs in heat. In other poems, as the following passages reveal, writers transmuted base impulse into high art.

The plan for a tryst:

Tell your mother:
"I was with my girlfriend."
Tell your mother:
"We were strolling in the square."
Tell your mother:

"We heard music and she danced with me."
All the while in the moonlight
I will sit on my bed,
loosening the combs from your hair,
holding you in my arms.
Lie to her and
lie with me.

Love's strategy:

As a general
advance against my position
and I shall withdraw to
the bedroom.

As a soldier
march against my lines
and I shall retreat to bed.

Forced entry:

Like a bridge
I will span you,
your waters
surging beneath me.

Like a threshold
I will cross you,
thrusting through your gate.

Counting the time:

You have wasted the day,
wasted the night.
You have squandered the
moon and stars.
For all these hours
my door stood unlocked.

The last sentry
rounds the walls.
Come to me now
before the dawn.

Recipe for passion:

Squeeze yourself into me
as the hand presses flour
into an open cup.

Pound yourself into me
as the fist rams flour into
a cup craving to be filled.

An elegy to a dead lover:

"Your lover is coming," she said. "Be ready!"

He comes from a far-away place now.
He comes by an alien road.
He comes like a dragonfly silent above the
    stream,
like a mist floating across the mountains.

I clothe his empty chair.

A second elegy (after Thorkild Jacobsen):

In the desert, by the early grass,
she cannot hold back her tears
from watering the dead husband
still growing in her mind.

If, as the Bible's Song of Songs claims, love
as is strong as death, then these erotic poems
will forever keep alive the spirit of a long-
dead world.

READING

The Great Decipherments

Cleator 1961, Daniels 1995, Friedrich 1957,
Gordon 1982 and 1986, Kahn 1967, and Pope
1998: the history of cuneiform's decipherment;
McLemee 2000: online library.

Major Languages

Edzard 1995: Sumerian language; Huehnergard 1995: Semitic languages; Nemet-Nejat
1998: the peoples and their languages.

Writing

Bienkowski and Millard 2000: scribes, libraries;
Black and Tait 1995: archives and libraries;
Chiera 1938: technique; Claiborne 1974: origins; Driver 1976: Semitic writing; Nemet-
Nejat 1998: scribes, archives, libraries; Pearson
1995: scribes; Saggs 1965: the scribe in Babylonian society; Schmandt-Besserat 1992 and
1996: tokens; Walker 1987: cuneiform.

Epic Poetry

Bottéro 1995: Akkadian literature; Bottéro et
al. 2001: *Epic of Gilgamesh*; Foster 1987: sex,
love, and knowledge in *Gilgamesh*; Foster
1995: translations: Gardner and Maier, translation of *Gilgamesh*; George 1999: translation
of *Gilgamesh* and Sumerian epics; Heidel
1949: *Gilgamesh* and Old Testament parallels;
Heidel 1951: the Babylonian *Epic of Creation*
and Old Testament parallels; Jackson 1997,
Kovacs 1989, Mason 1972: translation of *Gilgamesh*; Jacobson 1987: translation of Sumerian epics; Kramer 1963 and 1981: Sumerian
epic; Lambert 1987: Gilgamesh in literature
and art; Maier 1997: readings on *Gilgamesh*;
Pritchard 1969: translations of Sumerian and
Akkadian myths and epics; Saggs 1962:
Mesopotamian epic; Tigay 1982: evolution of
the *Gilgamesh* epic; Wolkstein and Kramer
1983: stories of Inanna.

Historical Chronicles

Bienkowski and Millard 2000: concise overview;
Contenau 1954: treatment, style, and validity;
Grayson 1975: Assyrian and Babylonian chroni-

cles; Greenstein 1995: autobiographies in ancient Western Asia; Kramer 1981: the first historian; Liverani 1995: the deeds of ancient Mesopotamian kings; Luckenbill 1924: Sennacherib's annals; Luckenbill 1926–27: Assyrian and Babylonian records; Pritchard 1969: Sumerian, Babylonian, and Assyrian historical texts; Thomas 1958: records of Assyria and Babylonia; Van Seters 1995: historiography of the ancient Near East.

Legal Documents

Driver and Miles 1935: Assyrian laws; Driver and Miles 1952–55: Babylonian laws; Gordon 1957: Hammurabi's Code; Greengus 1995: legal and social institutions of ancient Mesopotamia; Kramer 1981: the first "Moses" and the first legal precedent; Pritchard 1969: collections of laws from Mesopotamia; Roth 1997: law collections from Mesopotamia and Asia Minor; Saggs 1962: law and statecraft.

Divination Texts

Bottéro 2001: astrology; Buccellati 1995: "Prayer to the Gods of the Night"; Contenau 1954: astronomy, astrology, and divination; Johnson 1951: Dura Europos horoscope; Nemet-Nejat 1998: astronomy and divination; Olmstead 1938: Babylonian astronomy; Oppenheim 1977: astronomy, astrology, and extispicy; Pritchard 1969: Babylonian *Epic of Creation*; Rochberg 1995: astronomy and calendars; Rochberg-Halton 1992: Near Eastern calendars; Sachs 1952: Babylonian horoscopes; Saggs 1962: astronomy, divination, and horoscopes; Swerdlow 2000: ancient astronomy.

Hymns and Prayers

Bienkowski and Millard 2000: concise discussion with bibliography; Foster 1995, Pritchard 1969: translations.

Lamentations

Bienkowski and Millard 2000, Ferris 1992: the genre of lamentation; Cohen 1988: lamentations in Mesopotamia; Foster 1995: a city lament; Freedman 2000: lamentations in the Old Testament; Green 1978: Eridu lament; Green 1984: Uruk lament; Kramer 1940: Ur lament; Kramer 1981: Nippur lament and the motif of the weeping goddess; Michalowski: Sumer and Ur lament; Pritchard 1969: Ur lament, and Sumer and Ur lament.

Letters

Michalowski 1993, Oppenheim 1967: selected letters from Mesopotamia; Moran 1992: the Amarna letters; Pritchard 1969: Sumerian and Akkadian letters.

Proverbs

Barton 1937: Biblical parallels; Gordon 1959, Kramer 1963 and 1981: Sumerian proverbs; Marzal 1976: proverbs from Mari; Pritchard 1969: Akkadian proverbs.

Social Satire

Foster 1995: stories and humor; Foster 1995: humor and wit in the ancient Near East; Kramer 1981: Sumerian animal fables; Pritchard 1969: Akkadian fables.

Erotic Poetry

Alster 1985: Sumerian love songs; Foster 1995, Jacobsen 1987, Pritchard 1969: translations; Leick 1994: sex and eroticism in Mesopotamian literature; Kramer 1981: the first love song; Westenholz 1995: love lyrics from the ancient Near East; Wolkstein and Kramer 1983: translations of poems about Inanna.

6

ARCHITECTURE AND ENGINEERING

Through architecture and engineering, humanity leaves its mark upon the earth. Over the long course of time, however, the forces of nature and the destructive bent of man conspire to erase that mark, leaving only its remnants for the archaeologist to trace. This is especially true in a land like southern Mesopotamia that lacks stone, where structures could be built only of clay. Indeed, in all of Iraq there is not a single ancient monument still standing intact that dates to Sumerian, Babylonian, or Assyrian times. Unlike the Egyptologist who gazes at the pyramids of Giza and the columned splendor of Karnak, the student of Mesopotamia must sadly contemplate foundations in the dust.

As the author of the biblical book of Job once lamented (4: 19–20):

> How much less in them that dwell in houses
> of clay, whose foundation is in the dust . . .
> They are destroyed from morning to evening.

Yet the Mesopotamian archaeologist rises to the challenge, inspired by the conviction that there great civilizations once stood, that here civilization itself arose. If walls have fallen and bricks lie scattered, they must be reconstructed in the excavator's imagination with the help of keen observation and an imagery supplied by ancient literature and art. Through such effort, the lost world of Mesopotamia can once again assume three-dimensional form.

BUILDING MATERIALS AND HOUSES

The natural resources of Mesopotamia largely determined the structural materials used by its architects and engineers. In turn, the structural materials determined the basic size, shape, and style of the works they produced.

Limitations

Southern Mesopotamia was an alluvial plain that was bereft of stone. Indeed, it has been said that not a single pebble could be found in its soil that was not brought there from somewhere else. Building stone could be imported, but it was prohibitively expensive to do so. Only in the north was quarriable stone available, but even there it was used by the Assyrians exclusively for projects such as palaces and temples because of its limited supply.

Large forests that could yield construction-grade timber (of oak, pine, or cedar) were likewise lacking. In the south, the only local tree was the date-palm, more valuable alive than dead because its fruit was a staple of the Mesopotamian diet. When required, timber was imported from the mountains to the east and north, or from Lebanon to the west, famed for its forests of cedar.

In place of wood, Mesopotamian builders used bundles of river-grown reeds; in the place of stone, brick made from riverine clay.

Brick

The clayish soil of southern Mesopotamia was ideally suited to the manufacture of brick. The most durable brick was baked in kilns, but—in a country short of wood—the cost of heating the ovens made such brick very expensive. As a practical matter, then, oven-baked brick was reserved for prestigious buildings or for places like embankments or dikes where its greater durability made it essential. The most common brick was baked in the sun. It might not last as long as oven-baked brick, especially when subjected to rain and flood, but it was cheap and easy to replace.

The perfect time to make such brick was the summertime, when the sun was hot. For this reason, the ancient Mesopotamians called the first month of summer "the month of bricks." By that time, the winter rains and the spring floods would have done their maximum damage, and the need for repairs could be readily assessed and the work completed in timely fashion before wet weather returned.

If the required repairs were too extensive, the entire building might be leveled and a new one constructed atop its ruins. Such reconstructions, repeated throughout a community over the course of decades and centuries, led to its eventual elevation above the surrounding plain. In Arabic, the term for such an artificial mound is a "tell," a word that forms the common prefix found in the names of many abandoned sites from antiquity that dot the landscape of modern Iraq.

The actual making of the bricks was simple and similar, whether they were baked in ovens or in the sun. Though ordinary wet clay could be used by itself, it was usually blended with finely chopped straw to bind it and lend it extra strength (see Exodus 5: 10–14). The clay mixture would then be pressed into four-sided rectangular wooden molds. Next, the molds would be lifted up, much as a cake mold might be gingerly lifted off a freshly baked cake. The bricks would then be left out in the hot sun to dry, or transferred to the oven rack for baking.

When it came time for the finished bricks to be laid, they would be set in a mortar made of slushy clay or, better yet, made of an asphalt-like substance called bitumen.

The shape of Mesopotamian bricks changed over the course of history. The earliest examples are long and thin. Beginning in the fourth millennium B.C.E. and on into the third, they become uniformly rectangular, with their length double their width. In the Early Dynastic period, they retain their rectangular outline but acquire a convex side produced by rounding off the soft clay atop the mold. Such "plano-convex" bricks, with their rounded sides turned

outward, created a variegated wall surface. Still later, in the Akkadian period, the square brick, about 14 by 14 inches, came into its own.

Once their chronology was established, Mesopotamian bricks—like their clay cousins, the potsherds—helped archaeologists date the structures and strata where they occurred. Some Mesopotamian bricks, in fact, are stamped with the datable names of their royal builders.

A curiosity of etymology is that the word "adobe," which we normally associate with the architecture of Mexico and the American Southwest, is actually Near Eastern in origin. The Spaniards picked up the word from the Arabic language of the Moors, who occupied Spain in the eighth century C.E. In Arabic, *at-tub* meant

6.1 *Making sun-dried brick near the bank of the Tigris River.* (Rogers, *A History of Babylonia and Assyria*, 1915)

"the brick." But the word entered the Arabic language as a result of the Muslim conquest of Egypt in the seventh century C.E. There, the word for brick used by the native Copts was *tōbĕ*. The Copts, for their part, had preserved the linguistic memory of the ancient Egyptian word for brick, *djebat*. Egyptian *djebat* became Coptic *tōbĕ*, Coptic *tōbĕ* became Arabic *at-tub*, and eventually Arabic *at-tub* became Spanish *adobe*.

Bitumen

Bitumen is another name for ancient asphalt. It is a petroleum-like substance that occurs naturally in the Near East, especially in Iraq, where it seeps to the earth's surface and forms blackish, sticky deposits. The aboveground presence of this substance is, of course, connected to the underground presence of the oil that is the greatest source of Iraqi wealth today. Bitumen deposits are found along both of Iraq's major rivers, but in particular near the modern cities of Hit and Ramadi, west of Baghdad, on the southern bank of the Euphrates. The ancients who found these deposits discovered in them the properties of a powerful adhesive that bonded to brick better than did ordinary mortar and was, moreover, waterproof. Bitumen thereafter became the premium adhesive for laying brick walls and floors. Additionally, it was applied as a coating to make walls and pipes watertight. Among the ancient civilizations of the world, bitumen was used almost exclusively by the Mesopotamians, probably because it was found in their country in such abundance.

Waterproof though it was, bitumen could not prevent woe from seeping into the life of the average Mesopotamian. As one Babylonian long ago complained: "Here I am living in a house made of brick and bitumen and what do you know if a lump of mud doesn't land on my head!"

Reeds

Just as the land of the Tigris and Euphrates provided its people with the clay to make bricks and the bitumen to cement them together, so did it also provide them with the reeds they employed to fashion some of their earliest homes. Because of their natural buoyancy, bundles of reeds had long been used to build boats. But the early Mesopotaminas also used the same materials to construct their houses.

DOMESTIC ARCHITECTURE

Reed Houses

Digging a series of holes in the ground, the builders would insert a tall bundle of reeds in each hole. A circle of holes would be used to make a circular house; two parallel rows to make a rectangular one. Once the bundles were all firmly inserted, the ones opposite each other would be bent over and tied at the top to form a roof. For a front or back door, a reed mat would be draped over an opening (either at the ends of a rectangular house, or on the side of a circular one). Such primitive homes are still made and used by the marsh-dwellers of southern Iraq.

In a hot climate like Iraq's, a well-designed house must protect its dwellers from the sun's searing heat.

The reed houses accomplished this purpose by providing shade. In addition, the thick bundles of reeds provided some insulation. If the house was rectangular and there was an opening at either end, its owners may have enjoyed cross-ventilation as well, especially if

6.2   An early 20th-century view of reed houses being constructed in southern Iraq using age-old techniques and design.   (Rogers, *A History of Babylonia and Assyria*, 1915)

the axis of the house was orientated to take advantage of prevailing winds. But the temperature inside such a one-room house must have been high indeed during summer. During cold weather, portable brasiers or a small oven could have provided heat, but with the ever-present risk of fire due to the combustible nature of the materials from which the house was made.

Brick Houses

Superior to a reed house was one made of brick. The walls of such homes were as much as eight feet thick to keep out the summer's heat. For the same reason, there were few if any windows, and those that existed would have been small and fitted with a wooden grill for security. The exterior walls would have been whitewashed to reflect the radiant heat of the sun. In the walls, horizontal ducts, leading to the interior, admitted a small amount of fresh air.

Within, rooms were grouped around and opened onto a central courtyard, roofed over with flat planking and palm-fronds—again, to keep off the sun. Even if sunlight streamed down, the occupants could always sit against one of the courtyard's more shady walls. Against one wall of the courtyard a brick hearth might be built whose smoke would rise and exit through gaps in the roof. Often, the roof was packed down with earth. In such a case, using an exterior staircase, family members could ascend to sleep on the roof in the cool of a starlit evening.

Just as locally available raw materials dictated the structure of the Mesopotamian house, so—as we have seen—did local climate determine its design. (See also "Homes" in chapter 11.)

TECHNIQUES OF CONSTRUCTION

The builders of ancient Mesopotamia employed the same basic techniques of construction as other early peoples. Essentially, mass was piled on top of mass to create a solid form (such as the platformed base of a temple) or to create walls that enclosed space.

A major challenge ancient builders faced was creating doors and passageways. This was generally accomplished by the post-and-lintel system: a horizontal beam (the lintel) was supported atop two vertical posts. The opening, however, could be made only as wide as the longest available beam. In practical terms, this meant the height of a tree from which timbers were obtained or, in stone construction, the span of a quarried block. Yet if too much weight was placed on top of the lintel, the stress imposed could cause the lintel to crack and the structure to collapse. In stone construction, a lintel supported only at its ends could even crack from its own weight if its span was too great.

The engineering solution proved to be the arch, a Sumerian invention of the fourth millennium B.C.E. The arch created an opening while at the same time bearing weight. Its secret was to transfer that weight outward and then downward into the ground, rather than bearing it solely upon itself. By building a series of such arches back to back, engineers were able to construct vaults that served as tun-nels. In addition to forming passageways, the arch was a strong and efficient way of supporting a superstructure: because of its openness, it required less brick or stone than a wall of similar size carrying a similar weight.

The first arch to be designed in Mesopotamia was a corbel arch. Rather than consisting of a series of wedge-shaped blocks (voussoirs) curving around to either side of a central keystone, a corbel arch consisted of two slanting sets of stone steps that came closer and closer to each other as they rose until they met at the top to form the apex of a triangle.

The later true arch was a more sophisticated device both because of the correct slant needed for each voussoir and because of the critical role played by the keystone in maintaining the stability of the arch as a whole.

It is possible, but not at all certain, that the idea for the corbel arch was inspired by the stepped profile of the platforms used in building Mesopotamian temples. Another source for the idea of the arch may have been the curving outline of the bent-over bundles of reeds used to fashion homes.

Neither the Mesopotamians nor the Egyptians nor the Greeks—all of whom were familiar with the true arch—used it with the engineering and architectural bravado of the Romans. In part, this was so because Rome's legions needed bridges in order to traverse Europe's rivers. In part, it was so because the empire's cities needed elevated aqueducts to supplement local sources of water. But most of all, it was true because Roman leaders insured their own political survival by keeping the urban masses happy. As a result, on the backs of multiple arches rose towering amphitheaters and spas that provided tens of thousands of people with easy access to sensual pleasure. Though Mesopotamian engineers used arches to construct bridges and aqueducts, Mesopotamia's leaders never recognized the potential of the arch as a means of public persuasion.

From Village to City

Though humanity first expressed its artistic impulses in the Old Stone Age, architecture began in the New. The New Stone Age, or Neolithic Period, began in the Near East in the seventh millennium B.C.E. and was marked by a radical change in the way people lived. In earlier times, people had lived by hunting and gathering their food. But in the seventh millennium B.C.E., the principles of agriculture were discovered as well as the ways to domesticate animals. Practicing agriculture meant living in one place, and that in turn led to the construction of permanent dwellings and the beginning of village life. Farming produced not only a more settled way of life but a population explosion because of the abundant supplies of food it generated. As a result, clusters of primitive dwellings soon became large communities. In the fertile alluvial plains of the Tigris and Euphrates, once the methods of irrigation agriculture had been mastered these villages grew to the size of cities. Thus the "Neolithic Revolution" gave way to an "Urban Revolution" in which engineering and architecture came to play a larger and larger role. Cities arose that guarded their wealth behind moats and gated walls, while within these walls—amid winding streets and huddled dwellings and shops—stood administrative centers and temples, the new institutions of an invention called civilization.

Temples

"Mesopotamia is the birthplace of architecture," declared art historian Sigfried Giedion in his work, *The Eternal Present* (Giedion 1964: 176). In Mesopotamia "the age-old yearning to establish contact with invisible forces was, for the first time, given an architectural form" (Giedion 1964: 213).

If Giedion is correct, the churches, synagogues, and mosques of today ultimately owe their formal existence to structures that began in Sumer some 6,000 years ago.

When monumental architecture arose, its first utterance was a prayer. Just as the ancient Mesopotamians lived in houses, so did they build houses for their gods in the hope their gods would dwell among them and protect them. In these sacred houses, they set up images of their deities, and in them placed tables on which they laid offerings meant to obtain and insure divine blessing. In addition, they erected platformed shrines to coax their gods to descend to earth and to help their own human voices more readily reach heaven's heights.

Unlike today's places of worship, however, temple interiors were not intended to hold a congregation. Instead, the temple was the dwelling-place of the god's or goddess' holy statue, the repository of the deity's treasures, and the residence of its priestly attendants. On sacred occasions, the congregation might prayerfully gather in the courtyard in front of the sanctuary, but not pray within its darkened enclosure. Instead, priests or priestesses addressed the deity there on the community's behalf and offered up its gifts.

Origins and Development

The oldest example of a Mesopotamian temple yet found belongs to the southern city of Eridu. Dating as far back as the fifth millennium B.C.E., it consists of a single room measuring only 12 by 15 feet. At its center stood an offering table; in the wall before it was a niche with a plinth that once functioned as an altar or supported a god's statue. If that statue ever existed, it has never been found, nor do we know the name of the divinity it portrayed. The primitive sanctuary was approached through a simple doorway as though anyone in need could enter and commune with god.

By the fourth millennium B.C.E., temple architecture had changed, as revealed by a later temple at Eridu. The size of the structure had grown, and its interior was now subdivided into a floorplan that would become characteristic of temples at other sites: a central hall flanked on either side by a series of rooms, not unlike the nave of a church. In addition, the walls on the outside were strongly buttressed. The sanctuary, moreover, was raised on a terrace and had to be approached by a staircase. At times, the terrace was quite high, perhaps as much as 40 feet or more.

Some would see in this architectural transformation a transformation of religion itself: from a type of worship that was originally more intimate and personal to one that was later more hierarchical and remote. Commenting on this apparent transformation, archaeologist Walter Andrae wrote:

> Life in these [earlier] temples must be imagined as flowing freely through them. A coming and going is possible on every side, in strong contrast to the enclosure of the later Akkadian-Babylonian temple precincts which, with few exceptions, were built like a fortress with one single entry point. (Giedion 1964: 190)

Whether such an interpretation is justified we will never know. It is always a risky endeavor to extract a romantic homily from a pile of bricks. In the history of religion, however, the visionary prophet is eventually replaced by the myopic bureaucrat. Whether that was true in Mesopotamia, though, we cannot say. What is clear is that the temples them-

selves grew in size and complexity and with them, no doubt, the priestly colleges that supervised their activities.

Later in the Assyrian and Neo-Babylonian Empires, the temple was structurally integrated with the palace. On the one hand, such a step served to enhance the majesty of the king. On the other hand, it symbolized, through architecture, the subordination of sacred activities to secular control.

As time went on, Mesopotamian temples were renovated and rebuilt over the remains of their former selves. As this process continued, the sanctuaries rose higher and higher above the surrounding terrain.

Decorative fragments suggest their former splendor. Thanks to a coating of white gypsum plaster, the exterior walls of Uruk's "White Temple" must have shimmered in the sun. Meanwhile at Al Ubaid, a gleaming mosaic of colored stones and mother-of-pearl enveloped columns cut from the trunks of tall palms. Guardian leopards and geometric patterns adorned the interior of Tell Uqair's "Painted Temple." After a few hours of being exposed to the open air, their hues faded, but when the excavators first uncovered them, they were as vibrant as when they were first painted.

A city might well possess multiple temples. Sometimes, with the help of connecting courtyards, they formed religious complexes. A city's temples might be dedicated to a number of different deities, but usually the patron god or goddess of a city had a larger and more imposing temple than the rest. At Ur, the moon-god Nanna and his consort Ningal were so honored. At Ischali it was Ishtar, goddess of love and war. And at Babylon it was Marduk.

Markuk's temple precinct at Babylon was immense, stretching 470 feet in length and spreading over 60 acres. Initially built during the days of Babylon's First Dynasty, it was restored and refurbished a number of times before its final destruction in 479 B.C.E. under

6.3   Though headless, Gudea of Lagash still sits with his blueprints on his lap. The inscription on his skirt celebrates his pious penchant for erecting temples.   (E. de Sarzec, Découvertes en Chaldée, 1884–1912)

almost every Greek temple faced east, with the other sides facing west, north, and south. In Mesopotamia, however, it was the corners and not the sides that pointed in the cardinal directions, with the entry of the temple often located on its northeast or southeast side.

Mesopotamia's rulers took great pride in their role as builders of religious edifices. The stela that is inscribed with Ur-Nammu's code of law depicts him carrying tools on his shoulder, while a plaque portrays Ur-Nashe bearing on his head a basket of clay for the making of bricks. A statue of Gudea, now in the Louvre, shows him sitting with a ruler and the "blueprints" for a temple in his lap. Nabopolassar, for his part, boasts in an inscription how he rolled up his sleeves (actually, tucked up his gown!) and hauled clay and bricks for Marduk's temple. All of this is not very different from the posed photo of a politician turning up the first spadeful of dirt at the commencement of a civic project, except that our Mesopotamian examples involve places of worship.

One of the most fascinating aspects of temple construction was the insertion of a "foundation deposit," the ancient equivalent of a time capsule buried behind a modern cornerstone. Such a deposit would consist of an inscription recording the name of the royal builder and describing the circumstances of construction, including a list of any special materials that were employed, like the scented oils or honey sometimes added to the mortar or expensive woods like cypress and cedar used for the doors. The sixth century B.C.E. ruler Nabonidus even made a hobby of digging up old foundation deposits to see what they said, thereby bestowing upon himself the distinction of being the world's first archaeologist.

Foundation deposits were also incorporated into the construction of another type of religious structure, the ziggurat. Just as a campanile, or bell tower, stands next to an Italian

the Persians. After choosing Babylon as his new capital, Alexander the Great contemplated the temple's reconstruction, but after employing 10,000 laborers for two months just to clear away its rubble, he abandoned the project.

Some cities also featured a special temple located outside the city walls. Called a *bīt akītu* in Akkadian, it served as the destination for a religious procession that took place to celebrate the New Year.

One feature that set Mesopotamian temples apart from the ones Alexander knew in Greece was their cosmic orientation. The front of church, so did the ziggurat stand near the temple to the god it honored.

ZIGGURATS

The most distinctive architectural creation of ancient Mesopotamia was not the temple but the ziggurat. So far, over 30 of these structures have been found in various cities, the earliest at Eridu dating back to the end of the third millennium B.C.E.

The term ziggurat derives from the Akkadian word *zigguratu,* which meant a "peak" or "high place." Essentially, a ziggurat was a multistepped platform made of brick. The platform rested upon a terrace and presumably supported a shrine at its top—presumably, because no such shrine has ever been found. Indeed, even the massive earthen platforms themselves lie in ruins. But it is doubtless the case that in ancient times when they were intact, rituals involving the gods were enacted on their summits.

Ur

The best preserved ziggurat stands at Ur and dates to the late third millennium B.C.E. Its base is rectangular and measures 145 feet (on the northwest and southeast) by 190 feet (on the northeast and southwest). As our description suggests, its cosmic orientation is like that of most Mesopotamian temples, with its four corners pointing in the directions of east and west and north and south. Each side of the base is

6.4 *A restored view of the walls and ziggurat of ancient Babylon.* (M. Jastrow, *Babylonia and Assyria,* 1917)

6.5   *In this exterior view of the ziggurat at Ur, we can make out downspout channels and "weep holes" in the brick façade. These were designed to keep the interior of the structure dry.*   (University of Pennsylvania Museum)

actually convex, whether deliberately so to convey an impression of greater massiveness or the simple result of pressure from the weight above is hard to say.

The first level at Ur, the only one to survive intact, stands 50 feet high. Atop this are the walled outlines of a second higher level and the remains of a third, for a grand total of 70 feet from the bottom of the ziggurat to its current top. Jutting out from the northeast face is a grand staircase that is joined by two other staircases angling up from the building's corners. The staircases would bring the priestly worshiper up to the first floor, where other staircases would allow him to ascend to the second and then final levels.

In terms of construction, the Ur ziggurat consists of a core of sun-dried brick covered by an outer layer of oven-baked brick eight feet thick. It is this tough outer layer of weather-resistant brick that largely accounts for the ziggurat's survival. The core itself is interwoven with cables and mats woven from reeds. Weep-holes in the sides of the structure permit internal moisture to drip out, while channels running vertically drain off rainwater and direct it to the ground.

Originally, the first floor would have had its outer edges painted black, with red reserved for the second and third. At the top, the shrine may have been finished in an enameled brick with a deep blue glaze.

Babylon

Though only its foundations survive, Mesopotamia's largest ziggurat was located at Babylon. In ancient times it was called "Etemenanki," a name that means something like "the foundation of heaven and earth" or, perhaps better, "the link between heaven and earth." Originally, Babylon's ziggurat stood some 300 feet tall and rose up in seven stories. As a vertical triumph, its architectural audacity and the manpower and organization needed to execute it would later inspire the biblical tale of the Tower of Babel, for Babel is but another name for Babylon.

Seen from a distance, the ziggurat of Babylon would have appeared like a massive flight of multicolored stairs reaching for the heavens. If our ancient sources are reliable, each level was painted a different color: the first and lowest, white; the second, black; the third, red; the fourth, again white; the fifth, reddish orange; the sixth, silver; and the seventh and highest, glistening gold.

In addition to a cuneiform tablet that provides the measurements for Babylon's fabled ziggurat, we have an eyewitness account from the Greek traveler and historian Herodotus, who describes (*History* 1: 181–82) what he saw and was told during a visit in the mid-fifth century B.C.E.

> There was a tower of solid masonry, a little over 600 feet in length and width, upon which was raised a second tower, and on that a third, and so on up to eight. The ascent to the top is on the outside, by a path which winds round all the towers. When one is about half-way up, one finds a resting-place and seats, where persons are wont to sit some time on their way to the summit. On the topmost tower there is a spacious temple, and inside the temple stands a couch of unusual size, richly adorned, with a golden table by its side. There is no statue of any kind set up in the place, nor is the chamber occupied of nights by any one

> but a single native woman, who, as the Chaldaeans, the priests of this god [Jupiter Belus], affirm, is chosen for himself by the deity out of all the women in the land. They also declare—but I for my part do not credit it—that the god comes down in person into this chamber, and sleeps upon the couch. (Herodotus 1942 [1858]: 97–98, trans. George Rawlinson, revised)

Herodotus thus connects the shrine at the top with a rite of sacred marriage in which the god Marduk (identified by Herodotus with Zeus) mated with a mortal woman.

Additional details are provided by the first century B.C.E. historian Diodorus Siculus (2: 9).

> Now since with regard to this temple [of Zeus] the historians are at variance, and since time has caused the structure to fall into ruins, it is impossible to give the exact facts concerning it. But all agree that it was exceedingly high, and that in it the Chaldaeans made their observations of the stars, whose risings and settings could be accurately observed by reason of the height of the structure. Now the entire building was ingeniously constructed at great expense of bitumen and brick, and at the top of the ascent Semiramis [the builder, according to Diodorus] set up three statues of hammered gold . . . A table for all three statues, made of hammered gold, stood before them, forty feet long, fifteen wide, and weighing five hundred talents. And there were censers as well . . . and also three gold mixing bowls [for wine] . . . But all these were later carried off by the kings of the Persians, while as for the palaces and the other buildings, time has either entirely effaced them or left them in ruins; and in fact of Babylon itself but a small part is inhabited at this time, and most of the area within its walls is given over to agriculture. (Diodorus Siculus 1974: 381, trans. C. H. Oldfather)

Indeed, after Robert Koldewey stopped his excavations at the site in 1917, the peasants of the nearby village of Hilla stole all the bricks they could find, leaving behind only a large muddy hole where once had risen a tower that reached toward the heavens.

INSPIRATION AND FUNCTION

What, then, was the inspiration for the ziggurat? Herodotus gives one explanation: that it was designed as a lofty platform for a shrine that a god would descend to from heaven. Even more simply, the ziggurat could be viewed as an elaborate altar, elevated so that it might be closer to the gods' own realm. Diodorus offers yet another explanation: that it was meant to be a celestial observatory. Some, in fact, might see in the seven storys a symbolic representation of the five planets known to Babylonian astronomers, plus the Sun and Moon. Closer to Earth, others might alternately propose that, in a land ravaged by flood, the ziggurat was merely a monumental means to raise up a shrine and protect it from water damage. And if this explanation should seem too pedestrian, another explanation might suffice: that the ziggurat's form echoes the topography of the mountainous homeland from which the builders originally came, a land where gods were believed to dwell on mountaintops. Though we do not in fact know of such origins, some poetic names given to ziggurats—"house of the mountain" and "mountain of the storm"—tend to lend credence to the notion of the ziggurat as a man-made mountain.

Which explanation, then, is correct? The only valid answer I can give is that the various answers above are not mutually exclusive: more than one may have played a role in ministering to the ziggurat's birth.

ZIGGURATS AND PYRAMIDS

There is a saying in Arabic: "Man fears time, but time fears the pyramids." There is much truth in that saying, since the pyramids of Egypt have endured like no other monument of the ancient world. By their sheer mass they defy annihilation, and they will remain behind as a testament to human striving and ingenuity long after the human race itself has disappeared.

The durability of the pyramids is in great measure due to the natural resources of Egypt. The land of the Nile is rich in limestone, a stone ideal for quarrying and construction. Such, we know, was not the case in Mesopotamia, especially in the south. Ziggurats had to be made from brick, and brick—even oven-baked brick—is not as millennially lasting as stone. Hence most of Iraq's ancient ziggurats have dissolved into its landscape while the pyramids still tower above Egypt's desert.

Nevertheless, might the two—the pyramid of ancient Egypt and the ziggurat of ancient Iraq—be somehow related? Both arose in comparable cultural settings: riverine civilizations that flowered in the Near East in the fourth millennium B.C.E. Both required massive concentrations of manpower, organized and directed under centralized authority. Both were erected to honor the gods: in Egypt to honor the divine ruler, the pharaoh; in Mesopotamia to honor heavenly divinities that man had to serve. And both were vertical statements similar in form: four triangular sloping sides rising from a rectilinear base and made by piling mass upon mass. Indeed, before the Egyptians succeeded in building smooth-sided pyramids, they built ones that were stepped, and even afterward they continued to speak of their pyramids as "staircases to heaven."

While all these things are true, there are also significant differences between pyramids and ziggurats. Ziggurats were intended for the living; pyramids were built for the dead. Ziggurats were constructed in the hearts of bustling cities; pyramids were raised in the barren and desolate desert. Fundamentally, each pyramid was dedicated to a single pharaoh's quest for eternal life; each ziggurat, however, was dedicated to a god who was already eternal and would abide forever. Unlike the pyramid, which was built for a single individual and then sealed shut, the ziggurat was open to all to see and benefit from, not only during the generation that built it but also for all future time. In addition, the age of pyramid-building was relatively short, essentially the 450-year span of Egypt's Old Kingdom, but ziggurats continued to be built and rebuilt in Iraq for at least two thousand years.

Did one form influence the other? Could Pharaoh Zoser's Step Pyramid have inspired the earliest ziggurat? Could the ziggurat conversely have inspired the Egyptian architect Imhotep in his design of Zoser's monument? It is difficult to say. The earliest ziggurats of which we have traces (about 2100 B.C.E.) are centuries later than the date of Egypt's Step Pyramid (about 2650 B.C.E.). But still earlier ziggurats could have been built of which we no longer have physical evidence, especially since they were shaped from materials less durable than stone.

Of course, it is possible that Egypt and Mesopotamia arrived at their architectural concepts independently: Egypt piling rectangular tomb upon rectangular tomb, Mesopotamia raising platform upon platform, until the stepped profile emerged. We will never know.

What we do know is that each nation reached to the heavens, bending will and muscle to achieve transcendent goals. There is perhaps no more that a civilization can ask of itself.

PALACES

Like the earliest temple and ziggurat, Mesopotamia's earliest palace comes from Eridu. It dates to the early third millennium B.C.E.

While the developed temple is distinguished by its floorplan and the ziggurat by its elevation, the palace is marked by its multiplicity of rooms. Indeed, its name in Sumerian meant "big house."

Design

Just as the temple gradually gained rooms and the ziggurat storys, the palace took time in acquiring its characteristic form. That form consisted of two courtyards connected by a throne room that doubled as an audience hall. The outer courtyard was used for public events; the inner, for private ceremonies. Surrounding the outer courtyard were rooms that served as offices, workshops, and storage areas; surrounding the inner were residential quarters for the royal family and facilities to serve their domestic needs. A later addition was a Syrian-style columned portico known in Akkadian as a *bīt hilāni*. The walls of the palace might be decorated with paintings of ceremonial scenes or, in Assyrian times, with sculpted reliefs depicting the favorite pursuits of the monarch: hunting and war. The entire structure was usually surrounded by its own defensive wall. Some cities even boasted more than one royal palace, a tribute to the reigning monarch's egotism and vainglory.

Examples

One of the most extensive Mesopotamian palaces was that of the 18th-century B.C.E. ruler of Mari, Zimri-Lim, a contemporary of Hammurabi. Called "a jewel of archaic oriental architecture" (Lloyd, Müller and Martin 1974: 23), it contained about 300 rooms. When the eighth century B.C.E. Assyrian king Sargon II built his new capital city at Dur-Sharrukin, he designed its throne room with two special features: a spiral staircase leading to the roof for celestial observations and ceremonies, and a

6.6　A restored view (by James Fergusson) of the façade and grand entrance of Sennacherib's palace at Nineveh.　(Layard, *Discoveries in the Ruins of Nineveh and Babylon*, 1853)

floor with a stone track to guide the wheels of a portable brazier to comfort him with heat in winter. His successors, Sennacherib and Ashurbanipal, fitted out their palace at Nineveh with colossal pairs of sentries: stone-carved man-headed bulls that guarded its entranceways and stood 10 to 15 feet tall, enough to terrorize any visiting dignitary.

The most impressive Mesopotamian palace of all, however, may have been Nebuchadnezzar II's at Babylon, described in the king's own words as "the marvel of mankind, the center of the land, the shining residence, the dwelling of majesty." This palace had no fewer than five courtyards and a throne room measuring 55 by 140 feet. On the throne room's glazed-brick walls, lions with jaws agape paced nervously as the king contemplated his next military move.

The most stunning, and controversial feature of the palace were the Hanging Gardens of Babylon—controversial, because they may never have really existed or, at least, because no

incontrovertible proof of their existence has ever been found.

The Hanging Gardens were one of the Seven Wonders of the World, an ancient list of the seven greatest man-made marvels that a traveler in Hellenistic times could have beheld. Two were in Greece: the statue of Zeus at Olympia and the Colossus of Rhodes. Two were in Turkey: the Mausoleum at Halicarnassus and the Temple of Artemis at Ephesus. Two were in Egypt: the Great Pyramid at Giza and the Pharos, or Lighthouse, at Alexandria. And one in Mesopotamia: the Hanging Gardens of Babylon. Of these wonders, only one still stands: Egypt's Great Pyramid.

For a picture of what the Hanging Gardens looked like, we must go to the half-dozen ancient authors who described them, though none of these writers may have actually seen the gardens with his own eyes. Though their accounts differ in detail, they do agree in their basic outline: the gardens constituted an elevated

6.7 *Interior view of an Assyrian palace.*   (Rawlinson, *Seven Great Monarchies of the Ancient Eastern World,* 1884)

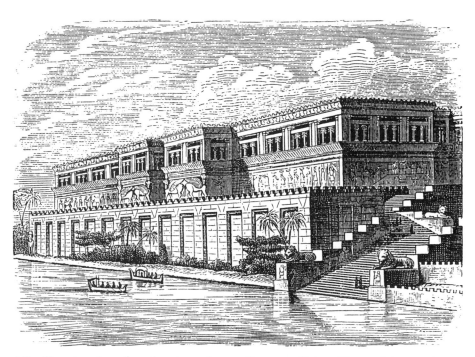

6.8 *Exterior view of an Assyrian palace.*   (Franz von Reber, *History of Ancient Art* [New York: Harper, 1882])

(hence "hanging") earth-covered terrace planted with trees, architecturally supported and mechanically watered. According to the ancient tale, their construction was ordered by Nebuchadnezzar because of his love for his wife (or concubine), who was homesick for the mountainous and tree-covered landscape of her Iranian homeland. The Greek historian Diodorus Siculus describes the gardens as resembling a stepped ziggurat; the Roman historian Quintus Curtius Rufus says the trees were about six feet in diameter and stood 50 feet tall, and the grove rested on a square base, each side of which was 400 feet long; while the Greek geographer, Strabo, and Philo of Byzantium describe the screw pump and hydraulic principles that were applied to raise the volume of water needed to irrigate the artificial forest. Whatever the case, the Hanging Gardens of Babylon were more than just the royal equivalent of a bouquet of long-stemmed roses! Though Robert Koldewey and others have searched for their massive remains, the exact location of the gardens, whether attached to the palace or beyond, remains a wondrous mystery.

CITY PLANNING

According to historian Marc Van de Mieroop, "Mesopotamia was . . . the most densely urbanized region in the ancient world" (Van de Mieroop 1999: 64). Yet, uncovering the plan of its cities is no easy matter. As Van de Mieroop points out, "Not a single urban site in Mesopotamia has been completely excavated. In fact, most excavations have uncovered only a very small percentage of the total area of the site under investigation" (Van de Mieroop 1999: 63).

The reasons for this are easy to understand. To begin with, archaeological excavation is a painstaking, time-consuming, and expensive undertaking. Second, most Mesopotamian sites are in a state of archaeological "melt-down" due to the decomposition of the building materials that were used in ancient times, especially in common houses. Short on time and money, the archaeologist will often zero in on obvious monumental remains in the hope of finding inscriptions and art, thereby ignoring the larger landscape where the everyday lives of ordinary people were lived out. Even aerial surveys offer only a skewed bird's-eye view of a site: not a snapshot of a day in the life of a city but a confusing montage of exposed ruins dating to different eras.

Fortunately, some ancient maps (in baked clay) survive, including one picturing Nippur as it appeared around 1500 B.C.E. In addition, there are cuneiform texts that cite the major monuments of various cities and list neighborhoods and the names of streets and city gates. With the help of these documents and the partial information gathered from a collection of sites, a composite portrait of a typical Mesopotamian city has emerged.

Our typical Mesopotamian city developed gradually. If it possessed a plan, it was not one that was imposed by logic with a neat grid-pattern of broad streets meeting at right angles. Instead, its "plan" arose organically from within as its population grew and their needs had to be met. Streets would tend to wind and be narrow, but that was acceptable since the shade their huddled buildings offered lent the pedestrian protection from the sun. At some point accessible to all by thoroughfare, a temple and ziggurat would be raised up in honor of the city's patron god. Elsewhere a palace would be constructed. In the cities of the south, the religious complex and palace would be centrally located; in the cities of the north, where terrain was uneven, both were enclosed within a strategically placed and well-fortified "upper city," while most of the population lived in the "lower" city below, or in the plains that stretched out beyond. In the south, suburbs probably existed outside the city walls, as well as harbors, fields, and orchards. In time of war, both in the south and the north, settlers would seek refuge inside the city's fortifications. To provide for just such a contingency, open spaces seem to have been reserved inside the city as a safe haven.

Of course, when a new capital city was constructed or an older city was given a facelift by an image-conscious king, efforts were made to impose regularity by substituting broad, intersecting avenues for the narrow, winding streets of an earlier era.

Though it is extremely difficult to estimate the population density of these ancient cities, it is possible to measure their general size. Ur covered 23.5 square miles; other Sumerian cities, almost 30. Nineveh, by comparison, covered nearly 290 square miles. According to the biblical book of Jonah (4:11), the sinful city of Nineveh was so broad it took three days to cross it, "that great city wherein more than 120,000 people dwell who cannot tell their right hand from their left." The largest city in Mesopotamia, however, was Babylon. Indeed, it was the largest city in the world until the days of imperial Rome. Babylon's expanse measured over 340 square miles. Describing Babylon, the Greek philosopher Aristotle once said (*Politics* 3: 3) that it was as big as a nation, "for when Babylon was captured, it took many of its citizens three days to learn the news" (Van de Mieroop 1999: 95).

WALLS

Mesopotamian cities were defined by their walls. Originally, especially in the south, those walls may have been built as dikes to protect early settlements, and the shrines of the gods, from the annual threat of flooding. But with the rise of imperialism, walls were principally designed to meet the danger of military attack.

Though little of them survives physically, their likeness is preserved in art, especially in Assyrian reliefs that depict cities under siege. There we see walls fitted out with zigzag crenelations, not unlike of those of medieval European castles. The crenelations enabled the defenders of a city to rain their arrows on the enemy below (taking aim through the open notches, or crenels) and then duck behind the tooth-like projections (or merlons) when the enemy returned fire with its own missiles.

Fortifications were constructed of brick (oven-baked on the outside of the wall; sun-dried, if necessary, within) and, wherever possible, of stone, at least on the lowest level. All of this was designed to prevent enemy sappers from burrowing through, and portable rams from piercing and smashing through, during time of siege. The city of Babylon had a double wall with rubble packed in between. The outer wall alone was between 20 and 25 feet thick, and defensive towers were set at 65-foot intervals along its 11-mile length, giving archers in each tower an overlapping field of fire. In addition, cities like Babylon provided themselves with an additional line of defense by surroundings themselves with moats fed by river water, or by using the river itself as an obstacle.

Citizens gained entry to their cities through imposing fortified gateways. Babylon probably had nine gates, of which only one has been excavated, the famous Ishtar Gate now on display in the Berlin Museum and decorated with lions and dragons executed in sculptured brick.

The greatest celebration of city walls, and of the promise of urban life itself, is to be found as a refrain in Mesopotamia's literary masterpiece, the *Epic of Gilgamesh*. After his labors are over and his travails past, the hero-king gazes toward the skyline of his city and says:

> Climb up and walk the length of Uruk's walls.
> Inspect its foundation. Make trial of the brick.
> Were not the bricks hardened in fire?
> Did not the Seven Sages lay their course?

With immortality denied him, Gilgamesh, with renewed vigor, commits himself to life in the here and now, to building a better existence for his people and himself, starting from the ground up.

CANALS AND AQUEDUCTS

Across the yawning gulf of 5,000 years, we see the sun-browned Sumerians beginning the endless task of breaking the rivers and the plain to the use of man. As century followed century, Mesopotamia came to be damascened by an azure web of canals, which tamed the mighty Euphrates, clothed the desert in rippling fields of golden grain, and moistened the roots of date palms planted along their banks in endless rows. (De Camp 1963: 52)

So L. Sprague de Camp depicts Mesopotamia in his book, *The Ancient Engineers*. Mesopotamia's land was blessed with life-giving water, and that is one of the leading reasons why civilization began there. Indeed, its very name means "the land between the rivers" (from the ancient Greek *potamos*, which meant "river," and the prefix *meso*, "between").

But it was not sufficient that the waters of the Tigris and Euphrates merely existed. The waters had to be bent to the "use of man" and delivered to his fields and pastures so that crops and herds could grow to sustain human life. As a result, the rivers of Mesopotamia inspired some of the earliest achievements in civil and mechanical engineering.

The Nature of the Rivers

When it came to water, the farmers of Egypt had an easier time than their ancient Iraqi brethren. The Nile flooded once a year with calendric precision, enabling farmers to prepare for its rise. When it did rise beginning in late July, its waters rose gradually, inundating the fields in August and September. And when they withdrew in early October, they left behind a fresh layer of rich silt that renewed the fertility of the land. It was then that the first seeds were sown and the agricultural cycle began. Indeed, there was time to plant both winter and summer crops before the Nile would rise again.

In Mesopotamia, however, the situation was very different. When the snows in the mountains to the north melted, the waters of the Tigris and Euphrates rose, but their annual flooding was unpredictable, occurring anytime between April and early June, too late to help any winter crops, and by then the seeds for summer crops had already been sown. And when the deluge came, it could arrive suddenly with an almost capricious fury, destroying the young plants as well as everything in its path. No wonder, then, that Mesopotamia was the home of the world's oldest story of a cataclysmic flood.

Of the two rivers, the Tigris was the more violent, flowing faster and flooding sooner. The Euphrates, on the other hand, with a shallower channel flowed more slowly and was less violent. Because of its more gentle nature, the Euphrates was more readily turned to by farmers for aid. Though the Tigris was used to water the lands that lay to its east, the waters of the more friendly Euphrates nourished most of Mesopotamia's cultivated soil.

Defensive Earthworks

Wherever feasible, levees were built to raise the height of the rivers' embankments, which were at times reinforced with reed mats or, for greater stability, with walls of baked brick set in bitumen. Dams were usually ineffectual because the earth out of which they were made eventually washed away.

Projects and Management

In addition to defensive earthworks to hold back floodwaters, networks of canals were constructed to distribute river water safely and efficiently. These public works projects could not have been accomplished without the efforts of an organized work force operating under centralized authority. To be sure, the populace knew their lives and welfare depended upon their collaborative efforts. But their kings also regarded flood control and irrigation as their highest responsibility and took the greatest pride in their hydraulic achievements. Hammurabi of Babylon, for example, devoted most of the last nine years of his reign to such projects and even ceremonially honored one of the years of his reign by naming it for a great canal he had built. In fact, three of the statutes in his famous code dealt specifically with the control of water, including punishments meted out to those who out of laziness failed to maintain the levees near their property.

Methods of Irrigation

Not only did canals need to be laboriously dug by hand; they also needed to be laboriously maintained. The fact is echoed in a favorite Babylonian curse: "May your canal become clogged with sand!"

The slope of a canal was critical to its operation because the flow of water depended upon gravity. If the slope was too steep, erosion from fast-flowing water would eat away the bed of the channel and make the level of the water too low for it to spill into the fields; if the slope was too gradual, silt would build up or reeds grow, clogging the flow. Thus, surveying played an important role in the construction of canals, just as regular dredging and reed-pulling did once they were dug. In addition, the embankments of canals had to be preserved to insure they would not collapse. When canals formed networks, the problems and challenges only multiplied.

At inlet points along the riverside, sluice gates controlled the entry of water into the canal system. But when the level of the water in the river dropped below the inlet point, the water had to be raised. This was accomplished by an ingenious device known in Arabic as a *shaduf*, a device still used in the Near East today.

A *shaduf* is a seesaw-like contraption consisting of a long pole with an empty bucket at one end and a counterweight at the other. The counterweight can be a bucket or sack filled with clay or rubble. The pole, for its part, rests horizontally atop a simple wooden framework that holds it loosely and allows it to swivel or bend as though on a fulcrum. Using his own body weight, the worker pulls the bucket end of the pole downward, swings it out over the water, and dips it into the river until the bucket is full. Loosening his grip on the pole, he then lets the counterweight raise the heavy bucket, and swings it out over the canal, into which he empties the water. Because the counterweight does the work of lifting the full bucket, the job is made easier. In fact, by using more than one *shaduf*, water can be raised from one level to another. Besides moving water from river to canal, the *shaduf* could help a farmer transfer water from a major canal and pour it into a minor one to irrigate his fields.

In addition to canals, wells have been found at a number of Mesopotamian sites. Here, a bucket would simply be lowered and then pulled up. This job too was made easier by an invention—the pulley—sometime before 1500 B.C.E. The pulley itself represented an application of an even earlier invention, the Sumerian wheel. For a more rapid water supply, King Nebuchadnezzar of Babylon installed a chain pump in the basement of his palace: a series of buckets attached to a continuous metal chain. As the buckets at the bottom filled up with water, the ones at the top emptied out.

Aqueducts

According to the Greek historian Herodotus, an Arabian king of the sixth century B.C.E. once transported water across the desert in a pipe sewn together from animal skins. The pipe was a long one: it would have taken 12 days to cover the same distance by camel caravan, a distance of more than 300 miles.

Whether the story is true or not, we'll never know. What we *do* know is that water was regularly transported for long distances across northern Mesopotamia by underground conduit, especially when a growing population center needed water and there was no handy river nearby. Once again an engineering solution solved a problem, in this case a solution even more ingenious than the *shaduf*.

On the one hand, transporting water over long distances in a closed conduit (to avoid evaporation) is not hard, for gravity will do the job. As long as the source of water—say, a mountain spring—is always higher than the point of delivery—say, a city in a valley, the water will reach its destination by simply flowing downhill. The problem, however, is to maintain the proper degree of slope. If the slope is not constant, for example, if the conduit goes up instead of down, flow will be impeded. If the slope is too gradual, flow will be too slow and sedimentation may clog the channel. If the slope is too steep, the rapid flow of the water may erode the channel and cause it to collapse. How, then, does one insure that the slope will be appropriate? Only by putting it underground, where its course is determined by excavation rather than by the landscape above. But how does one insure the right slope when the conduit is being cut many feet, perhaps even hundreds of feet, below ground? And, even if that can be accomplished, how can we be sure the workmen digging the conduit underground will point it in the right direction and keep it going straight? Besides, if we're talking about a conduit stretching for miles, how long will it take a few workmen in a crowded pit to cut through miles of solid bedrock? All of these frustrating questions show us why the underground water conduit, or subterranean aqueduct, was a long time in coming.

The solution was discovered by an eighth century B.C.E. Assyrian king named Sargon II during his conquest of Urartu, the ancient name for Armenia. Urartu was mining country, and the miners of Urartu had found the answers to all our questions. Once Sargon II learned them, he punished the Urartians by destroying all their aqueducts and then, when he returned triumphantly to Assyria, built underground aqueducts of his own. Later, the Persians would learn the secret, and in successive centuries it became common knowledge throughout the Mideast, where it is still in use today.

The device in question is called in Arabic a *qanat*, and in Persian a *kariz*. Basically, it is an underground water conduit with a constant slope. Not only that, but it has a regular series of access holes for maintenance (in case of blockages), holes that also release the air pressure that can build up and impede flow when the rush of water through the pipe becomes too fast.

But back to our problem: how, then, does one make a *qanat*?

The answer is to dig vertical channels into the rock at regular intervals. A surveyor on the ground marks out a straight line in the direction the water is meant to travel in. Wherever he then plants a stake, a hole is dug and a channel cut down through the rock. The straight up-and-downness of each channel can be easily monitored with a plumb line dropped down and dangled from the hole at the top. The proper depth of each channel can also be accurately predetermined by measuring from the horizontal plane above the series of holes. When different teams of miners have dug their vertical channels to the right depth, short horizontal channels can then be cut to connect them at the bottom. These short channels can be subsequently smoothed out to achieve a graduated slope. By employing multiple teams of diggers, the complete project can be executed more quickly and accurately than if a single set of miners burrowed slowly ahead in mole-like fashion.

In Afghanistan, such tunnels, dried out and abandoned, were exploited and expanded as hiding places and storage facilities by the militants of modern times.

Of course, the *qanat* could not be used in southern Mesopotamia's alluvial plain where the earth was soft and tunneling would have been risky. There, aboveground canals were the method of choice for moving water. But in the north where there was substantial bedrock, the *qanat* was the answer.

In later centuries, the ancient Romans excavated underground conduits to transport water to their cities, but they also carried the water through conduits supported far above ground by tall arches. The most remarkable of these aqueducts can still be seen in Spain at Segovia and in France at Nîmes. Nîmes's celebrated Pont du Gard was, in fact, originally designed to carry not traffic but water. In their heyday, the aqueducts of Rome—both underground and elevated—brought 250 million gallons of freshwater each day to the capital's urban masses. Amazingly, four are still in operation, including one that feeds the romantic Trevi Fountain. The Romans were able to erect aboveground aqueducts because they had access to large local supplies of quarriable stone, especially limestone, a luxury that the Mesopotamian engineer did not generally enjoy.

One Mesopotamian exception can be viewed near the modern city of Jerwan, located north of ancient Nineveh. A 30-mile-long underground conduit was built by the Assyrian king Sennacherib to supply Nineveh with water, but its slope required that it cross a small river valley. Sennacherib's solution was to build a 90-foot-long bridge to carry the conduit 30 feet above the stream. Ruins can still be seen of the five corbelled arches that supported the bridge, each constructed of cubic blocks of stone measuring 20 inches on each side. The whole aqueduct took a year and a quarter to complete, and Sennacherib planned a special ceremony to mark its opening. The monarch's thunder, however, was apparently stolen by a defective sluice-gate that allowed the water to flow before the ceremony could begin. Ever the opportunist, Sennacherib took this to be a sign from the gods validating his project and so he did not punish the seemingly negligent workers. Instead, as he proudly tells us in his annals, he rewarded them with fine clothes and golden rings and daggars.

Then and Now

Thanks to a complex and extensive system of irrigation that maximized the fertile potential of its soil, Mesopotamia enjoyed an abundance of agricultural produce. The land cultivated in southern Mesopotamia alone may have exceeded 12,000 square miles and the population density of the country as a whole may have even surpassed that of present-day Iraq.

This system was surely one of the glorious triumphs of ancient engineering. But what, then, became of it? And why must Iraq today import food to feed its people?

In part, the answer can be traced to the malevolence of man and nature.

Sennacherib, the same Assyrian king who built the aqueduct at Jerwan, was also capable of hydraulic destruction. Angry at Babylon for revolting against his rule, he massacred its people, dammed up the Euphrates, and then diverted its waters, sending them hurtling through the city. Later, he repented and rebuilt what he had destroyed, as did his son who succeeded him.

Less forgiving, however, were the Mongol hordes led by Hulagu Khan. After capturing Baghdad in 1258 C.E. and conquering Mesopotamia, they ravaged the country's canal system, leaving the people to starve. Politically and militarily vulnerable, Mesopotamia was plundered in successive centuries by foreign people as its population declined and social order broke down.

No enemy, however, foreign or domestic proved as unforgiving as nature itself.

Over time, the rivers meandered and their courses altered. Old canals became useless and were abandoned. With persistent neglect, even canals that still functioned slowly filled up with silt and reeds.

In prehistoric times, much of what is southern Iraq and Kuwait today lay submerged beneath the waters of the Persian Gulf. As a result, there are thick beds of sea salt beneath the soil. In ancient Mesopotamia, the intensive irrigation of the soil dissolved the salt and brought it to the surface. When the water evaporated, traces of salt were left behind, traces that accumulated over many centuries

and, over time, chemically inhibited seeds from germinating. The problem was compounded by the Tigris and Euphrates themselves, which carried dissolved salts they had picked up from the mountains to the north that were their source. As their waters flowed through Mesopotamia's canals and evaporated from its soil, the salts were left behind. Thus, what the Mongols and others had been incapable of achieving, salinization accomplished.

Today, parallel ridges can be seen traversing the landscape of Iraq, tracing in dry wasteland the lines of canals that once flowed with life-giving water. From outer space, satellite imagery can detect the remains of now-desiccated watercourses invisible at ground level to the naked eye. Nearby, a weary peasant bends over, lowering the pole of a *shaduf* just as his ancestors did 5,000 years ago. The Euphrates rolls silently by him, mindless of human struggle and folly.

BRIDGES

The building of the Jerwan aqueduct was necessitated by terrain: if water was to be carried in a conduit above a stream, the conduit had to be supported by a bridge. However, a bridge to transport vital water was one thing; one to transport people was another. Pedestrian bridges were rare in Mesopotamia because the rivers themselves provided the main means of transport. Where rivers were too broad or deep to be forded, ferries were used to convey passengers and cargo. In addition, rafts made of buoyant bundles of reeds were used, sometimes equipped with inflated animal skins for increased flotation when carrying heavy loads. The military used such rafts to cross rivers and, when necessary, built temporary pontoon bridges. The Assyrian king

Tiglathpileser I even employed a special corps of engineers to make emergency roadways on land and pontoon bridges over water for the use of his army.

Bridge construction in the land of the Tigris and Euphrates posed special engineering problems: the riverbeds, especially in the south, were soft and unstable; currents, especially on the Tigris, could be swift; and, over time, the very courses of the rivers shifted, making what otherwise would have been a permanent bridge obsolete. In addition, the proper materials for bridge construction—quarried stone and suitable timber—were in short supply locally, particularly in the south.

One remarkable exception was the bridge built over the Euphrates River at Babylon at the end of the seventh century B.C.E.

The bridge is described by two ancient historians: Herodotus, who lived during the Golden Age of Athens, and Diodorus Siculus, who lived during the Golden Age of Rome. Diodorus attributes its construction to the legendary Semiramis, ninth-century B.C.E. queen of Nineveh and early founder of Babylon; Herodotus, to Nitocris, the wife of Babylon's later sixth-century B.C.E. king, Nebuchadnezzar. As it turns out, Herodotus's version is closer to the truth, for, in an inscription that has been found, Nebuchadnezzar himself identifies the builder: his father, Nabopolassar.

Here then is Herodotus's account (*History* 1: 186) of the bridge's construction (with Nitocris playing the role of Nabopolassar).

The city . . . was divided by the river into two distinct portions. Under the former kings, if a man wanted to pass from one of these divisions to the other, he had to cross in a boat; which must, it seems to me, have been very troublesome. Accordingly, while she was digging [an artificial lake], Nitocris bethought herself of turning it to a use which should at once remove this inconvenience, and enable

her to leave another monument to her reign over Babylon. She gave orders for the hewing of immense blocks of stone, and when they were ready and the basin [of the lake] was excavated, she turned the entire stream of the Euphrates into the cutting, and thus for a time, while the basin was filling, the natural channel of the river was left dry. Forthwith she set to work, and in the first place lined the banks of the stream within the city with quays of burnt brick, and also bricked the landing places opposite the river-gates, adopting throughout the same fashion of brickwork which had been used in the town wall; after which, with the materials which had been prepared, she built, as near the middle of the town as possible, a stone bridge, the blocks whereof were bound together with iron and lead [clamps]. In the daytime square wooden platforms were laid along from pier to pier, on which the inhabitants crossed the stream; but at night they were withdrawn, to prevent people passing from side to side in the dark to commit robberies. When the river had filled the cutting [for the lake], and the bridge was finished, the Euphrates was turned back again into its ancient bed. (Herodotus 1942 [1858]: 100–1, trans. George Rawlinson)

Thanks to the fact that the Euphrates changed its course over time, archaeologists were able to excavate the actual ruins of the bridge. It was 380 feet long (Diodorus makes it almost a half mile in length) and was supported on seven piers made of stone, brick, and timber. Though massive (28 feet wide and 65 feet long), the piers were hydrodynamically designed like an airplane wing—rounded on the upstream side where the force of the current met the pier, and then sharply tapered toward the downstream. The flaw in the design was that their mass filled up half the river's width. This increased the velocity of the water flowing between them, especially at flood time, and led to the erosion of the riverbed around their foundations. But the bridge was still standing in Diodorus's time, more than 600 years after it was built, possibly because the riverbed repaired itself every year with fresh silt when the current was slow.

According to Diodorus, the superstructure of the bridge was 30 feet wide with a floor fashioned from palm-tree logs and planks of cypress and cedar, some of which—as Herodotus notes—could be removed for nighttime security.

Nabopolassar's bridge over the mighty Euphrates was unique in its day and continued to be so for centuries. It is the oldest permanent bridge of which we have any record, and rightly rivaled Babylon's Hanging Gardens in fame. If its span did not match New York's Verrazano or San Francisco's Golden Gate, it is only because Mesopotamian engineers dared in wood and brick what they could not yet dream in steel.

ROADS

Mesopotamia's rivers were its natural highways. Its cities dappled its riverbanks like green way stations in a wilderness, like gems strung along a riverine necklace hanging down toward the bosom of the sea.

As long as communal activities were circumscribed by a city's walls, and wheeled vehicles were few, there was little need for man-made roadways. The kingdoms of Mesopotamia were originally self-sufficient city-states, and therefore they did not need interconnection. Dirt pathways sufficed, especially for the caravans that brought trade goods overland.

Indeed, southern Mesopotamia's canal system inhibited the making of roads by setting up a series of watery barriers to movement by land. During winter rains dirt tracks turned to mud, and during spring floods they became impassable. Besides, the speediest beasts of burden were the obstinate donkey and, in later days, the lumbering camel.

In time of intercity war, armies traveled by water or along mercantile trails. Only with the rise of empire did the idea of permanent roads begin to appeal to Mesopotamia's rulers as a means to better communication and logistical control.

The Assyrians devoted particular attention to roads for a number of reasons. First, the terrain they inhabited was rough and hilly and required roadways to permit columned soldiers to pass. Second, their native river, the Tigris, was less navigable than the Euphrates and made water transport more difficult. And third, the extent of their conquests demanded a system that could expedite the transmission of administrative and military reports and orders and the rapid deployment of troops.

The Assyrian kings did not go so far as to build highways, but they did establish guardposts at regular intervals along desert tracks and dug wells for the use of travelers. In addition, they set up road signs to help them find their way. Sennacherib declared that roads should be well maintained and city streets well constructed, while Esarhaddon promised to reconstruct the infrastructure in conquered states so that their roads would be open and they could carry on commerce with neighboring nations. The Assyrians also established a royal messenger service, and they drew up maps for their couriers indicating the distances in hours between stops.

Paved roads were a rarity, but they did exist in Assyrian times, especially for processional ways that led to temples and were used during religious festivals. Also, the entryways to royal cities were paved to impress visitors. The pavement consisted of slabs of gypsum set in a bitumen mortar on top of a foundation of baked brick that rested on a layer of gravel. Main streets and market squares might also be paved. In earlier days especially in the south, brick in all likelihood took the place of stone.

It was the Persians who raised high-speed land travel to the level of an art. Herodotus (*History* 8: 98) recounted the method used by the kings of Persia to send official communiqués to the far-flung corners of their empire.

> Nothing mortal travels so fast as these Persian messengers. The entire plan is a Persian invention; and this is the method of it. Along the whole line of road there are men (they say) stationed with horses, in number equal to the number of days the journey takes, allowing a man and a horse to each day; and these men will not be hindered from accomplishing at their best speed the distance they have to go, either by snow, or rain, or heat, or by the darkness of night. The first rider delivers his dispatch to the second, and the second passes it to the third; and so it is borne from hand to hand along the whole line, like the light in the torch-race, which the Greeks celebrate to Hephaestus [the ancient god of technology]. (Herodotus 1942 [1858]: 633–34, trans. George Rawlinson)

The Persian system was duplicated by America's 19th century "Pony Express," but beat it by 24 centuries. Herodotus's description, incidentally, was adapted and inscribed on the façade of New York City's General Post Office ("Neither snow, nor rain, nor heat, nor gloom of night stays these couriers from the swift completion of their appointed rounds").

It was the Romans, however, who were antiquity's master road-builders. "All roads lead to Rome," went the saying, but it might more truly have said that all roads led from Rome, for the Romans understood the importance of land transportation for consolidation of their conquests. Their first highway was the famous Appian Way. Begun in

312 B.C.E., it led south from the city of Rome to the Italian seaport of Brundisium, a distance of 234 miles. By the time their empire had reached its zenith, Roman engineers had constructed 50,000 miles of all-weather, paved roads stretching from western Europe all the way to the Near East. So durable were they that some are still being used to this very day, including stretches of the venerable Appian Way. At places in the Near East, we can still see their neatly cut paving blocks pointing into the desert to vanished cities.

READING

Building Materials and Houses, Domestic Architecture, and Techniques of Construction

Contenau 1954: clay and brick making; de Camp 1963: house design; Forbes 1955–58: bitumen and quarrying; Kramer 1967: description and illustration of typical Sumerian house; Muller 1940, Stone 1997: houses; Saggs 1965: Babylonian and Assyrian houses.

From Village to City

Adams 1960, 1966, 1981: origins of cities; Childe 1951: the Neolithic and Urban Revolutions; Crawford 1977: early architecture; Lampl 1968: city planning in the ancient Near East; Leacroft 1974: illustrations of buildings; Oppenheim 1969: urban density and layout; Redman 1978: from farming to urban civilization; Roaf 1990: the evolution of agricultural villages; Roux 1992: the emergence of the city; Stone 1995: the development of cities in southern and northern Mesopotamia; Thesiger 1964: the marsh Arabs.

Temples

Contenau 1954: plan; Giedion 1964: evolution; Leacroft 1974: illustrations; Lloyd, Müller, and Martin 1974: plans; Roaf 1995: description.

Ziggurats

Contenau 1954: description; Giedion 1964: evolution and meaning; Leacroft 1974: illustrations; Ravn 1932: Babylon's tower; Van Buren 1952: construction.

Palaces

Bienkowski and Millard 2000: survey; Clayton and Price 1988, Romer 1995: Hanging Gardens of Babylon; Leacroft 1974: illustrations; Lloyd, Müller, and Martin 1974: plans; Roaf 1995: discussion; Russell 1998: Sennacherib's throne room; Stevenson 1992: irrigation of the Hanging Gardens; Winter 1993: the Near Eastern palace as ideological construct.

City Planning

Frankfort 1950: town planning in Mesopotamia; Gallery 1976: town planning and community structure; Lampl 1968: city planning; Oppenheim 1969: Mesopotamian cities; Rav 1932: Herodotus's description of Babylon; Stone 1995: development of cities in Mesopotamia; Van de Mieroop 1999: urban landscape.

Walls

Bienkowski and Millard 2000: walls in the ancient Near East.

Canals and Aqueducts

Adams 1981: irrigation and urban society; Borowski 1997: irrigation in the Near East; de Camp 1963: Mesopotamian engineering; Forbes 1955–58: irrigation, drainage, and water supply; Jacobsen 1982: salinity and irrigation; Jacobsen and Lloyd 1935: the Jerwan aqueduct; Landels 1978: the *shaduf* and *qanat*.

Bridges

De Camp 1963: triumphs of Mesopotamian engineering.

Roads

Forbes 1955–58: land transport and road-building.

7

SCULPTURE
AND OTHER ARTS

The Role of the Artist

Today when we think of an artist, we tend to think of an individualist who uses his or her talent for the purpose of self-expression, a nonconformist who may defy tradition even at the cost of financial security. Those who succeed are known by their names.

While this may be true of modern artists, it was not generally true of ancient ones except in Greece, where individualism shone. Rather than individualists and nonconformists, most ancient artists were the servants of society and tradition. Their employers were the state, centered in temple or palace, and the public at large, whose everyday needs they supplied. It may therefore be more useful to conceive of Mesopotamia's artists as craftsmen and artisans whose livelihoods were guaranteed by the utility and beauty of the objects their skill and talent produced: pottery, wall paintings, mosaics, glass, cylinder seals, carved ivory, and jewelry, as well as sculpture for the glorification of their kings and gods. Because of their subservient role, the great artists of Mesopotamia remain anonymous; only through their work does their identity survive.

Materials

The artists of Mesopotamia were challenged by the scarcity of locally available materials to develop and practice their craft. In measuring the technical achievement of Mesopotamia's artists, therefore, we must appreciate the natural obstacles they rose above to reach aesthetic heights.

In the south where civilization began, only clay was readily available; most other materials, especially minerals, had to be imported. It is for this reason that pottery became one of the very first of the country's arts, and architecture was first built with foundations and walls of brick. Only later in Assyria to the north could architects and sculptors avail themselves of ample local supplies of stone.

Sculpture

It is through sculpture that the faces of the past three-dimensionally emerge from the mists of time.

Art and Immortality

Life in ancient Mesopotamia, life anywhere and anytime, is as evanescent as flesh. For life to be preserved, it must be recorded in writing or art. But the preservation of life depends upon the permanence of the materials onto which its forms are transcribed.

We labor under an illusion if we assume our present age will be better remembered than antiquity. The average life expectancy of magnetic tapes, audio or video, is only about 10 years; of optical disks, 50; of archival quality microfilm, but a 100. In fact, average-quality CD-ROMs become unreadable or unreliable after only five years. Advances in technology, moreover, make older computer hardware and software obsolete; and as they grow obsolete, their data becomes unintelligible. Meanwhile, the film that recorded the images of the past is already crumbling; according to UNESCO, "three-quarters of the films which were made worldwide before 1950 have already disappeared." Thus our so-called Age of Information may be known to the future as an age of *missing* information.

The inhabitants of Mesopotamia's flood-plains were intimately familiar with imperma-nence. Like other peoples of antiquity they sought to imprint their identity on substances more durable than flesh, and—paradoxically—more durable than the electronic media we use today. For writing, they relied on clay; for sculpture, stone, copper, and bronze.

The scarcity of stone and metal, especially in the south, limited the quantity of portrait sculpture that could be produced. Combined with an autocratic government, the intrinsic value of these materials caused them to be used in art almost exclusively to portray the piety and power of political leaders.

Almost inexplicably, the faces of the gods rarely appear, unlike the situation in Egypt where the gods, along with the divine pharaoh, were one of sculpture's major subjects. One Mesopotamian exception found at Warka is a haunting almost life-size female head made of alabaster that today lacks its inlaid eyebrows and eyes. The "case of the missing idols" may per-haps be solved if we assume such statues were made of materials even more precious than stone or bronze: gold, for example, and/or ivory, materials that would be readily seized and car-ried off by an invading force. This is exactly what happened in classical Greece after the fall of the Roman Empire: the chryselephantine (gold and ivory) statues of Zeus at Olympia and Athena in Athens' Parthenon were cannibalized by iconoclastic vandals. During the European Dark Ages, even Greek and Roman bronze stat-ues were melted down wholesale for the usable metal they contained. Similarly, classical statues of marble were burnt in kilns to extract lime from the stone, lime that could then be used to make humble cement. It is the sheer quantity of classical sculpture that accounts for its partial survival against such great odds. Just as Greece was rich in marble, so in Egypt abundant quar-ries generated huge supplies of stone that were suitable for both architecture and monumental sculpture. Geology was not so kind to Mesopotamia, where the scarcity of raw materi-als severely limited artistic production.

Types and Techniques

Mesopotamian sculpture like sculpture every-where falls into two broad categories. First, there are statues, or "sculpture in the round," ranging in size from small figurines to larger than life-size pieces. Second, there are reliefs, works in which the stone on the surface of a slab is partially chiseled away, leaving raised figures set off against a lower background. When the figures dramatically stand out from the back-ground, we speak of "high relief"; when the dis-tance between planes is more subtle, we speak of "low" or (after the French) "bas-relief." In both statues and reliefs, details are incised into stone with hammer and chisel, and final finish-ing is achieved with the aid of abrasives. Copper and bronze statues were made by pouring molten metal into molds (if the statue was small) or by using the lost-wax, or cire perdue, method (if the statue was to be large). With this method, an original was shaped out of wax on a clay core and then covered in more clay. The wax was then melted out and displaced by molten metal that took on its form. At times, individual parts of a large statue might be cast separately and then fused together.

Traces of coloring show that Mesopotamian sculptors applied tinting to make stone statues and reliefs more life-like. Black was used for hair and beads, and for the rims and pupils of eyes, while the eyeball itself was painted white. Yellow paint was used to simulate golden jew-elry, and green to make the vegetation in land-scapes look more natural. Red was occasionally daubed on as well. In addition, statues might be enlivened with an inlay of stone in a contrast-ing or complementary color.

As evident in scenes carved in relief, Mesopotamian sculptors had not mastered the art of perspective. An object or person that realistically would have been behind another is often shown above.

Likewise, the parts of the body are not shown in true perspective. Generally, the face, legs, and feet are portrayed in profile, but the shoulders and chest full-front. The approach is one that attempts to capture not the naturalistic appearance of the body as a whole but the functional essence of each part. Thus, the locomotion generated by the lower limbs is best conveyed in relief not from the front but from the side where one leg and foot can be shown ahead of the other; in contrast, the muscular strength of the upper body can best be displayed not from the narrow side but from the broad front. This mode of anatomical representation parallels that employed by the artists of Egypt, as does the Mesopotamian portrayal of the eye, shown full and almond-shaped as though to communicate as completely as possible its vital structure.

Purposes and Subjects

Statues embodied the personality in order to communicate it to others in a religious or political setting. The statues might portray worshipers or rulers. In Assyrian times, paired statues of fantastic beasts flanked the entrances to palaces to inspire visitors with awe.

Reliefs served to commemorate important events such as a military victory, the completion of a major building, or the public proclamation of law. Reliefs could be carved on paneled walls for the purposes of decoration and propaganda, or could be carved on individual slabs of stone (known as stelae; sg., stela or stele) to signify a boundary or to record an episode from recent history. Stelae could combine pictures with inscriptions in cuneiform. A

technique principally employed by the Persians was to carve an inscribed relief on a prominent cliffside for all to see.

Statues from Sumer and Akkad

In 1932 while digging in the ruins of Tell Asmar (ancient Eshnunna), Henri (Hans) Frankfort and Seton Lloyd made a startling discovery. Mary Chubb, who was present, describes it:

> Seton and Hans were alone in the Abu temple when I reached it. They were crouching in front of the niche beside the altar, and a fresh pile of rubble lay all around them on the clean floor. . . . Down in the floor of the niche was a long oblong cavity—and in it I could see a gleaming, tightly packed mass of white and cream and gray and yellow stone statues. Here a strange eye stared up, then a hand, long fingers, curled round a cup, seemed to tremble with life as Seton gently brushed it with his fingers. . . . Most were over a foot in length. Many of them were broken, though all the pieces were in place; . . . it looked as if they had been complete when buried, but that the weight of the numerous rebuildings of the temple above must have cracked and crushed them. More statues came up, men and women, the men in fringed and tasseled kilts, the women with long cloaks thrown over one shoulder, leaving the other bare. All had their hands clasped before them, some holding cups. "They are worshipers, of course," Hans said. . . . Gazing up at us out of the shadows were two pairs of appalling eyes—huge black eyes with gleaming white eyeballs. They were set in the faces of a bearded man and a woman, each holding a cup. . . . We gazed at them, and they gazed back at us with vast, unseeing, nightmare eyes. (Chubb 1957: 142–44)

What Frankfort and Lloyd had found was a cache of 12 Sumerian figurines dating to about 2700 B.C.E. The largest, the "bearded man,"

7.1 *Votive statuettes discovered at Tell Asmar. Carved from limestone, alabaster, and gypsum, they stand reverently in prayer, even as they once stood in ancient Eshnunna almost 5,000 years ago.* (Oriental Institute, University of Chicago)

was 30 inches tall with large, staring eyes of lapis lazuli and shell set in bitumen glue. Similar statues have been found at other Sumerian sites. Inscriptions on them have been found as well, indicating—along with the statues' reverential poses and libation cups—that the figurines were meant to serve as pious surrogates for real-life worshipers. Says one inscription: "It offers prayers." Says another: "Statue, say to my lord . . ." By dedicating such a figurine to a deity and having it placed within the god's temple, the Sumerian worshiper expressed perpetual piety in anticipation of the god's blessings. As dutiful substitutes in art for the humble

humans they represented, these figurines resemble the mummy-like *shawabti* figurines that abound in the graves and tombs of Egypt.

From about 2100 B.C.E. come a series of statuettes portraying Gudea, the famous ruler of Lagash. At least 30 such portraits survive, suggesting that they were commissioned by Gudea himself both out of pride and out of a desire for self-glorification. In one marvelous example, now in the collection of the Detroit Institute of Arts, he stands $16^1/_8$ inches tall carved out of translucent gray-green paragonite. He wears a turban-like cap and a long shawl-like robe draped over his left arm, leaving his right shoulder bare. Over that shoulder and down his back runs an inscribed cuneiform "tattoo" recounting how he piously built temples to his patron god and his god's consort, and how he had a statue of the goddess created for her temple. As in his many portraits, Gudea stares ahead impassively, his hands clasped in studied and silent devotion.

In the field of relief sculpture, two stelae now in the Louvre commemorate other rulers of Lagash and their deeds. The stela of Ur-Nanshe (see figure 3.17, page 109) depicts the leader in the company of his family as he carries a basket filled with clay that he will use to make the first bricks for a new city temple. In a lower register, or level, he is shown celebrating together with his family the temple's completion. In both registers, the artist conveys Ur-Nanshe's social importance by making him twice as tall as his relatives. While the stela of Ur-Nanshe commemorates peacetime activities, the stela of Eannatum (also from the third millennium B.C.E.) celebrates victory in war. On one side of the stela, the ruler leads a tightly packed phalanx of warriors into battle and rides his chariot at the head of a column of light infantry. Eannatum's army advances over the corpses of the enemy. At the bottom, Lagash's own casualties are buried in a mass grave as Eannatum performs funeral rites. On the reverse side, Ningirsu, the god of Lagash, triumphantly holds enemy captives in a symbolic net.

From late third millenium B.C.E. Akkad comes the stela of Naram-Sin, also in the Louvre (see figure 3.12, page 98). The helmeted king holding bow and arrow appears at the foot of a mountain whose outline is echoed in the tall curved shape of the sculpted slab. As his troops ascend the slopes of the mountain, the king himself stands with his foot planted on enemy corpses while other enemy soldiers surrender and beg for mercy.

Dating to approximately the same period is the almost life-size copper portrait head of an anonymous Akkadian king, perhaps Sargon the Great (See figure 3.13, page 101). The hair on his head is carefully plaited, ending in a tight chignon held by three rings, duplicating the golden ones the king himself once wore. Beneath a diadem, locks of hair overlap in precise semicircles across his brow. His full and artfully curved lips are framed by a moustache above and a beard below, a long forked beard that descends in multiple cascading curls. The head was found in Nineveh's ancient city dump. The nose was bent when the statue tumbled to the ground, tossed

7.2   *Fashioned from jade-green paragonite, this reverential statue of Gudea of Lagash stands 16⅛ inches tall. Dating to the late third millennium B.C.E., the Sumerian statuette now calls Detroit its home.*   (Photograph © 1996, The Detroit Institute of Arts [Founders Society Purchase, Robert H. Tannahill Foundation Fund])

7.3   Art celebrated the military exploits of rulers. Here the Sumerian leader Eannatum spearheads an assault as a phalanx of his soldiers tramples the bodies of their enemies. (Rogers, *A History of Babylonia and Assyria*, 1915)

there perhaps by the vandals who savagely gouged out the gems that once brightened its eyes, leaving only empty holes where precious stones had been. Eyeless today in a Baghdad museum, this Iraqi Oedipus smiles. It is the smile of one who has outlived his enemies.

The Stela of Hammurabi

One of the world's oldest compendia of law is the Code of Hammurabi, named for the Babylonian king of the early eighteenth century B.C.E. This code comes down to us not in a book, nor on a clay tablet, but inscribed on the outside of a block of sculpted black diorite that

stands almost 7.5 feet tall and weighs four tons (See figure 3.3, page 69). At the top of the stela is a two-foot-high relief. On the right, sitting on his divine throne, is the bearded Babylonian god Shamash, waves of sunlight rising in rays from his shoulders. He wears a flounced gown and a spiraling turban, and he holds what appears to be a scepter in his hand. Facing him on the left like Moses is Hammurabi, one hand raised to his lips, portrayed as he receives legal enlightenment from his god. Diorite is one of the hardest stones to sculpt, but it is therefore also one of the most durable. The stone was chosen well to symbolize the everlasting nature of the king's divinely inspired laws, spelled out under the relief in 3,500 precisely incised lines of cuneiform. After the fall of Babylon, the stela was carried off by the Elamites to the city of Susa, where it remained buried until unearthed by French archaeologists at the dawn of the 20th century. It is today one of the treasured possessions of the Louvre.

Images from Assyria

Of the more than 100 kings who ruled Assyria, statues of only two exist: Ashurnasirpal II and his son Shalmaneser III. It is not through statues that the spirit of ancient Assyria still speaks, but through sculptural relief. According to Henri Frankfort:

> Reliefs constitute the greatest and most original achievement of the Assyrians. In fact, the history of Assyrian art is mainly the history of relief carving. (Frankfort 1997: 156)

A stone native to the north, gypsum, was the material from which these works of art were cut. Because of the tendency of this relatively soft stone to degrade when exposed to the elements, it was used mostly for the interiors, but sometimes for the façades and grand entranceways, of palaces. The reliefs date chiefly to the era of the Assyrian Empire's rise, from the ninth century to the fall of Nineveh in 612 B.C.E. The principal sites where the sculptures have surfaced are Nimrud (from the days of Ashurnasirpal II and Shalmaneser III), Khorsabad (from the days of Sargon II), and Nineveh (during the reigns of Sennacherib and Ashurbanipal). Additionally, from the site of Balawat near Nimrud come embossed bronze bands that once decorated the wooden doors of the ruined palace. Three sets of double doors survive, each girded with eight metal bands. The scenes in relief on the hammered and incised bronze bands duplicate in miniature the types of scenes executed elsewhere on gypsum panels.

As Julian Reade has observed, the pictures on Assyrian reliefs project "a man's world, where the secular themes were overwhelmingly war and sport" (Reade 1998 [1993]: 32). They are energized by action and the exercise of raw power, harnessed and rationally disciplined to achieve a single objective: domination. Whether showing battle or the hunt, the sculptures exude

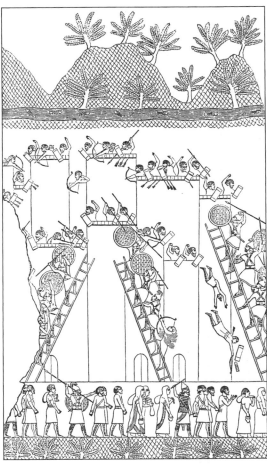

7.4   *Based on a sculptural relief, this drawing depicts in striking detail an Assyrian assault on an enemy city. As scaling soldiers storm the walls of the city, prisoners of war are led away into captivity. The eye and hand of the artist also capture the natural setting for man-made violence and suffering: trees and fish oblivious to war.* (Layard, *Nineveh and Its Remains*, 1849)

7.5 In this detail from a palace relief, fortification walls are attacked by a battering ram as archers fire at the defenders. Like a photojournalist, the sculptor also depicts the bodies of captives impaled on stakes. (M. Jastrow, *Babylonia and Assyria*, 1917)

delight in savagery, be it the slaughter of lions or the brutal butchery of men.

Notes Dominique Collon: "In all the scenes of battle depicted for over three centuries of Assyrian relief, no Assyrian is ever shown wounded or at a disadvantage" (Collon 1995: 36). Assyrian invincibility is the recurrent message of these works whose communicational intent was to fill Assyrian monarchs with self-confidence and subject peoples with dread.

The portraits of the kings, whatever their names, are monotonously the same. But such monotony can also have a purpose: to symbolize the unvarying power and constancy of Assyrian rule.

Nevertheless, throughout the sculpted scenes there is a meticulous attention to realistic detail. The Assyrian army crosses a river, cavalry and chariots charge, siege equipment advances, and another city falls and is sacked. Enemy soldiers and leaders inexorably die—

their chests pierced by spears, their throats slashed by swords, their limp bodies impaled on tall stakes or tied spread-eagle to the ground and flayed alive as their children watch. We see an aerial view of the Assyrian camp: while dinner is being prepared, the troops dance to the accompaniment of lutes and harps and play a game of ball with the decapitated heads of their victims. Meanwhile, the civilian survivors are herded on to deportation, their remaining possessions piled on carts and camels.

Violence and conquest also pervade scenes of the hunt, a diversion for Assyrian kings when they were not at war. A lioness, her hindquarters paralyzed by three arrows, rises up on her front legs in a defiant death agony, while a wounded lion vomits a torrent of blood.

7.6 The Assyrian artist's ability to portray the suffering of victims in war was paralleled by his capacity to render the pain of once-proud animals wounded in the hunt. Here we see a lioness whose body is pierced by arrows, and a dying lion that coughs up blood. (Bonomi, *Nineveh and Its Palaces*, 1875)

SCULPTURE AND OTHER ARTS

7.7 *A winged human-headed lion that once stood as a colossal sentinel at the Assyrian royal palace at Kalhu (Nimrud).* (Layard, *Nineveh and Its Remains,* 1849)

In the anatomy of both hunting and war, sinews are taut and muscles bulge.

Transfigured in the sculptor's imagination, lions rise to life in three-dimensional form as the multiton guardians of palace entrance-ways and gates. Like sphinxes, they are fitted out with the wings of great birds and the turbaned heads of bearded men to convey—as Austen Henry Layard perceived—the intelligence of man combined with the speed of a bird and the prowess of a lion (or, in other sculptural incarnations, the power of a bull). They stand in pairs, eyes fixed straight ahead like vigilant sentries, or with heads turned 90 degrees inward as if to inspect watchfully the stranger passing between them. Curiously, each block-like beast has five legs: four when viewed in profile, two when seen from the front, with one leg at the corner serving double duty.

Meanwhile inside the palace at Nineveh on a relief, Ashurbanipal and his queen enjoy a charming garden party, sampling delicacies to the strains of music while, from a nearby tree, hangs the severed head of an enemy king.

Some would claim the Assyrians were no more savage than other people; merely more honest. But their art betrays a pleasure taken in others' suffering that is unmatched in the art of

7.8 *An Assyrian sculptor carefully depicted the army of laborers needed to transport a multiton stone bull to its palatial site.* (Layard, *Discoveries in the Ruins of Nineveh and Babylon,* 1853)

any other nation. It is not simply horror we see, but horror celebrated. Comparable horrors are depicted in sketches that survive from Nazi concentration camps, but the sketches were drawn by anguished victims, not their tormentors. The only aesthetic analogue is a German lampshade made from Jewish skin, but even that was not meant for public display.

POTTERY

Compared to architecture, sculpture, and painting, pottery is often regarded as a "minor" art. Yet pottery combines within itself the defining virtues of the other arts. Like a work of architecture, a piece of pottery must have stability and structural integrity, and it serves utilitarian ends. Like sculpture, pottery is a tactile art that is shaped by hand. And like painting, the art of pottery may involve the decorative application of pigments to a smooth surface.

7.9 *Before this inscribed brick from Kalhu (Nimrud) dried, a dog leaped lightly over it, leaving his pawprints behind.* (Oriental Institute, University of Chicago)

Archaeological Value

Some may demean pottery because of its commonness and everyday use. Yet it is precisely because of these qualities that pottery is the archaeologist's best friend. Its commonplace nature means that its remains will be found throughout an ancient site, unlike other more precious artifacts that survive only in limited numbers. Though vases are fragile, once broken their fragments (known as potsherds or simply sherds) are virtually indestructible and can endure for millennia. The very breakability of pottery endears it to the archaeologist, for when a piece of pottery is broken, it must be replaced, not by one that is exactly the same but by one that may embody subtle stylistic changes of shape, fabric, or decoration that were introduced after the original piece was made. This stylistic mutability makes pottery an embodiment of change and, as such, a chronological marker that denotes the cultural period to which it belongs. Find enough datable pottery and you can date the cultural remains that surround it; find similar pottery at two sites and you know they are contemporary. Thus the humble art of pottery becomes the handmaid of history, offering its chronological services from the Neolithic Period (or New Stone Age) when ceramic ware began, down to the modern era. For Mesopotamia, pottery's story begins in the early seventh millenium B.C.E.

Aesthetic Value

For some ancient peoples, the Greeks in particular, pottery became a vehicle for intense and joyous artistic expression. Through the striking symmetry of their vases, the Greeks declared that order and beauty are synonymous; through dramatic vase-paintings of heroic myths, they proclaimed the cosmic centrality of man. To a poet like Keats, a Grecian urn could inspire an ode.

We would be far less than honest if we sought to make such a case for the pottery of Mesopotamia. Shapes are limited and pedestrian; designs are crude: lines, wavy or straight, and occasional silhouettes or outlines of birds, fish, or mammals including man, confined within geometric frames. Advances are largely technical: the introduction of the rapidly spinning potter's wheel (in the late fifth millennium B.C.E) that streamlined form and increased production; the ability (in the 14th century B.C.E.) to create delicate vessels, including cups, with walls almost as thin as an eggshell; and the capacity (in the same century) to make small bottles and jars with colorful glazes that sealed in the aroma of perfumes and scented oils.

When the ancient Greeks confronted the fragileness of human existence, their response was a defiant one: to take a medium as fragile as life itself and make it a work of beauty. When the ancient Mesopotamians confronted the same, potentially depressing fact, their answer was less bold but no less constructive: to reach down into the mud from which life had primordially sprung, harden the clay in fire, and use it to make existence more tolerable.

PAINTING

Bored by the monotony of a dusty and monochromatic landscape, a French tourist once described Iraq as *le pays beige*, "the beige country." Though we can readily understand how a compatriot of Monet might be less than thrilled with Iraq's dull visual appeal, we must be careful not to confuse modern topography with ancient character. However bland the land might seem today, in ancient times—thanks to extensive irrigation—much of the country around its population centers was verdant. But, more significantly, the land supported a vigorous culture that was rich in color.

It is the archaeologist's task to recapture that color in all its variety so it can be seen through the mind's eye. But the archaeologist's task is complicated by the nature of the objects unearthed. Rather than organic and alive, they are inorganic or dead. Skeletons, after all, are poor witnesses to the pleasures of the flesh, and inscribed words are a paltry substitute for visceral experience. Even art stumbles on its way to the witness box, since two main forms of art—architecture and sculpture—are made from colorless materials. Whatever decorative tinting they may have once enjoyed was long ago bleached away by the sun and stripped away by the forces of wind and water. As a result, the sculpted images of the dead stand before us almost as pale as stone. A chronic anemia seems to drain the past of its blood and transform the ancients into a race apart, remarkable perhaps but not human like ourselves.

It is the art of painting, however, that can put flesh back onto the old bones, add color to the complexion, enliven the costume, and revivify the settings in which ancient life was lived. But paintings, especially ones thousands of years old, are subject to the ravages of time. Colors fade and, in the case of murals, the plaster crumbles upon which the paint was applied, especially when the walls themselves come tumbling down. Here restorers must perform their duty, imaginatively reconstructing whole pictures where only fragments remain and faithfully re-creating the antique colors out of which they were composed.

Wall Paintings

Traces of paint still cling to Sumerian figures and Assyrian reliefs, demonstrating that the

Mesopotamians recognized the limitations of monotone clay and stone in portraying life, and accordingly sought to enhance them by adding color. Pottery, which in the hands of the classical Greek vase painter became a celebration of heroic myth and daily existence, never attained such stature in Mesopotamia; except for occasional abstract designs and figures in silhouette, the pottery of ancient Iraq was dully functional. Where painting shone was on the walls of Mesopotamia's palaces, and to a minor degree—judging by the limited evidence we possess—on the walls of its temples and private homes.

TECHNIQUES AND MATERIALS

In the earliest era of Mesopotamian wall painting, paints were applied to walls that had previously been coated with a plaster of mud, lime, or gypsum that had been allowed to dry. By the second half of the second millennium B.C.E., paints were applied while the plaster was still wet or fresh (*fresco* in Italian). The advantage of the fresco technique was that the pigments bonded better with the surface to which they were applied; the disadvantage was that the artist had to work rapidly while the undercoat was still damp. The practical solution was either to coat and paint a small area of wall at a time, or to keep the already plastered surface damp (perhaps with wet cloths) until it could be painted.

The wall painter's palette included black (made from lampblack or bitumen), white (from gypsum), and red (from iron oxide or mercuric oxide). Later, blue (made from copper oxide or lapis lazuli) and green (from malachite) made their appearance. Yellow seems to have been relatively rare. Before the artist painted, the mineral pigments were diluted in water to which egg white or casein from milk had been added as a binding agent so the paint would better adhere to the wall's

surface. The overall design was then sketched out on the wall with a sharp tool. After the colors were applied, figures were outlined in black.

SUBJECTS

The subjects of Mesopotamian wall paintings were traditional, featuring ceremonial tableaux and scenes of battle and hunting, much in the manner of stone reliefs. Like carved sealstones, the figures included animals both real and fantastic, gods and goddesses, and kings and attendants.

DISCOVERIES

Remains of wall paintings have been found in southern Iraq at Uruk, Nippur, Tell Uqair (with its painted temple), and Aqar Quf; in northern Iraq at Tepe Gawra, Nuzu, and Khorsabad; and in eastern Syria at Tell Sheikh Hamad. The best preserved and most extensive murals come from Mari, Til Barsip, and Dura-Europos.

Dating to the early 18th century B.C.E., the palace of King Zimri-Lim at Mari has yielded 26 rooms decorated with wall painting, the earliest murals to survive from any ancient Near Eastern palace. Ironically, the paintings were preserved by an act of war, for when Hammurabi destroyed the building, its second story collapsed on and sealed in its first, protecting the murals from further harm. When the city was abandoned, the ruined paintings survived until their recovery by French archaeologists in the 20th century.

The most striking scene shows the investiture of the king. He stands before the goddess Ishtar in the company of other gods and takes his oath of office. The central scene is flanked by griffins (symbols of awesome power) and by palm trees (symbols of fertility). Below, goddesses hold urns from which water magically leaps up and then flows down, nourishing the earth.

Til Barsip, located on the upper Euphrates in northern Syria, was the site of a palace constructed in the eighth century B.C.E. by the Assyrian king Tiglathpileser III. The well-preserved wall paintings show scenes of warfare and hunting. Prisoners of war tied to chariots are escorted to execution by armed soldiers. One Assyrian soldier leads an enemy prisoner by the beard. In a mural over 70 feet long, Tiglathpileser is shown enthroned in majesty, surrounded by members of his army and administrative staff. Elsewhere in the palace, in a bathroom of all places, we see a lion hunt indicative of the Assyrian fascination with power and domination.

The ruins of Dura-Europos lie at the outer edge of our study of Mesopotamia both geographically and chronologically. Situated in Syria at the northern end of the Euphrates, the city was founded about 300 B.C.E. and rose to become an important way station for Mideastern caravans. Among its remains are two synagogues and a church, all dating to the third century C.E. In one of the synagogues and in the church are frescoed walls that constitute, along with the paintings of Rome's catacombs, some of the earliest documented evidence of Jewish and Christian religious art. The wall paintings of the synagogue are extensive (unlike those of the Jewish catacombs) and portray episodes from the Old Testament, including Abraham contemplating the sacrifice of his son Isaac and Moses leading the Israelites across the Red Sea. Meanwhile, in the church, are portraits of Adam and Eve, on the one hand, and the Good Shepherd on the other, contrasting human mortality (in the person of Adam) with everlasting life (personified by Jesus as the Good Shepherd). The frescoes in the Dura-Europos church also include one of the earliest artistic portraits of Jesus, as a young, clean-shaven man with short hair.

Painted Cones and Enameled Brick

Murals were not the only way to enliven walls with color. Some Sumerian temples featured mud-brick columns implanted with clay cones, inserted into mortar-like nails with their heads painted black, white, or red.

In the Neo-Babylonian period, enameled brick was used for exterior walls. Unlike wall paintings which were only suitable for interior surfaces, enameled bricks created glossy and colorful pictures that were capable of withstanding weather. The brick was sculpted in low relief before being baked and was then coated with glazes in which pigments were blended with melted silica. The most renowned example is the almost 47-foot-tall Ishtar Gate and Processional Way that led into Babylon in the days of Nebuchadnezzar II. Against a blue background, bulls, lions, and giraffe-like dragons move in a stately parade.

Besides Babylon, enameled decoration was employed in Ashur and Nimrud in the time of the Assyrian Empire, and it was later adopted by the Persians at Susa to depict bodyguards in procession.

MOSAIC

In Hellenistic Greek art and in Roman art, mosaic played a prominent role. Mosaic pictures, composed of naturally colored stones or colorfully glazed tiles, decorated the floors of private homes and public buildings with images of gods and myths.

The infusion of Hellenistic culture into the Near East and the subsequent rise of Roman imperialism brought with them the influence of European ideas and art. But prior to the Hel-

7.10 This glazed tile, colored in red, brown, green, yellow, and black, and found at Kalhu (Nimrud), seems to show a cup, borne by a bodyguard, being presented to the king of Assyria (the fragmentary figure at the left). (von Reber, History of Ancient Art, 1882)

lenistic period, mosaics played almost no role in ancient Near Eastern architectural decoration.

In Sumerian times, terra-cotta cones with their heads colored in black, white, and red were inserted into mud-brick walls to create geometric designs known to archaeologists as "cone mosaics." Such designs included zigzags and diamond-shaped patterns. Another decorative technique used artificial flowers with black, white, and pink petals composed of alternating stones (for white and pink) and bitumen (for black).

The most famous and most elaborate example of Mesopotamian mosaic also dates to Sumerian days: the Royal Standard of Ur. Using bitumen as glue, an anonymous artist pieced together pictures with the help of blue lapis lazuli (for background) and bits of shell or mother of pearl (for the figures of people and animals). The Royal Standard consists of two back-to-back panels, each consisting of three horizontal registers of figures. One panel depicts the military victory of Ur and its leader over the city's enemies; the corollary panel depicts the celebration following the victory. Apart from its historic interest, the Royal Standard of Ur informs us about life in Sumer: the mode of battle (infantry and chariots), the brutal consequences of war (the corpses of soldiers trampled beneath the onrushing chariots; the prisoners of war taken captive), and the pleasures of peace (music, drinking, and the enjoyment of affluence). Enlightening as its content is in cultural terms, the Royal Standard of Ur is an aesthetic anomaly and, as far as we know, had no impact on the later history of Mesopotamian art. It is the sole surviving pictorial mosaic we possess from pre-Hellenistic Iraq.

7.11   *From Babylon's Ishtar Gate comes this bull executed in glazed brick.*
(Layard, *A Second Series of the Monuments of Nineveh*, 1853)

7.12   *Alternating with the bulls guarding Babylon's Ishtar Gate were fantastic
dragon-like creatures like this one.*   (Layard, *A Second Series of the Monuments of
Nineveh*, 1853)

Glass

Surely the most fragile material to survive from antiquity is glass. If cuneiform inscriptions are our "message in a bottle" from the Mesopotamian past, the bottle itself deserves our inspection. Considering the vicissitudes of history, it is a small miracle that a bottle of ancient glass should have floated intact across the sea of time to our own day, especially having come from a far-off land like Mesopotamia, so often ravaged by war and natural destruction.

History

In actuality, however, our oldest samples of Mesopotamian glass reach us not as intact artifacts but as lumps and fragments from primitive founderies. Crude as they are, they are nevertheless indisputable proof that glass was being manufactured as long ago as the late third millennium B.C.E. These examples are not only our earliest evidence of a Mesopotamian glass industry; they are, in fact, the oldest evidence of glass-making anywhere in the world.

By the second millennium B.C.E., we find glass beads scattered in Mesopotamia's soil. By 1600 B.C.E., new colors are being added to glass, and the first fragments of bottles occur. By the 12th century B.C.E. following the collapse of political stability in the Near East, the glass industry itself slips into decline due to social upheaval and the shrinkage of a market for luxury goods. In the eighth century B.C.E., a revival in the art takes place with Mesopotamia as one of the key centers of rebirth. During the centuries that follow, precious glass objects continue to be in demand. And by the first century B.C.E. with the advent of a new technique of mass production, even those of modest means could now afford glass ves-

sels that were once the prized possessions only of the rich.

Uses

In ancient Mesopotamia, glass was used to create pieces of jewelry, including beads, pendants, and amulets. Through the admixture of certain chemicals, the glassmaker could simulate the colors of precious stones, in particular lapis lazuli. Glass was also used for making vases and bottles, especially perfume bottles. Because only so much glass could be melted and worked at one time, these vessels were necessarily small. In addition, glass was employed in the art of sculpture: little figurines were made of molten glass, as well as the pupils of the realistic inlaid eyes in some statues.

Techniques

The prime ingredient for glassmaking is silica, obtained from sand or crushed quartz. When heated to the melting point with sodium compounds or plant ash, stabilized with lime, and then cooled, it becomes the translucent or transparent material known as glass.

The techniques employed in ancient glass-making depended upon whether the objects being manufactured were to be solid or hollow.

For solid objects the "open mold" method was used. Molten glass was simply poured into molds and, when cooled, took on their shape. This was the method used to make beads, pendants, amulets, and figurines.

For hollow objects like vases and bottles a different method was used, called "core-forming." A core was modeled out of mud mixed with straw or clay mixed with manure. A rod was then stuck into the top of the mass. Next, the artisan—holding the rod—dipped the core into molten glass. After it was extracted and while it was still hot and soft, the glass object would be rolled to make its surface more regular. Glass of different colors could also be dribbled over its exterior to create linear designs, or blobs of glass could be attached to its exterior to form a decorative pattern. After the vessel was totally cool, the rod would be removed and the core broken up and shaken out, leaving a hollow vessel whose interior could then be washed out and cleaned.

About 700 B.C.E. another method was introduced for making hollow objects. Known as the "lost wax technique," it was also used in antiquity for the manufacture of delicate jewelry and bronze statuary. Around a solid clay core, wax would be molded to the thickness and shape of the intended vessel. Then the wax would be covered with more clay. The inner core and outer layer of clay would be connected by small rods. Then the whole would be heated, melting the wax out and leaving a gap between the core and its outer envelope. Finally, molten glass would be poured into the gap, filling up the space where the wax had formerly been. Once the glass cooled, the outer layer of clay would be carefully peeled away, and the inner core (now "inside" the bottle) would be removed as well.

Interestingly, glassblowing was not introduced until the first century B.C.E. Thus most products of Mesopotamian glassmaking were created without the aid of this now-accepted method.

Colors and Designs

The favorite color for Mesopotamian glass was blue, perhaps in imitation of lapis lazuli's desirable hue. For decoration, other colors such as white and yellow were used. Coloration was achieved by blending chemicals with the basic silica mix. Crystal clear glass was not developed, however, until about 700 B.C.E.

The favorite designs were linear and wavy, accomplished by dribbling colored glass over an already formed vessel, probably while the vessel was being rotated on a wheel or, more likely, on a rod or lathe-like device. By carefully arranging pieces of colored glass on a soft glass surface, patterns such as chevrons could be formed as well as colorful mosaic designs.

Technology and Faith

One of the hallmarks of our own era is a faith in technology. But in ancient Mesopotamia—at least to judge by glassmaking—technology depended on faith.

A number of cuneiform tablets exist that give instructions for the making of glass. Most of these come from the library of the seventh-century B.C.E. Assyrian king Ashurbanipal. Before detailing the steps of manufacture, the tablets outline the spiritual prerequisites for producing good glass.

First, a propitious day in an auspicious month must be chosen for the commencement of work. Next, as soon as the kiln has been built but before the fire is lit, idols must be set up before which offerings must be made. A sheep must be sacrificed and juniper incense burnt, and a libation made of honey and melted butter. Furthermore, only those who are ritually clean can be allowed to be present at the worksite.

Some would claim these requirements simply prove the artisans were superstitious; others, that the craftsmen thought glassmaking was a form of magic that only the gods could perform. But a third possibility is that the glassmakers recognized the limitations of their own human powers and believed that their success was dependent upon divine help. In short, for technology to be truly effective, man must rely on more than practical knowledge.

If there is a modern lesson here, it is not that we must sacrifice a sheep or burn juniper incense or pour out honey and butter before taking a new technological step. Only that we should pause to reflect in humility upon our own smallness before undertaking new and great things.

CYLINDER SEALS

It is in miniature sculpture, or glyptic art (from Greek *glyphein*, "to carve"), that the artists of Mesopotamia especially excelled. The most culturally distinctive objet d'art from the land of the Tigris and Euphrates is the cylinder seal, a small (on average, 1–1.5 inches long), engraved cylinder of stone that was traditionally rolled on soft clay in order to leave its imprint as a signature or mark of ownership. Though cylinder seals were used throughout the ancient Near East wherever Mesopotamian influence was deeply felt, no other civilization in the world invented or perfected this art form.

Durability

The cylinder seal's career was a long one, covering three millennia of Mesopotamian history. Moreover, it journeyed across the millennia to our own day like a compact time capsule of ancient civilization. Unlike more fragile examples of human handiwork, the cylinder seal is made of durable stone. Its survival is further explained by its multiplicity. From a single thousand-year period of Mesopotamian history (3300–2300 B.C.E.: from the protoliterate period to the era of the early city-states), some 2,000 cylinder seals have been recovered. Based on the theory that for every archaeological object in a museum at least a hundred still lie buried, some 200,000 such seals from this one period alone still await excavation. And

where the seals themselves have not yet been located, their ancient impressions on clay persist and proclaim their existence.

Archaeological Value

As we will later see, cylinder seals and their imprints present us with pictures illustrating ancient Mesopotamia's myths, religious beliefs, and daily life. Their only shortcoming is that the pictures lack captions, but they are invaluable nonetheless as a pictorial record of a lost world. The seals supply information, moreover, about the chronology of ancient sites and their strata. Some, for example, bear a datable inscription naming a historic ruler. In addition—like pottery—the materials, size, shape, and decoration of cylinder seals changed over the course of time and thus denote when they were made. Finding a cylinder seal in a layer of ruins, even without an inscription, can be a clue as to the layer's age. One drawback, however, is that cylinder seals sometimes became heirlooms and as such were passed on from one generation to the next. As a result, the stratum in which a seal is found may be later than the era in which it was first made. Besides this, being a small object, a cylinder seal can easily tumble from the side of an excavation trench, down the slope of a mound during heavy rain, or even into a hole burrowed by a rodent, displacing itself from its original location and time period. But chronological limitations notwithstanding, inch for inch a cylinder seal packs more information and beauty into its compact size than any other object Mesopotamia produced.

Aesthetic Value

More than mere artifacts, cylinder seals are extraordinary examples of craftsmanly virtuosity.

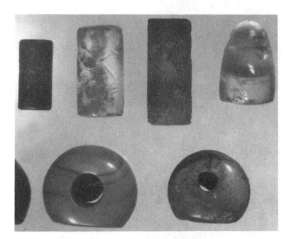

7.13 *Small disks and cylinders of stone, carved with religious and mythological images, were used by the ancient Mesopotamians as personal seals. Their impressions in clay served as signatures.* (Babylonian Collection, Yale University Library)

They carry engravings in miniature, executed—to our knowledge—without the aid of a magnifying glass. Indeed, magnification is required today to fully appreciate their detail, as are modern pressings in clay or plasticine through which the hollowed-out carvings assume their intended three-dimensional fullness as sculpture in relief. This technique of engraving is called intaglio, from Latin *intaliare*, "to cut." To achieve its desired effect, the ancient seal cutter had to think in reverse, imagining the positive shapes his negative cuttings would ultimately produce. Likewise, when inscriptions were required, the artist had to cut them as mirror images so they would read in the right direction when rolled onto clay. The actual engraving was further complicated by the fact that the surface of the seal was not flat, but curved.

Why would artists have engaged in an occupation fraught with such challenges? First, because sealcutting was a valued profession that bestowed upon the craftsman social esteem and honor. Second, because the products of his talent would be in constant demand. And third, because, like many an artist, he received pleasure from rising to a challenge to produce a work that was both useful and aesthetically pleasing.

At their finest, cylinder seal engravings exhibit in their detail and narrative arrangement what Edith Porada once called a "rhythmically ordered composition," that in rolled repetition is almost hypnotic in its overall effect.

History

The use of a seal (Sumerian *kishib*; Akkadian *kunukku*) to mark clay is attested as far back as the eighth millennium B.C.E. in Syria, when such objects served a decorative or possibly magical purpose. These seals were not cylindrical in shape, but circular and used like rubber stamps. By the middle of the sixth millennium B.C.E., stamp seals were being used in northern Iraq to imprint linear patterns or shapes onto clay tags and discs for identification purposes.

Perhaps by the fifth or certainly by the fourth millennium B.C.E., a new type of seal—the cylinder seal—was in use among the Sumerians of southern Mesopotamia and the Elamites of southwestern Iran, to judge by surviving impressions in clay. Its introduction antedates the birth of writing, but is contemporary with the discovery of metallurgy since metal tools were needed to engrave the stone.

The cylinder seal had a number of advantages over its predecessor, the stamp seal. By being rolled, a cylinder seal could cover a larger area in a shorter time. Its greater surface area admitted more room for designs which insured the individuality of the particular seal and therefore its effectiveness as a mark of personal identity and ownership. After the birth of writing, its greater surface area also allowed space for an inscription naming its owner. The more extensive design also appealed to the Mesopotamian aesthetic sense: its more elaborate imprint was literally more impressive than a stamp seal's, while its engraved embellishments made it a piece of jewelry as well as a unique mark of identity.

For three millennia, from Sumerian times down to the days of the Persian Empire, the cylinder seal surpassed the stamp seal in popularity. But by about 1000 B.C.E., it lost ground to the stamp seal, becoming obsolete by the end of the fifth century B.C.E. The reason was a change in language and script. Aramaic replaced Akkadian as the lingua franca of the Near East. While Akkadian was written in cuneiform on a clay tablet, Aramaic was written in ink on papyrus, parchment, or leather scrolls that were rolled up and tied with a cord secured by a small wad of clay. With no room for rolling a cylinder, the stamp seal became the seal of choice.

continuously in a single direction. Rather than cutting rough cylinders from stone, the sealcutters may have bought blanks from dealers, adding the finishing touches in their workshops.

Before or possibly after the engraving was done, a hole was drilled into each end of the cylinder. When the two holes met, they formed a longitudinal channel through which a cord could be threaded so the seal could be worn around the neck like a pendant. Sometimes a metal cap, usually of gold, was fastened with bitumen to one end of the cylinder. The cap featured a loophole through which the cord could be strung or a pin inserted to attach the seal to a garment. Just such a pinned seal was found resting on the skeletal chest of Queen Puabi in her grave at Ur. Judging by an ancient tale, such pins could be turned into lethal weapons: two of Mesopotamia's kings were assassinated by killers who tore off the royal pins and wielded them with deadly force.

Manufacture

The task of making seals belonged to the sealcutter (Sumerian *burgul*; Akkadian *purkullu*). An apprenticeship in making cylinder seals lasted at least four years, and masters and apprentices plied their craft in workshops, such as the one whose ruins were found in the Syrian city of Ugarit. From Tell Asmar, east of Baghdad, comes the toolkit of a worker. In a clay jar were found a small copper chisel, two pointed copper gravers (for detail), a whetstone, a borer (for drilling holes), and some seals that had not yet been completed. Engraving tools were also made of bronze and flint.

Drills and cutting blades were hand-powered: as the sealcutter's hand moved a bow back and forth, the bowstring caused a shaft it held to rotate back and forth. Later, a foot-operated wheel may have been used to make the shaft spin

Materials

The vast majority of cylinder seals were carved from stone, much of it imported. But some were made from other materials such as bone, ivory, shell, wood, clay, or metal (gold, silver, copper, and bronze).

The type of stone varied from period to period, depending on the vagaries of fashion and the availability of a particular stone from local or foreign sources. The earliest cylinders were carved from soft limestone, lapis lazuli, and rock crystal. Later, minerals with differing hues were employed, such as talc, diorite, and variegated agate. Colors were supplied by the greens of serpentine, chlorite, greenstone, and apple-green amazonite; the reds of carnelian, hematite goethite, and red-and-white mottled jasper; the purple of amethyst; and the blacks of black limestone, magnetite, and glassy obsidian. At one point late in the history of manufacture, a synthetic stone—composite, or "sinistered," quartz—was employed.

Some stones were believed to have magical properties and to bestow benefits upon their owner: lapis lazuli symbolized power and success, crystal conveyed happiness, and green marble insured continual blessings. According to Assyrian interpreters, to dream of being given a seal portended the birth of a son; a seal engraved with figures, sons and peace of mind; a red seal, sons and daughters; an ivory seal, one's heart's desire; and a royal seal, the protection of the gods.

Decorative Themes

In the decoration of cylinders seals a variety of themes was invoked, some predominating in one cultural period and others in another.

The earliest themes are economic in nature, depicting the production or display of foods and textiles. Accompanying these economic scenes are representations of rituals. Reflected in the cylinder seal's decoration at this early period, then, are two interconnected themes: material prosperity and piety. During the Early Dynastic period, perhaps in celebration of the heroic achievements of the age, new themes occur: mythic combat and banqueting; somewhat later, the gods themselves appear. In successive centuries, heroes and monsters, and gods and kings take their place on the miniature stage.

The seals inform us about Mesopotamian daily life (especially agricultural activities), dining and dress, music and dance, and transportation. We see deities just as the Mesopotamians saw them in their spiritual imagination, especially Utu (or Shamash), the god of the sun; Nanna (or Sin), the god of the moon; and Inanna (or Ishtar), the goddess of sexuality and battle. We also see illustrations of ancient myths, in particular struggles pitting one or more animals against a hero (Gilgamesh?) or

7.14   *Rolled onto clay (as here), a cylinder seal produced a raised design. This seal impression seems to portray the legendary comrades of Mesopotamian epic, Gilgamesh and Enkidu, shown here grappling with wild beasts. Both Gilgamesh and Enkidu are bearded, but Enkidu has horns and a tail, denoting his status as a creature of nature.*   (Babylonian Collection, Yale University Library)

against a creature that is half-man, half-bull (Enkidu?). Also populating the engravings are animals, birds, fish, and even insects, including some species of fauna that are extinct. The seals also provide us with our earliest pictorial evidence for temple design, domed buildings, the composite bow, and the lute.

Uses and Users

The Mesopotamian seal had a number of specialized uses.

Its earliest use, in the era before writing, was to mark hollow balls of clay that contained little clay tokens symbolizing goods (like sheep) involved in commercial transactions. Later, seals were used to secure jars and the valuables they contained: the mouths of the jars were covered and wound with cord; the cord was tied and knotted and wrapped in clay; and the clay was then imprinted with the seal. In similar fashion, seals were applied to doors leading to storage compartments and warehouses. The most frequent use of the seal, however, was to "sign" clay documents by rolling the seal across the tablet or across the clay envelope that contained it.

The function of the seal could be enhanced by a cuneiform inscription giving the name of the owner. Additional data might include the name of the owner's father, the owner's title and/or occupation, and the ruler or god he served. Such inscriptions were probably added after the pictorial design on the seal had been completed and the seal itself was purchased. The name of the purchaser would then be engraved, usually in a vertical space reserved for it. From such inscriptions we know that cylinder seals were owned and used by people in a great variety of occupations and social roles: men and (less commonly) women, rulers and priests, soldiers and scribes, royal cooks and servants, carpenters and other craftsmen, and the ubiquitous merchant. Even slaves who conducted business owned seals, as did the gods themselves who are sometimes shown wearing them. The same person could, in fact, own more than one seal, sometimes ordering a new one cut when he received a promotion or served a new ruler.

Seal impressions have been found on legal contracts, treaties, and letters. For a loan, the borrower or his cosigner would roll his seal acknowledging the amount borrowed. In a transfer of property, the seller would sign the bill of sale. Upon receiving goods, the recipient would sign the receipt. And in the case of mutual obligations—a marriage or a business agreement, for example—both contracting parties would sign. By the middle of the first millennium B.C.E., two copies of documents were generated, one for each party, much as it is done today.

If a cylinder seal were lost or stolen, it was a matter of great concern. The former owner would record the date and time of loss with an official to insure that transactions made after the loss would be invalid (not unlike the way we might call Visa or Mastercard to report a lost or stolen credit card). In one instance, we are told, a horn was sounded in a city to announce the loss of a seal.

The ancients were intimate with something that more and more has come to characterize our lives today: impermanence. In a land where a raging flood could wash away an entire city, the ancient Mesopotamian understood that few things—including life itself—are guaranteed and secure. Gilgamesh, we remember, held the fragile secret of eternal life in his hand only to see it snatched away. For the people of Mesopotamia then, the stone cylinder seal was the ultimate symbol of permanence in an impermanent world. Perhaps that is why it occupied such an important position in their lives and was worn as a badge of honor.

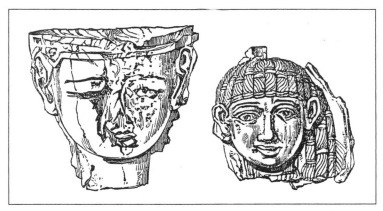

7.15   *Fragments of two miniature heads carved in ivory in the days of the Assyrian Empire.*   (Bonomi, *Nineveh and Its Palaces*, 1875)

CARVED IVORY

In the biblical Song of Solomon, the erotic protagonists praise each other's body in terms of glistening ivory. Says he: "Your neck is like a tower of ivory." Says she: "Your abdomen is ivory inlaid with sapphire." The books of Kings and Chronicles, for their part, tell how every three years a fleet of ships brought King Solomon a rich and exotic cargo of "gold, silver, ivory, apes, and peacocks."

Throughout the ancient Near East, ivory was regarded as a precious material, especially because it could be carved and made into ornaments. Its prime source was the elephant, hunted in the Near East until it became extinct there by the mid first millennium B.C.E. Yet as early as 2000 B.C.E., ivory was also being imported from India by the merchants of Ur.

The craft of carving ivory flourished especially in ancient Syria and Phoenicia, and the ornate products of these land traveled eastward to Mesopotamia by trade or, in the days of Assyrian imperialism, were acquired as tribute or booty from the lands Assyria conquered. In Mesopotamia itself, local workshops as well may have sprung up to transform raw ivory into works of art.

Ivory was used to make the handles of hand mirrors and fly whisks (de rigueur in the hot Near East) or was fashioned into luxurious containers for cosmetics. Ivory ornaments even adorned the bridles of royal horses. But ivory's prime function was to decorate furniture. Cut

7.16   *A woman of the ancient Near East gazes at us across the millennia through an ivory window.* (Bonomi, *Nineveh and Its Palaces*, 1875)

into small panels, the surface of the ivory was incised or sculpted in low relief with pictures and designs that might then be colored with paint or enlivened with an inlay of semi-precious stone. The panels were then attached to the wooden furniture with small nails.

Pictures on ivory objects included scenes of combat between man and lion, images of fantastic creatures, depictions of banqueting and entertainment, and portrayals of kings and courtiers. A favorite motif for panels was the "woman in the window," a woman's face set within a window-like frame. In addition, doll-sized female heads carved out of ivory have also been found. Whether they once actually belonged to dolls or perhaps to figurines of goddesses is unknown.

Though most of these ivory carvings were probably manufactured by foreign craftsmen before they ever reached Mesopotamia, they are numbered in the thousands, revealing the domestic popularity of this art form. Most of the remains date to Assyrian times, the ninth and eighth centuries B.C.E. A great cache was uncovered at Nimrud, but other finds have been made at Tell Halaf, Ashur, and Khorsabad.

One extraordinary piece, recovered at Nimrud from the bottom of a 70-foot-deep well, shows a young man being killed by a lioness. The Negroid features of the young man's face and his tightly curled hair suggest that he is Ethiopian or Nubian, though his skin is not black. He sits on the ground, his back bent back and supported by his arms as the lioness, standing over him, closes her jaws over his neck. Pain is not written on the young man's face, but rather surrender. Nor is the lioness savage, for she cradles his neck with one of her paws. The background is lush with flowers, papyrus and lily, inlaid in lapis lazuli and carnelian, gleaming with gilding. The scene might almost be an idyll of lovers coupling—she the tender aggressor, he the willing victim—but locked in fatal embrace.

7.17 This ivory panel from Kalhu (Nimrud), highlighted in gold, portrays an African man in the deadly grip of a lioness. (The British Museum)

"Love is as strong as death" the Song of Solomon reminds us. On this ivory panel, but four inches tall, we hear the same words. Yet we wonder why it was hurled down the mouth of a Nimrud well so long ago . . . and by whom.

JEWELRY

The survival of ancient jewelry is an enduring testament to humanity's love of beauty and its talent to fashion works of beauty from inert matter. The created ornaments become, in turn, a guarantor of the maker's and owner's immortality, for precious metal and stone that last for millennia are far more durable than flesh and blood. It is in graves that archaeologists most often find pieces of jewelry, for those who wore them in life wished to wear them also for all eternity in the life beyond. The presence of such objects in burials is in itself proof of an ancient belief in immortality, a belief that held out to the deceased the promise of enjoying earthly delights in the hereafter.

Materials and Manufacture

Along with that of Egypt, the jewelry of Mesopotamia is the world's oldest. As early as the seventh millennium B.C.E., necklaces, bracelets, and ornamental girdles were fashioned in Mesopotamia from shells, pieces of bone, and polished stones. When civilization began in the late fourth millennium B.C.E., the art of metallurgy began with it, expanding the jeweler's repertoire. But while Egypt could turn to the desert east of the Nile or southward to Nubia for sources of gold, the valleys of the Tigris and Euphrates were poor in minerals. In their hunger for adornment, the Mesopotamians sought out raw materials from other lands by trade. Gold and silver were obtained from Anatolia and northern Iran; orange-red carnelian from southeastern Iran, Pakistan, and India; and lapis lazuli, a precious blue mineral used for beads and inlay, from the Badakhshan district of northern Afghanistan and from eastern Pakistan.

One of the most remarkable techniques in the Mesopotamian goldsmith's arsenal was a process called granulation, which involved fusing masses of tiny gold globules onto a solid gold background. Also called "fusion welding," granulation used no solder but only heat to achieve its effects, a delicate procedure because at too high a temperature the golden globules could melt and lose their roundness. In addition to delicate hammering and granulation, jewelers employed such techniques as engraving, chasing, repoussé, filigree, and cloisonné, and they crafted hinges and clasps as well.

To produce different colors, gold was sometimes mixed with other metals such as copper. Blended with silver, it became an alloy known as electrum, which could also be found in a natural state.

Perhaps because it was so rare in Sumerian times, gold was not cast but instead hammered into thin sheets that were then cut, incised, and shaped. Heavier gold pieces became more common in the days of the Assyrians, either because their territory lay closer to sources of ore or because their armies were more effective in gathering gold from the peoples they conquered.

The Jewelry Trade

Jewelers played an important role in Mesopotamian society, serving the needs of both palace and temple. Such artisans are frequently mentioned in commercial documents and often by name along with the quantities of precious metals they were consigned for the execution of their commissions. Items once belonging to a jeweler from Larsa named Ilsu-Ibnisu were found in the ruins of his 18th-century B.C.E. temple workshop. Stored in a jar where Ilsu-Ibnisu had left them were some of his tools (including a tweezer, gravers, a stone for smoothing out metal, and a small anvil); 67 small weights; miscellaneous beads of agate, carnelian, hematite, and lapis lazuli; and scraps of precious metal that he intended someday to melt down and reuse. Among the Sumerians, the patron god of jewelers was none other than the god of wisdom, a testimonial to both the high level of expertise this craft demanded and the respect its practitioners received. Such respect, however, did not prevent a priestess named Bakhlatum from writing a letter of complaint to a goldsmith named Ili-iddinam. Preserved in the palace archives of Mari, a copy of her letter reproaches the jeweler for the four years that had passed since the priestess had paid him in full for a necklace and ornament that he had still not delivered.

Types and Uses

In Mesopotamia, jewelry was made for and used by both men and women. Among the favorite types that were worn by both sexes were rings, bracelets for wrists and ankles, armlets (worn on the upper arm), earrings, necklaces, and pins for holding garments or hair. Some necklaces were so heavy they required a counterweight at the back so the necklace would balance comfortably on the shoulders rather than pull on the nape of the neck. Such a device was also used by the bejeweled and top-heavy royals of Egypt. Another popular item of jewelry was something the Akkadians called a *tudittum*, or "breast ornament," though its exact shape and use remain unknown. It was just such an ornament that the priestess Bakhlatum had been waiting four years to wear!

Jewelry served many functions in Mesopotamian society. It was a favorite type of gift to celebrate a wedding or to honor a mother for the birth of a child. It could accompany a bride as part of her dowry, or it could be passed on as an heirloom on the occasion of a funeral. Pieces of jewelry were also exchanged between rulers to cement diplomatic relations, or they were bestowed on prostitutes by their Mesopotamian "Johns" to express appreciation. Nor were human beings the only ones to wear jewelry: the gods are described as wearing it as well, and their cult statues in temples were ritually adorned in similar fashion.

Although their prime purpose was legal and commercial, carved seal-stones used for "sign-ing" one's name were usually worn around the neck like the pendant of a necklace and thus became one of the most conspicuous types of jewelry during the course of Mesopotamia's long history.

Discoveries

The late fourth millennium B.C.E. tombs of Tepe Gawra, on the northern Tigris, have yielded a rich cache of ancient ornaments. The garments of the dead had been sewn with golden crescents and gold rosettes, the latter enhanced with centers of turquoise and lapis lazuli. Covering one body were 25,000 beads of semiprecious stone.

The richest find of jewelry ever made in southern Mesopotamia was at the Sumerian city of Ur. There, between 1926 and 1932, British archaeologist Sir Leonard Woolley uncovered the graves of 16 kings and queens who reigned during the middle of the third millennium B.C.E. Their servants were also buried with them (perhaps after having taken a sleeping potion) so they could tend to their lords' and ladies' needs in the afterworld. Especially noteworthy is the jewelry of Queen Puabi, featuring an elaborate headdress of golden flowers rising on stems above a canopy of golden beech leaves, while alongside each ear dangled huge golden earrings in the shape of twin crescent moons. In one mass grave, Woolley discovered the skeleton of a serving-maid still clasping in her hand a wound-up spool of silver hair ribbon, still coiled—Woolley deduced—because she had arrived at the ceremony late and hadn't had the time to put the ribbon on her hair.

Surpassing the royal treasures of Ur in weight is the golden jewelry found in 1988 and 1989 by Iraqi archaeologist Mazahim Mahmud Hussein at the Assyrian capital of Nimrud.

7.18 *The elaborate headdress and dramatic earrings of Queen Puabi of Ur. In this photograph they adorn a head sculpted in clay by the wife of Sir Leonard Woolley, who sought to capture the human presence of the queen, framed in her golden splendor.* (The British Museum)

Excavating beneath the floor of the Northwest Palace, Hussein unearthed the entombed remains of three queens of the ninth and eighth centuries B.C.E., all draped in golden jewelry. All told, some 1,500 pieces of jewelry were found weighing a total of 100 pounds. Among the pieces was a crown decorated with golden rosettes, a wide cuff-bracelet with lion's-head finials, and a necklace consisting of 28 golden pendants in the shape of teardrops.

The spirits of the dead queens still clutch at their regal baubles. As a cuneiform inscription on a stone tablet in the crypt of Queen Yaba declares: "If anyone lays his hand on my tomb . . . , opens my grave, or steals my jewelry, I pray to the gods of the netherworld that his soul shall roam in the scorching sun after death."

Yet if the Mesopotamian poem "The Descent of Ishtar" is to be believed, even Queen Yaba might have had to surrender her treasures someday. According to the poem, the goddess Ishtar was compelled to perform a divine striptease before gaining admission to the underworld. At each of its seven gates she had to remove an article of dress: her crown, her earrings, her beaded necklace, her breast ornaments, her girdle of birthstones, her wrist and ankle bracelets, and—finally—her clothing. As we were naked when we were born, she is told, so must we be naked when we pass through death's final door. Archaeological discoveries, however, argue to the contrary: Ishtar notwithstanding, the Mesopotamians believed—or, at least, hoped—that you *can* take it with you.

7.19 *In a drawing based upon a palace relief from Dur-Sharrukin (Khorsabad), the Assyrian king's cup-bearer wears a heavy earring of solid gold. The knobs of the earring accent the curls of his coiffure and the embroidered shoulder of his robe.* (Layard, *Nineveh and Its Remains*, 1849)

READING

The Role of the Artist

Bienkowski and Millard 2000: art and artists; Gunter 1990: artistic environments; Matthews 1995: artisans and artists in ancient western Asia.

Materials

Parrot 1961: Mesopotamian techniques; Sasson 1995: technology and artistic production.

Sculpture

Amiet 1977, Barnett 1976, Barnett and Lorenzini 1975, Collon 1995, Frankfort 1970, Groenewegen-Frankfort 1978, Lloyd 1961, Moortgat 1969, Parrot 1961, Reade 1976, 1998, Winter 1995, 1997: photographic illustrations in black-and-white and color, with discussion; Bertman 1986: art and immortality.

Pottery

Armstrong 1997: Mesopotamian pottery (with bibliography); Matson 1995: potters and pottery in the ancient Near East (with bibliography).

Painting

Amiet 1979, Parrot 1961: color illustrations; Castriota 1997: survey of ancient Near Eastern wall painting; Levine 1982: Dura Europos (with bibliography).

Mosaic

Parrot 1961: Sumerian mosaics; Moorey 1982: the Royal Standard of Ur.

Glass

Oppenheim et al. 1970: techniques of glassmaking, translations of cuneiform instructions, and illustrations of artifacts from the collection of the Corning (New York) Museum of Glass; Whitehouse 1997: survey of Near Eastern glassmaking.

Cylinder Seals

Buchanan 1981: photographs and translated inscriptions; Collon 1987 and 1993: illustrated survey; Frankfort 1965, Gibson and Briggs 1977: survey; Gordon 1957: glyptic art; Magness-Gardiner 1997: Near Eastern seals; Pittman 1995: survey of seals and scarabs; Porada 1976: Sumerian art in miniature; Porada 1980: mythological themes; Wiseman 1959: photographic enlargements and commentary.

Carved Ivory

Barnett 1975, 1982: ancient ivories in the Middle East; Bienkowski and Millard 2000: ivory carving; Herrmann 1986 and 1992: ivories from Nimrud; Lloyd 1961: Ethiopian slain by a lion (color illustration); Mallowan 1966–74, 1978: Nimrud ivories; Parrot 1961: photographs of ivories.

Jewelry

Bahrani 1995: survey; Harrington 1990: treasures from Nimrud; Maxwell-Hyslop 1971: detailed account; Moorey 1982: treasures from Ur.

8

ECONOMY

DEFINITION AND STRUCTURE

In the contemporary Western world, a nation's economy is conceptualized in secular terms: it is the product of human effort and choice, on the one hand, and the operation of impersonal forces such as supply and demand, on the other. In ancient Mesopotamia, however, the economy was ultimately a sacred entity: however human its participants might be, its success was dependent upon the favor of divine powers. Moreover, while today's economy is interpreted by specialists called economists, the ancient economy was guided by specialists called priests.

Because the economy of Mesopotamia was fundamentally agrarian, it was based on fertile soil and abundant water. The goddess Ninhursag was "Mother Earth"; the god Enki, the deity of freshwater beneath the soil. The archetypal farmer, Ninurta, was the son of Enlil, Mesopotamia's supreme god. In addition, each city worshiped its own patron divinity whose beneficence was sought through prayer and sacrifice.

In the beginning, the land belonged to the god of the city and was administered by a priesthood. Later, rulers and members of an aristocracy became landowners. Kinship groups came to own property as well, as did individuals who were awarded special grants. The land was worked by the owners themselves or by tenant farmers on behalf of the owners, especially when those owners held high social status.

SIGNIFICANCE

Were it not for Mesopotamia's productive economy, civilization itself could not have developed. The organization of land and the maintenance of irrigation canals led to the rise of law and government while food surpluses supported a complex division of labor and engendered a leisure that inspired the arts.

FARMING AND ANIMAL HUSBANDRY

The prime occupation in Mesopotamia was farming.

Agriculture originated in the ancient Near East around 9000 B.C.E. and marked a revolutionary change in people's lives. Whereas previously their subsistence had come from hunting and gathering, the raising of crops combined with the domestication of animals (another innovation), caused them to live a more settled rather than a nomadic existence. Mesopotamia, with its fertile soil and abundant water, offered the ideal environment for such a settled life to flourish, and small communities gradually grew to the size of cities. Thus the discovery of agriculture promoted the birth of urban civilization.

The chief crop in the valleys of the Tigris and Euphrates was grain, especially barley and emmer wheat, and the herb which yielded sesame seeds.

The farmers' tools were simple and mostly made of wood: a plow pulled by oxen, sickles fitted with flint blades for harvesting, a heavy sledge for threshing, and scoops or paddles for winnowing. The plow is depicted on cylinder seals from the fourth millennium B.C.E., but may have been invented as early as the fifth. By the second millennium B.C.E., a type of plow had been designed featuring a vertical funnel that allowed seeds poured in the top to drop into the furrows as they were cut by the blade.

The agricultural year began with sowing in the autumn or early winter. The chief dangers the farmer faced during the growing season were floods (often at the very time when crops were ripening), crop disease, locusts, and mice. In fact, farmers ritually recited a prayer to Ninkilim, the goddess of mice, imploring that the seed that had just been sown not be devoured. After the harvest (April and May and again, for some types, in summer), grain was stored in tall cylindrical silos built on decks to keep rodents away and to prevent underground moisture from coming into contact with and rotting the kernels.

We are fortunate to have a Sumerian "Farmer's Almanac" of over 100 lines dating back to 1700 B.C.E. In it, a father gives his son step-by-step instructions on how to bring in a good crop. Most critical, we are told, was the depth at which the seed was sown and the breaking up of heavy clods that might otherwise keep the seeds from sprouting. The farmer's son was also reminded to supervise his workers diligently. The Mesopotamian farmer understood the principle of crop rotation and the need to leave fields fallow so they could regain their fertility; he did not seem to have known, however, that fertility could be increased by adding manure to the soil.

8.1 At Nineveh, attendants carry delicacies for a royal Assyrian feast: pomegranates and locusts. (Layard, Discoveries in the Ruins of Nineveh and Babylon, 1853)

Orchards and Gardening

Mesopotamian farmers were adept at growing trees that yielded such fruits as apples, cherries, figs, pears, plums, pomegranates, and (in the Persian period) peaches, but the major cash crop was dates. Orchardists employed cuttings and graftings, and they recognized early on that the date-palm required sexual "mating" to produce its fruit.

The blazing sun and hot, dry winds of Iraq can quickly cause vegetables to wither in the parched soil. To combat the effects of oppressive heat, the ancient farmer invented "shade-tree gardening," using date-palms and other fruit trees to shield ground-level crops from excessive sun and wind. According to a myth, the technique was devised by a gardener named Shukallituda with the help of divine inspiration.

An illuminating text lists the varied vegetables and herbs that once grew in the gardens of king Merodach-baladan II of Babylon. The

8.2   A sow herds her young beside a bank of tall reeds.   (Layard, *Discoveries in the Ruins of of Nineveh and Babylon*, 1853)

scientific-mindedness of the scribe is expressed by the fact that the plants in the inventory are grouped according to species.

Irrigation

In northern Mesopotamia, farmers depended on rainfall to water their crops. In southern Mesopotamia, however, they used river water by digging and maintaining a system of irrigation canals (see chapter 6).

Sometimes the transportation of water was accomplished through the use of a *shaduf*, a long pole with a bucket at one end and a counterweight at the other, with the pole balanced on a fulcrum-like device. Swung out over a source of water, the *shaduf*'s bucket could be dipped in, easily raised (thanks to the counterweight), and then swiveled around and poured out into a nearby channel. The *shaduf*, as it is called in Arabic, is still being used by farmers in the Middle East today.

Animal Husbandry

The Neolithic discovery that plants could be grown for food occurred around the same time that people found they could raise animals as both sources of food and beasts of burden.

In ancient Mesopotamia the most important domesticated animals were oxen and donkeys, on the one hand, and sheep and cattle on the other. The former served as draught animals; the latter were raised for their milk, and for hides and wool that could be converted into clothing. A Sumerian temple frieze shows men milking cows and pouring the milk into jars that are thought to have been rocked back and forth to churn the milk into butter.

Farmyards also included ducks and geese raised for their eggs and meat. The chicken did not become popular until the first millennium B.C.E. And contrary to the Islamic prohibition against eating pork, there is evidence that the ancient Mesopotamians raised pigs.

The food supply of Mesopotamians was increased also by hunting (chiefly for game birds in the marshes) and fishing.

FISHING AND HUNTING

The waters of the Tigris and Euphrates nurtured fish, especially carp, that populated the rivers and their estuaries as well as the canals through which their waters flowed. Sometimes fish were also cultivated in ponds. Nets, spears, and harpoons were the fisherman's weapons depending on the size and weight of his quarry. Once caught, fish would be immediately cooked to prevent spoilage, or they were salted for later use. Documents show that royal and priestly authorities could control and lease fishing rights to commercial fishermen on the grounds that the waters as well as the land belonged to the state and its gods.

With the rise of agriculture and the domestication of animals, hunting ceased being a prime food-gathering activity. Hunting was used instead to kill animals that preyed on flocks and herds, or as a sport, especially in the

8.3 *An Assyrian lion hunt in progress. As a charioteer holds the reins and the team gallops over a fallen lion, an archer prepares to fire again.* (George Redford, *A Manual of Sculpture* [London: Sampson Low, Marston, Searle, and Rivington, 1882])

8.4 A wounded and vindictive lion gnaws on an Assyrian chariot-wheel during a hunt. (Rawlinson, *The Seven Great Monarchies of the Ancient Eastern World*, 1884)

days of the Assyrian kings, who hunted lions to demonstrate their own prowess.

CRAFTS

The accumulation of surplus food eventually meant that not everyone needed to be engaged in food production. As a result, individuals drew upon their talents and skills and traded the products of their labor for the food they required. Specialized crafts became more extensive as increased wealth led to the demand for luxury goods, and persons with social prestige called upon others to do their bidding. As a result, a whole variety of trades was soon practiced in ancient Mesopotamia.

The building trades employed architects, brickmakers, stone masons, and carpenters as well as decorative artists such as sculptors and painters. The food trades were practiced by such workers as fishermen, butchers, bakers, and brewers. Meanwhile, consumer goods were manufactured by bronze workers, silversmiths, goldsmiths, glassmakers, potters (the most common craft), leather workers and shoemakers, weavers, reed plaiters and basketmakers, jewelers, and seal-stone cutters. Transportation needs were met by wagonmakers, wagon drivers, shipwrights, and boatmen. In addition, there were street vendors, shopowners, and innkeepers, as well as prostitutes, some of whom were employed in the sacred service of the goddess of fertility in temples while others freelanced at the city gates and in taverns.

Most trades followed a system of male apprenticeship and were often passed on from father to son. Some trades may have been organized into guilds, and some traditionally occupied specific quarters of the city where their workshops were located and their wares were sold.

PROFESSIONS

In addition to the crafts and trades, there were also professions that required many years of dedication and were accompanied by high social status. Among these were the professions of the scribe, the physician, and the priest, including those who specialized in astronomy, divining, and exorcism. With the rise of imperialism and bureaucracy, a class of civil servants and career soldiers joined the ancient workforce.

WAGES AND PRICES

Surviving legal and business documents provide us with information about wages and prices in

Mesopotamia. However, because the history of the land stretched over thousands of years across diverse cultures that prospered in peace and suffered in war, generalizations about the ancient cost of living are hard to make, especially because the evidence we have is so fragmentary. But though the jigsaw puzzle on our table is incomplete, we can nevertheless be confident about many of the economic pieces we have been able to join together.

For example, during the second and first millennia B.C.E. the daily wage for an average worker seems to have held constant at about one-quarter of a bushel of barley. Workers were thus paid in a commodity rather than in money, since a money economy took many centuries to develop. But barley was a valuable commodity at that, since a worker could literally consume his wages. In addition to his salary in grain, the average worker would have also received a daily ration of about four and a half pounds of bread, a little over a gallon of beer, and (over the course of a year) approximately four pounds of wool that could be converted into enough cloth to make a small garment. On holidays, such as the festival of the New Year, a worker might receive an extra allowance of barley along with meat and sesame oil.

It would take the average worker between four to eight days to earn the equivalent of a shekel of silver (about $3/10$ of an ounce of this precious metal). What could he then buy for a lump of silver? The answer is: any one of the items below. The peculiarities of our shopping list reflect the eccentricities of our documentary evidence, but nevertheless convey the buying power of a few days' wages.

Depending, then, on the prevailing market price, which could and did vary over time, a shekel of silver might be traded for:

1 or 2 additional bushels of barley *or*
1 or 2 bushels of dates *or*
$1/8$–$1/12$ bushel of sesame seeds *or*

$6 3/4$–27 gallons of sesame oil *or*
$1/8$ jar of grape wine *or*
a little over a jar of date wine *or*
$2 1/4$ lbs. of plain wool *or*
$2 1/4$ oz. of purple-dyed wool *or*
50–100 bricks *or*
600 lbs. of asphalt *or*
25 small tools *or*
11 copper bowls.

A ram or a goat could be purchased for 2 shekels of silver, i.e., from the earnings generated by 8 to 16 days of work. An ox would go for 20 to 30 shekels, a donkey for 30, and a slave for 40 (at least in the days of Nebuchadnezzar). Moreover, for a shekel of silver a wagon and driver could be rented for three days, a boat for two days, and a small home or shop for half a year.

These "shekels," however, were not coins in the modern sense, since coinage had not yet been invented. As we will see in the next chapter, during Mesopotamia's long history most purchases were made by bartering one commodity for another, be it silver or produce, rather than by using money.

Though wages tended to hold steady, prices seem to have gradually escalated over the centuries, and efforts by kings such as Hammurabi to control them proved ineffective. Thus over time the cost of living went up and workers found it harder and harder to make ends meet. Wages, of course, would be supplemented by whatever goods an individual or family could raise or grow for personal consumption or sale, and therefore people tried to be as self-sufficient as possible. Naturally, the higher your social status, the higher your income. Thus an average laborer might earn the equivalent of a shekel every four to eight days, but a temple guard might earn as much as one and a half shekels in a single day. And those who sold commodities or the products of their specialized skills could earn still more.

Cuneiform tablets inscribed with the questions put to fortunetellers reveal that the poor longed to be rich, the rich feared becoming poor, and both worried about the tax collector!

READING

Definition, Structure, and Significance

Diakonoff 1991, Kramer 1963: land ownership; Jacobs 1985: wealth and cities; Lamberg-Karlovsky 1976: Sumerian economy; Oppenheim 1957: economic history; Postgate 1992: society and economy; Van de Mieroop 1999: urban economy; Yoffee 1995: economy of ancient western Asia.

Farming and Animal Husbandry

Braidwood R. J. 1960: origins of agriculture; Civil 1995, Kramer 1956: farmer's almanac; Crabtree, Campana, and Ryan 1989: domestication of animals; Crawford 1991, Hopkins 1997: agriculture; Dalley 1993, Gleason and Welch 1997: gardens; Gelb, Steinkeller, and Whiting 1991: land tenure; Hesse 1995: animal husbandry; Higham 1977: earliest farmers; LaBianca 1997, Schwartz 1995: pastoral nomadism; Leach 1982: kitchen gardening; Pollock 1999: pigs; Postgate and Payne 1975: shepherds and flocks; Schwartz 1995: pastoral nomadism; Zeder 1991: feeding cities; Zeuner 1963: domestic animals.

Fishing and Hunting

Anderson 1985, Contenau 1954: hunting; Bienkowski and Millard 2000: fishing and hunting; Nemet-Nejat 1998, Nun 1999: fishing.

Crafts

Armstrong 1997: ceramics; Bienkowski and Millard 2000: craftsmen; Matson 1995: pottery; Matthews 1995: artisans and artists; Moorey 1985: materials and manufacture; Nemet-Nejat 1998: crafts; Oppenheim et al. 1970: glassmaking; Oppenheim 1997: craftsmen and artists; Petzel 1987: textiles; Saggs 1965: crafts and industries; Zaccagnini 1983: mobility among craftsmen.

Professions

Contenau 1954, Nemet-Nejat 1998, Saggs 1965: various professions; Leemans 1960: the Babylonian merchant.

Wages and Prices

Contenau 1954: Babylonian and Assyrian weights, measures, and prices; Kramer 1963: Sumerian weights and measures.

9

TRANSPORTATION AND TRADE

TRANSPORTATION BY WATER

Characteristics of the Rivers

If Mesopotamia's water was the life's blood of its economy, its rivers were the arteries of its transportation and trade.

Because every community depended upon river water to drink and to irrigate its fields, no city was far from the Tigris or Euphrates. Indeed, if over the long course of time a winding river changed its path, the settlers it once served might be forced to abandon their homes. In this way, water could alter the flow of history.

The Tigris and the Euphrates are both navigable for most of their length, though the waters of the Euphrates are gentler and friendlier to boats. The relative shallowness of the rivers, however, and the shifting mud in their beds precluded the use of ships with deep draughts.

Both rivers flow from north to south, emptying into the Persian Gulf. Unfortunately, the prevailing winds blow in exactly the same direction. As a consequence, boats in ancient Iraq—except for short trips—could only travel south; journeys to the north, including return trips, had to be made by land. In this instance, ancient Egypt had a natural advantage over her sister civilization: while the Nile flows north into the Mediterranean, the prevailing winds in Egypt blow to the south. Thus, an Egyptian mariner had but to hoist his sails to head back home from the delta.

Expanding Mesopotamia's twin river system were multiple irrigation canals, many of which were broad and deep enough to carry boats along with passengers and cargo.

Types of Boats

Model boats are among the earliest objects found in Mesopotamian graves and tombs. From a grave at Eridu dug before 4000 B.C.E. comes the baked clay model of a broad-bottomed sailboat, complete with a socket for a mast; holes fore, aft, and amidships to tie the rigging; and a seat for the sailor to sit on. From a third millennium B.C.E. royal tomb at Ur comes a sleek rowboat crafted from silver with seven rowing benches and oars. Such model boats may have been intended to provide the ghosts of the dead with transportation in the spirit-world, like the more elaborate toy ships found in the treasure-filled tomb of pharaoh Tutankhamun. All these Near Eastern miniatures may also point to something far more mundane but just as illuminating: model-building as an ancient hobby. Additionally, just as Egyptian pieces of jewelry portray the gods sailing on a heavenly Nile, so do Mesopotamian cylinder seals depict the gods traveling in divine ships on similar voyages.

Of actual boats, the largest were barges and ferries that were hauled by ropes pulled from the banks of the rivers. The scarcity of timber in the land, however, limited the number of such large vessels.

Smaller vessels included the coracle and the kelek. The coracle is still in use in Iraq today where it goes by the Arabic name of *guffa*. Its shape led the ancients to call it a "turnip." Resembling a round reed basket, the coracle's natural buoyancy was enhanced by a watertight coating of bitumen. Both locomotion and direction were achieved with the help of a punting pole or oar, since Mesopotamian boats lacked a rudder.

Apart from the majestic city of Babylon, the most surprising thing the Greek traveler Herodotus saw during his visit to Mesopotamia was the kelek. Unlike the round coracle, the

9.1 *Transporting cargo in a kelek made more bouyant by inflated goatskins.* (von Reber, *History of Ancient Art*, 1882)

round kelek was made of hides stretched over a frame of willow branches, and it was ingeniously disassembled after it had served its purpose. (See Herodotus *History* 1: 194.)

Vessels could be made even more buoyant by attaching inflated goatskins to the hull. Where the goat's neck had been, the skin was sewn tight, as was the hide at the ends of three of the legs. The opening at the end of the fourth leg was then used like the mouth of a balloon to inflate the rest of the hide, after which the opening was tied shut. Assyrian art depicts soldiers clinging to goatskin "water wings" as they make their way across a river; if air leaked out, more could be added by blowing into the tightly gripped mouth of the "balloon." Assyrian art likewise shows enemies using such flotation devices to help them swim away and evade capture.

The importance of water transportation to Mesopotamia is evident in the Code of Hammurabi, where seven statutes apply to boats and boating. The code sets the price for caulking a boat as well as the penalty for not doing so properly. In addition, it sets the wage for a boatman and the punishment to be meted out for any accidents resulting from his carelessness.

TRANSPORTATION BY LAND

The Character of Roads

Unlike reliable rivers, paved roads were a rarity in ancient Mesopotamia. For most of the country's history, roads were simply the well-trodden and often winding trails flattened into broad pathways by centuries after centuries of commercial traffic. Occasionally they might be repaired locally by order of a city's ruler. It was imperialists, however, who were the first to recognize the strategic importance of good roads, which made possible the rapid deployment of troops and military equipment and the swift transmission of military intelligence. Those masters of territorial conquest, the Assyrians, were the first to institute, control, and maintain a nationwide system of highways with "Pony-Express" way stations for messengers set at regular intervals, a precedent later followed more extensively by the Persians. In order to reach their military objectives, the Assyrian army cut roads through rugged mountains, while outside cities their engineers paved royal highways with stone to impress visitors approaching the administrative centers of the empire. By the second millennium B.C.E., permanent bridges, albeit of wood, spanned the Euphrates; by the first millennium B.C.E., stone bridges graced Nineveh and Babylon.

As the imperialistic Romans would discover centuries later, roads built for war carry more than the tramping boots of soldiers; they also carry the material benefits of peace and thereby serve to homogenize culture, commercially unifying the conquerors with the conquered. Not only did merchants' wares widely travel these roads but also those invisible but invaluable commodities of cultural traditions and new ideas.

Vehicles

Sometime before 3000 B.C.E., the Sumerians became the first people in history to invent the wheel and dedicate it to the cause of transportation. By the third millennium B.C.E., they were constructing small two- and four-wheeled carts as well as covered wagons. The wheels of these vehicles were made of two half-discs of solid wood nailed together and covered with tires of leather, like those of a cart found in the tomb of Puabi at Ur. Many centuries later, the Assyrians manufactured metal tires out of sheets of copper, bronze, and ultimately iron, which afforded the wooden wheels better protection. Originally, the wheels of Sumerian vehicles were attached to the axle and turned with it. Later, they were designed to rotate separately around a rigid axle to make cornering easier. Four-wheeled vehicles, however, had a hard time turning because their front axles were not pivoted. The fastest vehicles were two-wheeled chariots, a clay model of which survives in a Sumerian grave.

The discovery around 1500 B.C.E. that wood could be bent with heat led to the development of wooden rims equipped with four to six spokes leading to a hub. Such lighter wheels meant faster vehicles, and faster vehicles accelerated the flow of commerce and the pace of battle. For passengers, however, wooden wheels, metal tires, and rough roads added up to a bumpy ride, especially when compared to a slow boat floating down a river.

Throughout, sledges—which antedated the wheel—continued to be used for dragging heavy loads over terrain that was too muddy or rocky for carts or wagons.

Beasts of Burden

The speed of wheeled transportation inevitably depended upon the speed of the animals pulling it. Prior to the domestication of the horse in the Near East (around 2300 B.C.E.), the draught animals of choice were the ox, the donkey, or the mule—slow going by any measure, especially in warfare. Donkey or mule caravans plied the trails of Mesopotamia for millennia, patiently hauling civilization's cargo. It was perhaps not until the ninth century B.C.E. that the horse, rather than the donkey, was used for riding.

Though our mental image of the Middle East is populated with camels (thanks to

9.2   This drawing, based on an Assyrian relief from Dur-Sharrukin (Khorsabad), portrays a groom leading two horses decked out with elegant harnesses.   (Layard, *Nineveh and Its Remains*, 1849)

Lawrence of Arabia), the camel made its historic appearance rather late in history, probably domesticated only shortly before 1000 B.C.E. Superior to other beasts of burden because it could carry five times the load of a donkey while requiring less frequent watering, the camel was used as a pack animal by the Assyrian military. Cyrus the Great of Persia, in fact, employed it as a surprise weapon against King Croesus of Lydia. Knowing horses couldn't stand the sight or smell of camels, Cyrus positioned his camels in front of his infantry and immediately threw the enemy's crack cavalry into disarray, winning the battle as a result. Or so reports Herodotus.

TRADE

Natural Resources

Despite the fact that Mesopotamia was agriculturally rich, it was poor in key natural resources that early civilizations thrived on. Chief among these were copper and tin, the two metals that were compounded to produce bronze, the metallic mainstay of the post–Stone Age world. Missing also, especially in the south, were two other resources: stone that could be quarried and cut into building blocks, and trees that could yield sufficient timber for large-scale construction.

To clothe themselves in the trappings of affluence, the ancient Mesopotamians initiated trade directly with the lands that possessed the resources they needed and, in addition, dealt with intermediaries who could supply them with these commodities. From these sources they also sought luxuries they lacked and raw materials that could be crafted into objects of fine art. From Anatolia and Iran they imported tin. From Bahrain and the Arabian coast they obtained copper, gold, ivory, pearls (called "fish eyes"), and a delicacy known as "Dilmun onions." From the territories that are today Oman and the United Arab Emirates they secured copper, diorite, ochre (for cosmetics), ivory, and semiprecious stones. From the African coast came gold, ebony, ivory, and carnelian; and from Phoenicia (today's Lebanon), timber (especially cedarwood) and aromatic oils. According to a poem, imported elephants and apes once jostled in the main city square of Akkad in the 23rd century B.C.E.

Mesopotamian ships were navigating the Red Sea by around 3000 B.C.E. and, even earlier, plying the waters of the Persian Gulf. There were also trade links with the far-off civilization of the Indus Valley, a prime source of carnelian and other semiprecious stones. Afghanistan was the ultimate source of lapis lazuli, a mineral for jewelry and ornaments, one that traveled over 1,300 miles to reach an eager Mesopotamian market. By the late 15th and early 14th centuries B.C.E., trade routes stretched to pharaonic Egypt, Syria, and the Hittite Empire of Turkey, enriching with their profits such commercial cities as Ugarit and Ebla in Syria and Mari in northern Mesopotamia.

In exchange for imported commodities, Mesopotamians offered such products as grain (barley, emmer wheat, or sesame seeds), other agricultural products like dates, and textiles both unfinished and tailored.

Merchants

The merchants (Akkadian *tamkarū*) of Mesopotamia belonged to one of three categories: those whose activities were purely domestic, whether retail or wholesale; those who were engaged in the import and export business; and those who busied themselves with the carrying trade, transporting materials or merchandise from one locale to another.

Until the rise of the enterprising Phoenicians in the eighth century B.C.E., the entrepreneurs of Babylonia were the most industrious traders of the ancient world. So widespread was their mercantile activity that their language, Akkadian, became the lingua franca of the Near East, employed not only for transacting business across national borders but also for the purposes of international diplomatic correspondence. Because of their mobility and foreign connections, Babylonian merchants also functioned as emissaries to foreign potentates, presenting gifts from Mesopotamian rulers and carrying messages on their behalf. As documents show, their commercial operations were at times carried out under treaties arranged between their homeland and the cities or countries where they conducted business.

For their mutual benefit, merchants formed cooperative trade organizations and collaborated in operating caravans that, because of their size, offered greater security against raids by marauders. Their commercial ventures were sometimes financed by loans from temple priesthoods or wealthy individuals who in turn were rewarded with interest on their financial investment or a share of the profits.

By the early second millennium B.C.E., checkpoints were set up on the Euphrates that allowed passage only to those merchant vessels that bore a "tablet of the king." Around the same time, the royal administration included a high official known as the "chief trader," or "secretary of commerce." Both facts testify to the realization by the government that the state should play an active role in commercial affairs.

Mediums of Exchange

One of the most remarkable aspects of business in the ancient world was that it was largely conducted without money. During the third and second millennia B.C.E. barter and not coinage constituted the basis of commercial exchange. Coinage was not invented until about 700 B.C.E., introduced first in the Turkish kingdom of Lydia. During that same century King Sennacherib of Assyria ordered that molten bronze be poured into clay molds to function as the first coinage of the land of the twin rivers. But coinage remained a novelty in conservative Mesopotamia until the kings of Persia and the monarchs of the Hellenistic Age promoted its use.

Coinage had a natural advantage over barter: unlike grain or livestock, coins were eminently portable and universally attractive as tokens of exchange, especially when the state, rather than individual merchants, guaranteed the weight and purity of the precious metal they contained. Indeed, the manufacture of a national coinage constitutes yet another step in the control of commerce by the state. At first, individual merchants put their own personal mark and guarantee on lumps of precious metal. But the larger the territory of a state became, the more it overlapped the wide commercial territory of merchants, and the more sense it made for the state to normalize and regulate transactions, especially if, by such regulation, commercial exchanges could be facilitated and accelerated to enhance the state's own wealth and power.

Prior to the introduction of coinage, the basic mediums of exchange in Mesopotamia were grain (measured by volume) and silver (measured by weight). Even the value of gold was expressed in terms of the more common metal, silver. In terms of relative value, first came gold (eight to 15 times more valuable than silver by weight); then silver; next lead; then copper; and finally iron, which became a common metal only in the first millennium B.C.E..

Weights and Measures

Commercial exchange necessitated uniformly accepted weights and measures. In all likelihood, such standards grew up informally in society's earliest days until centuries of usage and tradition fixed their meaning and value. Yet, even then, standards might vary from city-state to city-state. The rise of civilization and bureaucracy led to standardization, while the expansion of empire imposed uniformity over larger and larger geographical areas.

Ancient standards for weights and measures can be reconstructed with some degree of accuracy from surviving weights and commercial containers; measuring marks; deductions about basic units of measurement derived from the proportions of manufactured objects; and especially economic records, including private contracts and references found in law codes.

Babylonian and Assyrian weights and measures reveal their Sumerian origin in the non-Semitic, Sumerian names they bore and in the Sumerian counting system they embodied. The Sumerian mathematical system was a hybrid of a sexagesimal system (in which the basic number is 6 and multiples of 6) and a decimal system (based on the number 10 and its multiples). Like so many other things in Mesopotamian culture, counting owed its origins to the builders of the land's first civilization, the Sumerians. In Mesopotamia's system of linear measurement we can also see the operation of a universal human scale in which the joint of a finger or the length of a forearm serves as a basic unit.

Listed below are the Akkadian names and approximate values of Mesopotamian weights and measures along with their original Sumerian designations, the meanings of their names (where known), and their approximate values in today's terms.

Table of Weights

1 *she* (Sum. *sě*, "grain") = $\frac{1}{600}$ oz.
1 *shiklu* (Sum. *gin*, "shekel") – 180 *she* – $\frac{3}{10}$ oz.
1 *manû* (Sum. *ma-na*; "mina") = 60 *shiklu* = 18 oz.
1 *biltu* (Sum. *gu*; "talent") = 60 *manû* = 67 lb.

By Neo-Babylonian times, the *shiklu*, or "shekel," took the place of the *she* as the basic unit of weight. At $\frac{3}{10}$ of an ounce, a shekel of silver was approximately the weight of a U.S. quarter. The survival of the Sumerian sexagesimal system is evident in the multiples of 60 that function in the above table. Also, two of the four Akkadian names echo Sumerian ones.

Table of Lengths

1 *ubanu* (Sum. *shu-si*; "finger") = $\frac{2}{3}$ inch
1 *ammatu* (Sum. *kush*; "elbow" or "cubit") = 24 *ubanu* = 15½ inches
1 *kanu* (Sum. *gi*; "reed" or "cane") = 6 *ammatu* = 7'10½"
1 *gar* (Sum. *gar-(du)*) = 12 *ammatu* = 15'9"

1 *ashlu* (Sum. *esh;* "line") = 10 *gar* = 157½', or
   52½ yds.
1 *beru* (Sum. *danna;* "league") = 1800 *gar-(du)* =
   5¼ miles

The Sumerian *kush* equaled 30, rather than 24,
ubanu. Again, the multiples reveal the influence
of the Sumerian sexigesimal system and, to a
lesser extent, a decimal system. Replacing
Sumerian etymologies are Akkadian terms based
on standards of measurement from the natural
world the Babylonians knew: the length of a finger joint, the length of the forearm, and the
height of a tall reed. One of the most common
measures of length was the second, the so-called
cubit, the distance from the elbow to the tip of
the middle finger. Obviously, when purchasing
rope or cloth, it would have been advantageous
to buy it from a merchant with long arms!

Table of Area
1*musaru* (Sum. *sar;* "garden") = 1 sq. *gar* = 27½
   sq. yds.
1 *iku* (Sum. *iku;* "field") = 100 *musaru* = ⅚ acre
1 *buru* (Sum. *bur*) = 18 *iku* = 15 acres
1 *shar* = 1,080 *iku* = 25⅓ sq. miles

The Sumerians, as the first civilized people to
work the land, passed on their terminology for
land measurement to the later civilizations of
Mesopotamia. The sexigesimal and decimal
systems are again evident. Areas of land were
also calculated by the amount of grain required
to sow them: hence the terms *pi* and *imêru*
below, originally used to measure volumes,
were also applied to measuring land.

Table of Volumes
1 Sumerian *gin* = ⅖ oz.
1 *sila* or *qa* (Sum. *sila*) = 60 *gin* = 1½ pints
1 *massiktu* or *pi* = 60 *sila* or *qa* = 11 gallons or
   1⅓ bushels
1 *imêru* = 100 *sila* or *qa* = 18⅓ gallons or 2¼
   bushels
1 *qurru* or *gur* (Sum. *gur*) = 180 *sila* or *qa* = 33
   gallons or 4 1/10 bushels

Over the course of time, different values are
cited for the *sila* and *gur.* Cuneiform tablets
inform us that a typical donkey-load of grain
was an *imêru,* or 2¼ bushels, a mathematical
fact that the poor donkey was oblivious to!

READING

Transportation by Water

Bass 1995: sea and river craft in the Near East;
Beitzel 1992: travel and communication in Old
Testament times; Casson 1994: ancient travel;
Casson 1995: ancient ships and seamanship;
Nemet-Nejat 1998: water transportation; Price
1923: water transportation; Roaf 1990: models
of boats; Wachsman 1998: seagoing ships.

Transportation by Land

Beitzel 1992: travel and communication in Old
Testament times; Bulliet 1990: the camel and
the wheel; Crouwel and Littauer 1995: chariots
and the wheel; Crouwel and Littauer 1997, the
wheel; Dorsey 1995: carts and roads; Littauer
and Crouwel 1979: wheeled vehicles and ridden animals; Meadow and Uerpmann 1986,
1991, Wapnish and Hesse 1995, 1997: equids;
Meier 1988: the messenger in the ancient
Semitic world; Nemet-Nejat 1998: land transportation; Piggott 1983: earliest wheeled transport; Wapnish 1995, 1997: camels.

Trade

Astour 1995: overland trade routes; Contenau
1954: trade; Crawford 1973: invisible exports;
Groom 1981: frankincense and myrrh; Hawkins

1977: trade in the Near East; Joannès 1995: commerce and banking; Knapp 1991: spice, drugs, grain, and grog; Leemans 1960: merchants and foreign trade; MacDonald 1997: trade routes and goods; Moore and Lewis 1999: the birth of the multinational; Nemet-Nejat 1998: domestic economy and foreign trade; Polanyi 1957: trade and markets in early empires; Potts 1995: foreign trade; Snell 1995: exchange and coinage; Zaccagnini 1977: merchants at Nuzu.

Weights and Measures

Contenau 1954: Babylonian and Assyrian weights and measures; Hoyrup 1994: measure, number, and weight; Kramer, 1963: Sumerian measures; Powell 1981: money prior to coinage; Powell 1992: overview of weights and measures in the ancient Near East; Powell, 1995: sources and methods for reconstructing ancient measuring systems.

10

MILITARY AFFAIRS

THE INFLUENCE OF GEOGRAPHY

The geography of Mesopotamia encouraged war.

Mesopotamia is geographically defined by its mountains in the north, its alluvial plains in the south, and the rivers that connect them. The existence of not one but two major river valleys promoted the development of multiple settlements; the fertility of the valleys generated wealth; wealth, in turn, incited competition and greed; and the flatness of the plains made individual communities vulnerable to attack. The net effect in the south was a coalescence of power through imperialism: Akkad absorbed Sumer, and Babylon absorbed both. Eventually, mountainous Assyria in the north—which had always been topographically separate from the south and, because of its terrain, more defensible—marched upon the south and conquered it, and then went on to build an even wider empire. To life in Mesopotamia, therefore, warfare was a natural condition.

In Egypt, by contrast, the story was very different. There, there was one river, not two. The fertile singularity of the Nile and the forbidding deserts to its east and west promoted solidarity among the separate communities that grew up along the river's narrow banks. Conflict *did* exist: between the kingdom of the river valley to the south (Upper Egypt) and the kingdom of the delta to the north (Lower Egypt). But once the king of the south, Narmer, conquered the kingdom of the north around 3000 B.C.E., Egypt was united and would remain so, free for most of its history from internal war and the threat of external invasion.

The only similarity between the military histories of the two countries was that conquest followed the flow of water: in Egypt from south to north and in Mesopotamia from north to south.

EVIDENCE

While the goal of war is victory, its instrument is destruction. The physical effect of war, then, is to obliterate the factual proof of its very existence except through the survival of mute ruins. It is in its emotional aftermath that war is best remembered: in the celebratory propaganda of the winners and in the traumatic memories of the losers. But each of these—whether expressed in art or literature—is intrinsically subjective and prone to exaggeration. Yet if these are our main testimonies we must accordingly hear them out, measuring their veracity always against the objective bones and stones that archaeology can raise from the ground. At the same time, in assessing war, we must also be attuned to the silence and to the void that are war's truest fruits.

FORTIFICATIONS

Ancient warfare was essentially horizontal. Only in modern times with the advent of the airplane, bombs, and missiles, has attack become largely vertical. Consequently, ancient defenses were defenses against horizontal assault. Though they would be ineffective against today's aerial attack, the stout walls of an ancient city were a powerful deterrent against capture by its adversaries.

Because the earliest kingdoms of Mesopotamia were city-states, all power and legitimacy was concentrated in the fortified city; with its capture, the kingdom fell. Even when later doned, newer structures were built over their leveled remains. To keep pace with their rise, streets were resurfaced and rose as well. This process, carried out for a millennium or more, explains the abandoned mounds, or stratified "tells," that dot the landscape of Iraq today.

WEAPONS AND EQUIPMENT

Throughout the ancient Near East, the most common offensive weapon was the bow and

10.1   *An artist's reconstruction of the metropolis of Babylon as it would have looked around 600 B.C.E.*   (Oriental Institute, University of Chicago)

Mesopotamian states grew to the size of empires, the capital city remained the prime target of the enemy.

Because of the scarcity of building stone in the southern part of the country, city walls were made out of brick, especially baked, or burnt, brick for greater hardness and durability. Outside this wall might be a moat fed by river water; inside might be a second, or inner security wall guarding the king's palace. According to A. Leo Oppenheim "The walls of the cities in the ancient Near East . . . proclaimed the importance and might of the city." (Oppenheim 1977: 128). The strategic effect of the city walls was amplified by the height of the city above the surrounding plain. In the main, the verticality of the city was the product of continuous habitation at the same site for centuries. As houses made of sun-dried brick collapsed or were aban-

10.2   *This relief depicts some of the equipment carried by Assyrian troops: swords, a spear, a shield, arrows in a quiver, and a bow.*   (Rogers, *A History of Babylonia and Assyria*, 1915)

10.3 *Armed Assyrian soldiers. The two on the left hold spears and shields. One shield has already stopped two arrows fired by the enemy. The spearmen crouch to allow an archer behind them to fire. Assisting the archer is another spearman who holds a tall shield designed to protect the archer from enemy missiles.* (Layard, Nineveh and Its Remains, 1849)

arrow; the most common defensive armor, the helmet and shield. Other frequently used weapons were spears (for thrusting), javelins (for throwing), maces with stone heads, battle-axes with metal blades, and daggers. Surprisingly, the straight-bladed sword was rarely used in Mesopotamia before the first millennium B.C.E. Instead, for slashing, swords with sickle-shaped blades were preferred. Additional weapons included slingshots (with an effective range of over 300 feet) and mundane but effective digging tools for burrowing through or under enemy walls.

Soldiers wore helmets (first of relatively ineffective felt or leather, later of hammered metal), laced boots, and—in Sumer—a cloak of linen or leather to which metal discs were sewn for armored protection. By Assyrian times,

select troops were outfitted with body armor made of hundreds of overlapping metal scales that could flex and lend mobility in combat.

Offensive and defensive equipment evolved reciprocally and supported an ongoing arms race: developments in weaponry led to countermeasures in armor, and innovations in armor inspired further advances in weaponry. The introduction of the metal helmet, for example, led to the introduction of a battle-axe with a head like an adze to pierce the helmet's metal shell.

The most dramatic advance in Near Eastern weaponry occurred in Mesopotamia during the second half of the third millennium B.C.E.: the introduction of the composite bow. Unlike a simple bow carved from a single piece of wood, the composite bow consisted of multiple layers of material—wood, bone, and sinew—that were glued together. The composite nature of the bow increased its tensile strength, which was sometimes further enhanced by bonding together wood from different types of trees. The greater tensile strength of the bow increased the velocity and distance of the arrows it fired. With an accurate range of 300 to 400 feet (and a maximum range double that), the composite bow enabled archers to strike their targets while they themselves were still outside the range of their enemy's missiles. It is just such a weapon that may have allowed the army of Akkad to triumph over its otherwise well-equipped Sumerian adversaries. According to military historian Yigael Yadin: "the invention of the composite bow with its comparatively long range was as revolutionary, in its day, and brought comparable results as the discovery of gunpowder thousands of years later" (Yadin 1963: 48).

The materials out of which military equipment was constructed account in large part for its survival archaeologically. While perishable wood, linen, and leather disintegrated, the bronze and iron of arrowheads, spearpoints, axeblades, and armor endured. Yet even when the tools of war decomposed, their shapes and uses persisted in works of art that depicted ancient combat. Notable among such artworks are the victory monuments of Sumer and the battle scenes on the sculpted palace walls of Assyria.

THE ORGANIZATION OF THE ARMY

Begun as citizen militias, the armies of Mesopotamia eventually became large aggregations of trained professional soldiers with specialized skills and functions in battle. The expansion and professionalization of Mesopotamia's fighting forces went hand in hand with the growth of imperialism. The Sumerian army numbered its troops in the thousands, the Assyrian in the tens of thousands, and the Persian in the hundreds of thousands.

In the third millennium B.C.E., Sargon of Akkad became the first ruler in history to create a standing army. Shulgi, his successor, became the first to form specialized military units.

Command

Leading the Mesopotamian army in all periods was the king himself or his military surrogates, accompanied by the invisible protective presence of one or more state gods.

In its developed state, the Mesopotamian army consisted of both heavily armed assault troops and lightly armed auxiliaries deployed for tactical maneuvers. Specialists included archers (at times transported by chariot), sappers (to undermine enemy fortifications), and engineers (for the construction of military bridges and roads, and for building and supervising the operation of siege equipment). Expeditions also employed spies for reconnaissance and chaplains whose duty it was to sacrifice animals and inspect their entrails to determine if a given course of military action was divinely favored. Mobile units included chariots and, at a much later date, cavalry.

Chariots

According to Yigael Yadin, the "invention and development of the chariot was the most significant contribution to the art of warfare in the third millennium" (Yadin 1963: 36). Chariots were an innovation of the Sumerians who, in the absence of the horse, employed a donkey-like animal (perhaps the onager, or wild ass) for power. Though two-wheeled

10.4   A trio of Assyrian soldiers in a chariot. One drives, the second shoots arrows, and the third wields a shield for their protection.   (Layard, *Nineveh and Its Remains*, 1849)

chariots were used for transporting messengers with military intelligence or orders, the Sumerian war chariot was a heavy four-wheeled cart that carried a driver and a spearman. As a vehicle it was not easy to maneuver because the solid wheels were originally fixed to the axles and the front axle could not swivel during turns. Because of its clumsiness and the relative slowness of the draught animals that hauled it, the Sumerian battle-wagon was probably reserved for breaking up enemy formations in coordination with an infantry charge. Conceivably, it could also have been used for a kamikaze-style attack on the enemy commander in chief.

With the introduction of the horse from central Asia in the second millennium B.C.E., the chariot became a swift-moving two-wheeled mobile firing platform that carried a driver, an archer with spare quivers, and a shield-bearer to protect the rest of the crew. Centuries later, the Persians added to the deadliness of the Babylonian and Assyrian chariot by attaching scythe-like blades to the rims of the wheels to chop up enemy troops during a charge.

Cavalry

Because saddles and stirrups were unknown, it was extremely difficult for a rider to shoot arrows and control his mount at the same time. As a result, cavalry played a minor role in Near Eastern warfare until the first millennium B.C.E., when it was developed as a weapon by the Assyrians.

Logistical Support

Like every fighting force, the ancient Mesopotamian army traveled on its stomach, and required food supplies, cooks, and other types of logistical support.

SIEGE WARFARE

Siege warfare was raised to the level of an art by the Babylonians and Assyrians.

In addition to corps of sappers, their armies attacked walls with battering rams made of stout poles sheathed and capped in metal. Hung within wheeled and armored vehicles that were pushed by soldiers hidden inside for protection, rams fitted with pointed heads pierced city gates or penetrated walls at their base by prying building blocks apart. Rams were also pushed up specially constructed earthen ramps (limed or planked for traction) in order to pound the walls' thinner and therefore more vulnerable upper sections.

Meanwhile, scaling ladders were used for vertical assault. While the defenders within hastily braced the base of their walls with piles of earth and rubble and fired arrows, hurled stones, and poured flaming oil on the enemy below, the attackers advanced under the cover of leather shields. Portable siege towers enabled archers to focus their fire at the defenders at precisely those strategic points in the walls where sappers, battering rams, and ground forces were directing their energy.

During the Hellenistic period, siege technology in the Near East progressed even further in the hands of the Greeks and Romans, who introduced artillery-style crossbows and torsion catapults of various types that mechanically launched clusters of arrows, heaps of stones, and burning oil or naphtha at their hapless targets.

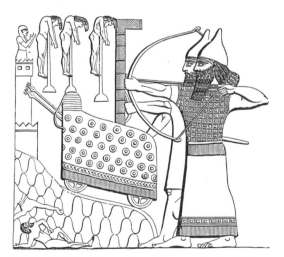

10.5 As Assyrian archers fire on a besieged city and a mobile battering ram does its work, impaled captives hang lifelessly. (Layard, Nineveh and Its Remains, 1849)

PSYCHOLOGICAL WARFARE

The Assyrians in particular were adept at psychological warfare.

When Sennacherib was trying to capture Jerusalem, his representative addressed the officials of the city in Assyrian, urging them to surrender in the face of Assyria's superior might. But when the officials refused, the Assyrian representative turned and shouted to the defenders on the walls, telling them directly in Hebrew what he knew their own leaders would never report. The point of the stratagem, of course, was to incite rebellion.

In conquering a territory, the Assyrians would frequently target small cities that could be easily captured. After achieving their military

10.6   At the right, scribes tally the severed heads of the enemy.   (Layard, *Nineveh and Its Remains*, 1849)

THE ART OF WAR

Warfare appears as a theme in the art of Mesopotamia, where it serves as a visual celebration of victory. As would be expected, such works of art were commissioned by the victors rather than the vanquished and consequently glorify the disciplined but brutal use of force to achieve political and economic ends.

From the world of the Sumerians come two particularly notable examples, both from the middle of the third millennium B.C.E.: the Royal Standard of Ur and the Stele of the Vultures.

The Royal Standard depicts a successful military campaign through the art of mosaic. On one side are scenes of battle: four-wheeled chariots with driver and spearman on board traverse a battlefield at increasing speed, rolling over the corpses of the enemy; later, infantrymen in cloaks advance and herd naked and bound prisoners of war in procession as the victorious king looks on. The opposite side of the Standard shows a victory banquet in progress as the spoils of war, chiefly livestock, are paraded past the king and his counselors, who drink beer and joyfully listen to music.

Only four fragments of the stone Stele of the Vultures survive. Together they commemorate in sculpture the triumph of a ruler of Lagash over the rival city-state of Umma. The largest fragment portrays the king of Lagash leading his forces into battle (See figure 7.3, page 219). Soldiers march with spears held high or move forward in tight formation with shields interlocked. The other fragments show the enemy falling in heaps before the army's onslaught. Vultures (from which the stele gets its name) fly by clutching in their talons the severed heads of executed prisoners. In an inscription, the humbled king of Umma vows never again to invade Lagash's borders.

objective, they would then proceed to loot and torch the houses, rape the women, burn the children alive, and kill or mutilate the men. The bodies or heads of their victims would be impaled on stakes erected atop the city walls, or their severed hands, noses, lower lips, or skulls would be heaped up in piles to demonstrate to others the price of resistance to Assyrian rule. Alternately, their corpses might be cut up into small pieces and fed to dogs, pigs, and vultures. Instead of butchering captives, the Assyrians would sometimes merely blind them and set them free so they could testify to the horrors they had last seen with their eyes.

Prisoners of war were often used by the Assyrians for forced labor. Beginning in the 13th century B.C.E., Assyria practiced the deportation of conquered peoples to prevent their insurrection in the future; by the ninth century B.C.E., mass deportation had attained the status of policy. The most famous such act was committed not by the Assyrians but by the Babylonians in the sixth century B.C.E., when king Nebuchadnezzar captured Jerusalem, destroyed its temple, and marched its rulers and people to Babylon in what became known as the "Babylonian Captivity."

10.7   *Discovered in the remains of Ur, the "Royal Standard" on one side depicts Ur's victorious army, composed of infantry and a corps of chariots. Near the center of the topmost register, prisoners of war are paraded before Ur's leader.*   (The British Museum)

10.8   *On the opposite side, the Royal Standard of Ur shows the fruits of victory. As enemy livestock are brought into the city, its leaders (at the top) take part in a victory celebration, drinking beer and listening to music.*   (The British Museum)

10.9　*The king of Assyria returns home from battle triumphant, riding in a chariot, his head covered by a parasol. In the foreground flows the fish-filled Tigris; in the background grow palm trees laden with dates.* (Layard, *Nineveh and Its Remains*, 1849)

To judge by the archaeological evidence, however, no people celebrated war more than the Assyrians. Though the plentiful evidence may simply be a result of sculptable stone being more available in the north, its extent also suggests that the Assyrians delighted in reflecting on their conquests.

Sculptural reliefs from Sennacherib's palace at Nineveh, for example, present panoramic pictures of siege operations conducted against enemy cities. As battering rams move into position, Assyrian archers and slingers fire their missiles. Meanwhile, defenders hurl blazing torches from the battlements, only to be shot and then tumble from their heights. All that is missing from these graphic carvings are the sounds of battle: the rumble of siege engines, the whiz of arrows, and the screams of the wounded. But even in silence such reliefs would cause the Assyrian king to swell with pride as he surveyed his palace walls and cause visiting dignitaries to

tremble at the prospect of Assyrian might turned against them.

ANCIENT MONUMENTS AND MODERN WARFARE

War can imperil not only the cities of the living but also the ghost towns of the dead.

In 1991 during the Persian Gulf War, the monuments of Mesopotamia were menaced by aerial bombardment because of the proximity of archaeological sites to strategic targets. The environs of ancient Ur, for example, served as a base for Iraqi planes while its ziggurat became a platform for anti-aircraft guns. Another anti-aircraft battery stood atop Tell Kuyunjik, ancient Babylon's main mound. Meanwhile, an air defense command center was moved to Nineveh, the ruined capital of the Assyrian Empire, from the modern city of Mosul. Indiscriminate bombing of these sites could have led to the wholesale destruction of historic remains. Indeed, the placement of military assets was likely designed to inhibit just such attacks.

Except for four bomb craters in its sacred precinct and bullet holes in the southeast face of its ziggurat, Ur escaped mostly unscathed. Elsewhere, the vibration from bomb blasts shook bricks loose from Ctesiphon's soaring arch (close to Iraq's largest bioweapons plant and a nuclear research facility) and cracked the walls of Nimrud's Northwest Palace.

At the Iraq Museum in Baghdad, portable antiquities were packed up and transported to provincial museums for safekeeping, but larger monuments—including colossal bulls from Khorsabad and a Sumerian mosaic wall—had to be left behind. Located next door to Saddam Hussein's presidential palace and the studios of Baghdad TV, the museum fortunately suffered only superficial damage.

In the chaos of war, outlying museums were reportedly attacked and looted by Kurdish and Shiite rebels. The Iraqi authorities, for their part, had already methodically looted the Kuwaiti National Museum before torching it. The illegal antiquities market may have benefited from such thefts.

Far more treasures, however, could not have been destroyed or stolen. They still lie securely buried beneath Iraq's soil—30, 40, or 50 feet deep in thousands of undiscovered cities and towns—where they have slept for millennia safe from the violence of a later age.

READING

The Influence of Geography

Hughes 1975: the physical environment of Mesopotamia.

Evidence

Editors of Time-Life Books 1993: illustrations of weaponry; Parrot 1961: Assyrian art; Pritchard 1969: texts.

Fortifications

Damerji 1992, Herzog 1997, Mazar 1995: fortifications; Yadin 1963: the art of warfare.

Weapons and Equipment

Boudet 1966: the ancient art of warfare; Chapman 1997: weapons and warfare; Gonen 1975: weapons of the ancient world; Hackett 1990: ancient warfare; Pfeiffer 1966: arms and weapons.

The Organization of the Army

Cook 1983: military communications; Dalley 1996: military organization; Henshaw 1969: soldiers; Kendall 1974: warfare and military matters in the Nuzu tablets; Sasson 1969: military establishments at Mari.

Siege Warfare

Editors of Time-Life Books 1995: illustrations; Hornblower and Spawforth 1996: artillery and siegecraft among the Greeks and Romans.

Psychological Warfare

Gelb 1973: prisoners of war; Nemet-Nejat 1998 (including notes): techniques and savagery; Oded 1979: mass deportations.

The Art of War

Editors of Time-Life Books 1993, Winter 1985: Stele of the Vultures; Moorey 1982: Royal Standard of Ur; Parrot 1961: Assyrian sculpture.

Ancient Monuments and Modern Warfare

Zimansky and Stone 1992: reports of war damage.

11

EVERYDAY LIFE

WORK

Because ancient Mesopotamia was fundamentally an agrarian society, the principal occupations were growing crops and raising livestock.

The Rise of Specialization

Because of the industriousness of the people and the fertility of the land, food surpluses soon arose. Such surpluses meant that not everyone needed to be self-sufficient, for anyone could now eat who had the means to barter food from those who produced it. As a result, a specialization of labor developed by which many traded the goods they made or the services they provided for the food and other commodities they desired.

Types of Work

With increasing specialization, a variety of occupations took shape, many of which reflected the growing complexity and sophistication of society.

Supplying the basic needs of domestic life were potters, weavers of cloth and baskets, leather workers and shoemakers, metalworkers (working copper and bronze and, later, iron), millers and brewers, and fishermen and boatmen. Manufacturing the material refinements of life were perfumers and confectioners as well as artisans like jewelers (goldsmiths and silversmiths) and carvers of that omnipresent marker of personal identity, the cylinder seal. And tending to the needs of body and mind were doctors, scribes, and teachers.

While those who practiced crafts usually sold their handiwork themselves, there were busy vendors and peddlers who sold commodities like salt and spices and sesame seed oil, and merchants who engaged in trade with distant cities and lands. Meanwhile in the streets, tavernkeepers and prostitutes, "the world's oldest profession," plied their trade.

While canal diggers kept the river water flowing to thirsty fields, others—architects and engineers, bricklayers and carpenters, sculptors and painters—applied their skills to building monumental works upon the urban landscape.

At the head of society were the kings and priests served by the populous staff of palace and temple. With the institution of standing armies and the spread of imperialism, military officers and professional soldiers took their place in Mesopotamia's expanding and diverse workforce.

SLAVERY

One of the early effects of civilization's expansion was the dehumanization of its members.

Causes of Slavery

With the rise of imperialism, prisoners of war became the slaves of their conquerors. The wholesale use of captives for forced labor reached its height under the Assyrian conqueror-kings, but its origins date back to at least the third millennium B.C.E. Thus the Sumerian ideogram for female slave is composed of two signs: one for woman, and the other for mountains—signifying the march of Sumer's armies beyond the river valleys and plains, and the subjugation of upland peoples.

Another explanation for ancient slavery besides conquest was financial desperation, for when families were hungry or in debt they often chose enslavement as the means of their economic salvation. An individual might sell himself into slavery, or sell his wife or children. Indeed, one of the most poignant testimonies to slavery is the clay impression of a child's foot dating to about 1200 B.C.E. Across the footprint runs a notation in cuneiform accompanied by the imprint of a seal—the bill of sale for an ancient child.

The Slave as Property

To be a slave was to be property. If a slave is hurt by someone, says Hammurabi's Code, it is the slaveowner not the slave who is to be compensated. Like property, a slave was marked with his owner's name: a brand on the hand. Should a slave escape and be caught, the punishment was severe; should someone help a slave escape, the punishment would be death for the abettor. If a barber shaved off the lock of hair that was the mark of a slave, the barber's hand could be cut off and the man who hired him impaled in his own doorway as a warning to others.

Employment

Most often, slaves were used for manual labor in households, but some served in temples as aids to priests. In Babylonia in the first millennium B.C.E., there may have been between two and three slaves in the average private home; in Assyria, perhaps between three and four; though poorer people owned none, and rich people more. Female slaves could serve a special purpose as their masters' concubines.

Some masters apprenticed their slaves to learn a trade or, if the slaves seemed clever, backed them financially in business. A Mesopotamian slave could even save money, rent property, and buy slaves of his own. But ultimately all his assets belonged to his master, who was merely making a shrewd investment in his own future. It is even questionable whether a slave could use his earnings to buy back his freedom.

MARRIAGE AND FAMILY

The ancient Mesopotamians believed that the family was of central importance to the stability of society.

The Business of Marriage

THE LEGAL FRAMEWORK

The belief in the centrality of marriage is clearly expressed in the Babylonian Code of Hammurabi. Of its 282 statutes, almost one-fourth are devoted to family law. This focus on the family is evident in even older Sumerian law codes, which influenced later Babylonian legal thinking.

In the language of the Sumerians, the word for "love" was a compound verb that, in its literal sense, meant "to measure the earth," that is, "to mark off land." To the Sumerians, then, the concept of love was related to the concept of possession and property. The Babylonians may well have shared this view: second only to the statutes of Hammurabi that deal with the family are statutes that deal with real estate. And even within the sphere of family law, questions concerning ownership and inheritance loom large.

Among both the Sumerians and the Babylonians (and very likely among the Assyrians as well) marriage was fundamentally a business arrangement designed to assure and perpetuate an orderly society. Though there was an inevitable emotional component to marriage, its prime intent in the eyes of the state was not companionship but procreation; not personal happiness in the present but communal continuity for the future.

Every marriage began with a legal contract. Indeed, as Mesopotamian law stated, if a man should marry without having first drawn up and executed a marriage contract, the woman he "marries" would not be his wife. Though such a couple might cohabit, without the formality of a contract neither they nor their offspring would be protected by the state and its laws.

Every marriage began not with a joint decision by two people in love but with a negotiation between the representatives of two families: between the prospective groom and his prospective father-in-law, or between the father of the prospective groom and the father of the bride-to-be. Once again it was the family that was paramount rather than the individual: more than uniting two individuals, the wedding would unite two families. Indeed, before the wedding (as is still the custom in certain traditional societies today) the bride and groom might not have known each other personally. The bride, in fact, could be considerably younger than her propertied husband-to-be; though betrothed, she might continue to live with her own family until coming of age.

CEREMONIES

The negotiation would have concluded with an amicable agreement involving betrothal gifts and a promised exchange of property. The groom would "purchase" his wife by paying a bride-price to her father; the father in turn would enrich his daughter with a dowry that might well exceed the value that the groom had paid. The terms of the prenuptial agreement would then be recorded in cuneiform by a scribe, "signed" by both parties with cylinder seals, and presented to each family for safekeeping.

Any debts either spouse had incurred before their wedding were their separate responsibilities, but debts incurred after their marriage were looked upon as their joint duty to repay.

Regrettably, almost no information comes down to us about the joyous celebration that no doubt would have followed (and even possibly have preceded) the formal signing of the marriage contract. For an idea of the feast, the richness of which would have been proportionate to the wealth of the two families, readers are invited to close their eyes after reading the sections in this chapter entitled "Food and Drink" and "Music," preferably after having partaken of authentic Mideastern food, drink, and music. (Even an authoritative text like this has its limitations!)

The veil, so prominent a symbol of the married woman in conservative Islamic societies today (and, in its absence, of her emancipation), owes its origin to ancient Mesopotamian practice. As part of the wedding ceremony, it is likely that the groom removed it from the face of his bride. Evidence suggests that married women wore it in public in ancient Assyria, but not in earlier Babylonia. Its use even earlier in Sumer is not attested.

THE SERIOUSNESS OF ENGAGEMENT

Engagements were serious business in Babylonia, especially for those who might have a change of heart. According to Hammurabi's Code, a suitor who changed his mind would forfeit his entire deposit (betrothal gift) and bride-price. If the prospective father-in-law changed *his* mind, he had to pay the disappointed suitor double the bride-price. Furthermore, if a rival suitor persuaded the father-in-law to change his mind, not only did the father-in-law have to pay double, but the rival wasn't allowed to marry the daughter. These legal penalties acted as a potent deterrent against changes of heart and a powerful incentive for both responsible decision making and orderly social behavior.

BRIDAL AUCTIONS

In addition to the arranged marriages described above, the marrying off of eligible young women may have been facilitated by public auction. The tradition is reported by Herodotus, who visited Mesopotamia in the fifth century B.C.E., as well as by other writers who lived during the Augustan Age of Rome. Herodotus (*History* 1: 196) writes:

> Of their customs . . . the following . . . is the wisest in my judgment. Once a year in each village the young women eligible to marry were collected all together in one place; while the men stood around them in a circle. Then a herald called up the young women one by one, and offered them for sale. He began with the most beautiful. When she was sold for a high price, he offered for sale the one who ranked next in beauty. All of them were then sold to be wives. The richest of the Babylonians who wished to wed bid against each other for the loveliest young women, while the commoners, who were not concerned about beauty, received the uglier women along with monetary compensation. When the herald had finished selling the most attractive women, he would call up the ugliest one, or perhaps one who was crippled, and would auction her off to the man who was willing to live with her for the least compensation. And the man who offered to take the smallest sum had her assigned to him. All the money came from the payments made for the beautiful women, and so those who were attractive financed the sale of those who were ugly or crippled. No one was allowed to give his daughter in marriage to the man of his choice, nor might any one take away and live with the young woman he had purchased without first having made a down payment; if, however, the parties did not agree on final arrangements, the money would be refunded. All who liked might come, even from distant villages, and bid for the women. This was the best of all their customs, but it has now fallen into disuse. (Herodotus 1942 [1858]: 105–6, trans. George Rawlinson, revised)

This tale reflects the Babylonian view, noted elsewhere in our discussion, that women were property to be bought and sold by men. The commercial ingenuity behind the auction also demonstrates the business acumen for which the Mesopotamian merchant was renowned.

Sterility, Divorce, and Marital Infidelity

As to the marriage bond itself, it was generally monogamous. But because the prime purpose of marriage was procreation, exceptions were made when a wife could not bear children. In such a case, the husband would be permitted to take a secondary wife, or use a handmaid, for the purpose of producing an heir. The husband, however, would be expected to honor and continue to support his wedded wife within his household. In the case of a wife's presumptive sterility, a husband would also have the option of divorce. Should he elect that option, he would have not only to refund his wife's dowry but pay her the full amount of her original marriage price, or, in lieu thereof, a substantial monetary settlement dictated by law—a persuasive financial disincentive against filing for divorce. Though the position of a wife was protected by the force of law, in cases of no progeny it was the woman, not the man, who was held responsible by society.

Besides sterility, Mesopotamian jurisprudence recognized other grounds for divorce. Furthermore, proceedings could be initiated by either husband or wife. If, for example, a wife was abused by her husband and denied him conjugal rights, and he then denounced her in public, she could win a divorce and secure the return of her dowry. Significantly though, the dowry would be repaid not to her directly but to her father from whom it had originally come. Two centuries before Hammurabi, the

Sumerian code of Lipit-Ishtar had protected wives by decreeing that a woman could not be arbitrarily divorced simply because her husband wanted to marry someone else; and the even earlier code of Ur-Nammu had specified alimony payments a husband must make.

But the man-made laws of Mesopotamia devoted more statutes to the sins of wives than they did to the faults of husbands. A woman, for example, who neglected her home and belittled her husband deserved to be summarily divorced without any financial settlement whatsoever, not even travel expenses. The most serious sin, however, was that of adultery. If a woman were accused of adultery by her husband, she could exonerate herself by swearing her fidelity before god; if accused by relatives or neighbors, she would be hurled into the river and left to its mercies; if caught in the sexual act, she would be tied to her paramour and drowned with him. If he wished, a forgiving husband could spare her; but, if so, the state could also then spare his wife's lover as well.

Incest

Incest within a family also incurred severe penalties. The harshest punishment was for a son and a mother who Oedipally slept together: both would be burned alive. A similar punishment was meted out to a father who slept with a son's virginal fiancée. But curiously, incest with one's own daughter was punishable only by exile from one's city.

Prolonged Separation

Other statutes dealt with the issue of missing husbands, especially soldiers who were captured in battle or merchants who were held hostage in foreign lands. If a husband had left sufficient provisions for his wife and family, she was obliged to remain faithful to him or suffer the penalty of being drowned. If no provisions remained or none had been left, she was free to live with another man for the sake of her and her children's welfare. But in the event of her husband's return, she had to return home with him. Any children born to the man she had been living with would then stay with that man. However, should a husband deliberately desert his family and forsake his city, he could reclaim neither wife nor progeny.

Death and Inheritance

In the event a married woman died, the dowry which she had brought with her when she married was applied to guarantee the proper upbringing of her children, both male and female. Indeed, the prime function of the dowry may have been to provide insurance of this very kind. Were a wife to die without bearing children, however, the dowry would revert to her father or brothers, who would then be responsible for refunding the original bride-price to her widowed husband so that he might marry again.

Were a married man to die, his estate would be passed on to his sons, the eldest son receiving the largest share. In Sumerian times, instead of dividing up a father's estate, the eldest son became the new head of the household under whose roof all the other family members could continue to live; in later times, however, the property (including land, buildings, furniture, slaves, and animals) was often divided.

Because Mesopotamian society was patriarchal, it was the sons, not the daughters, who inherited the estate. A father might make special bequests to his daughters or wife during his lifetime or in his will, but it was the sons (or, if they were dead, *their* sons) who were the automatic beneficiaries. These sons were in turn expected to look after their mother and unmarried sisters financially, including providing dowries for those of their sisters who were as yet unwed. Though a father could attempt to disinherit a son through his will, such action required court approval after the presentation of compelling evidence. In addition, as long as she did not remarry, a widow might continue to run her deceased husband's business.

As early as the Sumerian code of Ur-Nammu the law had extended special protection to widows and orphans, who otherwise might have been at the mercy of selfish and avaricious relatives. The Code of Hammurabi exhibits particular concern for the treatment children might receive at the hands of a hard-hearted stepfather who had children of his own from a prior marriage. To insure the proper upbringing of the new stepchildren, the Babylonian court demanded a full accounting of their deceased father's estate as well as guarantees of their future financial security before granting their widowed mother permission to remarry.

The Emotional Dimension of Marriage

While we have now examined most of the legal implications of marriage Mesopotamian-style, we have yet to explore its emotional side. Even if the marriage itself was in many ways a business arrangement, the partners in that business were human beings with feelings. The very survival of tons of legalistic clay tablets tends to bury and obscure the far more intangible aspect of emotion. To do real justice, then, to life in ancient Mesopotamia, we must learn to read between the cuneiform lines.

The physical act of love endures in works of erotic art retrieved from bedrooms, temples (for love was also divine), and tombs (for love was never meant to die). On plaques,

11.1   On this baked-clay model of a bed dating to the first half of the second millennium B.C.E., a couple sexually embraces. In addition to portraying an everyday act, the plaque may also have been symbolic in a religious sense, depicting a divine ritual of "sacred marriage" that insured the fertility of the land.   (The British Museum)

women of Mesopotamia kneel, their thighs invitingly outspread, or stand, proud in their nakedness, lifting their breasts as once they did for sculptors whose wet fingers caressed the soft clay of figurines. On terra-cotta beds, lovers look into each other's eyes, the woman's hand guiding penis to vagina, now the female on top, now the male.

Meanwhile, for those whose desire was unrequited, an appropriate magic spell was available. Use it, an Asssyrian sorcerer promised, and "she will speak to you the next time you see her and, powerless to resist your charms, will make love."

Or, with the help of another charm, "she will not keep you from her bed."

All the while, an elderly Sumerian couple sit side by side fused by sculpture into a single piece of gypsum rock: his right arm wrapped around her shoulder, his left hand tenderly clasping her right, their large eyes looking straight ahead to the future, their aged hearts remembering the past. "Though she has already borne me eight sons," the Sumerian couplet sings, "she is still ready to make love."

11.2 This seated figure of a Sumerian husband and wife dates to about 2700 B.C.E. and was found in the city of Nippur at the temple of Inanna, goddess of love. Both individuals stare ahead stiffly with wide-open eyes, like the subjects of turn-of-the-20th-century photographs. Affection is signified by the husband's right arm wrapped around his wife's shoulders and by his left hand resting on her wrist. (Oriental Institute, University of Chicago)

"A man's wife," declares a proverb, "is like a canteen in the desert."

Marriage, though, is a human institution, and like every human institution has its downside. Sumerian literature is replete with bits of proverbial wisdom that show the misgivings men had about matrimony:

The heart of a bride is filled with joy;
The heart of a groom with regret.

A marvelous idea: to marry;
A more marvelous idea: to divorce.

The complaints of Sumerian men, however, could be even more direct:

My wife is down at the temple;
My mother is down at the river;
And here I am starving!

Whoever hasn't supported a wife and a child
Doesn't know what it's like to have
A leash through his nose!

Sacred Marriage

Every year, however, the institution of marriage was celebrated amid great festivity. At the beginning of the New Year, it is believed, the king mated with a priestess who symbolized the incarnation of Inanna or Ishtar, the goddess of sexuality and procreation. By this sacred wedding, the future fertility of the womb and the soil was assured. In this rite the king played the role of the shepherd Dumuzi or Tammuz, the great goddess's divine lover.

As crowds of couples gathered about the temple and attended this rite, they would have received a spiritual confirmation of the cosmic rightness of the bond that connected them as man and woman, as husband and wife. Perhaps it is more than coincidental that the statue of the elderly couple we described was found in Nippur amid the ruins of the goddess's temple.

Birth, Death, and the Belief in an Afterlife

The Concept of Immortality

The ancient Egyptians fervently believed in a sensuous afterlife where the pleasures of this life would be eternally reexperienced in the next. Their spiritual confidence was sustained by the land in which they lived, a land whose abundance was made possible by the river Nile. Every year in July, the waters of the Nile rose gently and predictably, depositing a rich layer of silt on the farmers' fields, thereby renewing the valley's fertility. The benevolent dependability of the Nile coupled with the protective deserts on east and west that guarded Egypt from invasion encouraged its people to believe that beyond death's door lay a sunny vista radiant with promise.

But Mesopotamia was a different kind of land. Though it was watered by twin rivers, its flatness and openness left it vulnerable to invasion and attack. The Tigris and Euphrates, moreover, were potentially violent rivers. When the winter snows melted, the rivers could flood suddenly, savagely uprooting everything in their path. In a world where everything one had counted on could be suddenly swept away by war or natural disaster, an optimistic belief in the guaranteed happiness of the hereafter could hardly take root.

The certainty of death and the impossibility of immortality are the central themes of ancient Mesopotamia's greatest heroic tale, the *Epic of Gilgamesh*. In this story, the hero Gilgamesh, crushed by the death of his best friend, searches for the secret of eternal life only to have it snatched from his grasp. He learns that

Death cannot be seen
— not its face, not its voice —
until it shatters our lives
leaving nothing behind.

Death is what the gods gave man;
Life is what they kept for themselves.

Yet despite their innate pessimism, the people of Mesopotamia continued to hope that the soul could somehow live on after death. Their pessimism, however, tended to paint the landscape of that afterworld in gloomy tones. As Georges Contenau has written:

> In this region, illumined by no ray of light, wholly shrouded in dust, airless and lacking food and drink, the only sustenance of the spirits of the dead was the funerary offerings. If no man remembered them, then they returned to earth to plague the living, subsisting as best they might on such miserable scraps of food as they could find in the gutters. (Contenau 1954: 300)

Dwelling in a dark underworld called "the land of no return," the spirits of the dead hungered for the nourishment they had known in this life. In a world that was neither heaven nor hell but a realm of endless emptiness, the dead longed for the food of remembrance.

Death and Burial

PREPARATIONS

When the hour of death neared for an adult, the ancient Mesopotamian would lie in bed to await its coming in the company of loved ones, perhaps also with a priest in attendance. Beside the bed on the left sat an empty chair reserved for the spirit when it would rise invisibly from the corpse. Beside the chair lay the first spiritual offerings: beer and flat bread to strengthen the soul for its long journey to the underworld.

11.3 *This poignant photograph shows an infant burial at Tepe Gawra. Uncovered by the archaeologist, the skeleton of the child rests in a cracked pottery bowl where its parents placed it thousands of years ago.* (Estate of Cyrus H. Gordon)

11.4 *An Iraqi child stands beside an ancient sarcophagus that had just been excavated.* (Jastrow, *Babylonia and Assyria*, 1917)

When death finally came, the body would be washed, anointed in perfumed oils, and clothed, and laid out with jewelry and other favorite possessions.

INTERMENT

Burial would be in a baked-clay coffin set in a grave or in a mud-brick family crypt constructed beneath the house where the deceased had lived. A baby who had died might be buried in a large terra-cotta jar beneath the home's earthen floor; one such jar has been found shaped like a mother's breast. By their location the bodies of deceased relatives would remain close to their families and to the domestic settings they had known in their lifetimes. In cities, large public cemeteries have also been found.

Together with its possessions and offerings of food and drink, the body would be laid in the grave or crypt in a pose simulating the relaxed sleep from which its spirit would awaken, or in a fetal position foreshadowing its rebirth in the beyond. In humble graves the body might lie upon or be wrapped in a simple reed mat. In a niche a clay lamp might burn to light the soul's path through the darkness of the underworld.

Royal Tombs

For those of great social prominence and power, a much more prominent burial site would be chosen and a far more ostentatious funeral held. This was especially true of royalty, at whose death the entire city or kingdom would go into official mourning.

The most famous royal graves to be discovered in Mesopotamia are those of the Sumerian rulers buried at Ur around the middle of the third millennium B.C.E. and the Assyrian royals interred in stone sarcophagi at their palace at Ashur in the first millennium B.C.E. The royal graves at Ur are especially stunning because of their elaborate contents, which allow us to reconstruct the opulent lives of the dead. These contents, moreover, imply a level of confidence in a happy afterlife—at least for the mighty—that may antedate the dark pessimism of later times.

Unearthed by Sir Leonard Woolley in the 1920s, the royal cemetery at Ur contained the graves of 16 individuals, most probably kings and queens. The rulers were accompanied in death by the bodies of their guardians and servants who, by being buried with their masters, would live on to serve them in the next world. The poses of the servants and the absence of visible wounds point to the use of a sleeping potion or gentle poison administrated as they stood in the tomb, awaiting their spiritual journey.

BURIED TREASURE

These burials date to the middle of the third millennium B.C.E., the age when Egypt's pharaohs built the pyramids at Giza. Just as the pyramids would be robbed, so were the graves at Ur, violated by ancient thieves who broke into the tombs from above, sometimes in the course of digging later graves. Of the 16 tombs, only two survived intact. Yet even in the ransacked tombs evidence endures that illuminates life in ancient Sumer.

11.5   *A re-creation of the burial ceremony at the funeral of one of Ur's kings. In position are bodyguards and charioteers, musicians and servants, all waiting for the sleeping potion that will help them travel with the spirit of their dead king to the afterworld.*   (University of Pennsylvania Museum, Neg. # NC 35–8700; drawn by A. Forestier and originally published in *The Illustrated London News*, 1928)

In the tomb of a king, guarded by the skeletons of spear-carrying sentries, lay the corpses of nine women barren of their flesh but still adorned with ornate headdresses. Golden flower petals had once been poised over their heads as golden beech-leaves and beads of lapis lazuli and orange-red carnelian fringed their foreheads. Large earrings of beaten gold in the shape of crescent moons had once hung beside their ears.

The remains of two ox-drawn four-wheeled wagons lay on the earthen ramp where the funeral cortege had paused. The grain in the wood of the wheels was still impressed in the earth along with the traces of beaded reins and leather tires—the remains of the oldest wheeled vehicles in history ever found.

A queen's grave had been prepared over the site of her husband's. Beside her grasping hand lay a golden cup. A collar of variegated beads—gold, silver, lapis lazuli, carnelian, agate, and chalcedony—still hung from her neck. Near her lay shells filled with green eye shadow.

To occupy her idle hours in eternity there was the inlaid board and playing pieces of a royal parlor game like Parcheesi. While playing, she could sip a refreshing drink from a golden straw, and listen to the strains of a lyre strummed by her court musician, whose body rested nearby.

In another tomb, Woolley uncovered the remains of 28 serving-women. Two skulls still bore the traces of a purplish powder, silver chloride, the remnants of the silver ribbons they had once worn on their hair over 4,000 years ago.

As he knelt beside another skeleton, Woolley detected a flat gray disc about three inches across lying beside the maidservant's waist. Cleaning and inspecting it that night in his excavation headquarters, he realized what it was. As he would later write:

> It was the silver hair-ribbon, but it had never been worn—carried apparently in the woman's pocket, it was just as she had taken it from her room, done up in a tight coil with the ends brought over to prevent its coming undone; and since it formed thus a comparatively solid mass of metal and had been protected by the cloth of her dress, it was very well preserved and even the delicate edges of the ribbon were sharply distinct. Why the owner had not put it on one could not say; perhaps she was late for the ceremony and had not time to dress properly. (Woolley 1955: 72)

Perhaps she still holds it in her hand as she faithfully stands beside her queen in the land of no return. Or perhaps now, since she has had all eternity to catch her breath and fix her hair, she stands smiling with the ribbon finally and forever in place.

Birth

ANXIETY

If there is a theme that emerges from the Mesopotamian literature of childhood, it is fear. Perhaps this is only to be expected in a land where the consciousness of adults seems to have been so shadowed by pessimism. Our impression, of course, must be mollified by what we know has always been universally true of children, their joy in play, and by the testimony of the toys they have left behind, but the fear is there nonetheless, at least among adults who are the ones who have left us a record.

It begins in pregnancy with the litany of prayers and incantations and the hanging of amulets from the mother's neck to ward off evil spirits, chiefly the dread goddess Lamashtu, who threatens the expectant mother's life, can cause miscarriage and crib death, and may even steal the infant from its nurse. It continues in the prognoses of physicians who see evil omens at every turn. And it progresses through labor. (Will the child be born dead? Will it live only to become the one out of two that finally die? Will it be born deformed and need to be drowned in the river to avert evil? Will it be a girl that we must let die because she is not a boy who could support us when we grow old?) And it persists after delivery when lullabies are sung for fear the baby's crying will awake and anger the gods. As the incantation has it, a child is a ship that carries unknown cargo.

AN ANCIENT LULLABY

These sentiments are most poignantly revealed in a lullaby that survives in the tablets of Sumer. In fact, it is the oldest lullaby that exists in writing. In it a Sumerian mother tries to sing her son to sleep even as she fears the sickness that now grips him. She promises to feed him special treats once he gets well: leaves of fresh lettuce from her garden and sweet little cheeses. She sees him when he is older, taking a wife of his own, having a son to call his own. But her anxiety sweeps back, and in the future's darkness sees her baby already dead. Finally, hoping against hope, she prays for a guardian angel to watch over him in his sleep and bring him happiness in life and success. "Oo-a a-oo-a," she sings to comfort him. "Oo-a a-oo-a," she sings to still her own heart.

HOMES

Materials and Construction

The domestic architecture of Mesopotamia grew out of the soil upon which it stood. Unlike Egypt, Mesopotamia—especially in the south—was barren of stone that could be quarried for construction. Except for the date-palm, it was also poor in trees that could be cut down for lumber. Instead, the people of the Tigris and Euphrates turned to other natural

resources that lay abundantly at hand: the muddy clay of its riverbanks and the rushes and reeds that grew in their marshes. With them, the Mesopotamians created the world's first columns, arches, and roofed structures, as well as the world's first cities. Indeed, these same materials were the very ones out of which they invented the earliest tools of writing.

BUNDLES OF REEDS

To build a simple house, tall marsh plants would be uprooted, gathered together, and tied into tight bundles. After holes were dug in the ground, the bundles of reeds would be inserted, one bundle per hole. After the holes were filled in and firmly packed, pairs of bundles that faced each other would be bent over and tied together at the top, forming an archway. The remaining bundles would then be joined together in similar fashion. If the holes were dug in parallel rows, the archway would be long and the house rectangular; if they were dug in a circle, the resulting house would be round. Reed mats would then be draped over the top to cover the roof, or hung from a wall-opening to make a door. (See also Domestic Architecture, chapter 6.)

BRICKS OF CLAY

Another, even more popular alternative was to use sun-dried brick. Clay from the riverbanks would be mixed with straw for reinforcement and packed into small brick-shaped wooden molds, which would then be lifted off so the mud bricks could dry on the ground in the hot sun. Because a hot sun was essential for brick-making, the first month of summer was dubbed "the month of bricks."

Sun-dried brick was notoriously imperma-nent, especially as a consequence of yearly downpours. The alternative, oven-baked brick, was expensive, however, because of the fuel and skilled labor required for its manufacture. As a

11.6   *A native reed hut from Nuffar, Iraq, the site of ancient Nippur.*   (University of Pennsylvania Museum)

result, it tended to be used for the houses of kings and gods rather than the homes of ordinary people. Occasionally, though, it would be employed as tiles for floors in place of plain beaten earth, the usual surface families walked on in their homes.

WALLS, WINDOWS, AND DOORS

Before the walls of a house were raised, the ground at a building site would be leveled and beaten flat; since no foundation was used, level ground was critical for structural stability. The bricks would then be laid in rows with diluted clay serving as mortar. The walls would be made deliberately thick—sometimes as much as eight feet thick—to keep out the day's heat. Vertical channels might be left within the walls to permit the drainage of rainwater from roof to street. At the same time, horizontal ducts to the interior might be incorporated to allow for the circulation of air. These ducts would be blocked by perforated clay discs, with holes big enough to let air pass through but small enough to keep out rodents. Unfortunately, the occasional serpent might wend its way in, as well as other under-the-transom "guests," seeking relief from the oppressive heat: ants, beetles, cockroaches, scorpions, and lizards. Windows were small and rare but, if used, would be fitted with a wooden grillwork. The walls' exterior would be whitewashed—a further defense against radiant heat—and could feature a saw-toothed surface that in sunlight would create a pleasing vertical pattern of shadow and light. There would be only one exterior door, its frame painted bright red to keep out evil spirits.

Plan and Furnishings

A comfortable home made of brick would feature a central roofed courtyard around which smaller rooms would be grouped. In ancient Babylon, such a courtyard might have measured something like 8 by 18 feet or as much as 17 by 45 feet, giving the overall house plan a rectangular shape. The roof (which was also the ceiling) would have been flat and constructed of palmwood planks supporting palmleaves and rushes on top packed down with earth.

The kitchen could be a separate room, but often it was incorporated into the courtyard with an open brick hearth built against a wall. The kitchen's equipment would have included mortars for grinding spices, a stone handmill for grinding grain, knives, and terra-cotta cups, bowls, pots, and platters, some with a natural buff color, others glazed in blue, white, or yellow. There would be covered jars lined with bitumen to store food and semiporous jars to hold water and keep it cool by evaporation. Outside, depending on the locale, there might be a small garden and a livestock pen.

11.7   *Cut-away view of a brick home as found in Ur*   (after Sir Leonard Woolley).

Other rooms, some of which would interconnect, would have included a living room, bedrooms, a bathroom, and—in the case of the well-to-do—servants' quarters. Furniture would have been minimal, consisting of built-in benches of mud brick, chairs and low tables carved from palmwood, and—for special comfort—armchairs with curved backs woven of plaited reeds. The rich would have enjoyed high wooden beds to sleep on; the poor would have made do with reed mats, woolen throw rugs, or thin mattresses spread on the floor.

Lighting and Heating

In such homes made deliberately dark to keep out the heat of the day, artificial light would come from clay lamps. These were small and shaped like slippers, with a narrow pinched end to hold the wick. While Mediterranean cultures used olive oil to fuel their lamps, the olive was rare in Mesopotamia. Instead, sesame seed oil was used. Though the ancient Mesopotamians did know of crude oil (today's major source of Middle Eastern wealth), petroleum was seldom used because it was hard to extract from the ground. For more light than small lamps could provide, torches were used, especially in large buildings like palaces.

When heat was needed, portable braziers holding palm-wood embers would usually suffice.

Sanitation

Separate rooms with toilets date back to the third millennium B.C.E.. A tiled drain in the lowest part of the floor would carry away waste and wastewater to a cesspool or, if a primitive sewer system existed in a city, all the way to the river.

Garbage might be thrown into the streets for scavenging animals to dispose of or carried to a communal dump at the edge of the village or town.

Ruins and Resurrection

DECONSTRUCTION

Because of their fragile materials and the absence of standards governing construction, ancient homes often collapsed. To insure public safety, Hammurabi imposed the death penalty on builders who were guilty of negligence in a homeowner's death. Likewise, if a homeowner's son died in an accident due to faulty construction, the Babylonian builder's son would be executed by the state.

Despite these stern measures, archaeologists remain indebted to the Mesopotamians for the impermanence of what they built. The weakness of walls led to the destruction of houses, as did the risk of fire—always great when there are open fires inside living quarters, when structures have highly flammable ceilings and roofs, and when buildings are packed closely together along alley-like streets. Because of the fragile nature of the original building materials, the easiest way to rebuild involved leveling the loose rubble and building on top of it, thereby burying and preserving for all time broken artifacts and other fragments of everyday life.

GARBAGE AND ITS CONSEQUENCES

In addition, the absence of systematic garbage removal often dictated that refuse originally thrown on a floor would simply be covered up (when it became too unsightly) with a new layer of earth. Eventually, the floor level would rise so much that people would hit their heads on the ceiling (!)—a persuasive reason to rebuild. Even throwing the garbage into the street on a regular basis, and repaving the street with fresh dirt to cover it, resulted in street levels rising higher than the front stoop—creating a mess

inside when it rained outside and the rain poured in. Again, a reason to rebuild.

As a result of such events being repeated over centuries, whole Near Eastern communities grew not only horizontally but also vertically. Indeed, at a certain point the horizontal spread of a city was inhibited by its steep outer edge.

EXCAVATING INFORMATION

The net effect of all this is what archaeology calls "stratification," the superimposition of layers of occupational debris caused by continuous habitation at a site. The compressed garbage actually represents the compressed pages of a history book because every layer contains evidence in minute detail of day-to-day existence as it was lived during a particular period of time. By peeling away the layers, or strata, one at a time, and by carefully reading their "words," the skilled archaeologist can trace the course of human activities over millennia, not by surveying the consciously posed monumental portraits of the mighty but by examining the unpretentious minutiae of everyday life.

In Arabic, the raised ruins of a deserted city are called a "tell." But this Arabic word has a dual meaning, for it is the tells of the Near East that "tell" us of a vast and vanished world, a world that (to paraphrase Ecclesiastes) once hummed with life "before the silver cord was snapped, and the golden bowl was crushed, and the pitcher was shattered at the fountain, and the wheel fell split into the pit" (Ecclesiastes 12: 6).

CLOTHING

Invention and Symbolism

According to the Bible, the founders of the fashion industry were Adam and Eve. For when they ate the educational apple and for the first time recognized their nakedness, they set about sewing fig leaves together to hide the bare truth. If Sumer was the geographical inspiration for the Garden of Eden, as many believe, the world's first clothes were labeled "made in Mesopotamia."

Of course, tailoring was more than just the world's first craft. It also symbolically marked the distinction between technology and nature, between man and beast. Once Adam and Eve were garbed in knowledge, they were banished from Eden's naive simplicity. In effect, clothing was the outer garment of humanity that signaled man was a creature apart.

This same theme appears in the *Epic of Gilgamesh* in an episode that may well antedate the biblical book of Genesis. There, a savage named Enkidu is tempted by a prostitute to give up the ways of the wild. After she has sex with him, she clothes him and calls him a man. As a result, he is rejected by all the animals that had formerly been his friends.

Early Textiles

Archaeologists confirm that textiles were among the first of human inventions. Plant fibers may have been twisted, sewn, and plaited as far back as the Old Stone Age, some 25,000 years ago.

Some 10,000 years ago in the ancient Near East, New Stone Age farmers domesticated sheep and goats for their wool and hair, and they raised flax and cotton for yarn and thread. Wool seems to have been Mesopotamia's most common kind of cloth, along with linen, which was reserved for more expensive garments. Cotton wasn't introduced until the days of the Assyrians, who imported the plant from Egypt and the Sudan around 700 B.C.E.; and silk, perhaps not until the days of the Romans, who imported it from China.

Dyes

Though frequently employed with their natural hues, fabrics could be enlivened with colorful vegetable dyes. The most precious dye, however, a rich royal purple, came from a shellfish, the murex, which was harvested off the Lebanese and Syrian coasts. Thanks to the ancient Greeks who prized this dye, the land of its origin came to be called Phoenicia, or "Purpleland," from the Greek word for the color purple, *phoinix*.

Textile Production

Due to the abundance of raw materials, the industriousness of workers, and the energy of merchants, textile manufacture became a major industry in Mesopotamia and a prime source of its wealth. Rather than being based in factories, however, the manufacture of ancient textiles was most likely a cottage industry, but one conducted on a large scale. Though physical evidence is scant, looms and a spindle are depicted in surviving works of art.

Elusive Evidence

Though textiles are among the earliest of ancient products, they are also among the most elusive to document. Because of their organic substance, they readily perish and thus vanish from the archaeological record. If we are then to attempt a reconstruction of ancient clothing and fashions, we will need to turn to more durable materials like sculptured stone on which artists portrayed them. But even the most detailed of sculptures will leave us largely in the dark about the color and feel of the fabric. Moreover, since such monumental art normally commemorates only the rich and powerful, the clothing of the poor and humble will continue to be invisible. Though the Sermon on the Mount declares that the meek will inherit the earth, archaeologically speaking they usually inherit only the shroud of anonymity.

The Testimony of Art

Notwithstanding all these limitations, then, what can we learn about the clothing of ancient Mesopotamia?

THE SUMERIAN ELITE

As for the Sumerians, they stand before us as votive figurines in wide-eyed silence, their hands clasped reverentially below their hearts. The bearded men are dressed in long robes that leave one shoulder bare, or are wrapped in broadly pleated skirts of sheepskin or leather; the women are gowned in simple tunics that fall almost to their ankles. On the inlaid Royal Standard of Ur, the noblemen are clean-shaven with shaven heads, and they wear belted skirts. The soldiers, for their part, are uniformed in distinctive hooded capes.

BABYLONIAN AND ASSYRIAN ROYALTY

On the black Babylonian stele inscribed with Hammurabi's Code, the king stands attentively before the god of the sun. Hammurabi wears a long flowing robe, part of which he carries draped over his left arm. The god himself is seated in a gown that features a cascading skirt with five overlapping and flounced layers.

Mounted on a fleet horse and pursuing his quarry on a stone relief, the Assyrian king Ashurbanipal is decked out for the hunt in a belted tunic elaborately embroidered with flowers. Back in the garden of his palace, Queen Ashurharrat sits opposite him sharing wine while the two are fanned by servants and entertained by a harpist. The queen wears an elaborate embroidered outfit with a shawl and double tunic fringed with tassels. The locks of hair of both king and consort descend in tight ornate curls, once lustrous with oil.

THE CLOTHES OF COMMONERS

Paraphrasing King Arthur in Lerner and Loewe's *Camelot*, we might now pause to ask, "What did the simple folk wear?"

A tantalizing set of colorful clues comes not from Mesopotamia itself but from the land of the Nile. Dating from about 1900 B.C.E., the tomb of Khnumhotep at Beni Hasan offers us a series of colorful wall paintings portraying a group of Semitic immigrants to Egypt. A total of 37 individuals are depicted, including men, women, and children along with the donkeys that carry their baggage. The sandaled men, dark-haired with pointed beards, wear fringed kilts; the women, with long dark hair falling over their shoulders, are dressed in shifts resplendent with polka dots, geometric patterns, and variegated stripes in assorted colors. Though the hieroglyphic caption identifies their leader, Ibsha, as "the ruler of a foreign land," their simple possessions and their mode of transport suggest not a mighty potentate and his vassals but a tribal chieftain and his band.

Perhaps, then, this is how we might imagine the everyday dress of the common people of Mesopotamia throughout the centuries: a plain short skirt or kilt for men and a basic one-piece tunic for women, with some kind of wrap for colder weather. One thing in certain: rapid changes in fashion, designer labels, and mass-market merchandising were unknown to shoppers along the Tigris and Euphrates.

Our understanding is further enhanced by an eyewitness account of what Babylonians looked like in the fifth century B.C.E. Writing in the fifth century B.C.E., Herodotus (*History* 1: 195) reported:

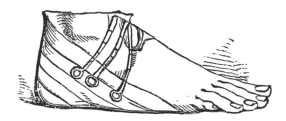

11.8   Two types of Assyrian sandals as depicted in palace reliefs from Kalhu (Nimrud) and Dur-Sharrukin (Khorsabad).   (Layard, *Nineveh and Its Remains*, 1849)

The dress of the Babylonians is a linen tunic reaching to the feet, and above it another tunic made in wool, besides which they have a short white cloak thrown around them, and shoes of a peculiar fashion . . . They have long hair, wear turbans on their heads, and anoint their whole body with perfumes. Every one carries a seal, and a walking stick, carved at the top into the form of an apple, a rose, a lily, an eagle, or something similar; for it is not their habit to use a stick without an ornament. (Herodotus 1942 [1858]: 105, trans. George Rawlinson)

COSMETICS AND PERFUME

The desire to enhance one's natural beauty and allure through the use of cosmetics and perfume is attested as far back as Sumerian times.

In Ur's Royal Cemetery a number of makeup kits were found containing a variety of pigments: white and black, yellow and red, and blue and green—all intended to help the dead look their best in the afterlife. Before traveling to the netherworld, we are told, the love-goddess Inanna/Ishtar applied an eyeliner (or possibly eyeshadow) called "Come Hither."

In Assyria and elsewhere, recipes existed for making perfumes by steeping aromatic plants in water and blending their essence with oil. A king of the Mitanni sent such perfume as a gift to his daughter in Egypt after she became one of the pharaoh's wives. And at Mari, perfume-makers used the resins of fragrant woods like cedar, cypress, juniper, myrtle, and storax, some of which were probably imported.

FOOD AND DRINK

Just as water was vital to the creation of organic life on this planet, so was it vital to the birth of civilization. The first civilizations of the world began in river valleys where abundant supplies of water made it possible to grow sufficient crops to support large populations. The world's first cities began in Mesopotamia, an event that could not have taken place had it not been for large-scale agriculture and the plentiful water upon which it depended.

Grain and Its By-Products

The staple crop of ancient farmers around the world was always grain: wheat, barley, rice, or corn. In Mesopotamia, the chief crop was barley. Rice and corn were unknown, and wheat flourished on a soil less saline than exists in most of Mesopotamia. Thus barley, and the bread baked from its flour, became the staff of life.

Mesopotamian bread was ordinarily coarse, flat, and unleavened, but a more expensive bread could be baked from finer flour. Pieces of just such a bread were, in fact, found in the tomb of Queen Puabi of Ur, stored there to provide her spirit with sustenance in the afterlife. Bread could also be enriched with animal and vegetable fat; milk, butter, and cheese; fruit and fruit juice; and sesame seeds.

Though bread was basic to the Mesopotamian diet, botanist Jonathan D. Sauer has suggested the making of it may not have been the original incentive for raising barley. Instead, he has argued, the real incentive was beer, first discovered when kernels of barley were found sprouting and fermenting in storage.

Whether or not Sauer is right, beer soon became the ancient Mesopotamian's favorite drink. As a Sumerian proverb has it: "He who does not know beer, does not know what is good." The Babylonians had some 70 varieties, and beer was enjoyed by both gods and humans who, as art shows, drank it from long straws to avoid the barley hulls that tended to float to the surface.

There was even a goddess of brewing, named Ninkasi, who was celebrated in a Sumerian hymn that dates to about 1800 B.C.E. Using the details of the brewing process recorded in this hymn, in 1989 the Anchor Brewing Company of San Francisco duplicated the recipe. According to one expert, the beer dubbed "Ninkasi" "had the smoothness and effervescence of champagne and a slight aroma of dates," which had been added as an ancient sweetening agent (Katz and Maytag 1991: 33).

11.9   *Courtiers hoist tankards of beer in the palace at Dur-Sharrukin. The bottoms of the handleless mugs are shaped out of metal to resemble the heads of lions.*   (Rawlinson, *The Seven Great Monarchies of the Ancient Eastern World*, 1884)

Fruits and Vegetables

The gardens of Mesopotamia, watered by irrigation canals, were lush with fruits and vegetables, whose ancient names survive in cuneiform dictionaries and commercial records.

Among the fruits were apples, apricots, cherries, figs, melons, mulberries, pears, plums, pomegranates, and quinces. The most important fruit crop, especially in southern Mesopotamia, was the date. Rich in sugar and iron, dates were easily preserved. Like barley, the date-palm thrived on relatively saline soil and was one of the first plants farmers domesticated.

Should you wish to sample a fruitcake fit for a Sumerian king or queen, the recipe survives: one cup butter, one-third cup white cheese, three cups first-quality dates, and one-third cup raisins, all blended with fine flour.

As for vegetables, the onion was king, along with its cousin, garlic. Other vegetables included lettuce, cabbage, and cucumbers; carrots and radishes; beets and turnips; and a variety of legumes, including beans, peas, and chickpeas, that could be dried for storage and later use. Together, the vegetables served as the basic ingredients for soup. Cooking oil, for its part, came from sesame seeds.

Curiously, two mainstays of the Mediterranean diet—olives and grapes (as well as wine)—were seldom found in Mesopotamian cuisine, largely because of the salinity of the river-valley soil and the absence of significant rainfall needed for their growth. Even honey was a luxury item since the Mesopotamians, unlike the Egyptians, did not keep bees but relied on hives found in the wild.

Spices and Herbs

Our contact with ancient Mesopotamia mostly takes place in the rarified atmosphere of museums, but to appreciate Mesopotamian daily life our imagination must breathe in the pungent aroma of the seasonings that once rose from ancient stoves and filled the air of once-populous cities. Coriander, cress, and cumin; fennel, fenugreek, and leek; marjoram, mint, and mustard; rosemary and rue; saffron and thyme once comprised the odoriferous litany of the Mesopotamian cook. Cumin, in fact, still echoes the Babylonian name, *kamūnu*, by which it was known 4,000 years ago.

Livestock and Fish

According to legend, prosperity came to Mesopotamia when the gods "made ewes give birth to lambs, and grain grow in furrows."

Sheep played an important role in the Mesopotamian economy. Shepherds tending their flocks are among the earliest images on seal-stones, and woolly rams are proudly pictured on the Royal Standard of Ur. The Sumerians, in fact, used 200 different words to describe sheep. Like goats and cows, ewes produced milk that was converted into butter and cheese, but sheep were also slaughtered for meat.

Beef was in short supply because meadowlands for grazing large herds were limited. The meat supply, however, was augmented by pork from pigs that foraged in marshlands. Game birds, deer, and gazelle were hunted as well. On farms, domesticated geese and ducks supplied eggs, while from the rivers and the sea, and from canals and private ponds, came some 50 types of fish, a staple of the Mesopotamian diet.

Generally, meats were either dried, smoked, or salted for safekeeping, or they were cooked by roasting, boiling, broiling, or barbecuing.

Housed at Yale University in New Haven, Connecticut, are the Yale Culinary Tablets, a collection of 35 recipes that seem to have survived from a "cordon bleu" cooking school that operated in Babylonia around 1700 B.C.E. Among the more exotic recipes is one for partridge sprinkled with vinegar and rubbed with salt and crushed mint.

The Good Life

Despite its abundance, the real Mesopotamia was no Garden of Eden, for our Sumerian Adam and Eve had to earn their living by the sweat of their brow. However, if the gods smiled and floods did not ravage the fields, life could indeed be good.

According to a legend, the hero Gilgamesh once went on a quest in search of immortality. In the course of his journey, he happened upon a tavern where a divine barmaid offered him some advice:

> Eat and drink your fill, Gilgamesh,
> And celebrate day and night.
> Make every day a festival;
> Day and night dance and play.

Thus, even if the people of Mesopotamia were denied immortality, they could still eat, drink, and be merry until they died thanks to the beneficence of their land.

MUSIC

Recapturing Sounds

"Heard melodies are sweet, but those unheard are sweeter," wrote John Keats in 1820 in his "Ode on a Grecian Urn." In this poem Keats attested to the power of the imagination to conceptualize a level of beauty loftier than that which reality can aspire to.

Ruins too possess such a power, romantically stimulating our imagination to construct a shining citadel out of scattered stones. Indeed, were it not for the romance of archaeology, those who have made it their career might be unable to endure the tedium of excavation. Nevertheless, the archaeologist's task is to retrieve an authentic picture of the past, not invent an imaginary one. Yet how challenging that task is when the evidence crumbles in one's hands; and how much more challenging still when it doesn't exist in matter at all.

In the whole body of the past there is perhaps no element more evanescent than music, an artifact written on the wind. How can we recapture the sounds of distant millennia when the civilizations that once heard them lie in the dust, especially if the particular civilization we are exploring is one of the earliest in human history?

The answer is to turn to media where the story of ancient music still resides: the written record of compositions and performance; works of art that depict musicians and their craft; and, where possible, the actual instruments themselves.

In the end we may still have to draw upon our imagination to bring the music fully to life, but it will be an imagination informed by archaeological fact.

The Importance of Music

One fact reverberates from the surviving works of art: though the ruins themselves may lie in silence, music was an integral part of ancient Mesopotamian life.

The images on inlaid plaques, carved sealstones, and sculpted reliefs transport us back to a world of sound. We watch a shepherd playing his flute as his dog sits and attentively listens. We revel with banqueters as a solo vocalist in the background raises her voice to the strains

11.10 An orchestra with strings and woodwinds marches out to greet an Assyrian army returning home in triumph. Bringing up the rear is a rhythm section with hands clapping. The figures with raised hands may be singers.

of a lyre. We repose in a palatial garden as a court harpist caresses his strings. We encamp with soldiers weary from a march as musicians play to soothe them. We clap our hands together with other spectators as two lines of dancers rhythmically advance toward one another and retreat. And we hear priests solemnly intone their temple hymns. So great, in fact, was a queen of Ur's love of music, she could not bear the thought of being in the afterworld without it; so, with the help of a sleeping potion in the tomb, she took her royal musicians with her into the beyond.

Types of Instruments

Works of art also show us in great detail the types of instruments musicians played and their great variety. They include percussion, wind, and string instruments.

PERCUSSION

Among the pictured percussions are bells. About a hundred have been dug up, their bronze clappers long ago stilled by corrosion. Large cymbals and castanets for the fingers of dancers are depicted as well as rattles and the sistrum, a type of metallic noisemaker that may have originated in Egypt. The sistrum resembled a slingshot, but, instead of an elastic band, it had one or more thick wires mounted horizontally that could be shaken and were sometimes strung with tiny cymbals or rings. Drums came in different shapes and sizes: shallow or deep; one- or two-sided; and made for setting on the floor, holding in the hands, or carrying suspended from a shoulder-strap. The biggest drum of all measured some five or six feet in diameter; known as "the great bull's hide," it was banged by priests during eclipses of the moon.

WIND

Wind instruments included single or double recorders (played vertically), the flute (played horizontally), panpipes, and horns. The horns were not used to make music but instead were blown to help signal large groups, such as soldiers in battle formation or laborers hauling colossal statues to their sites.

STRING

String instruments were of two main kinds: lyres and harps.

In a lyre, two arms rise up from a sound box. The strings, all of the same length, extend upward from the sound box to a crossbar where the strings are attached. Because they are the same length, the strings (made from animal gut

11.11 *This Assyrian musician has his harp attached by a belt to his waist, and he plays it with his left hand and a plectrum held in his right.* (Rawlinson, *The Seven Great Monarchies of the Ancient Eastern World*, 1884)

Discoveries at Ur

One of the most amazing finds in the entire history of music was made in the soil of Ur—the discovery of the world's oldest string instruments that are among the earliest musical instruments of any type ever found. They date to the mid third millennium B.C.E. A total of nine lyres and three harps lay buried in royal graves. Though the wooden frames had disintegrated, the inorganic ornamentation—of red limestone, white shell, and blue lapis lazuli—was intact, and it was recovered by pouring plaster of Paris into the outlines the frames had left so the pieces would stick together. Still shimmering was the gold, the one material that over the ages better than any other survives the ravages of

11.12 *The reconstructed Great Lyre from the "King's Grave" at Ur.* (University of Pennsylvania Museum)

or sinew) have the same pitch unless they are of different thicknesses or unless they are tuned. Tuning is accomplished by winding the strings around the crossbar to create proper tension or by turning adjustable metal pins that hold the strings in place.

Harps, on the other hand, have only one arm rising up from the sound box. The strings, of different lengths (and therefore of different pitches) extend diagonally from the sound box to the arm.

Traditionally, Mesopotamian lyres and harps seem to have had a maximum of 11 strings. In addition to lyres and harps, lutes are also portrayed.

11.13 *Detail from the front of the Great Lyre. The decorative bull's head is ornamented with gold foil and lapis lazuli. The bull is humanized with a beard, and below him, inlaid animals cavort like human beings, including a donkey that plays a lyre.* (University of Pennsylvania Museum)

Reconstructing Ancient Music

Attempts have been made by technicians at the British Museum and elsewhere to reconstruct a Sumerian lyre out of woods similar to those that would have once been used by ancient craftsmen. But, despite these reconstructions, the question still remains: what music did these ancient instruments once play?

Major clues have emerged from a series of cuneiform tablets dug up in Mesopotamian cities (including Ur) and in the Syrian coastal city of Ugarit, cities which flourished over 3,000 years ago. Called the "Song Tablet," the document from Ugarit contains the words and music for a hymn to the goddess Nikkal, consort of the moon god. The words are written in the languages of the Hurrians, a people who once dwelt in Mesopotamia. The Mesopotamian tablets, on the other hand, are so-called theory tablets, describing the mechanics of making music: the names of the strings of the lyre, the musical intervals between them, and the methods for tuning the lyre to different keys. The instructions for tuning reveal the use of a seven-note scale not unlike the "do-re-mi" of Western music. Combining the information from the theory tablets with the notations on the song tablet, musicologists have been able to play the song on a re-strung "ancient" lyre, reproducing melodies and harmonies of the remote past.

time. On the fronts of the body-like sound boxes, gold foil had been fashioned over wood to simulate the heads of bulls, probably to suggest the sonorous bellow that once resonated from the bass strings. To make the bulls' heads appear both more human and more divine, they were adorned with locks of hair and curly beards of purplish lapis. Below them were decorative panels portraying the hero Gilgamesh and various wild beasts. In one panel reminiscent of an Aesop's fable, a standing jackass strums a lyre and brays to the delight of his animal audience. The largest of the lyres—from the "Great Death Pit"—stood almost 5.5 feet tall.

Love Songs

Of course, not all the songs of Mesopotamia were sacred hymns. There were love songs too. We know this from a cuneiform list of their first lines, which also served as their titles. Among the top hits along the Tigris were tunes such as

"Your love, my lord, is like the aroma of cedarwood"; "How lush she is, how radiant" "Come to the royal gardens where cedars abound"; and "You are the keeper of the garden of desire."

Elvis Lives

One might well question how commercial such lyrics would be in today's pop music scene. But not to worry. A Finnish professor of literature, Jukka Ammondt, from the University of Jyväskylä might just have the answer. Professor Ammondt's claim to pop music fame is that he once recorded two albums of Elvis Presley songs in Latin. His latest release, you will be relieved to know, consists of songs of the "King" in Sumerian. The first cut is "Blue Suede Shoes," which translates into Sumerian as "E-sir Kush-za-gin-ga" ("Sandals of Leather of the Color of a Blue Gem"). Granted, something may be lost in translation, but it is comforting to know that—after all those millennia—the beat still goes on.

TOYS AND GAMES

Children's Toys

When we picture ancient civilizations in our minds, we seldom think of children. Perhaps it is because such civilizations are so old, or because their monuments—the remnants by which we know them—proclaim the glories of an adult world. But children there were, and their greatest testament is toys. Shaped from clay or wood, they remind us that the now silent streets and homes of ruined cities once rang with the shouts and laughter of the very young.

For infants and toddlers there were terracotta rattles, filled with pellets and pinched at the edges like piecrust, with a small hole for a string. For boys, dreaming of hunting or soldiering, there were slingshots and little bows and arrows and boomerangs to throw. For girls, hoping to raise their own children some day, there were dolls and miniature pieces of furniture (tables, stools, and beds) for playing house. Meanwhile, handheld ships and chariots, and tiny draught animals and wagons, let

11.14   *Though the children who played with them are long gone, these terra-cotta toys from ancient Mesopotamia survive.*   (University of Pennsylvania Museum)

the young travel through the world of their imagination. For more amusement there were also balls and hoops and a game of jump rope named curiously for the love goddess Ishtar.

Such toys as survive are now dutifully inked with museum acquisition numbers and locked up in glass cases. But on some Saturday should an errant child come by and gaze at them, her eyes may yet light up with an antique joy.

Board Games

One of the hazards of sentry duty on a long hot day is boredom. So it was over 27 centuries ago in the Assyrian city of Khorsabad. Two sentries, tired and bored, sought relief from the heat in the shade of a colossal winged bull, one of a pair of monstrous statues that guarded the entrance to King Sargon II's palace. Using the sharp point of his dagger, one of the sentries scratched out a rectangular pattern of 20 squares on the bull's stone pedestal. Then, with the aid of impromptu playing pieces and a pair of dice they had with them, he and his friend took turns playing a board game not unlike the ancient Indian game of Parcheesi or the modern Parker Bros. game of Sorry. Of course we don't know which guard won or lost, or how much they wagered on winning, but the scratches on the stone slab are still there for us to see.

The board game they played seems to have been a popular one in their day, for similar patterns have been found elsewhere scratched onto large clay bricks. Other game boards have been found with different numbers of squares or holes on their surface for playing other kinds of games, including one that may have been used for telling fortunes with the help of the 12 signs of the zodiac. A variety of playing pieces or "men" have been recovered, some abstract in shape and some in the shape of animals, as well as dice and throwing sticks used to determine moves. The dice are especially interesting since their opposite sides don't add up to seven like most numbers on modern dice (two and five, for example) but feature consecutive numbers (for example, one and two) on opposite sides. Some dice, in fact, are tetrahedral, with four triangular surfaces.

ETERNAL PASTIMES

Passing the time at work is one thing, but passing the time for all eternity is quite another. To supply recreation and alleviate ennui in the afterlife, Sumerian royalty had themselves buried with the means for their entertainment, just as did King Tutankhamun of Egypt. King Tut's tomb, in fact, was equipped with four game boards for playing the Egyptian game *senet*, the name of which meant "passage." A similar game was found by Sir Leonard Woolley in the Royal Cemetery at Ur, but dating to over a thousand years before Tut's time.

The Ur game board was originally made out of wood overlaid with a design composed of white shell, dark blue lapis lazuli, and red limestone set in a black bitumen cement. Measuring about $4\frac{3}{4}$ inches by $10\frac{5}{8}$ inches, the surface is composed of 21 squares of assorted design—some with dots, others with flowers, and still others with "eyes." The squares decorate an unusually shaped board that features a bigger rectangular zone and a smaller one joined by a narrow bridge. Guarding the outer edge is a band of hypnotic eyes.

The object of the game seems to have been to move your men from one end of the board to the other, while your opponent tried to block your passage across the bridge. Some of the marked squares may have been lucky ("Take another turn!") or unlucky ("Go back to Square One!"). As for the playing pieces, there are seven per player, one set with dark dots on a light background, the other set with light dots on dark.

RULES

The rules for all these games essentially remain an enigma. Knowing the rules themselves, the

11.15   *To while away the endless hours of eternity, Sumerian royals packed gameboards in their graves. This one from Ur comes complete with playing pieces but no set of rules.*   (The British Museum)

Mesopotamians saw no need to enclose a set of instructions. After all, it wasn't us they had in mind when they played!

SPORTS

Though other forms of competitive athletics may have existed in ancient Mesopotamia, the one sport for which there is considerable evidence—in art and literature—is wrestling. The wrestling match, for example, is a motif frequently found on cylinder seals. In fact, the most famous hero of Mesopotamian mythology, Gilgamesh, began his legendary career (see *The Epic of Gilgamesh*) by wrestling with a brute named Enkidu. As often happens in sports, the two competitors ended up becoming best friends.

In addition to wrestling, boxing is also depicted in Mesopotamian art, where it appears on decorative baked-clay plaques.

For kings, there was always the royal sport of hunting. The hunting exploits of Assyria's kings were celebrated in their annals and in sculptural relief on their palace walls.

EDUCATION

Just as the rivers of Mesopotamia fed its soil, the waters of knowledge nourished its civilization. And just as river water was transported to fields by a system of irrigation, so was knowledge transmitted to people by a system of education.

History of Schooling

The earliest schools of which we have record were developed by the ancient Sumerians.

The oldest evidence, lists of vocabulary words, survives from the ruins of the city of Uruk and dates to around 3000 B.C.E., close to the time when writing itself was invented. From 2500 B.C.E. come archaeological remains of the first real schools, at least two of which were established by royal edict. From between 2500 and 2000 B.C.E. sufficient remains exist to document the operation of a true school system. Additional proof comes in the form of hundreds of cuneiform tablets, the actual homework and classroom exercises of ancient students, ranging from beginner to advanced, along with directions and corrections from their teachers and even literary vignettes of everyday life in a Mesopotamian school. This abundant evidence dates to between 2000 and 1500 B.C.E., and it comes from a whole array of cities, including Uruk, Ur, Nippur, Shuruppak, and Abu Salabikh.

Schoolhouses

A Mesopotamian school was called a "tablet house" (Sumerian *edubba*; Akkadian *bît tuppi*) because of the clay tablets that were its stock-in-trade.

The first schools were probably attached to temples, which were the original communal centers of wisdom and learning. Later, schools were secularized and came to be located in private buildings.

Remains of ancient schoolhouses may have been uncovered at Ur, Nippur, Sippar, and Mari. The building uncovered at Mari featured two rooms, one of which had rows of benches made of baked brick that, depending on their length, could accommodate one, two, or four pupils at a time. In addition, large earthenware receptacles were found, probably intended for holding the damp clay out of which the students shaped their writing tablets. A complete schoolroom likely would have had shelves on which completed work was laid out to dry, storage chests for miscellaneous school supplies and for the safekeeping of "textbooks," and perhaps an oven to bake selected clay tablets in order to give them permanence.

Additional equipment may have included thin, slat-like writing boards made of wood and coated with wax that could be written upon with a sharp stylus and then later erased by rubbing the waxed surface smooth with the stylus's rounded edge.

Student Body

Students would have probably ranged in age from somewhere under 10 to their teens. Because schooling was privately paid and costly, students would have been the children of wealthy and prominent families. Except for the daughters of royalty or for girls being groomed as future priestesses, pupils would have been exclusively male. Accordingly, the student body of a Mesopotamian school would have been composed almost entirely of the sons of government officials, military officers, priests and scribes, and wealthy businessmen.

The Mesopotamian educational system thus differed from the modern Western model in three respects; it was private (rather than public), voluntary (rather than compulsory), and selective (rather than universal).

Faculty

In many ways, the Mesopotamian school was structured along the lines of the Mesopotamian family.

At the head of the Mesopotamian family was the father, and at the head of the Mesopotamian school was the "father of the tablet house," or principal (Sumerian *adda edubba*). Yet, even as every Mesopotamian family had to be obedient to the supreme authority of the state, there was an even higher authority in the school, the headmaster (Sumerian *ummia*, "expert" or "authority"). The students themselves were referred to as "the school's sons," while their work was supervised by older students called "big brothers," who acted as teachers' aids.

The disciplinary role of the father was played by an administrative officer who beat unruly pupils with a stick. Punishments were meted out for speaking without permission, getting up without permission, leaving without permission, dressing inappropriately, and not speaking in proper Sumerian.

The actual instructors were specialists in various subject areas. They included a math teacher ("the scribe of counting"), a teacher of surveying ("the scribe of the field"), and a language teacher ("the scribe of Sumerian").

Their salaries came out of the tuition paid by parents. They apparently were also not above being bribed: a Sumerian short story tells of the apple-polishing father of a lazy student who, at his son's prompting, invited the boy's teacher home to dinner and gave him fancy gifts including a fine ring. The teacher graciously responded by praising the boy effusively and expressing the hope that he would go to the head of his class and someday become a man of great leaning. (Whether he did or not, the tablets do not tell.)

School Calendar

The school day went from sunrise to sunset, with students eating lunch at school. Out of a typical 30-day month, school was in session 24, with three days off for vacation and three for religious holidays. Whether or not school was in operation year-round we do not know.

Curriculum

The prime purpose of schooling was to teach students the practical skills of literacy and numeracy so that, as adults, they could take their place in society and play a useful role.

Initially students were taught to recognize the meaning of basic cuneiform characters and to reproduce them on clay tablets with the aid of a blunt-ended reed "pen." They were also taught how to prepare blank clay tablets for the purpose of writing, by mixing, shaping, and smoothing the clay. Additionally, they were taught how to bake inscribed tablets to lend them permanence.

The mastery of cuneiform took many years because of the complexity of the script. Literacy was therefore not easy to come by, and required thousands of hours of specialized training to recognize and reproduce from memory the hundreds upon hundreds of characters and character combinations that were used. Because of the minuteness of these characters and the potential for confusion, training included the cultivation of a painstakingly accurate calligraphic style.

Formal education involved the mastery of literacy (for such tasks as maintaining business records, writing and reading contracts, composing letters, sending military messages, reciting prayers and incantations, and understanding medical texts) as well as the mastery of numeracy (for such jobs as measuring plots of land and their produce, determining taxes, projecting supplies for a military campaign, figuring out the amount of earth needed to construct a siege ramp, estimating the number of bricks required to erect a new palace, or making celestial calculations). Ultimately, specialized vocabulary would have to be mastered in such fields as astronomy, geography, mineralogy, zoology, botany, medicine, engineering, and architecture.

Furthermore, once the northerners of Akkad conquered the southerners of Sumer, becoming learned meant learning not one language but two: non-Semitic Sumerian and Semitic Akkadian. Though eventually Sumerian became a dead language like Latin, it was diligently studied because of the reverence in which it was held and the richness of its intellectual treasures, not unlike the position Latin later attained during the European Middle Ages and Renaissance and maintained until our own times. Advanced students might go on to study masterworks of Mesopotamian literature and, depending upon their chosen vocations, might continue such study during professional careers as priests or scholars.

Pedagogical Method

Repeated practice combined with the corrections of one's mistakes were the keys to learning in a Mesopotamian school. The teacher would begin by writing a sentence on the top of a tablet (or on the left side) and the student would be expected to copy it again and again below (or to the right). The teacher, or "big brother," would then make corrections. The student would then study his corrected work at home and on the next day would be expected to reproduce it without error. A new lesson would then follow. Not only do we have examples of written work with the teacher's corrections on them, but even one where the frustrated teacher crossed out all the student's work in exasperation!

Recitation as well as writing would be done to make sure the pupil was able not only to copy characters but also to comprehend their meaning. More advanced lessons would require the writing out and reading of more lengthy texts or extended mathematical calculations perhaps based on story problems. Throughout, the memorization of new vocabulary and mathematical procedures was stressed, while intellectual self-discipline was reinforced by maintaining a strict code of behavior in the classroom.

When appropriate, the teachers would explain material by lecture, and at intervals give tests, including comprehensive examinations. However, because the Mesopotamian school was really a kind of "one-room schoolhouse," pupils in a given classroom were simultaneously at different grade levels, an added reason to have an attentive "big brother" look over their shoulders.

For more advanced students, the drudgery was sometimes alleviated by the introduction of humorous story lessons about school (an episode, for example, in which a pupil and a big brother argue over who is really smarter, or in which a father complains about all the ways his errant son misbehaves). While poking fun at the educational system, these stories also served to point up the fact that going to school was a real privilege with an important purpose behind all the hard work.

Goals

VOCATIONAL TRAINING

The goal of this educational system was to turn a child into a scribe (Sumerian *tupshar*, "one who writes on tablets"). When grown up, the graduate of the Mesopotamian school system would be able to serve society by taking his place in the worlds of temple, palace, and business, drawing upon his skills in literacy and numeracy to excel at his job. Some might become professional scribes serving the practical needs of others; but others would follow their fathers' professions as government or temple officials or as businessmen.

SUSTAINING CIVILIZATION

Education also served a goal wider and deeper than mere vocationalism. Mesopotamia's system of schools was founded upon the principle that no civilization can prosper or long endure unless it draws upon the wisdom and experience of the past, however "dead" that past might superficially seem to be. Because that wisdom and experience was enshrined in writing, it was only through the instrument of literacy that its knowledge could be tapped. Moreover, it was only through literacy that the insights and achievements of the past and present could be passed on to the future. In short, the ancient Mesopotamians recognized that at its heart civilization is a vital continuum in which past, present, and future are organically linked. If a culture ceases to be literate, if it can no longer hear the guiding words of the past or speak them to the future, that chain is irrevocably broken.

The weakness of the Mesopotamian system may have been that it stressed memorization over creativity, conformity over individualism, and rote learning over invention. But its amazing durability shows that, despite this weakness, it also possessed enduring strength.

CULTIVATING HUMANITY

In an even larger sense, despite the seeming narrowness of its curriculum and pedagogy, education in Mesopotamia sought to inculcate what we must call, for want of a better word, "humanity." Indeed, this term appears for the first time in human history in Sumerian texts, and in ones that deal specifically with the goals of education. A student says to his headmaster: "I was like a puppy dog until you opened my eyes. You formed humanity inside me." A frustrated scribe writes to his son: "Because you did not have regard for your humanity, my heart was broken."

Through a respect for the past, through a reverence for learning, through the constant practice of self-discipline, and through an underlying commitment to service higher than to self, the Mesopotamians sought to reach education's highest goal: the fostering of humane sensibility and conduct.

HEALTH AND MEDICINE

The Beginnings of Medicine

The origins of the art of medicine are hidden in the mists of prehistory. It was in those earliest of days that human beings, in the palpable presence of death, sought the precious remedy for injury and illness by drawing upon the simple knowledge and skill they possessed and by invoking the invisible spiritual powers that inhabited their world. Trial and error were their teachers, and priests their guides, as ancestral wisdom was passed on from one generation to the next by word of mouth and example.

With the invention of writing, it became possible to give such wisdom tangible and permanent form, enabling it to be collected and stored for later use. With the advent of civilization, specialists arose who were trained in its study and application.

Early Texts

The oldest medical textbook in the world was uncovered in the ruins of the Sumerian city of Nippur. Dating to the close of the third millennium B.C.E., it consists of a single cuneiform tablet measuring 3¾ inches by 6¼ inches and inscribed with a dozen trusty prescriptions. To view the world's oldest medical library, however, we would need to travel north to the Assyrian city of Nineveh (or rather to London's British Museum, where its archives are now housed). There in Nineveh in the eighth century B.C.E., the acquisitive king Ashurbanipal assembled in his palace library a collection of some 800 clay tablets embodying the medical knowledge of his day, a valuable resource to have handy if ever he fell ill.

Types of Doctors

In ancient Mesopotamia there were two basic types of doctor you could turn to. First of all, there was the kind of doctor (*asu*) who as a rule relied upon medical substances to effect a cure. Second, there was the kind of doctor (*ashipu*) who traditionally trusted in spiritual remedies. On occasion, each type of doctor might apply the other's methods in addition to his own to assure a patient's recovery; and, in difficult cases, specialists of both types might collaborate.

It is noteworthy that the ancient Mesopotamians did not draw a sharp line between what we in the modern Western world would regard as the separate realms of science and religion. That modern medicine is increasingly recognizing the therapeutic function of the mind and spirit is a tribute to this ancient perception, however haltingly it may have once been uttered.

Divine Powers

A hymn has been discovered praising the Sumerian patron goddess of medicine, known variously as Bau, Gula, or Ninisina. Her opposite number among the Babylonians was Lamashtu, the goddess of disease and death. Significantly, among the Sumerians the insignia of the medical profession was a divine staff entwined with serpents, the origin of a similar symbol among the classical Greeks and the ultimate inspiration for the American Medical Association's logo.

To find a doctor in a Mesopotamian city you'd be well advised to head for the largest temple in town, which often doubled as a miniature medical center and school.

The Practice of Medicine

Cuneiform texts give us ample insights into the practices of Mesopotamian physicians.

PHARMACEUTICALS

The medical library of Ashurbanipal, for example, is a veritable *Physician's Desk Reference*, listing some 250 vegetable substances and some 120 mineral ones with ascribed medicinal properties. The most common mineral agents were potassium nitrate (or saltpeter), a known astringent, and sodium chloride (or salt), a recognized antiseptic. In addition, sulphur and alum are cited. Modern medicine also acknowledges the curative powers of many Mesopotamian extracts derived from seeds, fruits, roots, leaves, branches, barks, and gums. This natural pharmacopeia included asafoetida, belladonna, cannabis, cardamon, cassia, castor oil, cinnamon, colocynth, coriander, date, fig, fir, garlic, henbane, juniper, licorice, mandragora, mint, mustard, myrrh, myrtle, pear, poppy, thyme, and willow. Even the right time to pick herbs was noted in order to assure their maximum efficacy. The extraction and purification of minerals, moreover, points to an early but sophisticated understanding of chemistry.

PREPARATION AND USE OF MEDICINES

Medicinal agents may have been kept fresh or stored in a dry state until needed, when they would be prepared and blended with various substances for internal consumption or external application. The favorite Mesopotamian "mixer" was beer, but milk, honey, and wine served the same function. For external applications, such as salves and ointments, cedar oil, animal fat, or wax might be used. The combination of alkaline substances with fat yielded a kind of soap that had positive antiseptic benefits. Medicinal agents might also be put into poultices, inhaled in vapor, applied in drops to eyes and ears, or even—with the aid of a hollow reed or metal tube—blown into the vagina or penis. The use of emetics, enemas, suppositories, and hot baths is also attested.

Texts diligently cite the condition to be treated, the medicine to be used, and the method of administration. However, the quantities to be blended and the dosages to be administered regrettably are not recorded, perhaps because these depended upon the experience and judgment of the attending physician, or perhaps because they were closely guarded as professional secrets. Most significantly, the application of certain treatments for specific conditions is often in agreement with current medical practice.

DIAGNOSIS AND DISEASE

Before deciding upon treatment, the medical doctor would examine the patient, noting such things as pulse and temperature, reflexes, and the coloration of skin and urine. Following a flowchart of general symptoms, the physician would arrive at a diagnosis. Among the conditions diagnosed and treated are intestinal problems such as obstructions, colic, and diarrhea; neurological ones such as persistent headaches and epilepsy; rheumatism, jaundice, and gout; diseases such as tuberculosis, smallpox, typhus, and bubonic plague; infestations of lice; and venereal disease, including gonorrhea. The cuneiform literature also refers to mental illness and proposes a psychological explanation for sexual impotence.

By about 700 B.C.E. a pregnancy test had been developed for use by midwives. The test employed a woolen tampon soaked with a plant extract that reacted to changes in the pH value of vaginal secretions indicative of pregnancy. In effect, the tampon worked like a kind of gynecological "litmus paper."

Though there is no explicit reference to a germ theory of disease, at least one document reveals an awareness of contagion as a factor in the spread of illness. In a letter of concern sent to his wife, an 18th century B.C.E. king of Mari wrote:

> I've heard that lady Nanname is sick. She comes into contact with many people in the palace. Issue orders that no one should drink from the cup she drinks from, or sit on the seat she sits on, or sleep in the bed she sleeps in. Don't let her socialize with any other ladies in her house. What she has is catching.

MEDICAL SPECIALISTS

Specialists, so common a feature of medical practice today, are rarely mentioned in Mesopotamian literature, though a veterinarian and an ophthalmologist are cited. Mention is also made of a female doctor; though she may have been a gynecologist, this is by no means certain.

Spiritual Healing

Besides the physicians who used medicines to effect a cure, there were those who relied upon spiritual skills. Many illnesses, it was believed, were caused by evil spirits, or demons, that for one reason or another occupied the human body and made it sick. The job of the *ashipu*, or spiritual doctor, was to rid the body of such a spirit. The skilled practitioner was familiar with some 6,000 different demons by name, some of whom were held to be responsible for specific maladies. Once the malady had been determined and the demon identified, treatment could begin.

THE FUNCTION OF SIN

The premise was that an illness was caused by some kind of sin: a moral offense or crime, perhaps, or a failure to properly carry out a required religious ritual. To help the patient, the doctor might begin by reciting a list of typical sins in the hope that the patient would recognize the one that he had committed and which had led to his woes. Thus the Mesopotamian mind saw a connection between uprightness of character and uprightness of health, and Mesopotamians recognized what we might call illness of a psychosomatic nature, especially when induced by worry or guilt.

EXORCISM

Though he might well resort to using medicine to open up a second front against disease, the spiritual doctor essentially drew upon a store of magical spells and incantations. In some cases the demon was encouraged to leave its host and take up residence in an animal or an inanimate object. In other cases it was enticed to leave on the promise of gifts it would magically receive. At other times it would be chased away through the use of foul-smelling substances such as excrement.

GROUNDS FOR PROGNOSIS

Medical texts concerned with spiritual cures often list physical symptoms that can predict whether a patient will recover or die. If, for example, the patient is sick and gets out of bed on the third day of his illness, he will recover. But if on the third day he cries out from pain in his abdomen and his abdomen is hot, he will die. Other signs, however, which have no connection with a patient's physical state, are regarded as just as important. Thus if a patient

suffering from a long illness has a hallucination in which he sees a dog, he will recover, while if he sees a gazelle he will die. Moreover, if the doctor passes a white pig on his way to treat a patient, the patient will recover, but the patient will die if the pig is black.

MAGIC VERSUS MEDICINE

Based on his reliance on these latter signs and his dependence on magical spells to drive off demons, we might regard the *ashipu* as some sort of witch doctor, but his attention to physical symptoms and his willingness to use medicines when necessary is evidence of a more scientific approach. It is important to remember also that to a believer incantations could have a powerful psychological effect in promoting recovery. Furthermore, illnesses of psychogenic origin could well benefit from an *ashipu*'s ministrations, especially if those illnesses had been exacerbated by worry.

While it is easy to regard the art of spiritual healing as more primitive than the scientific use of medicines, it must be remembered that the search for medicinal agents may well have been as ancient as the application of spiritual remedies. Both methods may have grown up simultaneously, especially if the world of plants and minerals was viewed animistically as an expression of the divine.

Surgeons

In addition to the medical and spiritual physicians of ancient Mesopotamia, there was a third category of doctor: the surgeon.

LIABILITY

Surviving texts tell us very little about surgical practice, yet of all the doctors the surgeon is the one type singled out by Mesopotamia's legal system for government control. The Code of Hammurabi, for example, sets fees for operations and establishes penalties for surgical errors, the earliest recorded instance in history of legal consequences for medical malpractice.

FEES

The Babylonian surgeon's regulated fee structure was based on the patient's class, and thus on the ability to pay. For major surgery, including an eye operation, the surgeon would be paid 10 silver shekels by a member of the nobility, but only five shekels by a commoner. For a similar operation on a slave, the slave's owner would be expected to pay just two shekels. For setting a broken bone or tending to a sprained tendon, the fee would be five, three, or two shekels, respectively, again depending on the injured person's class. Veterinary operations cost even less.

PENALTIES

The penalties for surgical failure were substantial and, in the case of an aristocratic patient, severe. For causing a noble's death or blindness, for example, the surgeon's hand would be cut off. Such punitive measures and the greater scrutiny over surgery in general may be due to the fact that the consequences of surgery are more self-evident whereas the effects of medicines and magic spells are not so demonstrable.

OPERATIONS

Since dissection was forbidden by religion, surgeons would have had to learn their craft from practical experience, often in emergency situations. Their instrument of choice in a B.C.E. "O.R." would have resembled a straight razor and is casually referred to as a "barber's knife."

Dentistry

According to Mesopotamian tradition, a toothache was caused by a worm that had been given permission by the gods to feed on teeth and gums.

Our information comes from a cuneiform tablet that preserves an incantation against toothache. The document, in Akkadian, dates to the Neo-Babylonian period, but says it is based on an even more ancient text. A similar incantation, in the Hurrian language, has been found in the Old Babylonian records of Mari.

According to the Akkadian version, when the world was created a worm was spawned by the primordial mud. Racked by hunger, the worm tearfully pleaded to the gods for food. It rejected the ripe figs and apricots the gods offered, and instead asked if it could feed on teeth and gums. To our eternal grief, the gods acceded to the worm's request.

After telling the tale, the incantation instructs the doctor to grasp the base of the tooth with a surgical instrument (a forceps?) and curse the worm with divine retribution ("May the mighty hand of the god Ea strike you!"). The doctor is told to recite the tale and the curse three times. (An Ea-like yank probably came at the end of curse number three!) A prescription is then given for a postoperative mouthwash consisting mostly of beer and sesame seed oil. No mention is made of a preoperative anaesthetic.

Whether there were doctors specializing in dentistry, or whether dentistry was simply part of a doctor's general practice, we do not know.

Community Medicine

Like Internet users today who frequent medical chat-rooms to share experiences and information with others suffering from the same condition, the people of Mesopotamia practiced an early form of community medicine by giving each other tips on how to get better. According to the fifth century B.C.E. Greek historian Herodotus (*History* 1: 197):

> The following custom seems to me [one of] the wisest of their institutions. . . . [W]hen a man is ill, they lay him in the public square, and the passersby come up to him, and if they have ever had his disease themselves or have known any one who has suffered from it, they give him advice, recommending him to do whatever they found good in their own case, or in the case known to them; and no one is allowed to pass the sick man in silence without asking him what his ailment is. (Herodotus 1942 [1858]: 106–7, trans. George Rawlinson)

One may add that just being pelted with all that advice may have been enough to drive an ancient Babylonian into instant wellness.

READING

Work

Nemet-Nejat 1998: occupations; Powell 1987: labor.

Slavery

Dandmaev 1984, Saggs 1995: slaves.

Marriage and Family

Bottéro et al. 2001: love and sex in Babylon, women's rights; Derevenski 1994: children; Dosch 1996: family in Nuzu; Fenshaw 1962:

widows, orphans, and the poor; Finkelstein 1966: sex offenses; Gelb 1979: household and family; Gordon 1957: legal framework of married life in Hammurabi's Babylonia; Greenfield 1982: care for the elderly; Greengus 1966: marriage ceremonies; Greengus 1969–70, Westbrook 1990: adultery; Hallo 1976: women of Sumer; Harris 1990: literary images of women; Kramer 1963: love in Sumerian times; Kramer 1969: the sacred marriage ritual; Leick 1994: sex and eroticism; Mendelsohn 1949: the family in the ancient Near East; Roth 1987: marriage; Siebert 1984: women in the ancient Near East; Stol 1995: private life; Van der Toorn 1994: religion in women's lives; Westenholz 1990: role of women.

Birth, Death and the Belief in an Afterlife

Alster 1980: death; Bottéro 2001, Scurlock 1995: death and the afterlife; Bottéro et al. 2001, Moorey 1982: burials at Ur; Campbell and Green 1995: archaeology of death; Crawford 1991: life, death, and the meaning of the universe; Frankfort, Wilson, and Jacobsen 1946: discussion of the differing spiritual outlooks of the ancient Egyptians and Mesopotamians; Heidel 1949: the afterlife; Kramer 1956: the world's oldest lullaby; Jonker 1995: remembrance of the dead; Marks and Good 1987: love and death in the ancient Near East; Moorey 1982: tombs at Ur; Nemet-Nejat 1998: childbirth, infancy, and infant mortality; Saggs 1962: obstetric and pediatric medicine.

Homes

Baker 1966: furniture; Kramer 1967, Moorey 1982: description and illustrations of a typical

Sumerian home; Muller 1940, Stone 1997: houses; Saggs 1965: houses in Babylonia and Assyria; Simpson 1995: furniture.

Clothing

Bier 1995: textile arts; Collon 1995: clothing and grooming; Payne 1965: history of costume; Speiser 1953: color illustrations of life and dress in ancient Mesopotamia.

Cosmetics and Perfume

Bimson 1980: cosmetics from Ur; Dayagi-Mendels 1989: ancient perfumes and cosmetics.

Food and Drink

Badler, McGovern, and Michel 1992: beer; Bottéro 1992: recipes; Bottéro et al. 2001: cuisine, feasting, wine; Hartman and Oppenheim 1950: beer and brewing; Katz and Maytag 1991: brewing; Limet 1987: Sumerian cuisine; Milano 1994: drinking in ancient societies; Renfrew 1995: vegetables.

Music

Biblical Archaeology Review 1980: the world's oldest musical notation; Farmer 1957, Galpin 1955, Parrot 1961: ancient Mesopotamian music; Garfinkel 1998: dancing; Kilmer 1995: music and dance; Rimmer 1969: musical instruments; Woolley 1934: descriptions of harps and lyres found at Ur.

Toys and Games

Dales 1968: dice; Hübner 1997: games; Moorey 1982: illustration of game board from Ur; *Royal Game of Ur* 1991: reconstruction of game board.

Sports

Bienkowski and Millard 2000, Nemet-Nejat 1998: types of sports.

Education

Civil 1992: survey; Gadd 1956: the oldest schools; Kramer 1949, 1956, and 1963: education in Sumer; Landsberger 1960: scribal education; "Oldest School" 1952: archaeological evidence; Pearce 1995: scribes and scholars; Sjöberg 1975: the school; Vanstiphout 1995: memory and literacy.

Health and Medicine

Avalos 1995: illness and health care; Biggs 1969, Oppenheim 1962: survey; Biggs 1995: medicine, surgery, and public health; Contenau 1954: Babylonian medicine; Geller 1991: Talmudic evidence; James and Thorpe 1994: pregnancy test; Oppenheim 1960: Caesarian section; Powell 1993: drugs and pharmaceuticals; Ritter 1965: magical experts and physicians; Saggs 1962 and 1989; the practice of medicine, including translations of medical texts; Sigerist 1961: history of medicine; Wilson 1965, 1967: mental diseases and psychiatry.

12

MESOPOTAMIA AND SACRED SCRIPTURE

THE OLD TESTAMENT

Mesopotamian civilization had a far greater impact on the Old Testament than the New. Mesopotamia's cultural values and literary influence are especially evident in the book of Genesis, while its military and political history shaped the lives and times of the Hebrew prophets.

Geography made these influences inevitable: the land of the Bible was part of the "Fertile Crescent," the continuum of arable land that arced from the valleys of the Tigris and Euphrates to the valley of the Nile. This continuum was not only spatial but also cultural: ceaseless commerce and recurrent conquest brought into contact the different peoples of the Near East together with their languages and ideas. In short, the Bible was not born in a cultural vacuum. Though its spiritual message was unique, the experience and consciousness of its authors were conditioned by the Mesopotamian context in which they grew up.

Often the Old Testament appears to borrow material from the even older literary traditions of Mesopotamia. But even when this occurs, the differences are as telling as the similarities. Beneath the superficial parallelisms in imagery is a profound deviation in spiritual outlook. Identifying the similarities and appreciating the differences can help us better understand the ideological individuality of both the ancient Hebrews and their neighbors.

The Book of Genesis

CREATION

Date   In 1654, using chronological data found in scripture, Archbishop James Ussher of Armagh, Ireland, calculated the date when the universe was created by God: 4004 B.C.E. Later, Dr. John Lightfoot, vice chancellor of Cambridge University, refined this date and concluded the world had been created on October 23, 4004 B.C.E., at 9 o'clock in the morning. Long before the efforts of Ussher and Lightfoot, Jewish scholars had already calculated the year of creation at 3761 B.C.E., a date which became the starting point for the traditional Jewish calendar.

On the basis of scientific evidence, however, today's astronomers would argue that the universe was created not in 4004 or 3761 B.C.E., but between eight and 20 billion years ago.

Nevertheless, the chronological information in the Bible may reflect an historical fact: not the date for the creation of the universe but the date for the birth of civilization, an event that archaeologists say took place in the ancient Near East sometime in the fourth millennium B.C.E. Like an insect caught in prehistoric amber, this critical event in humanity's story may have been chronologically preserved in ancient memory, but confused in scripture with the world's own beginning.

Literary Precedents   Parallels exist between the story of creation in the biblical book of Genesis and an account of creation in the classic Babylonian epic, *Enuma Elish*.

Both Genesis and *Enuma Elish* are religious texts which detail and celebrate cultural origins: Genesis describes the origin and founding of the Jewish people under the guidance of the Lord; *Enuma Elish* recounts the origin and founding of Babylon under the leadership of the god Marduk. Contained in each work is a story of how the cosmos and man were created. Each work begins by describing the watery chaos and primeval darkness that once filled the universe. Then light is created to replace the darkness. Afterward, the heavens are made and in them heavenly bodies are placed. Finally, man is created.

These similarities notwithstanding, the two accounts are more different than alike.

Genesis is the product of a monotheistic religion; *Enuma Elish*, the product of a polytheistic one. But more spiritually significant than the quantity of gods a culture worships is their quality.

Enuma Elish tells how the gods savagely warred with each other for supremacy until Marduk emerged triumphant, splitting open the body of the goddess Tiamat to make the sky and draining the blood of the god Kingu to make man. Man, meanwhile, is merely fashioned out of divine self-interest by Mesopotamian gods who want someone to serve them. There is no paradise for man to lose, no original sin to commit, because man is not pure to begin with, having been made from the blood of a demon. The creation of man (woman is not even mentioned) is simply one episode among many in the tale of Marduk's rise to power. The tale's culminating event is the building of a great temple to his glory in Babylon.

In contrast, the story in Genesis builds toward the creation of man, and of woman, after which the Lord rests. God is portrayed as a singular and creative force, not battling with other gods for primacy, but intent upon creating through the power of His word a universe of rational order, beauty, and goodness.

THE GARDEN OF EDEN

Origin of the Name The word "eden" first appears in Sumerian literature, where it means "a fertile plain." Indeed, its origin may even be pre-Sumerian—borrowed from the language of those who lived in southern Mesopotamia before the Sumerians settled there. The word seems to recall in mythic terms the well-watered, garden-like paradise the earliest settlers would have encountered upon their arrival.

Location According to the book of Genesis (2:8), the Garden of Eden was located in the east. The garden was watered by a river that flowed out of Eden and then split into four branches (2:10–14): the Hiddekel, the Pherath, the Gihon, and the Pishon. Of these rivers, two are easy to identify: the Hiddekel is described as bordering Assyria and is the Hebrew name of the Tigris (Sumerian "Idiglat"); while the Pherath is the Hebrew name for the Euphrates (Sumerian "Buranum"). Thus the Bible locates Eden somewhere in or near Mesopotamia, a natural location for paradise given its verdant riverine landscape.

The other two rivers—the Gihon and Pishon—are harder to locate. The Bible says the Gihon flows around the land of Cush, a country normally identified with Ethiopia. Here, however, Cush may refer to a country east of the Tigris that was inhabited by a people called the Kashsha. The river in *that* Cush is the Karun, which rises in Iran and empties into the Persian Gulf. The fourth river, the Pishon, has now been identified thanks to an earth-orbiting satellite which detected traces of dry river beds (the Wadi Rimah and the Wadi Batin) down which the river's waters once coursed. The Arabian desert through which the Pishon long ago flowed was in fact once rich in gold, just as the Bible says.

One problem with our identifications is that our candidates for the biblical Gihon and Pishon do not, as the Bible states, originate from the same source as the Tigris and Euphrates. All four rivers, however, would have collectively emptied their waters into the same place, the Persian Gulf.

Ancient Sumerian literature once spoke of an Eden-like paradise. Called Dilmun, the land was pure, clean, and sunlit, a country where fresh water nourished the fields, predators were absent, and aging and sickness were unknown, a land inhabited by gods or by humans who had been made immortal. Like the biblical Garden of Eden, Dilmun was located in the east toward the rising sun. Some have searched for the remains of Dilmun on the island of Bahrain (though Bahrain lies south not east of Sumer), while others point to the Indus Valley, another early birthplace of civilization. Still others argue that Dilmun, and perhaps Eden itself, now lie submerged beneath the waters of the Persian Gulf, the result of a radical elevation in sea level that occurred between 5,000 and 4,000 B.C.E. The memory of such a paradise would have survived, they argue, long after the garden itself had sunk beneath the sea.

ADAM AND EVE

In the book of Genesis, Adam is enticed by Eve and, as a result, loses his claim to paradise. By eating the apple he gains knowledge, including the knowledge of his own nakedness. Enticed first by a serpent, Eve gains this knowledge too but, like Adam, pays the price of banishment from Eden's garden.

In the Mesopotamian *Epic of Gilgamesh*, a prostitute seduces Enkidu, a naive hero who had grown up in nature. As a result of the encounter, Enkidu gains knowledge, including a conscious awareness of his own nakedness, but he is forever banished from the companionship of the creatures of nature that had formerly been his friends. Later in the story, the hero Gilgamesh searches for the secret of eternal life. Given a magic plant that can provide rejuvenation, he loses this gift when it is stolen by a serpent.

In both Genesis and the *Epic of Gilgamesh* the attainment of knowledge is associated with a loss of innocence. In each story, sexual seduction and a serpent's wiles cause a male hero to fall from a state of grace.

Genesis, however, differs from the *Epic of Gilgamesh* in attributing the hero's fall to his disobedience to his god. The narrative in Genesis is thus distinguished by its moral framework. However painful the losses suffered by Enkidu and Gilgamesh, they do not stem from insubordination.

The story of Eve's birth is illuminated by a myth set in Dilmun, the Sumerian Eden. According to the tale, the goddess Ninhursag sought to cure the ailing god Enki. To cure his rib (Sumerian "ti"), she created a special goddess of healing called Nin-ti, "the lady of the rib." The creation of this goddess may underlie the story of how God created Eve from Adam's rib. Because the Sumerian word "ti" also means "to live," the goddess' name also meant "the lady who brings (someone) to life." Significantly, Eve's name in Hebrew, Havvah, means life.

THE FLOOD

The most compelling case for Mesopotamian literary influence on the Bible is the story of Noah and the ark, for the tale of a global flood and a divinely chosen survivor also occurs in the literary traditions of Sumer, Babylonia, and Assyria. These accounts strikingly parallel the biblical narrative both in their general outlines and in particular details. In its Akkadian incarnation as part of the classic *Epic of Gilgamesh*, the Mesopotamian flood-story was to become a staple of literature across the ancient Near East, including the land of the Bible.

Similarities   In the Mesopotamian versions, a god warns an individual of devastation from an impending flood. The god then gives directions for the construction of a vessel designed to save a select group of human beings and animals. Once the deadly rains have ceased, the boat comes to rest on a mountaintop. After the passage of time, the Mesopotamian Noah releases a series of birds in the hope they will fly back with evidence the flood is abating. Upon the receipt of this evidence, the passengers disembark and offer thanks to their god, who in turn promises never to send such a flood again.

12.1 The decipherment of this tablet—a Babylonian account of the Genesis-like Great Flood—revolutionized biblical studies and gave new impetus to the modern exploration of Mesopotamia. (The British Museum)

Differences Despite these similarities to the storyline in Genesis, there are also significant differences. While the biblical ark is made out of wood, the Mesopotamian one is made out of reeds, an abundant material used for construction in a land where wood was scarce. While the biblical ark is rectangular, the Mesopotamian one is a giant cube, with five times the displacement of Noah's vessel. As for the rain, it lasts for 40 days and nights in the Bible but only a week in the Mesopotamian account. The biblical ark comes to rest on the mountains of Ararat in Armenia; the Mesopotamian one, on Assyrian Mt. Nisir. And the species of birds sent out in the two stories are not exactly the same.

But the most illuminating difference between the two accounts is a moral one. In Genesis the Lord uses the flood to purge the earth of human sinfulness, singling out Noah for special treatment because he is righteous. The Mesopotamian Noah, on the other hand, is not explicitly saved because he is more righteous than his contemporaries. Nor does Enlil, the leader of the Mesopotamian gods, use the flood to punish sin. Instead, he floods the earth because a populous and noisy human race has been making him lose sleep. Throughout, the Biblical narrative has moral direction; indeed, after the flood God promulgates new ethical guidelines by which humankind must live. Conversely, Enlil is self-centered and concerned only with his own gratification; it is a divine subordinate, Ea, who warns the Mesopotamian Noah of the impending disaster.

The Name of Noah To the Sumerians the flood-hero was known as Ziusudra ("a life of long days"), spelled Xisouthros by the third century B.C.E. Babylonian priest, Berossus, in his retelling of the tale. In the Babylonian and Assyrian traditions, the hero was also known as Utnapishtim ("he found life") or as Atrahasis ("exceedingly wise"). Though Jewish tradition explains the name Noah as coming from the Hebrew root for "comfort," it may instead be a shortened form of the name Naahmuuliel, the name given to the flood-hero by the Hurrians, an ethnic group active in Mesopotamia in the second millennium B.C.E.

Historical Evidence for the Flood Unlike Israel, Mesopotamia was frequented by destructive floods, a persuasive reason for concluding that the biblical story of the flood originated not in Israel but in the valleys of the Tigris and Euphrates. Such a conclusion is supported by the fact that the ark was said to come to rest not on a mountain in Israel but on a mountain chain on Mesopotamia's northern frontier.

In his excavations at the Sumerian city of Ur, Sir Leonard Woolley believed for a time he had actually uncovered physical confirmation of the event: an eight-foot-thick layer of alluvial soil sandwiched between two layers of occupational debris, the remains of two cultures that had flourished before and after a great inundation. The layer of silt dated to the fourth millennium B.C.E. Later surveys of Sumer, however, revealed layers of silt at many sites, but all of them dated to different time periods ranging from 4000 to 2500 B.C.E. Thus, there had not been one universal flood, but many localized ones.

Nevertheless, in their ancient lists of kings, the Sumerians themselves divided their history into two main periods: before the Great Flood and after. Some modern scholars believe this division reflects the memory of an

12.2   The great "Flood Pit" at Ur. The discovery of a thick layer of mud sandwiched between layers of artifacts led Sir Leonard Woolley to speculate he had found evidence of the biblical flood.
(University of Pennsylvania Museum)

inundation that occurred some 10,000 years ago at the end of the Ice Age, when huge portions of land were covered by what are now the waters of the Persian Gulf. It was this cataclysmic event, they believe, that later became transfigured in myth.

THE TOWER OF BABEL

Genesis recalls an act of supreme arrogance, the building of a city with a lofty tower meant to reach to the heavens. To stop the project, God made human beings speak different languages so that, no longer being able to communicate with one another, they would be unable to collaborate. Accordingly, the Bible derives the word Babel from the Hebrew root *balal,* "to confuse."

The monument that inspired this story was, no doubt, the great *ziggurat,* or platformed temple, that once stood in the imposing city of Babylon. Babylon's name is in fact echoed in the Tower of Babel's name and is thus its true etymological source.

Because building stone was rare in southern Mesopotamia, ziggurats were built of brick, just as the Bible notes in its description of the Tower of Babel's construction.

In the Sumerian language, the stepped platform was called Etemenanki, "The House of the Foundation of Heaven and Earth," while the temple on top was called Esagila, "The House That Lifts Its Head." As though recalling these names, the Bible speaks of the Tower of Babel having "its head in heaven."

More than a disquisition on architecture, however, the story of the Tower of Babel is a moralistic tale that sees in the multiple languages of Mesopotamia's multicultural civilization the mark of divine vengeance.

ABRAHAM, ISAAC, AND JACOB

The "Patriarchal Narratives"—the stories of Abraham, Isaac, and Jacob—are a tapestry woven out of the cultural threads of the Mesopotamian world.

Origins Abraham's homeland was not Israel but ancient Iraq.

The Bible calls the city of his birth Ur of the Chaldees. This city may have been the Ur excavated by Sir Leonard Woolley in southern Mesopotamia, or its namesake, Ura, located in the northwest. Locating Abraham's birthplace in the north makes sense in terms of his ancestry: the names of his great-grandfather, grandfather, and brother are synonymous with the names of cities in the region, the same area from which Abraham later sought a wife for his son, Isaac. Moreover, an inscription found at the powerful city of Ebla reveals that one of its greatest kings bore the name Ebrum, the same name as Abraham's great-great-great-great-grandfather, the ancestor for whom the Hebrews were named. The language of Ebla was, in fact, the direct ancestor of the Hebrew language, and in its cuneiform tablets we read of people named Abraham, Esau, Ishmael, and Israel, a veritable "telephone directory" of Hebrew personal names.

Customs The folkways of the patriarchs, which once seemed peculiar and unique to the Bible, have now been shown to be consistent with practices in ancient Mesopotamian society during the second millennium B.C.E. Texts discovered at the northern Mesopotamian city of Nuzu have been especially instructive in this regard. Sarai's gift of a handmaid to Abram in order that her husband might produce an heir; Esau's sale of his birthright to his younger brother Jacob for a bowl of soup; the dying Isaac's oral will; and Rachel's theft of ritual objects called *teraphim* from her father Laban's home all find parallels in the legal documents of Nuzu, demonstrating that the patriarchs' lives were a fabric woven from the yarn of Mesopotamian cultural values.

The Book of Exodus

THE BIRTH OF MOSES

The story of the birth of Moses echoes elements in the legend of the birth of Sargon of Akkad, who ruled southern Mesopotamia approximately a thousand years before the probable date of the Exodus. Sargon's legend recounts how he was born in secret to a high priestess, who put him in a basket of rushes (the lid of which was sealed with bitumen) and placed the basket in a river. The basket was later found by a man named Akki, who was a drawer of water. Akki became the child's foster father and raised him. Later, the story says, the goddess Ishtar bestowed her love on the young Sargon and he rose to become king of the land. The secret birth, the deposit of the baby into a basket that is then floated on a river, the baby's discovery by an adult who becomes his foster parent, and the subsequent rise of the child to kingship under divine favor parallels the story of Moses in Exodus 2: 1–10. To be sure, there are differences: Moses' mother was not a priestess and his foster parent (an Egyptian princess) was not a lowly drawer of water; the social status of his birth mother and his foster mother are thus reversed in scripture.

These literary parallels may, of course, be merely a coincidence. The argument is further complicated by the fact that the basic outlines of the story are found in the Roman legend of Romulus and Remus, who were born to a priestess, set adrift in a river (the Tiber), found by a she-wolf and raised by a shepherd until they sought to become leaders of their people. It is hard to say whether the three stories arose from separate sources, or whether the Roman legend was in some way shaped by Near Eastern story motifs.

THE TEN COMMANDMENTS

The focus of Exodus is not Mesopotamia, the land of the Jewish people's origin, but Egypt, the country of its enslavement. Yet even in Exodus the presence of Mesopotamian cultural influence is palpable. While Egyptian society was governed by the oral pronouncements of the pharaoh, Mesopotamia was regulated by a long-standing tradition of written codes of law, from the Sumerian Code of Ur-Nammu to the Babylonian Code of Hammurabi. In concept as well as in content, the biblical "Ten Commandments" in Exodus are a lineal descendant of these codes. When Moses the leader stands atop Mt. Sinai to receive the Torah from the Lord, he becomes the Hebraic analogue to king Hammurabi who five centuries earlier had received the statutes of Babylon from the god Shamash seated upon his throne.

The Hebrew Prophets

Just as the earliest books of the Old Testament reflect the lifestyles and practices of ancient Mesopotamia, so do some of its last books bear the imprint of Mesopotamian militarism and politics. This is most clear in the book of Kings, I and II, and the writings of the Hebrew prophets.

HISTORICAL BACKGROUND

The key military events that had an impact on the prophets were the Assyrian king Shalmaneser's conquest of the Northern Kingdom of Israel in 722 B.C.E.; Sennacherib's siege of Jerusalem in 701 B.C.E.; the Babylonian king Nebuchadnezzar's capture of Jerusalem in 597 B.C.E. leading to the First Exile of the Jews; the city's recapture, the Temple's destruction, and the Second Exile in 586 B.C.E.; and the return of Jewish captives to Jerusalem in 536 B.C.E. under the reign of the Persian king Cyrus.

While the comments of the prophets often forecast the defeat of the Jewish nation or hold out the hope of its eventual renewal, their primary message is fundamentally moral

12.3 *This object, known as the "Black Obelisk," describes how the ninth-century B.C.E. Assyrian king, Shalmaneser III, prevailed over lesser kingdoms.* (Rogers, *A History of Babylonia and Assyria*, 1915)

His statutes, . . . I will send a fire upon Judah, and it shall devour the palaces of Jerusalem . . . because they sell the righteous for silver and the needy for a pair of shoes."

"They shall fall by the sword; their infants shall be dashed in pieces," said Hosea of the people of Israel who relied on foreign powers like Assyria rather than the Lord. "It hath been told thee, O man, what is good," proclaimed Micah, "and what the Lord doth require of thee: only to do justly, and to love mercy, and to walk humbly with thy God." Under the encroaching shadow of war, both Micah and Isaiah longed for the day when people "shall beat their swords into plowshares, and their spears into pruning-hooks. Nation shall not lift up sword against nation; neither shall they learn war any more. But they shall sit every man under his vine and under his fig tree, and none shall make them afraid." Meanwhile, the prophet Nahum railed against the savagery of Assyrian Nineveh, "the bloody city, the den of lions, the feeding place of the young lions," a city God would punish because of its brutality.

12.4   Detail from the Black Obelisk. In the second register from the top, King Jehu of Israel kneels in submission before Shalmaneser.   (Rogers, *A History of Babylonia and Assyria*, 1915)

in tone, viewing societal downfall as the inevitable consequence of ignoring or defying God's ethical teachings.

THE PROPHETS AND THEIR MESSAGE

The Hebrew prophets who lived before the days of exile derided the social injustices and religious hypocrisy that prevailed in their land under the influence of materialism. Amos, the earliest of the prophets, foresaw retribution:

"Thus saith the Lord: Because they have rejected the law of the Lord, and have not kept

12.5   In 701 B.C.E. the Assyrian king Sennacherib laid siege to the Judaean city of Lachish. The siege is described in detail in the Old Testament. Here, from a relief found at the site of the Assyrian capital, Jewish captives are shown begging for mercy. (Layard, *Discoveries in the Ruins of Nineveh*, 1853)

Nineveh and the Assyrian Empire did indeed fall in 612 B.C.E., but its conqueror, Babylon, proved an even greater threat to the Jewish nation. The prophet Habakkuk foresaw Jerusalem's coming destruction at the hands of the Babylonians, "that bitter and impetuous nation, that march through the breadth of the earth, to possess dwelling-places that are not theirs. They are terrible and dreadful. . . . Their horses are swifter than leopards, and are more fierce than the wolves of the desert." Both he and Jeremiah prayed for deliverance, but in the end Jerusalem fell, its Temple was sacked and burned, and its population was transported to Babylon to become slaves.

The sorrows of the captives are voiced in the book of Lamentations and in Psalm 137:

> By the waters of Babylon,
> There we sat down, yea, we wept,
> When we remembered Zion.
> Upon the willows in the midst thereof
> We hanged our harps.
> For there they that led us captive asked of us
>   words of song,
> And our tormentors asked of us mirth:
> "Sing us one of the songs of Zion."
>
> How shall we sing the Lord's song
> In a foreign land?
> If I forget thee, O Jerusalem,
> Let my right hand forget her cunning.
> Let my tongue cleave to the roof of my mouth,
> If I remember thee not;
> If I set not Jerusalem
> Above my chiefest joy.

Stripped of their Temple, the captives replaced empty ritual with heartfelt prayer, while their prophet Ezekiel envisioned the day when their dry bones would be revivified and their nationhood resurrected.

Released from captivity by the Persian king Cyrus, the Jews returned to their homeland and rebuilt their Temple, led by Ezra and Nehemiah and inspired by the words of the prophets Haggai and Zechariah. Yet, as the writings of Malachi show, prosperity would once again undermine a single-minded commitment to God's teachings. Once again, like a perpetual Greek tragedy, the ancient cycle of affluence, arrogance, folly, and vengeance was played out. To the eyes of the prophet Joel, the armies of destruction were already massing on the horizon like a vast swarm of locusts about to devour the land. Only God's mercy and love could and would save His people:

> And it shall come to pass in that day that the mountains shall drop down sweet wine, and the hills shall flow with milk . . . and a fountain shall come forth of the house of the Lord. . . . Judah shall be inhabited for ever, and Jerusalem from generation to generation.

THE BOOK OF JONAH

One of the most extraordinary books of the Old Testament is the book of Jonah. In the book, God instructs the prophet Jonah to preach to the people of Nineveh in order that they might turn from their wicked ways. Fearing the personal consequences of preaching to the Assyrians and assuming that God would eventually and mercifully spare them anyway, Jonah boards a ship heading in exactly the opposite direction. In the end, thanks to a divinely sent storm and sea monster (not a whale in the original Hebrew text!), Jonah accepts the mission and travels to Nineveh, "an exceedingly great city, of three days' journey [in scope]." In response to Jonah's message, the entire population of Nineveh, including man and beast, put on sackcloth and ashes and pray for deliverance. In turn, the Lord does not punish them.

The underlying theme of this story is the universality of Judaism's god. Not only do His powers reach out over the Mediterranean, but His judgment and mercy extend beyond the land of Israel to foreign lands, even to those inhabited by Israel's ancient enemies, who eventually acknowledge His power.

Psalms and Proverbs

Both the biblical book of Psalms and the biblical book of Proverbs are expressions of literary genres that long flourished in Mesopotamia and inspired their Hebrew analogues by example and form.

Job and Ecclesiastes

In addition, a Sumerian precedent exists for the book of Job, but a thousand years older than the biblical work. As Samuel Noah Kramer observes, "it represents man's first recorded attempt to deal with the age-old yet very modern problem of human suffering" (Kramer 1981: 112).

Similarly, a Babylonian dialogue exists that is colored by pessimism, anticipating the tone of the later biblical book of Ecclesiastes.

Both of these Mesopotamian works, however, are shorter and less complex than their analogues in the Bible. Rather than signifying direct literary influence, they may instead point to parallel efforts on the part of thinkers in both cultures to explain the human condition.

The Book of Esther

Although the geographical setting of the Book of Esther is Persia (Iran) rather than Mesopotamia (Iraq), the names of two of the stories' main characters are Mesopotamian in origin. The Hebrew name Mordecai echoes the name of the Babylonian god Marduk, and the Hebrew name Esther echoes the name of the love-goddess Ishtar.

The story states that Mordecai and Esther's families had previously lived in Babylon as a consequence of the Babylonian Captivity. Their Babylonian names could therefore be explained by their birthplace. When Cyrus II the Great of Persia released the Jews from their captivity in 536 B.C.E., some may have migrated to Persia, where our story takes place.

However, because Marduk and Ishtar are the names of Babylonian gods (and unlikely choices for the names of Jewish babies), the Book of Esther's characters may instead derive at least in part from Babylonian religious tradition. The marriage of the sexually attractive Esther to the Persian king may recall the ritual mating of the goddess Ishtar with Babylon's monarchs to ensure the earth's fertility (see Chapter 4). Furthermore, the role of Mordecai as the guardian of the king's life and his eventual adviser recalls the place of Marduk as the divine protector of Babylon's kings.

A key element in the story—the casting of lots by Persian diviners to determine the most auspicious date on which to exterminate the Jews—is reminiscent of the prominent place divination had in Mesopotamian society (see Chapters 4, 5, and 11). Even the Hebrew word for lot, *pur* (Esther 3: 7), the etymological origin of the Jewish holiday Purim, may stem from the Akkadian word for lot, *puru*.

The Book of Daniel

The theme of God's universality is also found not only in the book of Jonah but also in the book of Daniel, which dates to the second century B.C.E. In the story, Daniel and his three friends work for the Babylonian king Nebuchadnezzar and win his admiration because of their God-given wisdom and skill. Because of Daniel's ability to interpret a royal dream, Nebuchadnezzar declares the Lord to be the one true god. However, because Daniel and his friends refuse to worship a golden idol of the king, he throws them into a fiery furnace. When they emerge unscathed, he restores them to their position and reaffirms his faith in God, as he does again after Daniel interprets yet another dream.

Later, Nebuchadnezzar is slain and is replaced on the throne by Darius the Mede. Arrested for praying to someone other than Darius, Daniel is thrown into a lions' den, but through the power of prayer is saved once again. In recognition of this miracle, Darius then declares that Daniel's god should be worshiped throughout the empire.

The concluding portion of Daniel reports visions of successive conquerors who will rule the Near East: the Babylonians, the Medes, the Persians, Alexander the Great, and Alexander's Hellenistic successors. Ultimately, says the prophet, the Jewish people will stand supreme.

The acknowledgment of the Lord by foreign kings and the prophecy of the Jewish people's ultimate triumph over their enemies served to reassure the Jews with confidence in their own divinely ordained future in the face of centuries of conquest and oppression by others.

MESOPOTAMIA AND THE APOCRYPHA

The 13 ancient Jewish works known as the "Apocrypha" date to between 300 B.C.E. and 70 C.E. and they were not included in the canonical text of the Hebrew scriptures. Some of these works are connected with Mesopotamian civilization. *The Prayer of Azariah*, the *Song of the Three Young Men*, *Susanna*, and *Bel and the Dragon* supplement the canonical book of Daniel and are set in the court at Babylon, while the book of Tobit takes place in Nineveh. *Bel and the Dragon* tells how Daniel (1) cleverly proved that the food being offered to the idol Bel (Semitic for 'Lord') was actually being eaten by his priests and their families and (2) killed a dragon the Babylonians worshiped by feeding it a mix of pitch, fat, and

hair. The first episode exposes the fraudulence of Mesopotamian idolatry; the second, the vulnerability of a pagan deity pictured in Mesopotamian art. The book of Judith for its part tells the tale of a Jewish heroine who saved her country by beheading an Assyrian general named Holofernes, who was then besieging Jerusalem.

MESOPOTAMIA AND THE NEW TESTAMENT

While Mesopotamia plays a major role in the stories of the Old Testament, it plays only a minor role in the New. Instead, it is the culture, history, and thought of the Greco-Roman world that infuses the Gospels and their companion books. In short, while the Old Testament faces east (to Mesopotamia) and south (to Egypt), the New Testament looks westward to the civilizations of Greece and Rome.

Nevertheless, sporadic references to Mesopotamia do occur. In citing the genealogy of Jesus, Matthew refers three times to the Babylonian Captivity of 586 B.C.E., an event also referred to in the book of Acts. In his first letter the apostle Peter mentions Babylon once, referring to it only in passing. Indeed, only one story about Mesopotamia can be found in the Gospels: in Matthew we read how Jesus criticized the scribes and Pharisees for being less receptive to his message than the Ninevites had been to the message of Jonah.

In the book of Revelation, however, one Mesopotamian city assumes symbolic significance. In the book of Revelation, Babylon functions as a repugnant symbol of sin. Angels speak of its fall and prophesy its future destruction by God. In one powerful passage, an angel reveals the image of a prostitute bedecked in gaudy jewelry and holding a cup filled with moral contamination. On her head is written: "Babylon, the great, mother of harlots and of earth's abominations."

Revelation is the last book in the New Testament. Thus the Bible's final word on Mesopotamia is a curse.

MESOPOTAMIA AND THE KORAN

In the whole of the Koran, Mesopotamia is mentioned only once. The negative image of Babylon in the book of Revelation persists in the Koran's second Sura, where the angels of the city are described as masters of sorcery—a memory perhaps, albeit distorted, of ancient Babylonian magic.

In contrast to this single reference, the text of the Koran frequently refers to Egypt and its pharaoh, perhaps because in the seventh century C.E. when Mohammed lived the stone splendors of Egypt were still visible while the mud monuments of Mesopotamia had long since sunk into oblivion.

Yet in describing the paradise where the faithful will go after death, the prophet takes the biblical Eden and transmutes it into an idyllic land of pleasure where the immortal will forever dwell. In this Islamic image, Sumerian Dilmun awakens from its 3,500-year-long sleep. Says Mohammed:

> But whoever stands before Him in the purity of faith after performing good deeds will be raised to new heights—to the Gardens of Eden with flowing streams where he will dwell forever. (Sura 20: 75–76; trans. Ahmed Ali)

READING

Old Testament (General)

Barton 1937: archaeology and the Bible; Cornfeld 1976: archaeological commentary on biblical times and events; Dalley 1998: Mesopotamian influence; Gordon and Rendsburg 1997: the Near Eastern cultural context of the Bible; Keller 1981: the Bible as history; King 1969: Babylonian legends and Hebrew tradition; Kramer 1959: Sumerian literature and the Bible; Pritchard 1969: Mesopotamian texts.

The Book of Genesis

CREATION

Brandon 1963: Near Eastern stories; Clifford 1994, Tsumura 1994: comparisons; Dalley 1989 and 1991, McCall 1990: Mesopotamian myth of creation; Heidel 1951: Babylonian Genesis; Tsumura 1989: earth and waters.

THE GARDEN OF EDEN

Bibby 1972, Kramer 1944 and 1963, Potts 1983: Dilmun; Cornwall 1946: Dilmun; Hamblin 1987: location; Kramer 1956: Sumerian parallels; Rice 1985: Bahrain; Widegren 1951: tree of life.

ADAM AND EVE

Kramer 1956: Sumerian parallels.

THE FLOOD

Dalley 1991: Mesopotamian myth; Dundas 1988: literary parallels; Frymer-Kensky 1977, 1978: flood story; Heidel 1949: the Gilgamesh epic and parallels; Lambert and Millard 1969:

Atrahasis; Schmidt 1995: flood narratives; Tigay 1982: development of the Gilgamesh legend; Tsumura 1994: comparisons.

THE TOWER OF BABEL

Killick 1996: ziggurat; Koldewey 1915: excavations; Larue 1969, Oates 1986, Parrot 1955, Saggs 1962: tower; Van Buren 1952: construction.

ABRAHAM, ISAAC, AND JACOB

Berment and Weitzman 1979, Ebla; Eichler 1989, Gordon 1940, Gordon and Rendsburg 1992, Matthiae 1980, Pettinato 1981 and 1991, Starr 1939, Zaccagnini 1977: Nuzu; Gordon 1958 and 1963: Abraham as a merchant, and Ura as Ur; Greenberg 1955: the Hebrews and the Hab/piru; 1962: Rachel's theft of the *teraphim*; Liverani 1973: the Amorites; Malamat 1971 and 1992, Mendelhall 1948, Oppenheim 1952: Mari; Millard 2001, Schanks 2000: Abraham's Ur; Owen and Wilhelm 1981–: the Hurrians and Nuzu; Thompson 1974: historicity; Van Weters, 1972: Abraham in history and tradition; Wilhelm 1989: the Hurrians; Woolley 1950: Ur.

The Book of Exodus

Gordon 1957: the Code of Hammurabi; Kramer 1981: Sumerian law codes; Lewis 1980, Pfeiffer 1966, and Pritchard 1969: the Sargon legend.

The Hebrew Prophets

Hoenig and Rosenberg 1957: historical background and prophetic themes.

Psalms and Proverbs

Kramer 1956: commentary; Pritchard 1969: texts.

Job and Ecclesiastes

Kramer 1956: commentary; Pritchard 1969: texts.

The Book of Esther

Ausubel 1964: background to Purim.

The Book of Daniel

Freedman 2000: background and additions to text.

Mesopotamia and the Apocrypha

Freedman 2000: Bel and the Dragon; Wigoder 1986: summaries of books.

Mesopotamia and the New Testament

Keller 1981: Bible as history; Wigoder 1986: summaries of books.

Mesopotamia and the Koran

Babil 1995: Babylon's reputation in medieval Arabic literature; Ali 1988: text of the Koran.

13

THE LEGACY OF MESOPOTAMIA

What have the civilizations of ancient Mesopotamia bequeathed to us? What is their legacy to us, the inhabitants of a world they never could have imagined?

In his book, *History Begins at Sumer*, Samuel Noah Kramer lists 39 "firsts" in recorded history that can be credited to the Sumerians and the culture they created. Many of these belong to the field of religion: "Man's First Cosmogony and Cosmology," "Man's First Golden Age," "The First Moral Ideas," "The First Biblical Parallels," "The First 'Noah,'" "The First 'Moses,'" "The First 'Job,'" "The First Liturgic Laments," "The First Messiahs," "The First Mater Dolorosa," "The First Funeral Chants," "The First Tale of Resurrection," and "The First 'St. George.'" Others are landmarks in literature: "The First 'Farmer's Almanac,'" "The First Animal Fables," "The First Proverbs and Sayings," "Man's First Epic Literature," "The First Historian," "The First Love Song," "The First Sex Symbolism," "The First Literary Portrait of the Ideal Mother," "The First Lullaby," "The First Literary Imagery," "The First Case of Literary Borrowing," "The First Literary Debates," and "The First Library Catalogue." Still others are milestones in social history: "The First Legal Precedent," "The First Bicameral Congress," "The First Case of Tax Reduction," "Labor's First Victory," "The First 'War of Nerves,'" "The First 'Sick Society,'" "The First Schools," "The First Case of 'Apple-Polishing,'" and "The First Case of Juvenile Delinquency." Rounding out the 39 are "The First Aquarium," "The First Experiment in Shade-Tree Gardening," "The First Long-Distance Champion," and "The First Pharmacopoeia."

The length and variety of Kramer's list is a solid demonstration of the creative genius of the Sumerians, the founders of the world's earliest civilization.

But being first is not necessarily the same as having an enduring influence on later ages.

Some innovations may be forgotten, or may be reinvented later by others oblivious of their forebearers.

For example, in 1936 a clay jar was found in ancient ruins at Baghdad. Dating to between 250 B.C.E. and 250 C.E., the jar housed a hollow copper tube containing a vertical iron rod held in place by asphalt. If the empty space in the tube had been filled with an acid (such as vinegar), the object would have functioned as a primitive battery capable of generating a half-volt current. All that was missing were the wire connections. Yet the principle would be forgotten, and it would not be until 1800 that Alessandro Volta would "invent" the electric battery.

To assess the true legacy of Mesopotamia, then, we will need to trace the continuity of its ideas and the longevity of its accomplishments. Only then will we be able to determine Mesopotamia's actual influence upon us and our world. Yet to fully appreciate the answer, we must first understand the process of transmission that explains how these ancient concepts survived for millennia, often against great odds.

CONTINUITY AND CHANGE

The ancient lifeline that explains the transmission and survival of Mesopotamian lore is the writing system the Sumerians invented. Without writing that can give them permanence, ideas can perish along with the people who first conceived them; endowed with permanent form, however, they can transcend the millennia.

The cultures of Akkad, Babylon, and Assyria recognized the importance of writing and went on to master and adapt the system the Sumerians had devised. But, in addition to merely becoming literate in cuneiform, each successive nation also respected the cultural achievements of its predecessors. Thus the knowledge and wisdom of Mesopotamia were reverentially preserved by each new generation, and they grew by accumulation.

The Sumerian language posed a special challenge because the Sumerians, unlike their political successors, spoke and wrote a non-Semitic tongue. But so highly regarded were the Sumerians as the inventors of civilization, mastering their language and literature became a prerequisite for any Mesopotamian who wished to be considered educated and eligible for social advancement. As a consequence, Sumerian became the classic language of ancient Mesopotamia, with a status and longevity comparable to that of Latin in medieval and Renaissance Europe. The archaeological testimony to Sumerian's stature and persistence is found in bilingual cuneiform dictionaries, schoolroom exercises, royal libraries, and the durability of literary classics like the *Epic of Gilgamesh*. In the second millennium B.C.E., Semitic Akkadian became an international language of commerce and diplomacy, and the language helped spread cuneiform and its intellectual riches beyond the Tigris and Euphrates. Indeed, when the Indo-European Persians conquered the Neo-Babylonian Empire, they adopted the cuneiform script for their archives and public inscriptions, thereby embracing a visible symbol of continuity with the pre-Persian cultures they ruled.

Though cuneiform continued to be taught in academies and studied by Mesopotamian scholars as late as the first century C.E., it was eventually supplanted by the alphabet, a streamlined script that was far easier to learn and use. By that time Aramaic had become the new lingua franca of the Mideastern world, as would Arabic centuries later, and both were written in versions of the new script. As a consequence, the multimillennial chain of continuity with the linguistic and literary traditions of Mesopotamia was finally broken. Cuneiform inscriptions became illegible to the Mesopotamians themselves, who were now barred by illiteracy from drinking from the river of ancestral wisdom. Yet, like ancient time capsules, the baked clay tablets and stones would preserve this store of wisdom until it could be unlocked by the code-breaking scholars of a later world.

The Memory of Foreigners

Even though its most ancient languages and literatures might no longer be spoken or read by its own people, the cultural legacy of Mesopotamia was kept alive in the minds of foreigners.

BIBLICAL TRADITION

The first and most influential of these peoples were the ancient Hebrews. As we saw in the previous chapter, the Hebrew scriptures bear witness to the military power of Mesopotamia and its cultural impact. Because the Old Testament was preserved and revered by Jews and Christians, images of Mesopotamia—like cultural artifacts caught and irradiated in the spiritual amber of biblical prose and poetry—endured down through all later ages of Western civilization. As a result, the "Garden of Eden," the "Tower of Babel," "Noah and the Ark," and the fateful "Writing on the Wall" seen by King Belshazzar live on in our cultural memory to this day.

But the Hebrews were not the only foreign people to be influenced by Mesopotamia and to be impressed by its power. The classical Greeks and Romans also collaborated in preserving Mesopotamia's legacy.

THE FATHER OF HISTORY

Paradoxically, Mesopotamia is remembered thanks to one of the most celebrated wars in history, but a war in which the people of Mesopotamia played only a marginal role. In the fifth century B.C.E., the greatest conflict between Europe and Asia took place since the Trojan War made famous by Homer. Called the "Persian Wars" by the later Greeks, it was a David and Goliath conflict in which the massive might of the Persian Empire was pitted against the small city-states of Greece. The Persians attempted to swallow up Greece but were driven back by Greek patriots defending their native land and political freedom. Had Persia triumphed, the Golden Age of Athens and the artistic and literary achievements it inspired never would have taken place.

In the aftermath of the Hellenic victory, a Greek named Herodotus set about researching and writing a history of the war. Herodotus embodied a personality trait emblematic of his people: curiosity. Not content with just recording a list of battles, he probed the causes that had led to the war's origin. Since Persia in those days was the political and military master of the Near East, Herodotus wondered how the Persians had risen to such a position of preeminence. This, in turn, led him to wonder about the various cultures the Persians had triumphed over, including the kingdoms of Mesopotamia.

In the course of his investigation, Herodotus interrogated and read the works of Persian historians and traveled to the Near East to see its lands and peoples firsthand. He did not view the Persians and their allies as villains despite the fact that Babylonian and Assyrian troops had been part of the invasion force. Instead, he saw the high purpose of his inquiry "to preserve the remembrance of what men have done from decay and to prevent the great and marvelous actions of both the Greeks and the Barbarians (as he called them) from losing their full measure of glory." It is because of Herodotus's generosity of spirit that he recounted the achievements of those who had sought to rob his own people of their way of life. As human beings living a different way of life, the barbarians were a continuing source of fascination to him. Thus, in the very first volume of his history, he describes the land of Mesopotamia, the glorious city of Babylon and its rulers, and the curious customs of its people.

Western civilization would later call Herodotus "the father of history" because his was the first scientific attempt they knew of to assess the causes and consequences of historical events rather than merely to list them in chronological order. Herodotus not only influenced later historians of Greece and Rome but also subsequently the educated citizenry of Europe who regarded his work as a true classic of Western literature. For centuries, those who read the opening chapters of his history marveled, as did Herodotus himself, at the lands of the Tigris and Euphrates and their past glories.

ALEXANDER THE GREAT

After the Persian Wars, the next great confrontation between East and West came in the fourth century B.C.E. In retaliation for the invasion of Greece, Alexander, the 20-year-old king of Macedonia, declared war against Persia. But it was a personal war as well that Alexander waged, a war to prove his valor and gain incomparable glory. Having defeated the Persian king, Alexander developed a bold plan for ruling the largest empire the world had ever known, an empire that reached from Greece in the west to India in the east. His plan to insure its durability was to racially integrate the administration of both his army and his government, blending Persian with Macedonian and Greek into a new ethnic amalgam. In addition, he encouraged his soldiers to intermarry with native women and founded new cities throughout his realm to disseminate Hellenic culture under the stimulus of the East. For his administrative capital he chose Babylon, where he died in 323 B.C.E. just short of his 33rd birthday. Though his conquests were quickly divided up among his successors, the cultural revolution he had set in motion lived on in what is known as the Hellenistic Age.

LATER GREEK HISTORIANS

Before Alexander became king of Macedonia, a Greek physician named Ctesias served in the court of the Persian king Artaxerxes II. Fascinated with Persian civilization, he compiled a history of the empire and its rulers. He visited and described the city of Babylon, and he devoted special attention to the careers of two extraordinary Mesopotamian monarchs: Semiramis, Babylon's reputed founder and first queen, and Sardanapalus, reportedly Assyria's last king.

Semiramis played a man's role, supervising awesome works of engineering and construction and boldly and aggressively waging war; Sardanapalus, for his part, acted the role of a woman in dress and speech, until his deviancy and moral depravity brought ruin to his kingdom.

Ctesias was the first historian to explore Babylonian and Assyrian history in depth, but today his work survives only in fragments. Nevertheless, his account—especially his portraits of the power-loving Semiramis and the pleasure-loving Sardanapalus—made a lasting impression on later Greek historians.

Fragments survive of three other historians who were contemporaries of Alexander the Great: Cleitarchus, Aristobolus, and Berossus. A native of Mesopotamia, Berossus was the first writer to devote an entire work to the history of Mesopotamia. His purpose was to introduce the Greeks of the Hellenistic Age to his culture. As a priest of the god Marduk of Babylon, Berossus could read cuneiform and had access to temple archives.

In the third century B.C.E., Philo of Byzantium drew up a list of the "Seven Wonders of the Ancient World." Numbered among them were the astounding Hanging Gardens of Babylon, already celebrated by Ctesias.

Mesopotamia continued to attract the attention of a variety of Greek writers as a new power, Rome, began to flex its imperialistic muscles and cast its eyes to the east. Notable among these authors from the reign of Augustus Caesar were the historian Diodorus Siculus and the geographer Strabo, authors whose comprehensive works survive and who wrote extensively on Babylonia and Assyria.

Meanwhile, the erotic poets Propertius and Ovid chose Semiramis as a standard of irresistible femininity against which they measured their own mistresses' beauty. In the *Metamorphoses*, moreover, a poem that had a profound effect, in later centuries, on the creative imagination of Europe, Ovid placed the poignant love story of Pyramus and Thisbe in the city of Babylon, making the tomb of King Ninus the scene of their tragic tryst.

Roman prose writers themselves soon took up the theme of Mesopotamia, like the first century C.E. polymath, Pliny the Elder, who compiled an encyclopedia of the world in Roman times, and Quintus Curtius Rufus, who authored a biography of Alexander the Great.

Even the second century C.E. Christian philosopher Athenagoras got into the act by branding Semiramis lewd and diabolical.

All these classical writers helped to sustain Mesopotamia's reputation as a land of sensual riches and seductive wealth in an era when its actual cities were becoming mere tokens of their former selves. Through literature a myth of Mesopotamia was born that would nourish its legacy to later ages.

BORROWED WORDS

Long before classical authors were using words to describe Mesopotamia, Mesopotamian words were entering the languages of ancient Greece and Rome. Because Greek and Roman civilization shaped the later civilization of Europe, many of these same words are now a part of the English language. Thus the legacy of Mesopotamia is woven into the fabric of our thought and speech.

The main mechanism for this transfer was commerce, for as Mideastern commodities traveled west in caravans and ships, their names traveled with them as well.

Most are associated with plants: the crocus and the poppy; the cherry and the carob; and such ingredients as cumin and saffron, sesame and aromatic myrrh. Add to these the minerals jasper and gypsum, and naphtha. All in all, there are about 50 words in ancient Greek that are not Greek in origin but can be traced etymologically to Akkadian and, in some cases, back to Sumerian. Even the word "gum" may be Sumerian, a shortened form of ancient "shim-gam-gam-ma." Surprisingly, the common English words "sack" and "cane" may also have Sumerian ancestries.

It is hard to say how old the transfer is, but it may reach back to the second millennium B.C.E. and the age of Homer's heroes, when Mycenaean Greeks maintained a trading station on the Syrian coast at Ugarit, for the words "sesame" and "cumin" have been found inscribed in Linear B tablets uncovered in Bronze Age Greece. Still others may have made the journey across the Aegean in the holds of the eighth-century B.C.E. Phoenician merchant ships.

SURVEYING THE SKY

Before the earliest histories, the study of the stars may also have migrated from east to west. The pictures the Sumerians saw in the sky when they connected stellar dots became the names of their constellations, names which the astronomers of Babylonia reverentially repeated. Ten of these later became fixtures in the cosmic thinking of Greece and Rome: what the Sumerians perceived as a bull became Taurus; twins, Gemini; a crab, Cancer; a lion, Leo; balance-scales, Libra; a scorpion, Scorpio; an archer, Sagittarius; a creature resembling a goat, Capricorn; a man bearing water, Aquarius; and a dragon, Hydra. The Sumerians were also the first to describe the galactic stars spilling across the night sky as the "Milky Way." And when the three Magi followed the Star of Bethlehem, they were also following the celestial teachings and lore of the Babylonians who had preceded them in studying the heavens and their signs.

TRAVELERS IN AN ANTIQUE LAND

More than a thousand years after the Three Wise Men journeyed from Persia to Bethlehem, other travelers of the Middle Ages and Renaissance—like Benjamin of Tudela, John Eldred, and Leonhart Rauwolff—journeyed from Europe to the Near East. Informed by the teachings and stories of the Bible, they visited the once-proud cities of Mesopotamia—Babylon, Nineveh, and Khorsabad—and stood upon their ruins, conjuring up in their imaginations the Tower of Babel and the palaces of Babylon's kings. The memoirs of their travels would stir the imaginations of their readers with visions of lost splendor and fallen glory.

The 10th-century Arab geographer al-Masudi and the 14th-century Berber geographer Ibn-Battuta likewise had described and marveled at the crumbled gates of Nineveh and its toppled statues.

By the early 1700s the ruins of Mesopotamia were infused with new life thanks to the first European translation of the *Arabian Nights*. Viewed through the gauzy filter of fantasy "a strange but compelling landscape emerged,

Mesopotamian and Arabian, where Biblical Babylon and Nineveh flourished in the days of the great caliphs" (McCall 1998: 187).

ROMANTIC ESCAPE

Europe's fascination with the Mideast continued during the 19th century as Western imperialism brought the two worlds into proximity. For Europeans, the sensuous image of the Mideast offered an escape from the regimentation of the Industrial Revolution and, in England, from the emotional repression of the Victorian Age. As historian John Maier has written,

Orientalism, the fascination with an exotic East, intensified under the Romantic revolt against "civilization." . . . As the European nations came to exert dominance over the cultural "other," the East was available for the projection of primitive fears and desires (without the West's losing the assurance of its superiority). (Maier 1995: 11)

The public's fascination with the Orient was further intensified by the discoveries made in Mesopotamia by 19th-century explorers and archaeologists. Egypt's splendors had always been visible, but now a new world of awesome majesty and mystery—foreshadowed in the Bible—was being unearthed.

In the British Museum, the Louvre, and the Berlin Museum, the solemn sculptures of the Babylonians and Assyrians kept silent watch

13.1   *One of the colossal bulls of Nineveh shipped to London by Layard. It stands 14 feet high.*   (Layard, *A Second Series of the Monuments of Nineveh*, 1853)

alongside a philosophical bull that, in 1851, was miraculously endowed with the power of speech by an imaginative writer named W. H. Stone:

> I am the Bull of Nineveh. I was born in the quarries beside the river, the great river. . . . As a shapeless block was my substance borne to its place; there did the hands of cunning workmen fashion me; . . . the chisel carved my ear, and I heard; the tool opened my eyes, and I saw. . . . Beside me was a companion like myself; we two guarded the threshold . . . I felt myself the guardian of the nation's history, the emblem of its power, and the thought stamped itself on my features in a smile that has endured until now, proud at once and solemn. . . . The sound of music strikes my ear, singing and the voluptuous dance; no more the battle-car, the crash of armies, and the shout of victors. . . . Long did foreigners hold us; and by degrees the beauty of the ancient work faded: walls crumbled, roofs decayed. . . . At length, the building tottered and fell; elsewhere, fire had completed the work of the conqueror; we were left to silent ruin. . . . At length the shrouding earth fell. . . . Presently came one [the archaeologist] who seemed a lord. . . . Joy was in his face as he gazed on me . . . in the silent steady gaze, I read my changed condition . . . my long slumber, my inglorious waking, and I felt my fallen state. And my shame was clear . . . I was sad, for my pride was fallen. I was borne down beside my own ancient river . . . I was tossed many days on the heaving waters. Now I stand in a strange land [England]. . . . They say I am far from my violated home, in a city [London] prouder, greater, more glorious than my native realm; but boast not, ye vainglorious creatures of an hour. I have outlived many might kingdoms, perchance I may be destined to survive one more. (McCall 1995: 196–97)

Thus, an effusive bull from Nineveh bespoke the fate of the British Empire.

INSPIRATION AND IMAGINATION

Mesopotamia and Western Art

For many European artists living in an age of mercantile empire, the theme of the rise and fall of imperial power was expressed through the imagery of ancient Mesopotamia.

To those familiar with the Bible, the Tower of Babel taught a lesson about the consequences of reckless human ambition. But Pieter Breugel, both Elder and Younger, saw the Tower rising in the midst of the 16th-century Flemish city in which they lived, and so painted it in a Renaissance setting of a latter-day ambition. Other artists portrayed the famed tower with less moral relevance but with greater historical accuracy as a towering feature of Babylon's grandeur. The 17th-century Dutch engraver Olfert Dapper took his cue from descriptions of the Greek historians, while the 18th-century German engraver Johann Bernard Fischer von Erlach drew upon his training in the history of architecture.

In the 19th century, Gustave Doré through engraving and J. M. W. Turner through watercolor offered archaeological illustrations of the Bible, including scenes set in Mesopotamia. But in the Romantic age, sensual imagination won out over dry fact. In lush oils, Eugène Delacroix and Edgar Dégas retold the tales of Semiramis and Sardanapalus, and Dante Gabriel Rossetti and Sir Lawrence Alma-Tadema summoned up the goddess Astarte and fertile Spring. Of his visionary canvasses of Nineveh and Babylon, John Martin proclaimed: "Without demanding the clear daylight of truth, . . . the mind is content to find delight in the contemplation of the grand and the marvellous" (McCall 1995: 189).

Mesopotamia and Western Literature

The most famous European authors to be inspired by Mesopotamia were men of very different temperament: the 18th-century French satirist Voltaire and the 19th-century English Romantic poet Lord Byron.

Voltaire used ancient Babylonian life as a background for two satirical novels, *Zadig* and *The Princess of Babylon*. Like *Candide*, both these works pointed up the foibles of man and the absurdity of human society. Voltaire's most popular work on a Mesopotamian theme, however, was a tragedy entitled *Semiramis*.

Three of Byron's *Hebrew Melodies* dealt with Mesopotamia's connection with Jewish history: "The Destruction of Sennacherib," "By the Rivers of Babylon We Sat Down and Wept," and "Vision of Belshazzar." Like Voltaire, Byron's most popular work on a Mesopotamian theme was a tragedy. Entitled *Sardanapalus*, it explored the story of a man (not unlike Byron himself) who rose from indolence to action, from self-indulgence to self-sacrifice.

Both plays did not seek to recapture the authentic flavor of ancient times as much as they sought to use the past as a stage setting on which to comment upon contemporary society and the human condition.

The ancient artifacts and literature of Mesopotamia continued to inspire writers of the 20th century, among them Armand Schwerner, A. R. Ammons, John Gardner, and Denise Levertov. The modern translation of cuneiform texts had special impact as writers explored the primal power of vanished civilizations and the need to reclaim a lost truth hidden beneath the detritus of a forgotten world. Playing a distinctive role in the writers' quest were the literary figures of Ishtar (a symbol of womanly power) and Gilgamesh (a man who searched for permanence and saw it slip irretrievably from his grasp). As in centuries past, so in the modern—or even postmodern—era: the legacy of Mesopotamia has become a stimulus to articulate questions of enduring and transtemporal relevance.

Mesopotamia and Western Music

The legacy of Mesopotamia was also given a musical dimension by Western composers who were motivated to bring its "unheard melodies" back to life.

Relying on Herodotus and the Book of Daniel, Handel used the theme of Belshazzar to create his grandest oratorio.

Both Mozart and Beethoven planned, but never completed, works on Mesopotamian themes: Mozart, an opera based on the life of Semiramis (and inspired by Voltaire's play); and Beethoven, a companion piece to *The Ruins of Athens* set in Babylon.

Like Mozart who had been inspired by Voltaire's play, Rossini went on to complete an opera, *Semiramide*. And both Berlioz and Liszt wrote pieces about Sardanapalus: Berlioz, a prize-winning cantata, and Liszt, an opera. The most famous opera on a Mesopotamian theme, however, is by Verdi. Based on the career of Nebuchadnezzar, *Nabucco* features a noble chorus composed of Hebrew prisoners of war.

In the 20th century, Prokofiev and Martinu were among the composers who were influenced by the rediscovery of Mesopotamian civilization. As in the case of 20th-century literature, the century's music was especially affected by the images of Ishtar and Gilgamesh, whose personalities had been revived through new decipherments and translations.

Mesopotamia in the Movies

When it comes to movies, ancient Egypt has won more Oscars than Mesopotamia. There are no Tigris-and-Euphrates monarchs, not even Semiramis, who can hold a candle (or an oil lamp) to Cleopatra. And thanks to the disintegration of Mesopotamian corpses, no mummies endure to act out the role of monster.

Mesopotamia does, however, rank in cinematic history as the setting of one of the most famous silent films of all times, W. D. Griffith's classic epic *Intolerance*. Filmed on a 250-acre Hollywood lot, *Intolerance* literally had a cast of thousands, including 4,000 extras for Babylonian crowd scenes and 16,000 for battle scenes. The set included a mock palace with 50-foot columns topped by elephants, still standing to awe visitors as late as 1931.

The script of the film interwove four stories, the earliest set in Babylon, that illustrated the persistence of bigotry in human history.

AN ENDURING LEGACY

The works of art, literature, music, and cinema that we have already met represent creative acts on the part of individuals who were consciously influenced by the legacy of Mesopotamia. But the legacy of Mesopotamia also works its will upon individuals who are unconscious of its very existence. Indeed, it is in its unconscious

effects that Mesopotamia has exerted its most profound influence upon our culture.

Our culture, for example, would not be what it is without the Sumerians' invention of the world's first wheeled vehicles. Thus, not Henry Ford but a nameless Sumerian, is the ultimate father of the automobile and of the mechanical complications it has added to our everyday lives.

The Sumerians are also the first people we know of who sought to measure time with precision. Their sexigesimal system of counting is the basis of our 60-minute hour and, by extension, the 60-second minute. They or, according to Herodotus, the Babylonians were the first to invent the sundial and to divide day and night into multiples of six: 12 units of daylight, 12 units of night, and 24 hours of the two combined. As a result, the hand of Mesopotamia still determines the hourly length of the traditional workday and even the length of our electronic entertainment (half-hour or hour TV shows) when our workday has stopped. Indeed, not only our notion of time but also our concept of space is still sexigesimal: witness the 360-degree circle and its application to measurement and navigation.

Furthermore, the rapt attention millions give to their daily newspaper horoscopes is a form of unconscious homage that the 21st century pays to the priests who, unaided by telescope, scanned the skies of Babylonia 4,000 years ago and more. Some of the astrological signs we were born under still bear names, albeit in Latin, that recall the stellar images they drew.

On Earth, the idea of the city is theirs to claim as well. The teeming metropolis was born not along the thin edges of Egypt's Nile, but on the broad alluvial plains of the Tigris and Euphrates. It was the pulsing city that created the critical mass of talent out of which civilization grew and the arts first flourished. Indeed, so massive were ancient Babylon and

Nineveh that their muddy ruins still defy annihilation.

And what would civilization be without writing, another Sumerian invention? In fact, would civilization "be" at all without the ability to record and pass on the experience of the past? Though this book is printed in an alphabet, the oldest alphabet ever found (at Syrian Ugarit) was composed of cuneiform characters arranged in the same sequence that our own ABC's still follow. If, then, the Sumerians cannot claim to have invented the alphabet themselves, we must give them credit for discovering the raw materials out of which a true alphabet was later constructed.

But writing alone does not explain civilization. Civilization requires an abiding continuity for which education is essential so that the knowledge and values of the past can be transmitted to a new generation. For thousands of years the people of Mesopotamia recognized the social importance of education and conceived of it not in narrow vocational terms but in broader humanistic ones. "Because you didn't nurture your humanity," wrote one scribe to his son, "you broke my heart."

We cannot know if this respect for education was passed on to later ages. But the high value Judaism assigns to education—the word itself in Hebrew means "dedication"—and the veneration Judaism gives to the written word may in part stem from its contact with Mesopotamian beliefs. In similar fashion, we cannot know if the respect for law in Judaism and the classical world was, in part, a reflex of familiarity with Mesopotamian legal codes and the role of Mesopotamian law in building a more just and stable society. But even if Mesopotamian thought did not have such effects, the people of Mesopotamia were nevertheless trailblazers on the path to higher civilization. To the extent that we are their beneficiaries, we are enriched by their legacy and owe them our thanks.

DETROIT OF THE CHALDEES

Abraham, the peripatetic patriarch, traced his lineage to "Ur of the Chaldees," and thus proclaimed his Mesopotamian origins. Other Chaldaeans, but of a much later date, have traveled farther than Abraham could have ever dreamed. Not by caravan but by boat and plane they came, crossing both the Mediterranean and Atlantic to reach a new world of opportunity, the United States.

Today, they number over 75,000, a mere 10 percent of those still living in Iraq, but they form a vital component of America's population. They brought with them the sturdy equipment of most Old World immigrants, abiding family loyalty and a strong work ethic, coupled with a trait they shared with their mercantile ancestors from old Babylonia, a courageous entrepreneural spirit.

The Chaldaeans immigrated to America beginning in the early 1900s and then in greater numbers in the 1960s and 1970s when U.S. immigration laws were liberalized. Most settled in Detroit, Michigan, where auto assembly lines held out the promise of steady work. After the riots of 1967 when much of Detroit's inner city was torched, they took up the economic slack and became grocers and party-store owners in locations where others dared not open their doors. Today, 80 percent of America's Chaldaean families still live in metropolitan Detroit, where they play an important role in the city's business and professional life. Thanks to their contributions, a Chaldaean cultural center, the first in the Western Hemisphere, is being constructed in the Detroit suburb of West Bloomfield.

Like Abraham's father and grandfather, most of Detroit's Chaldaeans can trace their ancestry to northern Mesopotamia, to a cluster of villages north of Mosul centered around the village of Telkaif, a name in Arabic that means "the hill of good life."

But though many Chaldaeans can speak Arabic, the major language of Iraq, their native tongue is Aramaic, the language of their Babylonian ancestors. Nor is their religion Islam, the dominant religion of Iraq and most of the Middle East. Instead, it is Catholicism, because of the missionary activity of Thomas the Apostle and his disciples. In their liturgy, they use not the Latin of the Roman Church but the classic Aramaic that Thomas—and even Jesus himself—once spoke.

In Aramaic, in fact, the Arabic village of Telkaif, "the hill of good life," is called Telkeppe, "the hill of stones." To many Chaldaeans in decades past, "good life" was not to be found on a hill of stones but in a new nation across the sea. And so Mesopotamian life was transplanted from the Near East to the New World.

TWIN LEGACIES

In 1937 long before the atomic age, American author Stephen Vincent Benét wrote a science fiction tale about civilization's future. In the story a young man, the son of a priest, journeys across a nuclear wasteland toward the sacred ruins of the "Place of the Gods." What he finds is not a place of the gods at all but a city that was once inhabited by men, men who were hungry and "ate knowledge too fast," inviting their own destruction and the devastation of the world.

In a sealed room in a skyscraper, the young man finds the body of a "god" sitting in a chair, gazing out a window as he had done just before the final holocaust.

You could see that he would not have run away. He had sat at his window, watching his city die—then he himself had died. But it is better to lose one's life than one's spirit—and you could see from the face that the spirit had not been lost. I knew that, if I touched him, he would fall into dust—and yet, there was something unconquered in that face. (Benét 1942: 482)

Benét entitled his story "By the Waters of Babylon," recalling the ancient verse from Psalm 137: "By the rivers of Babylon, there we sat down, yea, we wept, when we remembered Zion."

The legacy of Mesopotamia is, on the one hand, a legacy of creative cooperation. Through such cooperation the first civilized communities arose. But the legacy of Mesopotamia is also a legacy of destructive conquest. The legacy of Mesopotamia is thus not one legacy but two, and between them the future leaders of modern Iraq—and the world—must choose.

Like a sword, every legacy has two edges.

The Middle East is the place where civilization began, but—according to biblical prophecy—it is also the place where civilization will end. Armageddon, the site of the final conflict, is an actual place in Israel: Har Megiddo, the mount ("har") that is all that is left of the ancient fortress-town of Megiddo.

Should a nuclear Armageddon ever come, life may someday return to our planet. In those remote days, the young may journey across an atomic wasteland, questing for a new home. Should that time ever come, it will be well-watered, fertile valleys that they will seek out on which to rebuild civilization. The valleys of the Tigris and Euphrates will then beckon to them even as they welcomed the first settlers on their soil millennia ago. And so, Mesopotamian life will be reborn, and new cities—hopefully, wiser cities—will rise again.

13.2   *A pile of architectural fragments dating to Roman times lie on the ground at Uruk, one of the most ancient of Sumer's cities.*   (William Kennett Loftus, *Travels and Researches in Chaldaea and Susiana,* 1857)

Someday, a postnuclear pioneer may uncover an ancient statue in the dust and, touching it, recognize "something unconquered in that face."

READING

Continuity and Change

Gordon 1987: *linguae francae* and forgotten scripts.

The Memory of Foreigners

Dalley 1998: influence on Israel and the Bible; influence in the Sassanian period and early Islam; Dalley and Reyes 1998: contact and influence in the Greek world; Drews 1973: the Greek historians; Geller 1995: influence on Hellenistic Judaism; Kuhrt 1995: influence on Greek and Hellenistic thought; Larsen 1995: "Babel/Bible" controversy; Lundquist 1995: Babylon in European thought; Maier 1995: the ancient Near East in modern thought; McCall 1998: rediscovery and aftermath; Schmandt-Besserat 1976: creativity and influence.

Inspiration and Imagination

Maier 1995: influence on creative thought; McCall 1998: inspirational power.

An Enduring Legacy

Black and Green 1998: zodiac; Kramer 1967: pillars of civilization; Kramer 1981: Sumerian innovations; Hallo 1996: modern Western institutions; James and Thorpe 1994: the "Baghdad battery"; Pingree 1998: astrology and astronomy; Thompsen 1960: the debt of Europe to Babylon, with special attention to vocabulary.

Detroit of the Chaldees

Kamoo 1999: bibliography of ancient and modern Chaldaean history; Sengsong 1999: Chaldaean-Americans and ethnic identity.

Twin Legacies

Benét 1942: short story.

CHRONOLOGICAL TABLE _____

The table below details the major technological changes and political and military events that affected people's lives in ancient Mesopotamia. Developments in other areas—such as literature and art or spiritual outlook—are described elsewhere in this book.

Because our evidence for chronology tends to be more hazy or incomplete the farther back into time we go, earlier dates cited in this table are generally less certain than later ones. Also, all rounded-off numbers should be regarded as approximations.

For further discussion of the events and personalities that are mentioned in the table, see chapter 2, "Archaeology and History," and chapter 3, "Government and Society."

Besides simplification and clarification, an additional virtue of this table is chronological compression. Viewing Mesopotamian history in "fast forward" reveals the devastating give-and-take that characterized the country's experience: repeatedly, invaders and armies swept across its landscape, leaving only destruction behind. In the light of such persistent destruction, the resilience of ancient Iraq's people is all the more remarkable. In the face of death and loss, life went on.

Palaeolithic Period (70,000–9000 B.C.E.)

The Palaeolithic is the earliest period for which evidence exists of human beings inhabiting Mesopotamia. During this period, people survive by gathering food through hunting, fishing, and picking wild edible plants, and they make their most durable tools from stone. The Palaeolithic is also the longest chapter of humanity's early history.

Mesolithic Period (9000–7000 B.C.E.)

The Mesolithic is a period of transition linking the Old Stone Age (Palaeolithic) with the revolutionary changes of the New Stone Age (Neolithic).

Neolithic Period (7000–5800 B.C.E.)

As they had been for tens of thousands of years, tools and weapons continue to be made of stone. But with the domestication of plants and animals, a more mobile life based solely on hunting, fishing, and gathering ends and a more settled village life based on farming and raising livestock begins. During this time, the first pottery and the first bricks are made.

Ubaid Period (5800–4000 B.C.E.)

Farmers in northern Mesopotamia employ irrigation canals to water and enlarge their cultivated fields. The earliest brick temples are built. Metallurgy begins as copper starts to replace stone as the principal material for tools and weapons.

5000 B.C.E.

Farmers from the north settle in southern Mesopotamia.

Uruk Period (3750–3150 B.C.E.)

Semitic nomads from the deserts of Syria and northern Arabia invade southern Mesopotamia, producing a mixed population.

3500 B.C.E.

The Sumerians settle in southern Mesopotamia. One of their communities, Uruk, develops into the world's first city. Other settlements become bustling urban centers as well. Writing is invented and cylinder seals are used. In addition, the plough, the potter's wheel, and the first wheeled vehicles are devised. Because of its added hardness and durability, bronze replaces copper in weapons and tools.

Early Dynastic Period (2900–2334 B.C.E.)

Hereditary monarchies arise in individual Sumerian city-states and vie for military supremacy in the south. Among the most powerful of these cities are Kish, Uruk, Ur, Lagash, and Umma. The Royal Graves of Ur (about 2600–2500 B.C.E.) date to this period.

2500 B.C.E.

The Elamites from Iran invade and briefly rule southern Mesopotamia but are driven out by an alliance of Sumerian cities.

Akkadian Period (2334–2193 B.C.E.)

Sargon the Great (2334–2279 B.C.E.), the king of Semitic Akkad, conquers the cities of Sumer and founds the world's first empire, with Agade as its capital. Under his grandson, *Naram-Sin* (2254–2218 B.C.E.), the empire extends to Armenia and Iran.

Invading Gutians from Iran conquer Sumer and destroy Agade. *Gudea* (2141–2122 B.C.E.) of Lagash leads his city to prosperity. Under the leadership of Uruk, the Gutians are expelled.

Neo-Sumerian Period (2112–2004 B.C.E.)

Ur-Nammu (2112–2095 B.C.E.) founds the glorious Third Dynasty of Ur. Under his son, *Shulgi* (2094–2047 B.C.E.), Ur's power reaches to Elam and the Zagros Mountains. Later, its power declines and the city is destroyed by the Elamites.

Old Babylonian and Old Assyrian Period (2000–1600 B.C.E.)

Individual city-states (Isin and Larsa in the south; Assur and Mari in the north) assert their autonomy.

Sumer is conquered by Semitic Amorites from the Syrian desert. Around 1900 B.C.E., the first Amorite dynasty is established in the city of Babylon. Despite competition from Mari, *Hammurabi* (1792–1750 B.C.E.), Babylon's sixth Amorite king, gains control over most of Mesopotamia. The dynasty ends, however, when Mesopotamia is invaded by the Hittites from Turkey.

Middle Assyrian Period (1600–1000 B.C.E.)

In the aftermath of Hittite destruction, the Kassites take control of Babylon.

In the north, the Hurrians establish a Mitannian empire and rule Assyria. But when they are defeated by the Hittites in the

14th century B.C.E., Assyria reclaims its independence.

The Assyrian king, *Tukulti-Ninurta I* (1244–1208 B.C.E.), captures Babylon, but it is later retaken by the Kassites.

The Elamites invade Babylonia, bringing an end to Kassite rule. Later, the Elamites are driven out by the Babylonian king, *Nebuchadnezzar I* (1124–1103 B.C.E.).

Assyria reaches new heights of imperialistic success under *Tiglathpileser I* (1115–1077 B.C.E.). Upon his death, his empire is smashed by Aramaean tribesmen and insurgents from the Zagros Mountains.

Iron supplants bronze as the metal for weapons and tools.

Neo-Assyrian Period (1000–605 B.C.E.)

Based in northern Mesopotamia, the Assyrians reestablish and expand their empire under a series of aggressive kings: *Ashurnasirpal II* (883–859 B.C.E.), *Shalmaneser III* (858–824 B.C.F.), *Tiglathpileser III* (744–727 B.C.E.), *Sargon II* (721–705 B.C.E.), *Sennacherib* (704–681 B.C.E.), *Esarhaddon* (680–669 B.C.E.), and *Ashurbanipal* (668–627 B.C.E.). Babylonia, Syria, Israel, and Egypt all surrender to their armies. However, the Assyrians overextend themselves, and the Assyrian Empire falls prey to a coalition of Medes from western Iran and Babylonian Chaldaeans who in 612 B.C.E. sack its capital, Nineveh.

Neo-Babylonian Period (625-539 B.C.E.)

From his capital city of Babylon, the Chaldaean king *Nebuchadnezzar II* (604–562 B.C.E.) regains control over Syria and Israel, destroying Jerusalem's Temple and transporting Jewish prisoners of war to Babylon (the "Babylonian Captivity"). During his 42-year reign, he builds the fabled "Tower of Babel" and presides over a Babylonian cultural renaissance.

The Persian Period (539-331 B.C.E.)

Nevertheless, in 539 B.C.E., the Persian king *Cyrus the Great* succeeds in capturing Babylon from *Nabonidus* (555–539 B.C.E.) and absorbs its former territories into his empire.

The Hellenistic Period (331–126 B.C.E.)

Leading a combined army of Macedonians and Greeks, *Alexander the Great* (356–323 B.C.E.) defeats the Persian army and takes Babylon, which he plans to make the capital of his new worldwide empire stretching from Greece to India. When he dies in Babylon eight years later at the age of 32, his generals divide up his conquests. One of these, Seleucus, establishes a dynasty that rules Mesopotamia until 126 B.C.F., when the Parthian king *Artabanus II* (128–124 B.C.E.) seizes Babylonia.

Parthian Period (126 B.C.E.–227 C.E.)

The Parthians rule Mesopotamia and Iran.

Sassanian Period (227–651 C.E.)

After defeating the Parthians, the Sassanians hold sway over Mesopotamia until its conquest by the militant forces of Islam.

LIST OF MUSEUMS WITH MAJOR MESOPOTAMIAN COLLECTIONS

France
Paris: The Louvre

Germany
Berlin: Staatliche Museen

Iraq
Baghdad: Iraq Museum

United Kingdom
London: British Museum

United States
Chicago: Oriental Institute (University of Chicago)
New York: Metropolitan Museum of Art
Philadelphia: University Museum (University of Pennsylvania)

BIBLIOGRAPHY

Note to the Reader

A number of general works are excellent sources of information about life in ancient Mesopotamia. Handy, one-volume works include P. Bienkowski and A. Millard, *Dictionary of the Ancient Near East* (Philadelphia: University of Pennsylvania Press, 2000); G. Contenau, *Everyday Life in Babylon and Assyria* (New York: St. Martin's Press, 1954); K. R. Nemet-Nejat, *Daily Life in Ancient Mesopotamia* (Westport, Conn.: Greenwood, 1997); Susan Pollock, *Ancient Mesopotamia* (New York: Cambridge University Press, 1999); and H. W. F. Saggs, *Everyday Life in Babylonia & Assyria* (New York: Dorset, 1965). Multivolume sets include E. M.

Meyers, ed., *The Oxford Encyclopedia of Archaeology in the Near East*. 5 vols. (New York: Oxford University Press, 1997), and J. M. Sasson, ed., *Civilizations of the Ancient Near East*. 4 vols. (New York: Scribner's, 1995). See also M. Roaf, *Cultural Atlas of Mesopotamia and the Ancient Near East* (New York: Facts On File, 1990).

Other general works of interest, as well as more specialized books and articles, are listed below.

Ongoing research and new discoveries can be followed in the pages of such periodicals as *Archaeology*, the *American Journal of Archaeology*, the *Journal of Cuneiform Studies*, the *Journal of Near Eastern Studies*, and the *Journal of the American Oriental Society*.

Adams, R. McC. *The Evolution of Urban Society: Early Mesopotamia and Prehispanic Mexico*. Chicago: Aldine-Atherton, 1966.

———. *Heartland of Cities*. Chicago: University of Chicago Press, 1981.

———. *Land behind Baghdad*. Chicago: University of Chicago Press, 1965.

———. "The Origin of Cities." *Scientific American* 203, no. 48 (September 1960): 153–55, 276+.

———, and H. J. Nissen, *The Uruk Countryside: The Natural Setting of Urban Societies*. Chicago: University of Chicago Press, 1972.

———. *The Age of God-Kings: TimeFrame 3000–1500 B.C.* (TimeFrame series). Alexandria, Va.: Time-Life Books, 1987.

Ahmed, S. S. *Southern Mesopotamia in the Time of Ashurbanipal*. The Hague: Mouton, 1968.

Aitkens, M. J. *Physics and Archaeology*. 2d ed. Oxford: Clarendon Press, 1974.

Albenda, P. "Assyrian Sacred Trees in the Brooklyn Museum." *Iraq* 56 (1994): 123–33.

———. *The Palace of Sargon, King of Assyria*. Paris: Éditions Recherche sur les Civilisations, 1986.

Albrektson, B. *History and the Gods: An Essay on the Idea of Historical Events as Divine Manifestations in the Ancient Near East and in Israel*. Lund, Sweden: CWK Gleerup, 1967.

Alcock, S. E., ed. *The Early Roman Empire in the East*. Oxford: Oxbow, 1997.

Alexander, S. M. "Notes on the Jewelry from Ur." In *The Legacy of Sumer*, edited by D. Schmandt-Besserat. Malibu, Calif.: Undena, 1976.

Algaze, G. *The Uruk World System: The Dynamics of Expansion of Early Mesopotamian Civilization*. Chicago: University of Chicago Press, 1993.

Ali, A., trans. *Islam: The Qur'an*. Princeton: Princeton University Press, 1988.

Alster, B. *Dumuzi's Dream*. Copenhagen: Akademisk Forlag, 1972.

———. "Epic Tales from Ancient Sumer: Enmerkar, Lugalbanda, and Other Cunning Heroes." In *Civilizations of the Ancient Near East*, edited by J. M. Sasson et al. New York: Scribner's, 1995.

———. "Ninurta and the Turtle." *Journal of Cuneiform Studies* 24 (1972): 120–25.

———. *The Proverbs of Ancient Sumer: The World's Earliest Proverb Collection*. Bethesda, Md.: CDL Press, 1997.

———. "Sumerian Love Songs." *Revue d'Assyriologie et d'Archéologie Orientale* 79 (1985), 127–59.

Amiet, P. *Art of the Ancient Near East*. New York: Abrams, 1977.

Anderson, J. "Layard, Sir Austen Henry." In *The Dictionary of Art*, edited by J. Turner. New York: Grove's Dictionaries, 1996.

Anderson, J. K. *Hunting in the Ancient World*. Berkeley: University of California Press, 1985.

Andrae, E. W., and R. M. Boehmer. *Sketches by an Excavator*. Berlin: Gebr. Mann Verlag, 1992.

Armstrong, J. A. "Ceramics: Mesopotamian Ceramics of the Neolithic through Neo-Babylonian Periods." In *The Oxford Encyclopedia of Archaeology in the Near East*, edited by E. M. Meyers. New York: Oxford University Press, 1997.

Arzt, J. "Near Eastern Royal Women." *Yale Graduate Journal of Anthropology*. 5 (1995), 45–56.

Astour, M. C. "Overland Trade Routes in Ancient Western Asia." In *Civilizations of the Ancient Near East*, edited by J. M. Sasson, et al. New York: Scribner's, 1995.

Aström P., ed. *High, Middle, or Low? Acts of the International Congress on Absolute Chronology*. 3 vols. Göteborg: Göteborg University, 1987–1989.

Ausubel, N. *The Book of Jewish Knowledge*. New York: Crown, 1964.

Avalos, H. I. *Illness and Health Care in the Ancient Near East: The Role of the Temple in Greece, Mesopotamia and Israel*. Atlanta: Scholars Press, 1995.

Azarpay, G. "Proportions in Ancient Near Eastern Art." In *Civilizations of the Ancient Near East*, edited by J. M. Sasson et al. New York: Scribner's, 1995.

Babil, the City of Witchcraft and Wine: The Name and Fame of Babylon in Medieval Arabic Geographical Texts. Winona Lake, Ind.: Recherches et Publications/Eisenbrauns, 1995.

Badawy, A. *Architecture in Ancient Egypt and the Near East*. Cambridge, Mass.: Massachusetts Institute of Technology Press, 1966.

Bahrani, Z. "Jewelry and Personal Arts in Ancient Western Asia." In *Civilizations of the Ancient Near East*, edited by J. M. Sasson et al. New York: Scribner's, 1995.

Baker, H. S. *Furniture in the Ancient World: Origins & Evolution, 3100–475 B.C.* London: The Connoisseur, 1966.

Banning, E. B. "The Neolithic Period: Triumphs of Architecture, Agriculture, and Art." *Near Eastern Archaeology* 61 (1998): 188–237.

Barag, D. *A Catalogue of Glass in the Department of Western Asiatic Antiquities in the British Museum. Vol. I: Ur III – A.D. 200*. London: British Museum, 1985.

Barbarian Tides: TimeFrame 1500–600 B.C. (TimeFrame series). Alexandria, Va.: Time-Life Books, 1987.

Barnett, R. D. *Ancient Ivories in the Middle East*. Jerusalem: Hebrew University Institute of Archaeology, 1982.

———. "Lady Layard's Jewelry." In *Archaeology in the Levant: Essays for Kathleen Kenyon*, edited by R.

Moorey and P. Parr. Warminster, United Kingdom: Aris & Phillips, 1978.

———. *A Catalogue of the Nimrud Ivories in the British Museum*. London: British Museum, 1975.

———. *Sculptures from the North Palace of Ashurbanipal at Nineveh*. London: British Museum, 1976.

———, E. Bleibtreu, and G. Turner. *Sculptures from the Southwest Palace of Sennacherib at Nineveh*. London: British Museum, 1998.

———, and A. Lorenzini, *Assyrian Sculpture in the British Museum*. London: British Museum, 1975.

Barton, G. A. *Archaeology and the Bible*. 7th ed. Philadelphia: American Sunday-School Union, 1937.

Bass, G. F. "Sea and River Craft in the Ancient Near East." In *Civilizations of the Ancient Near East*, edited by J. M. Sasson et al. New York: Scribner's, 1995.

Beaulieu, P.-A. "King Nabonidus and the Neo-Babylonian Empire." In *Civilizations of the Ancient Near East*, edited by J. M. Sasson et al. New York: Scribner's, 1995.

———. *The Reign of Nabonidus, King of Babylon, 556–539 B.C.* New Haven, Conn.: Yale University Press, 1990.

Beaumont, P. "Water Resources and Their Management in the Middle East." In *Change and Development in the Middle East: Essays in Honour of W. B. Fisher*, edited by J. I. Clarke and H. Bowen-Jones. London: Methuen, 1981.

———, G. H. Blake, and J. M. Wagstaff. *The Middle East: A Geographical Study*. 2d ed. New York: John Wiley, 1988.

Beek, M. A. *Atlas of Mesopotamia*. New York: Thomas Nelson, 1962.

Beitzel, B. "Travel and Communications, The Old Testament World." In *Anchor Bible Dictionary*, edited by D. N. Freedman. New York: Doubleday, 1992.

Bender, B. *Farming in Prehistory*. London: J. Baker, 1975.

Benét, S. V. *Selected Works of Stephen Vincent Benét*. New York: Farrar & Rinehart 1942.

Bermant, C., and M. Weitzman. *Ebla: A Revelation in Archaeology*. New York: Times Books, 1979.

Bersani, L. and U. Dutoit. *The Forms of Violence: Narrative in Assyrian Art and Modern Culture*. New York: Schocken, 1985.

Bibby, G. *Looking for Dilmun*. London: Penguin, 1972.

Biblical Archaeologist 47 (1984): 65–120 (articles on Mari by M.-H. Gates, D. Pardee, J. Glass, A. Lemaire, and J. Sasson).

Bickerman, E. J. *Chronology of the Ancient World*. London: Thames & Hudson, 1980.

Bienkowski, P., and A. Millard, eds. *Dictionary of the Ancient Near East*. Philadelphia: University of Pennsylvania Press, 2000.

Bier, C. "Textile Arts in Ancient Western Asia." In *Civilizations of the Ancient Near East*, edited by J. M. Sasson, et al. New York: Scribner's, 1995.

Biggs, R. D. "Ebla Texts." In *Anchor Bible Dictionary*, edited by D. N. Freedman. New York: Doubleday, 1992.

———. "Medicine in Ancient Mesopotamia." *History of Science* 8 (1969): 94–105.

———. "Medicine, Surgery, and Public Health in Ancient Mesopotamia." In *Civilizations of the Ancient Near East*, edited by J. M. Sasson et al. New York: Scribner's, 1995.

———. *ŠÀ. ZI.GA: Ancient Mesopotamian Potency Incantations*. Locust Valley, N.Y.: J. J. Augustin, 1967.

———, and McG. Gibson, eds. *The Organization of Power: Aspects of Bureaucracy in the Ancient Near East*. Chicago: University of Chicago Press, 1987.

Bigwood, J. M. "Ctesias' Description of Babylon." *American Journal of Ancient History* 3 (1978): 32–52.

Bimson, M. "Cosmetic Pigments from the 'Royal Cemetery' of Ur." *Iraq* 42 (1980): 75–79.

Bing, J. D. "Adapa and Mortality." *Ugarit-Forschungen* 16 (1984): 53–56.

Black, J. A. *Reading Sumerian Poetry*. Ithaca, N.Y.: Cornell University Press, 1998.

———, and A. R. Green. *Gods, Demons, and Symbols of Ancient Mesopotamia: An Illustrated Dictionary*. 2d ed. London: British Museum, 1998.

———, and W. J. Tait. "Archives and Libraries in the Ancient Near East." In *Civilizations of the Ancient Near East*, edited by J. M. Sasson et al. New York: Scribner's, 1995.

Bleibtreu, E. "Grisly Assyrian Record of Torture and Death." *Biblical Archaeology Review* (January/February 1991): 52–61, 75.

Boehmer, R. M. "Uruk-Warka." In *The Oxford Encyclopedia of Archaeology in the Near East*, edited by E. M. Meyers. New York: Oxford University Press, 1997.

Boiy, T., et al. *Changing Watercourses in Babylonia: Towards a Reconstruction of the Ancient Environment in Lower Mesopotamia*. Chicago: University of Chicago Press, 1999.

Borowski, O. "Irrigation." In *The Oxford Encyclopedia of Archaeology in the Near East*, edited by E. M. Meyers. New York: Oxford University Press, 1997.

Bottéro, J. "Akkadian Literature: An Overview." In *Civilizations of the Ancient Near East*, edited by J. M. Sasson et al. New York: Scribner's, 1995.

———. *Mesopotamia: Writing, Reasoning, and the Gods*. Chicago: University of Chicago Press, 1992.

———. *Religion in Ancient Mesopotamia*. Chicago: University of Chicago Press, 2002.

———. *Textes culinaires Mésopotamiens/Mesopotamian Culinary Texts*. Winona Lake, Ind.: Eisenbrauns, 1995.

———, et al. *Everyday Life in Ancient Mesopotamia*. Baltimore: Johns Hopkins University Press, 2001.

———, E. Cassin, and J. Vercoutter, eds. *The Near East: The Early Civilizations*. New York: Delacorte, 1967.

———, C. Herrenschmidt, and J-P. Vernant, eds. *Ancestor of the West: Writing, Reasoning, and Religion in Mesopotamia, Elam, and Greece*. Chicago: University of Chicago Press, 2000.

Boudet, J., et al. *The Ancient Art of Warfare*. 2 vols. London: Barrie & Rockliff, 1966.

Bower, B. "Vessel Residue Taps into Early Brewing." *Science News* 142 (November 7, 1992): 310.

Brackman, A. *The Luck of Nineveh: Archaeology's Great Adventure*. New York: McGraw-Hill, 1978.

Braidwood L. *Digging beyond the Tigris*. New York: Henry Schuman, 1953.

———, et al. *Prehistoric Archeology along the Zagros Flanks*. Chicago: University of Chicago Press, 1983.

Braidwood, R. J. "The Agricultural Revolution." *Scientific American* 203, no. 48 (September 1960): 130–34, 276.

———. *The Near East and the Foundations of Civilization*. Eugene, Oreg.: Oregon State System of Higher Education, 1952.

———. "The Background for Sumerian Civilization in the Euphrates-Tigris-Karun Drainage Basin." In *The Legacy of Sumer*, edited by D. Schmandt-Besserat. Malibu, Calif.: Undena, 1976.

———, and L. Braidwood "Jarmo: A Village of Early Farmers in Iraq." *Antiquity* 24 (1950): 189–95.

Brandon, S. G. F. *Creation Legends of the Ancient Near East*. London: Hodder & Stoughton, 1963.

Brentjes, B. "The History of Elam and Achaemenid Persia: An Overview." In *Civilizations of the Ancient Near East*, edited by J. M. Sasson et al. New York: Scribner's, 1995.

Brinkman, J. A. "Babylonian under the Assyrian Empire, 745–627 B.C." *Power and Propaganda: A Symposium on Ancient Empires (=Mesopotamia: Copenhagen Studies in Assyriology*, Vol. 7), edited by M. T. Larsen. Copenhagen: Akademisk Forlag, 1976.

———. "Mesopotamian Chronology of the Historical Period." In *Ancient Mesopotamia*, 2d ed., edited by A. L. Oppenheim. Chicago: University of Chicago Press, 1977.

———. *A Political History of Post-Kassite Babylonia, 1158–722 B.C.* Rome: Pontificium Institutum Biblicum, 1968.

———. *Prelude to Empire: Babylonian Society and Politics, 747–626 B.C.* Philadelphia: University Museum, 1984.

Brown, D. M., ed. *Mesopotamia: The Mighty Kings*. New York: Time-Life, 1995.

Buccellati, G. "Amorites." In *The Oxford Encyclopedia of Archaeology in the Near East*, edited by E. M. Meyers. New York: Oxford University Press, 1997.

———. *The Amorites of the Ur III Period*. Naples: Instituto Orientale di Napoli, 1966.

———. "Ethics and Piety in the Ancient Near East." In *Civilizations of the Ancient Near East*, edited by J. M. Sasson et al. New York: Scribner's, 1995.

Buchanan, B. *Early Near East Seals in the Babylonian Collection*. New Haven, Conn.: Yale University Press, 1981.

Bulliet, R. *The Camel and the Wheel.* Cambridge, Mass.: Harvard University Press, 1990.

Burney, C. A. *The Ancient Near East.* Ithaca, N.Y.: Cornell University Press, 1977.

Burstein, S. M. *The Babyloniaca of Berossus.* Malibu, Calif.: Undena, 1978.

Butzer, K. W. "Environmental Change in the Near East and Human Impact on the Land." In *Civilizations of the Ancient Near East,* edited by J. M. Sasson, et al. New York: Scribner's, 1995.

Cameron, G. C. "Darius Carved History on Ageless Rock." *National Geographic* 98 (December 1950): 825–44.

Campbell, S., and A. R. Green, eds. *The Archaeology of Death in the Ancient Near East.* Oxford: Oxford University Press, 1995.

Canby, J. V. "A Monumental Puzzle: Reconstructing the Ur-Nammu Stela." *Expedition* 29 (1988): 54–64.

Carter, E., and M. W. Stolper. *Elam: Surveys of Political History and Archaeology.* Berkeley: University of California Press, 1984.

Cassin, E., J. Bottéro, and J. Vercoutter, eds. *The Near East: The Early Civilizations.* New York: Delacorte, 1967.

Casson, L. *Ships and Seamanship in the Ancient World.* Rev. ed. Baltimore: Johns Hopkins University Press, 1995.

———. *Travel in the Ancient World.* Baltimore: Johns Hopkins University Press, 1994.

Castriota, D. "Wall Paintings." In *The Oxford Encyclopedia of Archaeology in the Near East,* edited by E. M. Meyers. New York: Oxford, 1997.

Caubet, A., and M. Bernus-Taylor. *The Louvre: Near Eastern Antiquities.* London: Scala Publications, 1991.

Caygill, J. *Treasures of the British Museum.* New York: Harry N. Abrams, 1985.

Ceram, C. W., ed. *Hands on the Past: Pioneer Archaeologists Tell Their Own Story.* New York: Knopf, 1966.

Chadwick, R. "Calendars, Ziggurats, and the Stars." *The Canadian Society for Mesopotamian Studies Bulletin* 24 (1992): 7–24.

Chapman, R. "Weapons and Warfare." In *The Oxford Encyclopedia of Archaeology in the Near East,* edited by E. M. Meyers. New York: Oxford University Press, 1997.

Charpin, D. "The History of Ancient Mesopotamia: An Overview." In *Civilizations of the Ancient Near East,* edited by J. M. Sasson et al. New York: Scribner's 1995.

Chiera, E. *They Wrote on Clay.* Chicago: University of Chicago Press, 1959.

Childe, V. G. *Man Makes Himself.* New York: New American Library, 1951.

Christie, A. *An Autobiography.* London: Collins, 1977.

Chubb, M. *City in the Sand.* New York: Crowell, 1957.

Civil, M. "Ancient Mesopotamian Lexicography." In *Civilizations of the Ancient Near East,* edited by J. M. Sasson et al. New York: Scribner's, 1995.

———. "Education in Mesopotamia." In *Anchor Bible Dictionary,* edited by D. N. Freedman. New York: Doubleday, 1992.

———. *The Farmer's Instructions: A Sumerian Agricultural Manual (=Aula Orientalis,* Supplemento 5). Barcelona: Editorial AUSA, 1994.

———. "A Hymn to the Beer Goddess and a Drinking Song." In *Studies Presented to A. Leo Oppenheim,* edited by R. D. Biggs and J. A. Brinkman. Chicago: University of Chicago Press, 1964.

———. "Lexicography." In *Sumerological Studies in Honor of Thorkild Jacobsen,* edited by S. J. Lieberman. Chicago: University of Chicago Press, 1976.

———. "Sumerian." In *The Oxford Encyclopedia of Archaeology in the Near East,* edited by E. M. Meyers. New York: Oxford University Press, 1997.

Claiborne, R., et al. *The Birth of Writing.* New York: Time-Life, 1974.

Clayton, P. A., and M. Price. *The Seven Wonders of the Ancient World.* London: Routledge, 1988.

Cleator, P. E. *Lost Languages.* New York: John Day, 1961.

Clifford, R. J. *Creation Accounts in the Ancient Near East and in the Bible.* (Biblical Quarterly Monograph Series, 26). Washington, D.C.: Catholic Biblical Association, 1994.

Clutton-Brock, J., and C. Grigson, eds. *Animals and Archaeology.* Vol 3: *Early Herders and Their Flocks.* Oxford: B.A.R., 1984.

Cohen, M. E. *The Canonical Lamentations of Ancient Mesopotamia.* Potomac, Md.: Capital Decisions, 1988.

———. *The Cultic Calendars of the Ancient Near East.* Bethesda, Md.: CDL Press, 1993.

Cohen, R., and R. Westbrook, eds. *Amarna Diplomacy: The Beginnings of International Relations.* Baltimore: John Hopkins University Press, 1999.

Colledge, M. A. R. *Parthian Art.* Ithaca, N. Y.: Cornell University Press, 1977.

———. *The Parthian Period.* Leiden: E. J. Brill, 1986.

———. *The Parthians.* London: Thames & Hudson, 1967.

Collon, D. *Ancient Near Eastern Art.* Berkeley: University of California Press, 1995.

———. "Clothing and Grooming in Ancient Western Asia." In *Civilizations of the Ancient Near East,* edited by J. M. Sasson et al. New York: Scribner's, 1995.

———. "Depictions of Priests and Priestesses in the Ancient Near East." In *Priests and Officials in the Ancient Near East* (=*Papers of the Second Colloquium on the Ancient Near East—The City and Its Life*), edited by K. Watanabe. Heidelberg: Universitätsverlag C. Winter, 1999.

———. *First Impressions: Cylinder Seals in the Ancient Near East.* London: British Museum, 1987 and 1993.

———. *Interpreting the Past: Near Eastern Seals.* London: British Museum, 1990.

———, M. Roaf, and V. S. Curtis. "Ancient Near East, § II, 7: Dress." In *The Dictionary of Art,* edited by J. Turner. New York: Grove's Dictionaries, 1996.

Contenau, G. *Everyday Life in Babylon and Assyria.* New York: St. Martin's Press, 1954.

Coogan, M. D. *The Oxford History of the Biblical World.* New York: Oxford University Press, 1998.

———. *Stories from Ancient Canaan.* Philadelphia: Westminster, 1978.

Cook, J. M. "The Armed Forces and Communications" Chap. 10 in *The Persian Empire.* London: J. M. Dent, 1983.

———. *The Persian Empire.* London: J. M. Dent, 1983.

Cooper, J. S. and W. Heimpel. "The Sumerian Sargon Legend." *Journal of the American Oriental Society* 103 (1983): 67–82.

Cornfeld, G., and D. N. Freedman. *Archaeology of the Bible: Book by Book.* New York: Harper & Row, 1976.

Cornwall, P. B. (with appendix by A. Goetze). "On the Location of Dilmun." *Bulletin of the American Schools of Oriental Research* 103 (1946): 3–11.

Cotterell, A., ed. *The Penguin Encyclopedia of Ancient Civilizations.* London: Penguin Books, 1980.

Cottrell, L. *The Anvil of Civilization.* New York: New American Library, 1957.

———. *Land of Shinar.* London: Souvenir Press, 1955.

———. *The Quest for Sumer.* New York: Putnam's, 1965.

Crabtree, P., D. Campana, and K. Ryan, eds. *Early Animal Domestication and Its Cultural Context.* Philadelphia: University of Pennsylvania Museum, 1989.

Crawford, H. *Sumer and the Sumerians.* Cambridge: Cambridge University Press, 1991.

Crawford, H. E. W. *The Architecture of Iraq in the Third Millennium B.C.* Copenhagen: Akademisk Forlag, 1977.

———. "Mesopotamia's Invisible Exports in the Third Millennium B.C." *World Archaeology* 5 (1973): 232–41.

Crawford, V. E. "Excavations in the Swamps of Sumer." *Expedition* 14, no. 2 (1972): 12–20.

———, P. O. Harper, and H. Pittman. *Assyrian Reliefs and Ivories in the Metropolitan Museum of Art: Palace Reliefs of Ashurnasirpal II and Ivory Carvings from Nimrud.* New York: Metropolitan Museum of Art, 1980.

Crenshaw, J. L. "The Contemplative Life in the Ancient Near East." In *Civilizations of the Ancient Near East,* edited by J. M. Sasson et al. New York: Scribner's, 1995.

Crouwel, J. H., and M. A. Littauer. "Chariots." In *The Oxford Encyclopedia of Archaeology in the Near East,* edited by E. M. Meyers. New York: Oxford University Press, 1997.

———. "Wheel." In *The Oxford Encyclopedia of Archaeology in the Near East,* edited by E. M. Meyers. New York: Oxford University Press, 1997.

Cryer, F. "Chronology: Issues and Problems." In *Civilizations of the Ancient Near East,* edited by J. M. Sasson et al. New York: Scribner's, 1995.

Cunningham, G. *"Deliver Me from Evil": Mesopotamian Incantations, 2500–1200 B.C.* Rome: Pontificium Institutum Biblicum, 1997.

Curtis, J. E. *Bronzeworking Centres of Western Asia, c.1000–539 B.C.* London: British Museum, 1988.

———, ed. *Fifty Years of Mesopotamian Discovery: The Work of the British School of Archaeology in Iraq, 1932–1982.* London: British School of Archaeology in Iraq, 1982.

———. *Later Mesopotamia and Iran.* London: British Museum Press, 1995.

———. "Nimrud." In *The Oxford Encyclopedia of Archaeology in the Near East,* edited by E. M. Meyers. New York: Oxford University Press, 1997.

———, and J. E. Reade, eds. *Art and Empire: Treasures from Assyria in the British Museum.* London: British Museum, 1995.

Dales, G. "Of Dice and Men." *Journal of the American Oriental Society* 88 (1968): 14–23.

Dalley, S. "Ancient Mesopotamian Gardens." *Garden History* 21 (1993): 1–13.

———. "Ancient Mesopotamian Military Organization." In *Ancient Near Eastern Civilizations,* edited by J. M. Sasson et al. New York: Scribner's, 1995.

———. *The Legacy of Mesopotamia.* Oxford: Oxford University Press, 1998.

———. *Mari and Karana: Two Old Babylonian Cities.* London: Longman, 1984.

———. *Myths from Mesopotamia.* Oxford: Oxford University Press, 1989.

———. *Myths from Mesopotamia: Creation, The Flood, Gilgamesh and Others.* New York: Oxford University Press, 1991.

———. "Nineveh, Babylon and the Hanging Gardens: Cuneiform and Classical Sources Reconciled." *Iraq* 56 (1994): 45–58.

———. "The Sassanian Period and Early Islam, c. A.D. 224–651." In *The Legacy of Mesopotamia,* edited by S. Dalley. New York: Oxford, 1998.

———, and A. T. Reyes. "Mesopotamian Contact and Influence on the Greek World." In *The Legacy of Mesopotamia,* edited by S. Dalley. Oxford: Oxford University Press, 1998.

Damerji, M. S. B. *The Development of the Architecture of Doors and Gates in Ancient Mesopotamia.* Tokyo: Institute for Cultural Studies of Ancient Iraq, Kokushikan University, 1987.

———. "Fortifications (Levant)." In *Anchor Bible Dictionary,* edited by D. N. Freedman. New York: Doubleday, 1992.

Dandamaev, M. A. *A Political History of the Achaemenid Empire.* Leiden: Brill, 1989.

———. *Slavery in Babylonia,* edited by M. A. Powell, and D. B. Weisberg. DeKalb: Northern Illinois University Press, 1984.

———, and V. G. Lukonin. *The Culture and Social Institutions of Ancient Iran.* Cambridge: Cambridge University Press, 1989.

Daniels, P. T. "The Decipherment of Ancient Near Eastern Scripts." In *Civilizations of the Ancient Near East,* edited by J. M. Sasson et al. New York: Scribner's, 1995.

———, and W. Bright, eds. *The World's Writing Systems.* Oxford: Oxford University Press, 1996.

David, R. *Handbook to Life in Ancient Egypt.* New York: Facts On File, 1998.

Dayagi-Mendels, M. *Perfumes and Cosmetics in the Ancient World.* Jerusalem: Israel Museum 1989.

De Camp, L. S. *The Ancient Engineers.* New York: Ballantine, 1963.

De Graeve, M.-C. *The Ships of the Ancient Near East (c. 2000–500 B.C.).* Louvain: Department Oriëntalistiek, University of Louvain, 1981.

De Sarzec, E., et al. *Découvertes en Chaldée.* Paris: E. Leroux, 1884–1912.

Deller, K. "Assyrian Eunuchs and Their Predecessors." In *Priests and Officials in the Ancient Near East (=Papers on the Second Colloquium on the Ancient Near East—The City and Its Life),* edited by K. Watanabe. Heidelberg: Universitätsverlag C. Winter, 1999.

Dentan R. C., ed. *The Idea of History in the Ancient Near East.* New Haven, Conn.: Yale University Press, 1955.

Derevenski, J. S. "Where Are the Children? Accessing Children in the Past." *Archaeological Review from Cambridge* 13 (1994): 7–20.

Deuel, L., ed. *The Treasures of Time: Firsthand Accounts by Famous Archaeologists of Their Work in the Near East.* New York: World, 1961.

Diakonoff, I. M., ed. *Ancient Mesopotamia: Socio-Economic History; A Collection of Studies by Soviet Scholars.* Moscow: Nauka, 1969.

———, ed. *Early Antiquity.* Chicago: University of Chicago Press, 1991.

———. "Main Features of the Economy in the Monarchies of Ancient Western Asia." In

Troisième conférence internationale d'histoire économique, 6. Munich, 1965.

———. "Media." In *Cambridge Ancient History of Iran*. Cambridge: Cambridge University Press, 1985.

———. "The Rise of the Despotic State in Ancient Mesopotamia." In *Ancient Mesopotamia, Socio-Economic History: A Collection of Studies by Soviet Scholars*, edited by I. M. Diakonoff. Moscow: Nauka, 1969.

———. "The Structure of Near Eastern Society," *Oikumene* 3 (1982): 7–100.

———. *Structure of Society and State in Early Dynastic Sumer*. Malibu, Calif.: Undena, 1974.

Diodorus Siculus. *Diodorus of Sicily*, I. Translated by C. H. Oldfather. Cambridge, Mass.: Harvard University Press, 1970.

Dion, P. E. "Aramaean Tribes and Nations of First-Millennium Western Asia." In *Civilizations of the Ancient Near East*, edited by J. M. Sasson et al. New York: Scribner's, 1995.

Dosch, G. "Houses and Households in Nuzi: The Inhabitants, the Family, and Those Dependent on It." In *Houses and Households in Ancient Mesopotamia*, edited by K. R. Veenhof. Istanbul: Nederlands Historisch-Archaeologisch Instituut te Istanbul, 1996.

Drews, R. *The Greek Accounts of Near Eastern History*. Cambridge, Mass.: Harvard University Press, 1973.

Driver, G. R. *Semitic Writing from Pictograph to Alphabet*. Rev. ed., edited by S. A. Hopkins. London: Oxford University Press, 1976.

———, and Sir J. C. Miles. *The Assyrian Laws*. Oxford: Clarendon Press, 1935; Aalen: Scientia Verlag, 1975.

———. *The Babylonian Laws*. 2 vols. Oxford: Clarendon Press, 1952 and 1955.

Dundes, A., ed. *The Flood Myth*. Berkeley: University of California Press, 1988.

Durand, J-M. *La Femme dans le Proche-Orient antique* (XXXIIIᵉ Rencontre Assyriologique Internationale). Paris: Éditions Recherche sur les Civilisations, 1987.

Dyson, R. H., Jr. "Sir Leonard Woolley and the Excavations at Ur." In *The Legacy of Sumer*, edited by D. Schmandt-Besserat. Malibu, Calif.: Undena, 1976.

The Editors of Time-Life Books. *Mesopotamia: The Mighty Kings*. New York: Time-Life, 1995.

———. *Sumer: Cities of Eden*. New York: Time-Life, 1993.

Edwards, I. E. S. et al., eds. *The Cambridge Ancient History*. 3d ed. Cambridge: Cambridge University Press, 1975–.

Edwards, M. "Eyewitness: Iraq." *National Geographic* 196, no. 5 (November 1999): 2–27.

Edzard, D. O. "Cuneiform." In *The Oxford Encyclopedia of Archaeology in the Near East*, edited by E. M. Meyers. New York: Oxford University Press, 1997.

———. *Gudea and His Dynasty*. Royal Inscriptions of Mesopotamia, Early Periods, *3.1* Toronto: University of Toronto Press, 1997.

———. "The Sumerian Language." In *Civilizations of the Ancient Near East*, edited by J. M. Sasson et al. New York: Scribner's, 1995.

Ehrich, R. W., ed. *Chronologies in Old World Archaeology*. 3d. ed. Chicago: University of Chicago Press, 1992.

Eichler, B. L. "Nuzi and the Bible: A Retrospective." In *DUMU-E₂-DUB-BA-A: Studies in Honor of Åke W. Sjöberg*, edited by H. Behrens, D. Loding, and M. T. Roth. Philadelphia: University Museum, 1989, 107–19.

The Electronic Corpus of Sumerian Literature (http://www-etcsl.orient.ox.ac.ok). 1997–.

Ellis, M. deJ. "An Old Babylonian Adoption Contract from Tell Harmal." *Journal of Cuneiform Studies* 27 (1975): 130–51.

Ellis, R. S. *A Bibliography of Mesopotamian Archaeological Sites*. Wiesbaden: Harrassowitz, 1972.

———. *Foundation Deposits in Ancient Mesopotamia*. New Haven, Conn.: Yale University Press, 1968.

Elmer-De Witt, P. "The Golden Treasures of Nimrud." *Time* 134 (October 30, 1989): 80–81.

Englund, R. K., and J. P. Grégoire. *The Proto-cuneiform Texts from Jemdet Nasr*. Berlin: Gebr. Mann Verlag, 1991.

Evans, J. *The History and Practice of Ancient Astronomy*. New York: Oxford University Press, 1998.

Eyre, C. J. "The Agricultural Cycle, Farming, and Water Management in the Ancient Near East." In *Civilizations of the Ancient Near East*, edited by J. M. Sasson et al. New York: Scribner's, 1995.

Fagan, B. M. *Return to Babylon: Travelers, Archeologists and Monuments in Mesopotamia.* Boston: Little, Brown, 1979.

Farber, W. "Witchcraft, Magic, and Divination in Ancient Mesopotamia." In *Civilizations of the Ancient Near East*, edited by J. M. Sasson et al. New York: Scribner's, 1995.

Farkas, A. E., P. O. Harper, and E. B. Harrison, eds. *Monsters and Demons in the Ancient and Medieval Worlds.* Mainz on Rhine: Philipp von Zabern, 1987.

Fensham, F. C. "Widow, Orphan, and the Poor in the Ancient Near Eastern Legal and Wisdom Literature." *Journal of Near Eastern Studies* 21 (1962): 129–39.

Ferguson, J. *Palaces of Nineveh and Persepolis Restored.* London: John Murray, 1851.

Ferris, P. W. *The Genre of the Communal Lament in the Bible and the Ancient Near East.* Atlanta: Scholars Press, 1992.

Ferry, D. *Gilgamesh: A New Rendering in English Verse.* New York: Farrar, Straus, & Giroux, 1992.

Finegan, J. *Archaeological History of the Ancient Middle East.* New York: Dorset, 1979.

Finkbeiner, O., and W. Röllig, eds. *Gamdat Nasr: Period or Regional Style?* Wiesbaden: Harrassowitz, 1986.

Finkel, I. L. "The Hanging Gardens of Babylon." In *The Seven Wonders of the Ancient World*, edited by P. A. Clayton and M. J. Price. London: Routledge, 1988.

———. "Necromancy in Ancient Mesopotamia." *Archiv für Orientforschung* 29, no. 3 (1983–84): 1–17.

———, and M. J. Geller, eds. *Sumerian Gods and Their Representations.* Groningen, Netherlands: Styx, 1997.

Finkelstein, J. J. "Mesopotamian Historiography." *Proceedings of the American Philosophical Society* 107 (1963): 461–72.

———. "Sex Offenses in Sumerian Laws." *Journal of the American Oriental Society* 86 (1966): 355–72.

Flannery, K. V. "The Ecology of Early Food Production in Mesopotamia." *Science* 147 (March 12, 1965): 1247–56.

Forbes, R. J. *Metallurgy in Antiquity.* Leiden: E. J. Brill, 1950.

———. *Studies in Ancient Technology.* 6 vols. Leiden: E. J. Brill, 1955–58.

———. "Water Supply." In *Studies in Ancient Technology.* 2d ed. Leiden: E. J. Brill, 1964.

Foster, B. R. "Akkadians." In *The Oxford Encyclopedia of Archaeology in the Near East*, edited by E. M. Meyers. New York: Oxford University Press, 1997.

———, ed. and trans. *Before the Muses: An Anthology of Akkadian Literature.* 2d ed. 2 vols. Bethesda, Md.: CDL Press, 1996.

———. *From Distant Past: Myths, Tales, and Poetry of Ancient Mesopotamia.* Bethesda, Md.: CDL Press, 1995.

———. "Gilgamesh: Sex, Love and the Ascent of Knowledge." In *Love and Death in the Ancient Near East*, edited by J. H. Marks and R. M. Good. Guilford, Conn.: Four Quarters, 1987.

———. "Humor and Cuneiform Literature." *Journal of the Ancient Near Eastern Society of Columbia University* 6 (1974): 69–85.

———. "Humor and Wit in the Ancient Near East." In *Civilizations of the Ancient Near East*," edited by J. M. Sasson et al. New York, Scribner's, 1995.

———. "Humor and Wit—Mesopotamia." In *Anchor Bible Dictionary*, edited by D. N. Freedman. New York: Doubleday, 1992.

———. "A New Look at the Sumerian Temple State." *Journal of the Economic and Social History of the Orient* 24 (1981): 225–241.

Frame, G. "Chaldaeans." In *The Oxford Encyclopedia of Archaeology in the Near East*, edited by E. M. Meyers. New York: Oxford University Press, 1997.

———. *Rulers of Babylonia from the Second Dynasty of Isin to the End of Assyrian Domination (1157–612 B.C.).* Toronto: University to Toronto Press, 1995.

Franke, S. "Kings of Akkad: Sargon and Naram-Sin." In *Civilizations of the Ancient Near East*, edited by J. M. Sasson et al. New York: Scribner's, 1995.

Frankel, D. *The Ancient Kingdom of Urartu.* London: British Museum, 1979.

Frankfort, H. *The Art and Architecture of the Ancient Orient.* 5th ed., revised by M. Roaf and D. Matthews. New Haven, Conn.: Yale University Press, 1997.

———. *The Birth of Civilization in the Near East.* New York: Doubleday, 1956.

————. *Cylinder Seals*. London: Gregg Press, 1965.

————. *Kingship and the Gods: A Study of Ancient Near Eastern Religion as the Integration of Society and Nature*. Chicago: University of Chicago Press, 1948.

————. *The Problem of Similarity in Ancient Near Eastern Religions*. (Frazier Lecture). Oxford: Clarendon Press, 1951.

————. "Town Planning in Ancient Mesopotamia." *The Town Planning Review* 21 (July 1950): 99–123.

————, and H. A. Frankfort, J. A. Wilson, and T. Jacobsen. *Before Philosophy: The Intellectual Adventure of Ancient Man*. Baltimore: Penguin, 1949.

————, and H. A. Frankfort, J. A. Wilson, T. Jacobsen, and W. A. Irwin. "Ancient Mesopotamian Religion: The Central Concerns." *Proceedings of the American Philosophical Society* 107 (1963): 473–84.

Frayne, D. R. *Sargonic and Gutian Periods (2334–2113 B.C.)*. Toronto: University of Toronto Press, 1993.

Freedman, D. N., ed. *The Anchor Bible Dictionary* Vol. 1. New York: Doubleday, 1992.

————, ed. *Eerdmans Dictionary of the Bible*. Grand Rapids, Mich.: Eerdmans, 2000.

Frick, F. S., et al. "Cities." In *The Oxford Encyclopedia of Archaeology in the Near East*, edited by E. M. Meyers. New York: Oxford University Press, 1997.

Friedrich, J. *Extinct Languages*. New York: Philosophical Library, 1957.

Frye, R. N. *The Heritage of Persia*. 2d ed. London: Cardinal, 1976.

————. *The History of Ancient Iran*. Munich: C. H. Beck, 1984.

Frymer-Kensky, T. "The Atrahasis Epic and Its Significance for Our Understanding of Genesis 1–9." *Biblical Archaeologist* 40 (1977), 147–155.

————. "What the Babylonian Flood Stories Can and Cannot Teach Us about the Genesis Flood." *Biblical Archaeology Review* 4, no. 4 (November/December 1978), 32–41.

Gadd, C. J. *Assyrian Sculptures in the British Museum, from Shalmanezer III to Sennacherib*. London: British Museum, 1938.

————. "Babylonian Myth and Ritual." In *Myth and Ritual*, edited by S. H. Hooke. Oxford: University Press, 1933.

————. "The Cities of Babylonia," In *The Cambridge Ancient History*. Rev. ed. Cambridge, U.K.: Cambridge University Press, 1962.

————. *The Fall of Nineveh*. London: The British Museum, 1923.

————. *Ideas of Divine Rule in the Ancient Near East*. London: Oxford University Press, 1948.

————. *The Stones of Assyria*. London: Chatto and Windus, 1936.

————. *Teachers and Students in the Oldest Schools*. London: School of Oriental and African Studies, University of London, 1956.

Gallery, J. A. "Town Planning and Community Structure." In *The Legacy of Sumer*, edited by D. Schmandt-Besserat. Malibu, Calif.: Undena, 1976.

Galpin, F. W. *The Music of the Sumerians and Their Immediate Successors, the Babylonians and Assyrians*. 2d ed. Strasbourg: Heitz, 1955.

Gardner, J., and J. Maier, trans. *Gilgamesh: Translated from the Sîn-leqi-unninī Version*. New York: Random House, 1985.

Garfinkel, Y. "Dancing and the Beginning of Art Scenes in the Early Village Communities of the Near East and South East Europe." *Cambridge Archaeological Journal* 8 (1998): 207–37.

Gasche, H., et al. *Dating the Fall of Babylon: A Reappraisal of Second-Millennium Chronology*. Chicago: University of Ghent and the Oriental Institute of the University of Chicago, 1998.

Gates, M.-H., et al. "The Legacy of Mari." *Biblical Archaeologist* 47 (1984).

Gelb, I. J. "The Ancient Mesopotamian Ration System." *Journal of Near Eastern Studies* 24 (1965): 230–43.

————. "Household and Family in Early Mesopotamia." In *State and Temple Economy in the Ancient Near East*. Vol. 1, edited by E. Lipiński. Louvain: Departement Oriëntalistiek, University of Louvain, 1979.

————. "On the Alleged Temple and State Economies in Ancient Mesopotamia." In *Studi in Onore di E. Volterra*, 6. Milan: A. Giuffrè, 1971, 137–54.

————. "Prisoners of War in Early Mesopotamia." *Journal of Near Eastern Studies* 32 (1973): 70–98.

————, P. Steinkeller, and R. M. Whiting. *Earliest Land Tenure Systems in the Near East: Ancient*

Kudurrus. Chicago: University of Chicago Press, 1991.

———, B. Landsberger, A. L. Oppenheim, and E. Reiner, eds. *The Assyrian Dictionary.* Chicago: Oriental Institute; Glückstadt: J. J. Augustin, 1956–.

Geller, M. J. "Akkadian Medicine in the Babylonian Talmud." In *A Traditional Quest: Essays in Honour of Louis Jacobs,* edited by D. Cohn-Sherbok. Sheffield: JSOT Press, 1991.

———. *Forerunners to Udug-hul: Sumerian Exorcistic Incantations.* Stuttgart: F. Steiner, 1985.

———. "The Influence of Mesopotamia on Hellenistic Judaism." In *Civilizations of the Ancient Near East,* edited by J. M. Sasson et al. New York: Scribner's, 1995.

George, A., trans., *The Epic of Gilgamesh.* London: Allen Lane, 1999.

———. *House Most High: The Temple in Ancient Mesopotamia.* Winona Lake, Ind.: Eisenbrauns, 1993.

Ghirshman, R. *Iran.* Baltimore: Penguin, 1954.

Gibbon, E. *The History of the Decline and Fall of the Roman Empire.* Edited by H. H. Milman. Philadelphia: Porter and Coates 1845 [1776].

Gibson, McG. *The City and Area of Kish.* Miami: Field Research Projects, 1972.

———. "By Stage and Cycle to Sumer." In *The Legacy of Sumer,* edited by D. Schmandt-Besserat. Malibu, Calif.: Undena, 1976.

Gibson, A. M., and R. D. Biggs, eds. *The Organization of Power: Aspects of Bureaucracy in the Ancient Near East.* Chicago: Oriental Institute, 1987.

———. *Seals and Sealings in the Ancient Near East.* Malibu, Calif.: Undena, 1977.

Giedion, S. *The Eternal Present: The Beginnings of Architecture.* New York: Pantheon, 1964.

Gilbert, A. S. "The Flora and Fauna of the Ancient Near East." In *Civilizations of the Ancient Near East,* edited by J. M. Sasson et al. New York: Scribner's, 1995.

Glassner, J.-J. "Progress, Science, and the Use of Knowledge in Ancient Mesopotamia." In *Civilizations of the Ancient Near East,* edited by J. M. Sasson et al. New York: Scribner's, 1995.

Gleason, K. L., and A. Welch. "Gardens." In *The Oxford Encyclopedia of Archaeology in the Near East,* edited by E. M. Meyers. New York: Oxford University Press, 1997.

Goetze, A. *The Laws of Eshnunna.* (*Annual of the American Schools of Oriental Research,* 31.) New Haven, Conn.: American Schools of Oriental Research, 1956.

Gonen, R. *Weapons of the Ancient World.* London: Cassell, 1975.

Gordon, C. H. "Abraham and the Merchants of Ura." *Journal of Near Eastern Studies* 17 (1958): 28–31.

———. "Abraham of Ur." In *Hebrew and Semitic Studies* (The G. R. Driver Festschrift), edited by D. W. Thomas and W. D. McHardy. Oxford: Clarendon Press, 1963.

———. *Adventures in the Near East.* Fairlawn, N.J.: Essential Books, 1957.

———. *The Ancient Near East.* New York: Norton, 1965.

———. "Biblical Customs and the Nuzu Tablets." *Biblical Archaeologist* 3 (1940): 1–12.

———. *The Common Background of Greek and Hebrew Civilizations.* New York: Norton, 1965.

———. *Ugaritic Textbook.* Rome: Pontifical Biblical Institute, 1967.

———. *Forgotten Scripts: Their Ongoing Discovery and Decipherment.* Rev. ed. New York: Dorset, 1987.

———. *Hammurapi's Code: Quaint or Forward-Looking?* New York: Rinehart, 1957.

———. "Homer and Bible." *Hebrew Union College Annual* 26 (1955): 43–108. (=*Homer and Bible.* Ventnor, N.J.: Ventnor Publishers, 1967.)

———. *The Pennsylvania Tradition of Semitics: A Century of Near Eastern and Biblical Studies at the University of Pennsylvania.* Atlanta: Scholars Press, 1986.

———. "Poetic Legends and Myths from Ugarit." *Berytus* 25 (1978): 5–135.

———. "Stratification of Society in Hammurapi's Code." *The Joshua Starr Memorial Volume: Studies in History and Philology.* New York: Conference on Jewish Relations 1953, 17–28.

———. *Ugaritic Literature.* Ventnor, N.J.: Ventnor Publishers, 1949.

———, and G. A. Rendsburg. *The Bible and the Ancient Near East.* 4th ed. New York: Norton, 1997.

———, and G. A. Rendsburg, eds. *Eblaitica: Essays on the Ebla Archives and Eblaite Language.* 3 vols. Winona Lake, Ind.: Eisenbrauns, 1992.

Gordon, E. *Sumerian Proverbs*. Philadelphia: University of Pennsylvania Museum, 1959.

Gorelick, L., and A. J. Gwinnett. "The Ancient Near Eastern Cylinder Seal as Social Emblem and Status Symbol." *Journal of Near Eastern Studies* 49 (1990): 45–56.

———. "Close Work without Magnifying Lenses?" *Expedition*, 22 (Winter 1981): 27–34.

———. "The Origin and Development of the Ancient Near Eastern Cylinder Seal: A Hypothetical Reconstruction." *Expedition* 22 (Summer 1981): 17–30.

Gray, J. *Near Eastern Mythology*. New York: Peter Bedrick, 1985.

Grayson, A. K. "Assyria and Babylonia." *Orientalia* 49 (1980): 140–94.

———. *Assyrian and Babylonian Chronicles*. Locust Valley, N.Y.: J. J. Augustin, 1975.

———. *Assyrian Royal Inscriptions*. 2 vols. Wiesbaden: Harrassowitz, 1972 and 1976.

———. "Assyrian Rule of Conquered Territory in Ancient Western Asia." In *Civilizations of the Ancient Near East*, edited by J. M. Sasson et al. New York: Scribner's, 1995.

———. *Assyrian Rulers of the Early First Millennium B.C.* 2 vols. Toronto: University of Toronto Press, 1991–96.

———. "Assyrians," In *The Oxford Encyclopedia of Archaeology in the Near East*, edited by E. M. Meyers. New York: Oxford University Press, 1997.

———. *Babylonian Historical/Literary Texts*. Toronto: University of Toronto Press, 1975.

———. "Eunuchs in Power: Their Role in the Assyrian Bureaucracy": In *Vom Alten Orient zum Alten Testament*, edited by M. Dietrich and O. Loretz. Neukirchen/Vluyn: Butzon & Bercker, 1995.

———. "Histories and Historians of the Ancient Near East: Assyria and Babylonia." *Orientalia* 49 (1980): 140–194.

———. "History and Culture of Babylonia." In *Anchor Bible Dictionary*, edited by D. N. Freedman. New York: Doubleday, 1992.

———. *Royal Assyrian Inscriptions*. 2 vols. Wiesbaden: Harrassowitz, 1972–76.

———. "The Struggle for Power in Assyria: Challenge to Absolute Monarchy in the Ninth and Eighth Centuries B.C." In *Priests and Officials in the Ancient Near East* (=Papers of the Second Colloquium on the Ancient Near East—The City and Its Life), edited by K. Watanabe. Heidelberg: Universitätsverlag C. Winter, 1999.

——— et al. *Royal Inscriptions of Mesopotamia Project*. Toronto: University of Toronto Press, 1987–.

Great Britain Naval Intelligence Division, *Iraq and the Persian Gulf*. London: H. M. Stationery Office, 1944.

Green, A. "Ancient Mesopotamian Religious Iconography." In *Civilizations of the Ancient Near East*, edited by J. M. Sasson et al. New York: Scribner's, 1995.

———. *Excavations at Nimrud: The Neo-Assyrian Foundation Figurines*. London: British Museum Press, 2002.

Green, M. R. "The Uruk Lament." *Journal of the American Oriental Society* 104 (1984): 253–79.

Green, M. W. "The Eridu Lament." *Journal of Cuneiform Studies* 30 (1978): 127–67.

Greenberg, M. "Another Look at Rachel's Theft of the Teraphim." *Journal of Biblical Literature* 81 (1962): 239–48.

———. *The Hab/piru*. New Haven: American Oriental Society, 1955.

Greenfield, J. C. "Adi baltu—Care for the Elderly and Its Rewards." *Archiv für Orientforschung* 19 (1982).

Greengus, S. "Legal and Social Institutions of Ancient Mesopotamia." In *Civilizations of the Ancient Near East*, edited by J. M. Sasson et al. New York: Scribner's, 1995.

———. "A Textbook Case of Adultery in Ancient Mesopotamia." *Hebrew Union College Annual* 40–41 (1969–70): 33–44.

———. "Old Babylonian Marriage Ceremonies and Rites." *Journal of Cuneiform Studies* 20 (1966): 55–72.

Greenstein, E. "Autobiographies in Ancient Western Asia." In *Civilizations of the Ancient Near East*, edited by J. M. Sasson et al. New York: Scribner's, 1995.

Groenewegen-Frankfort, H. *Arrest and Movement: An Essay on Space and Time in the Representational Art of the Ancient Near East*. London: Faber & Faber, 1951 (New York: Hacker, 1978).

Groom, N. *Frankincense and Myrrh: A Study of the Arabian Incense Trade*. London: Longman, 1981.

Guichard, M. "Mari Texts." In *The Oxford Encyclopedia of Archaeology in the Near East*, edited by E. M. Meyers. New York: Oxford University Press, 1997.

Gunter, A. C., ed. *Investigating Artistic Environments in the Ancient Near East*. Washington, D.C.: Smithsonian Institution, 1990.

———. "Material, Technology, and Techniques in Artistic Production." In *Civilizations of the Ancient Near East*, edited by J. M. Sasson et al. New York: Scribner's, 1995.

Gurney, O. R. *The Hittites*. Baltimore: Penguin, 1954.

———. "Sultan Tepe and Harran." In *Ancient Anatolia*, edited by R. Matthews. Madison, Wis.: University of Wisconsin Press, 1998.

Güterbock, H. G. "Narration in Anatolian, Syrian and Assyrian Art." *American Journal of Archaeology* 61 (1957): 62–71.

Gwinnett, A. J., and L. Gorelick. "The Change from Stone Drills to Copper Drills in Mesopotamia." *Expedition*, 29 (Fall 1987): 15–24.

Hackett, J., ed. *Warfare in the Ancient World*. New York: Facts On File, 1990.

Hallo, W. W. "Lamentations and Prayers in Sumer and Akkad." In *Civilizations of the Ancient Near East*, edited by J. M. Sasson et al. New York: Scribner's, 1995.

———. *Origins: The Ancient Near Eastern Background of Some Modern Western Institutions*. Leiden: E. J. Brill, 1996.

———. "Sumerian Literature." In *The Anchor Bible Dictionary*. Vol. 6. Edited by David Noel Freedman. New York: Doubleday, 1992.

———. "The Women of Sumer." In *The Legacy of Sumer*, edited by D. Schmandt-Besserat. Malibu, Calif.: Undena, 1976.

———, and W. K. Simpson. *The Ancient Near East: A History*. 2d ed. New York: Harcourt Brace, 1998.

———, and J. J. A. Van Dijk. *The Exaltation of Inanna*. New Haven, Conn.: Yale University Press, 1968.

Hamblin, D. J., and the editors of Time-Life Books. *The First Cities*. New York: Time-Life, 1973.

———. "Has the Garden of Eden Been Located at Last?" *Smithsonian* (June 1987): 127–35.

Hammurabi. *The Letters and Inscriptions of Hammurabi, King of Babylon, about B.C. 2200*. Edited by L. W. King. 3 vols. London: Luzac, 1989–1900; New York: AMS Press, 1976.

Handcock, P. S. P. *Mesopotamian Archaeology: An Introduction to the Archaeology of Babylonia and Assyria*. New York: Kraus Reprint, 1969.

Hansen, P. "Khorsabad." In *The Oxford Encyclopedia of Archaeology in the Near East*, edited by E. M. Meyers. New York: Oxford University Press, 1997.

———. "Royal Building Activity at Sumerian Lagash in the Early Dynastic Period." *Biblical Archaeologist* 55 (1992): 206–11.

Harcourt-Smith, S. *Babylonian Art*. Los Angeles: AMS Press, 1978 (1928).

Harper, P. O., et al. *Assyrian Origins: Discoveries at Ashur on the Tigris: Antiquities in the Vorderasiatisches Museum, Berlin*. New York: Metropolitan Museum of Art, 1995.

Harrak, A. "Mitanni." In *The Oxford Encyclopedia of Archaeology in the Near East*, edited by E. M. Meyers. New York: Oxford University Press, 1997.

———. "The Royal Tombs of Nimrud and Their Jewellery." *Bulletin of the Center for Syro-Mesopotamian Studies* 20 (1990).

Harris, R. "Images of Women in the Gilgamesh Epic." In *Lingering over Words: W. L. Moran A. V.*, edited by T. Abusch, J. Huehnergard, and P. Steinkeller. Atlanta: Scholars Press, 1990.

———. "The Organization and Administration of the Cloister in Ancient Babylonia." *Journal of the Economic and Social History of the Orient* 6 (1963): 121–57.

Hartman, L. F., and A. P. Oppenheim. "On Beer and Brewing Techniques in Ancient Mesopotamia." *Journal of the American Oriental Society*, Supplement 10 (1950).

Hawkes, J., ed. *The World of the Past*. Vol. 1. New York: Knopf, 1963.

Hawkins, D. "The Origin and Dissemination of Writing in Western Asia." In P. R. S. Moorey, *Origins of Civilization*. Oxford: Clarendon Press, 1979.

Hawkins, J. D. "Karkamish and Karatepe: Neo-Hittite City-States in North Syria." In *Civilizations of the Ancient Near East*, edited by J. M. Sasson et al. New York: Scribner's, 1995.

———. "Seton Howard Frederick Lloyd, 1902–1996." *Proceedings of the British Academy* 97 (1998): 359–77.

———. *Trade in the Ancient Near East.* = *Iraq* 39 (1977).

Healy, M., and A. McBride. *The Ancient Assyrians.* Oxford: Osprey, 1991.

Heidel, A. *The Babylonian Genesis.* 2d ed. Chicago: University of Chicago Press, 1951.

———. *The Gilgamesh Epic and Old Testament Parallels.* 2d ed. Chicago: University of Chicago Press, 1949.

Henrickson, R. C. "Elamites." In *The Oxford Encyclopedia of Archaeology in the Near East*, edited by E. M. Meyers. New York: Oxford University Press, 1997.

Henry, D. *From Foraging to Agriculture.* Philadelphia: University of Pennsylvania Press, 1989.

Henshaw, R. "The Assyrian Army and Its Soldiers, 9th–7th C. B.C." *Paleologia* 16 (1969): 1–24.

Herodotus. *The Persian Wars*, trans. George Rawlinson (1862), edited by F. R. B. Godolphin. New York: Modern Library, 1942.

Herrmann, G., ed. *The Furniture of Western Asia: Ancient and Traditional.* Mainz: Philipp von Zabern, 1996.

———. *Ivories from Nimrud, IV, 1: Ivories from Room SW 37 Fort Shalmaneser.* London: British School of Archaeology in Iraq, 1986.

———. *Ivories from Nimrud, V: The Small Collections from Fort Shalmaneser.* London: British School of Archaeology in Iraq, 1992.

———. "Lapis Lazuli: The Early Phases of Its Trade." *Iraq* 39 (1968): 21–37.

Hertzler, J. O. *The Social Thought of the Ancient Civilizations.* New York: McGraw-Hill, 1936.

Herzog, Z., et al. "Fortifications." In *The Oxford Encyclopedia of Archaeology in the Near East*, edited by E. M. Meyers. New York: Oxford University Press, 1997.

Hesse, B. "Animal Husbandry." In *The Oxford Encyclopedia of Archaeology in the Near East*, edited by E. M. Meyers. New York: Oxford University Press, 1997.

———. "Animal Husbandry and Human Diet in the Ancient Near East." In *Civilizations of the Ancient Near East*, edited by J. M. Sasson et al. New York: Scribner's, 1995.

Higham, C. *The Earliest Farmers and the First Cities.* Cambridge: Cambridge University Press, 1974; Minneapolis: Lerner, 1977.

Hillel, D. *Rivers of Eden: The Struggle for Water and the Quest for Peace in the Middle East.* New York: Oxford University Press, 1994.

Hinz, W. *The Lost World of Elam: Re-creation of a Vanished Civilization.* London: Sidgwick & Jackson, 1972.

Hitti, P. *A History of Syria.* London: Macmillan, 1957.

Hoenig, S. B., and S. H. Rosenberg. *Guide to the Prophets.* New York: Yeshiva University, 1957.

Hogarth, D. G. *Carchemish: Part I, Introductory.* London: British Museum, 1914.

Hole, F. *The Archaeology of Western Iran.* Washington, D.C.: Smithsonian Institution Press, 1987.

———. "Assessing the Past through Anthropological Archaeology." In *Civilizations of the Ancient Near East*, edited by J. M. Sasson et al. New York: Scribner's, 1995.

———. "Investigating the Origins of Mesopotamian Civilization." *Science* 153 (August 5, 1966): 605–11.

———, and R. F. Heizer. *Prehistoric Archaeology: A Brief Introduction.* New York: Holt, Rinehart, & Winston, 1977.

Hooke, S. H. *Babylonian and Assyrian Religion*, Oxford: Blackwell, 1962.

Hopkins, C. *The Discovery of Dura-Europos.* Edited by B. Goldman. New Haven, Conn.: Yale University Press, 1979.

Hopkins, D. C. "Agriculture." In *The Oxford Encyclopedia of Archaeology in the Near East*, edited by E. M. Meyers. New York: Oxford University Press, 1997.

Hornblower, S., and A. Spawforth, eds. *The Oxford Classical Dictionary.* 3d ed. New York: Oxford University Press, 1996.

Hornell, J. "The Role of Birds in Early Navigation." *Antiquity* 20 (1946): 142–49.

Hoyrup, J. *Measure, Number, and Weight.* Albany: State University of New York Press, 1994.

Hübner. U. "Games." In *The Oxford Encyclopedia of Archaeology in the Near East*, edited by E. M. Meyers. New York: Oxford University Press, 1997.

Huehnergard, J. "Akkadian." In *The Oxford Encyclopedia of Archaeology in the Near East*, edited by E. M. Meyers. New York: Oxford University Press, 1997.

———. *A Grammar of Akkadian*. Atlanta: Scholars Press, 1997.

———. "Semitic Languages." In *Civilizations of the Ancient Near East*, edited by J. M. Sasson et al. New York: Scribner's, 1995.

Huffmon, H. B. "Prophecy: Ancient Near Eastern Prophecy." In *Anchor Bible Dictionary*, edited by D. N. Freedman. New York: Doubleday, 1992.

Hughes, J. D. *Ecology in Ancient Civilizations*. Albuquerque, N.M.: University of New Mexico Press, 1975.

Hunger, H., ed. *Astrological Reports to Assyrian Kings*. Helsinki: Helsinki University Press, 1992.

Ichiro, K. *Deities in the Mari Texts*. Ann Arbor: University of Michigan Press, 1979.

Ionides, M. G. *The Régime of the Rivers Euphrates and Tigris*. London: E. & F. N. Spon, 1937.

Isaac, B. *The Limits of Empire: The Roman Army in the East*. Rev. ed. Oxford: Clarendon Press, 1992.

Jacobs, Jane. *Cities and the Wealth of Nations*. New York: Vintage, 1985.

Jacobsen, T. "An Ancient Mesopotamian Trial for Homicide." In *Toward the Image of Tammuz*, edited by W. L. Moran. Cambridge, Mass.: Harvard University Press, 1970.

———. "The Assumed Conflict between Sumerians and Semites in Early Mesopotamian History." *Journal of the American Oriental Society* 59 (1939): 485–95.

———. "Formative Tendencies in Sumerian Religion." In *The Bible and the Ancient Near East: Essays in Honor of William Foxwell Albright*, edited by G. Ernest Wright. Garden City, N.Y.: Doubleday, 1961.

———. "The Gilgamesh Epic: Romantic and Tragic Vision." In *Lingering over Words: Studies in Ancient Near Eastern Literature in Honor of William L. Moran*, edited by T. Abusch, J. Huehnergard, and P. Steinkeller. Atlanta: Scholars Press, 1990.

———, trans. *The Harps That Once. . . . : Sumerian Poetry in Translation*. New Haven, Conn.: Yale University Press, 1987.

———. "Pictures and Pictorial Language." In *Figurative Language in the Ancient Near East*, edited by M. Mindlin, M.-J. Geller, and J. E. Wansbrough. London: University of London School of Oriental and African Studies, 1987.

———. *Salinity and Irrigation Agriculture in Antiquity*. Malibu, Calif.: Undena, 1982.

———. "Searching for Sumer and Akkad." In *Civilizations of the Ancient Near East*, edited by J. M. Sasson et al. New York: Scribner's, 1995.

———. *The Sumerian King List*. Chicago: University of Chicago Press, 1939.

———. *The Treasures of Darkness: A History of Mesopotamian Religion*. New Haven, Conn.: Yale University Press, 1976.

———. *Toward the Image of Tammuz and Other Essays on Mesopotamian History and Culture*. Edited by W. L. Moran. Cambridge, Mass.: Harvard University Press, 1970.

———, and S. Lloyd. *Sennacherib's Aqueduct at Jerwan*. Chicago: University of University Press, 1935.

Jakob-Rost, L., et al. *The Museum of the Near East (National Museum of Berlin)*. Mainz: Philipp von Zabern, 1992.

James, P., et al. *Centuries of Darkness: A Challenge to the Conventional Chronology of Old World Archaeology*. New Brunswick, N.J.: Rutgers University Press, 1993.

———, and N. Thorpe. *Ancient Inventions*. New York: Ballantine, 1994.

Jeyes, U. "The Act of Extispicy in Ancient Mesopotamia: An Outline." *Assyriological Miscellanies* 1 (1980): 13–32.

Joannès, F. "Private Commerce and Banking in Achaemenid Babylon." In *Civilizations of the Ancient Near East*, edited by J. M. Sasson et al. New York: Scribner's, 1995.

Johansen, F. *Statues of Gudea, Ancient and Modern*. (*Mesopotamia: Copenhagen Studies in Assyriology*, vol. 6.) Copenhagen: Akademisk Forlag, 1978.

Johns, C. H. *Babylonian and Assyrian Laws, Contracts, Letters*. New York: Gordon, 1977.

Johnson, J. "Tell Time by the Stars." *Archaeology* 4 (Summer 1951): 76–82. Reprinted by *Archaeology*, Edited by S. Rapport and H. Wright. New York: Washington Square Press, 1964.

Jones, A. "The Horoscope Casters." *Archaeology Odyssey* (November/December 2000): 6f.

Jones, A. H. M. *Cities of the Eastern Roman Provinces*. 2d ed. Oxford: Clarendon Press, 1971.

Jones, T. B. "Bookkeeping in Ancient Sumer." *Archaeology* 9 (Spring 1956): 16–21.

———, ed. *The Sumerian Problem*. New York: John Wiley, 1969.

Jonker, G. *The Topography of Remembrance: The Dead, Tradition, and Collective Memory in Mesopotamia*. Boston: Brill Academic Publishers, 1995.

Kahn, D. *The Codebreakers*. New York: Macmillan, 1967.

Kamoo, R. *Ancient and Modern Chaldean History: A Comprehensive Bibliography of Sources*. Lanham, Md.: Scarecrow Press, 1999.

Katz, S. H., and F. Maytag, "Brewing an Ancient Beer." *Archaeology* 44 (July/August 1991): 24–33.

Keall, E. J. "Parthians." In *The Oxford Encyclopedia of Archaeology in the Near East*, edited by E. M. Meyers. New York: Oxford University Press, 1997.

Keller, W. *The Bible as History*. New York: William Morrow, 1981.

Kelly-Buccellati, M., ed. *Insight Through Images. . . . Edith Porada A. V.* Malibu, Calif.: Undena, 1986.

Kendall, T. "Warfare and Military Matters in the Nuzi Tablets" Ph. D. diss., Brandeis University, 1974.

Killick, R. G. "Ziggurat." In *The Dictionary of Art*, edited by J. Turner. New York: Grove's Dictionaries, 1996.

Kilmer, A. D. "Music and Dance in Ancient Western Asia." In *Civilizations of the Ancient Near East*, edited by J. M. Sasson et al. New York: Scribner's, 1995.

King, L. W. *Babylonian Boundary Stones and Memorial Texts in The British Museum*. London: British Museum, 1912.

———. *Bronze Reliefs from the Gates of Shalmaneser*. London: British Museum, 1915.

———. *History of Babylon from the Foundations of the Monarchy to the Persian Conquest*. Los Angeles: AMS Press, 1915.

———. *History of Sumer and Akkad: An Account of the Early Races of Babylonia from Prehistoric Times to the Foundation of the Babylonian Monarchy*. Westport, Conn.: Greenwood, 1970 (1916).

———. *Legends of Babylon and Egypt in Relation to Hebrew Tradition*. (Schweich Lectures on Biblical Archaeology, 1930.) Germantown, N.Y.: Periodicals Service, 1969.

———, and R. C. Thompson. *The Sculptures and Inscription of Darius the Great*. London: British Museum, 1907.

Klein, J. "The Birth of Kingship: From Democracy to Monarchy in Sumer." *Archaeology Odyssey*, January/February 2001, 17–25.

———. "Shulgi of Ur: King of a Neo-Sumerian Empire." In *Civilizations of the Ancient Near East*, edited by J. M. Sasson et al. New York: Scribner's, 1995.

Klengel, H. *Syria: 3000–300 B.C.: A Handbook of Political History*. Berlin: Akademie Verlag, 1992.

Klengel-Brandt, E. "Babylon." In *The Oxford Encyclopedia of Archaeology in the Near East*, edited by E. M. Meyers. New York: Oxford University Press, 1997.

———. "Babylonians." In *The Oxford Encyclopedia of Archaeology in the Near East*, edited by E. M. Meyers. New York: Oxford University Press, 1997.

Knapp, A. *The History and Culture of Ancient Western Asia and Egypt*. Illinois: Dorsey Press, 1988.

Knapp, A. B. "Spice, Drugs, Grain and Grog: Organic Goods in Bronze Age East Mediterranean Trade." In *Bronze Age Trade in the Mediterranean*, edited by N. H. Gale. Jonsered: P. Åströms, 1991.

Koch, H. "Theology and Worship in Elam and Achaemenid Iran." In *Civilizations of the Ancient Near East*, edited by J. M. Sasson et al. New York: Scribner's, 1995.

Kohl, P. L. "Central Asia and the Caucasus in the Bronze Age." In *Civilizations of the Ancient Near East*, edited by J. M. Sasson et al. New York: Scribner's, 1995.

Koldewey, R. *The Excavations at Babylon*. New York: Macmillan, 1915.

Kovacs, M. G., trans. *The Epic of Gilgamesh*. Stanford, Calif.: Stanford University Press, 1985.

Kraeling, C. H., and R. McC. Adams, eds. *City Invincible: A Symposium on Urbanization and Cultural Development in the Ancient Near East*. Chicago: University of Chicago Press, 1960.

Kramer, S. N. "The Death of Gilgamesh." *Journal of Cuneiform Studies* 21 (1967): 104–22.

———. "Dilmun, the Land of the Living." *Bulletin of the American Schools of Oriental Research* 96 (1944): 18–28.

———. *History Begins at Sumer: Thirty-Nine Firsts in Recorded History*. 3d rev. ed. Philadelphia: University of Pennsylvania Press, 1981.

———. *In the World of Sumer: An Autobiography.* Detroit: Wayne State University Press, 1986.

———. *Lamentation Over the Destruction of Ur.* Chicago: University of Chicago Press, 1940.

———. "Love, Hate and Fear: Psychological Aspects of Sumerian Culture." *Eretz-Israel* 5 (1958): 66–74.

———. "Mythology of Sumer and Akkad." In *Mythologies of the Ancient World*, edited by S. N. Kramer. New York: Doubleday, 1961.

———. "Poets and Psalmists: Goddesses and Theologians." In *The Legacy of Sumer*, edited by D. Schmandt-Besserat. Malibu, Calif.: Undena, 1976.

———. "Rivalry and Superiority: Two Dominant Features of the Sumerian Cultural Pattern." *Selected Papers of the Proceedings of the Fifth International Congress of Anthropological and Ethnological Sciences*, 1956, 287–91.

———. *The Sacred Marriage Rite: Aspects of Faith, Myth, and Ritual in Ancient Sumer.* Bloomington: Indiana University Press, 1969.

———. "Schooldays: A Sumerian Composition Relating to the Education of a Scribe." *Journal of the American Oriental Society* 69 (1949): 199–215.

———. "Sumerian Literature: A General Survey." In *The Bible and the Ancient Near East: Essays in Honor of William Foxwell Albright*, edited by G. Ernest Wright. Garden City, N.Y.: Doubleday, 1961.

———. "Sumerian Literature and the Bible." *Analecta Biblica* 12 (1959): 185–204.

———. *The Sumerians: Their History, Culture, and Character.* Chicago: University of Chicago Press, 1963.

———. *Sumerian Mythology.* New York: Harper and Row, 1972.

———, and the Editors of Time-Life Books. *Cradle of Civilization.* Alexandria, Va.: Time-Life Books, 1978.

———, and A. Falkenstein. "Ur-Nammu Law Code." *Orientalia* 23 (1954): 40–51.

Kubie, N. *Road to Nineveh: The Adventures and Excavations of Sir Austen Henry Layard.* London: Cassell, 1964.

Kuhrt, A. "Ancient Mesopotamia in Classical Greek and Hellenistic Thought." In *Civilizations of the Ancient Near East*, edited by J. M. Sasson et al. New York: Scribner's, 1995.

———. *The Ancient Near East, c. 3000–330 B.C.* 2 vols. New York: Routledge, 1995.

———. "Assyrian and Babylonian Traditions in Classical Authors: A Critical Synthesis." In *Mesopotamien und seine Nachbarn: Politische und kulturelle Wechselbeziehungen im alten Vorderasien vom 4. bis 1. Jahrtausend v. Chr.*, edited by H. J. Nissen and J. Renger. Berlin: D. Reimer, 1982.

———, and S. Sherwin-White. *Hellenism in the East: The Interaction of Greek and Non-Greek Civilizations from Syria to Central Asia after Alexander.* Berkeley: University of California Press, 1987.

Kuklick, B. *Puritans in Babylon: The Ancient Near East and American Intellectual Life, 1880–1930.* Princeton, N.J.: Princeton University Press, 1996.

La Bianca, Ø. S. "Pastoral Nomadism." In *The Oxford Encyclopedia of Archaeology in the Near East*, edited by E. M. Meyers. New York: Oxford University Press, 1997.

Laessøe, J. "Literacy and Oral Tradition in Ancient Mesopotamia." In *Studia Orientalia Ioanni Pedersen septuagenario . . . a collegis discipulis amicis dicata.* Copenhagen: Einar Munksgaard, 1953.

———. *People of Ancient Assyria: Their Inscriptions and Correspondence.* London: Routledge & Kegan Paul, 1963.

Lamberg-Karlovsky, C. C. "The Economic World of Sumer." In *The Legacy of Sumer*, edited by D. Schmandt-Besserat. Malibu, Calif.: Undena, 1976.

Lambert, W. G. *Babylonian Wisdom Literature.* Oxford: Clarendon Press, 1960; Winona Lake, Ind.: Eisenbrauns, 1996.

———. "The Cosmology of Sumer and Babylon." In *Ancient Cosmologies*, edited by C. Blacker and M. Loewe. London: Allen & Unwin, 1975.

———. "Destiny and Divine Intervention in Babylon and Israel." *Oudtestamentische Studiën* 17 (1972): 65–72.

———. "Divine Love Lyrics from Babylon." *Journal of Semitic Studies* 4 (1959): 1–15.

———. "Divine Love Lyrics from the Reign of Abi-Ešuh." *Mitteilungen des Instituts für Orientforschung* 12 (1966): 41–56.

———. "Gilgamesh in Literature and Art: The Second and First Millennia." In *Monsters and Demons in the Ancient and Medieval Worlds*, edited by A. Farkas et al. Mainz: Verlag Philipp von Zabern, 1987.

————. "Goddesses in the Pantheon." *Comptes rendus de Rencontre Assyriologique Internationale* 33 (1986): 125–30.

————. "The Historical Development of the Mesopotamian Pantheon: A Study in Sophisticated Polytheism." In *Unity and Diversity*, edited by H. Goedicke and J. J. M. Roberts. Baltimore: Johns Hopkins University Press, 1975.

————. "Morals in Ancient Mesopotamia." *Jaarbericht van het Vooraziatisch-Egyptisch Genootschap ex Orient Lux* 15 (1958): 184–96.

————. "Myth and Mythmaking in Sumer and Akkad." In *Civilizations of the Ancient Near East*, edited by J. M. Sasson et al. New York: Scribner's, 1995.

————. "Studies in Marduk." *Bulletin of the School of Oriental and African Studies* 47 (1984): 1–9.

————, and A. R. Millard. *Atra-Hasīs: The Babylonian Story of the Flood* (with *The Sumerian Flood Story* by M. Civil). Oxford: Clarendon Press, 1969.

Lampl, P. *Cities and Planning in the Ancient Near East.* New York: Braziller, 1968.

Landels, J. G. *Engineering in the Ancient World.* Rev. ed. Berkeley: University of California Press, 2000.

Landsberger, B. *The Fauna of Ancient Mesopotamia.* 2 vols. Rome: Pontificium Institum Biblicum, 1960 and 1962.

————. "Scribal Concepts of Education." In *City Invincible*, edited by C. H. Kraeling and R. M. Adams. Chicago: University of Chicago Press, 1960.

————. *Three Essays on the Sumerians.* Los Angeles: Undena, 1974.

Larsen, M. T. "The 'Babel/Bible' Controversy and Its Aftermath." In *Civilizations of the Ancient Near East*, edited by J. M. Sasson et al. New York: Scribner's, 1995.

————. *The Conquest of Assyria: Excavations in an Antique Land, 1840–1860.* New York: Routledge, 1996.

————. "The Mesopotamian Lukewarm Mind: Reflections on Science, Divination, and Literacy." In *Language, Literature, and History*, edited by F. Rochberg-Halton. New Haven, Conn.: American Oriental Society, 1987.

————. *The Old Assyrian City-State and Its Colonies.* Copenhagen: Akademisk Forlag, 1976.

————, ed. *Power and Propaganda: A Symposium on Ancient Empires* (=*Mesopotamia: Copenhagen Studies in Assyriology*, Vol. 7). Copenhagen: Akademisk Forlag, 1979.

————. "The Tradition of Empire in Mesopotamia." In *Power and Propaganda: A Symposium on Ancient Empires* (=*Mesopotamia: Copenhagen Studies in Assyriology*, Vol. 7), edited by M. T. Larsen. Copenhagen: Akademisk Forlag, 1976.

Larue, G. A. *Babylon and the Bible.* Grand Rapids, Mich.: Baker, 1969.

Layard, A. H. *Discoveries in the Ruins of Nineveh and Babylon.* 2 vols. London: John Murray, 1853.

————. *The Monuments of Nineveh.* London: John Murray, 1853.

————. *Nineveh and Babylon.* 2 vols. London: John Murray, 1853.

————. *Nineveh and Its Remains.* 2 vols. London: John Murray, 1867.

————. *A Popular Account of Discoveries at Nineveh.* New York: Harper & Bros., 1852.

————. *A Second Series of the Monuments of Nineveh.* London: John Murray, 1853.

Leach, H. "On the Origins of Kitchen Gardening in the Ancient Near East." *Garden History* 10 (1982): 1–16.

Leacroft, H., and R. Leacroft *Buildings of Ancient Mesopotamia.* Reading, Mass.: Addison Wesley, 1974.

Leemans, W. F. *The Old Babylonian Merchant: His Business and Social Position.* Leiden: E. J. Brill, 1960.

————. *Foreign Trade in the Old Babylonian Period as Revealed by Texts from Southern Babylonia.* Leiden: E. J. Brill, 1960.

Legrain, L. "The Boudoir of Queen Shubad." *Museum Journal* (University of Pennsylvania Museum) 20 (September/December 1929): 211–45.

————. "Nippur's Old Drug Store." *University [of Pennsylvania] Museum Bulletin* 8 (1940): 25–27.

Leichty, E. "Esarhaddon, King of Assyria." In *Civilizations of the Ancient Near East*, edited by J. M. Sasson et al. New York: Scribner's, 1995.

Leick, G. *A Dictionary of Ancient Near Eastern Architecture.* New York: Routledge, 1988.

———. *A Dictionary of Ancient Near Eastern Mythology*. New York: Routledge, 1991.

———. *Sex and Eroticism in Mesopotamian Literature*. New York: Routledge, 1994.

Leonard, J. N., and the Editors of Time-Life Books. *The First Farmers* (Emergence of Man series). New York: Time-Life Books, 1973.

Levey, M. *Chemistry and Chemical Technology in Ancient Mesopotamia*. Amsterdam: Elsevier, 1959.

Levine, L. I. *Ancient Synagogues Revealed*. Detroit: Wayne State University Press, 1982.

Lewis, B. *The Sargon Legend: A Study of the Akkadian Text and the Tale of the Hero Who Was Exposed at Birth*. Cambridge, Mass.: American Schools of Oriental Research, 1980.

Lewy, J. "The Late Assyro-Babylonian Cult of the Moon and Its Culmination at the Time of Nabonidus." *Hebrew Union College Annual* 19 (1945–46): 405–89.

Lieberman, S. J. "Of Clay Pebbles, Hollow Clay Balls and Writing." *American Journal of Archaeology* 84 (1980): 339–58.

———, ed. *Sumerological Studies in Honor of Thorkild-Jacobsen: On His Seventieth Birthday, June 7, 1974*. Chicago: University of Chicago Press, 1977.

Liebowitz, H. A. "The Impact of Sumerian Art on the Art of Palestine and Syria." In *The Legacy of Sumer*, edited by D. Schmandt-Besserat. Malibu, Calif.: Undena, 1976.

Lipinski, E., ed. *State and Temple Economy in the Ancient Near East*. 2 vols. Louvain: Departement Oriëntalistiek, University of Louvain, 1979.

Littauer, M. A, and J. H. Crouwel. *Wheeled Vehicles and Ridden Animals in the Ancient Near East*. Leiden: E. J. Brill, 1979.

Litvinsky, B. A. "Archaeology and Artifacts in Iron Age Central Asia." In *Civilizations of the Ancient Near East*, edited by J. M. Sasson et al. New York: Scribner's, 1995.

Liverani, M. *Akkad, the First World Empire: Structure, Ideology, Traditions*. Padua: Sargon, 1993.

———. "The Amorites." In *Peoples of Old Testament Times*, edited by D. J. Wiseman. Oxford. Clarendon Press, 1973.

———. "The Deeds of Ancient Mesopotamian Kings." In *Civilizations of the Ancient Near East*, edited by J. M. Sasson et al. New York: Scribner's, 1995.

———. "The Ideology of the Assyrian Empire." In *Power and Propaganda: A Symposium on Ancient Empires* (=*Mesopotamia: Copenhagen Studies in Assyriology*, Vol. 7), edited by M. T. Larsen. Copenhagen: Akademisk Vorlag, 1976.

———. *Prestige and Interest: International Relations in the Near East ca. 1600–1100 B.C.* Padua: Sargon, 1990.

Lloyd, S. *The Archaeology of Mesopotamia: From the Old Stone Age to the Persian Conquest*. London: Thames & Hudson, 1978.

———. *The Art of the Ancient Near East*. New York: Praeger, 1961.

———. "Excavating the Land between the Two Rivers." In *Civilizations of the Ancient Near East*, edited by J. M. Sasson et al. New York: Scribner's 1995.

———. *Foundations in the Dust: A Story of Mesopotamian Exploration*. Baltimore: Penguin, 1955.

———. *The Interval: A Life in Near Eastern Archaeology*. Faringdon: Lloyd Collon, 1986.

———. *Mounds of the Near East*. Chicago: Aldine, 1963.

———. *The Ruined Cities of Iraq*. Chicago: Ares, 1980.

———. *Twin Rivers: A Brief History of Iraq from the Earliest Times to the Present Day*. London: Oxford University Press, 1961.

———, H. W. Müller, and R. Martin. *Ancient Architecture: Mesopotamia, Egypt, Crete, Greece*. New York: Abrams, 1974.

———, and F. Safar. "Tell Hassuna." *Journal of Near Eastern Studies* 4 (1945): 255–89.

Loftus, W. K. *The Travels and Researches in Chaldaea and Susiana*. London: James Nisbet, 1857.

Loud, G., and C. B. Altman. *Khorsabad, Parts 1–2*. Chicago: University of Chicago Press, 1936–38.

Luckenbill, D. D. *Ancient Records of Assyria and Babylonia*. 2 vols. Chicago: University of Chicago Press, 1926–27.

———. *The Annals of Sennacherib*. Chicago: University of Chicago Press, 1924.

Lundquist, J. M. "Babylon in European Thought." In *Civilizations of the Ancient Near East*, edited by J. M. Sasson et al. New York: Scribner's, 1995.

Macdonald, M. C. A. "North Arabia in the First Millennium BCE." In *Civilizations of the Ancient Near East*, edited by J. M. Sasson et al. New York: Scribner's, 1995.

———. "Trade Routes and Trade Goods at the Northern End of the 'Incense Road' in the First Millennium B.C." In *Profumi d'Arabia*, edited by A. Avanzini. Rome: L'Erma di Bretschneider, 1997.

MacQueen, J. G. *The Hittites and Their Contemporaries in Asia Minor*. London: Thames & Hudson, 1986.

Madhloom, T. A. *The Chronological Development of Neo-Assyrian Art*. London: Athlone Press, 1970.

Magness-Gardiner, B. "Seals." In *The Oxford Encyclopedia of Archaeology in the Near East*, edited by E. M. Meyers. New York: Oxford University Press, 1997.

Magnusson, M. *Archaeology and the Bible*. New York: Simon & Schuster, 1977.

Maidman, M. P. "Nuzi: Portrait of an Ancient Mesopotamian Provincial Town." In *Civilizations of the Ancient Near East*, edited by J. M. Sasson et al. New York: Scribner's, 1995.

Maier, J. "The Ancient Near East in Modern Thought." In *Civilizations of the Ancient Near East*, edited by J. M. Sasson et al. New York: Scribner's, 1995.

———. *Gilgamesh: A Reader*. Wauconda, Ill.: Bolchazy-Carducci, 1997.

Maisels, C. K. *Early Civilizations of the Old World: Formative Histories of Egypt, the Levant, Mesopotamia, India, and China*. New York: Routledge, 1999.

———. *The Emergence of Civilization from Hunting and Gathering to Agriculture, Cities, and the State in the Near East*. London, New York: Routledge, 1990.

Malamat, A. "Mari." *Biblical Archaeologist* 34 (1971): 2–22.

———. *Mari and the Bible*. Boston: E. J. Brill, 1998.

———. *Mari and the Early Israelite Experience*. (Schweich Lectures on Biblical Archaeology.) New York: Oxford University Press, 1992.

Mallowan, A. C(hristie). *Come, Tell Me How You Live*. New York: Pocket, 1977.

Mallowan, M. E. L. *Early Mesopotamia and Iran*. New York: McGraw-Hill, 1965.

———. *Mallowan's Memoirs*. New York: Dodd, Mead, 1977.

———. *The Nimrud Ivories*. London: British Museum, 1978.

———. *Nimrud and Its Remains*. 3 vols. New York: Dodd, Mead, 1966.

———. "Noah's Flood Reconsidered." *Iraq* 26 (1964): 62–82.

———. *Twenty-Five Years of Mesopotamian Discovery, 1932–1956*. London: British School of Archaeology in Iraq, 1956.

——— et al. *Ivories from Nimrud*. 4 vols. London: British School of Archaeology in Iraq. 1966–74.

Marcus, D. "The Term 'Coffin' in the Semitic Languages." *Journal of the Ancient Near Eastern Society of Columbia University* 7 (1975): 85–94.

Marcus, M. I. "Art and Ideology in Ancient Western Asia." In *Civilizations of the Ancient Near East*, edited by J. M. Sasson et al. New York: Scribner's, 1995.

Margueron, J.-C. "Mari." In *The Oxford Encyclopedia of Archaeology in the Near East*, edited by E. M. Meyers. New York: Oxford University Press, 1997.

———. "Mari: A Portrait in Art of a Mesopotamian City-State." In *Civilizations of the Ancient Near East*, edited by J. M. Sasson et al. New York: Scribner's, 1995.

———. "Temples: Mesopotamian Temples." In *The Oxford Encyclopedia of Archaeology in the Near East*, edited by E. M. Meyers. New York: Oxford University Press, 1997.

Marks, J. H., and R. M. Good. *Love and Death in the Ancient Near East*. Guilford, Conn.: Four Quarters, 1987.

Marzahn, J. *The Ishtar Gate: The Processional Way/The New Year Festival of Babylon*. Mainz: Philipp von Zabern, 1992.

Marzal, A. *Gleanings from the Wisdom of Mari*. Rome: Biblical Institute Press, 1976.

Mason, H., trans. *Gilgamesh: A Verse Narrative*. With Afterword by J. H. Marks. New York: New American Library, 1972.

Matson, F. R. "Potters and Pottery in the Ancient Near East." In *Civilizations of the Ancient Near East*, edited by J. M. Sasson et al. New York: Scribner's, 1995.

Matthews, D. "Artisans and Artists in Ancient Western Asia." In *Civilizations of the Ancient Near East*, edited by J. M. Sasson et al. New York: Scribner's, 1995.

Matthews, R. J. *The Early Prehistory of Mesopotamia, 500,000 to 4,500 B.C.* Turnhout, Belgium: Brepols, 1999.

———. "History of the Field: Archaeology in Mesopotamia." In *The Oxford Encyclopedia of Archaeology in the Near East*, edited by E. M. Meyers. New York: Oxford University Press, 1997.

———. "Jemdet Nasr: The Site and the Period." *Biblical Archaeologist* 55 (1992): 196–203.

Matthiae, P. "Ebla." In *The Oxford Encyclopedia of Archaeology in the Near East*, edited by E. M. Meyers. New York: Oxford University Press, 1997.

———. *Ebla, An Empire Rediscovered*. London: Hodder & Stoughton, 1980.

Maxwell-Hyslop, K. R. *Western Asiatic Jewellery, c. 3000–612 B.C.* London: British Museum, 1971.

Mazar, A. "The Fortification of Cities in the Ancient Near East." In *Civilizations of the Ancient Near East*, edited by J. M. Sasson et al. New York: Scribner's, 1995.

McCall, H. *Mesopotamian Myths*. London: British Museum and Austin: University of Texas Press, 1990.

———. "Rediscovery and Aftermath." In *The Legacy of Mesopotamia*, edited by S. Dalley. New York: Oxford University Press, 1998.

McEwan, G. J. P. *Priest and Temple in Hellenistic Babylonia*. Wiesbaden: Stiener, 1981.

McGovern, P. E., S. J. Fleming, and S. H. Katz, eds.. *The Origins and Ancient History of Wine*. Amsterdam: Gordon and Breach, 1995.

McIntosh, J. *The Practical Archaeologist: How We Know What We Know about the Past*. New York: Facts On File, 1999.

McLemee, S. "Silicon Babylon." *Chronicle of Higher Education*, November 9, 2001, A14–15.

Meador, B. DeS. *Inanna, Lady of Largest Heart: Poems of the Sumerian High Priestess Enheduanna*. Austin: University of Texas Press, 2000.

Meadow, R. H., and H.-P. Uerpmann, eds. *Equids in the Ancient World*. 2 vols. Wiesbaden: Harrassowitz, 1986, 1991.

Meier, S. A. *The Messenger in the Ancient Semitic World*. Atlanta: Scholars Press, 1988.

———. "Women and Communication in the Ancient Near East." *Journal of the American Oriental Society* 111 (1991): 540–47.

Mellaart, J. *Earliest Civilizations of the Near East*. New York: McGraw-Hill, 1965.

———. *The Neolithic of the Near East*. London: Thames & Hudson, 1975.

Mendelhall, G. "Mari." *Biblical Archaeologist*, 11(1948): 1–19.

Mendelsohn, I. "The Family in the Ancient Near East." *Biblical Archaeologist* 11 (1948): 24–40.

———. *Slavery in the Ancient Near East*. New York: Oxford, 1949.

Merhav, R., ed. *Treasures of the Bible Lands: The Elie Borowski Collection*. Tel Aviv: Tel Aviv Museum and Modan Publishers, 1987.

Meyers, E. M., ed. *The Oxford Encyclopedia of Archaeology in the Near East*. 5 vols. Oxford: Oxford University Press, 1997.

Michalowski, P. "Early Mesopotamian Communicative Systems: Art, Literature, and Writing." In *Investigating Artistic Environments in the Ancient Near East*, edited by A. C. Gunter. Washington, D.C.: Smithsonian Institution, 1990.

———. *Lamentation over the Destruction of Sumer and Ur*. Winona Lake, Ind.: Eisenbrauns, 1989.

Michel, R. H., P. E. McGovern, and V. R. Badler. "Chemical Evidence for Ancient Beer." *Nature* 360 (November 5, 1992): 24.

———. *Letters from Early Mesopotamia*. Edited by E. Reiner. Atlanta: Scholars Press, 1993.

———. "Sumerian Literature: An Overview." In *Civilizations of the Ancient Near East*, edited by J. M. Sasson et al. New York: Scribner's, 1995.

———. "Sumerians." In *The Oxford Encyclopedia of Archaeology in the Near East*, edited by E. M. Meyers. New York: Oxford University Press, 1997.

Mikasa, H. I. H. Prince Takahito, ed. *Cult and Ritual in the Ancient Near East*. Wiesbaden: Harrassowitz, 1992.

Milano, L., ed. *Drinking in Ancient Societies: History and Culture of Drinking in the Ancient Near East*. Padua: Sargon, 1994.

———. "Ebla: A Third-Millennium City-State in Ancient Syria." In *Civilizations of the Ancient Near*

East, edited by J. M. Sasson et al. New York: Scribner's, 1995.

Millar, F. *The Roman Near East, 31 B.C.–A.D. 337.* Cambridge, Mass.: Harvard University Press, 1993.

Millard, A. R. "Abraham." In *Anchor Bible Dictionary*, edited by D. N. Freedman. New York: Doubleday, 1992.

———. "Babylonian King Lists." In *The Context of Scripture*, edited by W. W. Hallo and K. L. Younger. Leiden: E. J. Brill, 1997.

———. "Books in the Late Bronze Age in the Levant." In *Israel and Oriental Studies*, 18 (=*Past Links: Studies in the Languages and Cultures of the Ancient Near East*), edited by S. Izre'el, I. Singer, and R. Zadok. Winona Lake, Ind.: Eerdmans, 1998.

———. "Where Was Abraham's Ur? The Case for the Babylonian City." *Biblical Archaeology Review* 27, no. 3 (May/June 2001): 52–53, 57.

———, and D. J. Wiseman, eds. *Essays on the Patriarchal Narratives.* Leicester: Inter-Varsity Press, 1980.

Miller, N. F. "The Near East." In *Progress in Old World Palaeoethnobotany*, edited by W. van Zeis et al. Brookfield: A. A. Balkema, 1990.

Mirsky, J. *Sir Aurel Stein: Archaeological Explorer.* Chicago: University of Chicago Press, 1977.

Moore, K., and D. Lewis. *Birth of the Multinational: 2000 Years of Ancient Business History—From Ashur to Augustus.* Copenhagen: Copenhagen Business School, 1999.

Moorey, P. R. S. *Ancient Iraq: Assyria and Babylonia.* Oxford: Ashmolean Museum, 1976.

———. *Ancient Mesopotamian Materials and Industries: The Archaeological Evidence.* Oxford: Oxford University Press, 1994.

———. *The Ancient Near East.* Oxford: Ashmolean Museum, 1987.

———. *A Century of Biblical Archaeology.* Cambridge: Cambridge University Press, 1991.

———. "The Hurrians, the Mitanni and Technological Innovation." In *Archaeologia Iranica et Orientalis: Miscellanea in Honorem Louis Vanden Berghe*, edited by L. De Meyer and E. Haerinck. Ghent: Peeters, 1989.

———. *Kish Excavations, 1923–1933.* New York: Oxford University Press, 1978.

———. *Materials and Manufacture in Ancient Mesopotamia: The Evidence of Archaeology and Art: Metals, Metalwork, Glazed Materials and Glass.* Oxford: Oxford University Press, 1985.

———. *Ur 'of the Chaldees': A Revised and Updated Edition of Sir Leonard Woolley's Excavations at Ur.* Ithaca, N.Y.: Cornell University Press, 1982.

———. "What Do We Know about the People Buried in the Royal Cemetery?" *Expedition* 20 (1977): 24–40.

———. "Where Did They Bury the Kings of the IIIrd Dynasty of Ur?" *Iraq* 46 (1984): 1–18.

Moortgat, A. *The Art of Ancient Mesopotamia.* New York: Phaidon, 1969.

———. *Tammuz.* Berlin: W. de Gruyter, 1949.

Moran, W. L., ed. *The Amarna Letters.* Baltimore: Johns Hopkins University Press, 1992.

———. "The Gilgamesh Epic: A Masterpiece from Ancient Mesopotamia." In *Civilizations of the Ancient Near East*, edited by J. M. Sasson et al. New York: Scribner's, 1995.

Morrison, M. A., and D. I. Owen, eds. *Nuzi and the Hurrians.* Winona Lake, Ind.: Eerdmans, 1981.

Moscati, S. *An Introduction to the Comparative Grammar of the Semitic Languages.* Wiesbaden: Harrassowitz, 1964.

———. *The Face of the Ancient Orient.* Mineola, N.Y.: Dover, 2001 (1960).

Muhly, J. D. *Copper and Tin: The Distribution of Metal Resources and the Nature of the Metals Trade in the Bronze Age*, New Haven, Conn.: Connecticut Academy of Arts and Sciences, and Hamden, Conn.: Archon Books, 1973.

———. "Mining and Metalwork in Ancient Western Asia." In *Civilizations of the Ancient Near East*, edited by J. M. Sasson et al. New York: Scribner's, 1995.

———. *Supplement to Copper and Tin: The Distribution of Mineral Resources and the Nature of the Metal Trade in the Bronze Age.* Hamden, Conn.: Connecticut Academy of Arts and Sciences/Archon Books, 1976.

Muller, V. "Types of Mesopotamian Houses." *Journal of the American Oriental Society* 60 (1940): 151–80.

Muscarella, O. W. "Art and Archaeology of Western Iran in Prehistory." In *Civilizations of the Ancient Near East*, edited by J. M. Sasson et al. New York: Scribner's, 1995.

———. *Bronze and Iron: Ancient Near Eastern Artifacts in the Metropolitan Museum of Art*. New York: Metropolitan Museum of Art, 1988.

———, ed. *Ladders to Heaven: Art Treasures from Lands of the Bible*. Toronto: McClelland and Stewart, 1981.

Na'aman, N. "Amarna Letters." In *Anchor Bible Dictionary*, edited by D. N. Freedman. New York: Doubleday, 1992.

Nemet-Nejat, K. R. *Daily Life in Ancient Mesopotamia*. Westport, Conn.: Greenwood, 1998.

Neugebauer, O. "Ancient Mathematics and Astronomy." In *A History of Technology*, edited by C. Singer. Oxford: Clarendon Press 1954.

———. *The Exact Sciences in Antiquity*. New York: Harper & Row, 1962.

———. "A History of Ancient Astronomy." *Journal of Near Eastern Studies* 4 (1945): 1–38.

———. "The Survival of Babylonian Methods in the Exact Sciences of Antiquity and the Middle Ages." *Proceedings of the American Philosophical Society* 107 (1963): 528–35.

Nielsen, K. "Incense." In *Anchor Bible Dictionary*, edited by D. N. Freedman. New York: Doubleday, 1992.

Nissen, H. J. "Ancient Western Asia before the Age of Empires." In *Civilizations of the Ancient Near East*, edited by J. M. Sasson et al. New York: Scribner's, 1995.

———. *The Early History of the Ancient Near East, 9000–2000 B.C.* Chicago: University of Chicago Press, 1988.

———. "Short Remarks on Ancient State-Formation in Babylonia: An Answer to Steiner and Westenholz." In *Power and Propaganda: A Symposium on Ancient Empires (=Mesopotamia: Copenhagen Studies in Assyriology*, Vol. 7), edited by M. T. Larsen. Copenhagen: Akademisk Forlag, 1976.

———, P. Damerow, and R. K. Englund. *Archaic Bookkeeping. Writing and Techniques of Economic Administration in the Ancient Near East*. Chicago: University of Chicago Press, 1993.

———, and St. J. Simpson. "Mesopotamia." In *The Oxford Encyclopedia of Archaeology in the Near East*, edited by E. M. Meyers. New York: Oxford University Press, 1997.

Nun, M. "Fishing. In *The Oxford Encyclopedia of Archaeology in the Near East*, edited by E. M.

Meyers. New York: Oxford University Press, 1997.

Nutzel, W. "The Climate Changes of Mesopotamia and Bordering Areas, 1400 to 2000 B.C." *Sumer* 32 (1976): 11–24.

Oates, D. "Max Edgar Lucien Mallowan, 1904–1978." *Proceedings of the British Academy* 76 (1990): 499–511.

———. *Studies in the Ancient History of Northern Iraq*. London: Oxford University Press, 1968.

———, and J. Oates "Early Irrigation Agriculture in Mesopotamia." In *Problems in Economic and Social Archaeology*, edited by G. de G. Sieveking et al. London: Duckworth, 1976.

———. *The Rise of Civilization*. London: Phaidon & New York: Dutton, 1976.

———, and J. Curtis, eds. *Fifty Years of Mesopotamian Discovery*. London: British School of Archaeology in Iraq, 1982.

Oates, J. *Babylon*. Rev. ed. London: Thames & Hudson, 1986.

———. "Mesopotamian Social Organisation: Archaeological and Philological Evidence." In *The Evolution of Social Systems*, edited by J. Friedman and M. J. Rowlands. Pittsburgh: University of Pittsburgh Press, 1978.

———. "Ur and Eridu: The Prehistory." *Iraq* 22 (1960): 32–50.

———. "Urban Trends in Prehistoric Mesopotamia." In *La Ville dans le Proche-Orient ancien*, 81–92. Louvain: Peeters, 1983.

——— et al. "Seafaring Merchants of Ur?" *Antiquity* 5 (1977): 221–34.

Oded, B. *Mass Deportations and Deportees in the Neo-Assyrian Empire*. Wiesbaden: Reichert, 1979.

Ogden, J. *Jewellery of the Ancient World*. New York: Rizzoli, 1982.

Okada, Y. "An Architectural Innovation of the Temple Style: Sumerian to Babylonian." In *Priests and Officials in the Ancient Near East (= Papers of the Second Colloquium on the Ancient Near East—The City and Its Life)*, edited by K. Watanabe. Heidelberg: Universitätsverlag C. Winter, 1999.

"The Oldest School in the World." *Times Educational Supplement* (London), October 31, 1952.

Oller, G. H. "Messengers and Ambassadors in Ancient Western Asia." In *Civilizations of the*

Ancient Near East, edited by J. M. Sasson et al. New York: Scribner's, 1995.

Olmstead, A. T. *History of Assyria.* Chicago: University of Chicago Press, 1951.

———. "Babylonian Astronomy—Historical Sketch." *American Journal of Semitic Languages and Literatures* 55, no. 2 (April 1938): 113–29.

O'Neill, J. P., ed. *Egypt and the Ancient Near East.* New York: Metropolitan Museum of Art, 1987.

Oppenheim, A. L. *Ancient Mesopotamia: Portrait of a Dead Civilization.* Rev. ed., edited by E. Reiner. Chicago: University of Chicago Press, 1977.

———. "The Archives of the Palace of Mari." *Journal of Near Eastern Studies* 11 (1952): 129–39, and 13 (1954): 141–48.

———. "A Bird's-Eye View of Mesopotamian Economic History." In *Trade and Market in the Early Empires*, edited by K. Polanyi, C. M. Arensberg, and H. W. Pearson. Glencoe, Ill.: Free Press, 1957.

———. "A Caesarean Section in the Second Millennium B.C." *Journal of the History of Medicine and Allied Sciences* 15 (1960): 292–94.

———. *The Interpretation of Dreams in the Ancient Near East. With a Translation of an Assyrian Dream-Book.* Philadelphia: American Philosophical society, 1956.

———. *Letters from Mesopotamia: Official, Business, and Private Letters on Clay Tablets from Two Millennia.* Chicago: University of Chicago Press, 1967.

———. "Man and Nature in Mesopotamian Civilization." In *Dictionary of Scientific Biography*, edited by C. C. Gillispie et al. Vol. 15. New York: Scribner's, 1978.

———. "Mesopotamia—Land of Many Cities." In *Middle Eastern Cities*, edited by I. Lapidus. Berkeley: University of California Press, 1969.

———. "Mesopotamian Medicine." *Bulletin of the History of Medicine* 36 (1962): 97–108.

———. "On Royal Gardens in Mesopotamia." *Journal of Near Eastern Studies* 24 (1965): 328–33.

———. "Sea-Faring Merchants of Ur." *Journal of the American Oriental Society* 74 (1954): 6–17.

———. "Trade in the Ancient Near East." In *Vth International Congress of Economic History*, 1–37. Moscow: Nauka, 1970.

———, and L. F. Hartman. *On Beer and Brewing Techniques in Ancient Mesopotamia.* Baltimore: Johns Hopkins University Press, 1950.

———, R. H. Brill, D. Barag, and A. von Saldern. *Glass and Glassmaking in Ancient Mesopotamia: An Edition of the Cuneiform Texts Which Contain Instructions for Glassmakers with a Catalogue of Surviving Objects.* Corning, N.Y.: The Corning Museum of Glass, 1970.

Owen, D. I., and G. Wilhelm, eds. *Studies on the Civilization and Culture of Nuzi and the Hurrians.* Winona Lake, Ind.: Eerdmans, 1981–.

Paley, S. M. *King of the World: Ashur-nasir-pal II of Assyria 883–859 B.C.* Brooklyn, NY: Brooklyn Museum, 1976.

Pallis, S. A. *The Antiquity of Iraq: A Handbook of Assyriology.* Copenhagen: Munksgaard, 1956.

Parker, R. A., and W. Dubberstein. *Babylonian Chronology.* 3d ed. Chicago: University of Chicago Press, 1956.

Parker, S. B. *Ugaritic Narrative Poetry.* Atlanta, Ga.: Scholars Press, 1997.

Parpola, S., ed. *Assyrian Prophecies.* Helsinki: Helsinki University Press, 1997.

———. "Sons of God: The Ideology of Assyrian Kingship." *Archaeology Odyssey* 2 (November/December 1999): 16–27, 61.

———, *State Archives of Assyria*, Helsinki: Helsinki University Press, 1987–.

———, et al. *The Correspondence of Sargon II.* 2 vols. Helsinki: Helsinki University Press, 1987, 1990.

———, et al. *Letters from Assyrian and Babylonian Scholars.* Helsinki: Helsinki University Press, 1993.

Parrot, A. *The Arts of Assyria.* New York: Golden Press, 1961.

———. *Babylon and the Old Testament.* London: SCM Press, 1958.

———. *Nineveh and Babylon.* London: Thames & Hudson, 1961.

———. *Nineveh and the Old Testament.* New York: Philosophical Library, 1955.

———. *Tower of Babel.* New York: Philosophical Library, 1955.

———. *Sumer: The Dawn of Art.* Golden Press, 1961.

Paterson, A. *Assyrian Sculptures.* London: Kleinman & Co., 1904, 1911.

Paul, S. "Adoption Formulae: A Study of Cuneiform and Biblical Legal Codes." *Maarav* 2 (1979–80): 173–85.

Payne, B. *History of Costume: From the Ancient Egyptians to the Twentieth Century.* New York: Harper & Row, 1965.

Pearce, L. E. "The Scribes and Scholars of Ancient Mesopotamia." In *Civilizations of the Ancient Near East,* edited by J. M. Sasson et al. New York: Scribner's, 1995.

Peck, E. H., et al. *Gudea of Lagash* (exhibition guide). Detroit: Detroit Institute of Arts, 1982.

Pedersén, O. *Archives and Libraries in the Ancient Near East, 1500–300 B.C.* Bethesda, Md.: CDL Press, 1998.

Penglase, C. *Greek Myths and Mesopotamia: Parallels and Influence in the Homeric Hymns and Hesiod.* London: Routledge, 1994.

Perkins, A. L. *The Art of Dura-Europos.* Oxford: Clarendon Press, 1973.

———. *The Comparative Archaeology of Early Mesopotamia.* Chicago: University of Chicago Press, 1949.

———. "Narration in Babylonian Art." *American Journal of Archaeology* 61 (1957): 54–62.

Perlin, J. *A Forest Journey: The Role of Wood in the Development of Civilization.* New York: Norton, 1989.

Perna, M. *Administrative Documents in the Aegean and Their Near Eastern Counterparts* (=Centro Internazionale di Ricerche Archeologiche, Antropologiche e Storiche, 3). Turin: Archivi di Stato, Ministero per i Bene e le Attività Culturale, Uffico Centrale per i Beni Archivistici, 2000.

Peters, F. E. *The Harvest of Hellenism: A History of the Near East from Alexander the Great to the Triumph of Christianity.* New York: Simon & Schuster, 1972.

Pettinato, G. *The Archives of Ebla: An Empire Inscribed in Clay.* Garden City, N.Y.: Doubleday, 1981.

———. *Ebla: A New Look at History.* Baltimore: Johns Hopkins University Press, 1991.

Petzel, F. E. *Textiles of Ancient Mesopotamia, Persia, and Egypt.* Corvallis, Oreg.: F. E. Petzel, 1987.

Pfeiffer, C. F., ed. *The Biblical World: A Dictionary of Biblical Archaeology.* New York: Bonanza/Crown, 1966.

Pfeiffer, R. H. *State Letters of Assyria.* New Haven, Conn.: American Oriental Society, 1935 (repr. New York: Kraus Reprint Corporation, 1967).

———, and E. A. Speiser. "One Hundred New Selected Nuzi Texts." *Annual of the American Schools of Oriental Research* 16 (1935–36): 9–168.

Piggott, S. *The Earliest Wheeled Transport.* Ithaca, N.Y.: Cornell University Press, 1983.

Pinnock, F. "Erotic Art in the Ancient Near East." In *Civilizations of the Ancient Near East,* edited by J. M. Sasson et al. New York: Scribner's, 1995.

Pittman, H. "Cylinder Seals and Scarabs in the Ancient Near East." In *Civilizations of the Ancient Near East,* edited by J. M. Sasson et al. New York: Scribner's, 1995.

Place, V. *Nineve et l' Assyrie.* 3 vols. Paris, 1867–70.

Polanyi, K. *Trade and Market in the Early Empires.* Glencoe, Ill.: Free Press and the Falcon Wing's Press, 1957.

Polin, C. C. J. *Music of the Ancient Near East.* New York: Vantage Press, 1954.

Pollard, N. *Soldiers, Cities, and Civilians in Roman Syria.* Ann Arbor: University of Michigan Press, 2001.

Pope, M. *The Story of Decipherment: From Egyptian Hieroglyphic to Linear B.* London: Thames & Hudson, 1975.

Porada, E., ed. *Ancient Art in Seals.* Princeton, N.J.: Princeton University Press, 1980.

———. "Sumerian Art in Miniature." In *The Legacy of Sumer,* edited by D. Schmandt-Besserat. Malibu, Calif.: Undena, 1976.

———. "Understanding Ancient Near Eastern Art: A Personal Account." In *Civilizations of the Ancient Near East,* edited by J. M. Sasson et al. New York: Scribner's, 1995.

Porter, B. N. *Images, Power, and Politics: Figurative Aspects of Esarhaddon's Babylonian Policy (681–669 B.C.).* Philadelphia: American Philosophical Society, 1993.

———. "Sacred Trees, Date Palms, and the Royal Persona of Ashurnasirpal II." *Journal of Near Eastern Studies* 52 (1993): 129–39.

Postgate, J. N. *Early Mesopotamia: Society and Economy at the Dawn of History.* New York: Routledge, 1992.

———. "The Economic Structure of the Assyrian Empire." In *Power and Propaganda: A Symposium on*

Ancient Empires (=*Mesopotamia: Copenhagen Studies in Assyriology*, Vol. 7). Copenhagen: Akademisk Vorlag, 1976.

———. *The First Empires*. London: Phaidon, 1977.

———. "The Role of the Temple in the Mesopotamian Secular Community." In *Man, Settlement, and Urbanism*, edited by P. J. Ucko, R. C. Tringham, and G. W. Dimbleby. Cambridge, Mass.: Schenkman, 1972.

———. "Royal Ideology and State Administration in Sumer and Akkad." In *Civilizations of the Ancient Near East*, edited by J. M. Sasson et al. New York: Scribner's, 1995.

———. *Taxation and Conscription in the Assyrian Empire*. Rome: Biblical Institute Press, 1974.

———, and S. Payne. "Some Old Babylonian Shepherds and Their Flocks." *Journal of Semitic Studies* 20 (1975): 1–21.

———, and M. A. Powell, eds. *Trees and Timber in Mesopotamia* (=*Bulletin on Sumerian Agriculture* 6 [1992]).

Potts, D. T. *The Arabian Gulf in Antiquity*. Oxford: Oxford University Press 1990.

———, ed. *Araby the Blest: Studies in Arabian Archaeology*. Copenhagen: Museum Tusculanum Press, 1988.

———. *The Archaeology of Elam: Formation and Transformation of an Ancient Iranian State*. New York: Cambridge University Press, 1999.

———. *Dilmun: New Studies in the Archaeology and Early History of Bahrain*. Berlin: D. Reimer, 1983.

———. "Distant Shores: Ancient Near Eastern Trade with South Asia and Northeast Africa." In *Civilizations of the Ancient Near East*, edited by J. M. Sasson et al. New York: Scribner's, 1995.

———. *Mesopotamian Civilization: The Material Foundations*. Ithaca, N.Y.: Cornell University Press, 1997.

Powell, M. A. "Evidence for Agriculture and Waterworks in Babylonian Mathematical Texts." *Bulletin on Sumerian Agriculture* 4 (1988): 161–71.

———. "Drugs and Pharmaceuticals in Ancient Mesopotamia." In *The Healing Past: Pharmaceuticals in the Biblical and Rabbinic World*, edited by I. and W. Jacob. Leiden: E. J. Brill, 1993.

———. *Labor in the Ancient Near East*. New Haven, Conn.: American Oriental Society, 1987.

———. "Metrology and Mathematics in Ancient Mesopotamia." In *Civilizations of the Ancient Near East*, edited by J. M. Sasson et al. New York: Scribner's, 1995.

———. "Salt, Seed and Yields in Sumerian Agriculture." *Zeitschrift für Assyriologie* 75 (1985): 7–38.

———. "Weights and Measures." In *The Oxford Encyclopedia of Archaeology in the Near East*, edited by E. M. Meyers. New York: Oxford University Press, 1997.

Powell, M., Jr. "A Contribution to the History of Money in Mesopotamia Prior to the Invention of Coinage." In *Festschrift Lubor Matouš*, edited by B. Hruška and G. Komoróczy. Budapest: Eötvös Loránd Tudományegyetem, Ókori Történeti Tanszekek, 1978.

Price, I. M. "Transportation by Water in Early Babylonia." *American Journal of Semitic Languages* 40 (1923): 111–16.

Pritchard, J. B., ed. *The Ancient Near East: An Anthology of Texts and Pictures*. Princeton, N.J.: Princeton University Press, 1958.

———. *The Ancient Near East, Vol. II: A New Anthology of Texts and Pictures*. Princeton, N.J.: Princeton University Press, 1975.

———. *Ancient Near Eastern Texts Relating to the Old Testament*. 3rd ed. with Supplement. Princeton, N.J.: Princeton University Press, 1969.

———. *The Times Atlas of the Bible*. London: Times Books, 1987.

Quaegebeur, J., ed. *Ritual and Sacrifice in the Ancient Near East*. Louvain: Uitgeverij Peeters en Department Oriëntalistiek, 1993.

Quarantelli, E., ed. *The Land between Two Rivers*. Turin: II Quadrante Edizioni, 1985.

Radau, H. *Ninib, the Determiner of Fates*. Philadelphia: University of Pennsylvania Museum, 1910.

Rassam, H. *Asshur and the Land of Nimrod*. Farnborough: Gregg International Publishers, 1971 (1897).

Ravn, O. E. *Herodotus' Description of Babylon*. Copenhagen: Nyt Nordisk Forlag/Arnold Busck, 1942.

Reade, J. *Assyrian Sculpture*. 2d ed. London: British Museum, 1998 (1983).

———. "Hormuzd Rassam and His Discoveries." *Iraq* 55 (1993): 39–62.

———. "Ideology and Propaganda in Assyrian Art." In *Power and Propaganda: A Symposium on Ancient*

Empires (=*Mesopotamia: Copenhagen Studies in Assyriology*, Vol. 7). Copenhagen: Akademisk Vorlag, 1976.

———. *Mesopotamia*. London: British Museum, 1991.

Redford, D. B. *The Oxford Encyclopedia of Ancient Egypt*. New York: Oxford University Press, 2000.

Redman, C. L. *The Rise of Civilization: From Early Farmers to Urban Society in the Ancient Near East*. San Francisco: W. H. Freeman, 1978.

Reiner, E. *Letters from Early Mesopotamia*. Atlanta: Scholars Press, 1993.

———. *Your Thwarts in Pieces, Your Mooring Rope Cut: Poetry from Babylonia and Assyria*. Ann Arbor: University of Michigan, 1985.

———. *Astral Magic in Babylonia* (=*Transactions of the American Philosophical Society*, Vol. 8, Part 4). Philadelphia: American Philosophical Society, 1995.

Renfrew, C. *Archaeology: Theories, Methods, and Practice*. New York: Thames and Hudson, 1991.

———. "Before Babel: Speculations on the Origins of Linguistic Diversity." *Cambridge Archaeological Journal* 1 (1991): 3–23.

———, and P. Bahn. *Archaeology: Theories, Method and Practice*. London: Thames & Hudson, 1991.

Renfrew, J. M. "Cereals Cultivated in Ancient Iraq." *Bulletin on Sumerian Agriculture* 1 (1984): 32–44.

———. "Vegetables in the Ancient Near Eastern Diet." In *Civilizations of the Ancient Near East*, edited by J. M. Sasson et al. New York: Scribner's, 1995.

Renger, J. "Rivers, Water Courses, and Irrigation Ditches and Other Matters Concerning Irrigation Based on Old Babylonian Sources, 2000–1600 B.C." *Bulletin on Sumerian Agriculture* 5 (1990): 31–46.

Rice, M. *Search for the Paradise Land: An Introduction to the Archaeology of Bahrain and the Arabian Gulf, from the Earliest Times to the Death of Alexander the Great*. London: Longman, 1985.

Rich, C. J. *Memoir on the Ruins of Babylon*. London: Longman, 1815.

———. *Second Memoir on Babylon*. London: Longman, 1818.

———. *Narrative of a Residence in Koordistan, and on the Site of Nineveh*. London: Duncan & Malcomb, 1836.

———. *Narrative of a Journey to the Site of Babylon in 1811*. London: Duncan & Malcomb, 1839.

Rimmer, J. *Ancient Musical Instruments of Western Asia in the British Museum*. London: British Museum, 1969.

Ringgren, H. *Religions of the Ancient Near East*. Philadelphia: Westminster Press, 1973.

Ritter, E. K. "Magical Expert (=*Āšipu*) and Physician (=*Asû*): Notes on Two Complementary Professions in Babylonian Medicine." In *Studies in Honor of Benno Landsberger on his Seventy-Fifth Birthday, April 21, 1965*, edited by H. G. Güterbock and T. Jacobsen. Chicago: University of Chicago Press, 1965.

Roaf, M. *Cultural Atlas of Mesopotamia and the Ancient Near East*. New York: Facts On File, 1990.

———. "Media and Mesopotamia: History and Architecture." In *Later Mesopotamia and Iran*, edited by J. Curtis. London: British Museum Press, 1995.

———. "Palaces and Temples in Ancient Mesopotamia." In *Civilizations of the Ancient Near East*, edited by J. M. Sasson et al. New York: Scribner's, 1996.

Robertson, J. F. "The Social and Economic Organization of Ancient Mesopotamian Temples." In *Civilizations of the Ancient Near East*, edited by J. M. Sasson et al. New York: Scribner's, 1995.

Rochberg, F. "Astronomy and Calendars in Ancient Mesopotamia." In *Civilizations of the Ancient Near East*, edited by J. M. Sasson et al. New York: Scribner's, 1995.

Rochberg-Halton, F. *Aspects of Babylonian Celestial Divination: The Lunar Eclipse Tablets of Enuma Anu Enlil*. Horn: F. Berger, 1988.

———. "Babylonian Horoscopes and Their Sources." *Orientalia* 58 (1989): 102–23.

———. "Calendars: Ancient Near East." In *Anchor Bible Dictionary*, edited by D. N. Freedman. New York: Doubleday, 1992.

Rogers, R. W. *A History of Babylonia and Assyria*. 2 vols. North Stratford, N.H.: Ayer, 1977.

Romer, J., and E. Romer. *The Seven Wonders of the World: A History of the Modern Imagination*. New York: Henry Holt, 1995.

Root, M. C. "Art and Archaeology of the Achaemenid Empire." In *Civilizations of the*

Ancient Near East, edited by J. M. Sasson et al. New York: Scribner's, 1995.

Rostovtzeff, M. *Dura-Europos and Its Art*. New York: AMS Press, 1978 (1938).

Roth, M. T. "Age at Marriage and the Household: A Study of the Neo-Babylonian and Neo-Assyrian Forms." *Comparative Studies in Society and History* 29 (1987): 715–47.

Roth, T. *Law Collections from Mesopotamia and Asia Minor*. Atlanta: Scholars Press, 1995.

Rothman, M. S. "Tepe Gawra." In *The Oxford Encyclopedia of Archaeology in the Near East*, edited by E. M. Meyers. New York: Oxford University Press, 1997.

Roux, G. *Ancient Iraq*. 3d ed. New York: Penguin, 1992.

Rowton, M. B. "Chronology: Ancient Western Asia." In *The Cambridge Ancient History*, 1.1. 2d ed. Cambridge: Cambridge University Press, 1970.

———. "The Date of Hammurabi." *Journal of Near Eastern Studies* 17 (1958): 97–111.

———. *The Role of Watercourses in the Growth of Mesopotamian Civilization*. Neukirchen-Vluyn: Butzon & Bercker, 1969.

The Royal Game of Ur: A Game for 2 Players. London: British Museum, 1991.

Russell, J. M. "Assur." In *The Dictionary of Art*, edited by J. Turner. New York: Grove's Dictionaries, 1996.

———. *The Final Sack of Nineveh: The Discovery, Documentation, and Destruction of King Sennacherib's Throne Room at Nineveh, Iraq*. New Haven, Conn.: Yale University Press, 1998.

———. *From Nineveh to New York: The Strange Story of the Assyrian Reliefs in the Metropolitan Museum and the Hidden Masterpieces at Canford School*. New Haven, Conn.: Yale University Press, 1997.

———. *Sennacherib's Palace without Rival at Nineveh*. Chicago: University of Chicago Press, 1992.

———. *The Writing on the Wall: Studies in the Architectural Context of Late Assyrian Palace Inscription* (=*Mesopotamian Civilizations*, 9). Winona Lake, Ind.: Eisenbrauns, 1999.

Sabloff, J. A., and C. C. Lamberg-Karlovsky, eds. *Ancient Civilization and Trade*. Albuquerque: University of New Mexico Press, 1975.

Sachs, A. "Babylonian Horoscopes." *Journal of Cuneiform Studies* 6 (1952): 49–75.

Sack, R. H. *Images of Nebuchadnezzar: The Emergence of a Legend*. Cranbury, N.J.: Susquehanna University Press, 1992.

Safar, F., M. A. Mustafa, and S. Lloyd. *Eridu*. Baghdad: Iraq Ministry of Culture and Information, 1981.

Saggs, H. W. F. *Babylonians*. London: British Museum and Norman: University of Oklahoma Press, 1995.

———. *The Encounter with the Divine in Mesopotamia and Israel*. London: Athlone Press, 1978.

———. *Everyday Life in Babylonia and Assyria*. London: Batsford, 1965 and New York: Dorset, 1987.

———. *The Greatness That Was Babylon*. New York: Hawthorn Books, 1962.

———. "Introduction." In A. H. Layard, *Nineveh and Its Remains*. New York: Praeger, 1970.

———. *The Might That Was Assyria*. London: Sidgwick & Jackson, 1984.

———. "Some Ancient Semitic Conceptions of the Afterlife." *Faith and Thought* 90 (1958): 157–82.

Salvesen, A. "The Legacy of Babylon and Nineveh in Aramaic Sources." In *The Legacy of Mesopotamia*, edited by S. Dalley. New York: Oxford University Press, 1998.

Sancisi-Weerdenburg, H., et al. *Achaemenid History*. 8 vols. Leiden: E. J. Brill, 1987–94.

Sanders, N. K. *The Epic of Gilgamesh*. Baltimore: Penguin, 1972.

Sasson, J. M., ed. *Civilizations of the Ancient Near East*. 4 vols. New York: Scribner's, 1995.

———. "King Hammurabi of Babylon." In *Civilizations of the Ancient Near East*, edited by J. M. Sasson et al. New York: Scribner's, 1995.

———. *The Military Establishments at Mari*. Rome: Pontificium Institutum Biblicum, 1969.

———, ed. *Studies in Literature from the Ancient Near East Dedicated to Samuel Noah Kramer*. New Haven, Conn.: American Oriental Society, 1984.

———. *The Treatment of Criminals in the Ancient Near East*. Leiden: E. J. Brill, 1977.

Schlossman, B. "Portraiture in Mesopotamia in the Late Third and Early Second Millennium B.C." *Archiv für Orientforschung* 26 (1978/1979): 56–77, and 28 (1981/1982): 143–70.

Schmandt-Besserat, D. "An Ancient Token System: The Precursor to Writing and Numerals." *Archaeology* 39 (1986): 32–39.

———. *Before Writing*. 2 vols. Austin: University of Texas Press, 1992.

———. *How Writing Came About*. Austin: University of Texas Press, 1996.

———, ed. *The Legacy of Sumer*. Malibu, Calif.: Undena, 1976.

———. "Record Keeping before Writing." In *Civilizations of the Ancient Near East*, edited by J. M. Sasson et al. New York: Scribner's, 1995.

———. "Sumer—Art in an Urban Context." In *The Legacy of Sumer*, edited by D. Schmandt-Besserat. Malibu, Calif.: Undena, 1976.

Schmidt, B. "Flood Narratives of Ancient Western Asia." In *Civilizations of the Ancient Near East*, edited by J. M. Sasson et al. New York: Scribner's, 1995.

Schwartz, G. M. "Pastoral Nomadism in Ancient Western Asia." In *Civilizations of the Ancient Near East*, edited by J. M. Sasson et al. New York: Scribner's, 1995.

Scott, R. A. *Murder by Contrived Design: Babylon's Systematic Genocidal Plan and Strategies*. Decatur, Ga.: Cornerstone Productions, 1995.

Scurlock, J. "Death and the Afterlife in Ancient Mesopotamian Thought." In *Civilization of the Ancient Near East*, edited by J. M. Sasson et al. New York: Scribner's, 1995.

Searight, S. *The British in the Near East*. London: Weidenfeld & Nicholson, 1969.

Sengsong, M. C. *Chaldaean-Americans: Changing Conceptions of Ethnic Identity*. New York: Center for Migration Studies, 1999.

Severy, M. "Iraq: Crucible of Civilization." *National Geographic* 179 (May 1991): 102–15.

Seigel, B. J. *Slavery during the Third Dynasty of Ur* (=*American Anthropologist*, N.S. 49.1, Pt. 2, 1947).

Shanks, H. "Abraham's Ur: Is the Pope Going to the Wrong Place?" *Biblical Archaeology Review* 26 (March/April 2000): 62–63, 69.

Siebert, I. *Women in the Ancient Near East*. New York: A. Schram, 1974.

Sigerist, H. E. *A History of Medicine*. New York: Oxford University Press, 1961.

Silberman, N. A. *Between Past and Present: Archaeology, Ideology, and Nationalism in the Modern Middle East*. New York: Henry Holt, 1989.

Silverberg, R. *The Man Who Found Nineveh*. New York: Holt, Rinehart, & Winston, 1964.

Simons, G. L. *Iraq: From Sumer to Saddam*. New York: St. Martin's, 1994.

Simpson, E., "Furniture in Ancient Western Asia." In *Civilizations of the Ancient Near East*, edited by J. M. Sasson et al. New York: Scribner's, 1995.

Sjöberb, Å. W. "The Old Babylonian Edubba." *Assyriological Studies* 20 (1975): 159–79.

———, ed. *Sumerian Dictionary of the University Museum of the University of Pennsylvania*. Philadelphia: University of Pennsylvania Museum, 1985.

———, E. Bergmann, and G. B. Gragg. *The Collection of Sumerian Temple Hymns* and *The Keš Temple Hymn*. Locust Valley, N.Y.: J. J. Augustin, 1969.

Sladek, W. *Inanna's Descent to the Netherworld*. Philadelphia: University Microfilms International, 1974.

Smith, B. C. *The Emergence of Agriculture*. New York: W. H. Freeman, 1994.

Smith, G. *Assyrian Discovery: An Account of Explorations and Discoveries on the Site of Nineveh*. London, 1875.

Smith, S. "The Face of Humbaba." *[Liverpool] Annals of Archaeology and Anthropology* 11 (1924): 107–14.

Snell, D. C. *Life in the Ancient Near East, 3100–332 B.C.E.* New Haven, Conn.: Yale University Press, 1997.

———. "Methods of Exchange and Coinage in Ancient Western Asia." In *Civilizations of the Ancient Near East*, edited by J. M. Sasson et al. New York: Scribner's, 1995.

Solecki, R. *Shanidar: The First Flower People*. New York: Knopf, 1971.

Sollberger, E. *The Business and Administrative Correspondence under the Kings of Ur*. Locust Valley, N.J.: J. J. Augustin, 1966.

Sommerfeld, W. "The Kassites of Ancient Mesopotamia: Origins, Politics, and Culture." In *Civilizations of the Ancient Near East*, edited by J. M. Sasson et al. New York: Scribner's, 1995.

Speiser, E. A., trans. *The Anchor Bible: Genesis*. Garden City, N.Y.: Doubleday, 1982.

———. "Ancient Mesopotamia." In *The Idea of History in the Ancient Near East* (*American Oriental Series*, 38), edited by R. C. Dentan. New Haven, Conn.: Yale University Press and London: Oxford University Press, 1955.

———. "Ancient Mesopotamia, A Light That Did Not Fail." *National Geographic* 49 (1951): 41–105.

———. "Authority and Law in the Ancient Orient—Mesopotamia." *Journal of the American Oriental Society*, Supplement 17 (1954): 8–15.

———. *Excavations at Tepe Gawra*. Vol. 1. Philadelphia: University of Pennsylvania Press, 1935.

———. "Ethnic Movements in the Near East in the Second Millennium B.C." *Annual of the American Schools of Oriental Research* 13 (1931–32): 13–54.

Spence, Lewis. *Myths and Legends: Babylonia and Assyria*. Kila, Mont.: Kessinger, 1995.

———. *Myths and Legends of Babylonia and Assyria* (illus.). Detroit: Omnigraphics, 1998.

Spina, F. A. "Babel." In *Anchor Bible Dictionary*, edited by D. N. Freedman. New York: Doubleday, 1992.

Spycket, A. "Reliefs, Statuary, and Monumental Paintings in Ancient Mesopotamia." In *Civilizations of the Ancient Near East*, edited by J. M. Sasson et al. New York: Scribner's, 1995.

Starr, I. *Rituals of the Diviner*. Malibu, Calif.: Undena, 1983.

Starr, R. F. S. *Nuzi*. 2 vols. Cambridge, Mass.: Harvard University Press, 1939.

Stearns, J. B. *Reliefs from the Palace of Ashurnasirpal*. 2 vols. Osnabrück: Biblio, 1961.

Steele, F. R. "The Code of Lipit-Ishtar." *American Journal of Archaeology* 52 (1948): 425–50.

———. *The Code of Lipit Ishtar*. Philadelphia: University Museum, 1949.

Stein, D. L. "Hurrians." In *The Oxford Encyclopedia of Archaeology in the Near East*, edited by E. M. Meyers. New York: Oxford University Press, 1997.

———. "Nuzi." In *The Oxford Encyclopedia of Archaeology in the Near East*, edited by E. M. Meyers. New York: Oxford University Press, 1997.

Steinkeller, P. "Early Semitic Literature and Third-millennium Seals with Mythological Motifs." In *Literature and Literary Language at Ebla*, edited by P. Fronzaroli. Florence: Department of Linguistics, University of Florence, 1992.

———. "On Rulers, Priests, and Sacred Marriage: Tracing the Evolution of Early Sumerian Kingship." In *Priests and Officials in the Ancient Near East (=Papers of the Second Colloquium on the Ancient Near East—The City and Its Life)*, edited

by K. Watanabe. Heidelberg: Universitätsverlag C. Winter, 1999.

Steinmann, M. " 'Chicken Scratches' Written in Clay Yield Their Secrets." *Smithsonian* 19 (December 1988): 130–34+.

Stevenson, D. W. W. "A Proposal for the Irrigation of the Hanging Gardens of Babylon." *Iraq* 54 (1992): 35–55.

Stol, M. "Private Life in Ancient Mesopotamia." In *Civilizations of the Ancient Near East*, edited by J. M. Sasson et al. New York: Scribner's, 1995.

Stone, E. C. "Chariots of the Gods in Old Babylonian Mesopotamia (c. 2000–1600 BC)." *Cambridge Archaeological Journal* 3 (March 1, 1993): 83–107.

———. "The Development of Cities in Ancient Mesopotamia." In *Civilizations of the Ancient Near East*, edited by J. M. Sasson et al. New York: Scribner's, 1995.

———. "House: Mesopotamian Houses." In *The Oxford Encyclopedia of Archaeology in the Near East*, edited by E. M. Meyers. New York: Oxford University Press, 1997.

Strommenger, E. *5000 Years of the Art of Mesopotamia*. New York: Abrams, 1964.

Stronach, D., and K. Codella. "Nineveh." In *The Oxford Encyclopedia of Archaeology in the Near East*, edited by E. M. Meyers. New York: Oxford University Press, 1997.

Sullivan, R. D. *Near Eastern Royalty and Rome, 100–30 B.C.* Toronto: University of Toronto Press, 1990.

Swerdlow, N. M., ed. *Ancient Astronomy and Celestial Divination*. Cambridge, Mass.: MIT Press, 2000.

Tabouis, G. R. *Nebuchadnezzar*. New York: Gordon Press, 1977.

Teissier, B. *Ancient Near Eastern Cylinder Seals from the Marcopoli Collection*. Berkeley: University of California Press, 1984.

Thesiger, W. *The Marsh Arabs*. New York: Dutton, 1964.

Thomas, D. W. *Documents from Old Testament Times*. New York: Nelson, 1958.

Tigay, J. M. *The Evolution of the Gilgamesh Epic*. Philadelphia: University of Pennsylvania Press, 1982.

Thompsen, R. C. "The Debt of Europe to Babylon." In *The Cambridge Ancient History*. Vol. 3, chap. 11. Cambridge: Cambridge University Press, 1960.

———. *A Dictionary of Assyrian Botany.* London: British Academy, 1949.

———. *A Dictionary of Assyrian Chemistry and Geology.* Oxford: Clarendon Press, 1936.

———. *The Epic of Gilgamesh: Text, Transliteration, and Notes.* Oxford: Clarendon Press, 1930.

Thompson, T. L. *The Historicity of the Patriarchal Narratives.* Berlin: W. de Gruyter, 1974.

Thomsen, M. L. *The Sumerian Language: An Introduction to Its History and Grammatical Structure.* Copenhagen: Akademisk Forlag, 1984.

Tinney, S. J. *The Nippur Lament: Royal Rhetoric and Divine Legitimation in the Reign of Isme-Dagan of Isin (1953–1935 B.C.).* Philadelphia: University of Pennsylvania Museum, 1996.

Tobler, A. *Excavations at Tepe Gawra*, Vol. 2. Philadelphia: University of Pennsylvania Press, 1950.

Tomabechi, Y. "Wall Paintings from Dur Kurigalzu." *Journal of Near Eastern Studies* 42 (1983): 123–31.

Tosi, M. "Early Maritime Cultures of the Arabian Gulf and the Indian Ocean." In *Bahrain through the Ages*, edited by S. H. Khalifa and M. Rice. London: Routledge & Kegan Paul, 1984.

Trinkhaus, E. *The Shanidar Neandertals.* New York: Academic Press, 1983.

Tsumura, D. "Genesis and Ancient Near Eastern Stories of Creation and Flood." In *I Studied Inscriptions from before the Flood*, edited by R. S. Hess and D. T. Tsumara. Winona Lake, Ind.: Eerdmans, 1994.

Tsumura, D. T. *The Earth and the Waters in Genesis 1 and 2: A Linguistic Investigation.* Sheffield: Sheffield Academic Press, 1989.

Ungnad, A., L. Matouš, and H. A. Hoffner. *Akkadian Grammar.* Atlanta: Scholars Press, 1992.

Ussishkin, D. *The Conquest of Lachish by Sennacherib.* Tel Aviv: Tel Aviv University, 1982.

Van Buren, E. D. "The Building of a Temple-Tower." *Revue d'Assyriologie* 46 (1952): 65–174.

———. *Clay Figurines of Babylonia and Assyria.* New Haven, Conn.: Yale University Press, 1930.

———. *The Fauna of Ancient Mesopotamia as Represented in Art.* Rome: Pontificium Institutum Biblicum, 1939.

———. *Foundation Figurines and Offerings.* Berlin: H. Schoetz, 1931.

———. "Foundation Rites for a New Temple." *Orientalia* 21 (1952): 293–06.

———. "How Representations of Battles of the Gods Developed." *Orientalia* n.s. 24 (1955).

———. "Places of Sacrifice ('Opferstätten')." *Iraq* 14 (1952): 76–92.

———. "Representations of Fertility Divinities in Glyptic Art." *Orientalia* n.s. 23 (1954): 345–76.

———. *Symbols of the Gods in Mesopotamian Art.* Rome: Pontificium Institutum Biblicum, 1945.

Van de Mieroop, M. *The Ancient Mesopotamian City.* New York: Oxford University Press, 1999.

———. "The Government of an Ancient Mesopotamian City." In *Priests and Officials in the Ancient Near East (=Papers of the Second Colloquium on the Ancient Near East – The City and Its Life)*, edited by K. Watanabe. Heidelberg: Universitätsverlag C. Winter 1999.

———. "Old Babylonian Ur: Portrait of an Ancient Mesopotamian City." *Journal of the Ancient Near Eastern Society* 21 (1992): 119–30.

———. *Society and Enterprise in Old Babylonian Ur.* Berlin: Raimer, 1992.

———. "Women in the Economy of Sumer." In *Women's Earliest Records*, edited by Barbara Lesko. Atlanta: Scholars Press, 1987.

VanderKam, J. "Prophecy and Apocalyptics in the Ancient Near East." In *Civilizations of the Ancient Near East*, edited by J. M. Sasson et al. New York: Scribner's, 1995.

Van der Meer, P. *The Chronology of Western Asia and Egypt.* 2nd ed. Leiden: E. J. Brill, 1955.

Van der Toorn, K. *From Her Cradle to Her Grave: The Role of Religion in the Life of the Israelite and the Babylonian Woman.* Ithaca, N.Y.: Sheffield Academic/CUP Services, 1994.

———. *Sin and Sanction in Israel and Mesopotamia: A Comparative Study.* Assen: Van Gorcom, 1985.

———, B. Becking, and P. W. van der Horst, eds. *Dictionary of Deities and Demons in the Bible.* Leiden: E. J. Brill, 1995.

Van der Waerden, B. L. *Science Awakening, I: Egyptian, Babylonian, and Greek Mathematics.* Cranbury, N. J.: Scholars Bookshelf, 1988.

Van Dijk, J. *Early Mesopotamian Incantations and Rituals.* New Haven, Conn.: Yale University Press, 1985.

Van Driel, G., *The Cult of Assur*. Assen, Netherlands: Van Gorcum, 1969.

Van Seters, J. *Abraham in History and Tradition*. New Haven, Conn.: Yale University Press, 1975.

———. "The Historiography of the Ancient Near East." In *Civilizations of the Ancient Near East*, edited by J. M. Sasson et al. New York: Scribner's, 1995.

Vanstiphout, H. "Memory and Literacy in Ancient Western Asia." In *Civilizations of the Ancient Near East*, edited by J. M. Sasson et al. New York: Scribner's, 1995.

Veenhof, K. R., ed. *Cuneiform Archives and Libraries*. Leiden: E. J. Brill, 1986.

———. "Kanesh: An Assyrian Colony in Anatolia." In *Civilizations of the Ancient Near East*, edited by J. M. Sasson et al. New York: Scribner's, 1995.

———. "Libraries." In *The Oxford Encyclopedia of Archaeology in the Near East*, edited by E. M. Meyers. New York: Oxford University Press, 1997.

Villard, P. "Shamshi-Adad and Sons: The Rise and Fall of an Upper Mesopotamian Empire." In *Civilizations of the Ancient Near East*, edited by J. M. Sasson et al. New York, Scribner's, 1995.

Vincente, C. A. "The Tell Leilan Recension of the Sumerian King List." *Zeitschrift für Assyriologie* 85 (1995): 234–70.

Von Oppenheim, M. F. *Tell Halaf: A New Culture in Oldest Mesopotamia*. New York: Putnam's, 1933.

Von Soden, W. *The Ancient Orient: An Introduction to the Study of the Ancient Near East*. Grand Rapids, Mich.: Eerdmans, 1994 (1985).

Wachsman, S. *Seagoing Ships in the Bronze Age Levant*. College Station: Texas A&M University Press, 1998.

Waerden, B. L. van der. "History of the Zodiac." *Archiv für Orientforschung* 16 (1952–53): 216–30.

Wagstaff, J. M. *The Evolution of Middle Eastern Landscapes: An Outline to A.D. 1840*. Totowa, N. J.: Barnes & Noble, 1985.

Walker, C. B. F. *Cuneiform*. Berkeley: University of California Press, London: The British Museum, 1987.

Wapnish, P. "Camels." In *The Oxford Encyclopedia of Archaeology in the Near East*, edited by E. M. Meyers. New York: Oxford University Press, 1997.

———, and B. Hesse. "Equids." In *The Oxford Encyclopedia of Archaeology in the Near East*, edited by E. M. Meyers. New York: Oxford University Press, 1997.

Ward, A., and S. Joukowsky, eds. *The Crisis Years: The Twelfth Century BCE from Beyond the Danube to the Tigris*. Dubuque, Iowa: Kendall/Hunt, 1989.

Watanabe, K., ed. *Priests and Officials in the Ancient Near East* (= Papers of the Second Colloquium on the Ancient Near East—The City and Its Life), held at the Middle Eastern Culture Center in Japan [Mitaka, Tokyo], March 22–24, 1996). Heidelberg: Universitätsverlag C. Winter, 1999.

Waterfield, Gordon. *Layard of Nineveh*. New York: Frederick A. Praeger, 1963.

Waterman, L. *Royal Correspondence of the Assyrian Empire*. 4 vols. Ann Arbor: University of Michigan Press, 1930–36.

Weiss, H., ed. *From Ebla to Damascus: Art and Archaeology of Ancient Syria*. Washington, D. C.: Smithsonian Institute, Press, 1985.

———, ed. *The Origins of Cities in Dry-Farming Syria and Mesopotamia in the Third Millennium B.C.* Guilford, Conn.: Four Quarters, 1986.

———, and T. C. Young. "The Merchants of Susa." *Iran* 13 (1975): 1–18.

———, et al. "The Genesis and Collapse of Third Millennium North Mesopotamian Civilization." *Science* 261 (August 20, 1993): 995–1004.

Weissert, E. "Royal Hunt and Royal Triumph in a Prism Fragment of Ashurbanipal (82-5-22,2)." In *Assyria 1995*, edited by S. Parpola and R. M. Whiting. Helsinki: The Project, 1997.

Wellard, J. *Babylon*. New York: Saturday Review Press, 1972.

Wertime, T. A., and J. O. Muhly, eds. *The Coming of the Age of Iron*. New Haven, Conn.: Yale University Press, 1980.

West, M. L. "Akkadian Poetry: Metre and Performance." *Iraq* 59 (1997): 175–87.

Westbrook, R. "Adultery in Ancient Near Eastern Law." *Revue Biblique* 97 (1990): 542–80.

———. "The Enforcement of Morals in Mesopotamian Law." *Journal of the American Oriental Society* 104 (1984): 753–56.

———. "Ancient Near Eastern Myths in Classical Greek Religious Thought." In *Civilizations of the*

Ancient Near East, edited by J. M. Sasson et al. New York: Scribner's, 1995.

Westenholz, A. "The Old Akkadian Empire in Contemporary Opinion." In *Power and Propaganda: A Symposium on Ancient Empires (=Mesopotamia: Copenhagen Studies in Assyriology*, Vol. 7), edited by M. T. Larson. Copenhagen, Akademisk Vorlag, 1976.

Westenholz, J. G. "A Forgotten Love Song." In *Language, Literature, and History*, edited by F. Rochberg-Halton. New Haven, Conn.: American Oriental Society, 1987.

———. "Heroes of Akkad." *Journal of the American Oriental Society* 103 (1983): 327–36.

———. *Legends of the Kings of Akkade*. Winona Lake, Ind.: Eerdmans, 1997.

———. "Love Lyrics from the Ancient Near East." In *Civilizations of the Ancient Near East*, edited by J. M. Sasson et al. New York: Scribner's, 1995.

———. "Towards a New Concept of the Female Role in Mesopotamian Society." *Journal of the American Oriental Society* 110 (1990): 510–21.

Wheeler, M. *Archaeology from the Earth*. Baltimore: Penguin, 1954.

White, L. M. "Dura-Europos." In *The Oxford Encyclopedia of Archaeology in the Near East*, edited by E. M. Meyers. New York: Oxford University Press, 1997.

Whitehouse, D. "Glass." In *The Oxford Encyclopedia of Archaeology in the Near East*, edited by E. M. Meyers. New York: Oxford University Press, 1997.

Whiting, R. M., "Amorite Tribes and Nations of Second-Millennium Western Asia." In *Civilizations of the Ancient Near East*, edited by J. M. Sasson et al. New York: Scribner's, 1995.

Widengren, G. *The King and the Tree of Life in Ancient Near Eastern Religion*. Uppsala: Lundequistska Bokhandeln, 1951.

Wiesehöfer, J. *Ancient Persia: From 550 B.C. to 650 A.D.* London: I. B. Tauris, 1996.

Wiggermann, F. A. M. *Mesopotamian Protective Spirits: The Ritual Texts*. Groningen: Netherlands: STYX & PP Publications, 1992.

———. "Theologies, Priests, and Worship in Ancient Mesopotamia." In *Civilizations of the Ancient Near East*, edited by J. M. Sasson et al. New York: Scribner's, 1995.

Wigoder, G., P. M. Shalom, B. T. Viviano, and E. Stern, eds. *Illustrated Dictionary and Concordance of the Bible*. Jerusalem: G. G. The Jerusalem Publishing House and Pleasantville, N.Y.: The Reader's Digest Association, 1986.

Wilford, J. N. "Ancient Clay House Is Found in Syria." *New York Times*, January 3, 1993, I10.

———. "Jar in Iranian Ruins Betrays Beer Drinkers of 3500 B.C." *New York Times*, November 5, 1992, A16.

Wilhelm, G. *The Hurrians*. Warminster: Aris & Phillips, 1989.

Wilson, J. V. K. "An Introduction to Babylonian Psychiatry." In *Festschrift Benno Landsberger*. Chicago: University of Chicago Press, 1965.

———. "Mental Diseases in Ancient Mesopotamia." In *Diseases in Antiquity*, edited by D. R. Brothwell. Springfield, Ill.: C. C. Thomas, 1967.

Winnett, F., and W. L. Reed. *Ancient Records from North Arabia*. Toronto: University of Toronto press, 1970.

Winstone, H. V. F. *Uncovering the Ancient World*. New York: Facts On File, 1985.

———. *Woolley of Ur: The Life of Sir Leonard Wolley*. London: Secker & Warburg, 1990.

Winter, I. J. "Aesthetics in Ancient Mesopotamian Art." In *Civilizations of the Ancient Near East*, edited by J. M. Sasson et al. New York: Scribner's, 1995.

———. "After the Battle Is Over: The 'Stele of the Vultures' and the Beginning of Historical Narrative in the Art of the Ancient Near East." In *Pictorial Narrative in Antiquity and the Middle Ages*, edited by H. L. Kessler and M. S. Simpson. Washington, D. C.: National Gallery of Art, 1985.

———. "Art in Empire: The Royal Image and the Visual Dimension of Assyrian Ideology." In *Assyria 1995*, edited by S. Parapola and R. M. Whiting. Helsinki, 1997.

———. "The Body of the Able Ruler: Toward an Understanding of the Statues of Gudea." In *DUMU-E₂-DUB-BA-A: Studies in Honor of Åke W. Sjöberg*, edited by H. Behrens, D. Loding, and M. T. Roth. Philadelphia: University Museum, 1989.

———. "'Seat of Kingship'/'A Wonder to Behold': The Palace as Construct in the Ancient Near East." *Ars Orientalia* (1993): 27–55.

Wiseman, D. J. *Chronicles of Chaldean Kings.* London: British Museum, 1961.

———. *Cylinder Seals of Western Asia.* London: Batchworth, 1959.

———. *Nebuchadnezzar and Babylon.* London: Oxford University Press, 1985.

Wittfogel, K. A. *Oriental Despotism: A Comparative Study of Total Power.* New Haven, Conn.: Yale University Press, 1957.

Wohlstein, A. *The Sky-God An-Anu.* Jericho, N.Y.: P. A. Strook 1976.

Wolkstein, D., and S. N. Kramer. *Inanna, Queen of Heaven and Earth: Her Stories and Hymns from Sumer.* New York: Harper & Row, 1983.

Woolley, L. *The Art of the Middle East.* New York: Crown, 1961.

———. *Dead Cities and Living Men.* New York: Philosophical Library, 1956.

———. *Digging Up the Past.* Baltimore: Penguin, 1937.

———. *Excavations at Ur.* New York: Crowell, 1955.

———. *The Sumerians.* New York: AMS Press, 1970 (1929).

———. *Ur Excavations.* 8 vols. London: British Museum, 1934–1982.

———. *Ur of the Chaldees.* Rev. ed. Baltimore: Penguin, 1950.

Wright, G. E., and F. V. Filson. *The Westminster Historical Atlas to the Bible.* Rev. ed. Philadelphia: Westminster, 1956.

Yadin, Y. *The Art of Warfare in Biblical Lands.* 2 vols. New York: McGraw-Hill, 1963.

Yoffee, N. "The Economy of Ancient Western Asia." In *Civilizations of the Ancient Near East,* edited by J. M. Sasson et al. New York: Scribner's, 1995.

———, and J. J. Clark, eds. *Early Stages in the Evolution of Mesopotamian Civilization.* Tucson, Ariz.: University of Arizona Press, 1993.

Young, T. C., and L. Levine, eds. *Mountains and Lowlands: Essays in the Archaeology of Greater Mesopotamia.* Malibu, Calif.: Undena, 1977.

Zaccagnini, C. "The Merchant at Nuzi." *Iraq* 39 (1977): 171–89.

———. "Patterns of Mobility among Ancient Near Eastern Craftsmen." *Journal of Near Eastern Studies* 42 (1983): 245–64.

Zodok, R. *The Jews in Babylonia during the Chaldean and Achaemenian Periods.* Haifa: University of Haifa Press, 1979.

Zarins, J. "Camel." In *Anchor Bible Dictionary,* edited by D. N. Freedman. New York: Doubleday, 1992.

———. "The Early Settlement of Southern Mesopotamia: A Review of Recent Historical, Geological, and Archaeological Research." *Journal of the American Oriental Society* 112 (1992): 55–77.

Zeder, M. A. *Feeding Cities: Specialized Animal Economy in the Ancient Near East.* Washington, D.C.: Smithsonian Institution, 1991.

Zettler, R. L. "Nippur." In *The Oxford Encyclopedia of Archaeology in the Near East,* edited by E. M. Meyers. New York: Oxford University Press, 1997.

———, and L. Horne, eds. *Treasures from the Royal Tombs of Ur.* Philadelphia: University of Pennsylvania Museum, 1998.

Zeuner, F. E. *A History of Domesticated Animals.* London: Hutchinson, 1963.

Zimansky, P., and E. C. Stone. "Mesopotamia in the Aftermath of the Gulf War." *Archaeology* 45 (May/June 1992): 24.

INDEX

Boldface page numbers indicate major treatment of a subject. Page numbers in *italics* with suffix *f* denote a figure, suffix *m* denotes a map; and suffix *t* denotes a table.

Amentohep III 108, 177
Amentohep IV 108, 177
American School of Oriental
    Research 43
Ammi-ditana **75**
Ammi-saduqa **75–76**
Ammondt, Jukka 298
Ammons, A. R. 333
Amurru. *See* Martu
An **116**
Anabasis (Xenophon) 49
Anchor Brewing Company of
    San Francisco 292
The Ancient Engineers
    (de Camp) 203
Ancient Iraq (Roux) 54, 131
Ancient Near East 3*m*
ancient sites, names of 6–8
Andrae, Walter **40**, 192
animal husbandry **246–247**
    reading 250
animals
    autopsies **171–172**
    injured 221*f*
Anni **76**
Annunaki **116**
Annunitum **116**
Anshar and Kishar **116**
Antiochus I **76**, 101
Antiochus II **76**, 101
Antiochus III **76**
Antiochus IV **76**
Antiochus VII **76**
Antiochus XIII **76**
Anu. *See* An
Anunnaki. *See* Annunaki
Anzu. *See* Imdugud
Aphrodite 26, 129
Apil-Kin **76**
Apil-Sin **76**
Apocrypha **322**
    reading 324
Appian Way 210

Apsu 63–64
Aqar Quf 17
aqueducts. *See* canals and
    aqueducts
Arabian Nights 330
Aramaic language 233
Arbil **10**
archaeology and history
    39–59
    dating the past **49–51**,
        59
    digging **51–54**, 59
    discoverers **40–49**, 59
    narratives **54**, 59
    rulers, key **58–59**
    survey of history **54–58**,
        59
arch (construction) 190
arch (Ctesiphon) 16*f*
archers, warfare 267*f*
architecture and engineering
    185–211
    bridges **207–209**, 211
    building materials and
        houses **186–188**, 210
    canals and aqueducts
        203–207, 211
    city, transition from
        village to **191**,
        210–211
    city planning **201–202**,
        211
    domestic architecture
        188–190, 210
    palaces **198–201**, 211
    reading 210–211
    roads **209–210**, 211
    techniques of
        construction **190**
    temples **191–194**, 211
    walls **202–203**, 211
    ziggurats **194–198**, 211
archives **149**

Ardeshir **76**
Arik-den-ili **77**
army, organization of
    265–267
    cavalry 266
    chariots 265–266
    command 265
    logistic support 267
    reading 271
Arsaces (Arshak) **77**
art
    clothing, portrayal
        290–291. *See also*
        specific types of art
    marriage, portrayal
        279*f*, 280*f*
    Western art, legacy of
        Mesopotamia
        332–333
Artabanus I **77**
Artabanus II **77**
Artatama I **77**
Artatama II 108
Artaxerxes I (Persian king)
    77
Artaxerxes I (Sassanian ruler).
    See Ardeshir
Artaxerxes II **77**, 329
Artaxerxes III **77**
artist, role of **214**
    reading 241
arts
    materials **214**
    warfare, portrayal of
        267–270*f*, **268–270**,
        272
Aruru **116**
Asag **116**
Asarluhi **116–117**
Asharid-apal-Ekur **77**
ashipu 306
Ashnan **117**
Ashur **10–11**, 66, 91, **117**

livestock and fish 293–294

reading 310

spices and herbs 293

fortifications **262–263**

readings 271

walls, attack on 221*f*

Fort Shalmaneser 23

Four Quartets (Eliot) 157

fragmentary epics **162–165**

Frankfort, Henri 20, **42–43**, 216

Assyria, images from 220

fruits and vegetables **293**

fusion welding 238

G

Galla **118**

games. *See* toys and games

Gandash **86**

gardening **245–246**

Garden of Eden

Book of Genesis 313–314, 323

location 313–314

Gardner, John 333

"Gate of the Gods" 106

Gatumdug **118**

gazetteer

names of cities **6–8**

reading 37–38

Geme-Ninlila 105

Genesis. *See* Book of Genesis

geography 2–38

descriptions of cities **8–37**

military affairs and **262**, 271

names of cities **6–8**

natural resources **4–5**, 37

reading 37–38

rivers **2–4**, 37

surrounding countries **5–6**, 37

Geshtinanna **118**

Gibbon, Edward 16–17

Gibil **119**

Giedion, Sigfried 191

Gilgamesh 36, 64, 74, **86**, 129

cylinder seal, portrayed on 234*f*

The Epic of Gilgamesh 86, 129, **149–162**

literary figure 333

social satire 179

Girra. *See* Gibil

Girsu **20–21**, 25

Gishbare **119**

Giza 36

glass **229–231**

colors and designs 230

history 229

reading 241

techniques 229–230

technology and faith 230–231

uses 229

glazed tile 227*f*

gods. *See* religion and myth; *specific god*

Goetze, Albrecht **43**

Gordian III **86**

Gordon, Cyrus Herzl **43**

governance of world **115**

reading 135

government and society 61–112

justice and law **68–72**, 112

kingship **63–67**, 112

stratification of society **62–63**, 112

structure of civilization **62**, 111

taxation **67–68**, 112

grain and by-products **291–292**

"Great Death Pit" 36

great decipherments. *See* decipherments

Great Lyre 296–297*f*

Great Zab River 2, 10

Griffith, W. D. 334

groom leading two horses 255*f*

Grotefend, Georg Friedrich **43**, 139–140, 141

Guagamela 10

Gudea 21, **86**, 193*f*, 217, 218*f*

guffa 252

Gugulanna **119**

Gulkishar **86**

Gungunum **86**, 106

Gushkin-banda **119**

Guti 10

Guzana **21**

H

Hadad. *See* Ishkur

Al-Hadr 21

Hadrian 105

Haggai 320

Haia 29

Halaf 21

Hammurabi I 12, 22, 25–26, **86–87**

Code of Hammurabi. *See* Code of Hammurabi

death of 108

grandson 75

great-grandson 75

Mari, attack on 111

reign of 57
stela of Hammurabi
219–220
successor 89
wages 249
Hanging Gardens of Babylon
11, 201
Hanukkah 76
Hanun-Dagan **87**
Harbashihu **87**
harp 296*f*
Harran 36, 80, 82, 96, 99,
123, 125
Hassuna 32
Hatra **21**
health and medicine
304–309. *See also* medicine
reading 310
Hebrew Melodies (Byron) 333
Hebrew prophets **318–320**
historical background
318–319
message of 319–320
reading 324
Hellenistic Period **58**
warfare 267
Hellenistic Seleucid dynasty
16
Hendursanga **119**
Herodotus **43**
Babylon, described 11,
132
Egypt, on 4
"the father of history"
328
prostitution, on 129
Hezekiah 102
high priest 65
Hilal-Erra **87**
Hilprecht, Herman Volrath **43**
Hincks, Edward **43**
historical chronicles **165–167**
reading 182–183

History Begins at Sumer
(Kramer) 133–134
Hitler, Adolf 170
Hittites 15, 57, 74, 108
holy days and festivals
130–132
reading 136
Homer 135, 328
homes **285–288**
bricks 189–190,
285–286, 287*f*
deconstruction 288
excavating information
288
furnishing 287
garbage 288
heating and lighting 287
materials and
construction 285–286
native reed hut 286*f*
plans 287
reading 309–310
reeds, bundles of
188–189, 285
ruins and resurrection
288
sanitation 287–288
walls, windows, and
doors 286
horses, groom leading 255*f*
House of the Uplifted Head
13
Hulagu Khan 207
Humbaba. *See* Huwawa
hunting **247–248**
lion hunt 247*f*
reading 250
Hurrian language 143
Hussein, Mazahim Mahmud
43
Huwawa **119**
hymns and prayers **172–173**
reading 183

I

Iahdun-Lim **87**, 111
Iahsmah-Addad **87–88**
Ibal-pi-El I **88**
Ibal-pi-El II **88**
Ibbi-Sin **88**
Ibiq-Adad I **88**
Ibiq-Adad II **88**
Iblulsil **88**
Ibn-Battuta **40**
Iddin-Dagan **88**, 132
Iddin-Ilum **88**
Iddin-Sin 178
Ididish **88**
Iggid-Lim **87**
Igiga (or Igigu) **119**
Ikin-Shamagan **88**
Ikinum **88**
Ikum-Shamas **89**
Ilaba **119**
Ilshu **89**
Iluma-ilum 57, **89**
Ilum-Ishtar **89**
Ilushi-ilia **89**
Ilushuma **89**
Imdugud **119–120**
Imgur-Enlil **22**
Iminbi **120**
immortality, concept of
134–135, 281
art and **214–215**
reading 136, 309
Inanna 26, 28, 118, **120**,
126
New Year holiday 132
incest **278**
Indus Valley 255
infant burial 282*f*
infidelity **277–278**
inheritance **278–279**
inscriptions **139**
intaliare 232